Concepts of
Fitness and Wellness
A Comprehensive Lifestyle Approach

TWELFTH EDITION

Charles B. Corbin

Arizona State University

Gregory J. Welk

Iowa State University

William R. Corbin

Arizona State University

Karen A. Welk

Mary Greeley Medical Center, Ames, Iowa

Mc
Graw
Hill
Education

CONCEPTS OF FITNESS AND WELLNESS

Published by McGraw-Hill, a business unit of The McGraw-Hill Companies, Inc., 1221 Avenue of the Americas, New York, NY, 10020. Copyright © 2019 by The McGraw-Hill Companies, Inc. All rights reserved. Printed in the United States of America. Previous editions © 2016, 2013, 2011. No part of this publication may be reproduced or distributed in any form or by any means, or stored in a database or retrieval system, without the prior written consent of The McGraw-Hill Companies, Inc., including, but not limited to, in any network or other electronic storage or transmission, or broadcast for distance learning.

Some ancillaries, including electronic and print components, may not be available to customers outside the United States.

This book is printed on acid-free paper.

4 5 6 7 8 9 GPC 21

ISBN 978-1-260-08544-0
MHID 1-260-08544-9

Cover Image: ©Samuel Borges Photography/Shutterstock

All credits appearing at the end of the book are considered to be an extension of the copyright page.

The Internet addresses listed in the text were accurate at the time of publication. The inclusion of a website does not indicate an endorsement by the authors or McGraw-Hill, and McGraw-Hill does not guarantee the accuracy of the information presented at these sites.

mheducation.com/highered

Brief Contents

Contents

©Rubberball/Getty Images

©Chris Clinton/DigitalVision/Getty Images

©Comstock Images/Stockbyte/Getty Images

Section VI

Stress Management   343

©Caiaimage/Robert Daly/Getty Images

Section VII

Avoiding Destructive Behaviors   379

Section VIII

Making Informed Choices   435

Features

Concepts of Fitness and Wellness includes magazine-like features that help students integrate and apply information they may see in the news or read about on the Internet. These features have follow-up activities available in *Connect* and can be assigned online.

- *A Closer Look* provides information about new and sometimes controversial topics related to health, wellness, and fitness and encourages critical thinking.
- *Technology Update* describes emerging health and fitness technology, innovations, and research.
- *In the News* highlights late-breaking health, wellness, and fitness events, trends, and information.
- *HELP* personalizes fitness and health issues through brief narratives that relate to the defining elements of the HELP Philosophy (H: Health, E: Everyone, L: Lifetime, P: Personal)

A CLOSER LOOK

Technology Update

In the News

HELP Health is available to Everyone for a Lifetime, and it's Personal

Lab Activities

All end-of-concept Lab Activities are available in *Connect* and can be edited, assigned, completed, submitted, and graded online. Lab Resource Materials (extra materials for use in completing Lab Activities) are available for all fitness self-assessments.

50 Years of Success!

With the publication of this twelfth edition of *Concepts of Fitness and Wellness,* we celebrate the 50th anniversary of the publication of the first of the many *Concepts* books. The first book in this continuous franchise was published in 1968. Since that time, *Concepts of Physical Fitness,* published in 17 editions and winner of the McGuffey Award for Textbook Longevity, and *Concepts of Fitness and Wellness* have carried on the tradition started a half century ago. We are proud of the success of

the *Concepts* books and are thankful to those who have adopted these texts and who contributed to their success.

Into the Future

While we are pleased with our 50 years of success, it is our intent to continue to be at the forefront of the science movement that underlies the content of *Concepts of Fitness and Wellness.* Dr. Chuck Corbin, the founding author and past president of the prestigious National Academy of Kinesiology, continues to be actively involved in all facets of authorship. Dr. Greg Welk, a fellow in the National Academy of Kinesiology and an established fitness and wellness scholar, shares the leadership on the project and plays an increasing role in all aspects of content development. Dr. Will Corbin, a professor of clinical psychology with expertise in health psychology, leads the content related to stress management, alcohol, tobacco, drugs, and sexually transmitted infections. Dr. Karen Welk, an established physical therapist, provides expertise in flexibility, strength and conditioning, back care, and contraindicated exercises. Collectively, the author team addresses the research and technical jargon in a manageable format that provides instructors and students with access to the latest information about health, wellness, and fitness. Our goal is to achieve another 50 years of success.

In Tribute

We continue to pay tribute to Dr. Ruth Lindsey (1926–2005), one of the original authors of *Concepts of Fitness and Wellness.* She was a great leader and an outstanding advocate for healthy lifestyles, physical activity, and physical education and will long be remembered for her contributions to the *Concepts* program and our profession.

Dedication

The authors would like to dedicate this edition to our families (spouses, children, and grandchildren) for their continued support and sacrifices that enabled us to spend the time necessary to create this book.

Thank You

We are always listening to our users and to those who review *Concepts of Fitness and Wellness.* We greatly appreciate their feedback, which helps us make *Concepts* an even better resource for both students and instructors. We want to thank the instructors who provided insights regarding their course needs, which helped guide this edition's revisions:

Bob Amsberry, *Wartburg College*
Randall Anastasio, *University of South Alabama*
Janelle Anderson, *Arizona State University*
Joan Barch, *Lansing Community College*
JoAnne Barbieri Bullard, *Atlantic Cape Community College*
Kevin B. Kinser, *Tarrant County College*
Lindsey Nanney, *University of North Carolina–Wilmington*
Anthony Paul Parish, *Armstrong State University*
Michael Sergi, *Armstrong State University*
Deonna Shake, *Abilene Christian University*
Jamie Stanley, *Crowder College*
Adam Thompson, *Indiana Wesleyan University*
Bob Vezeau, *Kalamazoo Valley Community College*
Jesse Vezina, *Arizona State University*
Jason Vorwerk, *St. Ambrose University*
Kim Wathen, *Lansing Community College*
Greg S. Wimer, *Armstrong State University.*

To list everyone who has had an impact on the *Concepts* texts over the years would take several pages. Nevertheless, we feel that it is important to acknowledge those who have helped us. A list of the many contributors is available at **www.corbinconcepts.org,** as are additional resources we have provided that support the use of *Concepts of Fitness and Wellness* in your course. Thank you all!

Charles B. Corbin
Gregory J. Welk
William R. Corbin
Karen A. Welk
www.corbinconcepts.org

Courtesy Charles Corbin

Courtesy Greg and Karen Welk

Courtesy William Corbin

Courtesy Greg and Karen Welk

Educational Foundations

Fundamental to the success of any textbook is a strong educational foundation. First, it is important to have a strong philosophical foundation. *Concepts of Fitness and Wellness* is based on the "HELP" philosophy, which reinforces the power of personal behavior change and the self-management skills necessary for adopting and maintaining healthy lifestyles. Next, well-defined learning objectives are critical to understanding and applying the concepts that are clearly highlighted throughout *Concepts of Fitness and Wellness*. Finally, a strong visual program reinforces the content and facilitates multisensory learning.

Integrated HELP Philosophy

Health is available to Everyone
for a Lifetime, and it's Personal.

The HELP philosophy directs the content in *Concepts of Fitness and Wellness,* focusing on helping students achieve sound health (including fitness and wellness) through the adoption of healthy lifestyles. Particular emphasis is placed on various self-management skills that make it easier to sustain these lifestyle behaviors over time. The various lab activities in each Concept are designed to provide opportunities to learn these skills. Ultimately, the goal is for students to learn to prepare personal programs of health behavior change that address their own needs and interests.

Concepts-Based Framework

A novel and defining aspect of *Concepts of Fitness and Wellness* is the "concepts-based" approach to education. Specific learning objectives are provided at the beginning of each Concept to help focus and guide students to the most important information. Content within each Concept is organized into thematic sections and each includes several more concise "concepts" or principles. Carefully worded statements introduce each of these mini-sections to help students retain the key messages in the Concept. This modularized approach to learning offers advantages for student learning and retention since the important information is introduced and then directly reinforced.

LEARNING OBJECTIVES

After completing the study of this Concept, you will be able to:

▶ Identify the determinants of health, wellness, and fitness, and explain how they each contribute to health, wellness, and fitness.

▶ Differentiate between factors over which you have lesser and greater control.

▶ Use health behavior change strategies to carry out self-assessments of personal lifestyles and wellness perceptions.

Many factors are important in developing lifetime health, wellness, and fitness, and some are more in your control than others. A model that summarizes many of the factors that contribute to health, wellness, and fitness is provided in Figure 1 🔲 . Central to the model are health, wellness, and fitness because these are the states of being (shaded in green and gold) that each of us wants to achieve.

connect VIDEO 1

Learning Objectives (left) *introduce each concept and modularized "Concept Statements"* (right) *help guide student learning.*

Visual Enhancements for Learning

Students learn using many different types of sensory input. Accordingly, the visuals in *Concepts of Fitness and Wellness* include photos with concept-relevant captions, figures that convey conceptual materials in an easy-to-understand format, and exercise illustrations that show exactly how to perform exercises for important dimensions of health-related fitness.

Engaging graphics, diagrams, and exercise illustrations facilitate student learning.

Highlights of the Twelfth Edition: Innovations for Enhanced Learning

The twelfth edition of *Concepts of Fitness and Wellness* is designed to deliver a flexible and personalized approach to fitness and wellness education. The materials provide an integrated print and digital solution that enables instructors (and students) to explore options for applying the information.

Connect® Is Proven Effective

McGraw-Hill Connect® is a digital teaching and learning environment that improves performance over a variety of critical outcomes; it is easy to use; and it is proven effective. Connect empowers students by continually adapting to deliver precisely what they need, when they need it, and how they need it, so your class time is more engaging and effective. Connect for *Concepts of Fitness and Wellness* offers a wealth of interactive online content, including labs and self-assessments, video activities on timely health topics, and practice quizzes with immediate feedback.

New to this edition are assignable and assessable **Concept Clips**, which help students master key fitness and wellness concepts. Using colorful animation and easy-to-understand audio narration, Concept Clips provide step-by-step presentations to promote student comprehension. Topics include the stages of change model, diabetes types and metabolism, nutrition facts labels, the cardiorespiratory system, and the stress response.

Also new are **Newsflash** activities, which tie current news stories to key fitness and wellness fitness concepts. After interacting with a contemporary news story, students are assessed on their understanding and their ability to make the connections between real-life events and course content. Examples of Newsflash topics include food fads, stress and obesity, Pilates, and risks of sedentary behavior.

Personalized Learning SMARTBOOK®

Available within Connect, **SmartBook®** makes study time as productive and efficient as possible by identifying and closing knowledge gaps. SmartBook identifies what an individual student knows and doesn't know based on the student's confidence level, responses to questions, and other factors. SmartBook builds an optimal, personalized learning path for each student, so students spend less time on concepts they already understand and more time on those they don't. As a student engages with SmartBook, the reading experience continuously adapts by highlighting the most impactful content a student needs to learn at that moment in time. This ensures that every minute spent with SmartBook is returned to the student as the most value-added minute possible. The result? More confidence, better grades, and greater success.

New to this edition, SmartBook is now optimized for smart phones and tablets and accessible for students with disabilities using interactive features.

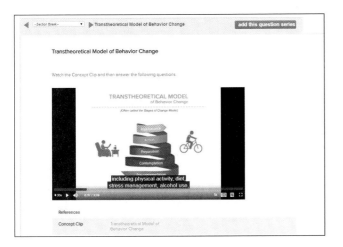

Advance Reporting

Connect Insight® is Connect's one-of-a-kind visual analytics dashboard—available for both instructors and students—that provides at-a-glance information regarding student performance, which is immediately actionable. By presenting assignment, assessment, and topical performance results together with a time metric that is easily visible for aggregate or individual results, Connect Insight gives the user the capability to take a just-in-time approach to teaching and learning, which was never before available. Connect Insight presents data that empower students and help instructors improve class performance in a way that is efficient and effective.

Dietary Analysis Tool

NutritionCalc Plus is a suite of powerful dietary self-assessment tools that help students track their food intake and activity and analyze their diet and health goals. Students and instructors can trust the reliability of the ESHA database while interacting with a robust selection of reports. This tool is provided at no additional charge inside Connect for Concepts of Fitness and Wellness, twelfth edition.

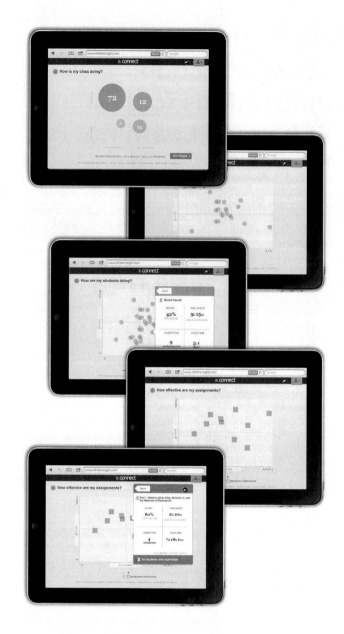

Highlights of the Twelfth Edition: Personal Responsibility, Self-Management, and Concept Updates

This edition of *Concepts of Fitness and Wellness* has been thoroughly updated with new elements aimed at enhancing student learning. Readers will find an even stronger focus on personal responsibility and self-management skills as these are critical for adopting and sustaining healthy lifestyles. Each Concept begins with *Learning Objectives* and a new element *Why It Matters!* to introduce key themes that help students see the direct relevance of the material. Each Concept ends with a new section *Using Self-Management Skills* to help the reader apply the information to everyday life. Updated descriptions in the *Strategies for Action* section then introduce the specific lab activities that provide opportunities to practice and learn these self-management skills.

The educational features in each Concept have also been completely updated, with new links and questions available in *Connect* to promote personal exploration of the content. A variety of video vignettes are embedded within the eBook and linked to Connect activities to help explain complex issues and provide opportunities for personal reflection and critical thinking. Updated *LearnSmart* lessons provide an adaptive learning resource that helps ensure that students master the intended learning objectives. Accessible and relevant resources and books are provided in the *Suggested Resources and Readings*, while scientific references are provided at the end-of-text *References* section. Although the content and resources provide a comprehensive framework for effective education, students have a variety of opportunities to learn and apply the information in ways that best match their interests and needs.

Each Concept includes many boxed features with engaging contemporary content that are useful for class discussions. *A Closer Look* provides information about new and sometimes controversial topics related to health, wellness, and fitness and encourages critical thinking. *Technology Update* describes advances in health and fitness technology and prompts exploration and personal evaluation. *In the News* highlights late-breaking health, wellness, and fitness information and provides opportunities for reflection. The *HELP* feature personalizes fitness and health issues to help students internalize the information.

Dynamic changes in the body of knowledge relating to health, wellness, and fitness are captured in the extensive updates to this edition. Details of the most recent nutrition guidelines and highlights of the new 2018 *Physical Activity Guidelines for Americans* are presented throughout. Changes in the American College of Sports Medicine (ACSM) exercise testing and prescription guidelines also prompted changes in exercise recommendations for several health-related fitness areas. Similarly, new regulations from the Food and Drug Administration (FDA) influence food labeling, tobacco, and drug policies and how products are marketed. Insights from medical research also led to changes in screening and treatment for various conditions. Other new research findings and public health updates are woven through each of the Concepts. Some of the updates are highlighted below:

1   Health, Wellness, Fitness, and Healthy Lifestyles: An Introduction
- Updates on the *Healthy People Initiative* (2020 and beyond)
- Updated statistics about health, longevity, and wellness
- Recent data regarding quality of life satisfaction and CDC population questionnaires
- Expanded emphasis on assessments and consumer skills in self-management section

2   Determinants of Lifelong Health, Wellness, and Fitness
- Refined model of factors influencing health, wellness, and fitness
- Mention of the CDC's Healthy Community Design Initiative to promote healthy environments
- Updated discussion of Americans' health status, including a recent report comparing developing countries
- Emphasis on the importance of personal actions and interactions in the self-management section

3   Self-Management Skills for Health Behavior Change
- Reformatted and expanded descriptions of self-management skills
- New perspectives on SMART goals
- Emphasis on self-planning skills in the self-management section

4   Preparing for Physical Activity
- Updated section on exercise screening guidelines, including the new PAR-Q+
- Updated material on the treatment of injuries (RICE model)
- New discussion on water versus fluid replacement drinks and their benefits
- New information on smartphone apps that help monitor environmental conditions
- Emphasis on building knowledge and balancing attitudes in the self-management section

5   The Health Benefits of Physical Activity

- New sections on descriptions/implications of sedentary behavior
- Overview of the American Heart Association's *Life's Simple 7* lifestyles
- Updates from the 2018 *Physical Activity Guidelines for Americans*
- Revised guidelines for hypertension
- Updated information on the benefits of muscular fitness
- Discussion of new technologies researchers are using to track health data
- Emphasis on building knowledge and changing beliefs in the self-management section

6   How Much Physical Activity Is Enough?

- New information from the 2018 *Physical Activity Guidelines for Americans*
- Clarifications about the "weekend warrior" approach to physical activity
- Updated statistics on adults meeting the latest physical activity guidelines
- Emphasis on building confidence and motivation in the self-management section

7   Adopting an Active Lifestyle

- New sections on terminology and guidelines related to sedentary behavior
- New content on the health risks of sedentary behavior, including mention of "is sitting the new smoking?"
- Emphasis on planning and monitoring in the self-management section

8   Cardiorespiratory Endurance

- New information based on the 2018 *Physical Activity Guidelines for Americans*
- Updates on studies that indicate the powerful benefits of vigorous exercise
- New explanation of online target heart rate calculators
- More detailed discussion on high-intensity interval training (HIIT)
- Discussion of research on developing medication to replace exercise
- Emphasis on monitoring and assessment in the self-management section

9   Vigorous Aerobics, Sports, and Recreational Activities

- New section clarifying the nature of vigorous exercises
- Updated information on patterns and trends in sports and recreation
- Highlights of the ACSM fitness trend report

- New discussion of "Fitness in the Parks" and group fitness trends
- New data on wearable fitness technology
- Emphasis on building confidence, motivation, and monitoring in the self-management section

10   Muscle Fitness and Resistance Exercise

- New information about health benefits from resistance exercise
- New descriptions of the multidimensionality of muscle fitness
- New discussion of "smart clothes"
- Emphasis on planning and assessment in the self-management section

11   Flexibility

- Completely updated section on the factors that influence flexibility
- Completely updated section on flexibility, injuries, and rehabilitation
- Revised section on stretching methods
- New section on functional fitness, posture, and flexibility-based activities
- Emphasis on consumer and performance skills in the self-management section

12   Body Mechanics: Posture, Questionable Exercises, and Care of the Back and Neck

- Revised section on descriptions and roles of the core musculature
- Revised content on causes and consequences of back and neck pain
- New content on the prevention of (and rehabilitation from) back and neck problems
- Updated explanations for why posture is important for back and neck health
- Emphasis on planning, assessment, and changing beliefs in the self-management section

13   Performance Benefits of Physical Activity

- New content on the importance of more focused and structured training for high-level performance
- New information on concussion awareness and education
- New discussion of WHOOP technology monitoring rest and recovery
- Emphasis on planning and consumer skills in the self-management section

14   Body Composition

- Updated information on the prevalence of obesity and extreme obesity

- New content on how to understand and interpret information about the obesity epidemic
- Consequences of the designation of obesity as a disease
- Updated content on obesity treatment guidelines
- Emphasis on assessment considerations in the self-management section

15 Nutrition

- Clarifications and descriptions of the latest *Dietary Guidelines for Americans*
- New section "Understanding Contemporary Nutrition Terms, Issues, and Food Preferences" that includes content on glucose intolerance and genetically modified foods
- Updated information on the FDA's prohibition on trans fats
- Emphasis on building knowledge, confidence, and motivation in the self-management section

16 Managing Diet and Activity for Healthy Body Fatness

- New information on consumer weight loss programs
- Updated content on losing body fat
- Strategies for confronting an obesogenic environment
- Emphasis on overcoming barriers, social support, and relapse prevention in the self-management section

17 Stress and Health

- New content on stress in contemporary society
- Updated information on the sources of stress
- Clarification on how stress affects health and wellness
- Emphasis on assessment and balancing attitudes in the self-management section

18 Stress Management, Relaxation, and Time Management

- Completely reorganized content to improve flow of information
- Updated descriptions and information on the principles of stress management
- New research on the impact of online social networks
- Emphasis on coping and consumer skills in the self-management section

19 The Use and Abuse of Tobacco

- Updated statistics on smoking patterns and trends
- New information on the impact of the media and marketing of tobacco
- Updated information on issues with e-cigarettes
- Emphasis on building self-confidence and motivation in the self-management section

20 The Use and Abuse of Alcohol

- Updated statistics and risks related to drinking and driving
- Updated information on campus strategies related to alcohol abuse
- Recent debates about college drinking and Greek life
- New apps designed to assist addiction treatment
- Emphasis on self-assessment and self-monitoring skills

21 The Use and Abuse of Other Drugs

- Completely reorganized structure to improve flow of information
- Updated statistics and graphics on the costs of drug abuse in society
- Patterns, trends, and consequences associated with legalized marijuana
- Emphasis on consumer skills in the self-management section

22 Preventing Sexually Transmitted Infections

- Updated statistics on the prevalence of different sexually transmitted infections
- Updates on progress with HIV treatment and vaccine development
- New discussion of the "Me Too" movement and sexual misconduct
- New information on the CDC's "Talk, Test, and Treat" STI-prevention campaign
- Emphasis on communication skills in the self-management section

23 Cancer, Diabetes, and Other Health Threats

- Updated statistics on prevalence and death rates from various cancers
- New screening guidelines for breast and prostate cancers
- New content on skin cancer and labeling of sunscreen products
- Revised content and descriptions of diabetes
- Emphasis on consumer skills and assessment in the self-management section

24 Evaluating Fitness and Wellness Products: Becoming an Informed Consumer

- Updates on quackery in the health and fitness industry
- Updated guidelines on use of vitamin and mineral supplements
- New examples of fraud in the dietary supplement industry
- Features and drawbacks of online personal training resources

- New information on the FDA's MedWatch alert system to report consumer fraud
- Emphasis on communication skills in the self-management section

25 Toward Optimal Health and Wellness: Planning for Healthy Lifestyle Change

- Updates on access to medical care and the physician's role in health
- Summary of self-management skills and links to enabling, predisposing, and reinforcing factors influencing behavior
- New research on the effects of optimism
- New data on Americans accessing health care
- New research on positive patient results from female doctors
- Emphasis on planning skills and practice in the self-management section

More Resources for Teaching with *Concepts of Fitness and Wellness*

Your Course, Your Way

McGraw-Hill Create® is a self-service website that allows you to create customized course materials using McGraw-Hill Education's comprehensive, cross-disciplinary content and digital products. You can even access third-party content such as readings, articles, cases, videos, and more.

- Select and arrange content to fit your course scope and sequence.
- Upload your own course materials.
- Select the best format for your students—print or eBook.
- Select and personalize your cover.
- Edit and update your materials as often as you'd like.

Experience how McGraw-Hill Education's Create empowers you to teach your students your way: **http://create.mheducation.com**

Learning Management System Integration

McGraw-Hill Education provides a one-stop teaching and learning experience available to users of any learning management system. This institutional service allows faculty and students to enjoy single sign-on (SSO) access to all McGraw-Hill Higher Education materials, including the award-winning McGraw-Hill *Connect*™ platform, from directly within the institution's website. The program provides faculty with instant access to all McGraw-Hill Higher Education teaching materials (e.g., eTextbooks, test banks, PowerPoint slides, animations, and learning objects), allowing them to browse, search, and use any instructor ancillary content in our vast library at no additional cost to instructors or students. Students enjoy SSO access to a variety of free products (e.g., quizzes, flash cards, narrated presentations) as well as subscription-based products (e.g., McGraw-Hill *Connect*™). With this program enabled, faculty and students never need to create another account to access McGraw-Hill products and services.

Instructor Resources

Instructors can access the following resources through the Library tab in *Connect:*

- PowerPoint presentations
- Instructor's manual
- Test bank
- Image bank

All test questions are available within TestGen™ software. PowerPoint presentations are WCAG compliant.

Health, Wellness, Fitness, and Healthy Lifestyles: An Introduction

LEARNING OBJECTIVES

After completing the study of this Concept, you will be able to:

▶ Describe the HELP philosophy and discuss its implications in making personal decisions about health, wellness, and fitness.

▶ Define the dimensions of health and wellness, and explain how they interact to influence health and wellness.

▶ Distinguish health-related and skill-related dimensions of physical fitness.

▶ Identify related national health goals and show how meeting personal goals can contribute to reaching national goals.

Good health, wellness, fitness, and healthy lifestyles are important for all people.

©Christopher Futcher/iStockphoto/Getty Images

Why it Matters!

Ninety-nine percent of American adults say that "being in good health" is of primary importance. In fact, people rate personal health (and health of loved ones) as being more important than money and other material things. This is because good health, wellness, and fitness can make us feel good, look good, and enjoy life fully. *Concepts of Fitness and Wellness* is specifically designed to help you learn the cognitive and behavioral skills needed to help you achieve good health, wellness, and fitness throughout life. In this first Concept you will learn about the distinctions between health, wellness, and fitness.

The HELP Philosophy

The HELP philosophy provides a basis for making healthy lifestyle change possible. The acronym *HELP* characterizes an important part of the philosophy: *Health* is available to *Everyone* for a *Lifetime*, and it's *Personal*. The HELP philosophy aids you as you apply the principles and guidelines that help you adopt and sustain healthy lifestyles. Throughout this edition, you will learn a variety of **self-management skills** that are critical for healthy living. The labs in each Concept provide opportunities to practice and apply these skills so that you can use them throughout your life. An overview of basic self-management skills is provided in a later Concept.

A personal philosophy that emphasizes health can lead to behaviors that promote it. The *H* in *HELP* stands for *health*. One theory that has been extensively tested indicates that people who believe in the benefits of healthy lifestyles are more likely to engage in healthy behaviors. The theory also suggests that people who state intentions to put their beliefs into action are likely to adopt behaviors that lead to health, wellness, and fitness.

Everyone can benefit from healthy lifestyles. The *E* in *HELP* stands for *everyone*. Anyone can change a behavior or lifestyle. Nevertheless, many adults feel ineffective in making lifestyle changes. Physical activity is not just for athletes—it is for all people. Eating well is not just for other people—you can do it, too. All people can learn stress-management techniques and practice healthy lifestyles.

Healthy behaviors are most effective when practiced for a lifetime. The *L* in *HELP* stands for *lifetime*. Young people sometimes feel immortal because the harmful effects of unhealthy lifestyles are often not immediate. As we age, however, unhealthy lifestyles have cumulative negative effects. Thus, adopting and sustaining healthy habits early in life is important for long-term health, wellness, and fitness.

Health and wellness are available to everyone for a lifetime.
©BananaStock/Getty Images

Healthy lifestyles should be based on personal needs. The *P* in *HELP* stands for *personal*. Each person has unique needs regarding health, wellness, and fitness. People also vary in attitudes, perceptions, and personal characteristics that influence healthy lifestyles. You will be provided with information about a variety of self-management skills, but it is up to each individual to take personal responsibility for learning and using these skills.

You can adopt the HELP philosophy. As you progress through these Concepts, consider ways that you can implement the HELP philosophy. In each Concept, HELP boxes are provided to stimulate your thinking about key health issues.

Self-Management Skills Skills that you learn to help you adopt healthy lifestyles and adhere to them.

National Health Goals

The *Healthy People Initiative* is a national public health program that establishes a comprehensive set of health promotion and disease prevention objectives with the primary intent of improving the nation's health. The objectives, developed by hundreds of experts from many different national organizations, provide benchmarks for determining **health** progress over each decade. The objectives also serve as goals to motivate and guide people in making sound health decisions as well as to provide a focus for public health programs. A complete list of *Healthy People* objectives (also referred to as goals) that relate to the content in *Concepts of Fitness and Wellness* is provided in this Concept to help you focus on relevant personal health goals.

In addition to helping change the health of society at large, the *Healthy People* objectives have implications for personal health behavior change. Societal changes can occur only when individuals adjust personal behaviors and work together to make changes that benefit other people. Not all objectives will have personal implications for each individual, but increased societal awareness of the objectives may lead to future changes in the health of our country.

A primary goal of the *Healthy People Initiative* is to help all people have high-quality, longer lives free of preventable disease, injury, and premature death. This goal makes distinctions between **lifespan** (life expectancy)

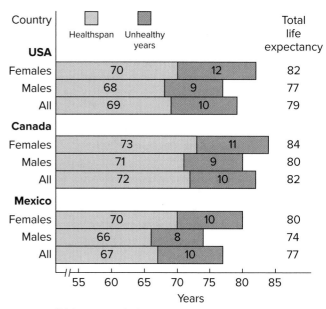

*Values rounded to nearest year.

Figure 1 ▶ Estimated healthspan and lifespan for many North Americans.*

Source: World Health Organization

and **healthspan** (healthy life expectancy). Lifespan refers to the number of years you live. Healthspan is the number of years in your life during which you experience good health that is free of chronic diseases and debilitating conditions that limit your daily activities and your wellness (quality of life).

Over the past century, the lifespan (life expectancy) of Americans has increased by 60 percent. As lifespan has increased, so has the number of unhealthy years. The expected lifespan for North American countries is shown in Figure 1. The green bars in Figure 1 depict the relative healthspan in each country and the orange bars show the number of years with poor health and low quality of life. The United States ranks 31st in expected lifespan compared to other countries in the world. Among North American countries, the United States ranks behind Canada (12th) and ahead of Mexico

Health is available to Everyone for a Lifetime, and it's Personal

National Health Goals: The *Healthy People Initiative*

The *Healthy People 2020* goals (established in 2010) represent the U.S. goals for health and health promotion. More than 1,200 objectives are currently specified, and in 2020, new *Healthy People 2030* goals will be established. Although there are some differences in the nature of the goals, the overarching vision of the *Healthy People Initiative* has remained the same over time: "a society in which all people achieve their full potential for health and well-being across the lifespan." Although the goals are set at the national level, they have implications for determining state and local funding, programming, and policy development.

The HELP philosophy emphasizes that health, wellness, and fitness are for eᴠeryone. Do you think public health goals can influence individual behavior? Conversely, do you think your individual choices and behaviors ultimately influence (or have an impact on) progress toward societal goals?

ACTIVITY

Health Optimal well-being that contributes to one's quality of life. It is more than freedom from disease and illness, though freedom from disease is important to good health. Optimal health includes high-level mental, social, emotional, spiritual, and physical wellness within the limits of one's heredity and personal abilities.

Lifespan The number of years you live (life expectancy).

Healthspan The number of healthy years in your life. It includes years free of illness and debilitating conditions and years of wellness (years with a good quality of life).

Healthy People Initiative: Goals for the Nation

The health goals listed in this table are from the *Healthy People Initiative* that establishes health goals for Americans. The specific goals listed below are those that are covered in *Concepts of Fitness and Wellness*. As you meet your personal goals, you contribute to the achievement of these national health goals.

General Health Goals

- Create a society in which all people live long, healthy lives.
- Promote quality of life, healthy development, and healthy behaviors (including being active, eating well, and avoiding destructive habits) across all stages of life.
- Attain high-quality, longer lives free of preventable disease, injury, and premature death.
- Achieve health equity, eliminate disparities, and improve the health of all groups.
- Create social and physical environments that promote good health for all.
- Increase public awareness and understanding of the determinants of health, disease, and disability.
- Increase health literacy of the population.
- Increase participation in employee wellness programs.
- Increase percentage of high-quality health-related websites.
- Increase percentage of people with health-care providers who involve them in decisions about health care.
- Increase recycling and environmental health efforts.

Fitness and Physical Activity Goals

- Reduce proportion of adults who do no leisure-time activity.
- Increase proportion of adults who meet guidelines for moderate to vigorous aerobic activity.
- Increase proportion of adults who meet guidelines for muscle fitness activity.
- Increase proportion of people who regularly perform exercises for flexibility.
- Increase access to employee-based exercise facilities and programs.
- Increase proportion of trips made by walking.
- Increase proportion of youth who meet guidelines for TV viewing and computer use and overuse (overuse is 2 hours a day or more).
- Increase schools with activity spaces that can be used in non-school hours.
- Increase percentage of physicians who counsel or educate patients about exercise.

- Decrease activity limitations, especially in older adults and disabled.

Hypokinetic Disease Goals

- Increase overall cardiovascular health; reduce heart disease, stroke, high blood pressure, and high blood cholesterol; increase screening; increase awareness; and increase emergency treatment by professionals or bystanders.
- Reduce cancer incidence and death rates, increase cancer patient longevity, increase survivor's quality of life, and increase cancer screening.
- Reduce diabetes incidence and death rates; increase diabetes screening, education, and care.
- Reduce osteoporosis (related hip fractures), pain of arthritis, and limitations from chronic back pain.
- Increase percentage of college students receiving risk factor information.
- Increase young adult awareness of CHD signs and symptoms.
- Reduce rate of sunburn among young people (tanning).

Body Composition/Weight Control Goals

- Increase proportion of adults with healthy weight.
- Reduce childhood overweight and obesity.
- Reduce disordered eating among adolescents.
- Increase worksites that offer nutrition and weight management classes and counseling.
- Increase physician counseling on nutrition and weight management.
- Increase BMI measurement by primary doctors.
- Increase weight-control efforts and activity levels of adults with high LDL.

Nutrition Goals

- Increase policies that give retail food outlets incentives to carry foods that meet dietary guidelines.
- Increase the contribution of fruits in the diet.
- Increase the variety and contribution of vegetables in the diet.
- Increase the contribution of whole grains in the diet.
- Reduce consumption of saturated fat in the diet.
- Reduce consumption of sodium.
- Increase consumption of calcium.
- Reduce iron deficiency.
- Reduce consumption of calories from solid fats and added sugars.

Healthy People Initiative

- Decrease the consumption of sugar-sweetened beverages.
- Increase food safety (variety of areas).

Mental and Emotional Health Goals

- Reduce depression and increase screening for depression.
- Increase screening for and treatment of mental health problems.
- Reduce suicide and suicide attempts.
- Increase availability of worksite stress-reduction programs.
- Reduce rates of depression and disordered eating.
- Increase levels of social support among adults.
- Increase the proportion of primary care facilities that provide mental health treatment.

Safety and Injury Prevention Goals

- Reduce sports and recreation injuries.
- Reduce injuries from overexertion.
- Reduce emergency department visits for nonfatal injuries.
- Increase the proportion of public and private schools that require students to wear appropriate protective gear when engaged in school-sponsored physical activities.
- Reduce injuries and accidental deaths (automobile, assault, drowning, firearms-related, homicides, motorcycle, pedestrian, poisonings).

Goals Related to Tobacco Use

- Increase the number of current smokers who try to quit.
- Reduce smoking during pregnancy.
- Increase the percentage of smoke-free homes.
- Reduce initiation of tobacco use among youth.
- Increase state and federal taxes on tobacco products.
- Reduce teen exposure to tobacco advertising.
- Increase tobacco screening in health-care settings.
- Increase indoor smoking bans in public places.
- Reduce secondhand-smoke exposure.

Goals Related to Sexually Transmitted Infections

- Promote responsible sexual behaviors to prevent sexually transmitted infections (STIs) and their complications.
- Reduce incidence of chlamydia, gonorrhea, syphilis, genital herpes, human papillomavirus (HPV), pelvic inflammatory disease (PID), and hepatitis B.

- Increase proportion tested for HIV.
- Increase percentage of sexually active women who are tested for chlamydia.
- Increase the number of health insurance plans that cover contraceptives.
- Increase proportion of young people who abstain from sexual intercourse, use condoms during sexual activity, and avoid risky sexual behaviors.
- Decrease the percentage of unintended pregnancies.
- Increase percentage of adolescents who receive formal instruction on reproduction before age 18.

Goals Related to Drug Use

- Reduce substance abuse to protect the health, safety, and quality of life for all, especially children.
- Reduce deaths and injuries caused by drug-related motor vehicle crashes.
- Increase availability of specialty treatment for substance abuse.
- Increase effectiveness of drug-abuse treatment programs.
- Reduce proportion of youth offered drugs or sold drugs at school.
- Reduce nonmedical use of prescription drugs.
- Reduce medical emergencies that occur from adverse events associated with medicines.
- Increase the age of onset and proportion of young people who remain drug free.
- Increase the proportion of adolescents who disapprove of substance abuse.
- Reduce steroid use by adolescents.
- Reduce adverse events from medical products.
- Reduce substance abuse to protect the health, safety, and quality of life for all, especially children.

Goals Related to Alcohol Use

- Reduce deaths and injuries caused by alcohol-related motor vehicle crashes.
- Reduce alcohol-related injuries and ER visits.
- Reduce the frequency of driving while intoxicated.
- Increase the proportion of adolescents who remain alcohol free.
- Reduce binge drinking and average alcohol consumption.
- Increase the number of adolescents who disapprove of alcohol consumption.

Source: Adapted from *Healthy People 2020.*

In the News

Healthiest Places to Live

Each year a number of organizations conduct surveys to determine which American cities rate highest in well-being and/or physical fitness. The American Fitness Index from the American College of Sports Medicine (ACSM) and the Gallup-Healthways Well-Being Index® are examples. A variety of criteria such as personal health behaviors, chronic health problems, recreational facilities, and community environmental factors are used to determine ratings. Search "well-being index" or "American Fitness Index" to learn more.

Do healthier people simply seek out healthier environments (and healthier cities) or are there unique attributes that help make an area or city healthier? How does your city rate?

connect
ACTIVITY

(47th). Although unhealthy years occur more often toward the end of the lifespan, they can happen at any time. Of concern is the fact that U. S. life expectancy *decreased* in recent years after more than 50 years of increases. Experts indicate that the dramatic increase in deaths from drug overdoses is one of the principal reasons for the recent decrease in life expectancy. Although these are national statistics, a goal of *Concepts of Fitness and Wellness* is to help you personally increase both your lifespan and your healthspan.

Achieving health equity, eliminating disparities, and improving the health of all groups is another primary goal of the *Healthy People Initiative.* Health varies greatly with ethnicity, income, gender, and age. As defined in the *Healthy People Initiative,* a health disparity is "a particular type of health difference that is closely linked with social, economic, and/or environmental disadvantage." To reduce health disparities, it is important to address underlying causes.

Another primary national health goal is to create social and physical environments that promote good health for all. The environment, both social and physical, has much to do with quality and length of life. Social environment refers to norms and values that influence our behavior, whereas physical environment refers to characteristics or features that may allow the healthier choice to be the easier choice. These features are known as "social determinants of health" and will be discussed in more detail later.

The final primary goal of the *Healthy People Initiative* is to promote health, wellness, and healthy behaviors across all stages of life. Health and wellness are products of a healthy lifestyle. Young adults generally have good health, but unhealthy lifestyles eventually take a toll and contribute to compromised health and wellness later in life. The subsequent sections will describe important distinctions between (and dimensions of) health, wellness, and fitness.

Health and Wellness

Health is more than freedom from illness and disease. Over 60 years ago, the World Health Organization defined health as more than freedom from illness, disease, and debilitating conditions. Prior to that time, you were considered to be "healthy" if you were not sick.

Regular physical activity can improve one's sense of well-being.
©Paul Bradbury/Getty Images

connect
VIDEO 1

HEALTH

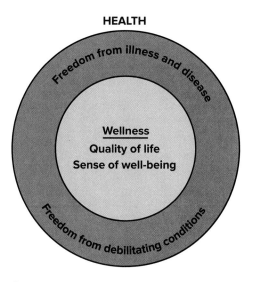

Figure 2 ▶ A model of optimal health, including wellness.

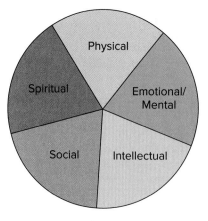

Figure 3 ▶ The dimensions of health and wellness.

Figure 2 illustrates the modern concept of health. This general state of being is characterized by freedom from disease and debilitating conditions (outer circle), in addition to wellness (center circle).

Wellness is the positive component of optimal health. Disease, **illness,** and debilitating conditions are negative components that detract from optimal health. Death can be considered the ultimate opposite of optimal health. **Wellness,** in contrast, is the positive component of optimal health. It is characterized by a sense of well-being reflected in optimal functioning, health-related **quality of life,** meaningful work, and a contribution to society. The term *health-related quality of life* also reflects a general sense of happiness and satisfaction with life.

Health and wellness are personal. Every individual is unique, and health and wellness are influenced by each person's unique characteristics. Making comparisons to other people on specific characteristics may produce feelings of inadequacy that detract from one's profile of total health and wellness. Each of us has personal limitations and strengths. Focusing on strengths and learning to accommodate weaknesses are essential keys to optimal health and wellness.

Health and wellness are multidimensional. The health and wellness dimensions include physical, emotional/mental, intellectual, social, and spiritual (see Figure 3). Each is important to optimal health and wellness.

Table 1 describes the various dimensions. Some people include environmental and vocational dimensions in addition to the five shown in Figure 3. Health and wellness are personal factors, so environmental and vocational health and wellness are not included in Table 1. However, the environment (including your work environment) is very important to overall personal wellness and, for this reason, environmental factors are prominent in the model of wellness described later.

Wellness reflects how one feels about life, as well as one's ability to function effectively. A positive total outlook on life is essential to each of the wellness dimensions. As illustrated in Table 2, a "well" person is satisfied in work, is spiritually fulfilled, enjoys leisure time, is physically fit, is socially involved, and has a positive emotional/mental outlook. He or she is happy and fulfilled.

The way one perceives each dimension of wellness affects one's total outlook. Researchers use the term *self-perceptions* to describe these feelings. Many researchers believe that self-perceptions about wellness are more important than actual circumstances or a person's actual state of being. For example, a person who has an  important job may find less meaning and job satisfaction than another person with a much less important job. Apparently, one of the important factors for a person who has achieved high-level wellness and a positive outlook on life is the ability to reward himself or herself. Some people, however, seem

Illness The ill feeling and/or symptoms associated with a disease or circumstances that upset homeostasis.

Wellness The integration of many different components (physical, emotional/mental, intellectual, social, and spiritual) that expand one's potential to live (quality of life) and work effectively and to make a significant contribution to society. Wellness reflects how one feels (a sense of well-being) about life, as well as one's ability to function effectively. Wellness, as opposed to illness (a negative), is sometimes described as the positive component of good health.

Quality of Life A term used to describe wellness. An individual with quality of life can enjoyably do the activities of life with little or no limitation and can function independently. Individual quality of life requires a pleasant and supportive community.

Table 1 ▶ Definitions of Health and Wellness Dimensions

Physical health—Freedom from illnesses that affect the physiological systems of the body, such as the heart and the nervous system. A person with physical health possesses an adequate level of physical fitness and physical wellness.

Physical wellness—The ability to function effectively in meeting the demands of the day's work and to use free time effectively. Physical wellness includes good physical fitness and the possession of useful motor skills. A person with physical wellness is generally characterized as fit instead of unfit.

Emotional/mental health—Freedom from emotional/mental illnesses, such as clinical depression, and possession of emotional wellness. The goals for the nation's health refer to mental rather than emotional health and wellness. However, mental health and wellness are conceptually the same as emotional health and wellness.

Emotional/mental wellness—The ability to cope with daily circumstances and to deal with personal feelings in a positive, optimistic, and constructive manner. A person with emotional wellness is generally characterized as happy instead of depressed.

Intellectual health—Freedom from illnesses that invade the brain and other systems that allow learning. A person with intellectual health also possesses intellectual wellness.

Intellectual wellness—The ability to learn and to use information to enhance the quality of daily living and optimal functioning. A person with intellectual wellness is generally characterized as informed instead of ignorant.

Social health—Freedom from illnesses or conditions that severely limit functioning in society, including antisocial pathologies.

Social wellness—The ability to interact with others successfully and to establish meaningful relationships that enhance the quality of life for all people involved in the interaction (including self). A person with social wellness is generally characterized as involved instead of lonely.

Spiritual health—The one component of health that is totally composed of the wellness dimension; it is synonymous with spiritual wellness.

Spiritual wellness—The ability to establish a values system and act on the system of beliefs, as well as to establish and carry out meaningful and constructive lifetime goals. Spiritual wellness is often based on a belief in a force greater than the individual that helps her or him contribute to an improved quality of life for all people. A person with spiritual wellness is generally characterized as fulfilled instead of unfulfilled.

Table 2 ▶ The Dimensions of Wellness

Wellness Dimension	Negative	Positive
Physical	Unfit	Fit
Emotional/mental	Depressed	Happy
Intellectual	Ignorant	Informed
Social	Lonely	Involved
Spiritual	Unfulfilled	Fulfilled
Total outlook	Negative	Positive

unable to give themselves credit for their successes. The development of a system that allows a person to perceive the self positively is essential, along with the adoption of positive **lifestyles** that encourage improved self-perceptions. The questionnaire in Lab 1A will help you assess your self-perceptions of the various wellness dimensions. For optimal wellness, it is important to find positive feelings about each dimension.

Health and wellness are integrated states of being. The segmented pictures of health and wellness shown in Figure 3 and Tables 1 and 2 are used only to illustrate the multidimensional nature of health and wellness. In reality, health and wellness are integrated states of being that can best be depicted as threads woven together to produce a larger, integrated fabric. Each dimension relates to each of the others and overlaps all the others. The overlap is so frequent and so great that the specific contribution of each thread is almost indistinguishable when looking at the total (Figure 4). The total is clearly greater than the sum of the parts.

It is possible to possess health and wellness while being ill or living with a debilitating condition. Many illnesses are curable and may have only a temporary effect on health. Others, such as Type 1 diabetes, are not curable but can be managed with proper nutrition, physical activity, and sound medical treatment. Those with manageable conditions may, however, be at risk for other health problems. For example, unmanaged diabetes is associated with a high risk for heart disease and other health problems.

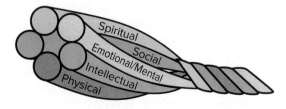

Figure 4 ▶ The integration of wellness dimensions.

A CLOSER LOOK

Population Surveys of Wellness and Quality of Life

Although the prevalence of obesity and chronic disease in adults is quite high, most adults still report a relatively high level of wellness. For example, a national poll indicates that 87 percent of Americans are very satisfied or somewhat satisfied with their overall quality of life. This finding suggests that even people experiencing the negative component of overall health—the presence of disease or illness—can experience wellness. Public health agencies use a variety of different measures to assess wellness (well-being), including questionnaires measuring overall life satisfaction, happiness, social support, and personal autonomy. (See Suggested Resources and Readings).

To what extent do you think your overall wellness is dependent on "freedom from disease and illness"? Do you think that maintaining wellness can help you cope with illness and disease?

Debilitating conditions, such as the loss of a limb or loss of function in a body part, can contribute to a lower level of functioning or an increased risk for illness and thus to poor health. On the other hand, such conditions need not limit wellness. A person with a debilitating condition who has a positive outlook on life may have better overall health (a long healthspan) than a person with a poor outlook on life but no debilitating condition.

Just as wellness is possible among those with illness and disability, evidence is accumulating that people with a positive outlook are better able to resist the progress of disease and illness than are those with a negative outlook. Thinking positive thoughts has been associated with enhanced results from various medical treatments and surgical procedures.

Wellness **is a term used by the uninformed as well as experts.** Unfortunately, some individuals and groups have tried to identify wellness with products and services that promise benefits that cannot be documented. Because well-being is a subjective feeling, unscrupulous people can easily make claims of improved wellness for their product or service without facts to back them up.

The term *holistic health* is similarly abused. Optimal health includes many dimensions; thus, the term *holistic* (total) is appropriate. In fact, the word *health* originates from a root word meaning "wholeness." Unfortunately, questionable health practices are sometimes promoted under the guise of holistic health. Care should be used when considering services and products that make claims of wellness and/or holistic health to be sure that they are legitimate.

Physical Fitness

Physical fitness is a multidimensional state of being. **Physical fitness** is the body's ability to function efficiently and effectively. It consists of at least six health-related and five skill-related dimensions (Figures 5 and 6), each of which contributes to total quality of life. Physical fitness is associated with a person's ability to work effectively, enjoy leisure time, be

The health-related dimensions of fitness are associated with enhanced health and wellness.
©*Syda* Productions/Shutterstock

healthy, resist **hypokinetic diseases or conditions,** and meet emergency situations. It is related to, but different from, health and wellness. Although the development of physical fitness is the result of many things, optimal physical fitness is not possible without regular physical activity.

Lifestyles Patterns of behavior or ways an individual typically lives.

Physical Fitness The body's ability to function efficiently and effectively. It consists of at least 11 health-related physical fitness and skill-related physical fitness components, each of which contributes to total quality of life. Physical fitness also includes metabolic fitness and bone integrity. Optimal physical fitness is not possible without regular exercise.

Hypokinetic Diseases or Conditions *Hypo-* means "under" or "too little," and *-kinetic* means "movement" or "activity." Thus, *hypokinetic* means "too little activity." A hypokinetic disease or condition is one associated with lack of physical activity or too little regular exercise. Examples include heart disease, low back pain, Type 2 diabetes, and obesity.

Body Composition

The relative percentage of muscle, fat, bone, and other tissues that make up the body. A fit person has a relatively low, but not too low, percentage of body fat (body fatness).

Muscular Endurance

The ability of the muscles to exert themselves repeatedly. A fit person can repeat movements for a long period without undue fatigue.

Cardiorespiratory Endurance

The ability of the heart, blood vessels, blood, and respiratory system to supply nutrients and oxygen to the muscles and the ability of the muscles to utilize fuel to allow sustained exercise. A fit person can persist in physical activity for relatively long periods without undue stress.

Dimensions of Health-Related Physical Fitness

Strength

The ability of the muscles to exert an external force or to lift a heavy weight. A fit person can do work or play that involves exerting force, such as lifting or controlling one's own body weight.

Power

The ability to transfer energy into force at a fast rate. Kicking in martial arts and throwing the discus are activities that require considerable power.

Flexibility

The range of motion available in a joint. It is affected by muscle length, joint structure, and other factors. A fit person can move the body joints through a full range of motion in work and in play.

Figure 5 ▶ Dimensions of health-related physical fitness.

Agility

The ability to rapidly and accurately change the direction of the movement of the entire body in space. Skiing and wrestling are examples of activities that require exceptional agility.

Reaction Time

The time elapsed between stimulation and the beginning of reaction to that stimulation. Reacting to a soccer ball and starting a sprint race require good reaction time.

Dimensions of Skill-Related Physical Fitness

Coordination

The ability to use the senses with the body parts to perform motor tasks smoothly and accurately. Juggling, hitting a tennis ball, and kicking a ball are examples of activities requiring good coordination.

Balance

The maintenance of equilibrium while stationary or while moving. Performing tai chi movements and performing stunts on the balance beam are activities that require exceptional balance.

Speed

The ability to perform a movement in a short period of time. Sprinters and wide receivers in football need good foot and leg speed.

Figure 6 ▶ Dimensions of skill-related physical fitness.

(Agility): ©Karl Weatherly/Stockbyte/Getty Images; (Reaction Time): ©John Lund/Drew Kelly/Blend Images LLC; (Coordination): ©Karl Weatherly/Photodisc/Getty Images; (Speed): ©JupiterImages/Brand X/Alamy Stock Photo; (Balance): ©Mangostar/Shutterstock

The health-related dimensions of physical fitness are directly associated with good health. The six dimensions of health-related physical fitness are body composition, cardiorespiratory endurance, flexibility, muscular endurance, power, and strength (see Figure 5). All health-related fitness dimensions have a direct relationship to good health and reduced risk for hypokinetic diseases. This is why they are emphasized in personal fitness programs.

Possessing a moderate amount of each dimension of health-related fitness is essential to disease prevention and health promotion, but it is not essential to have exceptionally high levels of fitness to achieve health benefits. High levels of health-related fitness relate more to performance than to health benefits. For example, moderate amounts of strength are necessary to prevent back and posture problems, whereas high levels of strength contribute most to improved performance in activities such as football and jobs involving heavy lifting.

The skill-related dimensions of physical fitness are associated more with performance than with good health. The dimensions of skill-related physical fitness are agility, balance, coordination, reaction time, and speed (see Figure 6). They are called skill-related because people who possess them find it easy to achieve high levels of performance in motor skills, such as those required in sports and in specific types of jobs. Power, a dimension that requires both strength and speed, was formerly considered a skill-related dimension of fitness but new evidence has linked power with good health.

Skill-related fitness has been called "sports fitness" or "motor fitness," but note that it is multidimensional and highly specific. For example, coordination could be hand-eye coordination, such as batting a ball; foot-eye coordination, such as kicking a ball; or many other possibilities. The five dimensions of skill-related fitness identified here are those commonly associated with successful sports and work performance. Additional information and self-assessments on skill-related fitness are included in later Concepts to help you understand the nature of total physical fitness and make important decisions about lifetime physical activity.

Metabolic fitness is a nonperformance dimension of total fitness. Physical activity can provide health benefits that are independent of changes in traditional health-related fitness measures. Physical activity promotes good **metabolic fitness,** a state associated with reduced risk for many chronic diseases. People with a cluster of low metabolic fitness characteristics are said to have metabolic syndrome (also known as Syndrome X). Metabolic syndrome is discussed in more detail in a later Concept.

Bone integrity is often considered to be a nonperformance measure of fitness. Traditional definitions do not include bone integrity as a part of physical fitness, but some experts feel they should. Like metabolic fitness, bone integrity cannot be assessed with performance measures the way most

There are many ways to train to improve functional fitness.
©Rido/Shutterstock

health-related fitness parts can. Regardless of whether bone integrity is considered a part of fitness or a component of health, strong, healthy bones are important to optimal health and are associated with regular physical activity and sound diet.

The many components of physical fitness are specific but are also interrelated. Physical fitness is a combination of several aspects, rather than a single characteristic. A fit person possesses at least adequate levels of each of the health-related, skill-related, and metabolic fitness components. Some relationships exist among various fitness characteristics, but each component of physical fitness is separate and different from the others. For example, people who possess exceptional strength may not have good cardiorespiratory endurance and those who have good coordination do not necessarily possess good flexibility.

Functional fitness is important for people of all ages. **Functional fitness** refers to the ability to perform activities of daily life. For adults, this includes performing work and household tasks as well as leisure activities without undue fatigue. It also includes having adequate fitness to meet the demands of emergency situations. For youth, functional fitness includes the ability to function in school and leisure activities without undue fatigue. For older adults, functional fitness plays key roles in enabling independence and in minimizing risks of falls.

Good physical fitness is important, but it is not the same as physical health and wellness. Good fitness contributes to the physical dimension of health and wellness by reducing risk for chronic diseases and by reducing the consequences of many debilitating conditions. Good fitness also contributes indirectly to other dimensions by helping us look our best, feel good, perform daily tasks, and enjoy life. However, other physical factors can also influence health and wellness. For example, having good physical skills enhances quality of life by allowing us to participate in enjoyable activities, such as tennis, golf, and bowling. Although fitness can assist us in performing these activities, regular practice is also necessary. Another example is the ability to fight off viral and bacterial infections. Although fitness can promote a strong immune system, other physical factors can influence our susceptibility to illness.

Using Self-Management Skills

Self-assessment is one of many self-management skills that can be learned to enhance lifelong healthy behaviors. Skills refer to the abilities you need in order to perform a specific task. Serving a tennis ball or typing on a computer are examples of physical or motor skills. Solving a math problem is an example of a mental or cognitive skill. A different set of skills—known as self-management skills—helps you adopt behaviors to enhance lifelong health, wellness, and fitness. *Self-assessment* (a specific self-management skill) refers to the ability to collect and evaluate personal information that will help you create a plan for improving your health, wellness, and fitness. You will conduct a variety of self-assessments as you work your way through this edition. For example, you will complete assessments for each dimension of health-related fitness and answer questionnaires to determine your wellness status, risk factors, attitudes, and health behavior patterns. To most effectively use self-assessments, consider the following guidelines:

- **Follow the same procedures each time you self-assess.** Read and follow the instructions to know how to do a self-assessment properly. Having written descriptions of the best way to perform an assessment reminds you of the proper techniques for assessment. Heeding an instructor's advice and following written descriptions of assessments helps ensure that each assessment is done the same way.

- **Use the same equipment or questionnaire each time you self-assess.** For example, when assessing your weight, use the same scale every time. Even if the scale isn't completely accurate, using the same scale helps you record fluctuations in weight over time. When assessing wellness with a questionnaire, use the same form each time to achieve consistent comparisons.

- **Practice.** Like all skills, self-assessment skills can be improved with practice. For example, if you regularly assess your fitness, you will get better at it and achieve more consistent results.

- **Be honest with yourself.** Many self-assessments require you to provide personal answers to questions. The results of your self-assessments are for you own use in establishing baseline information so that you can determine if you are improving your health, wellness, and fitness over time. The results will be meaningful only if you provide honest answers.

Use good consumer skills to evaluate information you read and hear about health, wellness, and fitness. The popularity and importance of health-related issues in our society make consumers vulnerable to mis-information, quackery, and fraud. A key to reducing your risk and to advancing your knowledge is to use good sources of information. See Technology Update for information about sound health-related websites.

Technology Update

Health Websites

The Internet provides a tremendous number of sources of information about health, wellness, and fitness. However, all online sources are not equally credible or useful. The best way to get accurate information is to use reliable sources. Focus on government agencies (.*gov*), prominent medical and public health associations, and established nonprofit agencies (.*org*). The first sites that come up in searches may not be the best, so check the source. A brief list of some prominent and credible Internet sites is provided below. Additional organizations and websites are referenced in other sections.

- Academy of Nutrition and Dietetics (AND)
- American College of Sports Medicine (ACSM)
- American Heart Association (AHA)
- American Medical Association (AMA)
- Center for Science in the Public Interest
- Centers for Disease Control and Prevention (CDC)
- Federal Trade Commission (FTC)
- Food and Drug Administration (FDA)
- Gallup-Healthways
- Harvard Health Publications
- Health Canada
- Healthy People 2020
- Mayo Clinic Health Letter
- MedlinePlus
- National Academy of Medicine (NAM)
- National Institutes of Health (NIH)
- Pew Research Center—Health
- President's Council on Fitness, Sports and Nutrition
- Quackwatch
- Robert Woods Johnson Foundation
- Society of Health and Physical Educators (SHAPE America)
- U.S. Consumer Information Center
- WebMD
- World Health Organization (WHO)

Do you consider the quality of sources when you access health-related information on the Internet? What features should you look for to ensure credibility?

Metabolic Fitness A positive state of the physiological systems commonly associated with reduced risk for chronic diseases such as diabetes and heart disease. Metabolic fitness is evidenced by healthy blood fat (lipid) profiles, healthy blood pressure, and healthy blood sugar and insulin levels.

Functional Fitness The ability to perform activities of daily life.

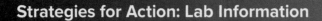

Strategies for Action: Lab Information

An initial self-assessment of your wellness will provide information for future self-comparison. In Lab 1A, you will estimate your wellness using a Wellness Self-Perceptions Questionnaire, which assesses the five wellness dimensions. Assessing each dimension will help you see areas of strengths and weaknesses and determine areas of priority as you set goals and make plans for improving. Answering the same questions at a later date can help you see if you have made progress. As each person makes progress toward improving wellness, collectively we move closer to the *Healthy People* goal of living long, high-quality lives.

Suggested Resources and Readings

The websites for the following sources can be accessed by searching online for the organization, program, or title listed. Specific scientific references are available at the end of this edition of *Concepts of Fitness and Wellness*.

- American College of Sports Medicine. American Fitness Index.
- Centers for Disease Control and Prevention. Well-Being Concepts.
- Centers for Disease Control and Prevention. National Health Information Survey. Online Information.
- Central Intelligence Agency. (2017). *The World Factbook.* Washington, DC: CIA.
- Gallup Poll. Well-Being Index.
- Johns Hopkins Medicine Library. *Reliable Health Information on the Internet* (pdf).

- National Academies of Sciences, Engineering, and Medicine. (2017). *Global Health and the Future Role of the United States.* Washington, DC: National Academies Press (pdf).
- National Institutes of Health. MedlinePlus Consumer Health Resources.
- Office of Disease Prevention and Health Promotion. *Healthy People 2020.*
- Office of Disease Prevention and Health Promotion. *Healthy People 2030.*
- Trust for America's Health. *Blueprint for a Healthier America 2016* (pdf).
- U.S. Department of Health and Human Services. HealthFinder.gov.
- U.S. Office of Disease Prevention and Health Promotion (Health.gov) (health literacy).
- World Health Organization. *World Health Statistics 2017.*

Lab 1A Wellness Self-Perceptions

Name	Section	Date

Purpose: To assess self-perceptions of wellness.

Procedures

1. Place an X over the appropriate circle for each question (4 = strongly agree, 3 = agree, 2 = disagree, 1 = strongly disagree).
2. Write the number found in that circle in the box to the right.
3. Sum the three boxes for each wellness dimension to get your wellness dimension totals.
4. Sum all wellness dimension totals to get your comprehensive wellness total.
5. Use the rating chart to rate each wellness area.
6. Complete the Results section and the Conclusions and Implications section.

Question	Strongly Agree	Agree	Disagree	Strongly Disagree	Score
1. I am physically fit.	4	3	2	1	
2. I am able to perform the physical tasks of my work.	4	3	2	1	
3. I am physically able to perform leisure activities.	4	3	2	1	
			Physical Wellness Total	**=**	
4. I am happy most of the time.	4	3	2	1	
5. I have good self-esteem.	4	3	2	1	
6. I do not generally feel stressed.	4	3	2	1	
			Emotional/Mental Wellness Total	**=**	
7. I am well informed about current events.	4	3	2	1	
8. I am comfortable expressing my views and opinions.	4	3	2	1	
9. I am interested in my career development.	4	3	2	1	
			Intellectual Wellness Total	**=**	
10. I have many friends and am involved socially.	4	3	2	1	
11. I have close ties with my family.	4	3	2	1	
12. I am confident in social situations.	4	3	2	1	
			Social Wellness Total	**=**	
13. I am fulfilled spiritually.	4	3	2	1	
14. I feel connected to the world around me.	4	3	2	1	
15. I have a sense of purpose in my life.	4	3	2	1	
			Spiritual Wellness Total	**=**	
			Comprehensive Wellness (Sum of five wellness scores)		

Results (Record your scores from the previous page; then determine your ratings from the Chart).

Wellness Dimension	Score	Rating
Physical		
Emotional/mental		
Intellectual		
Social		
Spiritual		
Comprehensive		

Wellness Rating Chart

Rating	Wellness Dimension Scores	Comprehensive Wellness Scores
High-level wellness	10–12	50–60
Good wellness	8–9	40–49
Marginal wellness	6–7	30–39
Low-level wellness	Below 6	Below 30

Conclusions and Implications: Rank each dimension of wellness. Place a 1 by the dimension you need to work on most and a 2 by the dimension needing the next most work. Rank the others as 3, 4, and 5. Then in the box below, briefly discuss your wellness ratings. Comment on your current level of wellness and dimensions that could use improvement.

◯ Physical   ◯ Emotional/mental   ◯ Intellectual   ◯ Social   ◯ Spiritual

Determinants of Lifelong Health, Wellness, and Fitness

LEARNING OBJECTIVES

After completing the study of this Concept, you will be able to:

► Identify the determinants of health, wellness, and fitness, and explain how they each contribute to health, wellness, and fitness.

► Differentiate between factors over which you have lesser and greater control.

► Use health behavior change strategies to carry out self-assessments of personal lifestyles and wellness perceptions.

Many factors contribute to health, wellness, and fitness, and some are more in your control than others.

©Rubberball/Getty Images

Why it Matters!

Your health, wellness, and fitness are influenced by many factors. These factors are often referred to as *determinants*. A key point is that you have more control over some determinants than others. In this Concept you will learn about the various determinants and how they contribute to your personal health, wellness, and fitness.

Determinants of Health, Wellness, and Fitness

Many factors are important in developing lifetime health, wellness, and fitness, and some are more in your control than others. A model that summarizes many of the factors that contribute to health, wellness, and fitness is provided in Figure 1. Central to the model are health, wellness,

and fitness because these are the states of being (shaded in green and gold) that each of us wants to achieve. Around the periphery are the factors that influence these states of being. Those shaded in dark blue are the factors over which you have the least control (heredity, age, and disability). Those shaded in light blue (environmental factors and health-care system) are factors over which you have some control but less than the factors shaded in red (personal actions and interactions and cognitions and emotions). Those shaded in light red are the factors over which you have greatest control (healthy lifestyles).

Determinants over Which You Have Little or Some Control

Heredity (human biology) is a determinant over which we have little control. Experts estimate that human biology, or heredity, accounts for 16 percent of all health problems, including early death. Heredity influences each dimension of health-related physical fitness, including our

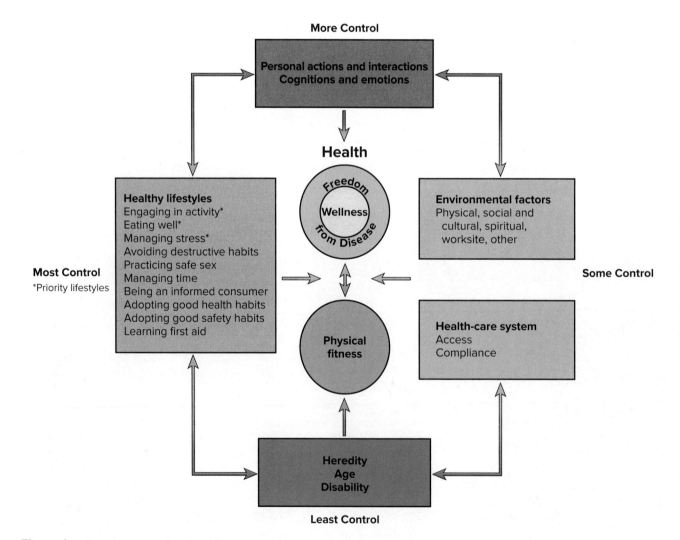

Figure 1 ▶ Determinants of health, wellness, and fitness.

Disabilities need not limit one's ability to experience an active, fulfilling life.
©PhotoAbility/Blend Images

tendencies to build muscle and to deposit body fat. Based on their genetics, individuals also respond and adapt differently to healthy lifestyles. Even more important is that predispositions to certain diseases are inherited. Some hereditary conditions are untreatable (e.g., congenital heart defects) while others are manageable with proper medical supervision and appropriate lifestyles (e.g., diabetes). Heredity is clearly a determinant over which you have little control (illustrated in dark blue in Figure 1) but you can take some preventive steps by being aware of your family history and by making efforts to manage factors that you can control.

Health, wellness, and fitness are influenced by age, but healthy lifestyles can delay and moderate the effect. In 2030, when all of the post–World War II baby boomers will be over the age of 65, adults 65 or older will make up 20 percent of the population. The number of people over 85 will triple by 2050. Data also indicate that there are more than 100,000 people over the age of 100 in the United States. The definition of *old* is clearly relative to your personal age, but societal perceptions of what constitutes "old age" are also changing. One survey reported that 25 percent of the population view that old age doesn't begin until a person hits 80 years or more.

Age is clearly a factor over which we have no control (shaded in dark blue in Figure 1) and it does directly influence our health status. The major health and wellness concerns of older adults include losing health, losing the ability to care for oneself, losing mental abilities, running out of money, being a burden to family, and being alone. Chronic pain is also a major problem among older adults with nearly 30 percent of adults over 65 experiencing chronic pain, as opposed to 3 percent of those under 30. The important message is that healthy lifestyles can dramatically reduce the effects of aging on health, wellness, and fitness. Thus, it is important to adopt and maintain healthy lifestyles to somewhat counter "normal" aging effects.

Disabilities can affect, but do not necessarily limit, health, wellness, and fitness. Disabilities typically result from factors beyond your control (shaded in dark blue in Figure 1). Many types of disabilities affect health, wellness, and fitness. An objective disability (e.g., loss of a limb, impaired intellectual functioning) can make it difficult to function in certain circumstances but need not limit health, wellness, and fitness. All people have a limitation of one kind or another. Societal efforts to help all people function within their limitations can help everyone, including people with disabilities, to have a positive outlook on life and experience a high quality of life.

The health-care system affects our ability to overcome illness and improve our quality of life. Approximately 10 percent of unnecessary deaths occur as a result of disparities in the health-care system. The quality of life for those who are sick and those who tend to be sick is influenced greatly by the type of medical care they receive. Health care is not equally available to all. Each year, thousands of people die because they lack health insurance. Uninsured individuals may not seek health care, and the quality of the care they do receive may not be high. Chronic conditions that go undetected can become untreatable or lead to additional complications. The passage of the Patient Protection and Affordable Care Act (shortened to the Affordable Care Act, or ACA) addressed this issue by enabling all Americans to have health insurance. According to the National Center for Health Statistics, the number of uninsured Americans dropped from 16 percent in 2010 to a record low of 8.8 percent in 2016.

Even with coverage, many people fail to seek medical help when warranted, and others fail to follow medical advice. For example, they do not take prescribed medicine or do not follow up with treatments. Men are less likely to seek medical advice than  women and this is a problem since some treatable conditions lead to bigger problems or become untreatable over time. This is why it is important to follow recommendations for regular screenings and seek medical advice when warranted.

Wellness as evidenced by quality of life is also influenced by the health-care system. Traditional medicine, sometimes referred to as the **medical model,** has focused primarily on the treatment of illness with medicine, rather than illness prevention and wellness promotion. Efforts to educate health-care personnel about techniques for promoting wellness have been initiated in recent years. Still, it is often up to the patient to find information about health promotion. For example, a patient with risk factors for heart disease might be advised to eat better or to exercise more, but little specific information may be offered. While you don't have full control over medical care, you do have some control over your access, use, and adherence to medical advice (see the light blue box in Figure 1).

The environment is a major determinant affecting our health, wellness, and fitness. Environmental determinants account for nearly one-fourth of all early deaths and affect quality of life in many ways. We do have more control over environmental factors than heredity, but you can't control all aspects of the environment. You do have some control

A bit of extra effort can help build physical activity into your daily routine
©Don Mason/Blend Images LLC

over how you interact with your environments and the extent with which you take advantage of available healthy opportunities. (See the light blue box in Figure 1.)

You can exert personal control by seeking out healthy environments that might enable you to be more active or to eat healthier. You can also look to avoid unhealthy or unsafe environments. Many people actively consider aspects of their environment when considering places to live or work since it

 **A CLOSER LOOK**

Determinants of Health in the United States

The United States is one of the wealthiest countries in the world but far from the healthiest. The report *U.S. Health in International Perspective: Shorter Lives, Poorer Health* found that Americans are less healthy than people in 16 other developed countries. This is attributed to a number of key determinants, including health systems (e.g., differences in access to health care), health behaviors (e.g., poor diet and exercise habits),

social and economic conditions (e.g., education system and high poverty), and unhealthy environments (e.g., walkability and fast food). (See Suggested Resources and Readings.)

What do you think is the most important determinant? Which of the determinants do you personally have most control over? Which one do you have least control over?

In the News

Healthy Community Design

Aspects of the "built environment"—the environment we live and work in—can directly impact our health. For example, access to healthy foods and the availability of walking routes make it easier to make healthy choices. The Centers for Disease Control and Prevention (CDC) has launched the Healthy Community Design Initiative as part of a broader campaign that is focused on improving environments for better health. Search "CDC Healthy Places" to learn more. (See Suggested Resources and Readings.)

How does the environment influence your ability to be active and to eat healthfully? What can you do to find healthier opportunities wherever you live?

has such a strong influence on their lifestyle. Circumstances may make it impossible for you to make the choices you would prefer, but it is important to at least be aware of the impact of your environment on your health and well-being. Also, consider broader influences on wellness from social, spiritual, and intellectual environments.

Determinants over Which You Have Greater Control

Personal actions, interactions, cognitions, and emotions all have an effect on health, wellness, and fitness. While you have no control over heredity, age, and disability (and limited control over health care and the environment), you can act (and interact) in ways to positively influence your lifestyle (shaded in dark red in Figure 1) . You can use your cognitive abilities to learn about your family history and use that information to limit the negative influences of heredity. You can learn how to adapt to disabilities and personal limitations, as well as to the aging process. You can research the health-care system and seek out healthy opportunities and options even in unhealthy environments.

Your personal interactions also influence your health, wellness, and fitness. You are not alone in this world. Your various environments, and how you interact with them, influence you greatly. You have a choice about the environments in which you place yourself and the people with whom you interact in these environments.

Humans have the ability to think (cognitions) and to use critical thinking to make choices and to determine the actions they take and the interactions they engage in. Emotions also affect personal actions and interactions. A major goal of *Concepts of Fitness and Wellness* is to help you use your cognitive abilities to solve problems and make good decisions about good health, wellness, and fitness, as well as to help you be in control of your emotions when taking action and making decisions that affect your health.

None of us makes perfect decisions all of the time. Sometimes we take actions and make choices based on inadequate information, faulty thinking, pressure from others, or negative influences from our emotions. While the focus of Concepts that follow is on healthy lifestyles, all of the factors that influence health, wellness, and fitness are important to consider. The goal is to help you consider all factors and to make informed decisions that will lead to healthful behaviors.

Lifestyle change, more than any other determinant, is the best way to prevent illness and early death in our society. Statistics show that more than half of early deaths are the result of chronic diseases caused by unhealthy lifestyles. Many of these chronic diseases are targeted in the Healthy People report, and many of the new health objectives focus on them. As shown in Figure 1, these lifestyles affect health, wellness, and physical fitness. The double-headed arrow between health/wellness and physical fitness illustrates the interaction between these factors. Physical fitness is important to health and wellness development and vice versa.

The major causes of early death have shifted from infectious diseases to chronic lifestyle-related conditions. Scientific advances and improvements in medicine and health care have dramatically reduced the incidence of infectious diseases over the past 100 years (see Table 1). Diphtheria and polio, both major causes of death in the 20th century, have been virtually eliminated in Western culture. Smallpox was globally eradicated in 1977.

Infectious diseases have been replaced with chronic lifestyle-related conditions as the major causes of death. Four of the top seven current causes of death (heart disease, cancer, stroke, and diabetes) fall into this category. While heart disease remains the leading killer among all adults, National Cancer Institute

Medical Model The focus of the health-care system on treating illness with medicine, with little emphasis on prevention or wellness promotion.

Table 1 ▶ Major Causes of Death in the United States

Current Rank	Cause	1900 Rank	Cause
1	Heart disease	1	Pneumonia*
2	Cancer	2	Tuberculosis*
3	Respiratory disease	3	Diarrhea/enteritis*
4	Accidents	4	Heart disease
5	Stroke	5	Stroke
6	Alzheimer disease	6	Liver disease
7	Diabetes	7	Injuries
8	Influenza/pneumonia*	8	Cancer
9	Kidney disease	9	Senility
10	Suicide	10	Diphtheria*

*Infectious diseases: The only diseases among the top 10 that are primarily infectious in nature today are influenza/pneumonia
Source: Data from the Centers for Disease Control and Prevention (CDC).

statistics indicate that cancer is the leading cause of death for adults under the age of 85. Death rates have recently decreased for 8 of the top 10 causes of death. The incidence of kidney disease was unchanged, and suicide increased 1 percent.

HIV, formerly in the top 10, has dropped from this list primarily due to the development of new treatments and prevention methods. It remains eighth among those aged 25–44. Many conditions in the top 10 list are sometimes referred to as chronic, or lifestyle-related, because healthy lifestyles can help reduce associated risks.

Healthy lifestyles are critical to wellness. Unhealthy lifestyles are the principal causes of modern-day illnesses, but healthy lifestyles (on the other hand) can result in the improved feeling of wellness that is critical to optimal health. The CDC uses the term *health-related quality of life* to describe the wellness benefits of healthy lifestyles. This well-being, or wellness, is associated with social, emotional/mental, spiritual, and physical functioning. Being physically active and eating well are two healthy lifestyles that can improve well-being and add years of quality living. Many of the healthy lifestyles associated with good physical fitness and optimal wellness will be discussed in detail later. The Healthy Lifestyle Questionnaire in Lab 2A gives you the opportunity to assess your current lifestyles.

Regular physical activity, sound nutrition, and stress management are priority healthy lifestyles. Three of the lifestyles listed in Figure 1 are considered to be priority

healthy lifestyles: engaging in regular **physical activity** or **exercise,** eating well, and managing stress. There are several reasons for placing priority on these lifestyles. First, they affect the lives of all people. Second, they are lifestyles in which large numbers of people can make improvement. Finally, modest changes in these behaviors can make dramatic improvements in individual and public health.

The other healthy lifestyles listed in Figure 1 are also important for good health. The reason they are not emphasized as priority lifestyles is that they do not affect everyone as much as the first three do. Many healthy lifestyles will be discussed in the Concepts that follow, but the focus is on the priority healthy lifestyles because virtually all people can achieve positive wellness benefits if they adopt them.

The "actual causes" of most deaths are due to unhealthy lifestyles. As illustrated in Table 1, chronic diseases (e.g., heart diseases, cancer) are the direct causes of most deaths in our society. Public health experts have used epidemiological statistics to show that unhealthy lifestyles such as tobacco use, inactivity, and poor eating actually cause the chronic diseases and for this reason are referred to as the "actual causes of death." A recent report of the National Research Council and the National Academy of Medicine indicates that inactivity and poor nutrition (combined) are the leading actual cause of death in the United States (see Table 2). Tobacco use,

Table 2 ▶ Actual Causes of Death in the United States

Rank	Actual Cause	Percentage of Deaths
1	Inactivity/poor nutrition	18
2	Tobacco use	15
3	Alcohol misuse	3
4	Medical errors	3
5	Toxic agents	2.5
6	Microbial agents	2
7	Firearms	1.5
8	Sexual behavior	1
9	Motor vehicles	1
10	Illicit drug use	<1

Note: Other factors account for the remaining 52 percent of the causes.
Source: National Research Council and Institute of Medicine (2015)

Technology Update

Online Health Information: Podcasts

Numerous health agencies post short audio podcasts to provide updated and credible information to professionals and consumers on health, wellness, and fitness topics. However, popular podcasts about "health" may not always be the most accurate or appropriate; thus, when searching online, pair your search with credible organizations to find better information. Examples of agencies with credible podcasts include the American Council on Exercise (ACE), the Centers for Disease Control and Prevention (CDC), the Food and Drug Administration (FDA), Johns Hopkins Medical Center, the *Journal of the American Medical Association,* Mayo Clinic, Medscape, National Public Radio (NPR), USA.gov, and the U.S. Department of Agriculture (USDA).

Do you think you would use podcasts for health-related information? Why or why not?

ACTIVITY

previously the leading cause of actual death, is now the second leading cause. Tobacco use has decreased over the past several decades, but poor dietary habits and lack of adequate exercise have increased. Destructive habits (tobacco use, alcohol misuse, illicit drug use, and unsafe sexual behavior) account for 20 percent, factors related to health care (medical errors and microbial agents) account for 5 percent, and accidents (firearms, toxic agents, motor vehicles) account for 5 percent of premature deaths in the United States. Most of these are determinants over which you have considerable control.

Using Self-Management Skills

Manage your personal actions and interactions to overcome barriers to healthy living. There are many reasons why people with good intentions fail to be active or fail to adhere to healthy lifestyles. In this Concept, you learned that environments can either enhance or inhibit healthy behaviors. However, by doing some research and planning ahead, you can take steps to address barriers and challenges imposed by your environment and become physically active.

- **Find convenient and safe places to be physically active.** Safety is a major deterrent to walking and biking for some people, but many communities have websites that provide information about safe places to participate in sports and active recreation. Search online for information about

bike, walking, or jogging paths and well-lighted parks for evening activity.

- **Consider walking inside when the weather is bad.** Extremely cold or hot weather can be a significant barrier to being active. However, malls and "big-box" stores can be alternative places to walk that are safe and climate controlled.

- **Advocate for safe and healthy environments.** Taking control over your health often necessitates being an advocate for change. The results may not be immediate, but advocating for parks or biking paths can lead to better opportunities for physical activity. Requesting healthier food choices at restaurants or grocery stores can also lead to gradual shifts in what is promoted or available.

Use self-management skills to adopt and sustain a variety of healthy lifestyles. Consider how to apply these specific self-management skills to help take positive actions related to health, wellness, and fitness.

- **Manage your time effectively.** Lack of time due to busy school and work schedules may make being physically active and eating healthfully a challenge. This makes learning how to manage your time even more important. Time management is a skill that can be learned to help you manage your lifestyle *and* your stress. In a later Concept, you will learn specific techniques for managing time.

- **Get help and social support from friends, family, and/or experts.** Research shows that support from others can be helpful to eating healthfully, performing regular exercise, and adopting other healthy lifestyles. However, friends and family may not know of your interests or values regarding health and wellness. Thus, it is important to manage your personal interactions. Also, sometimes the help of an expert may be necessary. Specific information about finding help is provided in many of the Concepts in this edition.

- **Build knowledge by learning the facts.** There is considerable misinformation on the Internet and in the media, so it is important to be an informed consumer. Too often people fall prey to health fraud because they lack good information. Learning facts can help you "do it right" and avoid failure resulting from trying things that are not based on solid research.

Physical Activity Generally considered to be a broad term used to describe all forms of large muscle movements, including sports, dance, games, work, lifestyle activities, and exercise for fitness. Although they have slightly different definitions, *exercise* and *physical activity* are sometimes used interchangeably to make reading less repetitive and more interesting.

Exercise Physical activity done for the purpose of getting physically fit.

Strategies for Action: Lab Information

Self-assessments of lifestyles will help you determine areas in which you may need changes to promote optimal health, wellness, and fitness. The Healthy Lifestyle Questionnaire in Lab 2A will help you assess your current lifestyle behaviors to determine if they are contributing positively to your health, wellness, and fitness. As you continue your study, refer back to this questionnaire to see if your lifestyles have changed.

Suggested Resources and Readings

The websites for the following sources can be accessed by searching online for the organization, program, or title listed. Specific scientific references are available at the end of this edition of *Concepts of Fitness and Wellness*.

- Centers for Disease Control and Prevention. *Impact of the Built Environment on Health* (pdf).
- Centers for Disease Control and Prevention. *Health-Related Quality of Life*. Atlanta. Website
- *Healthy People 2020.* Social Determinants of Health. Website.
- Johns Hopkins Medicine. PodMed Health and Medicine Podcasts. Online Resource.
- National Library of Medicine. Genetic Ancestry Testing. Online Resource.
- National Center for Health Statistics. (2017). *Health, United States, 2016: With Chartbook on Long-term Trends in Health*. Hyattsville, MD: USDHHS. pdf.
- National Research Council and Institute of Medicine. *U.S. Health in International Perspective: Shorter Lives, Poorer Health*. Institute of Medicine. Washington, DC: National Academies Press. pdf.
- National Research Council and Institute of Medicine. (2015). *Measuring the Risks and Causes of Premature Death*. Washington, DC: National Academies Press. Online Summary.

Lab 2A Healthy Lifestyle Questionnaire

Name	Section	Date

Purpose: To assess the current status of various lifestyle behaviors and to help you make decisions concerning good health and wellness for the future.

Procedures

1. Complete the Healthy Lifestyle Questionnaire on the next page by answering "Almost Never," "Sometimes," or "Almost Always" to each of the questions. If your behavior is not consistent, or you feel you are between the extremes, then choose the middle option ("Sometimes").
2. For each of the 10 lifestyle habits, sum the scores in the adjacent Total box.
3. Sum the 10 composite scores to create a Total Lifestyle Rating.
4. Record your scores in the Results section below.
5. Use the Healthy Lifestyle Rating Chart to determine your ratings. Add the ratings to the Results section.
6. Answer the question in the Conclusions and Implications section.

Results

Lifestyle Behavior	Score	Rating
Physical Activity Habits		
Nutrition Habits		
Stress-Management Habits		
Destructive Habits		
Safety Habits		
First Aid Habits		
Health Habits		
Medical Habits		
Consumer Habits		
Environmental Habits		
Total Score		

Healthy Lifestyle Rating Chart

Habit Rating	Score
Good Lifestyle	5–6
Neutral Lifestyle	3–4
Needs improvement	1–2

Total Score Rating	
Good Lifestyle	46–60
Neutral Lifestyle	30–45
Needs improvement	<30

Note: Your scores on the Healthy Lifestyle Questionnaire should be interpreted carefully. The statements are intended to provide a simple self-evaluation and are not designed as a screening or diagnostic tool. The various lifestyle behaviors pose different types of risks. For example, using tobacco or abusing drugs has immediate and significant negative effects on health and wellness, whereas other health lifestyles and skills, such as knowing first aid, may have subtler and less direct effects. Therefore, it is important not to compare scores on the different scales. The goal is to evaluate your overall profile and identify areas where you are doing well and areas that may need improvement.

Conclusions and Implications: In the space below, summarize the overall status of your lifestyle behaviors and indicate your strengths (areas where you are adopting healthy lifestyles) and concerns (areas where you may need to improve).

25

Healthy Lifestyle Questionnaire

Directions: Use the following ratings to determine your habits: 1 = Almost Never, 2 = Sometimes, 3 = Almost Always. Place that number in the box to the right of each question. Sum the two numbers to get a score for each lifestyle habit. Sum the lifestyle habit scores to get a total lifestyle rating.

Physical Activity Habits

1. I perform physical activity most days of the week (or vigorous 3 days). ☐

2. I perform some exercises for muscle fitness (at least 2 days a week). ☐ ☐ +

Nutrition Habits

3. I consume 4–5 servings of fruits and vegetables per day. ☐ ☐

4. I monitor the amount of fat in my diet. ☐ +

Stress-Management Habits

5. I am able to identify situations in daily life that cause stress. ☐ ☐

6. I take time out during the day to relax and recover from daily stress. ☐ +

Destructive Habits

7. I do *not* smoke or use other tobacco products. ☐ ☐

8. I do *not* binge drink or abuse alcohol. ☐ +

Safety Habits

9. I use seat belts and adhere to the speed limit when I drive. ☐ ☐

10. I avoid risky environments and situations. ☐ +

First Aid Habits

11. I can perform CPR if called on in an emergency. ☐ ☐

12. I can perform basic first aid if needed in an emergency. ☐ +

Health Habits

13. I brush my teeth at least twice a day and floss at least once a day. ☐ ☐

14. I get an adequate amount of sleep each night. ☐ +

Medical Habits

15. I do regular self-exams and have regular medical checkups. ☐ ☐

16. I seek and follow medical advice when needed and prescribed. ☐ +

Consumer Habits

17. I read product labels and make careful decisions before I buy. ☐ ☐

18. I avoid using questionable products or programs. ☐ +

Environmental Habits

19. I recycle paper, glass, and aluminum. ☐ ☐

20. I look for ways to conserve energy and protect the environment. ☐ =

Total Lifestyle Rating ☐

Note: These 10 habits capture only a sample of important lifestyle behaviors. A number of other potentially harmful behaviors are intentionally excluded due to their personal nature (such as the use and abuse of drugs, sexual practices, drinking and driving). Use the framework from this lab to think critically about your lifestyle behaviors and how you can work to improve them.

Self-Management Skills for Health Behavior Change

LEARNING OBJECTIVES

After completing the study of this Concept, you will be able to:

▶ Identify and define the five stages of change and explain how the stages relate to making lifestyle changes.

▶ Describe the four key factors that influence health behaviors, describe components in each category, and explain how the factors relate to stages of change.

▶ Identify and describe the self-management skills that predispose and enable you to change and to reinforce changes once you have made them.

▶ Identify and describe the six steps in self-planning and explain how they can be used to make personal plans for behavior change.

▶ Conduct self-assessments of your current stages for health behaviors and your self-management skills for making health behavior change.

Learning and regularly using self-management skills can help you adopt and maintain healthy lifestyles throughout life.

©JGI/Getty Images

Why it Matters!

Nearly everyone values good health, wellness, and fitness, but many people struggle to adopt the lifestyle patterns needed to achieve these outcomes. The focus in this Concept is on introducing different self-management skills that are needed to adopt and maintain healthy lifestyles. You may be good at some but not at others; this information will help you identify personal strengths and weaknesses. However, it is important to understand that self-management skills (like any skill) must be practiced and refined if they are to be useful. The labs and activities in this Concept (and others) provide opportunities to build these skills. However, it is up to you to learn from your experiences, apply the information, and adopt a long-term perspective for health behavior change that ultimately leads to healthy living throughout life.

Understanding Stages of Change

Many adults want to make lifestyle changes but find changes hard to make. Results of several national public opinion polls show that adults often have difficulty making desired lifestyle changes. Examples include those who believe that physical activity is important but do not get enough exercise to promote good health, those who have tried numerous times to lose weight but have failed, those who know good nutrition is good for health but do not eat well, and those who feel stress on a regular basis but have not found a way to become less stressed. Changes in other lifestyles are frequently desired but often not accomplished. While most people value health, many still seek shortcuts instead of learning how to adopt healthier lifestyles (see "In the News").

Practicing one healthy lifestyle does not mean you will practice another, though adopting one healthy behavior often leads to the adoption of another. College students are more likely to participate in regular physical activity than are older adults. However, they are also much more likely to eat poorly and abuse alcohol. Many young women adopt low-fat diets to avoid weight gain and smoke because they mistakenly believe that smoking will contribute to long-term weight maintenance. These examples illustrate the fact that practicing one healthy lifestyle does not ensure **adherence** to another. However, there is evidence that making one lifestyle change often makes it easier to make other changes. For example, smokers who have started regular physical activity programs often see improvements in fitness and general well-being and decide to stop smoking.

People progress—forward and backward—through several stages of change when making lifestyle changes. The widely used Transtheoretical Model suggests that lifestyle changes occur in at least five different stages, called **stages of change.** The stages of change model (see Figure 1) has been applied to many different lifestyles. For

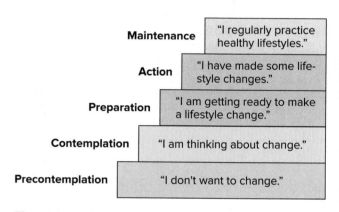

Figure 1 ▶ Stages of lifestyle change.

In the News

Myths and Medical Conspiracy Theories

There is considerable misinformation about health and medicine in society, fueled in part by web posts and media reports that popularize health myths or that reinforce unsubstantiated medical conspiracies. A prominent medical research study revealed that many Americans believe these conspiracy theories and have little trust in health information. For example, many people believe that agencies like the Food and Drug Administration intentionally keep information and medical treatments away from the public rather than serve and protect citizens. This misinformation adds to the confusion about what and whom to believe. (See Suggested Resources and Readings.)

Why do some people choose to believe in miracle cures and question the science related to health and medicine? How can you ensure that you get accurate health information?

example, smokers who are not considering quitting smoking are in the *pre-contemplation* stage, whereas those who are considering the need to change

are in the *contemplation* stage. These stages are very distinct, as is the next stage, *preparation*, which is characterized by specific efforts at changing. Individuals who have bought a nicotine patch or a book about smoking cessation are in the preparation stage; they have moved beyond contemplation and are preparing to take action. The *action* stage occurs when the smoker makes a change in behavior, even a small one, such as cutting back on the number of cigarettes smoked. The fifth stage, *maintenance,* is reached when a person finally stops smoking for a relatively long time (e.g., six months).

Although the stages model can be applied to any behavior, let's consider an example related to physical activity habits. Individuals who are totally sedentary may be in the precontemplation stage or in the contemplation stage if they are thinking about becoming active. A person at the preparation stage may have bought a pair of walking shoes and appropriate clothing for activity. Those who have started activity, even if infrequent, are at the stage of action. Those who have been exercising regularly for at least six months are at the stage of maintenance.

Whether the lifestyle is positive or negative, people move from one stage to another in an upward or a downward direction. Individuals in the action stage may move on to maintenance or revert to contemplation. Smokers who succeed in quitting permanently report having stopped and started dozens of times before reaching lifetime maintenance. Similarly, those attempting to adopt positive lifestyles, such as eating well, often move back and forth from one stage to another, depending on their life circumstances.

Once maintenance is attained, relapse is less likely to occur. Although complete relapse is possible, it is generally less likely after the maintenance stage is reached. At the maintenance stage, the behavior has been integrated into a personal lifestyle, and it becomes easier to sustain. For example, a person who has been active for years does not have to undergo the same thought processes as a beginning exerciser—the behavior becomes automatic and habitual. Similarly, a nonsmoker is not tempted to smoke in the same way as a person who is trying to quit.

Importance of Self-Management Skills

Learning self-management skills can help you alter factors that lead to healthy lifestyle change. Experts have determined that people who practice healthy lifestyles possess certain characteristics. Fortunately, these characteristics are attainable and the skills can be learned. The various skills needed to adopt and maintain healthy lifestyles are referred

to as "self-management skills" since they influence the way that you manage your behaviors. In this edition, 14 different skills are emphasized. Each is described in Table 1.

It takes time to change unhealthy lifestyles. People in Western cultures are used to seeing things happen quickly. We flip a switch, and the lights come on. We want food quickly, and thousands of fast food restaurants provide it. The expectation that we should have what we want when we want it has led us to expect instantaneous changes in health, wellness, and fitness. Unfortunately, there is no quick way to health. There is no pill that can reverse the effects of a lifetime of sedentary living, poor eating, or tobacco use. Changing your lifestyle is the key. But lifestyles that have been practiced for years are not easy to change. Environmental factors also influence options for healthy living (see "A Closer Look"). Learning self-management skills helps you overcome barriers and make positive lifestyle changes, but only if you implement them and practice them.

Blue Zones and Personal Responsibility

Lifestyles have a big impact on both quality and quantity of life. For his book *Blue Zones,* Dan Buettner researched communities across the world that had higher life expectancies and quality of life compared to other communities. The common characteristics in these healthy communities—including diet and activity—were identified and described as being important for healthy lifestyles. Although a healthy environment is important, each person ultimately has to make wise choices and manage his or her own lifestyle, regardless of the setting. (See Suggested Resources and Readings.)

Does your community provide a supportive environment for your health behaviors? Does the environment dictate your ability to be healthy, or is it your personal responsibility?

Adherence Adopting and sticking with healthy behaviors, such as regular physical activity or sound nutrition, as part of your lifestyle.

Stage of Change The level of motivational readiness to adopt a specific health behavior.

Table 1 ▶ Key Self-Management Skills

Overcoming Barriers	Ability to overcome problems and challenges in adopting or maintaining healthy lifestyles. By conquering challenges, you learn skills that help you overcome other barriers.
Building Self-Confidence and Motivation	Ability to act on your intentions and the discipline needed to stick to them.
Balancing Attitudes	Ability to balance positive and negative attitudes. Developing more favorable and optimistic outlooks can help you adhere to healthy lifestyles.
Building Knowledge and Changing Beliefs	Ability to interpret and apply information about health, wellness, and fitness. Knowledge doesn't always change beliefs, but awareness of the facts can play a role in achieving good health.
Goal-Setting Skills	Ability to establish (and focus on) what you want to achieve in the future.
Self-Assessment Skills	Ability to assess your own health, wellness, and fitness and to learn to interpret your own self-assessment results.
Self-Monitoring Skills	Ability to monitor behavior and to keep records. Many people think they adhere to healthy lifestyles but, in reality, do not. Self-monitoring gives you a true picture of your behavior and helps you track progress over time.
Self-Planning Skills	Ability to prepare and follow a plan for adopting or maintaining healthy lifestyle habits.
Performance Skills	Ability to learn lifestyle and physical skills needed to be physically active and healthy. These skills can help you feel confident and more successful in your efforts.
Coping Skills	Ability to handle change. This set of skills helps you see situations in different perspectives and have more control over your lifestyle.
Consumer Skills	Ability to understand and interpret health information and make sound decisions related to health, wellness, and fitness.
Time-Management Skills	Ability to devote time to the behaviors and activities that are most important to your personal health, wellness, and fitness.
Using Social Support	Ability to seek out and obtain support from others. By learning to find support, you are more likely to sustain motivation and drive when faced with challenges.
Preventing Relapse	Ability to return to healthy lifestyles despite challenges and setbacks. It is normal to have up and down phases, but this skill helps you avoid long-term relapses and return to healthy lifestyles when faced with barriers.

Making Lifestyle Changes

Various factors have been found to influence the adoption and maintenance of healthy lifestyles. A variety of theories have been proposed to understand health behavior (e.g., Social Cognitive Theory, Self-Determination Theory, Theory of Planned Behavior, Theory of Reasoned Action). Each theory offers some unique attributes or concepts, but they share many of the same components. The previously mentioned Transtheoretical Model integrates elements from multiple theories and can be viewed as a "meta-theory." The distinction between a "theory" and a "model" is important in this case. The Transtheoretical Model does not provide a new explanation of behavior (a theory) but rather a guide or map that makes using and applying the theories easier (a model). The unique advantage of the Transtheoretical Model is that it demonstrates that behavior is influenced in different ways depending on the stage of change a person has reached.

Another meta-theory used to explain the challenges of changing health behaviors is the Social-Ecological Model.

This model also integrates multiple theories, but a key point in this model is that a person's behavior is strongly influenced by the nature of the environment in which she or he lives. If you are in a supportive social environment and have access to healthy foods and activity resources, adopting healthier lifestyles is easier.

You do not need a thorough understanding of the theories and models, but you should be aware of the basic principles. Concepts from both the Transtheoretical and Social-Ecological models have been combined to provide a simpler way to understand the various factors that influence behavior. The various factors can be classified as **personal, predisposing, enabling,** and **reinforcing factors.** Personal factors refer to personal characteristics or conditions that may make it easier or more difficult to make change. Predisposing factors help initiate behavior change—moving toward contemplation or even preparation. Enabling factors help those in contemplation or preparation take a step toward action. Reinforcing factors move people from action to maintenance and help those in maintenance stay there. As depicted in Figure 2, there is a general progression in the relevance of factors across the various stages of change.

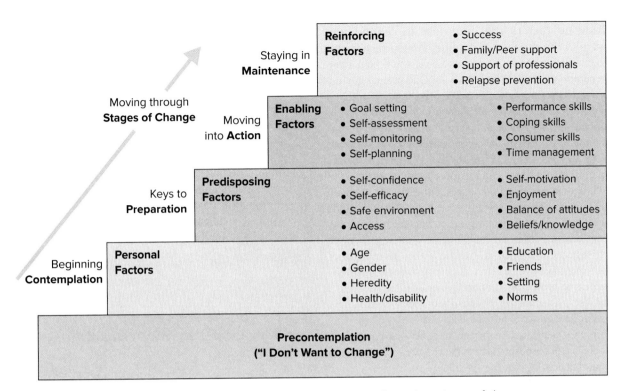

Staying in **Maintenance**	**Reinforcing Factors**	• Success • Family/Peer support • Support of professionals • Relapse prevention	
Moving into **Action**	**Enabling Factors**	• Goal setting • Self-assessment • Self-monitoring • Self-planning	• Performance skills • Coping skills • Consumer skills • Time management
Keys to **Preparation**	**Predisposing Factors**	• Self-confidence • Self-efficacy • Safe environment • Access	• Self-motivation • Enjoyment • Balance of attitudes • Beliefs/knowledge
Beginning **Contemplation**	**Personal Factors**	• Age • Gender • Heredity • Health/disability	• Education • Friends • Setting • Norms

Moving through **Stages of Change**

Precontemplation ("I Don't Want to Change")

Figure 2 ▶ Relevant factors and self-management skills to progress across the various stages of change.

Personal factors affect health behaviors but are often out of your personal control. Age, gender, heredity, social status, and current health and fitness levels are all personal factors that affect your health behaviors. Age effects are exemplified by differences in health behaviors across the lifespan. For example, young adults are more likely to smoke and drink excessively but to be more physically active than older adults. Gender differences are illustrated by the fact that women use health services more often than men. Women are more likely than men to have identified a primary care doctor and are more likely to participate in regular health screenings. Heredity can directly and indirectly influence lifestyle behaviors. For example, some people are more prone to addictions and hereditary predisposition may alter beliefs or attitudes about health and wellness.

Personal factors also capture other conditions that influence ability to make change. People with little education are more likely to have health problems and make less money. People with limited income often have less access to health care and healthy foods. Social interactions also affect your ability to change. People who have friends who practice healthy habits have an easier time adopting healthy behaviors than people who have friends or who have social interactions with people who practice destructive health behaviors. No matter what your circumstances are, you can take responsibility to change your health behaviors. Learning about predisposing, enabling, and reinforcing factors (see Figure 2) can help you overcome personal or social circumstances and help you to make the most of your efforts to change your lifestyles to promote health, wellness, and fitness.

Access to healthy foods is an important predisposing factor for good nutrition.
©Nicolas McComber/Getty Images

Personal Factors Factors, such as age or gender, related to healthy lifestyle adherence but not typically under personal control.

Predisposing Factors Factors that make you more likely to adopt a healthy lifestyle, such as participation in regular physical activity, as part of your normal routine.

Enabling Factors Factors that help you carry out your healthy lifestyle plan.

Reinforcing Factors Factors that provide encouragement to maintain healthy lifestyles, such as physical activity, for a lifetime.

Predisposing factors are important in getting you started with the process of change. Predisposing factors refer to characteristics, attributes, and beliefs that help a person prepare to adopt healthy behaviors. One particularly important predisposing factor is self-motivation (also called intrinsic motivation). People with intrinsic motivation tend to have greater levels of **self-confidence** and **self-efficacy**—terms that both have to do with having positive perceptions about your own abilities. People with positive self-perceptions are more predisposed to take action because they are confident in their ability to make behavior changes. Other factors that help you feel you are able to engage in a healthy behavior include easy access and a safe environment. For example, people who have easy access to exercise equipment at home or the workplace or who have a place to exercise within 10 minutes of home are more likely to be active than those who do not. Similarly, access to healthy food options is critical for adopting a healthy diet. A supportive physical and social environment can also make it easier to adopt healthy habits.

There are specific self-management skills that can help a person change predisposing factors (see Figure 2). Learning to overcome barriers in one lifestyle can build your confidence in being able to make other changes. Gaining knowledge and developing more favorable attitudes  can also help in adopting healthy lifestyles. Table 2 provides specific lifestyle examples of the various predisposing factors to help you understand how to apply them to your own lifestyle.

Enabling factors move you from the beginning stages of change to action and maintenance. Enabling factors refer to a range of self-management skills that help you follow through with decisions to make changes in behaviors. As shown in Figure 2, the ability to assess needs, set goals, make plans, and monitor progress are important in helping moving into the action stage on a particular behavior. Specific performance and consumer skills may be needed for some behaviors while coping and time-management skills can help you stick to your intended goals and plans. Table 3 provides illustrative examples for each of these enabling factors, and the labs in each

Concept provide opportunities for you to directly apply various self-management skills to your lifestyle.

Reinforcing factors help you adhere to lifestyle changes. Once you have reached the action or maintenance stage, it is important to stay at this high level. Reinforcing factors help you stick with a behavior change (see Figure 2).

Social support from family, peers, and health professionals can be an especially important reinforcing factor. There are, however, different kinds of support and some are more helpful than others. A supportive person might ask, "How can I help you meet your goals?" This type of support helps you take control of your own behavior and is not viewed as overly

---

HELP Health is available to Everyone for a Lifetime, and it's Personal

Do Your Friends Support or Hinder Your Efforts to Adopt Healthy Lifestyles?

Learning to find positive social support is an important self-management skill. Studies of social connections over time have shown that people are more likely to become obese if they have obese friends. Similar relationships have been shown among spouses. Researchers suggest that health behaviors tend to be shared within social groups, resulting in shared outcomes. (See link in Suggested Resources and Readings.)

Do your friends help you maintain a healthy lifestyle or do they make it more difficult to do so?

Self-Confidence The belief that you can be successful at something (for example, the belief that you can be successful in sports and physical activities and can improve your physical fitness).

Self-Efficacy Confidence that you can perform a specific task (a type of specific self-confidence).

Table 2 ▶ Lifestyle Examples of Self-Management Skills related to Predisposing Factors

Overcoming Barriers	You might find it hard to be physically active in the winter or bad weather. However, you can dress more appropriately or find alternate ways to be active indoors.
Building Confidence and Motivation	You may be tempted by snack foods and candy provided by coworkers. Resisting these foods takes discipline, but it builds confidence and motivation that helps keep focus on long-term goals.
Balancing Attitudes	You might have negative attitudes about physical activity from sports or experiences in school. Rather than focusing on negative memories or attitudes, focus on positive outcomes (e.g., enjoyment, social interactions, or how it helps you feel). Shifting the balance to positive attitudes can help in making change.
Building Knowledge and Changing Beliefs	You may doubt that eating habits influence health and wellness, but learning about nutrition and healthy lifestyles can increase knowledge and awareness and provide the basis for changes in beliefs and behavior.

Table 3 ▶ Lifestyle Examples of Self-Management Skills related to Enabling Factors	
Goal-Setting Skills	You decide to try to lose body fat. Setting a goal of losing 50 pounds makes success unlikely. Setting a more reasonable, behavioral goal of restricting 200 calories a day or expending 200 calories more each day for several weeks is a better strategy.
Self-Assessment Skills	You want to know your health strengths and weaknesses. The best process is to select good tests and self-administer them. Practicing the assessments in these Concepts will help you become good at self-assessment.
Self-Monitoring Skills	You can't understand why you are not losing weight despite your efforts. Keeping records may show that you are not counting all the calories you consume. Learning to keep records of progress contributes to adherence
Self-Planning Skills	You want to become more active, eat better, and manage stress. Self-planning skills will help in planning programs to meet different needs.
Performance Skills	You may avoid physical activity because you do not have the physical skills equal to those of peers. Learning sports or other motor skills allows you to choose to be active.
Coping Skills	You may often feel stressed and anxious. Learning stress-management skills, such as relaxation, can help you cope. Like all skills, stress-management skills must be practiced to be effective.
Consumer Skills	You may avoid seeking medical help when you are sick and instead take an unproven remedy. Learning consumer skills provides knowledge for making sound medical decisions.
Time-Management Skills	You want to spend more quality time with family and friends. Monitoring your time can help you reallocate it in ways that are more consistent with personal priorities.

controlling. However, other forms of feedback may be perceived as applying pressure and can hinder attempts to make healthy changes. For example, a statement such as "you are not going to get anywhere if you don't stick to your diet" will often be perceived as applying pressure. If you want to help friends and family make behavior changes, avoid applying pressure and attempt to provide positive forms of support. Learning how to seek and accept effective forms of social support from others is important for sustaining healthy lifestyles.

If you change a behavior and experience success, this makes you want to keep doing the behavior. However, if attempts to change a behavior result in failure, you may conclude that the behavior does not work and give up on it. Experts in behavior change have also determined that learning to overcome short-term setbacks or challenges is critical to long-term success. This self-management skill is often called *relapse prevention* since it is important to avoid reverting back to bad habits. With practice, you can learn to anticipate challenging situations that may make healthy lifestyles difficult. You can also learn to accept minor setbacks as temporary and return back to positive lifestyles with new insights. Table 4 provides specific lifestyle examples of how social support and relapse prevention can help to reinforce behavior change.

Adopting healthy lifestyle habits requires discipline and effort.
©Photodisc/Getty Images

Table 4 ▶ Lifestyle Examples of Self-Management Skills related to Reinforcing Factors	
Using Social Support	You have developed a plan to be more active. Friends encourage the change and help develop a schedule that will allow and encourage regular activity.
Preventing Relapse	You just quit smoking. To prevent relapse, you avoid situations where there is more temptation or pressure to smoke.

Using Self-Management Skills

Lifestyle change requires a personal commitment and the use of various self-management skills. As indicated in Figure 1, change occurs stage by stage and some behaviors may be harder for you to change than others. You may be in "action" or "maintenance" in some behaviors, but be at earlier "precontemplation" or "preparation" stages for others. Different skills are important, depending on your current stage and the lifestyle behavior you are attempting to change.

Self-planning is a self-management skill that requires the use of other self-management skills. The ability to set up and monitor your own lifestyle plans (i.e., self-planning skills) is particularly important in helping you take action or sustain your commitment to behavior change over time. A six-step self-planning process is introduced here to assist you in planning for lifestyle change (see Table 5). As you will note, several other self-management skills, including self-assessment, self-monitoring, and goal setting, are used within this process. Labs in each Concept will allow you to practice these skills and in the final Concept, after

Technology Update

Health Apps

Rapid changes in technology have created a huge market for customized applications (apps). There are apps for almost everything, including apps that help you manage and organize your lifestyle and that provide supportive prompts and reminders. Although these health-related apps offer consumers new ways to monitor their behavior, the effectiveness of most of these tools hasn't been established yet.

How useful are these types of health-related apps for promoting and maintaining healthy lifestyles? Are they simply fun technology, or do they support health behavior change?

you have studied a variety of concepts and self-management skills, you will develop a personal plan for several healthy lifestyles.

Table 5 ▶ Self-Planning Skills		
Self-Planning	**Description**	**Self-Management Skills**
1. Clarifying reasons	Knowing the general reasons for changing a behavior helps you determine the type of behavior change that is most important for you at a specific point in time. For example, if losing weight is the reason for wanting to change behavior, altering eating and activity patterns will be emphasized.	Results of the Self-Management Skills Questionnaire (Lab 3A) will help you determine which self-management skills you use regularly and the ones you might need to develop.
2. Identifying needs	Self-assessment is required to identify your needs. If you know your strengths and weaknesses, you can plan to build on your strengths and overcome weaknesses.	You will get the opportunity to practice *self-assessment* as you complete the lab activities. Examples include fitness, activity, dietary, stress, and attitude self-assessments.
3. Setting personal goals	Goal setting helps you develop a blueprint for planning.	In subsequent Concepts, you will have the opportunity to practice *setting goals* in a variety of healthy lifestyle plans as you complete the lab activities.
4. Selecting program components	A personal plan includes the specific program components that will meet your needs and goals. Examples include meal plans for nutrition and specific activities in your physical activity plan.	Several self-management skills, including *consumer skills, performance skills,* and *building knowledge,* will aid you in selecting program components.
5. Writing your plan	Your written plan provides "what" and "when" details. What are your going to do and when are you going to do it?	Effectively *managing time* is especially useful in preparing your written plan. You will get an opportunity to refine time-management skills in a lab activity later in this edition.
6. Evaluating progress	Once you have enacted your plan, you will know what works and what does not.	*Self-monitoring* is used in keeping records (logs) of your healthy behaviors (e.g., exercise, diet). Periodically *self-assessing* helps you determine if goals are met and how to modify the plan to make it better. You will get the opportunity to practice both as you complete the lab activities.

Step 1: Clarifying Reasons

Clarifying your reasons for behavior change is the first step in program planning. People at the precontemplation stage are not considering a change in behavior; they see no need. It's when they reach the contemplation stage that they consider changes in behavior. One of the most common and most powerful reasons for contemplating a change in a lifestyle is the recommendation of a doctor, often after a visit associated with an illness. Other common reasons are to improve personal appearance, lose weight, increase energy levels, improve the ability to perform daily tasks, and improve quality of life (wellness). Identifying your reasons for wanting to change helps you determine which behaviors to change first and helps you establish specific goals. Reflect on your reasons for wanting to make lifestyle changes before moving on to step 2.

Step 2: Identifying Needs

Self-assessments are useful in establishing personal needs, planning your program, and evaluating your progress. In the labs for this Concept (and others that follow), you will learn how to complete simple self-assessments of your behaviors and health/wellness status. The results of these assessments help you build personal profiles for a variety of health behaviors that can be used as the basis for program planning. With practice, self-assessments become more accurate. For this reason, it is important to repeat self-assessments and to pay careful attention to the procedures for performing them. If questions arise, get a professional opinion rather than making an error.

Periodic self-assessments can help determine if you are meeting health, wellness, and fitness standards and making progress toward personal health goals. When performed properly, self-assessments help you determine if you have met your goals and if you are meeting health standards (e.g., meeting health fitness standards, eating appropriate amounts of nutrients). Self-assessments also offer a measure of independence and can help you avoid unnecessary and expensive tests. They serve as a screening procedure to determine if you need professional assistance. However, because self-assessments may not be as accurate as tests by health and medical professionals, it is wise to have periodic tests by an expert to see if your self-assessments are accurate.

Self-assessments also have the advantage of consistent error rather than variable error. The best type of assessments are done by highly qualified experts using precise instruments. Following directions and practicing assessment techniques will reduce error significantly. Still, errors will occur. One advantage of a self-assessment is that the person doing the assessment is always the same—you. Even if you make an error in a self-assessment, it is likely to be consistent over time, especially if you use the same equipment each time you make the assessment. For example, scales have limitations for monitoring changes in weight (and fat). But if you measure your own weight using a home scale and your measurement

always shows your weight to be 2 pounds higher than it really is, you have made a consistent error. You can determine if you are improving because you know the error exists. Variable errors are likely when different instruments are used, when different people make the assessments, and when procedures vary from test to test. Differences in scores are harder to explain with variable forms of error because they are not consistent.

Step 3: Setting Personal Goals

There are differences between short-term and long-term goals. **Short-term goals** are goals that you can accomplish in days or weeks. **Long-term goals** take longer to accomplish—sometimes months or even years.

There are differences between general goals and SMART goals. **General goals** are broad statements of your reasons for wanting to accomplish something. Examples include changing a behavior such as eating better or being more active, or changing a physical characteristic such as losing weight or getting fit. **SMART goals** are less general and have several important characteristics. SMART goals are:

Specific: A specific goal provides details, such as limiting calories to a specific number each day.

Measurable: They allow you to perform assessments before you establish your goals and again later to see if you have met them.

Attainable: They are neither too hard nor too easy. If the goal is too hard, failure is likely, which is discouraging. If the goal is too easy, it is not challenging.

Realistic: They are your personal goals. If you put in the time and effort, you should have a realistic chance of meeting them. Realistic personal goals provide motivation.

Timely: Timely goals are especially meaningful when you begin a program for making personal changes. Choosing goals that are timely helps you focus on the most salient changes that you want to make.

There are differences between behavioral and outcome goals. A **behavioral goal** is associated with something you do. An example of a specific short-term behavioral goal is *to perform*

Short-Term Goals Statements of intent to change a behavior or achieve an outcome in a period of days or weeks.

Long-Term Goals Statements of intent to change behavior or achieve a specific outcome in a period of months or years.

General Goals Broad statements of your reasons for wanting to accomplish something. Examples include changing a behavior such as eating better or being more active, or changing a physical characteristic such as losing weight or getting fit.

SMART Goals Goals that are Specific (*S*), Measurable (*M*), Attainable (*A*), Realistic (*R*), and Timely (*T*).

Behavioral Goal A statement of intent to perform a specific behavior (changing a lifestyle) for a specific period of time. An example is "I will walk for 15 minutes each morning before work."

30 minutes of brisk walking six days a week for the next two weeks. It is a behavioral goal because it refers to a behavior (something you do). An **outcome goal** is associated with a physical characteristic (e.g., lowering your body weight, lowering your blood pressure, building strength). Typically, it takes weeks or months to reach outcome goals. This is because outcome goals depend on many things other than your behavior. For example, your heredity affects your body fat and muscle development.

Different factors influence your success in meeting goals. Consider these factors when setting your goals:

- *Behavioral goals are recommended for initial goal setting.* Typically, it takes weeks or months to reach outcome goals, so they make better long-term goals than short-term goals. Focus on changing behavior and outcomes will follow.

- *Outcome goals depend on many things other than your lifestyle behavior.* For example, your heredity affects your ability to achieve an outcome goal such as achieving a certain body weight and or achieving a fitness standard. The same lifestyle change program may produce different results for different people. For this reason, goals must vary from person to person, especially outcome goals. For example, two people may establish an outcome goal of losing 5 pounds over a six-week period. Because we inherit predispositions to body composition, one person may meet the goal, while another may not, even if both strictly adhere to the same diet. A similar example can be used for fitness and physical activity. People inherit not only a predisposition to fitness but also a predisposition to benefit from training. In other words, if 10 people do the same physical activities, there will be 10 different results. One person may improve performance by 60 percent, while another might improve by only 10 percent. This makes it hard for beginners to set realistic outcome goals. Too often, people set a goal based on a comparative standard rather than on a standard that is possible for the individual to achieve in a short time.

- *Use a series of short-term goals to make progress toward long-term goals.* Once short-term behavioral goals are reached, establish new ones. After meeting a series of short-term goals, consider goal-setting guidelines for more experienced people.

Goal-setting guidelines vary depending on past history and experience with the behavior. Beginners should consider these guidelines:

- *Start with general long-term goals in mind.* It is good to have your goals in mind when you begin a program. But beginners may want to use general rather than specific long-term goals. You may choose either behavioral or outcome goals, but keep them general. For example, choose a goal of losing weight or getting fit. Getting too specific can be discouraging for reasons discussed above.

- *Focus on SMART short-term behavioral objectives.* As noted previously, an example of a specific short-term behavioral goal is *to perform 30 minutes of brisk walking six days a*

A goal to consume more fruits and vegetables is an example of a behavioral goal.
©OMG/Stockbyte/Getty Images

week for the next two weeks. It is a behavioral goal because it refers to a behavior (something you do). It is a SMART goal because it is specific, measurable, attainable, realistic, and timely. When using behavioral goals the principal factor associated with success is your willingness to give effort. No matter who you are, you can accomplish a behavioral goal if you give regular effort. This type of goal will help you keep your motivation level high and prevent you from being discouraged.

- *Avoid frequent outcome self-assessments; focus on self-monitoring of behavior.* A self-assessment before setting goals helps you set SMART goals. Self-assessments can also help you see if you have met your goals. For beginners, however, frequent self-assessment—especially of outcomes— is discouraged. For example, if the long-term goal is to lose weight, frequent weighing can be discouraging and even deceiving. Self-monitoring of behavior is encouraged, however. For the walking goal discussed earlier, keeping an activity log of your daily participation will help you comply.

Experienced people should consider these guidelines:

- *Start with SMART long-term goals.* Experience helps people realize that it takes time to meet long-term goals, especially outcome goals. Both SMART behavioral and outcome goals can be considered.

- *Use a series of short-term SMART goals (both behavioral and outcome) as a means of accomplishing long-term goals.* Even experienced people are more likely to achieve success if they realize that setting and meeting a series of SMART short-term goals is important. For example, a person who has high blood pressure (160 systolic) may set a long-term outcome goal of lowering systolic blood pressure to 120 over a period of six months. Several behavioral goals can be established for the six-month period, including taking blood pressure medication (daily), performing 30 minutes of moderate physical activity each day, and

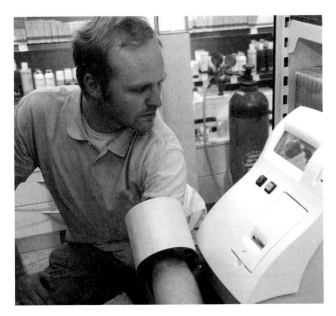

Periodic self-monitoring can help you track progress towards goals.
©wakila/Getty Images

limiting salt in the diet to less than 100 percent of the recommended dietary allowance. If the long-term outcome goal is realistic, adhering to SMART short-term behavioral goals will result in achieving the outcome goal.

- *Use self-assessments and self-monitoring to determine if you are making progress.* Self-assessments can be more frequent for the experienced. Still, avoid expecting too much, especially for outcome goals. Self-monitoring of behavioral goals is good, even for the experienced. If you commit to the behavior and stick to your plan, the outcomes will follow.

Maintenance goals are also appropriate once goals have been achieved or when improvements aren't necessary. For example, the person who lowers systolic blood pressure from 160 to 120 need not continue to lower the new healthy blood pressure. Once a healthy outcome goal has been achieved, a new outcome goal of maintaining a systolic blood pressure of 120 is appropriate. Behavioral goals will also have to be modified. For the person who has reduced blood pressure to a healthy level, medication levels might be reduced for maintenance.

Maintenance goals are appropriate in other areas as well. For example, nutrition and exercise strategies for weight maintenance will likely be different from those for losing weight. When a person reaches a healthy level of fitness (or a healthy body weight), maintenance may be the goal rather than continued improvement. You cannot improve forever; at some point, attempting to do so may be counterproductive to health.

Making improvement can motivate you to reach long-term goals. As noted earlier, setting short-term goals that are both attainable and realistic will help you reach your long-term goals. Meeting short-term goals encourages and motivates you to continue with your healthy lifestyle plan. Don't expect to set perfect goals all the time. No matter how much

self-assessing and self-monitoring you do, you may sometimes set goals too low or too high. If the goal is set too low, it is easily achieved, and a new, higher goal can be established. If the goal is set too high, you may fail to reach it, even though you have made considerable progress toward the goal.

Rather than becoming discouraged when a goal is not met, consider the improvement you have made. Improvement, no matter how small, means that you are moving toward your goal. Also, you can measure your improvement and use it to help set future goals. Of course, periodic self-assessments and good record keeping (self-monitoring) are necessary to keep track of improvements accurately.

Putting your goals in writing helps formalize them. If you don't write them down, your goals will be easy to forget. Putting goals in writing helps you establish a commitment to yourself and clearly establishes your goals. You can revise them if necessary. Written goals are not cast in concrete.

Step 4: Selecting Program Components

You can choose from many different program components to meet your goals. There are many different lifestyle changes that can be made to improve health, wellness, and fitness. They range from improving priority lifestyles (physical activity, nutrition, and stress management) to adopting positive safety and personal health habits to avoiding destructive habits. The changes you decide to make depend on your program goals. For example, if the goal is to become more fit and physically active, the program components will be the activities you choose. You will want to identify activities that match your abilities and that you enjoy. You will want to select activities that build the type of fitness you want to improve.

Other examples of program components are preparing menus for healthy eating, participating in stress-management activities, planning to attend meetings to help avoid destructive habits, and attending a series of classes to learn CPR and first aid. Preparing a list of program components that will help you meet your specific goals will prepare you for step 5, writing your plan.

Step 5: Writing Your Plan

Preparing a written plan can improve your adherence to the plan. A written plan is a pledge, or a promise, to be active. Research shows that intentions to be active are more likely to be acted on when put in writing. In the Concepts that follow, you will be given the opportunity to prepare written plans for becoming more active as well as for altering a variety of other lifestyles. A good written plan includes daily plans with scheduled times and other program details. For

Outcome Goal A statement of intent to achieve a specific test score (attainment of a specific standard) associated with good health, wellness, or fitness. An example is "I will lower my body fat by 3 percent."

Self-planning can help you implement a variety of changes to enhance health, wellness, and fitness.
©Erik Isakson/Blend Images LLC

Strategies for Action: Lab Information

The lab activity worksheets that accompany each Concept will help you learn the self-management skills necessary for behavior change. Self-assessing your current health, wellness, and fitness status, as well as a self-monitoring of your current lifestyles, can help you determine your reasons for making change and help you establish SMART goals for change. The questionnaire in Lab 3A will help you identify your stages of change for various behaviors and self-management skills you can use to change the behaviors. Like all skills, practice is necessary to improve self-management skills.

In the Concepts that follow, you will learn to self-assess a variety of outcomes (e.g., fitness, body fatness) and self-monitor behaviors (e.g., diet, physical activities, stress-management activities). In step 2 of the self-planning process, you used self-assessments to determine your needs and to help you plan your goals (step 3). Once you have tried your program, use the same self-assessments and self-monitoring strategies to evaluate the effectiveness of your program. You can see if you have met the goals you established for yourself.

example, the daily written plan for stress management could include the time of day when specific program activities are conducted (e.g., 15-minute quiet time at noon; yoga class from 5:30 to 6:30). An activity plan would include a schedule of the activities for each day of the week, including starting and finishing times and specific details concerning the activities to be performed. A dietary plan would include specific menus for each meal and between-meal snacks.

In the labs that accompany the final Concept, you will write plans for several different lifestyles. By then you will have learned a variety of self-management skills that will assist you.

Step 6: Evaluating Progress

Self-assessment and self-monitoring can help you evaluate progress. Once you have written a plan, you will want to determine your effectiveness in sticking with your plan. Keeping written records is one type of self-monitoring.

Self-monitoring is a good way to assess success in meeting behavioral goals. Keeping a dietary log or using a pedometer to keep track of steps are examples of self-monitoring. Self-assessments are a good way to see if you have met outcome goals.

Suggested Resources and Readings

The websites for the following sources can be accessed by searching online for the organization, program, or title listed. Specific scientific references are available at the end of this edition of *Concepts of Fitness and Wellness.*

- American Heart Association. Breaking Down Barriers to Fitness (online article).
- Blue Zones Project (website).
- Cash, R. M. (2016). *Self-Regulation in the Classroom.* Golden Valley, MN: Free Spirit Press.
- Centers for Disease Control and Prevention. Overcoming Barriers to Physical Activity.
- CNET Review. The Best Fitness Apps for Android and iPhone (online post).
- Glantz, K. & Rimer, B. K. (2015). *Health Behavior: Theory, Research, and Practice,* San Francisco: Jossey-Bass.
- National Public Radio. Medical conspiracy theories (online story).
- ProChange. Transtheoretical Model and Stages of Change.
- Prochaska, J. O. & Prochaska, J. M. (2016). *Changing to Thrive: Using the Stages of Change to Overcome the Top Threats to Your Health and Happiness,* Center City, MN: Hazelden Publishing.

Lab 3A Stages of Change and Self-Management Skills

Name	Section	Date

Purpose: To assess your current Stage of Change for three key priority lifestyle behaviors (physical activity, nutrition, and stress management) and your self-management skills related to each one.

Procedures

1. Complete the Stages of Change Questionnaire on the next page. Check one box for each of the three priority health behaviors (physical activity, nutrition, and stress management).
2. Complete the Self-Management Skills Questionnaire (pages 41–42). Each question reflects one of the self-management skills described in this Concept. Each of the 12 questions requires a response about three different healthy behaviors. Respond to each question by using a 3 for very true, a 2 for somewhat true, or a 1 for not true. Record the appropriate number in the box beside each question. After you have answered all 12 questions for all three healthy lifestyles, total the numbers in the three columns to get a total score for physical activity, nutrition, and stress management.
3. Record your Stages of Change for the three healthy lifestyles (the word by the box you checked) in the Results section.
4. Record your Self-Management Scores for the three healthy lifestyles in the Results section. Use the Self-Management Skills Rating Chart to determine a rating for each healthy behavior. Record your ratings in the Results section.
5. Provide the appropriate information in the Conclusions and Implications section.

Results

Health Behavior	Stage of Change	Self-Management Score	Self-Management Rating
Physical Activity			
Nutrition			
Stress Management			

Self-Management Skills Rating Chart

Rating	Score
Good	30–36
Marginal	24–29
Needs improvement	<24

Conclusions and Implications: Choose one of the three health behaviors (preferably a behavior for which you think you need improvement). In the space below, discuss your current ability to use the various self-management skills to help you change your stage for the health behavior. Which self-management skills did you score well on? Which ones could you possibly improve?

Health Behavior: _____

Stages of Change Questionnaire. Check only one box for each question.

1. **Physical Activity**
   ☐ Precontemplation—I am not active, and I do not plan to start.
   ☐ Contemplation—I am not active, but I am thinking about starting.
   ☐ Preparation—I am getting ready to become active.
   ☐ Action—I do some activity but need to do more.
   ☐ Maintenance—I have been active regularly for several months.

2. **Nutrition**
   ☐ Precontemplation—I do not eat well and don't plan to change.
   ☐ Contemplation—I do not eat well but am thinking about change.
   ☐ Preparation—I am planning to change my diet.
   ☐ Action—I sometimes eat well but need to do more.
   ☐ Maintenance—I have eaten well regularly for several months.

3. **Stress Management**
   ☐ Precontemplation—I do not manage stress well and plan no changes.
   ☐ Contemplation—I am thinking about making changes to manage stress.
   ☐ Preparation—I am planning to change to manage stress better.
   ☐ Action—I sometimes take steps to manage stress better but need to do more.
   ☐ Maintenance—I have used good stress-management techniques for several months.

Self-Management Skills Questionnaire	Very True	Somewhat True	Not True	Activity Score	Nutrition Score	Stress Score
1. I regularly self-assess: (self-assessment)						
personal physical fitness and physical activity levels	3	2	1	☐		
the contents of my diet	3	2	1		☐	
personal stress levels	3	2	1			☐
2. I self-monitor and keep records concerning: (self-monitoring)						
physical activity	3	2	1	☐		
diet	3	2	1		☐	
stress in my life	3	2	1			☐
3. I set realistic and attainable goals for: (goal setting)						
physical activity	3	2	1	☐		
eating behaviors	3	2	1		☐	
reducing stress in my life	3	2	1			☐
4. I have a personal written or formal plan for: (self-planning)						
regular physical activity	3	2	1	☐		
what I eat	3	2	1		☐	
managing stress in my life	3	2	1			☐
5. I possess the skills to: (performance skills)						
perform a variety of physical activities	3	2	1	☐		
analyze my diet	3	2	1		☐	
manage stress (e.g., progressive relaxation)	3	2	1			☐
6. I have positive attitudes about: (balancing attitudes)						
my ability to stick with an activity plan	3	2	1	☐		
my ability to stick to a nutrition plan	3	2	1		☐	
my ability to manage stress in my life	3	2	1			☐
7. I can overcome barriers that I encounter: (overcoming barriers)						
in my attempts to be physically active	3	2	1	☐		
in my attempts to stick to a nutrition plan	3	2	1		☐	
in my attempts to manage stress in my life	3	2	1			☐

Self-Management Skills Questionnaire (cont.)	Very True	Somewhat True	Not True	Activity Score	Nutrition Score	Stress Score
8. I know how to identify misinformation: (consumer skills)						
relating to fitness and physical activity	3	2	1	☐		
relating to nutrition	3	2	1		☐	
relating to stress management	3	2	1			☐
9. I am able to get social support for my efforts to: (social support)						
be active	3	2	1	☐		
stick to a healthy nutrition plan	3	2	1		☐	
manage stress in my life	3	2	1			☐
10. When I have problems, I can get back to: (relapse prevention)						
my regular physical activity	3	2	1	☐		
my nutrition plan	3	2	1		☐	
my plan for managing stress	3	2	1			☐
11. I am able to adapt my thinking to: (coping strategies)						
stick with my activity plan	3	2	1	☐		
stick with my nutrition plan	3	2	1		☐	
stick with my stress-management plan	3	2	1			☐
12. I am able to manage my time to: (time management)						
stick with my physical activity plan	3	2	1	☐		
shop for and prepare nutritious food	3	2	1		☐	
perform stress-management activities	3	2	1			☐
Total Activity Score				☐		
Total Nutrition Score					☐	
Total Stress Score						☐

Preparing for Physical Activity

LEARNING OBJECTIVES

After completing the study of this Concept, you will be able to:

▶ Identify and describe key factors for safely participating in a moderate to vigorous physical activity program.

▶ Describe the warm-up, the workout, and the cool-down and explain why each is important.

▶ Explain the potential risks associated with exposure to heat, cold, and altitude and describe precautions that can be taken to prevent problems.

▶ Identify the factors that contribute to soreness and injury from physical activity and describe steps that can be taken to recover from them.

▶ Identify and describe the common positive and negative attitudes about physical activity and explain how they relate to regular participation.

▶ Identify related national health goals and show how meeting personal goals can contribute to reaching national goals.

▶ Assess your readiness for physical activity and demonstrate appropriate warm-up activities.

Proper preparation can help make physical activity enjoyable, effective, and safe.

©John Lund/Drew Kelly/Blend Images LLC

43

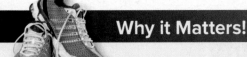

Why it Matters!

Engaging in physical activity is a priority lifestyle because it positively impacts multiple dimensions of health and wellness. There are few risks involved with moderate intensity physical activity, but it is important to start slowly and follow appropriate guidelines if you perform more vigorous activity or if you participate in outdoor activities. This Concept will provide guidelines for safe and effective physical activity. This information will help you prepare for and make physical activity a part of your normal routine.

Factors to Consider Prior to Physical Activity

Screening before beginning regular physical activity is important to establish medical readiness. The most recent guidelines for exercise testing and prescription of the American College of Sports Medicine (ACSM) suggest that that there are two types of pre-participation screening: self-screening and professional screening. In recent years, the ACSM has revised both methods of screening to simplify them and remove unnecessary barriers to adopting physically active lifestyles.

Individuals can self-screen using the Physical Activity Readiness Questionnaire for Everyone **(PAR-Q+).** This questionnaire was developed by the PAR-Q+ Collaboration team of investigators, with support from the Public Health Agency of Canada and the British Columbia Ministry of Health Services. It includes a seven-item screening questionnaire (see Lab 4A) and a two-page follow-up questionnaire with questions about medical conditions. People who answer "no" to all seven screening questions on the PAR-Q+ can skip the additional medical questions and begin participation as long as they follow the guidelines on the questionnaire. However, people who answer "yes" to one or more questions should complete the follow-up questions on pages 2 and 3 of the PAR-Q+ and consult a qualified exercise professional and/or a physician based on the nature of the medical condition. Many clinical, commercial, and worksite fitness programs also use the PAR-Q+ as a form of screening but they may also ask participants to sign a "participant declaration," included in the questionnaire. The full version is available online at eparmedx.com.

In addition to the PAR-Q+, the ACSM recommends that exercise professionals use a pre-participation screening system (professional screening) that considers a person's current and desired level of physical activity levels as well as the presence of signs or symptoms of cardiovascular, metabolic, or renal disease. There is insufficient evidence to indicate that risk factors (e.g., high blood pressure, high blood fat, high BMI) increase risk of adverse events in physical activity in those who do not have an actual disease, so risk factors are no longer of primary consideration by professionals when performing pre-participation screening.

Exercise professionals work closely with physicians when conducting a screening and may refer the participant to a physician for additional evaluation. The ACSM provides guidelines and indicates that health care providers may conduct a physical exam, a **clinical exercise test,** and/or laboratory tests.

For those resuming physical activity after an injury or illness, consultation with an exercise professional or a physician may be warranted, depending on the nature of the injury or illness. Consideration should also be given to altering exercise patterns if you have an illness or a temporary sickness, such as a cold or the flu. The immune system and other body systems may be weaker at this time, and medicines (even over-the-counter ones) may alter responses to exercise. It is best to work back gradually to your normal routine after illness.

There is no way to be absolutely sure that you are medically ready to begin a physical activity program. Even a thorough exam by a physician cannot guarantee that a person does not have some limitations that may cause a problem during exercise. However, new screening methods have been implemented because overly stringent methods used in the past have excluded some from exercise unnecessarily. Use of the PAR-Q+ (see Lab 4A) and adherence to the ACSM guidelines are advised to help minimize the risk while

encouraging maximum participation. Note that people over the age of 45 who are *not* accustomed to vigorous to maximal effort exercise are still encouraged to consult a qualified exercise professional before engaging in this intensity of exercise.

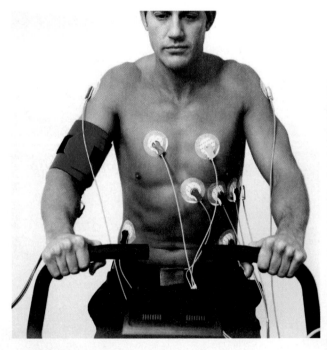

A standard exercise test—an example of professionally guided screening—is recommended for some individuals to ensure they can exercise safely.
©Digital Vision/PunchStock

Shoes are an important consideration for safe and effective exercise. Decisions about shoes should be based on intended use (e.g., running, tennis), shoe and foot characteristics, and comfort. Shoes are designed for specific activities, and performance will typically be best if you select and use them for their intended purpose and fit, rather than how they look. Hybrid shoes, known as "cross-trainers," can be a versatile option, but they typically don't provide the needed features for specific activities. For example, they may lack the cushioning and support needed for running and the ankle support for activities such as basketball. Features of common activity shoes are highlighted in Figure 1.

Most shoes have very thin sockliners, but supplemental inserts can be purchased to provide more cushioning and support. Custom orthotics can also be used to correct alignment

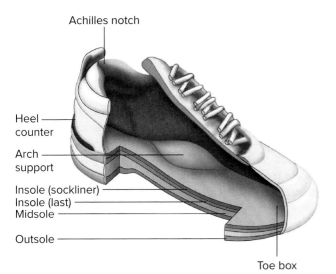

Achilles notch

Heel counter

Arch support

Insole (sockliner)
Insole (last)
Midsole

Outsole

Toe box

Achilles notch: Protects tendon

Heel counter: Cradles heel to provide movement control; reduces slippage and blistering; a stiff counter reduces pronation

Arch support: Supports arch; height and shape of arch should vary with foot characteristics

Insole (sockliner): Removable layer for additional shock and sweat absorption; can be replaced periodically and/or customized

Insole (last): Refers to shape of shoe bed; curved (allows more mobility; better for those with high, rigid arches); straight (controls excessive motion, better for those with abnormal pronation); or semicurved (moderate flexibility and stability)

Midsole: Provides cushion, stability, and motion control; important for shock absorption

Outsole: Provides traction; determines shoe flexibility; type depends on intended purpose of shoe

Toe box: Should have adequate height to wiggle toes and prevent rubbing on top of toes and adequate length so toes do not contact front of shoe

Figure 1 ▶ Anatomy of an activity shoe.

Table 1 ▶ Selecting Appropriate Clothing for Activity

General Guidelines
- Avoid clothing that is too tight or that restricts movement.
- Material in contact with skin should be porous.
- Clothing should protect against wind and rain but allow for heat loss and evaporation (e.g., GORE-TEX, COOLMAX).
- Wear layers so that a layer can be removed if not needed.
- Wear socks for most activities to prevent blisters, abrasions, odor, and excessive shoe wear.
- Socks should be absorbent and fit properly.
- Do not use nonporous clothing that traps sweat to lose weight; these garments prevent evaporation and cooling.

Special Considerations
- Consider eye protection for racquetball and other sports.
- Women should wear an exercise bra for support.
- Men should consider an athletic supporter for support.
- Wear helmets and padding for activities with risk of falling, such as biking or inline skating.
- Wear reflective clothing for night activities.
- Wear water shoes for some aquatic activities.
- Consider lace-up ankle braces to prevent injury.
- Consider a mouthpiece for basketball and other contact sports.

problems or minimize foot injuries (e.g., plantar fasciitis). A very important, and frequently neglected, consideration is to replace shoes after extended use. Runners typically replace shoes every four to six months (or 400 to 600 miles), even if the outer appearance of the shoe is still good. The main functions of athletic shoes are to reduce shock from impact and protect the foot. One of the best prevention strategies for avoiding injuries is to replace your shoes on a regular basis.

It is important to dress properly for physical activity. Clothing should be appropriate for the type of activity being performed and the conditions in which you are participating. Comfort is a much more important consideration than looks. Table 1 provides guidelines for dressing for activity.

Components of a Typical Bout of Physical Activity

The warm-up phase prepares the body for more vigorous activity. According to the ACSM, the **warm-up** can improve range of motion and may reduce injury risk. It

PAR-Q+ An acronym for Physical Activity Readiness Questionnaire for Everyone; designed to help determine if you are medically suited to begin an exercise program.

Clinical Exercise Test A test, typically administered on a treadmill, in which exercise is gradually increased in intensity while the heart is monitored by an EKG. Symptoms not present at rest, such as an abnormal EKG, may be present in an exercise test.

Warm-Up Light to moderate physical activity performed to prepare for a more vigorous workout.

increases body temperature, decreases risk of irregular heartbeats, and allows the body to transition into the workout that follows. The ACSM recommends a warm-up of *light-to-moderate aerobic and muscular endurance activities* prior to vigorous activities. However, some individuals (and athletes engaged in specific sports or activities) may benefit from different types of warm-up routines. A structured **stretch warm-up** includes exercises designed to stretch the muscles beyond their normal length. This is a traditional form of warm-up that is an enjoyable part of the regular exercise routine for many. In general, recent research has not confirmed the long-standing notion that a stretch warm-up reduces injury risk. Evidence that a stretch warm-up reduces post-exercise soreness is also uncertain. Athletes who participate in sports and activities requiring a larger-than-normal range of motion (e.g., gymnastics and diving) typically perform a stretch warm-up (after a general warm-up) as part of their pre-exercise routine. In these activities, the stretching is important for their performance. The stretch warm-up, however, can reduce strength, power, and/or speed performance, especially if the stretches last more than 60 seconds. For athletes and those concerned with high-level performance in activities that require strength, power, or speed, a stretch warm-up is not recommended. Typical exercisers who are not concerned with high-level performance, and who enjoy a stretch warm-up, may choose to perform a stretch warm-up after a general warm-up.

An alternative to a stretch warm-up is a **dynamic warm-up** that includes moderate intensity, calisthenic-type activities (see Lab 4B for examples). Unlike the stretch warm-up, the goal is not to lengthen the muscles, but to move the joints through a full range of motion. The dynamic warm-up can be substituted for a general warm-up in some cases and can be used instead of a stretch warm-up before strength, power, and/or speed activities (e.g., weight lifting, sprinting, or shot putting). A specific type of dynamic warm-up known as the *sport-specific warm-up* is recommended prior to sports. Examples include performing layups or shooting baskets before a basketball game or swinging a golf club or tennis racket before playing the actual game.

It is important to note that the stretch warm-up and dynamic warm-up are not the same as a workout to improve flexibility. A stretch warm-up prepares you for your workout, but stretching exercises designed to improve flexibility are considered part of a workout. (Additional information about stretching exercises is included in the Concept on flexibility.) The specific type of warm-up that you will perform depends on the nature of your workout. Table 2 provides information about types of warm-up activities for various types of physical activity.

The workout is the principal component of an activity program and occurs after the warm-up and before the cool-down. A **workout** can refer to physical activities designed as training for fitness and health, participation in sport or recreation for fun and enjoyment, or participation in moderate exercise for general health and wellness. If

Table 2 ▶ Warm-Up Guidelines for Different Physical Activities

Activity	Guidelines
Moderate Activity	• For walking and activities of equal intensity, no warm-up is necessary. • For moderate recreation, such as golf, a sport-specific warm-up may be performed. • Depending on intensity, a general, dynamic or, stretch warm-up (after the general or dynamic warm-up) can be performed.
Vigorous Aerobics	• For aerobic dance or similar dance activities, similar dance-related movements can be performed, with gradually increasing intensity, as a general warm-up. Some may choose a stretch warm-up (after the general warm-up). • For jogging, biking, swimming, and similar aerobic activities, performing the activity slowly and then with increased intensity can serve as a general warm-up. A dynamic warm-up can also be used as a general warm-up. A stretch warm-up can be performed after the general warm-up.
Vigorous Sports	• A general warm-up is recommended but can be done using dynamic exercises. Sport-specific exercises are appropriate. If a stretch warm-up is chosen, it should be done after the general warm-up. Stretches should not exceed 60 seconds. • For sports that require strength, speed, and power, you should choose a dynamic warm-up (it can double as a general warm-up). The stretch warm-up is not recommended.
Muscle Fitness Exercises	• Prior to training for muscle fitness, including speed training, choose a dynamic warm-up (it can double as a general warm-up). The stretch warm-up is not recommended.
Flexibility Exercises and Activities Requiring Flexibility	• Prior to performing flexibility exercises as part of your workout, a general warm-up is recommended. Some may choose to do dynamic exercises as the general warm-up. • Prior to performing activities such as gymnastics, diving, and dance, a stretch warm-up is recommended after the general warm-up.

performed as part of a more structured exercise routine, it is the component that provides the stimulus for adaptations and improved conditioning. The specific benefits from a workout depend on the type and intensity of activity that is performed (see the Concept on the health benefits of physical activity). Information about appropriate frequency, intensity, and length of time for different types of physical activities is included in subsequent Concepts (look for descriptions of the "physical activity pyramid").

A cool-down after the workout promotes an effective recovery from physical activity. After a more vigorous workout, it is wise to perform a **cool-down** to help the body transition back to a resting state. The ACSM recommends a 5- to 10-minute cool-down phase consisting of light to moderate physical activity, such as walking or slow jogging, and can also include stretching exercises. The moderate aerobic activity promotes effective recovery by aiding the return of blood from the working muscles to the heart. In addition to helping reduce metabolic by-products, the general cool-down helps the cardiovascular system (heart rate and blood pressure) return to a normal state.

Figure 2 depicts how muscle contractions influence circulation and why it is important to perform a cool-down following vigorous activity. During physical activity, the heart pumps a large amount of blood to supply the working muscles with the oxygen needed to keep moving. The muscles squeeze the veins, which forces the blood back to the heart. Valves in the veins prevent the blood from flowing backward. As long as exercise continues, muscles move the blood back to the heart, where it is once again pumped to the body. If exercise is stopped abruptly, the blood is left in the area of the working muscles and has no way to get back to the heart. In the case of a runner, the blood pools in the legs. Because the heart has less blood to pump, blood pressure may drop. This can result in dizziness and can even cause a person to pass out. The best way to prevent this problem is to slow down gradually after exercise and keep moving until blood pressure and heart rate have returned to near resting values. This phase is especially important for those with cardiovascular risk factors or disease.

Physical Activity in the Heat and Cold

Physical activity in hot and humid environments challenges the body's heat loss mechanisms. During vigorous activity, the body produces heat, which must be dissipated to regulate body temperature. The body has several ways to dissipate heat. *Conduction* is the transfer of heat from a hot body to a cold body. *Convection* is the transfer of heat through the air or any other medium. Fans and wind can facilitate heat loss by convection and help regulate

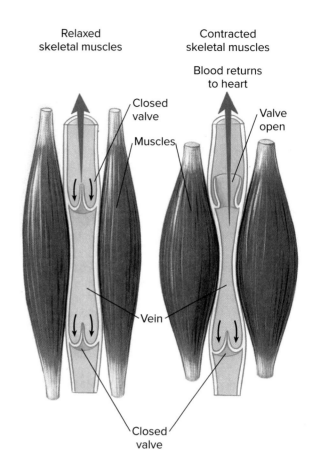

Figure 2 ▶ Muscle contractions help the veins return blood to the heart.

temperature. The primary method of cooling is through *evaporation* of sweat. The chemical process involved in evaporation transfers heat from the body and reduces the body temperature. When conditions are humid, the effectiveness of evaporation is reduced, since the air is already saturated with moisture. This is why it is difficult to regulate body temperature when conditions are hot and humid.

Heat-related illness can occur if proper hydration is not maintained. Maximum sweat rates during physical activity in the heat can approach 1–2 quarts per hour. If this fluid is not

Stretch Warm-up The performance of stretching exercises prior to a vigorous workout.

Dynamic Warm-up The performance of calisthenics of gradually increasing intensity prior to a vigorous workout (e.g., jumping jacks, jumping, skipping).

Workout The component of a total physical activity program designed to produce health, wellness, fitness, and other benefits using appropriate amounts of different types of physical activity.

Cool-Down Light to moderate activity performed after a more vigorous workout to help the body recover.

A CLOSER LOOK

CPR Guidelines and AEDs

To be prepared for physical activity, you also need to be prepared for emergencies. Active people in particular should know cardiopulmonary resuscitation (CPR) and how to use an automated external defibrillator (AED). Guidelines from the American Heart Association (AHA) use the letters C-A-B to guide a rescuer to remember the three key steps in CPR (C = Compressions; A = Airway; B = Breathing). If a person is unresponsive, a trained rescuer should first call for help (including dialing 911) and then begin chest compression immediately (30 times at a rate of 100 times per minute). Then open the airway and give mouth-to-mouth rescue breaths (2 times). Repeat the 30-2 compression-to-breath cycle. For the untrained rescuer, a "hands-only" approach (compression only) is recommended. Also, AEDs are available in many public places, including fitness centers and schools. The AHA offers free online training for CPR and AED devices at www.heart.org. (See link in Suggested Resources and Readings.)

How confident are you that you would be ready in an emergency? What steps would you take or have taken to be ready to perform CPR or use an AED if an emergency arises?

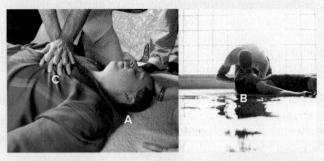

C = Compress
Push hard and fast in the center of the chest

A = Airway
Tip head back and lift the chin to open airway

B = Breath
Give mouth-to-mouth breaths

(left): ©Walter Lockwood/Photolibrary/Getty Images; (right): ©Steven Taylor/The Image Bank/Getty Images

---

replaced, **dehydration** can occur. If dehydration is not corrected with water or other fluid-replacement drinks, it becomes increasingly difficult for the body to maintain normal body temperatures. At some point, the rate of sweating decreases as the body begins to conserve its remaining water. It shunts blood to the skin to transfer excess heat directly to the environment, but this is less effective than evaporation. **Hyperthermia** and associated heat-related problems can result (see Table 3).

One way to monitor the amount of fluid loss is to monitor the color of your urine. Clear (almost colorless) urine produced in large volumes indicates that you are hydrated. As water in the body is reduced, the urine becomes more concentrated and is a darker yellow color. This indicates dehydration and a need for fluid replacement. Dietary supplements that contain amphetamine derivatives and/or creatine may contribute to undetected dehydration among some individuals.

Acclimatization improves the body's tolerance in the heat. Individuals with good fitness will respond better to activity in the heat than individuals with poor fitness. With

Table 3 ▶ Types of Heat-Related Problems

Problem	Symptoms	Severity
Heat cramps	Muscle cramps, especially in muscles most used in exercise	Least severe
Heat exhaustion	Muscle cramps, weakness, dizziness, headache, nausea, clammy skin, paleness	Moderately severe
Heatstroke	Hot, flushed skin; dry skin (lack of sweating); dizziness; fast pulse; unconsciousness; high temperature	Extremely severe

Adequate hydration is critical for safe exercise in the heat.
©Liquidlibrary/PictureQuest

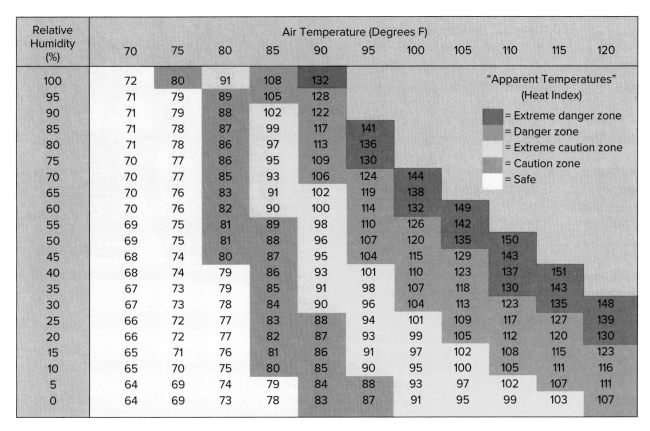

Relative Humidity (%)	Air Temperature (Degrees F)										
	70	75	80	85	90	95	100	105	110	115	120
100	72	80	91	108	132						
95	71	79	89	105	128						
90	71	79	88	102	122						
85	71	78	87	99	117	141					
80	71	78	86	97	113	136					
75	70	77	86	95	109	130					
70	70	77	85	93	106	124	144				
65	70	76	83	91	102	119	138				
60	70	76	82	90	100	114	132	149			
55	69	75	81	89	98	110	126	142			
50	69	75	81	88	96	107	120	135	150		
45	68	74	80	87	95	104	115	129	143		
40	68	74	79	86	93	101	110	123	137	151	
35	67	73	79	85	91	98	107	118	130	143	
30	67	73	78	84	90	96	104	113	123	135	148
25	66	72	77	83	88	94	101	109	117	127	139
20	66	72	77	82	87	93	99	105	112	120	130
15	65	71	76	81	86	91	97	102	108	115	123
10	65	70	75	80	85	90	95	100	105	111	116
5	64	69	74	79	84	88	93	97	102	107	111
0	64	69	73	78	83	87	91	95	99	103	107

"Apparent Temperatures" (Heat Index)

■ = Extreme danger zone
■ = Danger zone
■ = Extreme caution zone
■ = Caution zone
□ = Safe

Figure 3 ▶ Heat index values (apparent temperatures).

Source: Data from National Oceanic and Atmospheric Administration.

regular exposure, the body adapts to the heat. The majority of the adaptation to hot environments occurs in 7 to 14 days, but complete acclimatization can take up to 30 days. As you adapt to the heat, your body becomes conditioned to sweat earlier, to sweat more profusely, and to distribute the sweat more effectively around the body, and the composition of sweat is altered. This process makes it easier for your body to maintain a safe body temperature.

Precautions should be taken when doing physical activity in hot and humid environments. The **heat index** (also referred to as apparent temperature) combines temperature and humidity to help you determine when an environment is safe for activity. The combination of high temperature and humidity presents the greatest risk of heat-related problems in exercise. Physical activity is safe when the apparent temperature is below 80°F (26.7°C). Figure 3 shows the risk of exercise at progressively higher apparent temperatures.

Consider the following guidelines for exercising in the heat and humidity.

- Limit or cancel activity if the apparent temperature reaches the danger zone (see Figure 3).

- Drink fluids before, during, and after vigorous activity. Guidelines suggest about 2 cups before activity and about 1 cup for each 15–20 minutes during activity. After activity,

drink about 2 cups for each pound of weight lost. The thirst mechanism lags behind the body's actual need for fluid, so drink even if you don't feel thirsty. Fluid-replacement beverages (e.g., Gatorade, Powerade) are designed to provide added energy (from carbohydrates) without impeding hydration. If you choose to use one of these beverages, select one that contains electrolytes and no more than 4 to 8 percent carbohydrates (see HELP feature).

- Avoid extreme fluid intake. Drinking too much water can cause a condition called **hyponatremia,** sometimes referred to as "water intoxication." It occurs when you drink too

Dehydration Excessive loss of water from the body, usually through perspiration, urination, or evaporation.

Hyperthermia Excessively high body temperature caused by excessive heat production or impaired heat loss capacity. Heatstroke is a hyperthermic condition.

Heat Index An index based on a combination of temperature and humidity that is used to determine if it is dangerous to perform physical activity in hot, humid weather (also called apparent temperature).

Hyponatremia A condition caused by excess water intake, called "water intoxication," that results in a dilution of electrolytes, leading to serious medical complications.

HELP Health is available to Everyone for a Lifetime, and it's Personal

Water vs. Sports Drinks

There are many fluid replacement drinks on the market and consumers get confused about what to choose and when to drink. Water is typically the best choice for most exercisers since it is less expensive and doesn't contain extra calories. However, during longer bouts of exercise the extra calories and electrolytes (sodium, potassium, and chloride) help replace nutrients and improve performance. The benefits are generally not evident unless exercise is longer than 1-2 hours. The sugar content causes these drinks to empty slower from the stomach, but the electrolytes help it get absorbed faster from the intestine. Therefore, these drinks can be as effective as water for fluid replacement during longer bouts of exercise. While they are not needed for most people, the thirst-quenching aspects make them a popular choice for some exercisers.

What drinks do you prefer? Do you think you consume sufficient fluids before, during, and after exercise?

Wind, cold, and altitude present some additional challenges for winter exercise.
©Maridav/iStock/Getty Images

much water, resulting in the dilution of the electrolytes in the blood; interestingly, it has symptoms similar to those of dehydration. If left untreated, it can result in loss of consciousness and even death.

- Gradually expose yourself to physical activity in hot and humid environments to facilitate acclimatization.

- Dress properly for exercise in the heat and humidity. Wear white or light colors that reflect rather than absorb heat. Select wickable clothes instead of cotton to aid evaporative cooling. Rubber, plastic, or other nonporous clothing is especially dangerous. A porous hat or cap can help when exercising in direct sunlight.

- Watch for signs of heat stress (see Table 3). If signs are present, stop immediately, get out of the heat, remove excess clothing, and drink cool water. Seek medical attention if symptoms progress. Consider cold water immersion for heatstroke.

Physical activity in exceptionally cold and windy weather can be dangerous. Activity in the cold presents the opposite problems of exercise in the heat. In the cold, the primary goal is to retain the body's heat and avoid **hypothermia** and frostbite. Early signs of hypothermia include shivering and cold extremities caused by blood shunted to the body core to conserve heat. As the core temperature continues to drop, heart rate, respiration, and reflexes are depressed. Subsequently, cognitive functions decrease, speech and movement become impaired, and bizarre behavior may occur. Frostbite results from water crystallizing in the tissues, causing cell destruction.

In the News

Extreme Exercise and the Heart

Competition and personal challenge lead many individuals to push the limits of exercise performance. While moderate amounts of exercise are clearly beneficial, a prominent cardiologist has suggested that exercise beyond certain levels can actually increase your risk for developing cardiovascular disease. It has been well established that exercise can precipitate a heart attack in people who have cardiovascular disease risk factors, but the shocking conclusion in this study is that extreme exercise (e.g., ultramarathons or 24-hour exercise events) can cause cardiovascular disease. More research is needed to confirm this finding, but it may cause some athletes to rethink their exercise regimens. (See Suggested Resources and Readings.)

Do you agree with the notion that too much exercise can be harmful? Would this deter you from participating in extreme forms of exercise?

Actual Temperature Reading (Degrees F)	Estimated Wind Speed (mph)									Minutes to Frostbite
	Calm	5	10	15	20	25	30	35	40	
40	40	36	34	32	30	29	28	27	27	
30	30	25	21	19	17	16	15	14	13	
20	20	13	9	6	4	3	1	0	-1	
10	10	1	-4	-7	-9	-11	-12	-14	-15	
0	0	-11	-16	-19	-22	-24	-26	-27	-29	30
-10	-10	-22	-28	-32	-35	-37	-39	-41	-43	10
-20	-20	-34	-41	-45	-48	-51	-53	-55	-57	5
-30	-30	-46	-53	-58	-61	-64	-67	-69	-71	
-40	-40	-57	-66	-71	-74	-78	-80	-82	-84	

☐ = Caution Zone   ☐ = Risk Zone   ◼ = High Risk Zone   ◼ = Extreme Danger Zone

Figure 4 ▶ Windchill factor chart.

Source: National Weather Source

When doing activity in cold, wet, and windy weather, precautions should be taken. A combination of cold and wind (windchill) poses the greatest danger for cold-related problems during exercise. Research conducted in Canada, in cooperation with the U.S. National Weather Service, produced tables for determining **windchill factor** and the time of exposure necessary to get frostbite (see Figure 4). Consider the following guidelines for performing physical activity in cold and wind:

- Limit or cancel activity if the windchill factor reaches the danger zone (see Figure 4).

- Dress properly. Wear light clothing in several layers rather than one heavy garment. The layer of clothing closest to the body should transfer (wick) moisture away from the skin to a second, more absorbent layer. Polypropylene and capilene are examples of wickable fabrics. A porous windbreaker keeps wind from cooling the body and allows the release of body heat. The hands, feet, nose, and ears are most susceptible to frostbite, so they should be covered. Wear a hat or cap, mask, and mittens. Mittens are warmer than gloves. A light coating of petroleum jelly on exposed body parts can be helpful.

- Keep from getting wet in cold weather. If you get wet because of unavoidable circumstances, seek a warm place to dry off.  VIDEO 3

Physical Activity in Other Environments

High altitude may limit performance and require adaptation of normal physical activity. The ability to do vigorous physical tasks is diminished as altitude increases.

Technology Update

Apps for Monitoring Environmental Conditions

The environmental conditions can have a major impact on both the safety and enjoyment of outdoor physical activity. For example, individuals living in urban areas need to be aware of air pollution levels since exercise may be harmful under certain conditions. Simple smartphone apps can show pollution indicators in real-time and let people find better times to exercise. Exercising in extreme heat and cold can also be dangerous. Free apps now provide a quick way to check the composite heat index (based on heat and humidity) and the composite wind-chill (based on cold and wind). These can help you make decisions about your choice of exercise for the day or help you determine how to dress appropriately for the conditions.

Would you use these apps to help you make decisions about your choice of exercise for the day?

 ACTIVITY

Hypothermia Excessively low body temperature (less than 95°F), characterized by uncontrollable shivering, loss of coordination, and mental confusion.

Windchill Factor An index that uses air temperature and wind speed to determine the chilling effect of the environment on humans.

In addition, exercise at higher altitudes may produce symptoms such as a faster heart rate, shortness of breath, headache, dizziness, fatigue, and upset stomach (nausea and vomiting). With proper acclimation (gradual exposure), the body adjusts to the lower oxygen pressure found at high altitude, performance improves, and symptoms lessen. Nevertheless, performance ability at high altitudes, especially for activities requiring cardiorespiratory endurance, is usually less than would be expected at sea level. At extremely high altitudes, the ability to perform vigorous physical activity may be impossible without an extra oxygen supply. When moving from sea level to a high altitude, vigorous exercise should be done with caution. To minimize the effects of altitude on performance, spend at least two weeks at a higher altitude before performing high-intensity exercise, gradually increasing length and intensity of activity. Pace yourself, drink adequate water, take rest stops, listen to your body, and avoid alcohol.

Exposure to air pollution should be limited. Various pollutants can cause poor performance and, in some cases, health problems. Ozone, a pollutant produced primarily by the sun's reaction to car exhaust, can cause symptoms, including headache, coughing, and eye irritation. Similar symptoms result from exposure to carbon monoxide, a tasteless and odorless gas, caused by combustion of oil, gasoline, and/or cigarette smoke. The Environmental Protection Agency provides up-to-date pollution advisories based on an "air quality index" (see airnow.gov). Ratings range from "good" to "hazardous" to let people know if it is safe to be outside in their area. Exercisers wishing to avoid ozone and carbon monoxide may want to exercise indoors, early in the morning, or later in the evening and avoid areas with a high concentration of traffic.

Plant pollens, dust, and other pollutants in the air may cause allergic reactions for certain people. Weather reports of pollens and particulates may help exercisers determine the best times for their activities and when to avoid vigorous activities.

Soreness and Injury

Understanding soreness can help you persist in physical activity and avoid problems. A common experience for many exercisers is a certain degree of muscle soreness that occurs 24–48 hours after intense exercise. This soreness, termed delayed-onset muscle soreness **(DOMS)**, typically occurs when muscles are exercised at levels beyond their normal use. Some people mistakenly believe that lactic acid is the cause of muscle soreness. Lactic acid (a byproduct of anaerobic metabolism) is produced during vigorous exercise, but levels return to normal within 30 minutes after exercise, while DOMS occurs 24 hours after exercise. DOMS is caused by microscopic muscle tears that result from the excessive loads on the muscles. Soreness is not a

normal part of the body's response to exercise but occurs if an individual violates the principle of progression and does more exercise than the body is prepared for. While it may be uncomfortable to some, it has no long-term consequences and does not predispose one to muscle injury. To reduce the likelihood of DOMS, it is important to progress your program gradually.

The most common injuries incurred in physical activity are sprains and strains. A strain occurs when the fibers in a muscle are injured. Common activity-related injuries are hamstring strains that occur after a vigorous sprint. Other commonly strained muscles include the muscles in the front of the thigh, the low back, and the calf.

A sprain is an injury to a ligament—the connective tissue that connects bones to bones. The most common sprain is to the ankle; frequently, the ankle is rolled to the outside (inversion) when jumping or running. Other common sprains are to the knee, the shoulder, and the wrist.

Tendonitis is an inflammation of the tendon; it is most often a result of overuse rather than trauma. Tendonitis can be painful but often does not swell to the extent that sprains do. For this reason, elevation and compression are not as effective as ice and rest (Table 4). A physician should be consulted for an appropriate diagnosis.

Knowing how to treat minor injuries can help you reduce their negative effects. Minor soft tissue injuries, such as muscle strains and sprains, are common to those who are persistent in their exercise. If a serious injury should occur or if symptoms persist, it is important to get immediate medical attention. However, for minor injuries, there are some simple guidelines  that you can use. For years, experts have promoted the **RICE** formula as the accepted method of treatment. **R** stands for *rest*. **I** stands for *ice*. **C** stands for *compression*. **E** stands for *elevation*. In recent years there has been debate about the use of RICE exclusively. While many experts stick by the RICE formula, some experts have suggested that the formula should be amended to include **P** for *protection* (PRICE) and others have suggested the addition of both **P** for *protection* and **OL** for *optimal loading* (POLICE). Optimal loading refers to the gradual introduction of movement after a period of rest (R). The RICE formula works for all acronyms (see Table 4), however, PRICE and POLICE add to RICE by pointing out the need for injury prevention efforts and the need for gradual reintroduction of movement in the injury recovery process.

Some, but not all, athletic trainers and physicians recommend the use of over-the-counter pain remedies to reduce the pain of muscle strains and sprains. Nonsteroidal anti-inflammatory drugs (NSAID) have anti-inflammatory properties (e.g., ibuprofen). However, acetaminophen (e.g., Tylenol)

Table 4 ▶ The RICE Formula for Treating Minor Injuries	
RICE Components	**Application of Components**
Rest	For a day or two, rest helps you avoid further damage to the tissues. During this period, it is important to *protect* the injured body part using crutches and stabilizing devices (e.g., ankle brace). After a day or two, passive movement can begin to help retain (or prevent loss of) range of motion. This can be followed by light exercise over the next few days as appropriate (*optimal loading*). Gradually increasing the load can speed recovery.
Ice	The quick application of cold (ice or ice water) to a minor injury minimizes swelling and speeds recovery. Cold should be applied to as large a surface area as possible (soaking is best). If ice is used, it should be wrapped to avoid direct contact with the skin. Apply cold for 20 minutes, 3 times a day, allowing 1 hour between applications.
Compression	Muscle sprains and strains heal best if the injured area is rested. Rest helps you avoid further damage to the muscle. Wrapping or compressing the injured area also helps minimize swelling and speeds recovery. Elastic bandages or elastic socks are good for applying compression. Care should be taken to avoid wrapping an injury too tightly because this can result in loss of circulation to the area.
Elevation	Keeping the injured area elevated (above the level of the heart) is effective in minimizing swelling. If pain or swelling does not diminish after 24 to 48 hours, or if there is any doubt about the seriousness of an injury, seek medical help.

does not. It may reduce the pain, but will not reduce inflammation.

Muscle cramps can be relieved by statically stretching a muscle. Muscle cramps are pains in the large muscles that result when the muscles contract vigorously for a continued period of time. Muscle cramps are usually not considered to be an injury, but they are painful and may seem like an injury. They are usually short in duration and can often be relieved with proper treatment. Cramps can result from lack of fluid replacement (dehydration), from fatigue, and from a blow

directly to a muscle. Static stretching can help relieve some cramps. For example, the calf muscle, which often cramps among runners and other sports participants, can be relieved using the calf stretcher exercise, which is part of the warm-up in this Concept.

Using Self-Management Skills

Balancing attitudes is a self-management skill that can help you get started and stick with a physical activity program. Active people generally have more positive attitudes than negative ones. This  is referred to as a "positive balance of attitudes." Some self-management guidelines that will help you develop positive attitudes and limit negative attitudes are presented in the following paragraphs.

Knowing the most common negative attitudes can help you avoid them. Most people want to be active but negative attitudes can get in the way of regular physical activity adherence. The most common negative attitudes (excuses) for avoiding regular physical activity are listed in Table 5. Experts consider many of these attitudes to be barriers that can be overcome. Use the self-management strategies in Table 5 to overcome negative attitudes and limit excuses for being inactive.

Knowing the most common positive attitudes can motivate you to adopt them. Just as there are negative attitudes that limit activity, there are positive attitudes that encourage it.  The most common reasons people give for being physically active are highlighted in Table 6. The table also offers self-management strategies for adopting positive attitudes.

Assessing your attitudes can help you adopt strategies to change them. The first step in changing attitudes is becoming aware of your personal attitudes toward physical activity, both positive and negative. Becoming more aware of your attitudes can help you focus on strategies for eliminating negative attitudes and fostering positive ones. Like any behavior change, changing attitudes takes practice and effort.

> **DOMS** An acronym for delayed-onset muscle soreness, a common malady that follows relatively vigorous activity, especially among beginners.

Table 5 ▶ Negative Attitudes about Physical Activity

Negative Attitudes	Importance for Physical Activity Behavior	Strategy for Change
I don't have the time.	This is the number one reason people give for not exercising. Invariably, those who feel they don't have time know they should do more exercise. They say they plan to do more in the future when "things are less hectic."	Planning a daily schedule can help you find the time for activity and avoid wasting time on things that are less important.
It's too inconvenient.	Many people who avoid physical activity do so because it is inconvenient. They say, "It takes too long to get to the gym" and "It makes me sweaty and messes up my hair."	If you have to travel more than 10 minutes to do activity or if you do not have easy access to equipment, you will avoid activity. Locating facilities and finding a time when you can shower is important.
I just don't enjoy it.	Many people do not find activity to be enjoyable or invigorating. They may assume that all forms of activity have to be strenuous and fatiguing.	There are many activities to choose from. If you don't enjoy vigorous activity, try more moderate forms of activity, such as walking.
I'm no good at physical activity.	"People might laugh at me," "Sports make me nervous," and "I am not good at physical activities" are reasons some people give for not being active.	Selecting activities properly, avoiding comparisons to others, and learning skills can help anyone be more active.
I am not fit, so I avoid activity.	Some people avoid exercise because of health reasons. Some who are unfit lack energy. Starting slowly can build fitness gradually.	There are good medical reasons for not doing activity, but many people with problems can benefit from exercise if it is properly designed.
I have no place to be active, especially in bad weather.	Regular activity is more convenient if facilities are easy to reach and the weather is good. Most popular activities require little equipment and can be done in or near home.	If you cannot find a place, if it is not safe, or if it is too expensive, consider using low-cost equipment at home, such as rubber bands or calisthenics.
I am too old.	As people grow older, many begin to feel that activity is something they cannot do. Properly planned exercise for older adults is not only safe but also has many health benefits.	Older people who are just beginning activity should start slowly. Setting realistic goals can help, as can learning to do resistance training and flexibility exercises.

Strategies for Action: Lab Information

Pre-participation screening can help you safely participate in a physical activity program. Prior to participation, the use of the PAR-Q+ is recommended. In Lab 4A, answer the seven questions in the Par-Q+ to see if you are ready for participation. If you answer "yes" to any of the seven questions, you should follow up as indicated. Athletes and people who plan very vigorous training may require additional screening.

A proper warm-up can prepare your body for activity and a gradual cool-down can improve recovery. Lab 4B provides examples of dynamic exercises and stretching exercises that can

be considered when performing a warm-up. You can try these exercises and use the warm-up guidelines presented in the previous pages of this Concept to determine what works best for your needs.

Assessing your attitudes concerning physical activity can help you change them. Active people generally have more positive attitudes than negative ones. This is referred to as a "positive balance of attitudes." The questionnaire in Lab 4C gives you the opportunity to assess your balance of attitudes. If you have a "negative balance" score, you can analyze your attitudes and determine how you can change them to view activity more favorably.

Table 6 ▶ Positive Attitudes about Physical Activity

Positive Attitudes	Importance for Physical Activity Behavior	Strategy for Change
I am active because I simply enjoy it!	The sense of fun, well-being, and general enjoyment associated with physical activity is well documented.	Find activities that you enjoy. Many people find walking to be a simple and enjoyable activity because it doesn't require skill or extreme effort.
I enjoy being active because I care about my health.	Improving health is a primary reason for many people, and it takes only moderate amounts to benefit.	Learning about the powerful benefits of fitness can provide motivation to start.
I enjoy being active because it helps me look great.	Improving appearance is a major reason some people participate in regular exercise. Regular activity can help you look your best.	Setting realistic goals and avoiding comparisons with others can help you be more successful.
I enjoy being active because it helps me relax and reduces stress in my life.	Physical activity provides an outlet from daily frustrations and can help reduce depression and anxiety.	Build in time to take short activity breaks and allow your mind to be freed up from daily hassles while you are active.
I enjoy being active because it challenges me.	The challenge of doing something you have never done before can build a sense of personal accomplishment. This is a powerful motivator for physical activity.	Seek opportunities to learn new skills and try new things. Reward yourself for accepting challenges associated with physical activity.
I enjoy being active because it is a fun way to be with friends.	Physical activity provides opportunities to spend quality time with friends and family.	Find ways to be active with family and friends. Select partner or team activities that de-emphasize competition.
I enjoy being active because I like to compete.	Many people find "the thrill of victory" and "sports competition" very satisfying.	If you don't enjoy the "competing" aspect, focus on how you are improving versus winning or losing.
I enjoy being active because it helps me feel good about myself.	For many people, participation in physical activity is an important part of their identity. It can help you feel good about yourself, build your confidence, and increase self-esteem.	Physical activity is something that is self-determined and within your control. Schedule activity just as you would any important priority to accomplish during the week.
I enjoy being active because it is a fun way to enjoy the outdoors.	Spending time outside and experiencing nature pair well with many physical activities.	Seek out parks, bike and walking trails, and other outdoor settings for your activities.

Suggested Resources and Readings

The websites for the following sources can be accessed by searching online for the organization, program, or title listed. Specific scientific references are available at the end of this edition of *Concepts of Fitness and Wellness*.

- American College of Sports Medicine. Basic Injury Prevention Concepts.
- American College of Sports Medicine. Key position statements.

- American Heart Association. Heartsaver® First Aid CPR AED training.
- Environmental Protection Agency. Air Quality Index (AQI) from AirNow.gov.
- ePARmedx.com. Online physical activity readiness questionnaire.
- Institute of Medicine. (2012, September). *Fitness measures and health outcomes in youth.* National Academies Press (pdf).
- Reynolds, G. (2017, July 19). The toll of exercise on the heart (and why you may not need to worry). *The New York Times* (extreme exercise and the heart).
- WebMD. Understanding Heat-Related Illness Symptoms.

Lab 4A Readiness for Physical Activity

Name	Section	Date

Purpose: To help you determine your physical readiness for physical activity.

Procedures

1. Read the entire PAR-Q+ that follows.
2. After reading the PAR-Q+, answer the seven questions in the area bordered by the black box.
3. Record the number of "yes" answers in the Results section.
4. Discuss your medical readiness in the Conclusions and Implications section.

Results

Determine your PAR-Q+ score. Place an X over the circle that includes the number of "yes" answers that you had for the PAR-Q+ on the next page).

(0)　(1)　(2)　(3)　(4)　(5)　(6)　(7)

1. If you answered "no" to all seven questions, you are cleared for physical activity.
2. Follow the guidelines in the second section (inside the green border) of the PAR-Q+ before beginning physical activity.
3. If you answered "yes" to any of the questions, go to http://eparmedx.com to answer follow-up questions about medical conditions (pages 2 and 3 of the questionnaire) and inform your instructor of any limitations. If you have a temporary illness, are pregnant, or if your health changes delay activity (see information inside the yellow border at the bottom of the form).
4. If you answered "no" to all questions, you are cleared for participation in physical activity. If you plan to participate in physical activity at a fitness center or a health club, you may be asked to sign a separate declaration such as the one shown in the green area or on page 4 of the full PAR-Q+ form (see http://eparmedx.com).

Conclusions and Implications: In several sentences, discuss your readiness for physical activity. Base your comments on your questionnaire results and the types of physical activities you plan to perform in the future.

57

2018 PAR-Q+

The Physical Activity Readiness Questionnaire for Everyone

The health benefits of regular physical activity are clear; more people should engage in physical activity every day of the week. Participating in physical activity is very safe for MOST people. This questionnaire will tell you whether it is necessary for you to seek further advice from your doctor OR a qualified exercise professional before becoming more physically active.

GENERAL HEALTH QUESTIONS

Please read the 7 questions below carefully and answer each one honestly: check YES or NO.	YES	NO
1) Has your doctor ever said that you have a heart condition ☐ OR high blood pressure ☐?	☐	☐
2) Do you feel pain in your chest at rest, during your daily activities of living, **OR** when you do physical activity?	☐	☐
3) Do you lose balance because of dizziness **OR** have you lost consciousness in the last 12 months? Please answer **NO** if your dizziness was associated with over-breathing (including during vigorous exercise).	☐	☐
4) Have you ever been diagnosed with another chronic medical condition (other than heart disease or high blood pressure)? **PLEASE LIST CONDITION(S) HERE:** _____	☐	☐
5) Are you currently taking prescribed medications for a chronic medical condition? **PLEASE LIST CONDITION(S) AND MEDICATIONS HERE:** _____	☐	☐
6) Do you currently have (or have had within the past 12 months) a bone, joint, or soft tissue (muscle, ligament, or tendon) problem that could be made worse by becoming more physically active? Please answer **NO** if you had a problem in the past, but it *does not limit your current ability* to be physically active. **PLEASE LIST CONDITION(S) HERE:** _____	☐	☐
7) Has your doctor ever said that you should only do medically supervised physical activity?	☐	☐

☑ **If you answered NO to all of the questions above, you are cleared for physical activity.**
Please sign the PARTICIPANT DECLARATION. You do not need to complete Pages 2 and 3.

- ▶ Start becoming much more physically active – start slowly and build up gradually.
- ▶ Follow International Physical Activity Guidelines for your age (www.who.int/dietphysicalactivity/en/).
- ▶ You may take part in a health and fitness appraisal.
- ▶ If you are over the age of 45 yr and NOT accustomed to regular vigorous to maximal effort exercise, consult a qualified exercise professional before engaging in this intensity of exercise.
- ▶ If you have any further questions, contact a qualified exercise professional.

PARTICIPANT DECLARATION
If you are less than the legal age required for consent or require the assent of a care provider, your parent, guardian or care provider must also sign this form.

I, the undersigned, have read, understood to my full satisfaction and completed this questionnaire. I acknowledge that this physical activity clearance is valid for a maximum of 12 months from the date it is completed and becomes invalid if my condition changes. I also acknowledge that the community/fitness centre may retain a copy of this form for records. In these instances, it will maintain the confidentiality of the same, complying with applicable law.

NAME _____ DATE _____

SIGNATURE _____ WITNESS _____

SIGNATURE OF PARENT/GUARDIAN/CARE PROVIDER _____

🛑 **If you answered YES to one or more of the questions above, COMPLETE PAGES 2 AND 3.**

⚠ **Delay becoming more active if:**

- ✔ You have a temporary illness such as a cold or fever; it is best to wait until you feel better.
- ✔ You are pregnant - talk to your health care practitioner, your physician, a qualified exercise professional, and/or complete the ePARmed-X+ at **www.eparmedx.com** before becoming more physically active.
- ✔ Your health changes - answer the questions on Pages 2 and 3 of this document and/or talk to your doctor or a qualified exercise professional before continuing with any physical activity program.

Note: It is important that you answer all questions honestly. The PAR-Q+ is a scientifically and medically researched pre-exercise selection device. It complements exercise programs, exercise testing procedures, and the liability considerations attendant with such programs and testing procedures. PAR-Q+, like any other pre-exercise screening device, will misclassify a small percentage of prospective participants, but no pre-exercise screening method can entirely avoid this problem.

Lab 4B The Warm-Up

Name	Section	Date

Purpose: To familiarize you with possible warm-up and cool-down exercises.

Procedures

1. Consider the specific type of workout you are planning to perform and place a check in the Results section (e.g., walk, jog, slow jump rope). When completed, place a check in the box in the Results Section that corresponds to your planned workout.
2. Perform a general cardiovascular warm-up.
3. Perform each of the exercises in Chart 1. Perform dynamic exercises several times. Perform stretching exercises three times for 15–30 seconds each.
4. After you perform the specific warm-up exercises, place a check (Results section) beside the warm-up exercises that you think you would most likely include in your personal warm-up for the workout you checked.
5. Answer the questions in the Conclusions and Implications section.

Type of Workout (check one):

☐ Long jog

☐ Vigorous-intensity recreational activity

☐ Sports (game or practice)

☐ Other _____

☐ Cardiovascular Warm-Up

☐ Moderate-intensity recreational activity

☐ Vigorous aerobics

☐ Muscle fitness exercises

Warm-Up Exercises (check those that you would include in your warm-up):

Dynamic Warm-Up

☐ Grapevine

☐ Knee stride and reach

☐ High skip and reach

☐ Inchworm

☐ Backward jog

Stretch Warm-Up

☐ Calf stretch

☐ Hamstring stretch

☐ Seated side stretch

☐ Leg hug

Conclusions and Implications: In several sentences, explain the reasons for your selections.

Chart 1 The Warm-up

Dynamic Exercises. If you choose a dynamic exercise warm-up, perform the five exercises below and/or exercises from the Basic 8 for Calisthenics in the Concept on muscle fitness.

Grapevine

With feet at shoulder width and arms out at shoulder height, move sideways. With right leg, step across left leg, then step to left with left leg, right leg step behind left leg, step left leg to left. Repeat in the opposite direction, starting with left leg. Repeat several times.

Inchworm

From push-up position, walk the feet toward the hands several steps, keeping the hands still. Then walk the hands forward keeping the feet still. Repeat several times.

Knee Stride and Reach

Take a long stride forward with the right leg, touch the left knee to the floor. Reach up with both arms as you stride. Stand and repeat with left stride and right knee touch. Repeat 10–20 times.

Backward Jog

Jog backward slowly using moderately long steps. Pump your arms back and forth. Cover a distance of 10 yards, turn around, and backward jog in opposite direction. Repeat several times.

High Skip and Reach

Do a slow high skip. Alternate swinging one arm up and high above the head. Right arm up when on the right foot; left arm up when on the left foot. Repeat 10–20 times.

When performing a dynamic warm-up in the future you may want to consider the exercises from the Basic 8 for Calisthenics in the Concept on Muscle Fitness, as well as the exercises here.

Stretching Exercises. If you choose to do a stretch warm-up, perform the four stretching exercises below and/or other stretching exercises from the Concept on flexibility. Perform each stretch for at least 15–30 seconds.

Calf Stretch

This exercise stretches the calf muscles (gastrocnemius and soleus). Face a wall with your feet 2 or 3 feet away. Step forward on your left foot to allow both hands to touch the wall. Keep the heel of your right foot on the ground, toe turned in slightly, knee straight, and buttocks tucked in. Lean forward by bending your front knee and arms and allowing your head to move nearer the wall. Hold. Repeat with the other leg.

Seated Side Stretch

This exercise stretches the muscles of the trunk. Begin in a seated position with the legs crossed. Stretch the left arm over the head to the right. Bend at the waist (to right), reaching as far as possible to the left with the right arm. Hold. Do not let the trunk rotate. Repeat to the opposite side. This exercise can be done in the standing position but is less effective.

Hamstring Stretch

This exercise stretches the muscles of the back of the upper leg (hamstrings) as well as those of the hip, knee, and ankle. Lie on your back. Bring the right knee to your chest and grasp the toes with the right hand. Place the left hand on the back of the right thigh. Pull the knee toward the chest, push the heel toward the ceiling, and pull the toes toward the shin. Attempt to straighten the knee. Stretch and hold. Repeat with the other leg.

Leg Hug

This exercise stretches the hip and back extensor muscles. Lie on your back. Bend one leg and grasp your thigh under the knee. Hug it to your chest. Keep the other leg straight and on the floor. Hold. Repeat with the opposite leg.

When performing a stretch warm-up in the future, consider the four stretching exercises above and/or other stretching exercises from the Concept on flexibility.

Lab 4C Physical Activity Attitude Questionnaire

| | | | | | | | |

Name   Section   Date

Purpose: To evaluate your feelings about physical activity and to determine the specific reasons you do or do not participate in regular physical activity.

Directions: The term *physical activity* in the following statements refers to all kinds of activities, including sports, formal exercises, and informal activities such as jogging and cycling. Make an X over the circle that best represents your answer to each question.

		Strongly Disagree	Disagree	Undecided	Agree	Strongly Agree	Item Score	Attitude Score
1.	I should do physical activity regularly for my health.	1	2	3	4	5		Health and Fitness Score
2.	Doing regular physical activity is good for my fitness and wellness.	1	2	3	4	5	+	=
3.	Regular exercise helps me look my best.	1	2	3	4	5		Appearance Score
4.	I feel more physically attractive when I do regular physical activity.	1	2	3	4	5	+	=
5.	One of the main reasons I do regular physical activity is that it is fun.	1	2	3	4	5		Enjoyment Score
6.	The most enjoyable part of my day is when I am exercising or doing a sport.	1	2	3	4	5	+	=
7.	Taking part in physical activity helps me relax.	1	2	3	4	5		Relaxation Score
8.	Physical activity helps me get away from the pressures of daily living.	1	2	3	4	5	+	=
9.	The challenge of physical training is one reason I do physical activity.	1	2	3	4	5		Challenge Score
10.	I like to see if I can master sports and activities that are new to me.	1	2	3	4	5	+	=
11.	I like to do physical activity that involves other people.	1	2	3	4	5		Social Score
12.	Exercise offers me the opportunity to meet other people.	1	2	3	4	5	+	=
13.	Competition is a good way to make physical activity fun.	1	2	3	4	5		Competition Score
14.	I like to see how my physical abilities compare with those of others.	1	2	3	4	5	+	=
15.	When I do regular exercise, I feel better than when I don't.	1	2	3	4	5		Feeling Good Score
16.	My ability to do physical activity is something that makes me proud.	1	2	3	4	5	+	=
17.	I like to do outdoor activities.	1	2	3	4	5		Outdoor Score
18.	Experiencing nature is something I look forward to when exercising.	1	2	3	4	5	+	=

Procedures

1. Read and answer each question in the questionnaire.
2. Write the number in the circle of your answer in the box labeled "Item Score."
3. Add scores for each pair of scores and record in the "Attitude Score" box.
4. Record each attitude score and a rating for each score (use Rating Chart) in the chart below.
5. Record the number of good and excellent scores in the box provided. Use the score in the box to determine your rating using the Balance of Attitudes Rating Chart.

Results: Record your results as indicated in the Procedures section.

Physical Activity Attitude Questionnaire Results

Attitude	Score	Rating
Health and fitness		
Appearance		
Enjoyment		
Relaxation		
Challenge		
Social		
Competition		
Feeling good		
Outdoor		

How many good or excellent scores do you have?

Balance of Feeling Score

Having 5 or more in the box above indicates that you have a positive balance of attitudes (more positive than negative attitudes).

Attitude Rating Chart

Rating Category	Attitude Score
Excellent	9–10
Good	7–8
Fair	5–6
Poor	3–4
Very poor	2

Balance of Attitudes Rating Chart

Excellent	6–9
Good	5
Fair	4
Poor	2–3
Very poor	0–1

In a few sentences, discuss your "balance of attitudes" rating. Having more positive than negative scores (positive balance of attitudes) increases the probability of being active. Include comments on whether you think your ratings suggest that you will be active or inactive and whether your ratings are really indicative of your attitudes. Do you think that the scores on which you were rated poor or very poor might be reasons you would avoid physical activity? Explain.

The Health Benefits of Physical Activity

LEARNING OBJECTIVES

After completing the study of this Concept, you will be able to:

▶ Define the term *hypokinetic* and explain how physical activity can reduce risk of hypokinetic diseases and conditions.

▶ Identify several cardiovascular diseases/conditions associated with physical inactivity and explain how physical activity can help reduce risk.

▶ Describe metabolic syndrome and explain how physical activity can help reduce risk of this hypokinetic condition.

▶ Explain how physical activity can help reduce risk of other hypokinetic conditions.

▶ Explain the role of physical activity in preventing conditions associated with aging.

▶ Explain the role of physical activity in promoting optimal wellness.

▶ Present an overview of the health and wellness benefits of physical activity and fitness.

▶ Identify related national health goals and show how meeting personal goals can contribute to reaching national goals.

▶ Assess your heart disease risk factors.

Physical activity and good physical fitness can reduce the risk of illness and contribute to optimal health, wellness and fitness.

©JoseGirarte/Getty Images

Why it Matters!

The overarching goal of the *Healthy People* national health objectives is to help all people have high-quality, longer lives free of preventable disease, injury, and premature death. You can personally achieve these goals by committing to being physically active your entire life. Physical activity improves physical fitness and contributes to high-quality life (wellness, the positive component of good health). Regular physical activity also contributes to a longer life (lifespan) free of preventable disease and injury (healthspan). Physical activity is certainly not a panacea for all health issues, but it is likely the most important thing you can do to achieve good health, wellness, and fitness. This Concept will reinforce the importance of these tangible benefits associated with a physically active lifestyle.

Regular physical activity is good for the mind and body.
©Maridav/Shutterstock

Physical Activity, Fitness, and Wellness

Regular physical activity contributes to good physical fitness. Regular physical activity can lead to many physical fitness benefits (see Figure 1):

- Good physical fitness helps you function effectively (functional fitness). Although the need for each component of physical fitness is specific to each individual, every person requires enough fitness to perform normal daily activities without undue fatigue. Whether it be walking, performing household chores, or merely enjoying the simple things in life without pain or fear of injury, good fitness is important to all people.

- Good physical fitness can help an individual work more efficiently. A person who can resist fatigue, muscle soreness, back problems, and other symptoms associated with poor health-related fitness is capable of working productively and still has energy at the end of the day.

- Good physical fitness can help an individual enjoy leisure time. A fit person is more likely to get and stay involved in leisure-time activities than an unfit person. Enjoying your leisure time may not add years to your life, but it can add life to your years (wellness).

- Good physical fitness can help you handle unexpected emergencies. Emergencies often demand performance that requires good fitness. For example, flood victims may need to fill sandbags for hours without rest, and accident victims may be required to walk or run long distances for help.

- Good physical fitness is the basis for dynamic and creative activity. Although the following quotation by President John F. Kennedy is more than 50 years old, it clearly

points out the importance of physical fitness: *"The relationship between the soundness of the body and the activity*

of the mind is subtle and complex. Much is not yet understood, but we know what the Greeks knew: that intelligence and skill can only function at the peak of their capacity when the body is healthy and strong, and that hardy spirits and tough minds usually inhabit sound bodies. Physical fitness is the basis of all activities in our society."

Regular physical activity contributes to optimal wellness. Regular physical activity promotes high quality of life by contributing to each of the five dimensions of wellness.

- *Physical:* Regular physical activity enhances physical wellness by promoting good physical fitness (see previous section). Active people are less likely to miss work or school. Good fitness from regular physical activity helps you look your best.

- *Emotional/Mental:* Regular physical activity promotes emotional/mental wellness as evidenced by positive mood states, reduced anxiety and depression, improved self-concept, and greater independence.

- *Intellectual:* Regular physical activity fosters intellectual wellness by stimulating new brain cell development, enhancing higher-order brain functions such as attention and concentration, and improving cognitive performance (better short-term memory and better scores on tests).

- *Social:* Regular physical activity promotes social wellness through physical activities with friends in social settings. It can create camaraderie and teamwork through sports and

Health, Wellness, and Fitness Benefits of Physical Activity

Improved Cardiovascular Health
- Stronger heart muscle fitness and health
- Lower heart rate
- Better electric stability of heart
- Decreased sympathetic control of heart
- Increased O_2 to brain
- Reduced blood fat, including low-density lipoproteins (LDLs)
- Increased protective high-density lipoproteins (HDLs)
- Delayed development of atherosclerosis
- Increased work capacity
- Improved peripheral circulation
- Improved coronary circulation
- Resistance to "emotional storm"
- Reduced risk for heart attack
- Reduced risk for stroke
- Reduced risk for hypertension
- Greater chance of surviving a heart attack
- Increased oxygen-carrying capacity of the blood

Improved Strength and Muscular Endurance
- Greater work efficiency
- Less chance for muscle injury
- Reduced risk for low back problems
- Improved performance in sports
- Quicker recovery after hard work
- Improved ability to meet emergencies

Resistance to Fatigue
- Ability to enjoy leisure
- Improved quality of life
- Improved ability to meet some stressors

Other Health Benefits
- Decreased diabetes risk
- Quality of life for diabetics
- Improved metabolic fitness
- Extended life
- Decrease in dysfunctional years
- Aids for some people who have arthritis, PMS, asthma, chronic pain, multiple sclerosis, fibromyalgia, or impotence
- Improved immune system

Enhanced Mental Health and Function
- Relief of depression
- Improved sleep habits
- Fewer stress symptoms
- Ability to enjoy leisure and work
- Improved brain function

Improved Wellness
- Improved quality of life
- Leisure-time enjoyment
- Improved work capacity
- Ability to meet emergencies
- Improved creative capacity

Opportunity for Successful Experience and Social Interactions
- Improved self-concept
- Opportunity to recognize and accept personal limitations
- Improved sense of well-being
- Enjoyment of life and fun
- Improved quality of life

Improved Appearance
- Better figure/physique
- Better posture
- Fat control

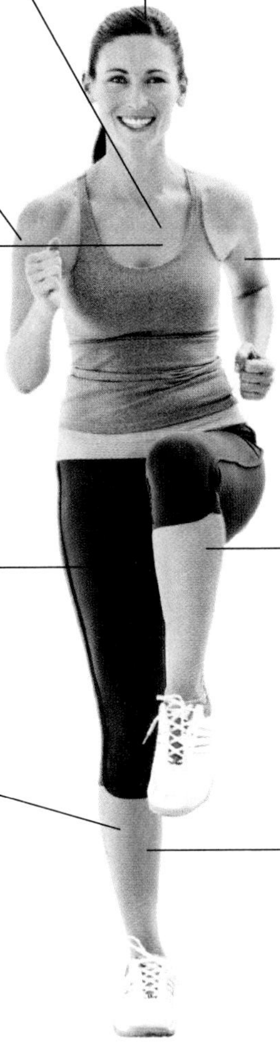

Greater Lean Body Mass and Less Body Fat
- Greater work efficiency
- Less susceptibility to disease
- Improved appearance
- Less incidence of self-concept problems related to obesity

Improved Flexibility
- Greater work efficiency
- Less chance of muscle injury
- Less chance of joint injury
- Decreased chance of developing low back problems
- Improved sports performance

Bone Development
- Greater peak bone density
- Less chance of developing osteoporosis

Reduced Cancer Risk
- Reduced risk for colon and breast cancers
- Possible reduced risk for rectal and prostate cancers

Reduced Effect of Acquired Aging
- Improved ability to function in daily life
- Better short-term memory
- Fewer illnesses
- Greater mobility
- Greater independence
- Greater ability to operate an automobile
- Lower risk for dementia

Figure 1 ▶ Health, wellness, and fitness benefits of physical activity.
(photo): ©Neustockimages/E+/Getty Images

recreational activities. In addition, it offers opportunities for group and individual challenges.

- *Spiritual:* Regular physical activity can promote spiritual wellness through outdoor and meditative activities.

Regular physical activity can improve fitness and functioning among older adults. Approximately 30 percent of adults aged 70 and over have difficulty with one or more activities of daily living. Women have more limitations than men, and low-income groups have more limitations than higher-income groups. Nearly one-half of these adults also get no assistance in coping with their limitations.

The inability to function effectively as you grow older is associated with lack of fitness and inactive lifestyles. This loss of function is sometimes referred to as "acquired aging," as opposed to "time-dependent" aging. Because so many people experience limitations in daily activities and find it difficult to get assistance, it is especially important for older people to stay active and fit.

In general, older adults are much less active than younger adults. Losses in muscle fitness are associated with loss of balance, greater risk of falling, and less ability to function independently. Studies also show that exercise can enhance cognitive functioning and perhaps reduce risk for dementia. Though the amount of activity performed must be adapted as people grow older, fitness benefits discussed in the next section and in later Concepts apply to people of all ages.

Regular physical activity can increase healthspan. An important national health goal is to increase the years of healthy life. Living longer is important, but being able to function effectively during all years of life (healthspan) is equally—if not more—important. *Compression of illness,* also called compression of morbidity, refers to shortening the total number of years that illnesses and disabilities occur. Healthy lifestyles, including regular physical activity, have been shown to compress illness and increase years of effective functioning. Inactive people not only have a shorter lifespan, but also have more years of illness and disability than active people.

Physical Activity and Hypokinetic Diseases

Regular physical activity reduces risk of the major chronic diseases. Most of the leading killers in our society are preventable chronic diseases (e.g., heart disease, cancer). These diseases are frequently referred to as **hypokinetic diseases or conditions** because regular physical activity reduces risk of these conditions. Virtually all **chronic diseases** that plague society are considered to be hypokinetic, though some relate more to inactivity than others. Nearly three-quarters of all deaths among those 18 and older are a result of chronic diseases. Leading public health officials have suggested that physical activity may offer the most promising public health solution to control chronic diseases, much as immunization controls infectious diseases. Many of the benefits of physical activity are summarized in Figure 1. Detailed descriptions of the various hypokinetic diseases and the benefits of regular physical activity are included in the sections that follow.

Regular physical activity over a lifetime may overcome the effects of inherited risk. People with a family history of disease may believe they can do nothing because their heredity works against them. There is no doubt that heredity significantly affects risk for early death from hypokinetic diseases. Studies of twins, however, suggest that active people are less likely to die early than inactive people with similar genes. This suggests that long-term adherence to physical activity can overcome other risk factors, such as heredity.

Physical Activity and Cardiovascular Diseases

The various types of cardiovascular disease are the leading killers in automated societies. There are many forms of **cardiovascular disease (CVD).** Some are classified as **coronary heart disease (CHD)** because they affect the heart muscle and the blood vessels that supply the heart. **Coronary occlusion** (heart attack) is a type of CHD. **Atherosclerosis** and **arteriosclerosis** are two conditions that increase risk for heart attack and are considered to be types of CHD. Angina pectoris (chest or arm pain), which occurs when the oxygen supply to the heart muscle is diminished, is sometimes considered to be a type of CHD, though it is really a symptom of poor circulation.

Stroke (brain attack), **hypertension** (high blood pressure), **peripheral vascular disease,** and **congestive heart failure** are other forms of CVD. In the United States, CVD accounts for more than 32 percent of all deaths. More than 83.5 million people currently have one or more forms of CVD. Men are more likely to suffer from heart disease than women, although the differences have narrowed in recent years. African American, Hispanic, and Native American populations are at higher than normal risk. Patterns are similar in other developed countries.

connect
VIDEO 2

Physical inactivity is a primary risk factor for CHD. The American Heart Association recognizes physical inactivity as one of seven primary risk factors for CHD. These risk factors are referred to as *Life's Simple 7* including smoking, inactivity, poor nutrition, overweight/obesity, high blood cholesterol, high blood pressure, and high blood sugar. The CDC indicates that eliminating three risk factors—smoking, inactivity, and poor eating—could prevent 80 percent of heart disease and stroke, 80 percent of Type 2 diabetes, and 40 percent of cancer cases. The economic costs of CHD are high. In fact, one of every 6 dollars spent on health care goes to CHD treatment. Campaigns such as *Life's Simple 7* (and the associated *My Life Check* assessment) are designed to promote awareness of CHD risks and contribute to reducing health care costs in society (see Technology Update).

Technology Update

My Life Check: A Tool to Evaluate Your Heart Health

While the risk factors for cardiovascular disease are well established, many people still struggle to make the needed changes to improve their health. The American Heart Association has developed a simple, effective, and free assessment called "My Life Check" that gives you a quick "heart score" based on your lifestyles. The assessment focuses on what are referred to as the "Simple 7" key risk indicators/behaviors: Manage Blood Pressure, Control Cholesterol, Reduce Blood Sugar, Get Active, Eat Better, Lose Weight, and Stop Smoking. (Search My Life Check or see the link in Suggested Resources and Readings.)

Would tracking these indicators help you maintain healthy lifestyles? If these data were linked to your physician's office, would it help you be more accountable for your lifestyle?

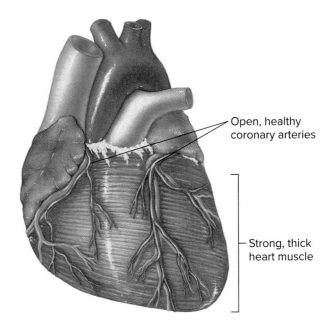

— Open, healthy coronary arteries

— Strong, thick heart muscle

Figure 2 ▶ The fit heart muscle.

Physical Activity and the Healthy Heart

Regular exercise increases the heart muscle's ability to pump oxygen-rich blood. A fit heart muscle can handle extra demands placed on it. Through regular exercise, the heart muscle gets stronger, contracts more forcefully, and therefore pumps more blood with each beat. The heart is just like any other muscle—it must be exercised regularly to stay fit. The fit heart also has open, clear arteries free of atherosclerosis (see Figure 2).

The "normal" resting heart rate is said to be 72 beats per minute (bpm). However, resting rates of 50 to 85 bpm are common. People who regularly do physical activity typically have lower resting heart rates than people who do no regular activity. Some endurance athletes have heart rates in the 30 and 40 bpm range, which is considered healthy or normal. Although resting heart rate is *not* considered to be a good measure of health or fitness, decreases in individual heart rate following training reflect positive adaptations. Low heart rates in response to a standard amount of physical activity *are* a good indicator of fitness. The bicycle and step tests presented later use your heart rate response to a standard amount of exercise to estimate your cardiorespiratory endurance.

Hypokinetic Diseases or Conditions *Hypo-* means "under" or "too little," and -*kinetic* means "movement" or "activity." Thus, *hypokinetic* means "too little activity." A hypokinetic disease or condition is one associated with lack of physical activity or too little regular exercise. Examples include heart disease, low back pain, Type 2 diabetes, and obesity.

Chronic Diseases Diseases or illnesses associated with lifestyle or environmental factors, as opposed to infectious diseases; hypokinetic diseases are considered to be chronic diseases.

Cardiovascular Disease (CVD) A broad classification of diseases of the heart and blood vessels that includes CHD, high blood pressure, stroke, and peripheral vascular disease.

Coronary Heart Disease (CHD) Diseases of the heart muscle and the blood vessels that supply it with oxygen, including heart attack.

Coronary Occlusion The blocking of the coronary blood vessels; sometimes called heart attack.

Atherosclerosis The deposition of materials along the arterial walls; a type of arteriosclerosis.

Arteriosclerosis Hardening of the arteries due to conditions that cause the arterial walls to become thick, hard, and nonelastic.

Stroke A condition in which the brain, or part of the brain, receives insufficient oxygen as a result of diminished blood supply; sometimes called apoplexy or cerebrovascular accident (CVA).

Hypertension High blood pressure; excessive pressure against the walls of the arteries that can damage the heart, kidneys, and other organs of the body.

Peripheral Vascular Disease A lack of oxygen supply to the working muscles and tissues of the arms and legs, resulting from decreased blood flow.

Congestive Heart Failure The inability of the heart muscle to pump the blood at a life-sustaining rate.

Physical Activity and Atherosclerosis

Atherosclerosis, which begins early in life, is implicated in many cardiovascular diseases. Atherosclerosis is a condition that contributes to heart attack, stroke, hypertension, and peripheral vascular disease. Deposits on the walls of arteries restrict blood flow and oxygen supply to the tissues. Atherosclerosis of the coronary arteries, the vessels that supply the heart muscle with oxygen, is particularly harmful. As arteries become progressively narrower, the blood supply to the heart muscle is diminished. Individuals may experience a sharp chest pain called *angina pectoris* to alert them to a problem. However, atherosclerosis can also precipitate a heart attack because a fibrous clot is more likely to obstruct a narrowed artery than a healthy, open one.

Current theory suggests that atherosclerosis begins when damage occurs to the cells of the inner wall, or endothelium, of the artery (see Figure 3). Substances associated with blood clotting are attracted to the damaged area. These substances seem to cause the migration of smooth muscle cells, commonly found only in the middle wall of the artery (media), to the endothelium. In the later stages, fats and other substances form plaques, or protrusions, that progressively diminish the internal diameter of the artery.

Physical activity can help prevent atherosclerosis by lowering blood lipid levels. There are several kinds of **lipids** (fats) in the bloodstream, including **lipoproteins,** phospholipids, triglycerides, and cholesterol. Cholesterol is the most well known, but it is not the only culprit. Many blood fats are manufactured by the body itself, whereas others are ingested in high-fat foods, particularly saturated fats (fats that are solid at room temperature).

As noted earlier, blood lipids are thought to contribute to the development of atherosclerotic deposits on the inner walls of the artery. One substance, called **low-density lipoprotein (LDL),** is a major contributor to the development of atherosclerosis. LDL is basically a core of cholesterol surrounded by protein and another substance that makes it water soluble. The benefit of regular exercise is that it can reduce blood lipid levels, including LDL-C (the cholesterol core of LDL). People with high total cholesterol and LDL levels have a higher than normal risk for heart disease (see Table 1). However, there are subtypes of LDL cholesterol (characterized by their small size and high density) that pose even greater risks. These subtypes are hard to measure and not included in most current blood tests, but future research will no doubt help us better understand and measure them.

Triglycerides are another type of blood lipid. Elevated levels of triglycerides are related to heart disease. Triglycerides lose some of their ability to predict heart disease with the presence of other risk factors, so high levels are more difficult to interpret than other blood lipids. Normal levels are considered to be 150 mg/dL or less. Values of 151 to 199 are borderline, 200 to 499 are high, and above 500 are very high. It would be wise to include triglycerides in a blood lipid profile. Physical activity is often prescribed as part of a treatment for high triglyceride levels.

Physical activity can help prevent atherosclerosis by increasing HDL in the blood. Whereas LDLs carry a core of cholesterol that is involved in the development of atherosclerosis, **high-density lipoprotein (HDL)** picks up cholesterol and carries it to the liver, where it is eliminated from the body. HDL is often called the "good cholesterol" and is desirable. When having a blood test, ask for information about HDL as well as the other measures included in Table 1. Individuals who have regular physical activity usually have lower total cholesterol, lower LDL, and higher HDL levels than inactive people.

Physical activity can help prevent atherosclerosis by reducing blood coagulants. Fibrin and platelets (types of cells involved in blood coagulation) deposit at the site of an injury on the wall of the artery, contributing to the process of plaque buildup, or atherosclerosis. Regular physical activity has been shown to reduce fibrin levels in the blood. The breakdown of fibrin seems to reduce platelet adhesiveness and the concentration of platelets in the blood.

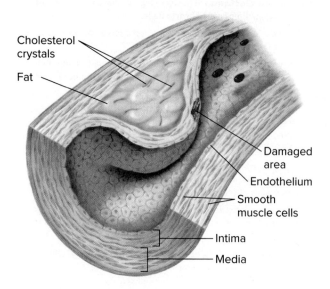

Cholesterol crystals
Fat
Damaged area
Endothelium
Smooth muscle cells
Intima
Media

Figure 3 ▶ Atherosclerosis.

Table 1 ▶ Cholesterol Classifications (mg/dL)

	Total (TC)	LDL-C	HDL-C	TC/HDL-C
Optimal	—	<100	—	
Near optimal	—	100–129	—	—
Desirable	<200	—	60+	—
Borderline	200–239	130–159	40–59	3.6–5.0
High risk	240+	160–189	<40	5.0+
Very high risk	—	>190	—	—

Source: Third Report of the National Cholesterol Education Program.

Other indicators of inflammation of the arteries are predictive of atherosclerosis. A number of other constituents in the blood have been shown to be associated with risk for cardiovascular disease. These compounds are not necessarily causes of atherosclerosis, but they are indicators of inflammatory processes that lead to plaque formation. Inflammatory processes also soften existing plaque and increase the likelihood of plaque rupture or the formation of clots, which can directly precipitate heart attacks.

A number of inflammatory markers have been studied, but a recent AHA/CDC position statement indicates that most are "not yet applicable for routine risk assessment" for a variety of reasons. The position statement indicates that C-reactive protein (CRP) is the one inflammatory marker recommended for use in screening. CRP values above 3.0 mg/L are considered high risk and values below 1.0 mg/L are considered low risk. You may want to ask your physician about inflammatory markers at your next physical exam.

Physical Activity and Heart Attack

Physical activity reduces the risk for heart attack, the most prevalent and serious of all cardiovascular diseases. A heart attack (coronary occlusion) occurs when a coronary artery is blocked (see Figure 4). A clot, or thrombus, is the most common cause, reducing or cutting off blood flow and oxygen to the heart muscle. If the blocked coronary artery supplies a major portion of the heart muscle, death will occur within minutes. Occlusions of lesser arteries may result in angina pectoris or a nonfatal heart attack.

People who perform regular physical activity have half the risk for a first heart attack, compared with those who are sedentary. Possible reasons are less atherosclerosis, greater diameter of arteries, and less chance of a clot forming.

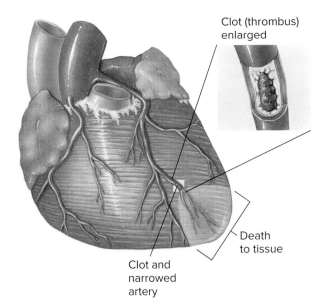

Figure 4 ▶ Heart attack.

Clot (thrombus) enlarged

Death to tissue

Clot and narrowed artery

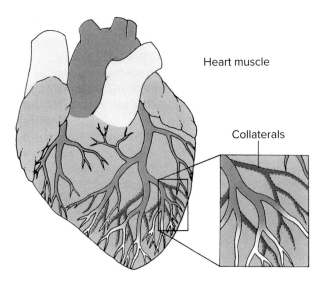

Figure 5 ▶ Coronary collateral circulation.

Heart muscle

Collaterals

Physical activity can improve coronary circulation and, thus, reduce the chances of having a heart attack or dying from one. Within the heart, many tiny branches extend from the major coronary arteries. All of these vessels supply blood to the heart muscle. Active people are likely to have greater blood-carrying capacity in these vessels, probably because the vessels are larger and more elastic. Also, active people may have more profuse distribution of arteries within the heart muscle (see Figure 5), which results in greater blood flow. There is evidence that physical activity may promote the growth of "extra" blood vessels, which are thought to open up to provide the heart muscle with the necessary blood and oxygen when the oxygen supply is diminished, as in a heart attack. Blood flow from extra blood vessels is referred to as **coronary collateral circulation.**

Improved coronary circulation provides protection against heart attacks since healthier vessels are larger and less occluded. The development of collateral blood vessels supplying the heart may also diminish the effects of a heart attack, as these extra (or collateral) blood vessels may take over the function of regular blood vessels if another vessel gets clogged.

Lipids All fats and fatty substances.

Lipoproteins Fat-carrying proteins in the blood.

Low-Density Lipoprotein (LDL) A core of cholesterol surrounded by protein; the core is often called "bad cholesterol."

Triglycerides A type of blood fat associated with increased risk for heart disease.

High-Density Lipoprotein (HDL) A blood substance that picks up cholesterol and helps remove it from the body; often called "good cholesterol."

Fibrin A sticky, threadlike substance that, in combination with blood cells, forms a blood clot.

Coronary Collateral Circulation Circulation of blood to the heart muscle associated with the blood-carrying capacity of a specific vessel or development of collateral vessels (extra blood vessels).

The heart of an inactive person is less able to resist stress and is more susceptible to an emotional storm that may precipitate a heart attack. The heart is rendered inefficient by one or more of the following circumstances: high heart rate, high blood pressure, and excessive stimulation. All of these conditions require the heart to use more oxygen than is normal and decrease its ability to adapt to stressful situations.

The inefficient heart beats rapidly because it is dominated by the **sympathetic nervous system,** which speeds up the heart rate. Thus, the heart continuously beats rapidly, even at rest, and never has a true rest period. High blood pressure also makes the heart work harder and contributes to its inefficiency.

Research indicates that regular physical activity can:

- lead to dominance of the **parasympathetic nervous system,** which slows the heart rate and helps the heart work efficiently;

- help the heart rate return to normal faster after emotional stress;

- strengthen the heart muscle, making it better able to weather an **emotional storm;**

- reduce hormonal effects on the heart, thus lessening the chances of circulatory problems; and

- reduce the risk of sudden death from ventricular fibrillation (arrhythmic heartbeat).

Regular physical activity is one effective means of rehabilitation for a person who has coronary heart disease or who has had a heart attack. Not only does regular physical activity seem to reduce the risk of developing coronary heart disease, but also those who already have the condition may reduce the symptoms of the disease through regular exercise. For people who have had heart attacks, regular and progressive exercise can be an effective prescription when carried out under the supervision of a physician. Remember, however, that exercise is not the treatment of preference for all heart attack victims. In some cases, it is harmful.

Physical Activity and Other Cardiovascular Diseases

Regular physical activity is associated with a reduced risk for high blood pressure (hypertension). "Normal" **systolic blood pressure** is less than 120 mm Hg, and normal **diastolic blood pressure** is less than 80 mm Hg. However, new guidelines from the American Heart Association and the American Stroke Association have changed the way that hypertension is categorized. The term *Stage 1 Hypertension* is now used to define an elevated blood pressure between 130/80 and 139/89 (see Table 2). This replaces the previous categorization of "Prehypertension" that was defined as values between 120/80 and 140/90. The new categorization

Table 2 ▶ Blood Pressure Classifications for Adults

Category	Systolic Blood Pressure (mm Hg)		Diastolic Blood Pressure (mm Hg)
Normal	<120	and	<80
Elevated	120–129	and	<80
Stage 1 Hypertension	130–139	or	80–89
Stage 2 Hypertension	140 and up	or	90 and up
Hypertensive Crisis	>180	and/or	>120

Source: www.heart.org/hbp.

will increase the estimated percentage of Americans with hypertension up to 46 percent compared with about 32 percent with the past definitions that started above 140/90. High blood pressure scars the vessel walls and increases the risks for heart attack, stroke, kidney damage, and other health problems. Evidence suggests that the risks are already doubled by the time readings reach 130/80; thus, the new guidelines are intended to draw attention to the risks and to promote behavior change. Because higher levels of blood pressure create greater risks, *Stage 2 Hypertension* is now defined as systolic BP at 140 or higher, or diastolic at 90 or higher. A new category of "Hypertensive Crisis" has also been added for values above 180 or 120, respectively, to denote a stronger alarm (see Table 2).

Hypertension is sometimes referred to as the "silent killer" because many people do not know they have it. African Americans, Hispanics, and Native Americans have higher incidence than White non-Hispanics, but incidence increases for all groups with age. Exceptionally low blood pressures (below 100 systolic and 60 diastolic) do not pose the same risks to health as high blood pressure but can cause dizziness, fainting, and lack of tolerance to change in body positions. It is important to be aware of your blood pressure levels and to monitor them over time, particularly with age. With practice and good equipment, you can accurately measure your own blood pressure. Because blood pressure can be elevated by emotions and circumstances, a single measurement may not be accurate. At least two separate measurements are recommended. While self-assessments can be helpful, they are not a substitute for periodic assessments by a qualified medical person.

Regular physical activity helps keep blood pressure in healthy levels and can reduce levels for individuals with hypertension. Exercise increases blood pressure on a short-term basis, but it imposes a positive stress on the heart by challenging it to pump higher volumes of blood. This leads to desirable adaptations that improve cardiac function and lower resting heart rate and blood pressure. Inactive, less fit individuals have a 30 to 50 percent greater chance of being hypertensive than active, fit people.

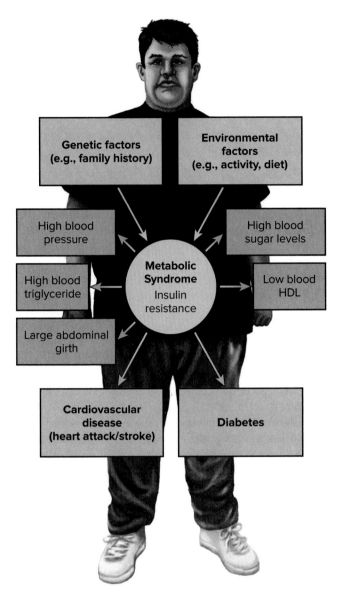

Figure 6 ▶ Mechanism and effects of metabolic syndrome.
Source: www.heart.org/hbp

Regular physical activity can help reduce the risk for stroke. Stroke is a major killer of adults. People with high blood pressure and atherosclerosis are susceptible to stroke. Since regular exercise and good fitness are important to the prevention of high blood pressure and atherosclerosis, exercise and fitness are considered helpful in the prevention of stroke.

Physical activity decreases risk factors for metabolic syndrome. Metabolic syndrome is a metabolic disorder that is characterized by a clustering of various metabolic risk factors. People with at least three of the following characteristics are considered to have metabolic syndrome: blood pressure above 130/85, a fasting blood sugar level of 100 or higher, blood triglycerides of 150 or above, a low blood HDL level

(less than 40 for men and less than 50 for women), and/or a high abdominal circumference (equal to or above 40 inches for men or 35 inches for women). As shown in Figure 6, metabolic syndrome is typically associated with insulin resistance (i.e., the body does not use insulin effectively). It directly impacts risk for diabetes as well as cardiovascular disease.

As with many conditions, family history and other genetic factors can predispose a person to metabolic syndrome (see Figure 6). However, healthy lifestyle and other environmental factors can positively impact all of the underlying precursors of metabolic syndrome. Thus, physical activity can reduce risk of metabolic syndrome as well as the various chronic conditions associated with it (e.g., diabetes, heart disease, and stroke). Lab 5A can be used to screen for possible risk of metabolic syndrome. A periodic physical exam with blood profiles and a metabolic syndrome assessment is recommended, especially as you get older.

Regular physical activity is helpful in preventing peripheral vascular disease. People who exercise regularly have better blood flow to the working muscles and other tissues than inactive, unfit people. Since peripheral vascular disease is associated with poor circulation to the extremities, regular exercise can be considered one method of preventing this condition.

Physical Activity and Other Hypokinetic Conditions

Physical activity reduces the risk of some forms of cancer. According to the American Cancer Society (ACS), cancer is a group of many different conditions characterized by abnormal, uncontrolled cell growth. The initial factors that contribute to the abnormal cell growth are not well understood. However, as the abnormal cells divide, they get larger and form **malignant tumors (carcinomas).** If the abnormal cells reach the blood, they can spread, causing tumors

Sympathetic Nervous System The branch of the autonomic nervous system that prepares the body for activity by speeding up the heart rate.

Parasympathetic Nervous System The branch of the autonomic nervous system that slows the heart rate.

Emotional Storm A traumatic emotional experience that is likely to affect the human organism physiologically.

Systolic Blood Pressure The upper blood pressure number, often called working blood pressure. It represents the pressure in the arteries at its highest level just after the heart beats.

Diastolic Blood Pressure The lower blood pressure number, often called resting pressure. It is the pressure in the arteries at its lowest level just before the next beat of the heart.

Malignant Tumors (carcinomas) An uncontrolled and dangerous growth capable of spreading to other areas; a cancerous tumor.

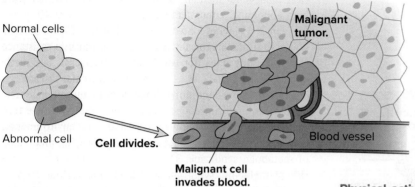

Normal cells

Abnormal cell   **Cell divides.**

Malignant cell invades blood.

Malignant tumor.

Blood vessel

Figure 7 ▶ The spread of cancer (metastasis).

elsewhere in the body (see Figure 7). **Benign tumors** are generally not considered to be cancerous because their growth is restricted to a specific area of the body by a protective membrane. The first editions of this book did not include any form of cancer as a hypokinetic disease. We now know, however, that overall death rates from some types of cancer are lower among active people than among those who are sedentary. In fact, the ACSM indicates that inactivity is linked to 13 different types of cancer. Possible reasons why physical activity reduces the risk of four common forms of cancer are described in Table 3. They are listed in order based on strength of evidence.

As previously indicated, cancer is the second leading cause of death. In the United States, cancer causes nearly 600,000 deaths annually. However, the  five-year survival rate for people diagnosed with cancer is up 50 percent over the past three decades. Many factors are responsible, including early diagnosis and improved medical treatments. Healthy lifestyles can also play a role. The ACS

Table 3 ▶ Beneficial Effects of Physical Activity on Cancer

Cancer Type	Effect of Physical Activity
Colon	Exercise speeds movement of food and cancer-causing substances through the digestive system, and reduces prostaglandins (substances linked to cancer in the colon).
Breast	Exercise decreases the amount of exposure of breast tissue to circulating estrogen. Lower body fat is also associated with lower estrogen levels. Early life activity is deemed important for both reasons. Fatigue from therapy is reduced by exercise.
Rectal	Similar to colon cancer, exercise leads to more regular bowel movements and reduces "transit time."
Prostate	Fatigue from therapy is reduced by exercise. Regular exercise, especially vigorous exercise, may reduce death rate.

guidelines highlight the importance of regular physical activity and a healthy diet in preventing cancer and early death. Physical activity is also considered to be important to the wellness of the cancer patient in many ways, including improved quality of life, physical functioning, and self-esteem, as well as less dependence on others, reduced risk for other diseases, and reduced fatigue from disease or disease therapy.

Physical activity plays a role in the management and treatment of Type 2 diabetes. Diabetes mellitus (diabetes) is a group of disorders that results when there is too much sugar in the blood. It occurs when the body does not make enough **insulin** or when the body is not able to use insulin effectively.

Type 1 diabetes, or insulin-dependent diabetes, accounts for a relatively small number of the diabetes cases and is not considered to be a hypokinetic condition. Type 2 diabetes (often not insulin-dependent) was formerly called "adult-onset diabetes." Reports indicate more cases of Type 2 diabetes among children than in the past, in part because of better record keeping but also because of increases in obesity among children in recent years.

Diabetes is the seventh leading cause of death among people over 40. It accounts for at least 10 percent of all short-term hospital stays and has a major impact on health-care costs in Western society. According to the American Diabetes Association (ADA), there are more than 30 million people who have been diagnosed as diabetic. Unfortunately another 7 million are diabetic and do not know it. An estimated additional 84 million are prediabetic.

There are several tests for diabetes and pre-diabetes. The most commonly used are the oral glucose tolerance test (OGTT) that assesses your ability to regulate blood sugar at the time of the  test and a blood test (A1C) that assesses your blood sugar levels over the past two to three months. Consult your physician to see what test is most appropriate for you.

Medical intervention is clearly essential for people with Type 2 diabetes, but healthy lifestyles are important for effective treatment. Regular physical activity can help reduce body fatness, decrease **insulin resistance,** improve **insulin sensitivity,** and improve the body's ability to clear sugar from the blood in a reasonable time. With sound nutritional habits and proper medication, physical activity can be useful in the management of both types of diabetes.

Physical activity is important to maintaining bone density and decreasing risk for osteoporosis. Some experts consider bone integrity to be a health-related component of physical fitness. Bone density cannot be self-assessed. It is measured using a dual X-ray absorptiometry (DXA) machine, an expensive and sophisticated form of X-ray machine that can also be used to measure body fatness. Healthy bones

In the News

Stronger Evidence for Benefits of Physical Activity

Every ten years the national Physical Activity Guidelines for Americans are revised. The most recent guidelines were published in 2018. Many of the "major findings" are similar to those described in this Concept. For example, the guidelines continue to emphasize that regular physical activity reduces the risk of a large number of diseases and conditions (e.g., heart disease, hypertension, cancer, diabetes, bone mineral loss) and that it is beneficial in maintaining a healthy weight and minimizing risk of overweight/obesity. However, the review also documented additional benefits. Some other major findings related to the health benefits of physical activity include:

• Physically active individuals sleep better, feel better (reduced depression and anxiety), function better (improved cognition), and have a better quality of life (more energy, less fatigue, ability to perform daily tasks, maintenance of independence).

• Single bouts of moderate to vigorous activity can produce some immediate benefits such as lower blood pressure, improved insulin sensitivity, improved sleep, reduced anxiety symptoms, and improved cognition.

• There is strong evidence that regular physical activity reduces the risk of dementia and improves some aspects of cognitive functioning.

For the first time, there is evidence that regular physical activity provides health benefits for children as young as 3 years of age. Search "2018 Physical Activity Guidelines for Americans" online to learn more about the revised guidelines.

Do you think the benefits of physical activity get enough attention? With the benefits being so strong, why is it hard for some people to justify the effort to fit in regular exercise?

are dense and strong. When bones lose calcium and become less dense, they become porous and are at risk for fracture. The bones of young children are not especially dense, but during adolescence and early adulthood (see Figure 8), bones increase in density to a level higher than at any other time in life (peak bone density). Though bone density often begins to decrease in young adulthood, it is not until older adulthood that bone loss becomes dramatic. Over time, if bone loss continues, older adults become susceptible to a condition called **osteoporosis** (bone density drops below the osteoporosis threshold). Some will have crossed the fracture threshold, putting them at risk for fractures, especially to the hip, vertebrae, and other "soft" or "spongy" bones of the skeletal system. Active people have a higher peak bone mass and are more resistant to osteoporosis (see blue line in Figure 8) than sedentary people (see red line in Figure 8).

Women, especially postmenopausal women, have a higher risk of osteoporosis than men, but it is a disease of both sexes.

Although Figure 8 reflects the combined bone density status for men and women, males typically have a higher peak bone mass than females, and for this reason, males can lose more bone density over time without reaching the osteoporosis or fracture threshold. More women reach the osteoporosis and fracture thresholds at earlier ages than men. Other risk factors for osteoporosis are age, family history/heredity, frame size, smoking, caffeine use, alcohol use, current or previous eating disorders, early menstruation, low dietary calcium intake, low body fat, amenorrhea, and extended bed rest.

The National Osteoporosis Foundation (NOF) recommends five steps to bone health and osteoporosis prevention:

1. Get your daily recommended amounts of calcium and vitamin D. Eat a diet rich in both nutrients. Exposure to the sun provides a source of vitamin D. The NOF recommends 1,000 mg of calcium daily for people under 50, and 1,200 mg for those over 50. Adults under age 50 need 400–800 IU of vitamin D, and adults over 50 need

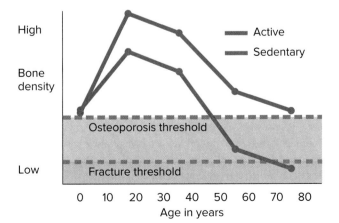

Figure 8 ▶ Changes in bone density with age.

Benign Tumors An abnormal growth of tissue confined to a particular area; not considered to be cancer.

Insulin A hormone that regulates blood sugar levels.

Insulin Resistance A condition that occurs when insulin becomes ineffective or less effective than necessary to regulate sugar levels in the blood.

Insulin Sensitivity A person with insulin resistance (see previous definition) is said to have decreased insulin sensitivity. The body's cells are not sensitive to insulin, so they resist it and sugar levels are not regulated effectively.

Osteoporosis A condition associated with low bone density and subsequent bone fragility, leading to high risk for fracture.

800–1,000 units. If you have difficulty getting enough of these nutrients from food or sunlight, your health-care provider may recommend a supplement.

2. Engage in regular weight-bearing exercise. Weight-bearing exercise (e.g., walking, dancing, jogging) and resistance training are good choices. Recent evidence indicates that activities that build power, such as jumping and performing explosive movements, are especially valuable in building strong bones. The load bearing and pull of muscles build bone density.

3. Avoid smoking and excessive alcohol.

4. Talk to your health-care provider about bone health.

5. When appropriate, have a bone density test and take medication. There is no cure for osteoporosis, but the FDA has approved a variety of treatments for osteoporosis to help reduce bone loss over time. When appropriate, a physician may prescribe FDA-approved medications such as raloxifene (sold as Evista), alendronate (sold as Fosamax), or other approved drugs. Hormone  treatments such as thyroid-based calcitonin treatments and estrogen are approved. Estrogen replacement therapy (ERT), also known as hormone replacement treatment (HRT), can reduce risk of osteoporosis among postmenopausal women, but may increase risk for cancer and other diseases. Medical consultation based on individual factors is recommended.

Muscle fitness exercise provides a number of important health benefits. It is now well established that muscle fitness exercise has benefits that add to those provided by other forms of moderate and vigorous physical activity. It reduces risk of early death and reduces many metabolic and cardiovascular risk factors (e.g., body composition, blood pressure, blood sugar, blood lipids). It is especially beneficial in reducing risk of osteoporosis.

Active people who possess good muscle fitness are also less likely to have back and musculoskeletal problems than are inactive, unfit people. Because few people die from it, back pain does not receive the attention given to such medical problems as heart disease and cancer. But back pain is the second leading medical complaint in the United States, second only to headaches. Only the common cold and the flu cause more days lost from work. At some point in our lives, approximately 80 percent of all adults experience back pain that limits the ability to function normally. It is by far the most frequently injured of all body parts.

The great majority of back ailments are the result of poor muscle strength, low levels of endurance, and poor flexibility. Tests on patients with back problems show weakness and lack of flexibility in key muscle groups. Lack of fitness is probably the leading reason for back pain in Western society. Other factors also increase the risk of back ailments, including poor posture, improper lifting and work habits, heredity, and diseases such as scoliosis and arthritis.

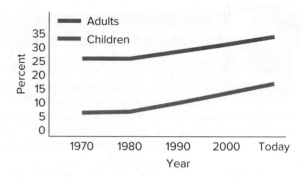

Figure 9 ▶ Incidence of obesity.
Source: National Center for Health Statistics.

Physical activity is important in maintaining a healthy body weight and avoiding the numerous health conditions associated with obesity. National studies indicate that more than two-thirds of adults are overweight and more than one-third are obese (34.9 percent). Nearly a third of children are either overweight or obese. From 1950 through 1980, obesity and overweight were fairly stable but increased dramatically from 1980 to the present. In the past few years the rate of increase in overweight and obesity has not been as dramatic as during the previous decade (see Figure 9). Research has shown that fat people who are fit are not at especially high risk for early death. However, when high body fatness is accompanied by low cardiorespiratory endurance and low metabolic fitness, risk for early death increases substantially.

Physical activity reduces the risk and severity of a variety of common emotional/mental health disorders. Nearly half of adult Americans will report having a mental health disorder at some point in life. A recent summary of studies revealed that there are several emotional/mental disorders associated with inactive lifestyles.

Depression is a stress-related condition experienced by many adults. Thirty-three percent of inactive adults report that they often feel depressed. For some, depression is a serious disorder that physical activity alone will not cure; however, research indicates that activity, combined with other forms of therapy, can be effective.

Anxiety is an emotional condition characterized by worry, self-doubt, and apprehension. More than a few studies have shown that symptoms of anxiety can be reduced by regular activity. Low-fit people who do regular aerobic activity seem to benefit the most. In one study, one-third of active people felt that regular activity helped them cope better with life's pressures.

Physical activity is also associated with better and more restful sleep. People with insomnia (the inability to sleep) seem to benefit from regular activity if it is not done too vigorously right before going to bed. Regular aerobic activity is associated with reduced brain activation, which can result in greater ability to relax or fall asleep.

A final benefit of regular exercise is increased self-esteem. Improvements in fitness, appearance, and the ability to perform new tasks can improve self-confidence.

Physical activity can help the immune system fight illness. Until recently, infectious disease and other diseases of the immune system were not considered to be hypokinetic. However, evidence now indicates that regular moderate to vigorous can actually aid the immune system in fighting disease. Each of us is born with an "innate immune system," which includes anatomical and physiological barriers, such as skin, mucous membranes, body temperature, and chemical mediators that help prevent and resist disease. We also develop an "acquired immune system" in the form of special disease-fighting cells that help us resist disease. Figure 10 shows a J-shaped curve that illustrates the benefits of exercise to acquired immune function. Sedentary people have more risk than those who do moderate activity, but with very high and sustained vigorous activity, such as extended high performance training, immune system function actually decreases.

Regular moderate and reasonable amounts of vigorous activity have been shown to reduce incidence of colds and days of sickness from infection. The immune system benefit may extend to other immune system disorders as well. There is evidence that regular physical activity can enhance treatment effectiveness and improve quality of life for those with HIV/AIDS. However, as Figure 10 indicates, too much exercise may cause problems rather than solve them.

Recent evidence indicates that Alzheimer disease and dementia are hypokinetic conditions. More than a few studies indicate that factors relating to heart health also contribute to brain health. The studies indicate that physical and challenging mental activities are especially important for preventing decline in cognitive function and reducing the risk of developing Alzheimer disease and dementia. Although additional research is needed, this is important news for physicians and public health officials looking for ways to reduce the prevalence of Alzheimer disease. (*Note:* Although many

HELP   Health is available to Everyone for a Lifetime, and it's Personal

This Is Your Brain on Exercise

A prominent research review of more than 400 studies supports the relationship between exercise and academic performance. Physical activity and fitness are associated with creative abilities, improved concentration and attention, better short-term memory, reduced risk of Alzheimer disease, and better test-taking abilities. New research indicates that regular activity *causes* positive changes in cognitive performance over time. (See link in Suggested Resources and Readings.)

Although the HELP philosophy emphasizes "health" as a target, exercise can help with many other aspects of life. Do you think that exercise helps you with cognitive performance?

Source: C. H. Hillman.

organizations retain the use of the term *Alzheimer's disease,* leading scholars and journals in the field use the term *Alzheimer disease* because the German physician and scientist for whom the disease was named discovered the disease but did not have it. We use the term *Alzheimer disease* in deference to the recommendation of the experts.)

Physical activity during pregnancy can benefit both the mother and the child. In the not too distant past, exercise during pregnancy was discouraged. Over the years, evidence has shown that appropriate exercise (including resistance training and moderate to vigorous aerobic exercise) by pregnant women can help prevent excess weight gain, help retain prepregnancy fitness levels, and result in shorter, less complicated labor. Physical activity does not cause miscarriage or damage to the baby and may help the baby developmentally.

Pregnant women are nearly twice as likely as other women to be sedentary (fail to meet current activity guidelines) in spite of the fact that guidelines from the American College of Obstetricians and Gynecologists indicate that most women should meet national guidelines as described. More intense exercise is appropriate in many cases but should be done with "close medical supervision."

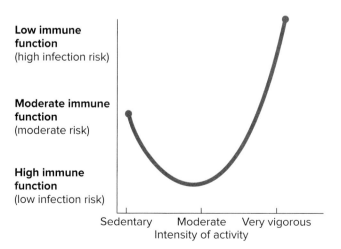

Low immune function
(high infection risk)

Moderate immune function
(moderate risk)

High immune function
(low infection risk)

Sedentary   Moderate   Very vigorous
Intensity of activity

Figure 10 ▶ Physical activity and immune function.

Source: National Center for Health Statistics

Physical activity can have positive effects on some non-hypokinetic conditions. Physical activity helps resolve symptoms and improve function and quality of life in people with the following conditions:

• *Arthritis.* Many, if not most, people with arthritis are in a deconditioned state resulting from a lack of activity. The traditional advice that those with arthritis should avoid physical activity is now being modified in view of the findings that carefully prescribed exercise has a variety of benefits. Common problems for those with either rheumatoid arthritis or osteoarthritis are decreased strength, loss of range of motion, and poor cardiovascular endurance. Well-planned exercise, designed to meet the needs of the specific type of arthritis of the individual, can be beneficial in preventing and treating impairments, and enhancing function, general fitness, and well-being.

• *Asthma.* People with asthma often have physical activity limitations, but with proper management, activity can be part of their daily lives. In fact, when done properly, activity can reduce airway reactivity and medication use. Because exercise can trigger bronchial constriction, it is important to choose appropriate types of activity and to use inhaled medications to prevent bronchial constriction caused by exercise or other triggers, such as cold weather. People with asthma should avoid cold weather exercise.

• *Premenstrual syndrome (PMS).* PMS, a mixture of physical and emotional symptoms that occur prior to menstruation, has many causes. However, changes in lifestyle, including regular exercise, may be effective in relieving PMS symptoms.

• *Cystic fibrosis.* A recent review indicates that exercise helps cystic fibrosis patients by facilitating systemic improvements and, more important, enhancing quality of life.

• *Other conditions.* Low- to moderate-intensity aerobic activity and resistance training are prescribed for some people who have chronic pain (persistent pain without relief) and/or fibromyalgia (chronic muscle pain). Evidence also suggests that active people have a reduced chance of having gallstones, compared to inactive people. Activity may also decrease the risk of impotence.

Physical Activity as a Treatment

Physical activity is now recognized as effective "medicine" for prevention of chronic disease. Since physical activity is still not widely prescribed or promoted by medical professionals, the American College of Sports Medicine (ACSM) initiated a program called Exercise Is Medicine (EIM) designed to "encourage primary care physicians, and other health-care providers, to assess and review every patient's physical activity program at every visit." The initiative has taken off both in the United States and internationally. The website (www.exerciseismedicine.org) provides information to the general public, health-care providers, health and fitness professionals, and the media.

Physical activity is a major part of worksite and school health promotion programs. Companies realize the importance of promoting healthy lifestyles among their employees. Worksite health promotion programs typically focus broadly on promoting a variety of healthy lifestyles, but physical activity is considered the mainstay of most programs. To facilitate active lifestyles, many companies build their own fitness centers inside the workplace or provide free or reduced-cost memberships for employees. Worksite programs that promote activity can reduce risk factors in employees and help companies save money and control the high cost of health care. Employees miss less work (i.e., reduced absenteeism), are more productive while at work (i.e., increased "presenteeism"), and have higher morale. Schools, including many universities, also recognize the importance of physical activity, resulting in the expansion of fitness centers on many campuses. The expansion of worksite and school health physical activity programming can provide benefits to individuals while also advancing public health.

Physical activity is an effective treatment for rehabilitation of hypokinetic diseases and injury. Physical activity is used to help people rehabilitate after a heart attack, to cope with cancer treatments, and to recover from injuries (e.g., sports, accidents) and surgeries (e.g., knee, hip, and shoulder replacements).

Many factors promote health and wellness and reduce the risk for disease. Inactivity, poor nutrition, smoking, and inability to cope with stress are all risk factors associated with various chronic diseases. These factors are in your control, and changing them can dramatically reduce your risk for chronic diseases. Other risk factors over which you have some control include weight/body composition, blood lipids and other blood constituents, and blood pressure. You also have some control over your health care. Recent reductions in chronic disease have resulted because of improved health care. For example, heart disease rates have decreased dramatically in recent years because of better detection (e.g., exercise tests, angiograms, CT scans), better emergency care, and improved medications.

Some risk factors, however, are not within your control (e.g., age, heredity, and gender). Table 4 summarizes the risk factors that are within your control as well as those that are not. By adopting healthy lifestyles, you can take control over some of the preventable disease risks. For example, by being physically active you can reduce your risk for heart disease and diabetes (even if you are overweight). Altering your diet can reduce the chances of developing high levels of blood lipids and reduce the risk for atherosclerosis (even if you have a family history of the condition). Adopting healthy lifestyles is a proactive approach to health and wellness but it does not assure disease immunity. Even so, studies of twins suggest that active people are less likely to die early than inactive people with similar genes. This finding suggests that long-term adherence to physical activity can overcome risk factors considered to be out of your control, such as heredity. Lab 5A helps you assess your heart disease risk factors, both those

Table 4 ▶ Hypokinetic Disease Risk Factors

Factors That Cannot Be Altered

1. *Age.* As you grow older, your risk of contracting hypokinetic diseases increases. For example, the risk for heart disease is approximately three times as great after 60 as before. The risk of back pain is considerably greater after 40.
2. *Heredity.* People who have a family history of hypokinetic disease are more likely to develop a hypokinetic condition, such as heart disease, hypertension, back problems, obesity, high blood lipid levels, and other problems. African Americans are 45 percent more likely to have high blood pressure than Caucasians; therefore, they suffer strokes at an earlier age with more severe consequences.
3. *Gender.* Men have a higher incidence of many hypokinetic conditions than women. However, differences between men and women have decreased recently. This is especially true for heart disease, the leading cause of death for both men and women. Postmenopausal women have a higher heart disease risk than premenopausal women.

Factors That Can Be Altered

4. *Regular physical activity.* Regular exercise can help reduce the risk for hypokinetic disease.
5. *Diet.* A clear association exists between hypokinetic disease and certain types of diets. The excessive intake of saturated fats, such as animal fats, is linked to atherosclerosis and other forms of heart disease. Excessive salt in the diet is associated with high blood pressure.
6. *Stress.* People who are subject to excessive stress are predisposed to various hypokinetic diseases, including heart disease and back pain. Statistics indicate that hypokinetic conditions are common among those in certain high-stress jobs and those having Type A personality profiles.
7. *Tobacco use.* Smokers have five times the risk of heart attack as nonsmokers. Most striking is the difference in risk between older women smokers and nonsmokers. Tobacco use is also associated with the increased risk for high blood pressure, cancer, and several other medical conditions. Apparently, the more you use, the greater the risk. Stopping tobacco use even after many years can significantly reduce the hypokinetic disease risk.
8. *Body (fatness).* Having too much body fat is a primary risk factor for heart disease and is a risk factor for other hypokinetic conditions as well. For example, loss of fat can result in relief from symptoms of Type 2 diabetes, can reduce problems associated with certain types of back pain, and can reduce the risks of surgery.
9. *Blood lipids, blood glucose, and blood pressure levels.* High scores on these factors are associated with health problems, such as heart disease and diabetes. Risk increases considerably when several of these measures are high.
10. *Diseases.* People who have one hypokinetic disease are more likely to develop a second or even a third condition. For example, if you have diabetes,* your risk of having a heart attack or stroke increases dramatically. Although you may not be entirely able to alter the extent to which you develop certain diseases and conditions, reducing your risk and following your doctor's advice can improve your odds significantly.

*Some types of diabetes cannot be altered.

not in your control and those in your control. Although the lab focuses on heart disease risk factors, many of the factors are also risk factors for other chronic diseases.

Too much activity can lead to hyperkinetic conditions. The information presented in this Concept points out the health benefits of physical activity performed in appropriate amounts. When done in excess or incorrectly, physical activity can result in **hyperkinetic conditions,** the most common being overuse injury to muscles, connective tissue, and bones. Recently, anorexia nervosa and body neurosis have been identified as conditions associated with inappropriate amounts of physical activity. These conditions are discussed in the Concept on performance.

Using Self-Management Skills

Building knowledge is important to making sound decisions about health, wellness and fitness. Acquiring knowledge can help you become motivated to make change and be sure that the changes you make are effective. Changes based on bad information can produce poor results and loss of motivation and confidence. The

information in this Concept is based on sound scientific evidence and provides you with information for making good decisions about fitness and health. However, every day new information becomes available. For this reason, it is important to keep your "knowledge" up to date by accessing accurate information. All fitness and health information is not equal. For example, one of the most common sources of fitness and health information on the web is Wikipedia. Yet studies show that information on Wikipedia is often incorrect—especially information about drugs, medicines, and supplements. There is much misinformation in the media as well. Be skillful in acquiring knowledge. When selecting sources (e.g., books, articles, Internet links) use your investigative skills. Check the credentials of the authors, the organization sponsoring the website, and so on. Additional information is provided in the Concept on consumerism and at websites such as MedlinePlus (search "evaluating health information" online).

Hyperkinetic Conditions Diseases/illnesses or health conditions caused, or contributed to, by too much physical activity.

Changing your beliefs is important to behavior change. Experts indicate that in addition to acquiring knowledge it is important to examine our beliefs if we are to make behavior (lifestyle) changes. If we hold beliefs that are inconsistent with the facts, what are the reasons? Why are we resisting the facts? Why do we do things that are against our health interests? For example, many people know that smoking is bad for them but still smoke. The "facts" may seem abstract leading to statements such as, "it takes a long time for smoking to cause cancer and I can stop anytime I want to." Some actually believe that they are special, that smoking affects others but not "me."

More than a few prominent people have made similar statements about exercise. Mark Twain is credited with the saying, "whenever I get the urge to exercise, I lie down until the feeling passes" and astronaut Neil Armstrong is credited with saying, "I believe that every human has a finite number of heartbeats. I don't intend to waste any of mine running around doing exercises." There is some question about the origin of these statements but, regardless, they have been widely circulated. They illustrate the point that well-informed people can still hold beliefs that are counter to the facts and that limit healthy lifestyle change. In some cases, help from others (social support) is necessary (e.g., smoking cessation assistance) to make positive changes.

Strategies for Action: Lab Information

A self-assessment of risk factors can help you modify your lifestyle to reduce risk for heart disease. The Heart Disease Risk Factor Questionnaire in Lab 5A will help you assess your personal risk factors for heart disease. It is not a substitute, however, for a regular medical exam that includes an assessment of other cardiovascular disease risk factors, such as cholesterol and blood glucose. This will allow you to use more sophisticated and accurate risk factor assessments (see the My Life Check tool highlighted in the Technology Update feature).

It is never too early to start being active to improve health. Many of the studies presented in this Concept indicate that being "active for a lifetime" prevents health problems. Young adults often think "I'll worry about these problems when I get older." But what you do early in life has much to do with your current health, as well as your health later in life.

Subsequent Concepts cover the different components of health-related fitness and the type and amount of activity needed to improve these components. The lab activities in each of these Concepts are designed to help you begin planning *now* for lifelong physical activity.

connect
ACTIVITY

A CLOSER LOOK

23 and ½ Hours

Even though the benefits associated with regular physical activity are enormous, participation in exercise and physical activity still remains low. A YouTube video by Dr. Mike Evans called *23 and ½ Hours* presents a compelling challenge to viewers: Commit 30 minutes a day to physical activity to ensure that you get the basic health benefits that come from physical activity. (See link in Suggested Resources and Readings.)

With so many powerful benefits of physical activity, why do so many people fail to put a high priority on it?

connect
ACTIVITY

Suggested Resources and Readings

The websites for the following sources can be accessed by searching online for the organization, program, or title listed. Specific scientific references are available at the end of this edition of *Concepts of Fitness and Wellness*.

- American College of Sports Medicine. Exercise Is Medicine initiative.
- American Heart Association. My Life Check heart health screener.
- American Heart Association. Recommendations for Physical Activity in Adults.
- Centers for Disease Control and Prevention. Health and Academic Achievement (pdf).
- ePARmedx.com. Online physical activity readiness questionnaire.
- Harvard Nutrition Source. Simple Steps to Preventing Diabetes.
- National Institutes of Health. All of Us Lifestyle Study.
- U.S. Department of Health and Human Services. U.S. Physical Activity Guidelines.

Lab 5A Assessing Heart Disease Risk Factors

Name	Section	Date

Purpose: To assess your risk of developing coronary heart disease. See next page for directions.

Heart Disease Risk Factor Questionnaire

Risk Points

	1	2	3	4	Score
Unalterable Factors					
1. How old are you?	30 or less	31–40	41–54	55+	
2. Do you have a history of heart disease in your family?	None	Grandparent with heart disease	Parent with heart disease	More than one with heart disease	
3. What is your gender?	Female		Male		
			Total Unalterable Risk Score		
Alterable Factors					
4. Do you get regular physical activity?	4–5 days a week	3 days a week	Fewer than 3 days a week	No	
5. Do you have a high-fat diet?	No	Slightly high in fat	Above normal in fat	Eat a lot of meat and fried and fatty foods	
6. Are you under much stress?	Less than normal	Normal	Slightly above normal	Quite high	
7. Do you use tobacco?	No	Cigar or pipe	Less than 1/2 pack a day or use smokeless tobacco	More than 1/2 pack a day	
8. What is your percentage of body fat?*	F = 17–28% M = 10–20%	29–31% 21–23%	32–35% 24–30%	>35% >30%	
9. What is the systolic number in your blood pressure?	<120	121–140	141–160	>160	
10. Do you have other diseases?	No	Ulcer	Diabetes**	Both	

Extra Points: Add points for as many of the following test results as you have available: 1 point for CRP above 3, 1 point for homocysteine above 100, 3 points for LDL above 130, 3 points for TC/HDL-C above 4. If only total cholesterol is available, add 1 point for a score of 200–240 or 3 points for scores above 240.

Total Alterable Risk Score	
Extra Points	
Grand Total Risk Score	

*If unknown, estimate your body fat percentage or see Lab 14A.

**Diabetes is a risk factor that is often not alterable.

Source: Adapted from *CAD Risk Assessor,* William J. Stone. Reprinted by permission.

Procedures

1. Answer the 10 questions in the Heart Disease Risk Factor Questionnaire and determine whether you should add the extra points by circling the answer that is most appropriate for *you*.
2. For each of your answers, look at the top of the column. In the box provided at the right of each question, write down the number of risk points for that answer.
3. Determine your unalterable risk score by adding the risk points for questions 1, 2, and 3.
4. Determine your alterable risk score by adding the risk points for questions 4 through 10.
5. Determine your total heart disease risk score by adding the scores obtained in steps 3 and 4.
6. Look up your risk ratings on the Heart Disease Risk Rating Chart and record them in the Results section. Answer the questions in the Conclusions and Implications section.

Results: Write your risk scores and risk ratings in the appropriate boxes below.

Heart Disease Risk Scores and Ratings

	Score	Rating
Unalterable risk		
Alterable risk		
Total heart disease risk		

Heart Disease Risk Rating Chart

Rating	Unalterable Score	Alterable Score	Total Score
Very high	9 or more	21 or more	31 or more
High	7–8	15–20	26–30
Average	5–6	11–14	16–25
Low	4 or less	10 or less	15 or less

Conclusions and Implications: The higher your score on the Heart Disease Risk Factor Questionnaire, the greater your heart disease risk. In several sentences, discuss your risk for heart disease. Which of the risk factors do you need to control to reduce your risk for heart disease? Why?

How Much Physical Activity Is Enough?

LEARNING OBJECTIVES

After completing the study of this Concept, you will be able to:

▶ Describe each of the key principles of physical activity and explain how the principles relate to each other in helping you achieve health, wellness, and fitness.

▶ Name the four elements of the FITT formula and explain how the formula relates to the concepts of *threshold of training* and *target zones* for different types of physical activity.

▶ List the five steps in the physical activity pyramid and identify the FIT formula for each.

▶ Describe the physical activity patterns of adults, differentiating among groups based on age, gender, and ethnicity.

▶ Describe the four fitness zones used for self-assessments of physical fitness and explain how each level relates to health and performance.

▶ Identify related national health goals and show how meeting personal goals can contribute to reaching national goals.

▶ Self-assess your current activity level for each step of the physical activity pyramid and estimate your current health and skill-related physical fitness.

There is a minimal and an optimal amount of physical activity necessary for developing and maintaining good health, wellness, and fitness.

©Stockbyte/Getty Images

Concept 6

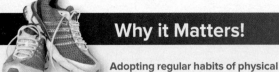

Why it Matters!

Adopting regular habits of physical activity is critical for achieving and maintaining good health, wellness, and fitness. However, for physical activity to have an optimal effect, it is important to perform appropriate amounts and to progress your training in appropriate ways. This Concept describes the foundational principles of physical activity and explains key concepts such as the FITT formula, the *threshold of training,* and *target zones.* Important guidelines and recommendations are summarized in the conceptual *physical activity pyramid* to help you understand and remember physical activity guidelines for different types of activities.

▼

The Principles of Physical Activity

Overload is necessary to achieve the health, wellness, and fitness benefits of physical activity. The **overload principle,** the most basic of all physical activity principles, indicates that doing "more than normal" is necessary if benefits are to occur. In order for a muscle (including the heart muscle) to get stronger and more powerful, it must be overloaded, or worked against a load greater than normal. To increase flexibility, a muscle must be stretched longer than is normal. To increase muscular endurance, muscles must be exposed to sustained exercise for a longer than normal period. The health benefits associated with metabolic fitness seem to require less overload than for health-related fitness improvement, but overload is required, just the same.

Increase physical activity progressively for safe and effective results. The **principle of progression** indicates that overload should occur in a gradual progression rather than in major bursts. Failure to adhere to this principle can result in excess soreness or injury. Although some tightness or fatigue is common after exercise, it is not necessary to feel sore in order to improve. Training is most effective when the sessions become progressively more challenging over time.

The benefits of physical activity are specific to the form of activity performed. The **principle of specificity** states that to benefit from physical activity you must overload specifically for that benefit. For example, strength-building exercises may do little for developing cardiorespiratory endurance, and stretching exercises may do little for altering body composition or metabolic fitness.

Overload is also specific to each body part. If you exercise the legs, you build fitness of the legs. If you exercise the arms, you build fitness of the arms. Some gymnasts, for example, have good upper body development but poor leg development, whereas some soccer players have well-developed legs but lack upper body development.

Specificity is important in designing your warm-up, workout, and cool-down programs for specific activities. Training is most effective when it closely resembles the activity for which you are preparing. For example, if your goal is to improve performance in putting the shot, it is not enough to strengthen and improve power in the arm muscles. You should train using exercises that require overload of all muscles used and that require motions similar to those used in putting the shot.

The benefits achieved from overload last only as long as overload continues. The **principle of reversibility** is the overload principle in reverse. To put it simply, if you don't use it, you lose it. Some people have the mistaken impression that if they achieve a health or fitness benefit it will last forever. Although there is evidence that you can maintain health benefits with less physical activity than it took to achieve them, if you do not engage in regular physical activity, any benefits attained will gradually erode.

In general, the more physical activity you do, the more benefits you receive. Just as there is a correct dosage of medicine for treatment of illness, there is a correct dosage of physical activity for promoting health benefits and the development of physical fitness. Research indicates that benefits from physical activity follow a *dose-response relationship*—the more moderate to vigorous physical activity (MVPA) that you perform, the more benefits you gain.

Figure 1 illustrates the overall pattern of the dose-response relationship. The red bar indicates the high risk for hypokinetic disease and early death for those who are inactive. A modest increase in physical activity, such as the 150 minutes of moderate activity per week, results in a substantial decrease in risk and early death (green bar). Additional activity (blue bar) has extra benefits, but the benefits are not as great as those that come from making the change from being inactive to doing some activity. As the black bar indicates, further reductions are possible with even higher amounts of activity, but the relative gain is much smaller. The committee that developed the *Physical Activity Guidelines for Americans 2018,* indicated that "*risk appears to continue to decrease with increased exposure up to at least 5 times the current recommended levels of MVPA*". However, it is important to point out that increased activity also comes with risks. Therefore, the benefits may not always outweigh the costs.

It is also important to note that "dose" of activity necessary to get one benefit is not the same as the "dose" for

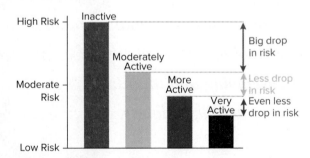

Figure 1 ▶ Decreases in hypokinetic disease risk with increases in dose of activity.

another. For example, changes in cholesterol levels resulting from physical activity may change at a different rate than changes in blood pressure. Many benefits in health, wellness, and fitness are obtained with moderate amounts of activity, so the key is to be at least active enough to obtain these benefits. However, as noted above, the accumulated evidence indicates that MVPA above the minimally recommended levels provides additional benefits for health, wellness and fitness.

The rate of improvement levels off as you become more fit, and at some point maintenance is an appropriate goal. The **principle of diminished returns** explains the rate and degree of improvement decrease as a person gets more fit. Beginners (people in the low and marginal fitness zones) often see relatively large fitness improvements when they begin an exercise program. However, people with higher levels of fitness must do considerably more activity to continue to improve. For example, a person who runs a mile in 15 minutes may cut several minutes from his or her running time in the first month or two of training. A fitter person who currently runs a mile in 5 minutes would have to do considerably more training to cut his or her time by even a few seconds. For most people, reaching the good fitness zone is a worthwhile goal. As the principle of diminishing returns indicates, those interested in high-level competition requiring high levels of fitness will have to follow high-volume exercise regimens.

Rest is needed to allow the body to adapt to exercise. The **principle of rest and recovery** indicates that you should allow time for recuperation after overload. Proper rest is needed within intense periods of activity, and appropriate rest is needed between training sessions. Rest provides time for the body to adapt to the stimulus provided during the workout. Failure to take sufficient rest can lead to overuse injuries, fatigue, and reduced performance. For recreational exercisers, rest generally implies taking a day off between bouts of exercise or alternating hard and easy days of exercise.

All people benefit from physical activity, but the benefits are unique for each person. Heredity, age, gender, ethnicity, lifestyles, current fitness and health status, and a variety of other factors make each person unique at any point in time. The **principle of individuality** indicates that the benefits of physical activity vary from individual to individual based on each person's unique characteristics.

Physical Activity Guidelines and the FITT Formula

The *Physical Activity Guidelines for Americans* provides recommendations for the types and amounts of physical activity needed for good health. The first guidelines (published in 2008) recommended a minimum of 150 minutes of moderate activity (5 or more days per week) or 75 minutes of vigorous activity (3 or more days per week). The revised 2018 guidelines have retained the focus on the total volume of physical activity. They also continue to provide flexibility with how guidelines are met. Rather than requiring activity on 5 different days, the guidelines specify that 150 minutes of moderate physical activity can be accumulated during the week. If you fail to meet the 30-minute target on one day, you can make it up on another and still meet the guideline. You can also achieve the guidelines with 75 minutes of vigorous intensity activity or a combination of both moderate and vigorous. Additional insights about flexibility in meeting guidelines are included in the HELP feature.

The acronyms FITT and FIT help you remember important variables for applying the overload principle. For physical activity to be effective, each type of activity must be done with enough frequency, with enough intensity, and for a long enough time. The first letters from four words spell **FITT** and can be considered as the formula for achieving health, wellness, and fitness benefits.

Frequency (how often)—Physical activity must be performed regularly to be effective. Most benefits require 3 to 5 days of activity per week, but frequency ultimately depends on the specific activity and the benefit desired.

Intensity (how hard)—Physical activity must be intense enough to require more exertion (overload) than normal to produce benefits. The appropriate intensity varies with the desired benefit. Health benefits from metabolic fitness require only moderate activity, but performance benefits require more vigorous activity.

Time (how long)—Physical activity must be done for an adequate length of time to be effective. The length of the activity session depends on the type of activity and the expected benefit.

Type (kind of activity)—The benefits derived depend on the type of activity performed. For example, moderate activity must be done at least 5 days a week, while muscle fitness activity may be done as few as 2 days a week.

Overload Principle You must perform physical activity in greater than normal amounts (overload) to improve physical fitness or obtain health benefits.

Principle of Progression You need to gradually increase overload to achieve optimal benefits.

Principle of Specificity Specific types of exercise are needed to improve each fitness component or the fitness of a specific part of the body.

Principle of Reversibility Disuse or inactivity results in loss of benefits achieved as a result of overload.

Principle of Diminished Returns The more benefits you gain as a result of activity, the harder additional benefits are to achieve.

Principle of Rest and Recovery You need adequate rest to allow the body to adapt to and recover from exercise.

Principle of Individuality Overload provides unique benefits to each individual based on the unique characteristics of that person.

FITT, FIT A formula used to describe the frequency, intensity, time, and type of physical activity necessary to produce benefits. When the type of activity has been determined, the second T is dropped and the shorter acronym FIT is used.

HELP   Health is available to Everyone for a Lifetime, and it's Personal

Flexibility in Meeting the 2018 Physical Activity Guidelines

One of the "major findings" reported in the latest *Physical Activity Guidelines for Americans* is that "*the benefits of physical activity can be achieved in a variety of ways.*" Some specific conclusions are listed below:

- People who perform little or no moderate to vigorous activity can get health benefits by replacing sedentary behavior with light-intensity activity.
- People who perform little or no moderate to vigorous activity, no matter how sedentary, can get many health benefits by adding some or more moderate activity.
- People who are already in the target area for moderate to vigorous activity can benefit from doing more moderate to vigorous activity.

The 2018 guidelines emphasize that moderate and vigorous physical activity can be combined to meet recommendations. They also document the added value of performing additional physical activity beyond the minimal levels. Health benefits from resistance training and activities such as yoga and Tai Chi are also highlighted. Finally, the new guidelines consider the unique needs of different sub-groups (e.g., youth, adults, older adults, challenged individuals, pregnant women). Search *"2018 Physical Activity Guidelines for Americans"* online to learn more about the revised guidelines.

Based on your personal interests, would you lean toward the moderate or the vigorous guideline or a combination of both?

connect
ACTIVITY

When determining the formula for each type of activity, the shorter acronym (FIT) can be used because you have already determined the activity type. In the following section, you will learn more about the **FIT** formula for each activity in the physical activity pyramid. In subsequent Concepts, each formula is described in greater detail.

The volume and progression of physical activity are important considerations. The American College of Sports Medicine (ACSM) uses the acronym FITT-VP to illustrate the importance of volume and progression in planning your exercise program. *Volume* refers to the total amount of physical activity that you perform each day. It is a combination of the frequency, intensity, and total amount of time spent in exercise. For example, a short but more intense bout of activity can provide a volume of activity similar to a longer, moderate exercise bout. Various combinations of frequency,

connect
VIDEO 2

intensity, and time of physical activity (volume) can be used in a gradual progression to reach personal goals based on individual needs. *Progression,* in this context, refers to the application of the principle of progression described earlier in this Concept. Essentially, to continue to improve you have to progress (i.e., increase) any or all of the FIT components. However, being patient is important, too. Attempts to get fit fast will probably be counterproductive, so the key is to start slowly and progress gradually using the FITT formula.

Various patterns can be used to achieve the overall daily and weekly goals for physical activity, but consistency is recommended. The recommended daily volume of exercise for achieving health benefits is a minimum of 30 minutes but this can be accumulated in several short bouts or in one longer bout. Guidelines are less specific about how activity should be performed over a week. A recent study in *JAMA Internal Medicine* reported that people who exercised regularly on only 1 or 2 days a week had many of the same benefits as those who exercised more frequently as long as they met the overall goal (i.e., 150 minutes of moderate activity or 75 minutes of vigorous activity per week). This evidence could lead some to believe that the "weekend warrior" approach is a sound strategy. However, it is important to note that physical activity in this study was assessed only at the beginning of this study and researchers assumed that participants continued the same level of activity over the many years of the study. More important is the fact that the weekend warriors in this study reported that they regularly met the recommended standards for minutes of moderate and vigorous physical activity per week. They just did the activity (frequently sporting activities) on fewer days per week (1 to 2 days) instead of the recommended (3 or more days per week). More than half (55 percent) were active on 2 days so the total volume of activity was likely sufficient to maintain a level of fitness needed to safely perform their activities.

The researchers concluded that both approaches had similar outcomes, but the preponderance of evidence supports the national activity guidelines that call for regular more frequent activity. Regular physical activity promotes better metabolic health outcomes and also has advantages for mental health. Performing aerobic activity on a more regular basis—not too many days apart—provides a better approach to fitness, health, and injury prevention. While some activity is better than none, evidence does not support the use of occasional vigorous activity for those who are unfit and those who have not been regularly active. (See A Closer Look.)

connect
VIDEO 3

Threshold of training and *target zone* help you use the FIT formula. The **threshold of training** is the minimum amount of activity (frequency, intensity, and time) necessary to produce benefits. Depending on the benefit expected, slightly more than normal activity may not be enough to

The Weekend Warrior

A "weekend warrior" refers to someone who participates in unusually strenuous physical activity only on weekends or on random days. Many adopt that lifestyle because they are too busy on weekdays, but others do so by choice since it may be part of their recreation time. However, fitness experts have consistently warned against being a weekend warrior, suggesting that occasional vigorous physical activity can be dangerous and is not effective in producing the health benefits of more frequent physical activity. A recent study showed that the daily patterns may not matter as long as you meet the overall recommended minutes per week, but the analyses only focused on certain health indicators. Participating less regularly may also limit other social, mental, and physiological benefits. (See Suggested Resources and Readings.)

Do you identify with the weekend warrior mentality, or do you prefer more consistent patterns of physical activity throughout the week?

promote health, wellness, or fitness benefits. The **target zone** begins at the threshold of training and stops at the point where the activity becomes counterproductive. Figure 2 illustrates the threshold of training and target zone concepts.

Some people incorrectly associate threshold of training and target zones with only cardiorespiratory endurance. As the principle of specificity suggests, each component of fitness, including metabolic fitness, has its own FIT formula and its own threshold and target zone. The target and threshold levels for **health benefits** are different from those for achieving **performance benefits** associated with high levels of physical fitness.

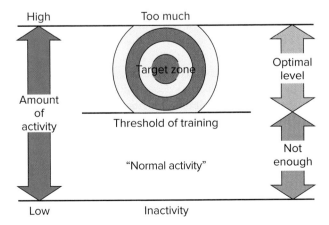

Figure 2 ▶ Physical activity target zone.

The Physical Activity Pyramid

The physical activity pyramid classifies activities by type and associated benefits. The physical activity pyramid (see Figure 3) was created to help readers better understand the five basic *types* of physical activity (e.g., the last *T* in FITT). Over the years, it has proven to be a useful model for illustrating how each type of activity contributes to the development of health, wellness, and fitness. The pyramid depicts five different steps. Each step represents a step toward achieving health, wellness, and fitness. Inactivity is shown below the pyramid because it does not represent a step toward active living. Placement in the pyramid is not meant to suggest that higher steps are more important than lower steps. Activities from all steps are important for optimal health, wellness, and fitness. Key concepts illustrated by the physical activity pyramid include the following:

- Each type of activity has its own FIT formula and unique health, wellness, and fitness benefits.
- The different types of physical activity can be combined to meet activity guidelines.
- Extended periods of inactivity can be harmful to your health.
- Eating well (sound nutrition) is an important companion behavior to physical activity (see energy balance scale at the top of Figure 3).

Each of the five steps of the physical activity pyramid are discussed in greater detail in the paragraphs that follow as well as in later Concepts.

Inactivity can be hazardous to your health. The steps in the physical activity pyramid show the five different types of physical activity (Figure 3). The words "Avoid Inactivity" appear below the pyramid in bold black letters. This is important because current evidence indicates that people who are inactive for large portions of the day have an increased risk of chronic disease. Even active people are at risk if they are sedentary for long periods of time when not involved in activity. (See the Concept on adopting active lifestyles for additional information.)

Threshold of Training The minimum amount of physical activity that will produce health and fitness benefits.

Target Zone The amounts of physical activity that produce optimal health and fitness benefits.

Health Benefits The results of physical activity that provide protection from hypokinetic disease or early death.

Performance Benefits The results of physical activity that improve physical fitness and physical performance capabilities.

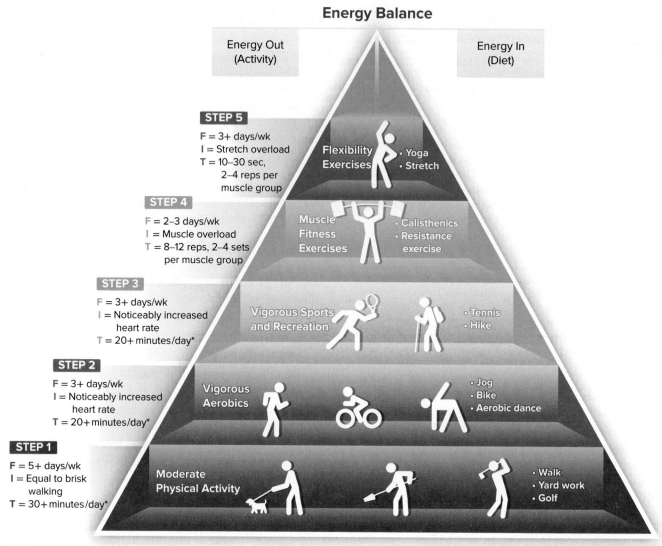

Figure 3 ▶ The physical activity pyramid.

Source: Charles B. Corbin.

Moderate activities provide many benefits for modest amounts of effort. **Moderate aerobic activities** equal in intensity to brisk walking provide significant health benefits. For a variety of reasons, they are depicted as step 1 of the physical activity pyramid (see Figure 3). The broad bottom of the pyramid illustrates that moderate activities are the most widely performed activities among adults. For optimal benefits, moderate activities are performed 5 or more days per week compared to 2 to 3 days per week for activities in steps 2 to 5. Finally, and perhaps most important, moderate activities provide many benefits for a modest amount of effort (see Figure 1). Moderate aerobic activities, such as walking to and from work, climbing the stairs rather than taking an elevator, or doing brisk housework when done as part of the normal daily routine

are often referred to as lifestyle physical activities. Moderate activities that are not part of the normal daily routine, such as taking a walk or a bike ride, can also be planned specifically to increase activity levels.

Studies indicate that individuals with active jobs have reduced risks for many chronic conditions. Those who actively commute (bike or walk) to work or to run errands have also been found to have better health profiles. The regular accumulation of activity as a part of one's lifestyle is sufficient to promote positive improvements in metabolic fitness, and these improvements can positively impact health. Additional activity from the other layers of the pyramid are strongly recommended. Moderate activity can be viewed as the baseline, or minimal, activity that should be performed. A summary of the FIT formula for moderate activity is illustrated in step 1 of Figure 3.

Vigorous aerobic activity provides additional health benefits. Vigorous aerobic activities (step 2) are of greater intensity than moderate activities (step 1). The greater intensity results in significantly higher heart rates and higher oxygen consumption. Because of its greater intensity, vigorous aerobics can be performed as few as 3 days a week and is especially good for building cardiorespiratory endurance and helping control body fatness. Examples of vigorous aerobic activities, sometimes referred to as active aerobics, are jogging, biking, and aerobic dance. Vigorous aerobic activities can provide metabolic fitness and health benefits similar to moderate activities and can be performed instead of, or in combination with, moderate activities to meet national activity guidelines.

Vigorous sports and recreation activities can provide similar benefits as vigorous aerobic activity. Vigorous sports and recreation are activities of similar intensity to vigorous aerobics. Some sports, such as golf and bowling, can be classified as moderate aerobic activities because they are of a lower intensity. Vigorous sports and recreation activities (see Figure 3, step 3) can be performed instead of, or in combination with, vigorous aerobic activities or moderate activities, to meet national activity guidelines.

Muscle fitness exercises are important for optimal fitness and health. There are muscle fitness benefits from many different activities, including vocational activities that require lifting, active sports such as gymnastics and wrestling, and recreational activities such as rock climbing. Various muscle fitness activities, such as resistance training, plyometrics, and calisthenics, are included at step 4 of the pyramid and they contribute to strength, muscular endurance, and power. The many health and performance benefits of muscle fitness exercises are described in the Concept on muscle fitness. A general description of the FIT formula for muscle fitness exercises is included in Figure 3 (step 4).

Flexibility exercises are important for building and maintaining flexibility. There are flexibility benefits from many different activities, including sports such as gymnastics

Adhering to physical activity guidelines can help you enjoy active recreation.
©Fuse/Getty Images

and diving. The flexibility exercises included at step 5 of the pyramid are those that are planned specifically to build flexibility, such as stretching exercises and yoga. The many benefits of flexibility exercises are described in the Concept on flexibility. A general description of the FIT formula for flexibility exercises is included in Figure 3 (step 5).

Energy balance is important for maintaining a healthy body composition. Weight management requires that energy intake be matched by energy expenditure. The FIT formula messages in the physical activity pyramid provide general information about the amounts of activity (energy expenditure) necessary for general health and fitness benefits. But these amounts may not be enough for weight management (or weight loss). Current physical activity guidelines suggest that 45 to 60 minutes of daily moderate activity may be necessary (as opposed to 30 minutes).

The balance scale at the top of the pyramid in Figure 3 illustrates the importance of balancing energy intake with energy expenditure. (More information about maintaining energy balance for body composition is included in the Concepts on nutrition and diet.)

Some important factors should be considered when using the physical activity pyramid. The physical activity pyramid is a useful model for describing different types of activity, their benefits, and the FIT formula for each level. However, it shouldn't be interpreted too rigidly. The following statements summarize the most important points:

- *No single activity provides all of the benefits.* Many people wonder, "What is the perfect form of physical activity?" There is no single activity that can provide all of the health, wellness, and fitness benefits. It is best to perform activities from all steps of the pyramid because each type of activity has different benefits.

- *Something is better than nothing.* Some people may say, "I just don't have time to do all of the activities in the pyramid." This could lead some to throw up their hands in despair, concluding, "I just won't do anything at all." Evidence indicates that something is better than nothing, so try to do a little activity and add more as time allows.

- *Activities from steps 2 and 3 can be used instead of, or in combination with, those from step 1 to achieve health and fitness benefits.* While more people typically perform moderate activities (step 1), many prefer more vigorous activities from

Moderate Aerobic Activities Aerobic activities equal in intensity to a brisk walk are referred to as moderate activities (see step 1 of the activity pyramid).

Vigorous Aerobic Activities Vigorous aerobic activities that elevate the heart rate and are greater in intensity than a brisk walk (see step 2 of the activity pyramid).

Vigorous Sports and Recreation Sports such as soccer and volleyball, or recreational activities such as hiking, that elevate the heart rate and are of greater intensity than a brisk walk. (See step 3 of the physical activity pyramid.)

steps 2 and 3 of the pyramid. Both provide health benefits and the two can be combined to meet activity guidelines.

- *Activities from steps 4 and 5 are useful even if you are limited in performing activities at other levels.* It is best to include some activities from steps 1, 2, and 3, but muscle fitness exercise and flexibility exercise do provide benefits on their own.

- *Good planning will allow you to schedule activities from all steps in a reasonable amount of time.* In subsequent Concepts, you will learn more about each step of the pyramid, as well as how to plan a total physical activity program.

- *Specific activity recommendations exist for youth.* According to guidelines, children should accumulate at least 60 minutes, and up to several hours, of age-appropriate physical activity on most, if not all, days of the week. The guidelines also recommend minimizing periods of inactivity (periods of 2 or more hours). Adults play a major role in shaping children's current and future activity patterns.

- *Specific guidelines exist for older adults.* Specific activity guidelines are available for adults 65 and older. The guidelines are similar to those for younger adults but differ in some important ways. The guidelines for intensity of aerobic activity take into account the older adult's activity level. Also, older adults typically do more repetitions and use less resistance when doing muscle fitness exercise, flexibility exercises become more important, and exercise for balance is recommended.

Technology Update

Medical Applications for Consumer Monitors

The consumer marketplace is flooded with a variety of physical activity monitors designed to help people track their exercise behaviors (e.g., Fitbit, Apple Watch, Garmin). Most link wirelessly with associated smartphone apps so that users can get real-time reports of their physical activity behaviors. While consumers are familiar with applications for personal activity tracking, many new medical applications are also being explored. Some apps with integrated wearable sensors are being developed to monitor certain vital signs. For example, it may be possible for an app to spot irregular heart rhythms that may be indicative of an impending heart attack. This is just one example of new medical applications planned with consumer activity monitors and wearable technology.

Where do you see the future going with consumer wearable monitors?

Physical Activity Patterns

The percentage of adults who meet physical activity goals varies by gender, age, and ethnicity. National physical activity goals have been established for moderate to vigorous aerobic physical activity as well as for muscle fitness exercise. As noted in Table 1, only about half of Americans meet national goals for aerobic activity and less than a third meet national goals for muscle fitness activity (30 percent). For aerobic activity, men are more active than women and non-Hispanic Whites are more active than non-Hispanic Blacks and Hispanics. The age groups that are most likely to meet aerobic activity goals are the youngest group (18–24) and the oldest (65+). For muscle fitness activity, non-Hispanic Blacks meet the goal more often than non-Hispanic Whites and Hispanics. Muscle fitness activity decreases with age with young people being twice as likely to meet the national goals. The good news is that the numbers in Table 1 show higher percentages of adults meeting aerobic activity goals than in the past: 51 percent as compared to 43 percent 10 to 15 years earlier.

Too many Americans (26 percent) still report performing no regular leisure-time activity. This pattern is more common in females (27 percent) than males (25 percent), more likely in non-Hispanic Blacks (31 percent) and Hispanics (31 percent) than non-Hispanic Whites (24 percent), and

Table 1 ▶ Percentages of Adults Who Meet National Activity Goals

Classification	Aerobic Activity	Both Aerobic and Muscle Fitness Activity
Gender	Percentage	Percentage
Male	52%	35%
Female	50	26
Age	Percentage	Percentage
18–24	53%	47%
25–34	49	37
35–44	49	31
45–54	50	27
55–64	51	24
65+	49	23
Ethnicity	Percentage	Percentage
Non-Hispanic White	53%	30%
Non-Hispanic Black	44	32
Hispanic	45	29

Source: National Health Interview Survey.

In the News

Activity Levels of College-Age Students Are Similar to 60-Year-Old Adults

A recent study of the activity levels of American adults of all ages showed that the total volume of activity for 19-year-olds was equal to that of older adults (age 60). This study was unique because activity was assessed objectively using activity monitors (accelerometers) rather than more subjective questionnaires (see Table 1). While young adults did more moderate and vigorous activity than older adults, when total volume (all activity per day) was counted, 19-year-olds were the least active segment of the adult population (i.e., people over 18). The authors noted different groups were active or inactive at different times of the day. Teens and young adults typically have low activity levels early in the day. (See Johns Hopkins press release in Suggested Resources and Readings.)

What factors do you think explain these patterns? Do these findings surprise, inspire, or confuse you?

connect
ACTIVITY

---

more likely with increases with age (17 percent for 18–24 compared with 31 percent for 65+).

The proportion of people meeting national health goals varies based on age. Children are the most active group in Western society. During adolescence, activity starts to decrease, but teens still do more activity than young adults. Activity levels of all types decrease from young adulthood to ages 65 and over (see Table 1).

The proportion of adults meeting national health goals varies based on income, education, and disability status. People at or near poverty levels are more than twice as likely to be totally inactive during leisure time, compared with those with high income. Low-income people are also much less likely to meet national health goals for activity than middle- to high-income people. High school dropouts are nearly three times more likely to be totally inactive than college graduates. Adults with one or more physical disabilities have a high probability of being inactive.

Physical Fitness Standards

Health-based criterion-referenced standards are recommended for rating your fitness. This Concept has focused on the amount of physical activity necessary to get health and fitness benefits. Another question to be answered is "How much physical fitness is enough?" Most experts recommend **health-based criterion-referenced standards** to rate your current fitness. These standards are based on how much fitness is needed for good health. Other standards use norms or percentiles that compare a person's fitness against a reference population. Knowing how you compare with other people is not that important. In fact, such comparisons have been shown to be discouraging to many people. Determining if your fitness is adequate to enhance your health and wellness is more relevant.

connect
VIDEO 6

Table 2 ▶ The Four Fitness Zones

High-Performance Zone

Reaching this zone provides additional health benefits and is important to high-level performance. However, high performance scores are hard for some people to achieve, and for many people high-level performance is not important. So reaching this zone may be more important to some than others.

Good Fitness Zone

If you reach the good fitness zone, you have enough of a specific fitness component to help reduce health risk. However, staying active (in addition to reaching this fitness zone) is important.

Marginal Fitness Zone

Marginal scores indicate that some improvement is in order, but you are nearing minimal health standards set by experts.

Low Fitness Zone

If you score low in fitness, you are probably less fit than you should be for your own good health and wellness.

In the Concepts that follow, you will perform many different self-assessments to determine your fitness zone for each dimension of fitness. Four different rating zones are used (see Table 2). The long-term goal is to achieve the "good fitness zone," a standard associated with good health. People in the low fitness zone have a higher risk than those in the other three zones and a goal should be to first strive to move out of the low zone into the marginal fitness zone. Those in the marginal zone are at lower risk than those in the low fitness zone, but they should strive to move into the good fitness zone.

connect
VIDEO 7

Health-Based Criterion-Referenced Standards The amount of a specific type of fitness necessary to gain a health or wellness benefit.

With reasonable amounts of physical activity over time, most people should be able to improve their fitness enough to make it into the good fitness zone. For personal reasons, some may wish to aim for the high-performance zone. Reaching the high-performance zone is important for those interested in high-level performance, but should not be a goal of those in the low or marginal fitness zones until the good fitness zone is reached. Reaching this level provides additional health benefits, but considerable effort is necessary to reach it.

Using Self-Management Skills

Knowledge is important to making sound decisions about fitness and health. Building knowledge is a self-management skill needed to help you make good decisions about healthy lifestyles. The information in this Concept is based on the most recent research and guidelines from professional and governmental organizations. Keep up-to-date on current and new recommendations, such as those in the most recent *Physical Activity Guidelines for Americans*. Knowing and applying the physical activity guidelines, such as those described in this Concept, can help you get active and stay active.

Self-confidence is especially important in becoming more active. People who lack self-confidence typically don't think that they can do something that they actually can do. To build self-confidence, set small, realistic goals that ensure success in order to encourage effort. Basically, "the little train that could" was right. If you set a realistic goal ("I think I can") and achieve several small goals, you gradually accomplish larger goals ("I know I can"). The example used in an earlier Concept applies here. A person says, "I would like to be more active, but I have never been good at physical activities." By starting with a small but reasonable goal, a 10-minute walk, the person sees that "I can do it." Over time, the person becomes confident and increases activity. Getting positive feedback from others (social support) is also effective in building self-confidence.

Intrinsic motivation increases exercise adherence. Intrinsic motivation refers to doing a behavior because it is satisfying to you rather than doing it for an external reward (extrinsic motivation). People who are intrinsically motivated will participate because they enjoy it or because it provides them with a level of satisfaction. For some, previous experiences in physical activity have not been satisfying and this has reduced their intrinsic motivation. Some things that can be done to improve intrinsic motivation include examining your attitudes in order to reduce negative attitudes and increase positive attitudes. You can also do an assessment of your current activities and then try new activities that provide a fresh perspective. Building self-confidence through meeting small and manageable goals can also boost intrinsic motivation by improving your self-perceptions.

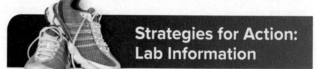

Strategies for Action: Lab Information

A self-assessment of your current activity at each level of the pyramid can help you determine future activity goals. Lab 6A provides you with the opportunity to assess your physical activity at each level of the pyramid.

Self-assessments of physical fitness can help you prepare a fitness profile that can be used in program planning. In the Concepts that follow, you will learn to perform a variety of self-assessments of fitness and will learn the scores that are necessary on these assessments to reach the good fitness zone, as described in Table 2. In the meantime, you can complete Lab 6B. This lab will help you understand the nature of each part of fitness and estimate your current fitness level for each type of fitness. When you complete the more detailed self-assessments later in this edition, you will be able to determine the accuracy of your estimates.

Suggested Resources and Readings

The websites for the following sources can be accessed by searching online for the organization, program, or title listed. Specific scientific references are available at the end of this edition of *Concepts of Fitness and Wellness*.

- American College of Sports Medicine. (2018). *ACSM's Guidelines for Exercise Prescription and Testing*. Philadelphia: Wolters Kluwer. Chapter 1, pp. 6–10
- Buckworth, J. (2017). Promoting self-efficacy for healthy behaviors. *ACSM's Health and Fitness Journal, 21*(5), 40–42.
- Centers for Disease Control and Prevention. CDC Physical Activity Trend Maps,
- Feibus, M. (2017, December 7). New health trackers warn of heart-attack risks, discretely. *USA Today* (online article).
- JAMA Network. (2017, January 9). Do Exercise "Weekend Warriors" Lower Their Risk of Death? (online press release).
- Johns Hopkins School of Public Health. 19-Year-Olds as Sedentary as 60-Year-Olds (press release).

Lab 6A Self-Assessment of Physical Activity

Name	**Section**	**Date**

Purpose: To estimate your current levels of physical activity from each category of the physical activity pyramid.

Procedures

1. Place an X over the circle that characterizes your participation in each category in the pyramid. Place an X over one circle, at the bottom of the pyramid, to indicate days of inactivity.
2. Determine if you met the national goal for each type of activity. In the Results section, place an X over the "yes" circle if you meet the goal in each area or an X over the "no" circle if you do not meet the goal.

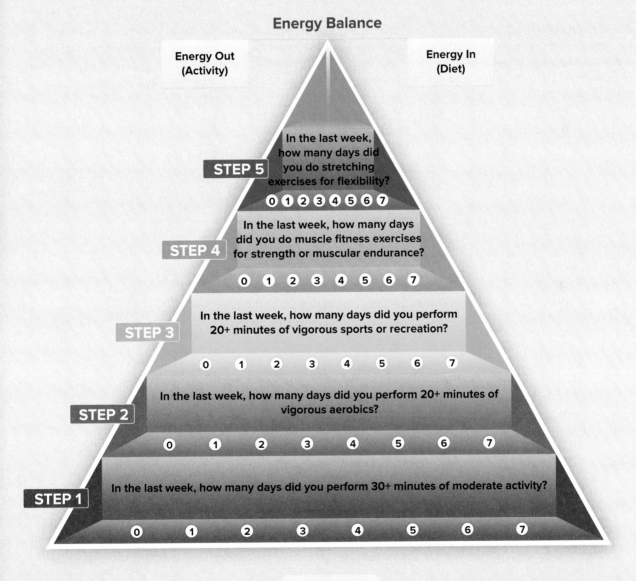

Energy Balance

Energy Out (Activity)   **Energy In (Diet)**

STEP 5 In the last week, how many days did you do stretching exercises for flexibility?
0 1 2 3 4 5 6 7

STEP 4 In the last week, how many days did you do muscle fitness exercises for strength or muscular endurance?
0 1 2 3 4 5 6 7

STEP 3 In the last week, how many days did you perform 20+ minutes of vigorous sports or recreation?
0 1 2 3 4 5 6 7

STEP 2 In the last week, how many days did you perform 20+ minutes of vigorous aerobics?
0 1 2 3 4 5 6 7

STEP 1 In the last week, how many days did you perform 30+ minutes of moderate activity?
0 1 2 3 4 5 6 7

Inactivity

In the last week, how many days did you fail to do any activities from the 5 steps above?
0 1 2 3 4 5 6 7

Results

Activity Type	Step	National Goal	Did You Meet the National Health Goal?	
Moderate activity	1	5 days or more	Yes	No
Vigorous activity	2 and 3	3 days or more	Yes	No
Muscle fitness	4	2 days or more	Yes	No
Flexibility exercises	5	3 days or more	Yes	No
Inactivity	—	Avoid total inactivity	Yes	No

Conclusions and Implications: In the space below, describe your current physical activity patterns. Do you meet the national health goals in all areas? If not, in what types of activity from the pyramid do you need to improve? Are the answers you gave for the past week typical of your regular activity patterns? If you meet all national health goals, explain why you think this is so. Do you think that meeting the goals in the pyramid on the previous page indicates good activity patterns for you?

Lab 6B Estimating Your Fitness

Name	**Section**	**Date**

Purpose: To help you better understand each of the 11 dimensions of health-related and skill-related physical fitness.

Procedures

1. Consider a warm-up before and cool-down after. Perform each of the activities described in Chart 1 on the next page.
2. Estimate your current fitness levels. Place a check in the appropriate circle for each fitness dimension in the Results section below. If the activity was difficult or if past tests suggest it, check the "low fitness" circle; if the activity was somewhat difficult or if you think you need improvement, check the "marginal fitness" circle; if the task was relatively easy or if past tests indicate it, check the "good fitness" circle; and if you think your fitness in an area is sufficient, check the "high performance" circle.

Special Note: The activities performed in this lab *are not intended as valid tests of physical fitness.* Completing the activities will help you better understand each dimension of fitness. You should not rely primarily on the results of the activities to make your estimates. Consider previous fitness tests you have taken and your own best judgment of your current fitness. In later Concepts, you will learn how to perform accurate assessments of each fitness dimension that will help you assess the accuracy of your estimates.

Results

Fitness Zones

Fitness Component	Low Fitness	Marginal Fitness	Good Fitness	High Performance
Body Composition	○	○	○	○
Cardiorespiratory Endurance	○	○	○	○
Flexibility	○	○	○	○
Muscular Endurance	○	○	○	○
Power	○	○	○	○
Strength	○	○	○	○
Agility	○	○	○	○
Balance	○	○	○	○
Coordination	○	○	○	○
Reaction Time	○	○	○	○
Speed	○	○	○	○

Conclusions and Implications: Describe the information you used to make your estimates of physical fitness. How confident are you that these estimates are accurate?

Directions: Attempt each of the activities in Chart 1. Place a check in the circle next to each component of physical fitness to indicate that you have attempted the activity.

Chart 1 Physical Fitness Activities

Body Composition ◯

1. *The pinch.* Have a partner pinch a fold of fat on the back of your upper arm (body fatness), halfway between the tip of the elbow and the tip of the shoulder.

   Men: no greater than 3/4 inch

   Women: no greater than 1 inch

Cardiorespiratory Endurance ◯

2. *Run in place.* Run in place for 1.5 minutes (120 steps per minute). Rest for 1 minute and count the heart rate for 30 seconds. A heart rate of 60 (for 30 sec.) or lower passes. A step is counted each time the right foot hits the floor.

Flexibility ◯

3. *Backsaver toe touch.* Sit on the floor with one foot against a wall. Bend the other knee. Bend forward at the hips. After three warm-up trials, reach forward and touch your closed fists to the wall. Bend forward slowly; do not bounce. Repeat with the other leg straight. Pass if fists touch the wall with each leg straight.

Muscular Endurance ◯

4. *Side leg raise.* Lie on the floor on your side. Lift your leg up and to the side of the body until your feet are 24 to 36 inches apart. Keep the knee and pelvis facing forward. Do not rotate so that the knees face the ceiling. Perform 10 with each leg.

Power ◯

5. *Standing long jump.* Stand with the toes behind a line. Using no run or hop step, jump as far as possible. Men must jump their height plus 6 inches. Women must jump their height only.

Strength ◯

6. *Push-up.* Lie face down on the floor. Place the hands under the shoulders. Keeping the legs and body straight, press off the floor until the arms are fully extended. Women repeat once; men, three times.

Agility ◯

7. *Paper ball pickup.* Place two wadded paper balls on the floor 5 feet away. Run until both feet cross the line, pick up the first ball, and return both feet behind the starting line. Repeat with the second ball. Finish in 5 seconds.

Balance ◯

8. *One-foot balance.* Stand on one foot; press up so that the weight is on the ball of the foot with the heel off the floor. Hold the hands and the other leg straight out in front for 10 seconds.

Coordination ◯

9. *Paper ball bounce.* Wad up a sheet of notebook paper into a ball. Bounce the ball back and forth between the right and left hands. Keep the hands open and palms up. Bounce the ball three times with each hand (six times total), alternating hands for each bounce.

Reaction Time ◯

10. *Paper drop.* Have a partner hold a sheet of notebook paper so that the side edge is between your thumb and index finger, about the width of your hand from the top of the page. When your partner drops the paper, catch it before it slips through the thumb and finger. Do not lower your hand to catch the paper.

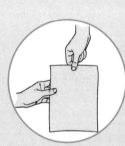

Speed ◯

11. *Double-heel click.* With the feet apart, jump up and tap the heels together twice before you hit the ground. You must land with your feet at least 3 inches apart.

Adopting an Active Lifestyle

LEARNING OBJECTIVES

After completing the study of this Concept, you will be able to:

▶ Define moderate physical activity and differentiate it from light and vigorous physical activity.

▶ Describe the health benefits of moderate physical activity, and explain why moderate physical activity is the most popular form of physical activity.

▶ Describe and explain the FIT formula for moderate physical activity.

▶ Plan a personal moderate physical activity program based on SMART goals, and self-monitor your plan.

▶ Evaluate your current environment and determine ways to modify it to encourage moderate physical activity.

▶ Describe the risks associated with inactivity, including excessive sitting.

ctivity has many health risks that can be overcome with regular moderate-intensity physical activity.

©Blend Images/Michael DeYoung/Getty Images

Why it Matters!

Humans are clearly meant to move, but the nature of our society has made it difficult for many people to lead active lifestyles. Cars, motorized golf carts, riding lawn mowers, elevators, remote control devices, and email are just some of the modern conveniences that have reduced the amount of activity in our daily lives.

Finding ways to get regular physical activity is critical for optimal health, wellness, and fitness; but it is now clear that avoiding inactivity is also important. In fact, evidence suggests that excessive inactivity (especially too much sitting) puts your health at risk even if you are physically active. In this Concept, you will learn about the risks associated with excessive sedentary behavior as well as the benefits of moderate activity (sometimes referred to as moderate-intensity activity). You will also learn strategies to help you avoid sedentary living and incorporate moderate activity into your daily routine.

Moving from Inactivity to Active Living

Inactivity can be distinguished from sedentary behavior. The five steps in the physical activity pyramid illustrate the different types of physical activity (Figure 1). The activities in the pyramid provide health, wellness, and fitness benefits that we will describe in detail. However, it is now clear that sedentary behavior presents a risk to a person's health, independent of the level of activity. In other words, there are health risks even for active people who sit too much. The words *Avoid Inactivity* are included in bold black type below the pyramid to emphasize the independent risks associated with sedentary lifestyles.

The term *inactivity* is used intentionally in the pyramid as the opposite of physical activity, but it is important to clarify some terminology. Research leaders in the field actually make distinctions between being "inactive" and being "sedentary." Inactivity refers to a lack of physical activity while being sedentary reflects excessive time spent sitting or lying down. A person can meet guidelines for physical activity but still spend too much time being sedentary. Another person can be labeled as "inactive" but he or she may not be truly "sedentary" if the person doesn't spend much time sitting or lying down. Thus, it is important to learn to distinguish these words and behaviors. See the In the News feature for more details.

Moderate physical activity can be distinguished from "light" activity and "vigorous" activity. Scientists have devised a method to classify levels of activity by intensity. With this system, all activities are compared against the amount of energy expended at rest. Resting energy expenditure is defined as 1 "metabolic equivalent" or 1 **MET.** Other activities are then assigned values in multiples of METs. For generally healthy adults, activities that require an energy expenditure of 3.0 to 6.0 METs are classified as **moderate physical activities.** This means that they require between three and six times the energy expended while at rest. Moderate-intensity activities are often referred to as aerobic physical activities because the aerobic metabolism can typically meet the energy demand of the activity. This allows moderate-intensity (aerobic) activities to be performed comfortably for extended periods of time by most people.

Activities above 6 METs are considered to be **vigorous physical activities,** and these cannot usually be maintained as easily unless a person has a good level of fitness. Examples include more structured

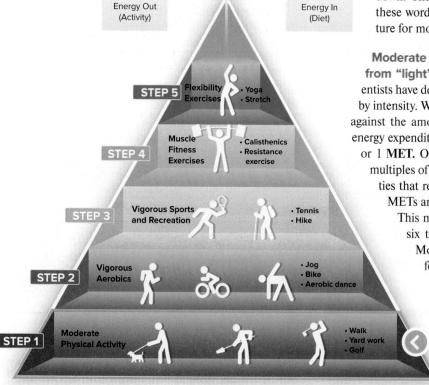

Figure 1 ▶ The physical activity pyramid, step 1: moderate physical activity.
Sources: Charles B. Corbin

In the News

Standardization of Research on Sedentary Behavior

An international team of researchers have collaborated to develop standardized terminology and guidelines to advance research on sedentary behavior. The published paper, co-authored by 84 scientists from 20 countries, aims to promote standardization in the ways that terms such as *physical inactivity, stationary behavior, sedentary behavior,* and *screen time* are used. The differences may seem subtle to nonresearchers, but the standardization will help in further studying the independent influences. (See links for Sedentary Behaviour Research Network in the Suggested Resources and Readings.)

Do you understand the differences between inactivity *and* sedentary behavior? *Do you currently take steps to limit sedentary behavior in your own lifestyle?*

aerobic activities (e.g., jogging, biking, swimming) or vigorous sports (e.g., soccer). Activities below 3.0 METs can be classified as "light intensity," but researchers now distinguish **light activity** (1.5 to 3.0 METs) from **sedentary behavior** (1.0 to 1.5 METs), which primarily captures sitting and lying time. Examples of light activities include lower-intensity activities of daily living such as showering, grocery shopping, washing dishes, and casual walking. Distinctions among the types of activities are summarized in Table 1.

Activity classifications vary depending on one's level of fitness. Normal walking is considered light activity for a person with good fitness (see Table 2), but for a person with low to marginal fitness the same activity is considered moderate. Similarly, brisk walking may be a vigorous activity (rather than moderate) for individuals with low fitness. Table 2 helps you determine the type of lifestyle activity considered moderate for you. Beginners with low fitness should start with normal rather than brisk walking, for example. In later Concepts, you will learn to assess your current fitness level. You may want to refer back to Table 2 after you have made self-assessments of your fitness.

Moderate physical activity is the foundation of an active lifestyle. Moderate physical activity is included at the base of the physical activity pyramid (see Figure 1) because it can be performed by virtually all people, regardless of fitness level or age. Moderate activities include some activities of daily living as well as less intense sports and recreational activities. Taking a brisk walk is a simple and logical way to incorporate moderate activity into daily living. However, activities of daily living, such as walking the dog, gardening, mowing the lawn, doing carpentry, or doing housework can count as moderate activities. Moderate sports and recreational activities not considered to be vigorous enough to be placed at step 3 of the physical activity pyramid can also be used to meet the moderate physical activity guideline (e.g., playing catch, shooting baskets, doing recreational bike riding, and doing casual rollerblading).

Because moderate activities are relatively easy to perform, they are popular among adults. Walking is the most popular of all leisure-time activities among adults. Women walk more than men, and young adults (aged 18–29) walk less

Table 1 ▶ Classification of Physical Activity Intensities for Generally Healthy Adults

Classification	Intensity Range	Examples
Sedentary	1.0–1.5 METs	Sitting, lying
Light	1.5–3.0 METs	Showering, grocery shopping, playing musical instrument, washing dishes
Moderate	3.0–6.0 METs	Walking briskly, mowing lawn, playing table tennis, doing carpentry
Vigorous	>6.0 METs	Hiking, jogging, digging ditches, playing soccer

MET One MET equals the amount of energy a person expends at rest. METs are multiples of resting activity (2 METs equal twice the resting energy expenditure).

Moderate Physical Activities Activities equal in intensity to brisk walking; activities three to six times as intense as lying or sitting at rest (3–6 METs), also referred to as moderate-intensity physical activity.

Vigorous Physical Activities Activities that are more vigorous than moderate activities with intensities at least six times as intense as lying or sitting at rest (>6 METs).

Light Activities Activities that involve standing and/or slow movements with intensities 1.5 to 3.0 times as intense as lying or sitting at rest (1.5–3.0 METs).

Sedentary Behavior Activities that involve lying or sitting with intensities similar to or just slightly higher than rest (1.0–1.5 METs).

Table 2 ▶ Classification of Moderate Physical Activities for People of Different Fitness Levels				
	Activity Classification by Fitness Level			
Sample Lifestyle Activities	**Low Fitness**	**Marginal Fitness**	**Good Fitness**	**High Performance**
Washing your face, dressing, typing, driving a car	Light	Very light or light	Very light	Very light
Normal walking, walking downstairs, bowling, mopping	Moderate	Moderate	Light	Light
Brisk walking, lawn mowing, shoveling, social dancing	Vigorous	Moderate/vigorous	Moderate	Moderate

Brief walks throughout the day can help you meet recommended levels of moderate activity.
©PureStock/Getty Images

than older adults, probably because of more involvement in sports and other vigorous activities. As many as 40 to 50 percent of adults say they walk, but less than half that number report walking 30 minutes or more at least 5 days a week.

While overall activity levels tend to decline with age, involvement in lifestyle activity actually tends to increase. This is because many older adults move away from vigorous sports and recreation and spend more time in lifestyle activities, such as gardening and golf. Older adults tend to have more time and money for these types of recreational activities, and the lower intensity may be appealing. The advantage of moderate activity is that there are many opportunities to be active. Finding enjoyable activities that fit into your daily routine is the key to adopting a more active lifestyle.

Health Risks of Sedentary Behavior

Sedentary behavior is an established risk factor for many chronic diseases. Extended periods of sedentary time have been associated with obesity, diabetes risk, and a number of other conditions, even if a person gets sufficient amounts of physical activity. A recent longitudinal study provided the strongest evidence to date to support a direct relationship between time spent sitting and risk of early mortality. The study monitored lifestyle patterns in a sample of over 8,000 adults (aged 45 and older) using objective activity monitors. The monitors captured both the total sedentary time as well as the extent of prolonged sitting. By monitoring the same participants over time, the researchers were able to examine associations between sedentary behavior and various health risks. In the primary analyses, risk of death was greater for those with more sitting time (and longer sedentary bouts) even after controlling for age, weight status, and exercise habits.

Research has also clarified the biochemical mechanisms that explain health risks associated with sedentary living. Interestingly, the mechanisms are similar to the established pathways that link hypertension and high cholesterol to cardiovascular disease. In both cases, blood vessel inflammation is a precursor to impaired arterial health which then contributes to cardiovascular disease. Reducing or minimizing extended bouts of sedentary time is important for reducing common health risks.

Guidelines are still evolving for quantifying sedentary behavior. The guidelines for physical activity have been refined over many years, but parallel work on sedentary behavior is still in the early phases. The American Academy of Pediatrics has had a long-standing recommendation aimed at minimizing excessive screen time for children. A related objective of the *Healthy People Initiative* is to reduce the proportion of youth who are inactive for long periods of time (defined as viewing television and videos or playing computer games more than 2 hours a day). These recommendations and objectives have increased awareness about the risks of sedentary behavior, but official guidelines are still being refined in the U.S.

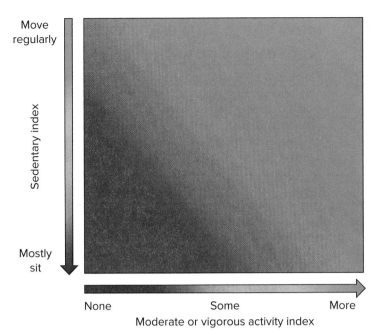

Figure 2 ▶ Conceptual model showing combined health risks of high levels of sedentary behavior and low levels of physical activity. (Adapted from J. Jakicic)

Experts who worked to establish the 2018 *Physical Activity Guidelines for Americans* emphasized the importance of reducing sedentary behavior among adults; however, additional research is needed to provide more specific guidelines. Evidence suggests that the health effects are dependent on both the total amount as well as the length of continuous periods of sedentary time. Therefore, the best advice is to minimize the total amount of sedentary time and to break up extended periods of sitting by standing up and moving about more often. Obtaining physical activity from the five steps of the physical activity pyramid is ideal, but minimizing time spent being sedentary provides independent benefits.

The importance of both physical activity and sedentary behavior is captured in the heat-map image in Figure 2. The section in the lower left corner (Red area) is the high risk zone since that area reflects low physical activity and high sedentary behavior. The area to the upper right corner (Green area) is the low risk zone since it reflects high physical activity and low sedentary behavior. Additional details on the benefits of moderate activity are discussed in the next section.

The Health and Wellness Benefits of Moderate Physical Activity

Moderate activity provides significant health benefits. Research has clearly shown that even modest amounts of moderate activity have significant health benefits. Two early studies paved the way for this line of research. One study reported that postal workers who delivered mail had fewer health problems than workers who sorted mail. Another study reported that drivers of double-decker buses in England had more health problems than conductors who climbed the stairs during the day to collect the tickets. The studies controlled for other lifestyle factors, so the improved health was attributed to the extra activity accumulated throughout the day. Since then, hundreds of studies have further confirmed the importance of moderate activity for good health. However, additional health benefits are possible if vigorous physical activity is also performed.

Moderate activity promotes metabolic fitness. Metabolic fitness is fitness of the systems that provide the energy for effective daily living. Indicators of good metabolic fitness include normal blood lipid levels, normal blood pressure, normal blood sugar levels, and healthy body fat levels. Moderate physical activity promotes metabolic fitness by keeping the metabolic system active. Building and maintaining cardiorespiratory endurance requires a regular challenge to the cardiovascular system, and building metabolic fitness requires a similar regular challenge to the metabolic system. Individuals with good levels of fitness will receive primarily **metabolic fitness benefits** from moderate activity, but those with low fitness will likely receive metabolic and cardiorespiratory endurance benefits. Moderate activity is particularly important for the large segments of the population that do not participate in other forms of regular exercise. As previously described, some activity is clearly better than none.

Moderate physical activity has wellness benefits. The health benefits from physical activity are impressive, but the **wellness benefits** may have a bigger impact on our daily lives. Numerous studies have shown that physical activity is associated with improved quality of life (QOL), but it has proven difficult to determine the contributing factors or underlying mechanisms. The influence may be due to reduced stress, improved cognition, better sleep, improved self-esteem, reduced fatigue, or (more likely) a combination of many different effects. Research suggests that college students who are more physically active have more positive feeling states ("pleasant-activated feelings") than students who are less physically active, even after controlling for sleep and previous days' activity and feeling states. They also noted that feeling states improved on days when people reported performing more activity than normal. The wellness benefits can impact young people every day, whereas health benefits may not be noticed until a person gets older.

Metabolic Fitness Benefits Improvements in metabolic function that reduce risks of diabetes and metabolic syndrome.

Wellness Benefits Increases in quality of life and well-being.

Regular activity is important to achieving health, wellness, and fitness benefits. For the benefits of activity to be optimal, it is important to exercise regularly. The specific benefits from moderate activity tend to be more dependent on frequency than on intensity. This is sometimes referred to as the **last bout effect** because the effects are short term (i.e., attributable to the last bout of activity performed). For example, regular exercise promotes metabolic fitness by creating the stimulus that helps maintain insulin sensitivity and improve glucose regulation. Another example is the beneficial effect of exercise on stress management. In this case, the periodic stimulus from exercise helps directly counter the negative physical and physiological responses to stress. To maximize the benefits of physical activity, it is important to try to get some activity every day.

Sustained light-intensity activity provides benefits by keeping metabolism active. The new physical activity guidelines have recommended that activities be at least moderate in intensity. However, researchers have also become interested in the accumulation of light-intensity activity since it may reflect time that is not spent in sedentary activities. Essentially, a person who accumulates a lot of light activity would likely also have lower amounts of sedentary behavior.

Because light activity has a higher metabolic cost, there has also been considerable interest in the potential implications for weight loss. Some researchers referred to light activity as *Non-Exercise Activity Thermogenesis (NEAT)* to emphasize the substantial number of calories that can be burned by performing more light-intensity activity. Research on uses of standing desks in worksites has not documented major benefits on weight status, but this may be due to the relatively small metabolic difference between sitting and standing. A person would also not likely lose weight with a standing regimen unless it was part of a planned, intentional weight reduction program. Additional research is clearly needed, but standing more at work helps break up sedentary time and keeps the metabolism more active. While moderate-intensity activity is preferable, light activity probably provides some tangible benefits, especially for a highly sedentary person.

How Much Moderate Physical Activity Is Enough?

There is a FIT formula for moderate physical activity. The term *threshold of training* is used to describe the minimum activity needed for benefits. Public health guidelines endorsed by the ACSM, the AHA, and the CDC have recommended that adults accumulate 150 minutes of moderate-intensity activity each week, an amount equal to 30 minutes 5 days a week. The recommendation highlighted in the original *Surgeon General's Report on Physical Activity* called for adults to accumulate about 1,000 kcal/week (or about 150 kcal/day) from moderate activity. Table 3 summarizes the threshold levels for frequency, intensity, and time (duration). Note that these are considered minimal, or threshold, levels. The target zone calls for the accumulation of 30 or more minutes a day. Physical activity above the recommended minimum provides additional health benefits.

Vigorous activity can substitute for moderate activity. The *Physical Activity Guidelines for Americans* focus on the volume of physical activity performed. Moderate intensity activity is sufficient to meet the guidelines, but vigorous-intensity activity can also be substituted to meet the weekly targets. According to the guidelines, each minute of vigorous activity counts as 2 minutes of moderate activity. Therefore, the guideline can also be met by performing 75 minutes of vigorous activity instead of 150 minutes of moderate activity.

The guidelines can also be expressed in total "MET-minutes." To compute MET-minutes, you simply multiply the MET level of the activity you performed by the number of minutes. For example, a 60-minute brisk walk (approximately 3 METs) would yield 180 MET-minutes (3 METs × 60 minutes). However, note that this same volume can also be achieved with a 30-minute run that requires approximately 6 METs (6 METs × 30 minutes). A total of 500 MET-minutes per week is recommended to meet the minimum guidelines.

Sustained bouts of activity are recommended, but accumulating moderate activity throughout the day also provides benefits. Previous guidelines suggested that

Table 3 ▶ The FIT Formula for Moderate Physical Activity		
	Threshold of Training (minimum)[a]	**Target Zone (optimal)**
Frequency	At least 5 days a week	5–7 days a week
Intensity[b]	• Equal to brisk walking[b] • Approximately 150 calories accumulated per day • 3 to 5 METs[b]	• Equal to brisk to fast walking[b] • Approximately 150–300 calories accumulated per day • 3 to 6 METs[b]
Time (duration)[c]	30 minutes or three 10-minute sessions per day	30–60 minutes or more accumulated in sessions of at least 10 minutes

[a]The recommendation of 150 minutes can be accumulated throughout the week, but these thresholds provide a good target.
[b]Heart rate and relative perceived exertion can also be used to determine intensity.
[c]Depends on fitness level (see Table 2).

HELP   Health is available to Everyone for a Lifetime, and it's Personal

Is Walking a Means to an End or an End in Itself?

Walking is by far the most commonly reported moderate activity, but some people often go out of their way to avoid walking (such as waiting for campus buses, driving around parking lots to get closer to a store, or taking an elevator rather than climbing a few flights of stairs).

Do you view walking as a "means to an end" (i.e., simply as a way to get around) or as an "end in itself" (i.e., as a way to get more physical activity)? How might this perception influence your activity patterns?

connect
ACTIVITY

moderate activity bouts should be 10 minutes in length or longer for optimal health and fitness benefits. However, the evidence is not compelling for the specific 10-minute recommendation. Aiming for extended bouts of activity is best, but short-duration moderate activity accumulated throughout the day is also beneficial. The intermittent activity can also be helpful for breaking up sedentary time.

Special moderate activity guidelines have been developed for children, older adults, and adults with chronic health conditions. Guidelines for physical activity depend on the unique needs of the target population. Children need more physical activity than adults (at least 60 minutes and up to several hours of activity each day).

Guidelines are also different for older adults and adults with chronic conditions. As previously described (see Table 2), activity that is moderate for young adults may be too intense for some older individuals or those with health problems. Because of this, the guidelines recommend that these individuals focus on tracking minutes of activity. This allows the intensity to be a self-determined level that corresponds to a person's relative level of fitness.

Monitoring Physical Activity and Sedentary Behavior

A variety of methods can be used to accumulate moderate physical activity for health benefits. Finding 30 minutes or longer for continuous physical activity may be difficult, especially on very busy days. However, the physical activity guidelines emphasize that moderate activity can be accumulated throughout the day. Figure 3 illustrates the activity profiles for three different people. The pink line profiles a person who is

connect
VIDEO 4

inactive except for brief walks from the car to the office in the morning and from the office to the car in the evening. This person is sedentary and does not meet the moderate activity guidelines. Because some activity is better than none, the brief walks are better than no activity at all. The blue line represents a person who is sedentary most of the day but meets the moderate activity guideline by taking a long walk on a treadmill during the noon hour. The green line represents the activity of a person who meets the moderate activity standard in multiple bouts, including lifestyle activities such as walking to and from work, walking to lunch, and climbing the stairs. You can accumulate activity using the method that you prefer as long as you meet the recommended guidelines.

Energy expenditure can be used to monitor physical activity. As shown in Table 3, an energy expenditure of between 150 and 300 kcal/day from physical activity is sufficient for meeting physical activity guidelines. While not as simple as tracking time, calories expended from physical activity can be estimated if the approximate MET value of the activity is known. The energy cost of resting energy expenditure (1 MET) is approximately 1 calorie per kilogram of body weight per hour (1 kcal/kg/hr). An activity such as brisk walking (4 mph) requires an energy expenditure of about 4 METs, or 4 kcal/kg/hr. A 150-lb person (~70 kg) walking for an hour would expend about 280 kcal (4 kcal/kg/hr × 70 kg × 1 hr). Note that a 30-minute walk would burn approximately 150 calories and satisfy the guideline.

Commercial fitness equipment can provide energy expenditure estimates. The devices use an estimated MET level based on the selected intensity or a measured heart rate (if a heart rate sensor is used). The timer on the machine then tracks the time of the workout, and this allows calories to be estimated during the workout. The accuracy of the estimate will depend on the internal calculations, but energy expenditure can't be estimated unless body weight is entered during the setup process. If this wasn't obtained, the calorie estimates are probably based on some reference value of weight and therefore may not be accurate. Table 4 lists estimated METs for different activities, along with calorie estimates (per hour of exercise) for people of different body weights.

Step counts can help monitor physical activity patterns. Steps have become a popular and well-understood metric to quantify physical activity. Digital pedometers have been used for years to provide an easy way for people to track steps, but step counts can be reported on other monitoring devices, including various consumer activity monitors and smartphone apps. Steps provide a good indicator of activity for most people since most forms of activity involve some locomotor movement (major exceptions would be swimming and cycling).

Last Bout Effect A short-term effect associated with the last bout of activity. Typically related to improvements in metabolic fitness.

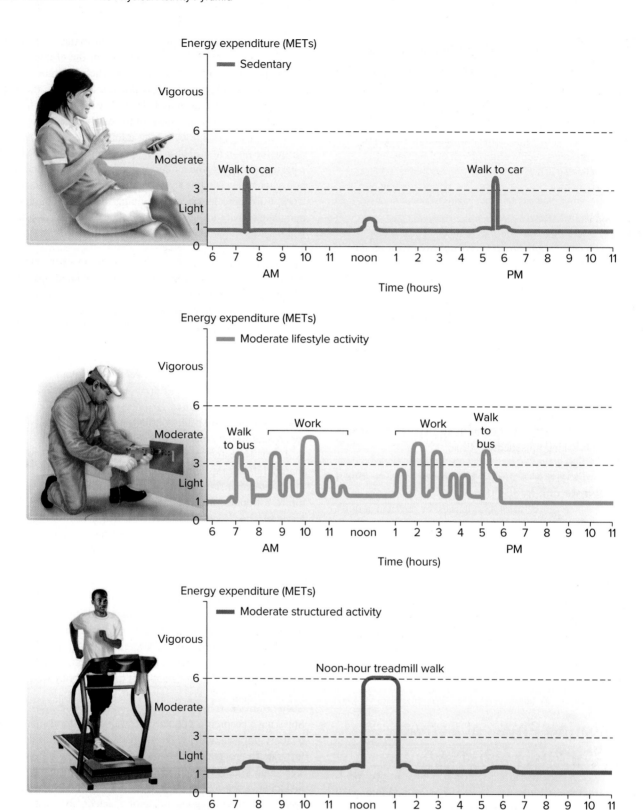

Figure 3 ▶ Comparison of people performing moderate activity in different ways.

Table 4 ▶ Calories Expended in Lifestyle Physical Activities

Activity Classification/Description	METs[a]	Calories Used per Hour for Different Body Weights					
		100 lb (45 kg)	120 lb (55 kg)	150 lb (70 kg)	180 lb (82 kg)	200 lb (91 kg)	220 lb (100 kg)
Gardening Activities							
Gardening (general)	5.0	227	273	341	409	455	502
Mowing lawn (hand mower)	6.0	273	327	409	491	545	599
Mowing lawn (power mower)	4.5	205	245	307	368	409	450
Raking leaves	4.0	182	218	273	327	364	401
Shoveling snow	6.0	273	327	409	491	545	599
Home Activities							
Child care	3.5	159	191	239	286	318	350
Cleaning, washing dishes	2.5	114	136	170	205	227	249
Cooking/food preparation	2.5	114	136	170	205	227	249
Home/auto repair	3.0	136	164	205	245	273	301
Painting	4.5	205	245	307	368	409	450
Strolling with child	2.5	114	136	170	205	227	249
Sweeping/vacuuming	2.5	114	136	170	205	227	249
Washing/waxing car	4.5	205	245	307	368	409	450
Leisure Activities							
Bocci ball/croquet	2.5	114	136	170	205	227	249
Bowling	3.0	136	164	205	245	273	301
Canoeing	5.0	227	273	341	409	455	501
Cross-country skiing (leisure)	7.0	318	382	477	573	636	699
Cycling (<10 mph)	4.0	182	218	273	327	364	401
Cycling (12–14 mph)	8.0	364	436	545	655	727	799
Dancing (social)	4.5	205	245	307	368	409	450
Fishing	4.0	182	218	273	327	364	401
Golf (riding)	3.5	159	191	239	286	318	350
Golf (walking)	5.5	250	300	375	450	500	550
Horseback riding	4.0	182	218	273	327	364	401
Swimming (leisure)	6.0	273	327	409	491	545	599
Table tennis	4.0	182	218	273	327	364	401
Walking (3.5 mph)	3.8	173	207	259	311	346	387
Occupational Activities							
Bricklaying/masonry	7.0	318	382	477	573	636	699
Carpentry	3.5	159	191	239	286	318	350
Construction	5.5	250	300	375	450	500	550
Electrical work/plumbing	3.5	159	191	239	286	318	350
Digging	7.0	318	382	477	573	636	699
Farming	5.5	250	300	375	450	500	550
Store clerk	3.5	159	191	239	286	318	350
Waiter/waitress	4.0	182	218	273	327	364	401

Note: MET values and caloric estimates are based on values listed in *Compendium of Physical Activities.*
[a]*Based* on values of those with "good fitness" ratings.
Source: Source: Ainsworth et al., "2011 Compendium of Physical Activities: a second update of codes and MET values". *Medicine and Science in Sports and Exercise,* 2011;43(8):1575-1581.

Table 5 ▶ Activity Classification for Pedometer Step Counts in Healthy Adults

Category		Steps/Day
Sedentary		<5,000
Low active		5,000–6,999
Somewhat active	Threshold	7,000–9,999
Active	Target Zone	10,000–12,500
Very active		>12,500

Source: Based on values from Tudor-Locke.

The ability to easily monitor daily step counts provides a helpful reminder to many people about the importance of being active during the day.

Studies on large numbers of people provide data to help classify people into activity categories based on step counts (see Table 5), but it is beneficial to set goals on your own baseline. Wear the pedometer (or similar monitoring device) for 1 week to establish a baseline step count (average steps per day). Then, set a goal of increasing steps per day by 1,000 to 3,000 steps. Keep records of daily step counts to help you determine if you are meeting your goal. Setting a goal that you are likely to meet will help you find success. As you meet your goal, increase your step counts gradually.

There are some limitations in using steps as indicators of total physical activity. A person with longer legs will accumulate fewer steps over the same distance than someone with shorter strides (due to a longer stride length). A person running will also accumulate fewer steps over the same distance than a person who walks. There is considerable variability in the quality (and accuracy) of monitors and step counting apps, so it is also important to consider this when interpreting data.

Activity monitors and cell phone apps can track and record sedentary time. Behavioral feedback from monitors can help remind users to stand up and move more during the day. The available consumer monitors do this in different ways. Some have prompts or start vibrating if the monitor has been stationary for more than 60 minutes. Other devices provide visual cues or feedback on the screen. The Apple Watch, for example, has an interface designed to help remind users about the dual goals of being active and minimizing sedentary time. The display features concentric rings that are completed if the individual meets the intended goals. The "exercise" ring is completed when you accumulate 30 minutes of physical activity, but to complete the "stand" ring you have to accumulate at least some movement in each of the 12 waking/active hours in the day.

Smartphone apps provide feedback to help track active and sedentary time.
©Apgeo Design, LLC

Adopting and Sustaining an Active Identity

Seek ways to reduce and/or break up sedentary time. Much time in our daily lives is spent being sedentary (e.g., reading/studying, working at computers, driving in cars, eating). A key for healthy living (and weight control) is to minimize time spent being sedentary. The popularity of standing desks has increased in recent years as a way to promote more activity at work (see the Technology Update feature). Minimizing time spent watching television or standing while on the phone can also help reduce total sedentary time. The negative effects of sedentary time can also be minimized with periodic breaks. Research suggests that the risks are due to prolonged sitting, so take periodic standing breaks.

Seek out and promote active environments. Most people would like to be more active, but the nature of our society and our environment often makes this difficult. Studies have demonstrated conclusively that the physical, or **built, environment** has important influences on physical activity patterns, but ultimately you must take responsibility for your lifestyle and find ways to be active. Try to take stock of your lifestyle (and your environment) and determine ways to take advantage of what is available. You can also seek out ways to be a local advocate for walkability and biking issues in your community.

Technology Update

Standing Desks and Treadmill Desks

New designs and options in office furniture have enabled people to be less sedentary while at work. For example, electronic desks allow standard sitting desks to transform into "standing desks" with the push of a button. A company called TrekDesk sells desks that mount over standard treadmills to enable people to walk while they work. These devices offer considerable potential for promoting activity in worksite settings. (See www.trekdesk.com.)

Would you take advantage of an active workstation if it was available on campus or at your work setting? Why or why not?

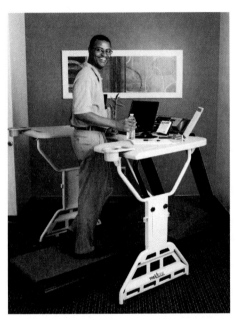

©TrekDesk

Seek out ways to add physical activity into your day. Active commuting is one way to add physical activity to your lifestyle. It takes additional preparation and the logistics can be challenging, but it is a great way to build activity into your day. In addition to providing beneficial amounts of physical activity, this can save time, reduce gas, save money, and help the environment. Another option is to take more active trips to the store. Research suggests that the overwhelming majority of our car trips are 1 mile or less. Walking or biking even a few of these trips can have a big impact. The ability to walk or bike to work or to the store may not be possible for you because of the nature of

Built Environment A term used to describe aspects of our created physical environment (e.g., buildings, roads).

Bike commuting is an effective way to add physical activity to your day.
©Image Source/Getty Images

A CLOSER LOOK

Is Sitting the New Smoking?

Most people know that physical activity is important for their health, but some are just becoming aware of the potential risks of excessive time being sedentary. The question *Is Sitting the New Smoking?* has been picked up by the media as they release information about this issue. Many organizations are also working to change societal perceptions and habits related to sedentary behavior. JustStand.org says its mission is to lead

the "uprising (literally and figuratively) to sit less, stand up and move more."

Has the emphasis on sedentary behavior in the popular press influenced your behavior? Do you agree with the label of sitting as the "new smoking" or do you think this is overstated?

your community or the safety of the roads. However, there are a number of other strategies you can use to get more activity in your day. Consider parking farther away from store entrances, using the stairs rather than the elevator, taking walking breaks, and even standing (instead of sitting) when convenient. Adopting an active lifestyle in a sedentary society is challenging, but it is within your control.

Using Self-Management Skills

Preparing a moderate physical activity plan requires the use of multiple self-management skills. You can use the six steps in program planning outlined in the Concept

devoted to self-management skills to prepare a moderate physical activity plan. Preparing a plan requires the use of a variety of self-management skills including self-assessment, goal setting, and self-monitoring. Preparing a plan also gives you a chance to practice using these skills.

Self-monitoring your sedentary behaviors can aid in reducing them and increasing activity levels. The advent of activity monitors has made it easy to objectively self-monitor physical activity patterns. The monitors also provide information about the amount of time spent doing nothing (being inactive). (See the Strategies for Action: Lab Information for alternate methods of assessing sedentary behavior.)

Strategies for Action: Lab Information

Preparing a plan of moderate physical activity, including SMART goals, is a good place to start. Moderate physical activity is something that virtually anyone can do. In Lab 7A, you will set moderate physical activity goals and plan a 1-week moderate physical activity program. As you prepare your goals and plan, keep in mind the guidelines on SMART goals. For some people, this plan may be the main component of a lifetime plan. For others, it may be only a beginning that leads to the selection of activities from other levels of the physical activity pyramid. Even the most active people should consider regular moderate physical activity because it is a type of activity that can be done throughout life.

Self-monitoring moderate physical activity can help you stick with it. The self-monitoring chart in Lab 7A not only helps

you keep a log of moderate activities (or step counts), but it also lets you hone your self-management skills. Charts like this can be copied to make a log book for long-term activity self-monitoring.

Self-monitoring of sedentary behavior can help you minimize sedentary time. In Lab 7B, you will conduct an assessment of your sedentary behavior. You will determine time spent being inactive and also calculate a Sedentary Behavior Index based on the ratio of your sedentary to light activity. Reducing time spent in sedentary behavior takes conscious effort, but the lab will provide a way to examine it.

Suggested Resources and Readings

The websites for the following sources can be accessed by searching online for the organization, program, or title listed. Specific scientific references are available at the end of this edition of *Concepts of Fitness and Wellness*.

- Active Living Research MOVE. A Blog about Active Living.
- American College of Sports Medicine. (2017). *ACSM's Guidelines for Exercise Testing and Prescription* (10th ed.). Philadelphia: Lippincott Williams & Wilkins.
- American College of Sports Medicine. Physical Activity 360.
- American College of Sports Medicine. Sit Less/Move More (pdf).
- American Heart Association. Sitting Less for Adults (pdf).
- Bureau of Labor Statistics. American Time Use Survey.
- CNN. Yes, Sitting Too Long Can Kill You (online resource).
- JustStand.org. The Body Is Designed to Move (pdf).
- JustStand.org. Sit Less, Stand More Infographics (pdf).
- Levine, J. A. (2014). *Get Up! Why Your Chair Is Killing You and What You Can Do About It.* New York: Palgrave Macmillan.
- Sedentary Behaviour Research Network. What is sedentary behaviour? http://www.sedentarybehaviour.org
- U.S. Department of Health and Human Services. (2018). *Physical Activity Guidelines for Americans.* Washington, DC.

Lab 7A Setting Goals for Moderate Physical Activity and Self-Monitoring (Logging) Program

Name   **Section**   **Date**

Purpose: To set moderate activity goals and to self-monitor (log) physical activity.

Procedures

1. Read the five stages of change questions below. Place a check by the stage that best represents your current moderate physical activity level. If you are at stages 1–3 (precontemplation, contemplation, or preparation), you may want to set goals below the threshold of 30 minutes per day to get started. Those at the action or maintenance stage should consider goals of 30 minutes or more per day.
2. Determine moderate activity goals for each day of a 1-week period. In the columns (Chart 1) under the heading "Moderate Activity Goals," record the total minutes per day that you expect to perform **OR** the total steps per day that you expect to perform. Record the specific date for each day of the week in the "Date" column.
3. The goals should be realistic for you, but try to set goals that would meet current physical activity guidelines. If you choose step goals, you will need a pedometer. Use Table 5 in this Concept to help you choose daily step goals.
4. If you choose minutes per day as your goals, use Chart 2 to keep track of the number of minutes of activity that you perform on each day of the 7-day period. Record the number of minutes for each bout of activity of at least 10 minutes in length performed during each day (Chart 2). Determine a total number of minutes for the day and record this total in the last column of Chart 2 and in the "Minutes Performed" column of Chart 1.
5. If you choose steps per day as your goals, determine the total steps per day accumulated on the pedometer and record that number of steps in the "Steps Performed" column for each day of the week (Chart 1).
6. Answer the questions in the Conclusions and Implications section (use full sentences for your answers).

Determine your stage for moderate physical activity. Check only the stage that represents your current moderate activity level.

☐ Precontemplation: I do not meet moderate activity guidelines and have not been thinking about starting.

☐ Contemplation: I do not meet moderate activity guidelines but have been thinking about starting.

☐ Preparation: I am planning to start doing regular moderate activity to meet guidelines.

☐ Action: I do moderate activity, but I am not as regular as I should be.

☐ Maintenance: I regularly meet national goals for moderate activity.

Chart 1 Moderate Physical Activity Goals and Summary Performance Log

Select a goal for each day in a 1-week plan. Keep a log of the activities performed to determine if your goals are met.

	Date	Moderate Activity Goals		Summary Performance Log	
		Minutes/Day	**Steps/Day**	**Minutes Performed**	**Steps Performed**
Day 1					
Day 2					
Day 3					
Day 4					
Day 5					
Day 6					
Day 7					

Chart 2 Moderate Physical Activity Log (Daily Minutes Performed)

If you choose minutes per day as goals, write the number of minutes for each bout of moderate activity performed each day. Record a daily total (total minutes of moderate activity per day) in the "Daily Total" column. Record daily totals in Chart 1.

	Date	Moderate Activity Bouts					Daily Total
		Bout 1	Bout 2	Bout 3	Bout 4	Bout 5	
Day 1							
Day 2							
Day 3							
Day 4							
Day 5							
Day 6							
Day 7							

Did you meet your moderate activity goals for at least 5 days of the week? (Yes) (No)

Do you think you can consistently meet your moderate activity goals? (Yes) (No)

What activities did you perform most often when doing moderate activity?
List the most common activities in the spaces below.

Conclusions and Implications

1. Do you feel that you will use moderate physical activity as a regular part of your lifetime physical activity plan, either now or in the future? Use several sentences to explain your answer.

2. Did setting goals and logging activity make you more aware of your daily moderate physical activity patterns? Explain why or why not.

Lab 7B Estimating Sedentary Behavior

Name **Section** **Date**

Purpose: To estimate time spent in sedentary behavior.

Procedures

1. Pick a day of the week to evaluate.
2. Use the Sedentary Behavior Assessment to estimate the time spent in different intensities of activity during the day.
3. Summarize the results for the time spent in each category and be sure your daily total = 24 hours.
4. Calculate the ratio of sedentary to light activity and use the Rating Chart to determine your Sedentary Behavior Index. *Note:* There are no absolute guidelines, but a smaller ratio is desirable.
5. Calculate the average breaks in sedentary time across the five categories and use the Rating Chart to determine your Sedentary Break Index. *Note:* There are no absolute guidelines, but a larger number of average breaks is desirable.
6. Record your scores and the indexes in the Results section.
7. Answer the questions in the Conclusions and Implications section.

Sedentary Behavior Index Rating Chart

Sedentary Behavior Index	Sedentary/Light Ratio
Low Sedentary	<1
Moderate Sedentary	1.0–2.0
High Sedentary	>2.0
Sedentary Break Index	**Average Break Score**
Frequent Breaks	4–5
Moderate Breaks	2–3
Infrequent Breaks	0–1

Results Summarize your activity/inactivity profile by completing the following:

Sleep Time (hr)	=	_____	Sleep %	=	_____
Sedentary Time (hr)	=	_____	Sedentary %	=	_____
Light Time (hr)	=	_____	Light %	=	_____
Moderate Activity Time (hr)	=	_____	Moderate %	=	_____
Vigorous Activity Time (hr)	=	_____	Vigorous %	=	_____
Total Hours	=	_____			
Sedentary/Light Ratio	=	_____	Average Break Score	=	_____
Sedentary Behavior Index	=	_____	Sedentary Break Index	=	_____

Conclusions and Implications: Summarize the overall assessment of your sedentary behaviors by describing both the total time you spend sedentary and the calculated sedentary/light ratio. Comment on the frequency of breaks in sedentary behavior and explain how changing the frequency of your breaks would influence your Sedentary Behavior Index. Do you feel you are effectively minimizing sedentary time, or do you think you may have room for improvement?

Based on categories and constructs used in the Workforce Sitting Questionnaire (Chau et al., 2011).

Sedentary Behavior Assessment (complete these steps in order):

1. Estimate the total time you spend in sedentary or light activity (Sedentary + Light) by subtracting from 24 (hours) the estimated time you spend (in hours) sleeping, engaged in moderate physical activity (MPA), and engaged in vigorous physical activity (VPA). The formula below will give you an estimate of the combined time spent in sedentary or light activities.

Sedentary + Light (hr) = 24 − ⬚ − ⬚ − ⬚ = ⬚
                          Sleep (hr)   MPA (hr)   VPA (hr)   Sedentary + Light

2. Estimate the time you spend being sedentary (i.e., sitting or lying) in five major categories or settings and then sum for the whole day. For each category, estimate the frequency of breaks in the sedentary behavior for that category.

The categories below represent key time periods when people spend significant time being sedentary.

Estimate the total time spent sitting or lying in each of these categories throughout the day (not sleeping).

Estimate how many breaks from sitting you take during 1 hour of sitting in each of these settings (e.g., standing up, stretching, walking). Put an X that best captures the frequency of breaks.

	(hr)	(min)						
Traveling to/from places (e.g., bus/car)	⬚	⬚	5	4	3	2	1	0
At school and work (e.g., class, meetings, presentations, work)	⬚	⬚	5	4	3	2	1	0
Watching TV or using other media (e.g., TV, video games)	⬚	⬚	5	4	3	2	1	0
Computer use at home (e.g., homework, Web searching, email)	⬚	⬚	5	4	3	2	1	0
Other leisure activities (e.g., reading, relaxing, talking)	⬚	⬚	5	4	3	2	1	0

Total Sedentary Time =   = _____ hr + _____ min   Average Break Score = _____

3. Calculate the time spent in light activity by subtracting your estimated sedentary time (step 2) from the estimated time spent in Sedentary 1 Light (step 1).

Estimated Light Activity = ⬚ − ⬚ = ⬚
                     Sedentary + Light (step 1)   Sedentary Time (step 2)   Light Time

4. Calculate a ratio of sedentary to light activity by dividing Sedentary Time (step 2) by Light Time (step 3). Use the formula below to make your calculations.

Estimated Sedentary/Light Ratio = ⬚ / ⬚ = ⬚
                           Sedentary Time (step 2)   Light Time (step 3)   Sedentary/Light Ratio

Based on categories and constructs used in the Workforce Sitting Questionnaire (Chau et al., 2011).

Cardiorespiratory Endurance

LEARNING OBJECTIVES

After completing the study of this Concept, you will be able to:

▶ Describe the different components of the cardiovascular and respiratory systems.

▶ List the health benefits of cardiorespiratory endurance.

▶ Outline the FIT formula for moderate to vigorous physical activity designed to promote cardiorespiratory endurance.

▶ Identify several methods of determining exercise intensity levels for promoting cardiorespiratory endurance, select the method you think is most useful to you, and explain the reasons for your choice.

▶ Describe key guidelines for monitoring aerobic exercise, including self-monitoring heart rate.

▶ Indicate several self-assessments for cardiorespiratory endurance, select the self-assessment you feel is most useful to you, and explain the reasons for your choice.

Cardiorespiratory endurance is probably the most important aspect of physical fitness because it has a major impact on health and greatly influences physical performance.

©Ryan McVay/Getty Images

Why it Matters!

Cardiorespiratory endurance is generally considered to be the most important aspect of physical fitness. The fitness of the cardiovascular and respiratory systems is central to good health since your heart and lungs need to be healthy to efficiently pump blood and oxygen through your entire body. The heart is a muscle and, like other muscles, it gets stronger and more efficient if it is regularly trained. Healthy blood vessels are also critical for carrying blood and nutrients to the tissues; but without a healthy respiratory system, the circulatory system would be ineffective in providing oxygen to the body. Regular physical activity is essential for keeping both the cardiovascular and respiratory systems working properly, reducing the risk of heart disease and stroke as well as providing additional health and wellness benefits that extend well beyond reducing risks for disease. This Concept describes the function of the cardiovascular and respiratory systems and explains how to determine the appropriate intensity of exercise needed to promote cardiorespiratory endurance. Thus, it can be viewed as an owner's manual for your cardiovascular and respiratory systems.

Elements of Cardiorespiratory Endurance

The term *cardiorespiratory endurance* has several synonyms. Cardiorespiratory endurance is the ability of the heart, blood vessels, blood, and respiratory system to supply nutrients and oxygen to the muscles, and the ability of the muscles to utilize fuel to allow sustained exercise. A person with good cardiorespiratory endurance can persist in physical activity for relatively long periods without undue stress. Cardiorespiratory endurance is the preferred name for this component of fitness, but it is sometimes referred to as cardiovascular fitness, cardiovascular endurance, or aerobic fitness. The laboratory measure of this component of fitness is referred to as **aerobic capacity** (discussed later in this Concept). Field tests such as those in Lab 8B measure cardiorespiratory endurance, but scores are sometimes used to estimate aerobic capacity.

Good cardiorespiratory endurance requires a fit heart muscle. The heart is a powerful muscle that pumps blood through the body. The heart of a normal individual beats reflexively about 40 million times a year. In a single day, the heart pumps over 4,000 gallons of blood through the body. To keep the cardiovascular system working effectively, it is crucial to have a strong and fit heart.

Like other muscles in the body, the heart becomes stronger if it is exercised. The size and strength of the heart increases, and it can pump more blood with each beat, accomplishing the same amount of work with fewer beats. Typical resting heart rate (RHR) values are around 70–80 beats per minute, but a highly trained endurance athlete may have a resting heart rate in the 40s or 50s. There is some individual variability in RHR, but a decrease in your RHR with training indicates clear improvements in cardiorespiratory endurance.

Good cardiorespiratory endurance requires a fit vascular system. The heart has four chambers, which pump and receive blood in a rhythmical fashion to maintain good circulation (see Figure 1). Blood containing a high concentration of oxygen is pumped by the left ventricle through the aorta (a major artery), where it is carried to the tissues. Blood flows through a sequence of arteries to capillaries and to veins. Veins carry the blood containing lesser amounts of oxygen back to the right side of the heart, first to the atrium and then to the ventricle. The right ventricle pumps the blood to the lungs. In the lungs, the blood picks up oxygen (O_2), and carbon dioxide (CO_2) is removed. From the lungs, the oxygenated blood travels back to the heart, first to the left atrium and then to the left ventricle where it is pumped out to the rest of the body.

A dense network of arteries distributes the oxygenated blood to the muscles, tissues, and organs. Healthy arteries are elastic, are free of obstruction, and expand to permit the flow of blood. Muscle layers line the arteries and control the size of the arterial opening upon the impulse from nerve fibers. Unfit arteries may have a reduced internal diameter (atherosclerosis) because of deposits on the interior of their walls, or they may have hardened, nonelastic walls (arteriosclerosis).

The blood in the four chambers of the heart does not directly nourish the heart. Rather, numerous small arteries within the heart muscle provide for coronary circulation. Poor coronary circulation precipitated by unhealthy arteries can be the cause of a heart attack.

Deoxygenated blood flows back to the heart through a series of veins. The veins are intertwined in the skeletal muscle, and this allows normal muscle action to facilitate the return of blood to the heart. When a muscle is contracted, the vein is squeezed, and this pushes the blood back to the heart. Small valves in the veins prevent the backward flow of the blood, but defects in the valves can lead to pooling of blood in the veins. Regular physical activity keeps the valves of the veins healthy and helps reduce pooling of blood in the veins.

Capillaries are the transfer stations where oxygen and fuel are released, and waste products, such as carbon dioxide, are removed from the tissues. The veins receive the blood from the capillaries for the return trip to the heart.

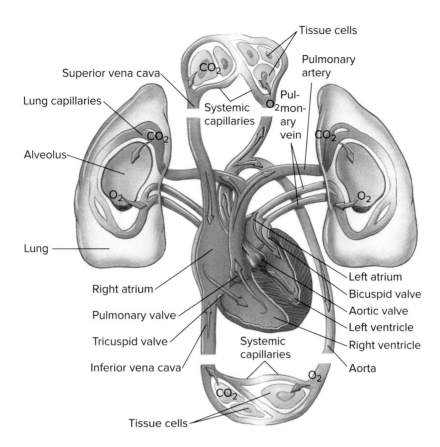

Figure 1 ▶ Cardiovascular and respiratory systems.

Good cardiorespiratory endurance requires healthy blood and a fit respiratory system. The process of taking in oxygen (through the mouth and nose) and delivering it to the lungs, where it is picked up by the blood, is called external respiration. External respiration requires fit lungs as well as blood with adequate **hemoglobin.** Hemoglobin carries oxygen through the bloodstream. Lack of hemoglobin reduces oxygen-carrying capacity—a condition known as **anemia.**

Delivering oxygen to the tissues from the blood is called internal respiration. Internal respiration requires an adequate number of healthy capillaries. In addition to delivering oxygen to the tissues, these systems remove carbon dioxide. Good cardiorespiratory endurance requires fitness of both the external and internal respiratory systems.

Cardiorespiratory endurance requires fit muscle tissue capable of using oxygen. Once the oxygen is delivered, the muscle tissues must be able to use oxygen to sustain physical performance. Physical activity that promotes cardiorespiratory endurance stimulates changes in muscle fibers that make them more effective in using oxygen. Outstanding distance runners have high numbers of well-conditioned muscle fibers that can readily use oxygen to produce energy for sustained running. Training in other activities would elicit similar adaptations in the specific muscles used in those activities.

During exercise, the performance and function of the cardiovascular and respiratory systems are maximized. During exercise, a number of changes occur to increase the availability of oxygen to the muscles. Breathing rate and depth increase, allowing the body to take in more oxygen. The heart beats faster and pumps more blood with each beat (increased stroke volume). The higher heart rate and larger stroke volume allow more blood to be pumped each minute (increased cardiac output).

Aerobic Capacity The ability to supply oxygen during very vigorous physical activity typically measured by a laboratory test ($\dot{V}O_2$ max).

Hemoglobin The oxygen-carrying protein (molecule) of red blood cells.

Anemia A condition in which hemoglobin and the blood's oxygen-carrying capacity are below normal.

During exercise, the blood passing through the lungs picks up more oxygen and distributes it more quickly. Activation of the sympathetic nervous system also leads to a redistribution of the blood flow, so that more of it gets shunted to the working skeletal muscle. During rest, the muscles get about 20 percent of the available blood flow, but this increases to about 70 percent during vigorous exercise. Within the muscles, a larger percentage of the available oxygen is also extracted from the muscles during exercise. Collectively, these changes help provide the muscles with the oxygen needed to maintain aerobic metabolism (see Table 1).

Aerobic capacity is evaluated using an indicator known as maximum oxygen uptake, or $\dot{V}O_2$ max. A person's **maximum oxygen uptake ($\dot{V}O_2$ max),** commonly referred to as aerobic capacity, is determined in a laboratory by measuring how much oxygen a person can use in maximal exercise. The test is usually done on a treadmill using specialized gas analyzers to measure oxygen use. The treadmill speed and grade are gradually increased, and when the exercise becomes very hard, oxygen use reaches its maximum. The test is a good indicator of the ability of the cardiovascular and respiratory systems to function effectively.

Elite endurance athletes can extract 5 or 6 liters of oxygen per minute from the environment, and this high aerobic capacity is what allows them to maintain high speeds in both training and competition without becoming excessively tired. In comparison, an average person typically extracts about 2 to 3 liters per minute. $\dot{V}O_2$ max is typically adjusted to account for a person's body size because bigger people may have higher scores due to their larger size. Values are reported in milliliters (mL) of oxygen (O_2) per kilogram (kg) of body weight per minute (mL/kg/min).

The field tests in Lab 8B assess your cardiorespiratory endurance. They are functional fitness tests that determine your ability to persist in exercise for relatively long periods of time. Some, such as the Bicycle Test, allow you to estimate your aerobic capacity ($\dot{V}O_2$ max).

Adaptations to regular aerobic exercise result in improved cardiorespiratory endurance. Specific adaptations occur within each of the systems shown in Figure 2. The heart muscle gets stronger and pumps more blood with each beat, allowing the heart to pump less frequently to deliver the same amount of oxygen. The lungs and blood function more efficiently in picking up oxygen and delivering it to the muscles. The vessels more effectively deliver the blood and the muscles adapt to use oxygen more efficiently. These adaptations allow a person to take in and use more oxygen during maximal exercise (increased aerobic capacity or $\dot{V}O_2$ max). The adaptations contribute to improved endurance performance as well as health benefits.

Table 1 ▶ Changes in Cardiovascular and Respiratory Function Between Rest and Exercise for a Person with Good Cardiorespiratory Endurance

		Rest	Maximal Exercise
Lungs	Breathing Rate (breaths/min)	12	30
Heart	Heart Rate (beats/min)	70	190–200
	Stroke Volume (mL/beat)	75	150
	Cardiac Output[a] (L/min)	5.2	28.5
Arteries	Blood Flow Distribution (%)	20%	70%
Muscle	Oxygen Extraction (%)	5%	20%
System	$\dot{V}O_2$ (mL/kg/min)[b]	3.5	60

[a]Cardiac output = heart rate × stroke volume.
[b]$\dot{V}O_2$-oxygen consumption = CO × oxygen extraction.

Cardiorespiratory Endurance and Health Benefits

Good cardiorespiratory endurance reduces risk for heart disease, other hypokinetic conditions, and early death. Numerous studies over the past 30 to 40 years have confirmed that good cardiorespiratory endurance is associated with a reduced risk for heart disease as well as a number of other chronic, hypokinetic conditions. The consensus is that low-fitness individuals are three to six times more likely to develop symptoms of heart disease, metabolic syndrome, or diabetes than high-fitness individuals. While the specific amount of fitness needed to reduce risks varies by condition and population, evidence clearly supports the need for at least a moderate level of fitness. As shown in Figure 3, there are dramatic reductions in risk in moving from the low fitness category to the moderate fitness category for both males and females. Thus, this should be the goal for most people.

The drop in risk associated with moving from moderate to high fitness is not as great as the drop from low to moderate fitness. However, a new study published in the medical journal *Lancet* demonstrates that the gains are tangible and clinically important. The study, likely the largest study ever conducted on the health benefits of physical activity,

Maximum Oxygen Uptake ($\dot{V}O_2$ max) A laboratory measure of aerobic capacity. Commonly referred to as $\dot{V}O_2$ max, or the volume (V) of oxygen used when a person reaches his or her maximum (max) ability to supply it during exercise.

Major Blood Vessels

Cardiorespiratory Endurance Characteristics

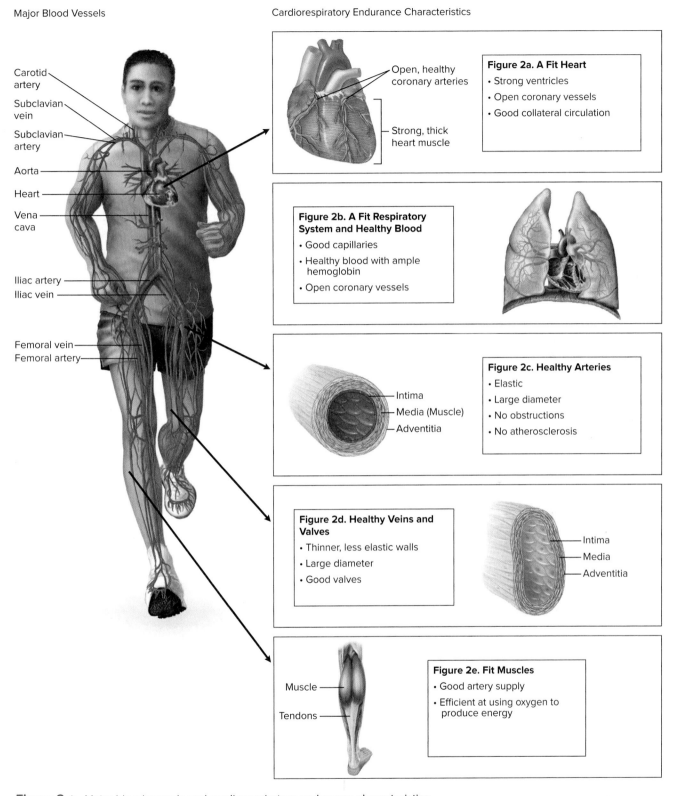

Figure 2 ▶ Major blood vessels and cardiorespiratory endurance characteristics.

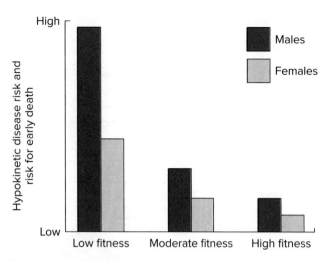

Figure 3 ▶ Risk reduction associated with cardiorespiratory endurance.

Source: Adapted from Blair et al.

evaluated associations between fitness and health in more than 130,000 people from 17 countries. The researchers divided the diverse sample into three groups based on activity habits: *low activity* (those not meeting the World Health Organization recommendation of 150 minutes of activity per week), *moderate activity* (those meeting the recommendation), and *high activity* (those exceeding the recommendation). People meeting the recommendation had a lower early death rate (28 percent less) and lower heart disease rate (20 percent less) than those who did not exercise at the recommended level. However, those in the high activity group received additional health benefits. They were less likely to die early (15 percent less) or have heart disease (19 percent less) than those who were in the moderate activity group. The benefits of activity were consistent across all income groups

and were independent of the type of activity performed. Thus, it didn't matter if the activity came as part of recreation or through work. Clearly, doing some activity is better than doing none, but doing more than the minimum has added benefits. To get into the high activity group, participants could do additional moderate activity or additional vigorous activity. Vigorous activity takes less time and has the added advantage of improving cardiorespiratory endurance.

The benefits of cardiorespiratory fitness are independent of its beneficial effect on other risk factors. Physical activity has been shown to have beneficial effects on some other established heart disease risk factors, such as cholesterol, blood pressure, and body fat. It is important to note that the beneficial effects of cardiorespiratory endurance on risk for heart disease and early death are considered to be independent of these other effects. This means that active/fit people would still have lower health risks even if their cholesterol, blood pressure, and body fat levels were identical to those in a matched set of inactive/unfit people. This evidence contributed to the labeling of physical inactivity as a major, independent risk factor for heart disease. The risk associated with physical inactivity is as large as (or larger than) risks associated with any of the other established risk factors.

Good fitness reduces risks for normal weight, overweight, and obese people. Some people think they cannot be fit if they are overweight or overfat. It is now known that appropriate physical activity can build cardiorespiratory endurance in all types of people, including those with excess body fat. In fact, numerous studies have demonstrated that a fit, overweight person is at lower risk of

In the News

Exercise in a Pill

Some people wish that the benefits of exercise could be bottled up in a pill. A new study reports on the existence of a chemical compound that appears to do just that. The chemical acts to influence a metabolic pathway that promotes improved cardiovascular endurance and increased fat metabolism (similar to how exercise impacts these outcomes). Mice that were bred to have a high amount of the chemical were better able to perform tasks requiring cardiorespiratory endurance and they also were better able to resist weight gain. When the chemical was injected into normal mice, they were found to be more resistant to weight gain but did not have enhanced endurance. No cellular changes were observed in the muscle fibers so the

effects were attributed to an enhancement of fatty acid utilization which spares the use of glucose. It is premature to draw conclusions and tests are also needed in humans; however, the authors concluded that the ability to chemically alter energy pathways may make it possible to preserve glucose utilization and enhance endurance. Previous reports of "exercise in a pill" have not panned out, so it is still prudent to be skeptical. (See Suggested Resources and Readings.)

If an "exercise pill" was ever developed, do you think it could replace the need for regular physical activity? Would you still participate in physical activity if it wasn't important for your health?

chronic disease than an unfit person who is normal weight. These findings demonstrate that for chronic disease prevention, low fitness is a greater risk than excess body fatness. The greatest risk is among people who are both unfit and overfat.

Good cardiorespiratory endurance enhances the ability to perform various tasks, improves the ability to function, and is associated with a feeling of well-being. Moving out of the low fitness zone is of obvious importance to disease risk reduction. Achieving the good fitness zone on tests further reduces disease and early death risk and provides wellness benefits, including the ability to enjoy leisure activities and meet emergency situations. In older adults, achievement of good fitness results in an improved ability to function and maintain independence. Cardiorespiratory endurance in the high-performance zone provides benefits that may be important for success in certain athletic events and in occupations that require high performance levels (e.g., firefighters).

The FIT Formula for Cardiorespiratory Endurance

The FIT formula for cardiorespiratory endurance varies for people of different activity levels. Adaptations to physical activity are based on the overload principle and the principle of progression. It is important to provide an appropriate challenge to the cardiovascular and respiratory systems (overload), but the challenge should be progressive, increasing gradually as fitness improves. For most people, vigorous physical activity from steps 2 and 3 (see Figure 4) is necessary to improve cardiorespiratory endurance. However, for people with low fitness, moderate physical activity (step 1) produces improvements.

An important point is that the perceived intensity of physical activity depends on a person's level of fitness. Table 2 presents the FIT formulas for people of five different fitness and activity levels. While the *frequency* of exercise is similar for the different levels, the *intensity* and amount of

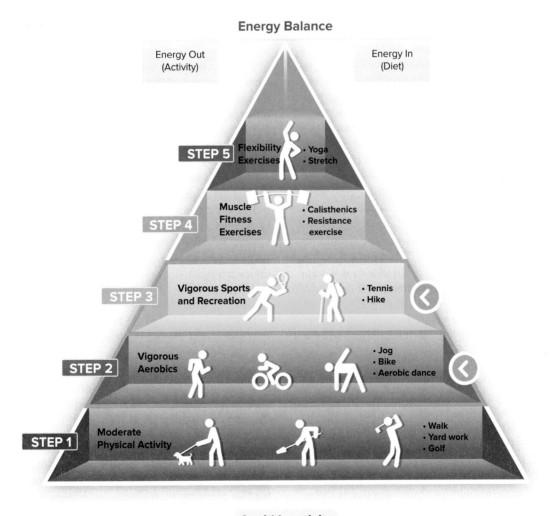

Figure 4 ▶ Select activities from steps 2 and 3 of the pyramid for optimal cardiorespiratory endurance.

Source: Charles B. Corbin

Table 2 ▶ FIT Formula for Cardiorespiratory Endurance for People of Different Fitness and Activity Levels

Fitness Level	Very Low	Low	Marginal	Good	High Performance
Activity Level	Sedentary	Some light to moderate activity	Sporadic moderate to vigorous activity	Regular moderate to vigorous activity	Habitual moderate to vigorous activity
F = Frequency (days per week)	3–5	3–5	3–5	3–5	3–5
I = Intensity					
Heart Rate Reserve (HRR)	30–40%	40–55%	55–70%	65–80%	70–85%
Max. Heart Rate (maxHR)	57–67%	64–74%	74–84%	80–91%	84–94%
Relative Perceived Exertion (RPE)	12–13	12–13	13–14	13–15	14–16
T = Time (minutes per day)	20–30	30–60	30–90	30–90	30–90

time spent in activity vary considerably. Individuals with lower fitness levels should use lower intensities since their maximal capacity is also lower. As fitness improves, the intensity should be increased to maintain or improve fitness. The sections that follow provide added information about the FIT formula.

The frequency (F) of physical activity to build cardiorespiratory endurance ranges from 3 to 5 or more days a week. The ACSM guidelines for building cardiorespiratory endurance suggest a frequency of at least 5 days a week for low-fit people who do primarily moderate physical activity. Moderate activity can be safely performed every day and can provide additional benefits. For more active people (and those with higher levels of cardiorespiratory endurance), vigorous physical activity at least 3 days a week is recommended. Vigorous physical activity provides additional benefits (compared to moderate activity); however, it can increase risk for orthopedic injury if it is done too frequently. Therefore, 5 days a week is the maximal recommended dose for most people. Healthy people who are fit and regularly active and have no evidence of joint problems or injuries may train up to 6 days a week, but most experts agree that at least 1 day off a week is beneficial. Use Table 2 to determine the appropriate frequency of exercise for you based on your current activity and fitness level. Complete the fitness assessments at the end of this Concept before making your decision. The ACSM guidelines focus on exercise for building cardiorespiratory endurance but are similar to national guidelines designed to produce health and wellness benefits.

The intensity (I) of physical activity necessary to produce cardiorespiratory endurance depends on a person's level of fitness. Consistent with the overload principle and the principle of progression, you need to exercise at a gradually increasing level of intensity that is higher than normal to improve cardiorespiratory endurance. To determine the appropriate intensity, it is important to have

some indicator of a person's overall fitness. If the maximal aerobic capacity is known, an appropriate intensity can be set at a percentage of the maximum level. Because these values cannot be calculated without special equipment, other indicators of relative intensity are more commonly used.

Heart rate provides a good indicator of the relative challenge presented by a given bout of exercise. Therefore, guidelines for the intensity of physical activity to build cardiorespiratory endurance are typically based on percentages of **heart rate reserve (HRR)** or maximal heart rate (maxHR). Current guidelines as outlined in Table 2 specify different intensity levels based on current fitness and activity levels. Calculations of HRR and maxHR will be described in detail later, but the general range for HRR is 30 to 85 percent and for maxHR, 57 to 94 percent.

Ratings of perceived exertion (RPE) refers to the assessment of the intensity of exercise based on how the participant feels; a subjective assessment of effort. RPE has been shown to be useful in assessing the intensity of aerobic physical activity. The RPE scale ranges from 6 (very, very light) to 20 (very, very hard), with 1-point increments in between. If the values are multiplied by 10, the RPE values loosely correspond to HR values (e.g., 60 = rest HR and 200 = maxHR). Details will be provided later, but the target zone for aerobic activity is from 12 to 16 (see Table 2).

Regardless of what method is used, the important point is that lower intensities provide a cardiorespiratory endurance benefit for low-fit inactive and/or sedentary people, but higher intensities are needed for more fit people. Use Table 2 to determine the appropriate *intensity of exercise* based on your current activity and fitness level.

The amount of time (T) for building cardiorespiratory endurance is typically based on minutes of activity per day. The ACSM, the American Heart Association, and the U.S. Department of Health and Human Services all recommend a minimum of 150 minutes of moderate activity per week, or 75 minutes of vigorous activity per week (or a combination of minutes from moderate and vigorous activity). Extending the length of time for exercise bouts has additional benefits for health and wellness, as well as cardiorespiratory endurance. For example, 150 to 300 minutes of moderate activity per week is beneficial in losing body fat and maintaining a healthy body weight. For fit and active people, extending bouts of vigorous activity from 20 up to 90 minutes provides health and wellness benefits and enhances cardiorespiratory endurance. Use Table 2 to determine the appropriate length of time for daily exercise for you based on your current activity and fitness level.

Different patterns of activity can be used to achieve the recommended dose of exercise. Some people may prefer to perform regular 30-minute bouts of exercise but others may prefer to accumulate it throughout the day. A pattern of three 10-minute bouts provides similar benefits to one 30-minute session. The  number of days per week can vary from 3 to 6 days per week, but exercising one day a week with no regular activity in between (i.e., being a weekend warrior) is discouraged. The prescriptions in Table 2 are aimed at improving cardiorespiratory endurance based on individual characteristics of typical people. Specialized training regimens are typically needed for those interested in high-performance events (e.g., running races, triathlons) and competitive sports.

Threshold and Target Zones for Intensity of Activity to Build Cardiorespiratory Endurance

There is a minimum intensity and an optimal intensity range for activity designed to develop cardiorespiratory endurance. As noted earlier, monitoring heart rate and making ratings of perceived exertion are the most practical methods of determining the intensity of activity necessary to build cardiorespiratory endurance. The threshold of training (minimum intensity) and the target zone (optimal intensity range) can be determined using several methods. Most methods are based on heart rate, so the target zone is typically referred to as *target heart rate zone*. Ratings of perceived exertion (RPE) can also be used to define the target zone for exercise intensity. This section provides details of using these methods.

An estimate of maximal heart rate (maxHR) is needed to determine appropriate target heart rate zones for aerobic exercise. Your maxHR is the highest heart rate attained in maximal exercise. It could be determined using an electrocardiogram while exercising to exhaustion; however, it can also be estimated with formulas. MaxHR is known to decrease with age, so one simple and commonly used approach is to subtract your age from 220 (i.e., maxHR = 220 − age). However, studies have shown that this formula leads to inaccurate estimates for most people. A number of

Aerobic activities provide an ideal stimulus for improving cardiorespiratory endurance.
©Purestock/SuperStock

A CLOSER LOOK

High-Intensity Interval Training (HIIT)

Although the use of High-Intensity Interval Training (HIIT) continues to be a popular topic among fitness enthusiasts, most consumers don't understand the basis for it. Interval training has been used by athletes for many years to increase the intensity of training and to help elicit stronger gains in performance. However, it is now widely promoted to the general public as a way to squeeze exercise into a busy schedule. The alternating segments of high and low intensity can help achieve fitness gains, but experts caution that it may increase risk of injury, particularly for beginning exercisers, low-fit individuals, and older adults. The high intensity may also detract from the enjoyment of exercise and limit long-term adherence. Research "HIIT" to learn more about the pros and cons.

Does this type of routine make exercise seem like work rather than play? Does this type of routine appeal to you or not?

Heart Rate Reserve (HRR) The difference between maximal heart rate (highest heart rate in vigorous activity) and resting heart rate (lowest heart rate at rest).

Ratings of Perceived Exertion (RPE) The assessment of the intensity of exercise based on how the participant feels; a subjective assessment of effort.

more specialized, nonlinear equations have been developed to avoid this problem. For example, a new formula for women was recently developed (maxHR = 206 × [.88 × age]). There is currently no consensus on the most accurate method, but evidence supports the utility of a relatively simple nonlinear method known as the Tanaka formula: maxHR = 208 − (.7 × age). Calculations made at a variety of ages show little, if any, differences between the formulas, so it is recommended for most applications. Table 3 illustrates the calculations for determining maxHR for a 22-year-old.

The heart rate reserve (HRR) method is the preferred way to calculate target heart rate zones. Table 2 provides five different intensity ranges for activity designed to build cardiorespiratory endurance. After you have assessed your fitness using fitness tests (see the Lab Resource Materials section and Lab 8B), determine which of the five intensity ranges is best for you based on your current activity and fitness.

Table 3 provides a worked example for calculating heart rate target zones using the HRR method. The example is for a 22-year-old with good cardiorespiratory endurance who does regular moderate-to-vigorous physical activity and who has a resting heart rate of 68 beats per minute. The target heart rate zone for this hypothetical person is 65 to 80 percent. To determine the threshold of training (minimum heart rate for building cardiorespiratory endurance), use 65 percent of the

working heart rate, and then add that value to the resting heart rate. To determine the upper limit of the target zone, use 80 percent of the working heart rate and add that value to the resting heart rate.

Because target zone heart rates vary for people of different fitness and activity levels and because resting and maximal heart rates vary, each person will have a unique range of heart rates defining the target heart rate zone. The chart in Figure 5 allows you to look up similar threshold and target heart rate zones based on your resting heart rate and age (up to age 65). Locate your resting heart rate on the left and your age across the top. The values at the point where they intersect represent your target heart rate (based on 65 percent and 80 percent of HR reserve). Look across the columns for a given row to see how the target zone changes with age. Look down the rows for a certain column and see how the target zone changes with fitness. The chart shows that fit individuals (lower rest HR values) have lower target heart rate zones than unfit individuals (higher rest HR values). This may seem somewhat paradoxical, but the reason is that fit individuals start exercise with a lower HR value and therefore have a larger HRR.

The percentage of maximal heart rate method is an alternative way to calculate target heart rate zones. The percentage of maxHR method is simpler to use than the HRR method, but it is not as accurate. This procedure takes maximal heart rate into account but does not factor in individual differences in resting heart rate. People with a typical resting HR of 60 to 70 bpm will tend to get similar values with both methods, but the percentage of maxHR method tends to be less accurate for people with high or low resting heart rates.

To use the percentage of maxHR method, first find your maximum HR with the formula (maxHR = 208 − [.7 × age]). Then multiply your maxHR by the appropriate percentages from Table 2. For a person with good fitness and who performs regular moderate-to-vigorous activity, the percentages would be 80 to 91 percent. The maxHR for a 22-year-old is 193, so the target heart rate zone would be 154 to 176 using this method (.80 × 193 = 154 and .91 × 193 = 176). As illustrated in Table 3, this procedure yields somewhat similar but higher values for the maxHR method than for the HRR method. The differences between the two methods vary for people of different ages, resting heart rates, and fitness/activity levels. The percentage of maxHR method is considered an acceptable alternative method, but the HRR method is more precise. Threshold and target zone heart rates should be used as general guidelines for aerobic exercise. You should check your resting heart rate and learn to calculate your target heart range based on the HRR method. It is important to understand how to make the calculations, since the process explains the relationships.

The target heart ranges should be used as just that, a general target to try for during your exercise session. By bringing your heart rate above the threshold and into the target zone, you will provide an optimal challenge to your cardiovascular and respiratory systems and maintain/improve your

Table 3 ▶ Sample Target Heart Zone Calculations for a 22-Year-Old, Using the Percentage of Heart Rate Reserve Method

Calculating Maximal Heart Rate

Maximal heart rate	= 208 − (.7 × age)
	= 208 − (.7 × 22)
	= 208 − 15.4
	193

Calculating Heart Rate Reserve

Maximal heart rate	193 bpm
Minus resting heart rate	− 68 bpm
Equals heart rate reserve (HRR)	125 bpm

Calculating Threshold Heart Rate

HRR	125 bpm
×65%	×.65
Equals	81 bpm
Plus resting heart rate	+68 bpm
Equals threshold heart rate	149 bpm

Calculating Upper Limit Heart Rate

HRR	125 bpm
×80%	×.80
Equals	100 bpm
Plus resting heart rate	+68 bpm
Equals upper limit heart rate	168 bpm

Rest HR	Threshold	20	25	30	35	40	45	50	55	60	65
Effect of Age and Resting Heart Rate on Target Heart Range											
50	65%	144	141	139	137	135	132	130	128	125	123
	80%	165	162	160	157	154	151	148	146	143	140
55	65%	145	143	141	139	136	134	132	129	127	125
	80%	166	163	161	158	155	152	149	147	144	141
60	65%	147	145	143	140	138	136	133	131	129	127
	80%	167	164	162	159	156	153	150	148	145	142
65	65%	149	147	144	142	140	137	135	133	131	128
	80%	168	165	163	160	157	154	151	149	146	143
70	65%	151	148	146	144	142	139	137	135	132	130
	80%	169	166	164	161	158	155	152	150	147	144
75	65%	152	150	148	146	143	141	139	136	134	132
	80%	170	167	165	162	159	156	153	151	148	145

Figure 5 ▶ Effect of age and resting heart rate on target heart range.

cardiorespiratory endurance. Guidelines for heart rate monitoring are provided in the next section.

Ratings of perceived exertion can be used to monitor the intensity of physical activity. The ACSM suggests that regularly active people can use RPE to determine if they are exercising in the target zone (see Table 4). Ratings of perceived exertion have been shown to correlate well with

Technology Update

Online Target Heart Rate Calculators

Keeping up with fitness terminology and recommendations can be challenging, but it is especially difficult when you get different information from different sources. For example, many people have misconceptions about exercise heart rate calculations and this confusion is compounded by how it is described in various online sources. As described in this Concept, target heart zones should take into account your age and your resting heart rate as well as existing fitness level. Internet-based calculators vary considerably in quality and may not take these factors into account. You can check online calculators by searching "Target Heart Rate Calculators" and comparing results with calculations made using the information in this Concept.

Did you find online calculators to be accurate? Do you think that they would be accurate for low-fit or older people?

ACTIVITY

Table 4 ▶ Ratings of Perceived Exertion (RPE)

Rating	Description	Target Zone
6		
7	Very, very light	
8		
9	Very light	
10		
11	Fairly light	
12		X
13	Somewhat hard	X
14		X
15	Hard	X
16		X
17	Very hard	
18		
19	Very, very hard	
20		

Source: Data from Borg.

HRR. For this reason, RPE can be used to estimate exercise intensity, avoiding the need to stop and count heart rate during exercise. A rating of 12 is equal to threshold, and a rating of 16 is equal to the upper limit of the target zone. With practice, most people can recognize when they are in the target zone using ratings of perceived exertion.

Guidelines for Heart Rate and Exercise Monitoring

Learning to count heart rate can help you monitor the intensity of your physical activity. Each time your heart beats, it pumps blood into the arteries. The surge of blood causes a pulse, which can be felt by holding a finger against an artery. The major arteries that are easy to locate and are frequently used for pulse counts are the radial, just below the base of the thumb on the wrist (see Figure 6), and the carotid, on either side of the Adam's apple (see Figure 7). Counting the pulse at the carotid is the most popular procedure, probably because the carotid pulse is easy to locate. The radial pulse is a bit harder to find because of the many tendons near the wrist, but it works better for some people.

To count the pulse rate, simply place the fingertips (index and middle finger) over the artery at the wrist or neck location. Move the fingers around until a strong pulse can be felt. Press gently so as not to cut off the blood flow through the artery. Counting the pulse with the thumb is *not* recommended because the thumb has a relatively strong pulse of its own, and it could be confusing when counting another person's pulse.

Counting heart rates during exercise presents some additional challenges. To obtain accurate exercise heart rate values, it is best to count heartbeats or pulses while moving; however, this is difficult during most activities.

The most practical method is to count the pulse immediately after exercise. During physical activity, the heart rate increases, but immediately after exercise, it begins to slow and return to normal. In fact, the heart rate has already slowed considerably within 1 minute after activity ceases. Therefore, you must locate the pulse quickly and count the rate for a short period in order to obtain accurate results. For best results, keep moving while quickly locating the pulse; then stop and take a 15-second count. Multiply the number of pulses by 4 to convert heart rate to beats per minute.

You can also count the pulse for 10 seconds and multiply by 6, or count the pulse for 6 seconds and multiply by 10 to estimate a 1-minute heart rate. The latter method allows you to calculate heart rates easily by adding 0 to the 6-second count. However, short-duration pulse counts increase the chance of error because a miscount of 1 beat is multiplied by 6 or 10 beats rather than by 4 beats.

The pulse rate should be counted after regular activity, not after a sudden burst. Some runners sprint the last few yards of their daily run and then count their pulse. Such a burst of exercise will elevate the heart rate considerably. This gives a false picture of the actual exercise heart rate. Everyone should learn to determine resting heart rate accurately and to estimate exercise heart rate by quickly and accurately making pulse counts after activity (see Lab 8A).

Declines in resting heart rate and exercise heart rate signal improvements in cardiorespiratory endurance. As described in this Concept, the heart beats to provide the body (and working muscles) with oxygen. Oxygen is used to produce energy using aerobic metabolism. During rest, the

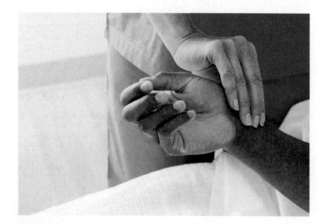

Figure 6 ► Counting your radial (wrist) pulse.
©XiXinXing/Shutterstock

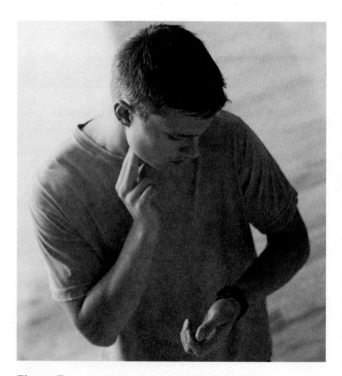

Figure 7 ► Counting your carotid (neck) pulse.
©Duncan Smith/Getty Images

heart can beat relatively slowly to provide sufficient oxygen to the body. During exercise, the demand for energy increases, so the body increases heart rate (and respiration) to help distribute more oxygen to the body. Changes in resting heart rate and exercise heart rate provide good indicators of improvements in fitness because they indicate that the heart can pump fewer times to provide the same amount of blood flow to the body. A fit individual has a stronger heart and can pump more blood with each beat.

A comparison of resting and exercise heart rates for three hypothetical individuals performing the same bout of exercise is shown in Figure 8. The column labeled "A" shows the response of an unfit person. This person has a high resting heart rate of 90, and this increases to 160 during the exercise. This intensity would feel pretty hard, so an RPE would likely be about 17. Compare this response to the results for a moderately fit (B) or highly fit (C) person. Both have a lower resting heart rate and a lower exercise heart rate, so exercise is easier and can be maintained more easily.

Using Self-Management Skills

Self-monitoring physical activity intensity (heart rate or perceived exertion) helps you determine the effectiveness of activity for building cardiorespiratory endurance. A variety of self-monitoring techniques were provided in this Concept for ensuring that physical activity levels are of sufficient intensity to promote cardiorespiratory endurance improvement or maintenance. These methods include heart rate monitoring and the use of ratings of perceived exertion (RPE). To use these methods effectively it is important to practice self-monitoring using one or both techniques.

Learning to self-assess cardiorespiratory endurance is important to setting goals and program planning. For an activity program to be most effective, it should be based on personal needs. Some type of self-assessment is necessary to determine your personal need for cardiorespiratory endurance. The best measure is a laboratory assessment of $\dot{V}O_2$ max, but this is not possible for most people. To provide alternatives, researchers have developed other tests that give reasonable estimates. Commonly used tests are the step test, the swim test, the 12-minute run, the Astrand-Ryhming bicycle test, and the walking test. These tests are developed based on comparisons with measured $\dot{V}O_2$ max and are good general indicators of cardiorespiratory endurance. Learning about each method will allow you to choose one that you can use as you set physical activity goals and plan your physical activity program.

The self-assessment you choose depends on your current fitness and activity levels, the availability of equipment, and other factors. The walking test is probably best for those at beginning levels because more vigorous forms of activity may cause discomfort and discourage future participation. The step test is somewhat less vigorous than the running test and takes only a few minutes to complete. The bicycle test is also submaximal or relatively moderate in intensity. It is quite accurate but requires more equipment and expertise than the other tests. You may need help from a fitness expert to do this test properly. It does allow you to

HELP   Health is available to Everyone for a Lifetime, and it's Personal

Does Your Current Activity Level Predict Your Future Activity Level?

College students have some unique opportunities to be active on campus. Students typically have easy access to a well-equipped recreation center and they can also enroll in various intramural programs. However, it is not clear how activity patterns may change during college. Students who were athletes in high school may move away from exercise and sports to pursue other things, while those who were not in high school sports may find new interest in physical activity. Building physical activity into your routine in college can help you sustain or develop an active identity. Finding time to exercise now can also help you make similar adjustments to changing obligations and priorities later in life.

How have your physical activity patterns changed since you entered college? Do you take advantage of campus opportunities to be active? How confident are you that you will be able to be physically active later in life?

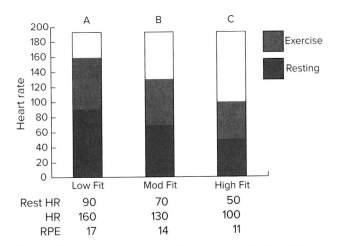

Figure 8 ▶ Comparison of resting and exercise heart for three 22-year-old individuals (maxHR = 193) with different levels of fitness (A = low fitness, B = moderate fitness, C = high fitness).

	Low Fit	Mod Fit	High Fit
Rest HR	90	70	50
HR	160	130	100
RPE	17	14	11

estimate your aerobic capacity ($\dot{V}O_2$ max). The swim test is especially useful to those with musculoskeletal problems and other disabilities. The running test is the most vigorous and for this reason may be best for more advanced exercisers with high levels of motivation.

Results on the walking, running, and swimming tests are greatly influenced by the motivation of the test taker. If the test taker does not try hard, fitness results are underestimated. The bicycle and step tests are influenced less by motivation because one must exercise at a specified workload and at a regular pace. Because heart rate can be influenced by emotional factors, by exercise prior to the test, and other factors, tests using heart rate can sometimes give incorrect results. Thus, do your self-assessments when you are relatively free from stress and are rested. Prior to performing any of these tests, be sure that you are physically and medically ready.

Prepare yourself by doing some regular physical activity for 3 to 6 weeks before actually taking the tests.

Building knowledge is important to persistence in future physical activity. Every January 1, many people make New Year's resolutions to become more active. Making a commitment does increase the odds of sticking with a plan, but too many people drop out of activity after only a few months, failing to meet their resolution. Lack of knowledge is one reason why people drop out. Too often people choose to do activities without having a good understanding of how to do the activity properly. They often have expectations that are not realistic. Learning the facts about exercise, such as those presented in this Concept, can help you know how to exercise properly and provide you with expectations that you can reasonably expect to meet.

Strategies for Action: Lab Information

Practicing self-monitoring of physical activity intensity can help you make sure that activity improves cardiorespiratory endurance. In Lab 8A you will have the opportunity to practice counting heart rate at rest and after exercise to see if the exercise bout gets you into the heart rate target zone. You will also get the opportunity to practice using RPE to determine if the exercise is of adequate intensity to build cardiorespiratory endurance. Practice increases the accuracy of your self-monitoring and provides information that will allow you to select one or both of these techniques for use in the future.

Practicing self-assessments for cardiorespiratory endurance can help you choose a test that is best for you. In Lab 8B you will have the opportunity to self-assess your cardiorespiratory endurance using one or more tests. Trying several tests will help you make an informed choice about which test will be most useful to you in the future. A non-exercise estimate of cardiorespiratory endurance is also provided for comparison. Although this self-report tool has limitations, it is increasingly being used as a screening tool by physicians to determine if patients have risks associated with poor fitness.

Suggested Resources and Readings

The websites for the following sources can be accessed by searching online for the organization, program, or title listed. Specific scientific references are available at the end of this edition of *Concepts of Fitness and Wellness*.

- American College of Sports Medicine. (2018). *ACSM's Guidelines for Exercise Prescription and Testing*. Philadelphia: Walters Kluwer. Chapter 6, pp. 147–161.
- American Heart Association. AHA Recommendations for Physical Activity in Adults (download the infographic).
- Biddle, S. J., & Batterham, A. M. (2015). High-intensity interval exercise training for public health: A big HIT or shall we HIT it on the head? *International Journal of Behavioral Nutrition and Physical Activity*, *12*(1), 95 (published debate).
- Healthline.com. What Is Cardiorespiratory Endurance and How Can You Improve It? (online resource).
- Livestrong. A List of the Benefits of Cardiorespiratory Endurance (online resource).
- Salk Institute. (2017, May). "Exercise-in-a-Pill" Boosts Athletic Endurance by 70 Percent. *Science Daily* (online press release).
- VeryWell.com. What Is Cardiorespiratory Endurance? (online resource).

Lab Resource Materials: Evaluating Cardiorespiratory Endurance

The Walking Test

- Warm up; then walk 1 mile as fast as you can without straining. Record your time to the nearest second.
- Immediately after the walk, count your heart rate for 15 seconds; then multiply by four to get a 1-minute heart rate. Record your heart rate.
- Use your walking time and your postexercise heart rate to determine your rating using Chart 1.

Chart 1 Walking Ratings for Males and Females

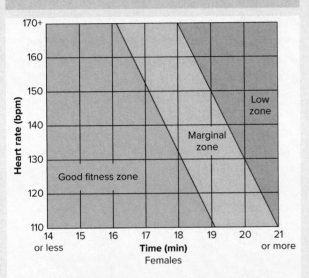

Females

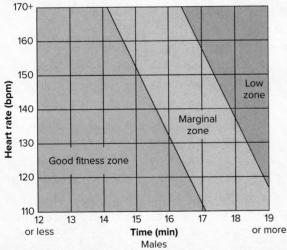

Males

Source: James M. Rippe, M.D.

The ratings in Chart 1 are for ages 20 to 29. They provide reasonable ratings for people of all ages.

Note: The walking test is not a good indicator of high performance; the running and bicycle tests are recommended.

The Step Test

- Step up and down on a 12-inch-tall bench for 3 minutes at a rate of 24 steps per minute. One step consists of four beats—that is, "up with the left foot, up with the right foot, down with the left foot, down with the right foot."
- Immediately after the exercise, sit down on the bench and relax. Don't talk.
- Locate your pulse or have someone locate it for you.
- Five seconds after the exercise ends, begin counting your pulse. Count the pulse for 60 seconds.
- Your score is your 60-second heart rate. Locate your score and your rating on Chart 2.

Chart 2 Step Test Rating Chart

Classification	60-Second Heart Rate
High-performance zone	84 or less
Good fitness zone	85–95
Marginal fitness zone	96–119
Low fitness zone	120 and above

Source: Kasch and Boyer.

As you grow older, you will want to continue to score well on this rating chart. Because your maximal heart rate decreases as you age, you should be able to score well if you exercise regularly.

The Astrand-Ryhming Bicycle Test

- Ride a stationary bicycle ergometer for 6 minutes at a rate of 50 pedal cycles per minute (one push with each foot per cycle). Cool down after the test.
- Set the bicycle at a workload between 300 and 1,200 kpm. For less fit or smaller people, a setting in the range of 300 to 600 is appropriate. Larger or fitter people will need to use a setting of 750 to 1,200. The workload should be enough to elevate the heart rate to at least 125 bpm but no more than 170 bpm during the ride. The ideal range is 140–150 bpm.
- During the sixth minute of the ride (if the heart rate is in the correct range—see previous step), count the heart rate for the entire sixth minute. The carotid or radial pulse may be used.
- Use Chart 3 (males) or 4 (females) to determine your predicted oxygen uptake score in liters per minute. Locate your heart rate for the sixth minute of the ride in the left column and the work rate in kp · m/min across the top. The number in the chart where the heart rate and work rate intersect represents your predicted O_2 uptake in liters per minute. The bicycle you use must allow you to easily and accurately determine the work rate in kp · m/min.

- Ratings are typically assigned based on milliliters per kilogram of body weight per minute. To convert your score to milliliters per kilogram per minute (mL/kg/min), the first step is to multiply your score from Chart 3 or 4 by 1,000. This converts your score from liters to milliliters. Then divide your weight in pounds by 2.2. This converts your weight to kilograms. Finally, divide your score in milliliters by your weight in kilograms. This gives you your score in mL/kg/min.

- Example: An oxygen uptake score of 3.5 liters is equal to a 3,500-milliliter score (3.5 × 1,000). If the person with this score weighed 150 pounds, his or her weight in kilograms would be 68.18 kilograms (150 divided by 2.2). The person's oxygen uptake would be 51.3 mL/kg/min (3,500 divided by 68.18).
- Use your score in mL/kg/min to determine your rating (Chart 5).

Chart 3 Determining Oxygen Uptake Using the Bicycle Test—Men (liters O_2/min)

Heart Rate	Work Rate (kp·m/min)			
	450	600	900	1,200
123	3.3	3.4	4.6	6.0
124	3.3	3.3	4.5	6.0
125	3.2	3.2	4.4	5.9
126	3.1	3.2	4.4	5.8
127	3.0	3.1	4.3	5.7
128	3.0	3.1	4.2	5.6
129	2.9	3.0	4.2	5.6
130	2.9	3.0	4.1	5.5
131	2.8	2.9	4.0	5.4
132	2.8	2.9	4.0	5.3
133	2.7	2.8	3.9	5.3
134	2.7	2.8	3.9	5.2
135	2.7	2.8	3.8	5.1
136	2.6	2.7	3.8	5.0
137	2.6	2.7	3.7	5.0
138	2.5	2.7	3.7	4.9

Heart Rate	Work Rate (kp·m/min)				
	450	600	900	1,200	1,500
139	2.5	2.6	3.6	4.8	6.0
140	2.5	2.6	3.6	4.8	6.0
141	2.4	2.6	3.5	4.7	5.9
142	2.4	2.5	3.5	4.6	5.8
143	2.4	2.5	3.4	4.6	5.7
144	2.3	2.5	3.4	4.5	5.7
145	2.3	2.4	3.4	4.5	5.6
146	2.3	2.4	3.3	4.4	5.6
147	2.3	2.4	3.3	4.4	5.5
148	2.2	2.4	3.2	4.3	5.4
149	2.2	2.3	3.2	4.3	5.4
150	2.2	2.3	3.2	4.2	5.3
151	2.2	2.3	3.1	4.2	5.2
152	2.1	2.3	3.1	4.1	5.2
153	2.1	2.2	3.0	4.1	5.1
154	2.0	2.2	3.0	4.0	5.1

Heart Rate	Work Rate (kp·m/min)				
	450	600	900	1,200	1,500
155	2.0	2.2	3.0	4.0	5.0
156	1.9	2.2	2.9	4.0	5.0
157	1.9	2.1	2.9	3.9	4.9
158	1.8	2.1	2.9	3.9	4.9
159	1.8	2.1	2.8	3.8	4.8
160	1.8	2.1	2.8	3.8	4.8
161	1.7	2.0	2.8	3.7	4.7
162	1.7	2.0	2.8	3.7	4.6
163	1.7	2.0	2.8	3.7	4.6
164	1.6	2.0	2.7	3.6	4.5
165	1.6	1.9	2.7	3.6	4.5
166	1.6	1.9	2.7	3.6	4.5
167	1.5	1.9	2.6	3.5	4.4
168	1.5	1.9	2.6	3.5	4.4
169	1.5	1.9	2.6	3.5	4.3
170	1.4	1.8	2.6	3.4	4.3

Chart 4 Determining Oxygen Uptake Using the Bicycle Test—Women (liters O_2/min)

Heart Rate	Work Rate (kp·m/min)				
	300	450	600	750	900
123	2.4	3.1	3.9	4.6	5.1
124	2.4	3.1	3.8	4.5	5.1
125	2.3	3.0	3.7	4.4	5.0
126	2.3	3.0	3.6	4.3	5.0
127	2.2	2.9	3.5	4.2	4.8
128	2.2	2.8	3.5	4.2	4.8
129	2.2	2.8	3.4	4.1	4.8
130	2.1	2.7	3.4	4.0	4.7
131	2.1	2.7	3.4	4.0	4.6
132	2.0	2.7	3.3	3.9	4.6
133	2.0	2.6	3.2	3.8	4.5
134	2.0	2.6	3.2	3.8	4.4
135	2.0	2.6	3.1	3.7	4.4
136	1.9	2.5	3.1	3.6	4.3
137	1.9	2.5	3.0	3.6	4.2
138	1.8	2.4	3.0	3.5	4.2

Heart Rate	Work Rate (kp·m/min)				
	300	450	600	750	900
139	1.8	2.4	2.9	3.5	4.0
140	1.8	2.4	2.8	3.4	4.0
141	1.8	2.3	2.8	3.4	3.9
142	1.7	2.3	2.8	3.3	3.9
143	1.7	2.2	2.7	3.3	3.8
144	1.7	2.2	2.7	3.2	3.8
145	1.6	2.2	2.7	3.2	3.7
146	1.6	2.2	2.6	3.2	3.7
147	1.6	2.1	2.6	3.1	3.6
148	1.6	2.1	2.6	3.1	3.6
149	1.5	2.1	2.6	3.0	3.5
150	1.5	2.0	2.5	3.0	3.5
151	1.5	2.0	2.5	3.0	3.4
152	1.4	2.0	2.5	2.9	3.4
153	1.4	2.0	2.4	2.9	3.3
154	1.4	2.0	2.4	2.8	3.3

Heart Rate	Work Rate (kp·m/min)			
	400	600	750	900
155	1.9	2.4	2.8	3.2
156	1.9	2.4	2.8	3.2
157	1.8	2.3	2.7	3.2
158	1.8	2.3	2.7	3.1
159	1.8	2.3	2.7	3.1
160	1.8	2.2	2.6	3.0
161	1.8	2.2	2.6	3.0
162	1.8	2.2	2.6	3.0
163	1.7	2.2	2.5	2.9
164	1.7	2.1	2.5	2.9
165	1.7	2.1	2.5	2.9
166	1.7	2.1	2.5	2.8
167	1.6	2.0	2.4	2.8
168	1.6	2.0	2.4	2.8
169	1.6	2.0	2.4	2.8
170	1.6	2.0	2.4	2.7

Chart 5 Bicycle Test Rating Scale (mL/O$_2$/kg/min)

Age	Men 17–26	27–39	40–49	50–59	60–69
High-performance zone	50+	46+	42+	39+	35+
Good fitness zone	43–49	35–45	32–41	29–38	26–34
Marginal fitness zone	35–42	30–34	27–31	25–28	22–25
Low fitness zone	<35	<30	<27	<25	<22

Age	Women 17–26	27–39	40–49	50–59	60–69
High-performance zone	46+	40+	38+	35+	32+
Good fitness zone	36–45	33–39	30–37	28–34	24–31
Marginal fitness zone	30–35	28–32	24–29	21–27	18–23
Low fitness zone	<30	<28	<24	<21	<18

The 12-Minute Run Test

- Locate an area where a specific distance is already marked, such as a school track or football field, or measure a specific distance using a bicycle or automobile odometer.
- Use a stopwatch or wristwatch to accurately time a 12-minute period.
- For best results, warm up prior to the test; then run at a steady pace for the entire 12 minutes (cool down after the test).
- Determine the distance you can run in 12 minutes in fractions of a mile. Depending on your age, locate your score and rating in Chart 6.

Chart 6 Twelve-Minute Run Test Rating Chart

Classification—Men	Men (Age) 17–26 Miles	Km	27–39 Miles	Km	40–49 Miles	Km	50+ Miles	Km
High-performance zone	1.80+	2.90+	1.60+	2.60+	1.50+	2.40+	1.40+	2.25+
Good fitness zone	1.55–1.79	2.50–2.89	1.45–1.59	2.35–2.59	1.40–1.49	2.25–2.39	1.25–1.39	2.00–2.24
Marginal fitness zone	1.35–1.54	2.20–2.49	1.30–1.44	2.10–2.34	1.25–1.39	2.00–2.24	1.10–1.24	1.75–1.99
Low fitness zone	<1.35	<2.20	<1.30	<2.10	<1.25	<2.00	<1.1	<1.75

Classification—Women	Women (Age) 17–26 Miles	Km	27–39 Miles	Km	40–49 Miles	Km	50+ Miles	Km
High-performance zone	1.45+	2.35+	1.35+	2.20+	1.25+	2.00+	1.15+	1.85+
Good fitness zone	1.25–1.44	2.00–2.34	2.20–1.34	1.95–2.19	1.15–1.24	1.85–1.99	1.05–1.14	1.70–1.84
Marginal fitness zone	1.15–1.24	1.85–1.99	1.05–1.19	1.70–1.94	1.00–1.14	1.60–1.84	.95–1.04	1.55–1.69
Low fitness zone	<1.15	<1.85	<1.05	<1.70	<1.00	<1.60	<.95	<1.55

Source: Based on data from Cooper.

The 12-Minute Swim Test

- Locate a swimming area with premeasured distances, preferably 20 yards or longer.
- After a warm-up, swim as far as possible in 12 minutes using the stroke of your choice.

- For best results, have a partner keep track of your time and distance. A degree of swimming competence is a prerequisite for this test.
- Determine your score and rating using Chart 7.

Chart 7 Twelve-Minute Swim Rating Chart

	Men (Age)							
	17–26		27–39		40–49		50+	
Classification—Men	Yards	Meters	Yards	Meters	Yards	Meters	Yards	Meters
High-performance zone	700+	650+	650+	600+	600+	550+	550+	500+
Good fitness zone	600–699	550–649	550–649	500–599	500–599	475–549	450–549	425–499
Marginal fitness zone	500–599	450–549	450–459	400–499	400–499	375–475	350–449	325–424
Low fitness zone	Below 500	Below 450	Below 450	Below 400	Below 400	Below 375	Below 350	Below 325

	Women (Age)							
	17–26		27–39		40–49		50+	
Classification—Women	Yards	Meters	Yards	Meters	Yards	Meters	Yards	Meters
High-performance zone	600+	550+	550+	500+	500+	450+	450+	400+
Good fitness zone	500–599	450–549	450–549	400–499	400–499	375–449	350–449	325–400
Marginal fitness zone	400–499	350–449	350–449	325–399	300–399	275–375	250–349	225–324
Low fitness zone	Below 400	Below 350	Below 350	Below 325	Below 300	Below 275	Below 250	Below 225

Source: Based on data from Cooper.

Non-Exercise Estimate of Cardiorespiratory Endurance

- Follow the steps in Lab 8B to determine your score.
- Use Chart 8 to determine your rating.

Chart 8 Non-Exercise Fitness Assessment Rating Chart

Rating	Score
Needs Improvement	1–4
Marginal	5–9
Good Conditioning	10–13
Highly Conditioned	131+

Lab 8A Counting Target Heart Rate and Ratings of Perceived Exertion

Name	**Section**	**Date**

Purpose: To learn to count heart rate accurately and to use heart rate and/or ratings of perceived exertion (RPE) to establish the threshold of training and target zones.

Procedure

1. *Resting Heart Rate:* Practice counting the number of pulses felt for a given period of time at both the carotid and radial locations while sitting still. Then, use a clock or watch to count for 15, 30, and 60 seconds using both sites. Record the values in the Results section and complete calculations of heart rate. *Note:* The practice in locating your carotid and radial pulses quickly is important when trying to count your pulse after exercise.
2. *Run 1:* Run a quarter mile at a comfortable pace; then count your heart rate at the end of the run. Use 15-second pulse counts (choose either carotid or radial) and multiply by four to get heart rate in beats per minute (bpm).
   * Rate your perceived exertion (RPE) for the run (see RPE chart below). Record your results.
   * Record the bpm in the Results section.
3. *Run 2:* Repeat the run a second time. This time, try to intentionally run at a speed that gets you in the heart rate and RPE target zone. Record your heart rate and RPE results.

Results: Record your *resting* heart rates in the boxes below.

Carotid Pulse   **Heart Rate per Minute**   **Radial Pulse**   **Heart Rate per Minute**

15 seconds × 4 =   15 seconds × 4 =

30 seconds × 2 =   30 seconds × 2 =

60 seconds × 1 =   60 seconds × 1 =

Record your heart rate and rating of perceived exertion for run 1.

Pulse Count   **Heart Rate per Minute**

15 seconds × 4 =

Rating of Perceived Exertion

Record your heart rate and rating of perceived exertion for run 2.

Pulse Count   **Heart Rate per Minute**

15 seconds × 4 =

Rating of Perceived Exertion

Ratings of Perceived Exertion (RPE)		
Rating	**Description**	**Target Zone**
6		
7	Very, very light	
8		
9	Very light	
10		
11	Fairly light	
12		X
13	Somewhat hard	X
14		X
15	Hard	X
16		X
17	Very hard	
18		
19	Very, very hard	
20		

Source: Data from Borg.

Answer the following questions:

Which pulse-counting technique did you use after the runs?   Carotid ◯   Radial ◯

What is your heart rate target zone (to calculate, see Table 3) [   ] bpm

Was your heart rate for run 1 enough to get in the heart rate target zone?   Yes ◯   No ◯

Was your RPE for run 1 enough to get in the target zone (12–16)?   Yes ◯   No ◯

Was your heart rate for run 2 enough to get in the heart rate target zone?   Yes ◯   No ◯

Was your RPE for run 2 enough to get in the target zone (12–16)?   Yes ◯   No ◯

Conclusions and Implications: In several sentences, discuss your results, including which method you would use to count heart rate and why. Also discuss heart rate versus RPE for determining the target zone.

Lab Supplement:* You may want to keep track of your exercise heart rate over a week's time or longer to see if you are reaching the target zone in your workouts. Shade your target zone with a highlight pen and plot your exercise heart rate for each day of the week (see sample).

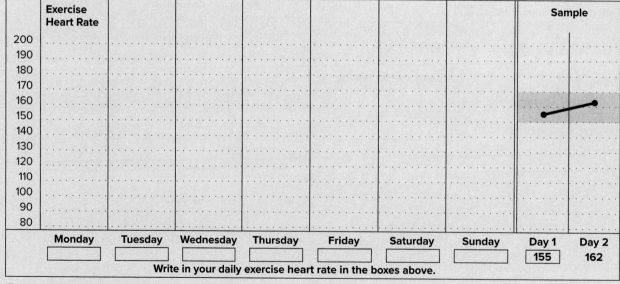

Write in your daily exercise heart rate in the boxes above.

*Thanks to Ginnie Atkins for suggesting this lab supplement.

Lab 8B Evaluating Cardiorespiratory Endurance

Name	Section	Date

Purpose: To acquaint you with several methods for evaluating cardiorespiratory endurance and to help you evaluate and rate your own cardiorespiratory endurance.

Procedure

1. Perform one or more of the five cardiorespiratory endurance tests and determine your ratings using the information in the Lab Resource Materials.
2. Perform each of the steps for the Non-Exercise Estimate of Cardiorespiratory Endurance, using the information on the next page. Learning this technique will allow you to estimate your fitness when you are injured or for some other reason cannot do a performance test.

Results

1. Record the information from your cardiorespiratory endurance test(s) in the spaces provided.
2. After you have completed the steps for the Non-Exercise Estimate of Cardiorespiratory Endurance, use Chart 8 in the Lab Resource Materials to determine your fitness rating.

Walking Test

Time		minutes
Heart rate		bpm
Rating		(see Chart 1)

Bicycle Test

Workload		kpm
Heart rate		bpm
Weight		pounds
Weight in kg*		
$mL/O_2/kg$		
Rating		(see Chart 5)

Non-Exercise Test

Score		
Rating		(see Chart 8)

Step Test

Heart rate		bpm
Rating		(see Chart 2)

12-Minute Run Test

Distance		miles
Rating		(see Chart 6)

12-Minute Swim Test

Distance		yards
Rating		(see Chart 7)

Non-Exercise Estimate of Cardiorespiratory Endurance

Record your scores and do the calculations to determine scores for A to E below.

- Look up your activity score on Chart 1 (below). Record score in box A. ☐ (A)

- Record your gender (female = 0/male = 1) _____ × 2.77 = ☐ (B)

- Determine your resting heart rate (Lab 8A), record here _____ × 0.03= ☐ (C)

- Calculate your BMI (see Lab 14B), record here _____ × 0.17 = ☐ (D)

- Record your age in years. _____ × 0.10 = ☐ (E)

Use the following formula to calculate your score. Use Chart 8 on page 128 to get your rating; record this below.

18.07   +   **A**   +   **B**   −   **C**   −   **D**   −   **E**   =   **Estimated Cardiorespiratory Endurance (METs)**

18.07   +   ☐   +   ☐   −   ☐   −   ☐   −   ☐   =   ☐

Chart 1 Self-Reported Activity Score (for Step 1 Above)

Activity Score	Choose the Score That Best Describes Your Physical Activity Level
0.00	I am inactive or do little activity other than usual daily activities.
0.32	I regularly (>5 d/wk) participate in physical activities requiring low levels of exertion that result in slight increases in breathing and heart rate for at least **10 minutes** at a time.
1.06	I participate in aerobic exercises (e.g., brisk walking, jogging) or other activities (e.g., sports or active recreation) requiring similar levels of exertion for **20 to 60 minutes per week.**
1.76	I participate in aerobic exercises (e.g., brisk walking, jogging) or other activities (e.g., sports or active recreation) requiring similar levels of exertion for **1 to 3 hours per week.**
3.03	I participate in aerobic exercises (e.g., brisk walking, jogging) or other activities (e.g., sports or active recreation) requiring similar levels of exertion for **over 3 hours per week.**

Conclusions and Implications

1. In several sentences, explain why you selected the tests you selected. Discuss your current level of cardiorespiratory endurance and steps you will need to take to maintain or improve it. Comment on the effectiveness of the tests you selected.

2. In several sentences, explain your results from the non-exercise assessment by comparing the results with the other test(s). Did the self-report version classify you into the same fitness category? Try to explain any differences you noted.

Vigorous Aerobics, Sports, and Recreational Activities

LEARNING OBJECTIVES

After completing the study of this Concept, you will be able to:

▶ Explain the difference between moderate and vigorous physical activity and describe the unique benefits of vigorous physical activity.

▶ Identify several different types of vigorous aerobic activities and describe the advantages of each as possible activities in a personal activity program.

▶ Identify several different types of vigorous sports activities, describe the advantages of sports activities in a personal activity program, and explain the importance of skill learning to sports performance.

▶ Identify several different types of vigorous recreational activities and explain how they differ from vigorous aerobic and sports activities.

▶ Plan and self-monitor a vigorous physical activity program, and evaluate the factors that will help you adhere to it.

Vigorous physical activity—including vigorous aerobics, sports, and recreational activities—promotes health, wellness, fitness, and enhanced performance.

©Ingram Publishing

Why it Matters!

Vigorous aerobic physical activity provides many health benefits and there are many ways to be active. Some people enjoy the challenge and thrill of sports while others prefer the independence and freedom of individual aerobic exercise. Some people like exercising with friends or in groups while others like to exercise alone. In this Concept, you will learn about the different types of vigorous physical activity as well as strategies to help you adopt and maintain an active identity over time.

build cardiorespiratory endurance and for enhancing performance, but it is also a great way to meet national physical activity guidelines. You can achieve the recommended volume of activity using combinations of moderate activity or vigorous activity, but an advantage of vigorous activity is that you can meet the guidelines in fewer days or with less overall time. Another advantage of vigorous activities is that they provide a good workout for the cardiovascular and respiratory systems. This additional stimulus is important for promoting cardiorespiratory endurance.

Three different types of vigorous physical activity are described in this Concept: vigorous aerobics, vigorous sports, and vigorous recreational activities. The importance of these vigorous forms of physical activity for health and fitness is emphasized by placement near the foundation of the physical activity pyramid (see Figure 1), with vigorous aerobic activities at step 2 and vigorous sports and recreational activities at step 3.

Foundations of Vigorous Physical Activity

A variety of vigorous activities can be used to meet physical activity guidelines. In the past, vigorous physical activity was recommended for people who wanted to

Figure 1 ▶ Vigorous aerobics, sports, and recreational activities are included at the second and third steps of the physical activity pyramid.

Source: Charles B. Corbin

Vigorous aerobic activities provide an effective stimulus to build cardiorespiratory endurance. The word aerobic literally means "with oxygen." Aerobic activity is generally defined as activity that is rhythmical, uses the large muscles, and is performed in a continuous manner. Many moderate-intensity activities meet these criteria but it is generally used to refer to more vigorous forms of activity. Dr. Ken Cooper of the Cooper Institute in Dallas popularized the term *aerobics* in his book *Aerobics,* published in 1968. His book emphasized the importance of **vigorous aerobic activities** such as those in step 2 of the physical activity pyramid (e.g. jogging, aerobic dance, and cycling). The activities included in this step of the pyramid are at least 6 METs (six times more intense than resting) and significantly elevate the heart rate. The nature of these vigorous aerobic activities provides a good stimulus to the cardiorespiratory system and promotes positive training adaptations if performed regularly. Many people refer to these types of exercise sessions as "cardio" workouts.

Vigorous sports and recreation can provide the same benefits as vigorous aerobic activities. Vigorous sports typically involve intermittent activity with bursts of activity and short periods of rest. They are not continuous like vigorous aerobic activities, but they provide similar benefits due to the high intensity. Examples of vigorous sports include basketball, soccer, hockey, and tennis. Swimming and cycling are also popular activities that can be considered sports. However, most people do these activities noncompetitively, so they are typically considered as vigorous aerobic activities. Sports such as golf, bowling, and billiards/pool are aerobic but are light to moderate in intensity. For this reason, they are classified as moderate physical activities.

Vigorous recreational activities can provide similar benefits as vigorous sports and vigorous aerobic activities. Recreational activities are generally pursued for reasons other than fitness. The term reflects the notion of "re-creation" since it helps people relax and enjoy themselves. Because many of these activities can be performed at intensities suitable for building cardiorespiratory endurance, some can be categorized as **vigorous recreational activities.** Hiking, skiing, kayaking, canoeing, hunting, and rock climbing are examples of recreational activities that may also be vigorous in nature. Therefore, many recreational activities can help meet guidelines for moderate or vigorous activity.

Physical activities at steps 2 and 3 of the pyramid produce improvements in cardiorespiratory endurance and health in addition to those produced by moderate physical activities. Participation in moderate activity provides important health benefits, but vigorous aerobic activity results in additional health benefits, such as improved cardiorespiratory endurance and improved performance (see Table 1). To get the benefits outlined in Table 1, vigorous activity should be performed at least 3 days a week for 20 minutes

Table 1 ▶ Benefits of Vigorous Physical Activity*

- Vigorous activity meets national guidelines for physical activity and reduces risk of many chronic diseases and early death.
- Vigorous activity provides greater health benefits than moderate activity even when the total volume or calorie expenditure is the same.
- Vigorous activity provides additional health benefits (in a dose-response manner) when performed beyond the minimal guidelines.
- Vigorous activity contributes to many wellness benefits including improved quality of life, reduced risk of depression, reduced anxiety, and improved cognitions.
- Vigorous activity improves cardiorespiratory endurance and enhances ability to perform activities that require good cardiorespiratory endurance.

*Benefits depend on regular participation (at least 3 days a week) and appropriate intensity and duration (at least 20 minutes at target intensity).

at the appropriate target intensity. Additional activity above this minimum amount has added benefits, but the amount depends on the specific health indicator, your baseline level of fitness, and other factors. The point of maximum health benefits has not been established, but the added benefits from additional vigorous exercise were emphasized by the expert panel that developed the 2018 *Physical Activity Guidelines for Americans.*

All forms of aerobic activity provide the same generalized benefits for the cardiovascular system. However, a recent review has concluded that running may be particularly beneficial. In one major study, runners had a 45 percent lower risk of death from heart disease or stroke and a 30 percent lower risk of early death than non-runners, after controlling for overall levels and intensity of activity. Runners were also found to live 3 years longer than non-runners. Those who run for 6 years or more had the largest benefit. Perhaps most important is the fact that even short bouts of running (5–10 minutes) have health benefits. The results demonstrate that there are many benefits of running, but there are also greater risks of injury associated with

Vigorous Aerobic Activities Aerobic activities of an intensity at least six times that of resting (6 METs), commonly defined as activities with enough intensity to produce improvements in cardiorespiratory endurance.

Vigorous Sports Sports are competitive activities that have an organized set of rules, along with winners and losers. Vigorous sports are those of similar intensity to vigorous aerobic activities.

Vigorous Recreational Activities Recreational activities are those that are done during leisure time that do not meet the characteristics of sports. Vigorous recreational activities are of similar intensity to vigorous aerobics.

running. The effects may also be due to the other underlying explanations. Thus, the main message is that participation in vigorous physical activity provides additive benefits over participation in moderate-intensity activities.

Moderate and vigorous physical activity can be combined to meet national guidelines. National guidelines specify the total amount of activity that should be performed rather than having separate recommendations for moderate and vigorous activity. This approach helps people incorporate both moderate and vigorous activity into their lifestyle. The guidelines are based on tracking the total MET-minutes of physical activity performed. Because vigorous activity is performed at higher intensities (higher MET values), it makes a larger contribution to total activity than moderate-intensity activity performed for the same time. As discussed in the Concept on adopting active lifestyles, to determine MET-minutes, you multiply the MET value of an activity by the number of minutes that you perform it. For example, if a person walked for 10 minutes at 4 mph (4 METs), the MET-minutes would be 40 (4 METs × 10 minutes). If the person also jogged for 20 minutes at 5 mph (8 METs), the MET-minutes for jogging would be 160 (8 METs × 20 minutes); the total MET-minutes for the day would be 200.

To meet the physical activity guidelines, a person must accumulate a minimum of 500 MET-minutes per week. These are considered to be minimal levels, and the physical activity guidelines encourage people to move toward the target of 1,000 MET-minutes per week for additional benefits. Activity should be done at least 3 days a week when the combined method is used, even though the MET-minute standard could be met with large amounts of activity performed on 1 or 2 days. Bouts of activity must be at least 10 minutes in length to be counted toward the recommendation. MET values for a variety of moderate activities are included in the Concept on moderate physical activity. A complete list of the MET values for a variety of activities can be found online (search "Compendium of Physical Activities"). In Lab 9C you will learn more about how to combine moderate and vigorous activity to meet national goals.

Not all activities at levels 2 and 3 of the pyramid are equally safe. Sports medicine experts indicate that certain types of physical activities are more likely than others to result in injury.

Walking and low-impact dance aerobics are among the least risky activities. Skating, an aerobic activity, is the riskiest, followed by basketball and competitive sports. Among the most popular aerobic activities, running has the greatest risk, with cycling, high-impact dance aerobics, and step aerobics having moderate risk for injury. Swimming and water aerobics are among those least likely to cause injuries because they do not involve impact, falling, or collision. In general, activities that require high-volume training (aerobics and jogging), collision (football, basketball, and softball), falling (biking, skating, cheerleading, and gymnastics), the use of specialized

HELP   Health is available to Everyone for a Lifetime, and it's Personal

Vigorous Exercise Boosts Metabolism Long after the Workout

The benefits of vigorous exercise persist even after the workout is over. For example, a vigorous 45-minute bike workout burns approximately 330 calories, but you can expect to burn perhaps 500 total calories (a 37 percent increase) due to the heightened metabolism following the workout. This extra boost to the metabolism can have important implications for energy balance and weight control.

How does this information influence your perception about the importance of vigorous exercise?

equipment that can fail (biking), and repetitive movements that stress the joints (tennis and high-impact aerobics) increase risk for injury. These statistics reinforce the importance of using proper safety equipment, proper performance techniques, and proper training techniques.

Vigorous physical activity is not for everyone! While some people enjoy pushing their body to the limits or appreciate the challenge of intense sporting competitions, other people may not. The key is to find activities that you enjoy and that provide meaning and value to your life since these are the activities that you are most likely to adhere to over time. There is considerable hype in the fitness industry about optimizing training regimens to achieve high fitness. Examples include the CrossFit movement and the allure of "Ninja Warrior" type competitions. While this may appeal to some, it may be overly structured or too intense for others. Other hype in the fitness industry is about new workout methods that promise faster gains through shorter and more intense workouts. An example is with the promotion of high-intensity interval training, or HIIT. Proponents suggest that HIIT helps people by providing them with a way to get maximal benefit in the shortest possible time. However, many experts are concerned that the high-intensity "work-like" regimens make exercise less enjoyable and discourage future involvement in the long run. While HIIT and vigorous activity may work for some, the most important consideration is to find forms of physical activity that you intrinsically enjoy.

Vigorous Aerobic Activities

A variety of vigorous aerobic activities are available for meeting individual needs and interests. Because there are so many choices, many beginning exercisers want to know which type of aerobic exercise is best. The best form of exercise is clearly whatever form you enjoy and will do

regularly. Some people tend to be very consistent in performing their favorite form of activity, while others stay active by participating in a variety of activities. Seasonal differences are also common with physical activity participation. Many people choose to remain indoors during very hot or very cold weather and perform outdoor activities when temperatures are more moderate.

Vigorous aerobics can be done either continuously or intermittently. We generally think of vigorous aerobics as being continuous. Jogging, swimming, and cycling at a steady pace for long periods are classic examples. Experts have shown that aerobic exercise can be done intermittently as well as continuously. Both **continuous** and **intermittent aerobic activities** can build cardiorespiratory endurance. For example, studies have shown that three 10-minute exercise sessions in the target zone are as effective as one 30-minute exercise session. Still, experts recommend bouts of 20 to 60 minutes in length, with several 10- to 15-minute bouts being an acceptable alternative when longer sessions are not possible.

Modern exercise equipment can store personal settings, track progress, and link to the Internet and social media applications.
©Technogym, Inc

Vigorous aerobic activities are often rhythmical and typically involve the large muscle groups of the legs. The rhythmical nature of aerobic activity allows it to be performed continuously and in a controlled manner. The activation of a large muscle mass is important in providing an appropriate challenge to the cardiovascular and respiratory systems. Examples of popular aerobic activities include running, swimming, biking, cross-country skiing, and inline skating. Many exercise enthusiasts embrace **cross training,** in which a number of different activities are used to meet the aerobic exercise guidelines.

Exercise machines can provide an engaging indoor alternative to traditional aerobic exercises. Many people prefer aerobic exercise machines because of their ease of use, safety, and convenience. Treadmills have historically been the most commonly used exercise machine, but elliptical devices and an array of stair-climbing devices are also extremely popular. Bike, rowing, and skiing machines are also commonly used but they may be most popular among individuals that specifically enjoy these activities. An advantage of contemporary machines is that users can specify different types of workouts and watch TV or listen to music to pass the time. Most machines provide estimates of calories expended based on the self-selected intensity, but these may not be accurate unless it incorporates your body weight. Thus, these numbers should not be considered especially accurate.

A drawback of exercise machines is that interest and novelty may wear off over time. However, new features have been developed to enhance interest and ease of use. For example, some machines have personalized key systems, which automatically record your settings and the details of your workout each time you use the machine. This information can then be downloaded onto computers for automatic logging. Newer machines have also started to utilize gaming technology to further enhance the user experience. Interactive displays in these machines allow you to feel like you are exercising outdoors and you can compete against virtual or real opponents. Through wireless computer networks, it is now possible for users to save their data on websites and/or share their results through social media applications. See Technology Update to explore interactive machines.

Continuous Aerobic Activities Aerobic activities that are slow enough to be sustained for relatively long periods without frequent rest periods.

Intermittent Aerobic Activities Aerobic activities, relatively high in intensity, alternated with frequent rest periods.

Cross Training A term used to describe the performance of a variety of activities to meet exercise goals.

Technology Update

Interactive Gaming in Exercise Equipment

Interactive games are popular entertainment at home, but interactive technology has also impacted exercise equipment and fitness centers. For example, the Expresso Interactive Gaming bikes are designed to create a realistic and engaging indoor biking experience. The user chooses a course and then navigates through the virtual terrain by turning the handlebars and shifting the gears. The display provides updates of your progress, and completed workouts can be saved on the Internet or sent to an associated smartphone app. If you want competition, you can try to set the course record or share your workout and performance on Facebook to challenge your friends.

Would this type of technology motivate you to exercise? Why or why not?

Many people enjoy the social interactions of group exercise classes.
©Christopher Futcher/Getty Images

Vigorous exercise in a group setting provides a social exercise experience. Although most vigorous aerobics can be done individually, many people prefer the social interactions and challenge of group exercise classes. Many fitness centers and community recreation centers offer group exercise classes.

An advantage of group exercise classes is that there is a social component, which helps increase motivation and promote consistency. A disadvantage is that all participants are generally guided through the same exercise. A vigorous routine can cause unfit people to overextend themselves, while an easy routine may not be intense enough for experienced exercisers. A well-trained group exercise leader can help participants adjust the exercise to their own level and ability. Check the qualifications of the exercise leader to be sure that he or she is certified to lead group exercise. Descriptions of the most common individual forms of aerobic activity are provided below:

- *Dance aerobics: A choreographed series of movements done to music.* There are a variety of forms of dance aerobics. In *high-impact dance aerobics,* both feet leave the ground simultaneously for a good part of the routine. Although this provides a good workout, it may not be ideal for everyone. In *low-impact dance aerobics,* one foot stays on the floor at all times, making risk of injury lower and a good choice for beginners or older exercisers. In *step aerobics,* the participant steps up and down on a bench while doing various dance steps. Step aerobics is typically low impact but relatively higher in intensity due to the stepping.

- *Rhythmic dance: A more fluid dance-oriented form of aerobics.* Rhythmic dance evolved naturally out of the aerobic dance movement, and there are many examples of dance-based classes. Jazzercise is one of the more long-lasting and well-known forms, and it paved the way for more hybridized group exercise classes. Classes in hip-hop aerobics have been popular for a while as well as Zumba and other Latin-based dance classes.

- *Martial arts: Popular, vigorous aerobic activities.* In addition to traditional martial arts, such as karate and tae kwon do, a number of other alternative forms have been developed, including kickboxing, aerobic boxing, cardio karate, box fitness, and Tae Bo. These activities involve intermittent bouts of high-intensity movements and lower-intensity recovery. Because martial arts involve a lot of arm work, they can be effective in promoting good overall fitness. Some activities are more intense than others, so consider the alternatives to find the best fit for you.

- *Spinning classes: Attracting new people to bicycling.* A spinning class is a group cycling class performed on specialized indoor bike trainers. A group leader typically leads participants through routines that involve intermittent bursts of high-intensity intervals followed by spinning at lower resistance to recover. While specific to cycling, the format has appealed to a broader set of fitness enthusiasts who just enjoy the challenge it provides.

- *Water-based classes: Taking advantage of the resistive properties of water.* Water walking and water exercise classes are popular alternatives to swimming. Although these activities can be done alone, they are typically conducted in group settings and are especially good for people with arthritis, musculoskeletal problems, or high body fat. The body's buoyancy in water assists the participant and reduces injury risk. The resistance of the water provides an overload that helps the activity promote health and cardiorespiratory benefits. Exercises done in shallow water tend to be low in impact, while deeper-water exercises are considered to be higher-impact activities. Neither type requires the ability to swim. Water activity also serves as a way of rehabilitating from injury.

- *Hybridized "combo" classes: Cross-training applications.* Hybrid combo classes combine aerobics, resistance exercise, plyometrics, and/or calisthenics. They offer a complete workout in a structured and engaging group environment. Classes are marketed with customized names to reflect the nature of the activities involved (e.g., CardioPump, PowerPump, Cardio Sculpt, BodyJam, BodyAttack). There are a number of certification programs for combo classes designed to ensure consistency and quality of programming.

- *Individualized small-group fitness centers: A personal focus.* Large commercial fitness centers remain popular, but many small private fitness centers provide an appealing alternative for some people. An example is the Curves franchise that provides a structured group exercise format, allowing people to exercise in a more convenient, small-group setting. A similar line of centers branded under the name Kosama offers shorter enrollments and personalized attention over a set period of time rather than an ongoing membership.

A CLOSER LOOK

Group Fitness and "Fitness in the Parks"

Although group exercise classes have been popular for many years, the recent ACSM Worldwide Fitness Trend survey identified "group exercise training" as one of the top 10 fitness trends. This was labelled as a general trend for larger exercise classes and not for specific types of classes, which were tracked separately. A possible reason for the trend is the growing popularity of large-scale outdoor group exercise events. The movement started with yoga in the park, and now many communities offer a variety of vigorous group classes under the broader moniker of "Fitness in the Parks." Programming typically includes yoga and Pilates as well as more vigorous exercise classes, such as kickboxing and Zumba® (a dance-based, interval exercise program blended with Latin rhythms). The appeal is that people can come out for a free class without committing to a membership at a fitness center. Exercising in a group can also increase accountability and promote social connectedness.

Do you see the appeal of outdoor group exercise? Would it help motivate you to be more active? Why or why not?

ACTIVITY

Vigorous Sports and Recreational Activities

Some sports are more vigorous than others. Sports typically involve brief intermittent periods of sprinting or high-intensity activity but they vary in the type, nature, and intensity of movement involved. Soccer involves many muscle groups and is high in intensity but does not emphasize the use of the arms. The action in basketball, tennis, and soccer involves bursts of activity followed by rest, but they require persistent, vigorous activity over a relatively long time. Golf requires little vigorous activity. Sports that have characteristics similar to those of basketball, tennis, and soccer have benefits like those of vigorous aerobic activities. Of course, any sport can be more or less active, depending on how you perform it. Shooting baskets or even playing half-court basketball is not as vigorous as playing a full-court game.

The most popular sports share characteristics that contribute to their popularity. The most popular sports are often considered to be lifetime sports because they can be done at any age. The characteristics that make these sports appropriate for lifelong participation probably contribute significantly to their popularity. Often,  the popular sports are adapted so that people without exceptional skill can play them. For example, bowling uses a handicap system to allow people with a wide range of abilities to compete. Slow-pitch softball is much more popular than fast-pitch softball or baseball because it allows people of all abilities to play successfully.

One of the primary reasons sports participation is so popular is that sports provide a challenge. For the greatest enjoyment, the challenge of the activity should be balanced by the person's skill in the sport. If you choose to play against a person

Volleyball is a popular competitive and recreational sport that can be played for a lifetime.
©Christopher Futcher/iStockphoto/Getty Images

with lesser skill, you will not be challenged. On the other hand, if you lack skill or your opponent has considerably more skill, the activity will be frustrating. For optimal challenge and enjoyment, learn the skills of a given sport before competing. Likewise, choose an opponent who has a similar skill level.

Some recreational activities can also be classified as vigorous. Activities that you do in your free time for personal enjoyment or to "re-create" yourself are considered recreational activities. Recreational activities that exceed threshold intensity for cardiorespiratory endurance are considered vigorous. They are more vigorous than activities such as fishing, bowling, and golf, which are typically classified as lifestyle or moderate activities (step 1 in the pyramid). Examples of vigorous recreational activities include common snow activities (downhill skiing, snowboarding), water activities (surfing, wakeboarding, kayaking, canoeing), and mountain activities (hiking, mountain biking). As with sports, recreational activities can be done at different intensities. If done for a sufficient length of time, vigorous recreational activities can provide the same benefits as vigorous sports or other vigorous activities. Note that vigorous activities such as cycling, jogging, and skiing could be classified in both the vigorous recreational and vigorous aerobic activities sections. Sports can also be considered vigorous recreational activities, depending on how the individual views them. Many people view recreation as simply time to relax and be outdoors, and find the resulting improvements in fitness to be just an additional benefit. This is a healthy attitude since activities pursued purely for enjoyment are easier to maintain than activities pursued purely for fitness.

Patterns and Trends in Physical Activity Participation

Vigorous aerobics, sports, and recreational activities are among the most popular types of activity. Each year a number of different organizations conduct surveys to determine which activities are the most popular. Results vary based on how the questions are asked and who asks them. Regardless of the group doing the poll, vigorous individual activities rank high (among top 25). For example, running, aerobic exercise machines, biking, and dance aerobics are consistently in the top 10 activities. Some vigorous individual sports and recreational activities also rank among the most popular (e.g., tennis, hiking). Basketball and slow-pitch softball are among the most popular team sports, but participation is lower in other team sports. Fishing, bowling, and golf are popular but are not vigorous in nature. In many polls, walking ranks number one, but it is moderate rather than vigorous in nature, except for older people or people with health problems. Individual muscle fitness activities rank high (e.g., calisthenics, machines, barbells, and dumbbells), as do flexibility exercises (e.g., stretching, yoga).

Participation in physical activity varies by age group. Results of a new poll by the Sports and Fitness Industry Association (SFIA) are illustrated in Figure 2. Overall, fitness activities are the most popular among all age groups except Gen Z (born after 2000). Outdoor sports are next, being

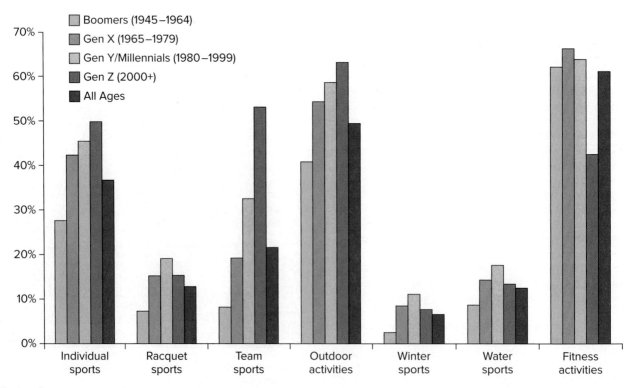

Figure 2 ▶ Patterns of physical activity by age group.

Source: Sports and Fitness Industry Association (formerly National Sporting Goods Association).

most popular among young age groups. Individual sports also rank high, especially among younger age groups.

Team sports are less popular than other activities among adults, but are among the most popular activities for youth (i.e., Gen Z). Racquet sports, water sports, and winter sports were the least popular general activity types, probably because of their need for special facilities and equipment, their relatively high cost, and requirements for specific weather (e.g., snow for skiing) and geographical conditions (e.g., lakes for boating).

Casual participation is different from regular participation. Some polls seek to capture the relative popularity of activities by asking participants to indicate which ones they have performed in the past year. A person who has done the activity once can check "yes" for that activity but casual participation (once to a few times a year) does not provide the same health, wellness, and fitness benefits as regular participation.

Not surprisingly, far more people are casual exercisers than regular participants. For example, over 25 million Americans report jogging/running for exercise, but only 10 million report running regularly (about 6 million males and 4 million females). Distinctions in participation and regular participation are even more evident for other activities. An estimated 50 million Americans report riding their bike for recreation, but only 15 million report frequent recreational bike riding, and a still smaller segment of the population (about 2 million) participates in regular fitness bicycling. Nearly 100 million people report participating in recreational swimming; however, the number of people who report regular fitness swimming is only about 2.5 million.

Fitness trends are different than fitness fads. The ACSM's *Health and Fitness Journal* conducts annual surveys of growing trends in fitness to help capture the pulse of the fitness field. Data are collected from a sample of more than 2,800 health and fitness professionals worldwide who complete a standardized survey. The compiled results seek to differentiate between trends (generalized changes in a situation or in the way people are behaving) and fads (a temporary notion that is taken up with great enthusiasm for a brief period). The reports have been useful in informing consumers and fitness leaders of shifts in activity preferences.

The most recent report highlights wearable technology as the number one trend (see In the News). Body weight (using body weight calisthenics) was second. Also high on the list was high-intensity interval training (HIIT), but it is premature to see if this interest will remain over time. Other activity trends include strength training, group training, and yoga. Zumba, a group dance program that combines Latin rhythms with interval-type exercise, indoor cycling (spinning), and structured "boot camp" fitness classes that were popular in previous years have since dropped in the ratings. The top 10 trends are summarized in Table 2. (Search "Worldwide Survey of Fitness Trends for 2017" for

Table 2 ▶ ACSM's *Health and Fitness Journal's* Top 10 Fitness Trends

Rank	Product/Trend	Description
1	Wearable technology	Wearable activity trackers, smart watches, heart rate monitors, and GPS tracking devices continue to be popular for monitoring activity.
2	Body weight training	Body weight training builds on the popularity of "core" training and applied fitness regimens popular in CrossFit and other programs.
3	High-intensity interval training (HIIT)	The short bursts of activity followed by short periods of rest or recovery in HIIT allow users to maximize the intensity and efficiency of workouts.
4	Educated and experienced fitness professionals	Stronger certification and credentialing programs have increased access to more qualified fitness professionals with better skills for planning and facilitating exercise.
5	Strength training	Strength training continues to be a popular fitness trend as many people enjoy the challenges and variety from this type of training.
6	Group training	Group exercise remains popular since it can help promote motivation while also providing reinforcing and supportive social networks.
7	Exercise is Medicine (EIM)	This global health initiative that encourages physicians and other health-care providers to assess and prescribe physical activity is taking root and can impact future programming.
8	Yoga	The attention on mind–body awareness and specific body postures can help promote health and relaxation.
9	Personal training	The growth in kinesiology degree programs has enhanced education and training of personal trainers and more effective use in health and fitness facilities.
10	Exercise and weight loss	Exercise programming focused on weight loss continues to be in high demand as more individuals realize the importance of activity for weight control.

In the News

Growth and Evolution of Wearable Fitness Technology

Consumer interest in wearable technology continues to grow and this interest is being met with an array of new products, services, and technologies. The marketplace has undergone considerable change from year to year as companies jockey for position in this dynamic growth area. Established leaders include FitBit, Apple, and Garmin, and many other large companies are poised to engage. Market researchers reported a 20% increase in the sale of wearable monitors from 2016–2017 and projections suggest that it will double by 2021. However, most of the growth is expected in the smartwatch market with manufacturers competing to increase functionality and utility of data from wearable devices.

Do you enjoy trying to keep up with the latest fitness trends? Do you see advantages or disadvantages with regard to the growth of wearable technology?

---

complete details from the survey.) While trends in fitness preferences and methods change, the importance of regular exercise remains constant.

Using Self-Management Skills

Becoming skillful will help you enjoy sports and recreation. Improving your skill can increase the chances that you will participate in the activity or sport for a lifetime. The following self-management strategies can help you improve your sport performance:

- *When learning a new activity, focus on the general idea of the skill first; worry about details later.* For example, a diver who concentrates on pointing the toes and keeping the legs straight at the end of a flip may land flat on his or her back. To make it all the way over, the diver should concentrate on merely doing the flip. When the general idea is mastered, then concentrate on details.

- *The beginner should be careful not to emphasize too many details at one time.* After the general idea of the skill is acquired, the learner can begin to focus on the details, one or two at a time. Concentration on too many details at one time may result in **paralysis by analysis.** For example, a golfer who is told to keep the head down,

the left arm straight, and the knees bent cannot possibly concentrate on all of these details at once. As a result, neither the details nor the general idea of the golf swing is performed properly.

- *Once the general idea of a skill is learned, a skill analysis of the performance may be helpful.* Be careful not to over-analyze; it may be helpful to have a knowledgeable person help you locate strengths and weaknesses. Watching videos of skilled performances can be helpful to learners.

- *In the early stages of learning a lifetime sport or physical activity, it is not wise to engage in competition.* Beginners

Learning new skills can be challenging but rewarding.
©JupiterImages/Creatas/Alamy Stock Photo

who compete are likely to concentrate on beating their opponent rather than on learning a skill properly. For example, in bowling, you may abandon the newly learned hook ball in favor of a straight ball to ensure hitting pins. This may help your score in the present game, but is not likely to improve bowling skills for the future.

- *To be performed well, sports skills must be overlearned.* Often, when you learn a new activity, you begin to play the game immediately. The best way to learn a skill is to overlearn it, or practice it until it becomes habit. Frequently, games do not allow you to overlearn skills. For example, it is not effective to learn to serve during a tennis match since there may be only a few opportunities to do so. For the beginner, it is much more productive to hit many serves (overlearn) with a friend until the general idea of the serve is well learned. Focus on the basic mechanics of the skill when learning something new. Accuracy, power, and finesse will come with practice of a properly performed skill.

- *When unlearning an old (incorrect) skill and learning a new (correct) skill, a person's performance may get worse before it gets better.* For example, you may have learned how to score well in golf with a flawed swing. Accept that your performance may get worse initially as you try to learn better technique. As the new swing pattern is refined and overlearned, your skill will improve, as will your golf score.

- *Mental practice may aid skill learning.* Mental practice (imagining the performance of a skill) may benefit performance, especially if the performer has had previous experience in the skill. Mental practice can be especially useful in sports when the performer cannot participate regularly because of weather, business, or lack of time.

- *For beginners, practicing in front of other people may be detrimental to learning a skill.* An audience may inhibit learning of a new sports skill. This is especially true if you feel that your performance is being evaluated, judged, or critiqued by others.

- *There is no substitute for good instruction.* Getting good instruction, especially at the beginning level, will help you learn skills faster and better. Instruction will help you apply these rules and use practice more effectively.

Preparing a vigorous physical activity plan requires the use of multiple self-management skills. You can use the six steps in program planning outlined in the Concept on self-management to prepare a vigorous physical activity plan. Preparing a plan requires the use of a variety of self-management skills including self-assessment, goal setting, and self-monitoring. Preparing a plan also helps you manage your time—an important self-management skill. Lack of time is a common reason for not exercising. Preparing a plan helps you fit your activity into your daily schedule. (More information is provided in Strategies for Action: Lab Information.)

Choosing activities that are self-promoting can enhance confidence and fun. Self-promoting activities are activities that make you feel successful. They require relatively little skill and can be done in a way that avoids comparison with other people. They allow you to set your own standards of success and can be done individually or in small groups that are suited to your personal needs. Examples include wheelchair distance events, jogging, resistance training, swimming, bicycling, and dance exercise.

A key for long-term exercise adherence is to find exercises that you enjoy and that fit into your lifestyle. Sports are a common form of activity for younger people, but other aerobic and recreational activities have become more common among adults. This is partially because of changing interests, but also because of changing opportunities and lifestyles.

Choose effective monitors and apps for activity tracking. A variety of consumer activity monitors are available to assist in tracking the volume and intensity of exercise. Various smartphone apps can also be used to help prompt you to stay active and to help you chart progress. The devices are only designed to provide estimates of movement, heart rate, and steps, so don't focus too much on the actual numbers. Use the information primarily to remind yourself of your goals and to track progress over time. Research is still evolving with monitors, but many people find that regular use keeps them more engaged in their exercise programs.

Paralysis by Analysis An overanalysis of skill behavior. This occurs when more information is supplied than a performer can use or when concentration on too many details results in interference with performance.

Strategies for Action: Lab Information

Understanding the factors that influence physical activity adherence will improve your chances of staying active throughout life. In Lab 9A, you will evaluate predisposing, enabling, and reinforcing factors that may help you identify the types of activity best suited to you and that enhance the chances that you will stay active over time.

Preparing a vigorous physical activity plan can help you with adherence. Lab 9B is designed to help you plan and perform a 1-week physical activity program. It helps you practice the steps in program planning and provides an opportunity to self-monitor adherence to your plan. This initial plan focuses on short-term activity goals. Future plans can focus more on

long-term goals for both fitness and physical activity. If you like, you can copy the lab worksheet to make a log book for long-term self-monitoring.

Consider combining moderate and vigorous physical activity to meet activity guidelines. *Cross training* is a term used to describe the performance of a variety of activities to meet exercise goals. For example, on different days you can do a moderate activity such as walking, a vigorous aerobic activity such as jogging on a treadmill, a vigorous sport such as tennis, and a vigorous recreational activity such as mountain biking. These activities from different levels on the activity pyramid can be combined to meet activity guidelines. Lab 9C will help you learn and use this MET-minute system.

Suggested Resources and Readings

The websites for the following sources can be accessed by searching online for the organization, program, or title listed. Specific scientific references are available at the end of this edition of *Concepts of Fitness and Wellness*.

- American College of Sports Medicine. Worldwide Survey of Fitness Trends for 2017 (pdf).

- Bureau of Labor Statistics. Leisure Time Use Survey.
- Physical Activity Council. 2017 Participation Report—The Physical Activity Council's Annual Report Tracking Fitness, Sports and Recreation in the U.S. (online report).
- Sports and Fitness Industry Association (SFIA). Sports, Fitness, and Leisure Participation Report (pdf).
- U.S. Department of Health and Human Services. *Physical Activity Guidelines for Americans* (health.gov website).

Lab 9A The Physical Activity Adherence Questionnaire

Name	Section	Date

Purpose: To help you understand the factors that influence physical activity adherence and to see which factors you might change to improve your chances of achieving the action or maintenance level for physical activity.

Procedures

1. The factors that predispose, enable, and reinforce adherence to physically active living are listed below. Read each statement. Place an X in the circle under the most appropriate response for you: very true, somewhat true, or not true.
2. When you have answered all of the items, determine a score by summing the four numbers for each type of factor. Then sum the three scores (predisposing, enabling, reinforcing) to get your total score.
3. Record your scores in Chart 1 of the Results section (using Chart 2 to determine the ratings). Answer the questions in the Conclusions and Implications section.

	Very True	Somewhat True	Not True	
Predisposing Factors				
1. I am very knowledgeable about physical activity.	3	2	1	
2. I have a strong belief that physical activity is good for me.	3	2	1	
3. I enjoy doing regular exercise and physical activity.	3	2	1	
4. I am confident of my abilities in sports, exercise, and other physical activities.	3	2	1	
			Predisposing Score =	
Enabling Factors				
5. I possess good sports skills.	3	2	1	
6. I know how to plan my own physical activity program.	3	2	1	
7. I have a place to do physical activity near my home or work.	3	2	1	
8. I have the equipment I need to do physical activities I enjoy.	3	2	1	
			Enabling Score =	
Reinforcing Factors				
9. I have the support of my family for doing my regular physical activity.	3	2	1	
10. I have many friends who enjoy the same kinds of physical activities that I do.	3	2	1	
11. I have the support of my boss and my colleagues for participation in activity.	3	2	1	
12. I have a doctor and/or an employer who encourages me to exercise.	3	2	1	
			Reinforcing Score =	
			Total Score (Sum 3 Scores) =	

Results: Record your scores in the "Score" column. Use your score and the Physical Activity Adherence Ratings Chart to determine your ratings. Record your ratings in the "Rating" column below.

Chart 1 Physical Activity Adherence Ratings

Adherence Category	Score	Rating
Predisposing		
Enabling		
Reinforcing		
Total		

Chart 2 Physical Activity Adherence Ratings Chart

Classification	Predisposing Score	Enabling Score	Reinforcing Score	Total Score
Adherence likely	11–12	11–12	11–12	33–36
Adherence possible	9–10	9–10	9–10	27–32
Adherence unlikely	<9	<9	<9	<27

Conclusions and Implications: In several sentences, discuss your ratings from this questionnaire. Also discuss the predisposing, enabling, and reinforcing factors you may need to alter in order to increase your prospects for lifetime activity.

In several sentences, discuss what type of activity you find most enjoyable (vigorous aerobics, vigorous recreation, or vigorous sports). Comment on *why* you enjoy the activities that you have selected.

Lab 9B Planning and Logging Participation in Vigorous Physical Activity

Name		Section	Date

Purpose: To set 1-week vigorous physical activity goals, to prepare a plan, and to self-monitor progress in your 1-week vigorous aerobics, sports, and recreation plan.

Procedures

1. Consider your current stage of change for vigorous activity using the questions provided below. Read the five stages of change questions below and place a check by the stage that best represents your current vigorous physical activity level.
2. Determine vigorous activity (active aerobics, active sports, or active recreation) goals for each day of a 1-week period. In Chart 1, under the heading "Vigorous Activity Goals," record the total minutes per day that you expect to perform. Record the specific date for each day of the week in the "Date" column, and the activity or activities that you expect to perform in the "Activity" column.
3. Only bouts of 10 minutes or longer should be considered when selecting your daily minutes goals. The daily goals should be at least 20 minutes a day in the target zone for vigorous activity for at least 3 days of the week.
4. Use Chart 2 to keep track of the number of minutes of activity that you perform on each day of the 7-day period. Record the number of minutes for each bout of activity of at least 10 minutes in length performed during each day in Chart 2. Determine a total number of minutes for the day and record this total in the last column of Chart 2 and also in the last column ("Summary Performance Log") of Chart 1.
5. After completing Charts 1 and 2, answer the questions and complete the Conclusions and Implications section (use full sentences for your answers).

Determine your Stage of Change for vigorous physical activity. Check only the stage that represents your current vigorous activity level.

☐ Precontemplation. I do not meet vigorous activity guidelines and have not been thinking about starting.

☐ Contemplation. I do not do vigorous activity but have been thinking about starting.

☐ Preparation. I am planning to start doing regular vigorous activity to meet guidelines.

☐ Action. I am regularly doing vigorous activity but have been doing it only recently (less than 6 months)

☐ Maintenance. I regularly perform vigorous activity and have been doing it consistently for a while (more than 6 months).

Results

Chart 1 Vigorous Physical Activity Goals and Summary Performance Log

Select a goal for each day in a 1-week plan. Keep a log of the activities performed to determine if your goals are met (see Chart 2), and record total minutes performed in the chart below.

	Date	Vigorous Activity Goals		Summary Performance Log Total Minutes Performed/Day
		Minutes/Day	Activity	
Day 1				
Day 2				
Day 3				
Day 4				
Day 5				
Day 6				
Day 7				

Chart 2 Physical Activity Adherence Ratings Chart

Record the number of minutes for each bout of vigorous activities performed each day. Add the minutes in each column for the day and record a daily total (total minutes of vigorous activity per day) in the "Daily Total" column. Record your daily totals in the last column of Chart 1.

	Date	Vigorous Activity Bouts					Daily Total
		Bout 1	Bout 2	Bout 3	Bout 4	Bout 5	
Day 1							
Day 2							
Day 3							
Day 4							
Day 5							
Day 6							
Day 7							

Did you meet your vigorous activity goals for at least 3 days of the week? Yes No

Do you think that you can consistently meet your vigorous activity goals? Yes No

What activities did you perform most often when doing vigorous activity? List the most common activities that you performed in the spaces below.

Vigorous Aerobics _____ Vigorous Sports _____ Vigorous Recreation _____

Conclusions and Implications

Are the activities that you listed above ones that you think you will perform regularly in the future? Yes No

Did setting goals and logging activity make you more aware of your daily vigorous physical activity patterns? Explain why or why not.

Lab 9C Combining Moderate and Vigorous Physical Activity

Name	Section	Date

Purpose: To learn about MET-minutes and how to combine moderate and vigorous physical activity to meet physical activity guidelines and goals.

Procedures

1. National guidelines recommend at least 150 minutes of moderate or 75 minutes of vigorous physical activity as the minimum amount per week. The guidelines indicate that you can combine the two forms to meet your activity goal. When combining moderate and vigorous activities, MET-minutes are used. The minimum goal for beginners is 500 MET-minutes, and 1,000 MET-minutes is the minimum goal for a reasonably fit and active person. Consider this information as you complete the rest of this lab.
2. In Chart 1 below list several moderate activities and several vigorous activities for each day of one week. Next to the activities indicate the number of minutes you plan to perform each activity. Be sure to choose both moderate and vigorous activities.
3. Use the information in Chart 2 to determine a MET value for each activity or use the list of MET values found by searching the Internet for "Compendium of Physical Activities" to determine values for those not listed in Chart 2. Record the MET value in the space provided for each activity.
4. Multiply the MET values for each activity by the number of minutes you plan to perform each activity to determine MET-minutes for each activity.
5. Total the MET-minute columns for both moderate and vigorous activities to be performed during the week.
6. Answer the questions in the Conclusions and Implications section.

Results

Chart 1 Moderate and Vigorous Activity Plan for One Week

Day	Date	Moderate Activity				Vigorous Activity			
		Activity	Min	METs	MET-min	Activity	Min	METs	MET-min
1									
2									
3									
4									
5									
6									
7									
Totals									

Total MET-mins = Moderate MET-mins + Vigorous MET-mins =

Did you meet the 500 MET-minute recommendation for beginners? (Yes) (No)

Did you meet the 1,000 MET-minute recommendation for more active people? (Yes) (No)

Which is your weekly activity plan most likely to include?

☐ Moderate activity only

☐ Vigorous activity only

☐ Both moderate and vigorous activity

Chart 2 MET Values for Selected Moderate and Vigorous Physical Activities

Moderate Activities	METs		Vigorous Activities	METs
Bowling	3.0		Shoveling Snow	6.0
Vacuuming/Mopping	3.0		Walking (4.5 mph)	6.3
Walking (3 mph)	3.0		Aerobic Dance	6.5
Child Care	3.5		Bricklaying	7.0
Golf (riding)	3.5		Cross-Country Skiing (leisure)	7.0
Biking (10 mph flat)	4.0		Soccer (leisure)	7.0
Fishing (moving, not stationary)	4.0		Basketball (game)	8.0
Raking Leaves	4.0		Biking (12–17 mph)	8.0
Table Tennis	4.0		Hiking Terrain (pack)	8.0
Volleyball (non-comp.)	4.0		Jogging (5 mph)	8.0
Working as Waiter/Waitress	4.0		Tennis (singles)	8.0
Ballroom dance (social)	4.5		Volleyball (games)	8.0
Basketball (shooting)	4.5		Digging Ditches	8.5
Mowing Lawn (power)	4.5		Step Aerobics	8.5
Painting	4.5		Cross-Country Skiing (fast, 5–7 mph)	9.0
Tennis (doubles)	5.0		Swimming Laps (varies with strokes)	9.0
Walking (4 mph)	5.0		Jogging (6 mph)	10.0
Construction	5.5		Racquetball (games)	10.0
Farming	5.5		Soccer (competitive)	10.0
Golf (walking)	5.5		Running (11.5 mph)	11.5
Softball (games)	5.5		Handball (games)	12.0
Swimming (leisure)	5.5			

Note: MET values are based on the Compendium of Physical Activities Tracking Guide (available at http://prevention.sph.sc.edu/tools/docs/documents_compendium.pdf).

Conclusions and Implications: In the space provided below discuss the MET-minute method of combining activities to meet goals. Do you think that this method will be useful to you? Explain why or why not.

Muscle Fitness and Resistance Exercise

LEARNING OBJECTIVES

After completing the study of this Concept, you will be able to:

▶ Identify and explain the factors that influence strength, muscular endurance, and power.

▶ List the health benefits of fitness and resistance exercise.

▶ Describe the types of progressive resistance exercise (PRE) and their advantages and disadvantages, including some basic exercises for each type of PRE.

▶ Describe different types of PRE equipment and the advantages and disadvantages of each.

▶ Determine the amount of exercise necessary to improve muscle fitness and explain the FIT formulas for the different types of PRE.

▶ Describe how to design PRE programs for optimal effectiveness.

▶ Evaluate facts and fallacies about PRE and the risks of performance-enhancing drugs, supplements, and steroids.

▶ Describe several self-assessments for muscle fitness, understand the self-assessments that help you identify personal needs, and plan (and self-monitor) a personal PRE program.

Progressive resistance exercise promotes muscle fitness that permits efficient and effective movement, contributes to ease and economy of muscular effort, promotes successful performance, and lowers susceptibility to some types of injuries, musculoskeletal problems, and illnesses.

©SG Hirst/Getty Images

Concept 10

Why it Matters!

Muscle fitness provides a number of benefits for both health and wellness. Like other dimensions of fitness, the key to building and sustaining good muscle fitness is regular exercise. Current guidelines call for resistance exercise at least 2 days a week, but specific training plans and prescriptions depend on whether your primary goals are to improve strength, muscular endurance, power, or for general conditioning. The varying quality of fitness information on the Internet has led many people to have misconceptions about progressive resistance exercise. This Concept covers the scientific basis and health benefits of muscle fitness as well as principles, guidelines, and specific exercises that can help you establish an appropriate muscle fitness program.

Progressive resistance exercises are used in programs designed to build muscle fitness.
©Fuse/Corbis/Getty Images

Factors Influencing Muscle Fitness

Muscle fitness is a multidimensional construct. The three components of muscle fitness (strength, muscular endurance, and power) each reflect different capacities of human movement. Strength is the amount of force you can produce with a single maximal effort of a muscle group. Muscular endurance is the capacity of the skeletal muscles, or group of muscles, to continue contracting over a long period of time. Muscle power is the ability to exhibit strength quickly and it depends on the combination of strength and speed. Power is associated with enhanced sports performance and has historically been considered a skill-related component of fitness. However, it is now considered to be a health-related component because of its link to bone health and other health factors.

Progressive resistance exercise is the principal method of improving muscle fitness. Exercise that gradually and systematically increases overload to the muscles is called **progressive resistance exercise (PRE).** *Weight training* and *progressive resistance training (PRT)* are often used as synonyms for *PRE*, but they should not be confused with the various competitive events related to resistance exercise. Weight lifting is a competitive sport that involves two lifts: the snatch and the clean and jerk. Powerlifting, also a competitive sport, includes three lifts: the bench press, the squat, and the dead lift. Bodybuilding is a competition in which participants are judged on the size and **definition** of their muscles. Participants in these competitive events rely on highly specialized forms of PRE to optimize their training. Individuals interested in general muscular fitness also rely on PRE but do not need to follow the same routines or regimens to achieve good results.

Skeletal muscle tissue has unique properties that are important to muscle fitness. The three types of muscle tissue—smooth, cardiac, and skeletal—have different structures and functions. Smooth muscle tissue consists of long, spindle-shaped fibers, with each fiber containing only one nucleus. The smooth muscle fibers are located in the walls of the esophagus, stomach, and intestines, where they contract involuntarily to move food and waste products through the digestive tract. Cardiac muscle tissue is also involuntary and, as its name implies, is found only in the heart. These fibers contract in response to demands on the cardiovascular system. The heart muscle contracts at a slow, steady rate at rest but contracts more frequently and forcefully during physical activity. Skeletal muscle tissues consist of long, cylindrical, multinucleated fibers. They provide the force needed to move the skeletal system and can be controlled voluntarily.

Muscle fiber types influence adaptations to training and muscle fitness performance. There are three distinct types of muscle fibers: slow-twitch (Type I), fast-twitch (Type IIb), and intermediate (Type IIa). Each responds and adapts differently to PRE. Therefore, muscle fitness is influenced directly by fiber type distribution and the extent to which they have adapted as a result of training.

The slow-twitch fibers are generally red in color and are well suited to produce energy with aerobic metabolism. Slow-twitch fibers generate less tension but are more resistant to fatigue. Endurance training leads to adaptations in the slow-twitch fibers that allow them to produce energy more efficiently and to better resist fatigue. Fast-twitch fibers are generally white in color and are well suited to produce energy with anaerobic processes. They generate greater tension than slow-twitch fibers, but they fatigue more quickly. These fibers are particularly well suited to fast, high-force activities that require strength and power, such as explosive weight-lifting movements, sprinting, and jumping. Resistance exercise enhances strength primarily by increasing the size (muscle **hypertrophy**) of fast-twitch fibers, but cellular adaptations also take place to enhance various metabolic properties. Intermediate fibers have biochemical and physiological properties that are between those of the slow-twitch and fast-twitch fibers. A distinct property of these intermediate fibers is that they are highly adaptable, depending on the type of training that is performed.

An example of fast-twitch muscle fiber in animals is the white meat in the flying muscles of a chicken. The chicken is heavy and must exert a powerful force to fly a few feet up to a perch. A wild duck that flies for hundreds of miles has dark meat (slow-twitch fibers) in the flying muscles for better endurance.

People who want large muscles will use PRE designed to build strength (fast-twitch fibers). People who want to participate in activities for a long period of time without fatigue will want to use PRE programs designed to build muscular endurance (slow-twitch fibers).

Leverage is an important mechanical principle that influences muscle fitness. The body uses a system of levers to produce movement. Muscles are connected to bones via tendons, and some muscles (referred to as "primary movers") cross over a particular joint to produce movement. When a muscle contracts, it physically shortens and pulls the two bones connected by the joint together to produce movement. Figure 1 shows the two heads of the biceps muscle inserting on the forearm. When the muscle contracts, the forearm is pulled up toward the upper arm (elbow flexion). The muscle on the opposite side (triceps) relaxes or lengthens to allow the movement. Figure 2 shows a related image of knee flexion and extension to show the distinctions between

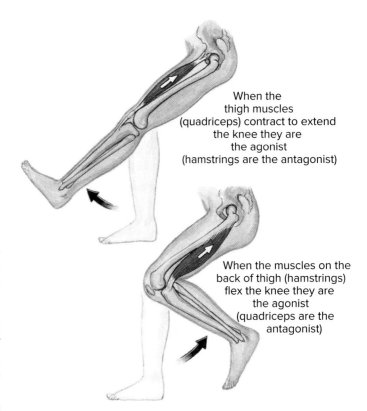

When the thigh muscles (quadriceps) contract to extend the knee they are the agonist (hamstrings are the antagonist)

When the muscles on the back of thigh (hamstrings) flex the knee they are the agonist (quadriceps are the antagonist)

Figure 2 ▶ Muscles work in pairs to coordinate movement.

agonist muscles and **antagonist muscles** that work together to coordinate movement.

A person with long arms and legs has a mechanical advantage in most movements, since the force that is exerted can act over a longer distance. Although it is not possible to change the length of your limbs, it is possible to learn to use your muscles more effectively. The ability of elite golfers to hit a golf ball 350 yards, for example, is due primarily to the ability to generate torque and power rather than due to strength.

Genetics, gender, and age affect muscle fitness performance. Each person inherits a certain proportion of muscle fiber types in his or her skeletal muscle. This allocation influences the potential a person has for muscle fitness activities. Regardless of genetics, all people can improve their strength and muscular endurance with proper training.

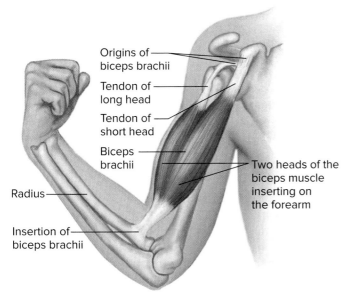

Origins of biceps brachii

Tendon of long head

Tendon of short head

Biceps brachii

Two heads of the biceps muscle inserting on the forearm

Radius

Insertion of biceps brachii

Figure 1 ▶ Muscles contract (shorten) to produce movement.

Progressive Resistance Exercise (PRE) The type of physical activity done with the intent of improving muscle fitness.

Definition The detailed external appearance of a muscle.

Hypertrophy Increase in the size of muscles as a result of strength training; increase in bulk.

Agonist Muscles Muscle or muscle group that contracts to cause movement during an isotonic exercise.

Antagonist Muscles Muscle or muscle group on the opposite side of the limb from the agonist muscles.

Women generally are smaller than men, have smaller amounts of the anabolic hormone testosterone, and, therefore, have less muscle mass than men. Because of this, women typically have 60 to 85 percent of the absolute strength  of men. However, when expressed relative to lean body mass, women have similar relative strength as men. For example, a 150-pound female who lifts 150 pounds has relative strength equivalent to that of a 250-pound male who lifts 250 pounds, even though she has less absolute strength. Gender differences between males and females for both absolute and relative power are similar to those for strength. Absolute muscular endurance tends to be greater for males, but the difference again is negated if relative muscular endurance is considered.

Measures of **relative muscle fitness** are typically better indicators of performance (regardless of gender) since they take into account differences in size and muscle mass. However, for some activities, **absolute muscle fitness** may be more important. Maximum strength and power are usually reached in the 20s and typically decline with age. However, after age 30, people who are physically inactive can lose as much as 3 to 5 percent of their muscle mass per decade, a phenomenon known as **sarcopenia.** Muscular endurance also typically declines as people grow older, but the decrease is less dramatic for muscular endurance than for strength and power. Regardless of age or gender, PRE helps prevent loss of muscle mass and maintain absolute and relative muscle fitness. This suggests that PRE is one antidote to premature aging.

The components of muscle fitness are interrelated. Most activities rely on various combinations of strength and muscular endurance; thus, it is important to have sufficient amounts of both. Training protocols are specific for each, but a person who trains for strength will develop some endurance and a person who trains for endurance will develop some strength. Power is sometimes referred to as "explosive strength" because it is the product of both strength and speed. Strength contributes to power, but specific training is necessary for building power.

While not a component of muscle fitness, cardiorespiratory endurance is conceptually related to muscular endurance. Both are necessary for performing exercise for extended periods of time. Cardiorespiratory endurance depends primarily on the efficiency of the circulatory and respiratory systems, while muscular endurance depends primarily on the efficiency of the local skeletal muscles.

Health Benefits of Muscle Fitness Exercise

Good muscle fitness and regular muscle fitness exercise contribute to the prevention of chronic diseases and early death. Muscle fitness (often described as the functional outcome of muscular strength, muscular endurance, and power) provides key benefits to the skeletal system, the cardiovascular system, and the metabolic system. Progressive resistance exercise (PRE) that promotes muscle fitness also enhances bone density and bone strength,  which are important in countering the loss of bone mass with osteoporosis. Muscle fitness is critical across the lifespan, but it is especially important for older adults. The following list summarizes some of the established health benefits associated with good muscle fitness:

- Lower risk of all-cause mortality
- Fewer heart attacks; a better heart disease risk profile
- Lower incidence of high blood pressure (hypertension)
- Reduced risk of some cancers
- Healthier blood lipid profile
- Better insulin sensitivity and improved blood glucose
- Reduced risk of metabolic syndrome
- Better body composition (i.e., less body fat and more lean muscle)
- Greater bone mass and less risk of osteoporosis
- Lower risk for osteoarthritis and musculoskeletal disorders

Good muscle fitness and regular muscle fitness exercise contribute to weight control. The primary determinant of daily energy expenditure is lean body mass since it influences your overall basal metabolic rate. Gradual increases in body fatness with age are attributable (in large part) to declines in muscle mass and corresponding declines in metabolism. Regular PRE can preserve muscle mass and contribute to improved weight control. For each pound of muscle gained, a person can burn approximately 35 to 50 calories more per day. Physical activity has been shown to be critical for maintaining weight loss and a recent longitudinal study confirmed that muscle fitness exercise is especially important for controlling excess abdominal body fatness.

Good muscle fitness and regular muscle fitness exercise help maintain the ability to function effectively in daily life. The National Strength and Conditioning Association (NSCA) indicates that PRE increases muscle fitness, reducing the demands on the muscular, skeletal, cardiorespiratory, and metabolic systems. With good muscle fitness, you have the energy needed to perform daily work efficiently and effectively and the reserve energy to enjoy leisure time.

Regular muscle fitness exercise is important for both prevention and treatment of injuries and chronic conditions. Muscle balance is important in reducing the risk for injury so resistance training should build both agonist and antagonist muscles. For example, if you do resistance exercise to build the quadriceps muscles (front of the thigh), you should also exercise the hamstring muscles (back of the thigh). In this instance, the quadriceps are the agonist (muscle being used), and the hamstrings are the antagonist. If the quadriceps become too strong relative to the antagonist hamstring muscles, the risk for injury increases (see Figure 2).

Muscle fitness exercise provides the cornerstone for effective physical therapy and is prescribed for injury rehabilitation and recovery after a variety of musculoskeletal surgeries. Individuals with cancer and other chronic conditions have also been shown to benefit in different ways from muscle fitness exercise. For example, women with breast cancer report fewer symptoms after performing PRE.

Good muscle fitness is associated with good posture and reduced risk for back problems. When muscles in specific body regions are weak or underdeveloped, poor posture can result. Lack of fitness of the abdominal and low back muscles is particularly related to poor posture and potential back problems. Muscle fitness of the core (e.g., abdominal, paraspinal [back] and gluteal muscles) also influences posture and may reduce the risk of injuries and back problems. (Review the Concept on body mechanics for more comprehensive information on posture and back care.)

Good muscle fitness and regular muscle fitness exercise are associated with wellness and quality of life. Recent research has documented a number of wellness and mental health benefits associated with resistance exercise including increased vigor, improved cognition, improved mood states, reduced depression, reduced anxiety, and reduced fatigue. A recent meta-analysis concluded that regular resistance exercise was associated with reduced anxiety symptoms among both healthy participants and participants with a

physical or mental illness. Another systematic review specifically examined the psychological benefits of strength exercise in people who are overweight. The results showed small but consistent benefits in a variety of psychological outcome measures with effects comparable to or sometimes stronger than those found in aerobic and diet interventions. Thus (similar to aerobic exercise), resistance exercise can increase healthspan (years of quality of life) as well as lifespan. (See HELP feature for a related story.)

Types of Progressive Resistance Exercise

There are different types of PRE, and each has its advantages and disadvantages. The main types of PRE are isotonic, isometric, plyometric, and isokinetic. All use overload progressively to build muscle fitness, each in a unique way. The advantages of each type are summarized in Table 1.

- **Isotonic** exercises are the most common type of PRE. They include calisthenics (body weight exercise), resistance machine exercises, free weight exercises, and exercises using other types of resistance such as exercise bands. The defining feature of isotonic exercise is that the muscle shortens and lengthens to cause movement. Isotonic exercise allows for the use of resistance through a full range of joint motion and provides an effective stimulus for muscle development.

When performing isotonic exercise, both **concentric contractions** (shortening) and **eccentric contractions** (lengthening) are important. For example, in a standard biceps curl, the biceps contract concentrically to lift the

Relative Muscle Fitness Muscular performance (strength, endurance, or power) adjusted for body size.

Absolute Muscle Fitness A maximum performance for strength (e.g., number of pounds lifted at one time), muscular endurance (e.g., number of times a specific weight can be lifted), or power (e.g., maximum distance in putting the shot).

Sarcopenia An age-related decline in muscle mass that is due, in part, to declines in physical activity.

Isotonic Type of muscle contraction in which the muscle changes length, either shortening (concentrically) or lengthening (eccentrically).

Concentric Contractions Isotonic muscle contractions in which the muscle gets shorter as it contracts, such as when a joint is bent and two body parts move closer together.

Eccentric Contractions Isotonic muscle contractions in which the muscle gets longer as it contracts—that is, when a weight is gradually lowered and the contracting muscle gets longer as it gives up tension. Eccentric contractions are also called *negative exercise*.

Table 1 ▶ Advantages and Disadvantages of Isotonic, Isometric, Plyometric, and Isokinetic Exercises

	Advantages	Disadvantages
Isotonic	• Can effectively mimic movements used in sport skills • Enhance dynamic coordination • Challenge muscles through full range of motion	• Does not offer equal resistance at all joint angles • May require equipment or machines
Isometric	• Can be done anywhere • Require only low-cost/little equipment • Can rehabilitate an immobilized joint	• Build strength at only one position • Cause less muscle hypertrophy • Are a poor link or transfer to sport skills
Plyometric	• Build power that is especially useful in sports • Typically do not require expensive equipment • Facilitate bone development when used appropriately	• Can be risky for the untrained • Require good knowledge of training technique to be safe • Require good strength for safe and effective use
Isokinetic	• Offer equal resistance at all joint angles • Are beneficial for rehabilitation and evaluation • Are safe and less likely to promote soreness	• Require specialized equipment • Cannot replicate natural acceleration found in sports • Are more complicated to use and cannot work all muscle groups

weight and then eccentrically to lower the weight back down to the starting position. Many people emphasize only the lifting (concentric) phase, but isotonic exercises are most effective when weights are lowered in a slow and controlled manner. Depending on the resistance used, isotonic exercises can build both **dynamic strength** and **dynamic muscular endurance.** *Dynamic* refers to movement, so strength and muscular endurance that causes movement are referred to as dynamic.

- **Isometric** exercises are those in which no movement takes place while a force is exerted against an immovable object. When properly done, isometric exercise can build **static strength** or **static muscular endurance.** However, isometric exercises are not emphasized in PRE programs because the gains are evident only at the angle of the joint used in the exercise.

- **Plyometric** exercises are a form of isotonic exercises that involves a stretch-shortening cycle: an active prestretch (eccentric phase) followed by a fast powerful contraction (concentric phase). An example is landing following a jump (eccentric phase) and then jumping again (concentric phase). More aggressive forms include "depth jumping," such as jumping up off a box to landing (eccentric phase) and then jumping back on top of the box (concentric phase). The loading or eccentric phase stretches the muscle before it contracts, allowing the muscle to contract with greater force. Less aggressive forms include activities such as repetitive hopping, sequential jumping, jumping rope, and medicine ball throws. Plyometrics build power (explosive strength). A foundation in strength is necessary prior to performing plyometric exercises.

- **Isokinetic** exercises are isotonic–concentric muscle contractions performed on machines that keep the velocity of the movement constant through the full range of motion.

Resistance exercise can promote lean body mass and contribute to a healthy appearance.
©Tom Grill/Corbis/Getty Images

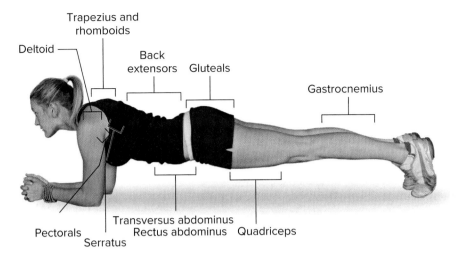

Deltoid
Trapezius and rhomboids
Back extensors
Gluteals
Gastrocnemius
Pectorals
Serratus
Transversus abdominus
Rectus abdominus
Quadriceps

Figure 3 ▶ The plank is a core exercise that strengthens the abdominals, back, shoulders, and a number of other stabilizing muscles of the core.
©Mark Ahn Creative Services

Isokinetic machines essentially match the resistance to the effort of the performer, permitting maximal tension to be exerted throughout the range of motion. Isokinetic exercises are effective, but they are typically found only in sport training or rehabilitation settings.

Core training uses a variety of resistance training methods to build the core muscles of the body. **Core training** is not a specific type of resistance training such as isokinetics, isometrics, or plyometrics. It can be done with a variety of methods. However, specific types of exercises are used to more effectively engage the core musculature. Inadequate development of these muscles has been shown to be a risk factor for back pain, so it is important to incorporate specialized core exercises into a resistance training program.

The plank is one of the most common isometric core training exercises as it effectively activates a number of stabilizing core muscles. In the front plank, a person holds a horizontal push-up position, bearing the body weight on the forearms, elbows, and toes. The plank strengthens primarily the abdominals, back, and shoulders, but a variety of stabilizing muscles are engaged to resist the pull of gravity and keep the body horizontal (see Figure 3). Many variations of the plank exist and they can be modified to fit different fitness levels.

Functional fitness training focuses on improving movements used in real life. Interest in functional fitness has increased dramatically in recent years, and it is now widely promoted in both fitness centers and rehabilitation facilities. The ACSM recommends the use of neuromotor exercises designed to improve motor skills, balance, coordination, gait, and agility for the maintenance and improvement of functional fitness. Balance tends to deteriorate with age, partly due to corresponding declines in muscle strength, range of motion, and a reduced ability to coordinate muscle movements.

Therefore, neuromuscular exercise and functional fitness are especially important for older individuals.

Functional balance training is a specific training method designed to improve balance and mobility. It is beneficial to older people but is also used in rehabilitation and in specialized training regimens for sports. This type of training is typically conducted with specialized devices, such as exercise balls (Swiss balls), BOSU platforms, and balance boards. Because these devices challenge you to remain balanced, they recruit muscles that are not typically worked in most strength training regimens. Core fitness exercises are also important for functional fitness training because of their importance to coordination and agility.

Dynamic Strength A muscle's ability to exert force that results in movement. It is typically measured isotonically.

Dynamic Muscular Endurance A muscle's ability to contract and relax repeatedly. This is usually measured by the number of times (repetitions) you can perform a body movement in a given period. It is also called *isotonic endurance.*

Isometric Type of muscle contraction in which the muscle remains the same length. Also known as *static contraction.*

Static Strength A muscle's ability to exert a force without changing length; also called *isometric strength.*

Static Muscular Endurance A muscle's ability to remain contracted for a long period. This is usually measured by the length of time you can hold a body position.

Plyometrics A training technique used to develop explosive power. It consists of isotonic–concentric muscle contractions performed after a prestretch or an eccentric contraction of a muscle.

Isokinetic Isotonic–concentric exercises done with a machine that regulates movement velocity and resistance.

Core Training A specialized training regimen designed to improve the strength and functionality of core muscles.

Progressive Resistance Exercise: How Much Is Enough?

PRE is the best type of training for muscle fitness. PRE is the most common and effective type of training for building muscle. It is sometimes referred to as progressive resistance training (PRT). The word *progressive* is used because the frequency, intensity, and length of time of muscle overload are gradually, or progressively, increased as muscle fitness increases. Moderate and vigorous physical activity do not provide an appropriate stimulus for maintaining or improving muscular fitness. Specific exercises from step 4 of the pyramid are needed to improve strength, muscular endurance, and power (see Figure 4).

There is a FIT formula for each type of PRE. The FIT formula varies for each type of isotonic PRE, depending on the expected benefit. Days of exercise per week are used to determine frequency (F). Intensity (I) is determined using a percentage of your **1 repetition maximum (1RM)** for isotonic and isokinetic exercises and percentage of maximum exertion for isometric exercises (see Lab 10A). Time (T) is determined by the number of repetitions and sets (groups of repetitions)

of an exercise. Table 2 illustrates the FIT formulas for PRE designed primarily to build different components of muscle fitness (strength, muscular endurance, general muscle fitness, and power). Most people will benefit from the general muscle fitness regimen, but customized programs may be needed for more specific goals.

There is an optimal frequency of PRE for building muscle fitness. As illustrated in Table 2, the recommended frequency of exercise for muscle fitness varies based on the expected outcomes. For beginners and older people, 2–3 days per week is recommended. For most everyone else, 3 days per week is recommended. The ACSM recommends 48 hours of rest between exercise sessions to provide appropriate time for recovery. The great proportion of potential strength gains can be accomplished with 2 days of training per week. Exercise done on a third day results in additional increases, but the amount of gain is relatively small, compared with gains resulting from 2 days of training per week. For people interested in health benefits rather than performance benefits, 2 days a week saves time and may result in greater adherence to a strength training program. For people interested in performance benefits, more frequent training may be warranted

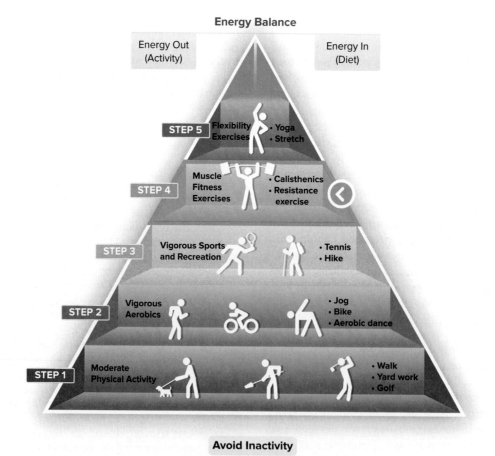

Figure 4 ▶ To build muscle fitness, activities should be selected from step 4 of the physical activity pyramid.

Source: Charles B. Corbin

Table 2 ▶ Threshold of Training and Fitness Target Zones for Different Components of Muscular Fitness		
	Threshold of Training	**Fitness Target Zones**
Muscular Strength Training		
Frequency	2 days a week for each muscle group	2–3 days a week for each muscle group
*Intensity**	40–60% of 1RM	60–80% of 1RM
Time (sets and repetitions)	1–2 sets of 8–12 reps	2–4 sets of 8–12 reps
Muscular Endurance Training		
Frequency	2 days a week for each muscle group	2–3 days a week for each muscle group
*Intensity**	<50% of 1RM	50% of 1RM
Time (sets and repetitions)	1–2 sets of 15–25 reps	2–4 sets of 15–25 reps
General Muscle Fitness Training (combined strength and muscular endurance)		
Frequency	2 days a week for each muscle group	2–3 days a week for each muscle group
*Intensity**	40–60% of 1RM	60–80% of 1RM
Time	1 set of 8–12 reps	1–3 sets of 8–12 reps
Power Training (plyometrics are recommended only for those with a sufficient base of fitness)**		
Frequency	2 days a week	2–3 days a week
*Intensity**	Body weight	Body weight or with load
Time	1 set of jumps or movements	1–3 sets of jumps or movements

*Recommendations are for typical exercisers. Beginners or older individuals may benefit from loads of even 20–40% of 1RM for all parts of muscle fitness, including power. Advanced lifters may need to use higher intensities and with different formats.
**Plyometrics is an effective way to build power, but it is recommended only for those with a sufficient base level of fitness. Body weight may be sufficient for most people but intensity can be increased with added weight or medicine balls. Exercises may include depth jumps or bounding calisthenics.

(4 to 6 days a week). Rotating exercises so that certain muscles are exercised on one day and other muscles are exercised the next allows for more frequent training. For example, upper body exercises can be performed on alternating days so that each can be performed 2-3 days per week.

There is an optimal intensity of PRE for building muscle fitness. The amount of resistance (intensity of exercise) used in a PRE program is based on a percentage of your 1 repetition maximum (1RM)—the maximum amount of resistance you can move (or weight you can lift) one time. The 1RM value provides an indicator of your maximum strength, but desired levels of resistance are determined using percentages of the 1RM value. The specific prescription depends on the program goals (see Table 2). For strength, the percentages typically vary 60 to 80 percent of the 1RM value depending on experience and fitness level. For older adults, the percentage of 1RM is less (40 to 50 percent). For muscular endurance, the recommended percentage is 50 percent of 1RM for most adults, with slightly lower ranges recommended for older adults (40-50%).

Sets and repetitions are typically used for determining the optimal amount of time for building muscle fitness. For cardiorespiratory endurance exercise, the recommendations for time (T) refers to minutes but, with PRE, the T refers to sets and repetitions. Each set should be performed to muscle fatigue, but not to muscle failure as this can result in increased injury risk and muscle soreness that reduces adherence to regular training.

The recommended number of repetitions varies with the type of PRE. The stimulus for strength is high-level exertion, so the goal is to select a load that can be lifted a maximum of 8-12 times. A total of 1-3 sets are recommended with at least 2-3 minutes between sets. For muscular endurance the stimulus is more related to volume, so the focus should be on lighter

1 Repetition Maximum (1RM) The maximum amount of resistance you can move a given number of times—for example, 1RM = maximum weight lifted one time; 6RM = maximum weight lifted six times.

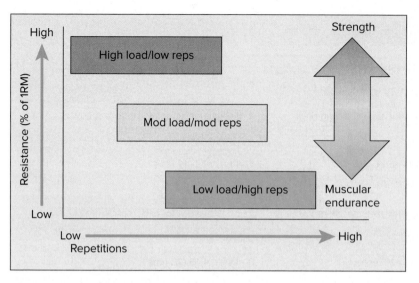

Figure 5 ▶ Comparison of muscular endurance with muscle strength by different repetitions and resistance.

weights that can be lifted 15-25 times. A total of 2-4 sets are recommended with rest intervals of approximately 1 minute. Individuals interested in general muscle fitness can select weights that allow an intermediate range of reps (10-18). Advanced lifters may need to select higher intensities and perform more sets to provide a stimulus that continues challenging the muscles.

The graph in Figure 5 illustrates the relationship between strength and muscular endurance. Training that requires high resistance and low repetitions (top bar) results in the least gain in endurance but the greatest gain in strength. Training with moderate resistance and moderate repetitions (second bar) results in moderate gains in both strength and endurance. Training that requires a high number of repetitions and a relatively low resistance (third bar) results in small gains in strength but large increases in muscular endurance.

The FIT formula for power varies based on the type of exercise and the abilities of the person performing it. Even though power is viewed as a dimension of health-related fitness, achieving power requires a good foundation of strength. This is because power reflects both the force and speed of movement. Beginners should build strength before trying to improve power. Following the FIT formula for strength (see Table 2) for 6 weeks would provide a sound foundation of strength.

Once a foundation of strength is achieved, more specific power training can be used as part of an overall strength program. Guidelines from the ACSM recommend heavy loading (85-100 percent of 1RM) to increase the force component of the power equation and light to moderate loading (30-60 percent of 1RM) performed at an explosive velocity to enhance the speed component of power. Therefore, multi-set routines are often used to enable training in both strength and speed. Exercises for power can be done with free weights or pulleys to simulate sport-related movements more effectively.

A training technique that is specifically designed to improve power is plyometric exercise. This technique takes advantage of a quick prestretch prior to a movement to increase power. By repeatedly doing these movements in training, it is possible to provide a greater stimulus to the muscles and improve the body's ability to perform power movements over time. Examples of plyometric drills for leg power are hopping drills or depth jumps. During these exercises, the leg muscles lengthen in an eccentric contraction to absorb the force of the drop and then follow immediately with a strong concentric contraction to complete the next jump or stride. The prestretch of the muscle during landing adds an elastic recoil that provides extra force to the push-off (see Figure 6). A push-up that thrusts the hands and arms off the floor is an example of the same principle applied to upper body exercise. A medicine ball throw provides another good option to build power in the upper body.

Dropping off the box requires eccentric contractions (shortening of muscle fibers) to slow the body during the landing phase.

The subsequent explosive leap challenges the muscle to transition to a concentric contraction (lengthening of muscle fibers) to land on the box.

Figure 6 ▶ Plyometric exercise—a technique for developing power.

Circuit resistance training (CRT) is an effective way to build muscular endurance as well as cardiorespiratory endurance. CRT consists of the performance of high repetitions of an exercise with low to moderate resistance, progressing from one station to another, performing a different exercise at each station. The stations are usually placed in a circle to facilitate movement. CRT typically uses about 20 to 25 reps against a resistance that is 30 to 40 percent of 1RM for 45 seconds. Fifteen seconds of rest is provided while changing stations. Approximately 10 exercise stations are used, and the participant repeats the circuit two to three times (sets). Because of the short rest periods, significant cardiovascular benefits have been reported in addition to muscular endurance gains.

CRT strategies are commonly used in new hybridized group fitness classes aimed at building both muscular fitness and aerobic fitness. CRT strategies are also commonly used in functional fitness training programs since various real-world movement tasks can be easily added to a base of aerobic activity. Thus, CRT can be broadly viewed as a method of integrating resistance exercise with aerobic exercise.

Programs intended to slim the figure/physique should be of the muscular endurance type. Many men and women are interested in exercises designed to decrease girth measurements. High-repetition, low-resistance exercise is suitable for this because it usually brings about some strengthening and may decrease body fatness, which in turn changes body contour. Exercises do not spot-reduce fat, but they do speed up metabolism, so more calories are burned. However, if weight or fat reduction is desired, aerobic (cardiorespiratory) exercises are best. To increase girth, use strength exercises.

Endurance training may have a negative effect on strength and power. Some studies have shown that for athletes who rely primarily on strength and power in their sport, too much endurance training can cause a loss of strength and power because of the modification of different muscle fibers. Strength and power athletes need some endurance training, but not too much, just as endurance athletes need some strength and power training, but not too much.

Resistance Training Equipment

Free weights are the most commonly used equipment for resistance exercise. Free weight equipment consists of weights that are typically loaded onto a barbell or a dumbbell. They have often been considered to be the domain of serious weight lifters, but now they are widely used by more casual fitness enthusiasts. Based on 3-year-trend data from the Sports and Fitness Industry Association (SFIA), use of free weight equipment has increased by 5 to 15 percent while use

Exercise balls can be used to enhance or facilitate resistance exercises.
©Blend Images/Getty Images

Technology Update

Can Clothing Sense Your Workouts?

Scientists have used a method called electromyography (EMG) to study the function and coordination of muscles. It is widely used in clinical evaluations to test heart function but new applications have placed sensors in clothing to monitor athletic performance, to detect risks of injury, and to aid in rehabilitation. By monitoring muscle use and training load more precisely, it might be possible to optimize training, minimize muscle imbalances, or reduce the risk of injuries. This technology was previously available only at high-level training facilities, but it is now available in "smart clothes" that link to smartphones for use by consumers. The potential value of this technology for consumer applications is uncertain.

Do you support these types of technology advances, or are they just commercial ventures aimed at making money from individuals interested in fitness?

ACTIVITY

Table 3 ▶ Advantages (+) and Disadvantages (−) of Free Weights and Machine Weights

		Free Weights		Machine Weights
Isolation of Major Muscle Groups	−/+	Movements require balance and coordination; more muscles are used for stabilization.	+/−	Body stabilizes during lift, allowing isolation, but muscle imbalances can develop.
Applications to Real-Life Situations	+	Movements can be developed to be truer to real life.	−	Movements are determined by the paths allowed on the machine.
Risk for Injury	−	There is more possibility for injury because weights can fall or drop on toes.	+	They are safer because weights cannot fall on participants.
Need for Assistance	−	Spotters are needed for safety with some lifts.	+	No spotters are required.
Time Requirement	−	More time is needed to change weights.	+	It is easy and quick to change weights or resistance.
Number of Available Exercises	+	Unlimited number of exercises is possible.	−	Exercise options are determined by the machine.
Cost	+	They are less expensive, but good (durable) weights are still somewhat expensive.	−	They are expensive; access to a club is usually needed.
Space Requirement	+/−	Equipment can be moved, but loose weights may clutter areas.	−/+	Machines are stationary but take up large spaces.

of machines has decreased by 2 to 5 percent. Factors that contribute to their popularity are their versatility, the ability to change weight in gradual increments, and the ability to modify exercises for specific muscles or movements (see Table 3). Because free weights require balance and technique, they may be more difficult for beginners to use.

Resistance training machines offer many advantages for overall conditioning. Resistance training machines can be effective in developing strength and muscular endurance if used properly. They can save time because, unlike free weights, the resistance can be changed easily and quickly. They may be safer because you are less likely to drop weights. A disadvantage is that the kinds of exercises that can be done on these machines are more limited than free weight exercises. They also may not promote optimal balance in muscular development, since a stronger muscle can often make up for a weaker muscle in the completion of a lift. Some machines have mechanisms that provide variable, or accommodating, resistance. These features allow the machine to provide a more appropriate resistance across the full range of motion. New lines of equipment allow the arms and legs to work more independently and enable the exercises to better simulate free living movements.

A variety of resistance devices are available to aid in plyometric and functional fitness training. To improve functional fitness, it is important to mimic movements that occur in real life. Kettlebells, for example, are now widely available in fitness centers. While kettlebells are not really different from a traditional dumbbell, the handles make them more versatile for more dynamic, functional fitness

A CLOSER LOOK

CrossFit Controversy

CrossFit has increased in popularity over time and is sometimes promoted as the "sport of fitness." Although CrossFit gyms are found all over the United States, and competitions frequently air on television, there is still some controversy regarding CrossFit safety. Some experts remain concerned that CrossFit may push people to perform exercises they are not ready for or that increase their risk of injury. There have been numerous instances of people getting injured while participating in CrossFit as well as reports of poor credentials at some CrossFit gyms. Advocates argue that consumers have a choice regarding physical activity and that the media highlights isolated events. (See link in Suggested Resources and Readings.)

Do you support the CrossFit movement, or do you think that it pushes people too hard or puts them at risk?

connect
ACTIVITY

movements. Other simple resistance devices used in functional fitness training include weighted "medicine balls," weighted bars (e.g., Bodybar), and sand/water bag resistance cords. The same equipment can be used in plyometric training for power.

Body weight exercises have become increasingly popular due to their simplicity and utility for functional fitness training. Recent polls have consistently identified body weight exercises as a recent fitness trend. New devices such as the TRX Suspension Trainer are now used in many gyms to facilitate body weight exercise. Because the TRX system leverages gravity, it is possible to easily change resistance by adjusting body position. Advocates emphasize the flexibility of the system and the ability to adapt it to build strength and endurance as well as balance and core function.

Calisthenics, such as curl-ups and push-ups, can also provide simple and flexible options for body weight exercise. Many variations can be added to increase the difficulty of various calisthenic exercises. For example, push-ups can be made more challenging by elevating your feet. Elastic tubes or bands available in varying strengths may be substituted for the weights and for the pulley device used in many resistance training machines to impart resistance.

Principles of Muscle Fitness Training

Apply the overload principle to determine appropriate workloads. For the body to adapt and improve, the muscles and systems of the body must be challenged. As noted earlier, the concept behind PRE is that the frequency, intensity, and duration of lifts are progressively increased to maintain an effective stimulus as the muscle fitness improves. When the overload principle is followed, the muscles are progressively challenged and the body adapts with structural and metabolic improvements that lead to increases in strength and endurance. Progress may be hard to detect, and this may contribute to the many misconceptions about resistance training. Table 4 summarizes some common myths and fallacies about resistance exercise (e.g., "no pain, no gain") and explains what really happens with correctly planned resistance exercise.

Apply the principle of progression to adapt and change the program. An effective PRE program should build progressively over time as your fitness level improves.

Table 4 ▶ Fallacies and Facts about Resistance Training

Fallacies	Facts
Resistance training will make you muscle-bound and cause you to lose flexibility.	Normal resistance training will not reduce flexibility if exercises are done through the full range of motion and with proper technique. Powerlifters who do highly specific movements have been shown to have poorer flexibility than other weight lifters.
Women will become masculine-looking if they gain strength.	Women will not become masculine-looking from resistance exercise. Women have less testosterone and do not bulk up from resistance training to the same extent as men. Women and men can make similar relative gains in strength and hypertrophy from a resistance training program, however. The greater percentage of fat in most women prevents the muscle definition possible in men and camouflages the increase in bulk.
Strength training makes you move more slowly and look uncoordinated.	Strength training, if done properly, can enhance sport-specific strength and increase power. There are no effects on coordination from having high levels of muscular fitness.
No pain, no gain.	It is not true that you have to get to the point of soreness to benefit from resistance exercise. It may be helpful to strive until you can't do a final repetition, but you should definitely stop before it is painful. Slight tightness in the muscles is common 1 to 2 days following exercise but is not necessary for adaptations.
Soreness occurs because lactic acid builds up in the muscles.	Lactic acid is produced during muscular work but is converted back into other substrates within 30 minutes after exercising. Soreness is due to microscopic tears or damage in the muscle fibers, but this damage is repaired as the body builds the muscle. Excessive soreness occurs if you violate the law of progression and do too much too soon.
Strength training can build cardiorespiratory endurance and flexibility.	Resistance exercise can increase heart rate, but this is due primarily to a pressure overload rather than a volume overload on the heart that occurs from endurance (aerobic) exercise. Gains in muscle mass do cause an increase in resting metabolism that can aid in controlling body fatness.
Strength training is beneficial only for young adults.	Studies have shown that people in their 80s and 90s can benefit from resistance exercise and improve their strength and endurance. Most experts would agree that resistance exercise increases in importance with age rather than decreases.

A variety of training methods can be used to improve functional fitness.
©Monkey Business Images/Shutterstock

Many beginning resistance trainers experience soreness after the first few days of training. The reason for the soreness is that the principle of progression has been violated. Soreness can occur with even modest amounts of training if the volume of training is considerably more than normal. In the first few days or weeks of training, the primary adaptations in the muscle are due to motor learning factors rather than to muscle growth. Because these adaptations occur no matter how much weight is used, start your program slowly with light weights. After these adaptations occur and the rate of improvement slows down, the intensity and volume of training can increase to achieve proper overload.

The most common progression used in resistance training is the double progressive system, so called because this system periodically adjusts both the resistance and the number of repetitions of the exercise performed. For example, if you are training for strength, you may begin with three repetitions in one set. As the repetitions become easy, additional repetitions are added. When you have progressed to eight repetitions, increase the resistance and decrease the repetitions in each set back to three and begin the progression again.

Apply the principle of specificity to get specific results. The adaptations resulting from exercise are specific to the type and intensity of exercise performed. If you are not training for a specific task, but merely wish to develop muscle fitness for daily living, a general fitness program (or a functional fitness program) will provide good, overall benefits. However, specific training is needed if you have specific goals. Factors that can be varied in your program are the type of muscle contraction (isometric or isotonic), the speed or cadence of the movement, and the amount of resistance being moved. For example, if you want strength in the elbow extensor muscles (e.g., triceps) so that you can more easily lift heavy boxes onto a shelf, you can train using isotonic contractions, at a relatively slow speed, with a relatively high resistance. If you want muscle fitness of the fingers to grip a heavy bowling ball, much of your training should be done isometrically using the fingers the same way you normally hold the ball. If you are training for a skill that requires explosive power, such as in throwing, striking, kicking, or jumping, your strength exercises should be done with less resistance and greater speed. If you are training for a skill that uses both concentric and eccentric contractions, you should perform exercises using these characteristics (e.g., plyometrics).

Apply the principle of diminishing returns for program efficiency. To get optimal strength gains from progressive resistance training, several sets of exercise repetitions should be performed. However, research indicates that considerable fitness (and health benefits) can be achieved with a single set. The first set produces approximately 50 percent of the available gain, with successive sets yielding smaller incremental benefits. A single set is recommended for beginners, but 2 or more are recommended for most people (see Table 2). For those interested in high-level performance, extra benefits from additional sets may be worth the effort. However, for many people this may not be the case.

Apply the principle of rest and recovery to avoid overtraining. Rest is an important part of the body's adaptation to exercise. The frequency guidelines proposed in Table 2 are based on the need for rest following vigorous resistance training exercise. For most people, 3 days of resistance training provides an appropriate amount of overload and rest. If PRE is done more often than this, injuries and overtraining are more likely.

While often not appreciated, an adequate rest period between workouts ensures that there is appropriate time for cellular adaptations to occur. The repeated repetitions in a PRE workout create some minor damage to the outer layers of the contracting muscle fibers. With adequate rest, these muscle fibers rebuild and become stronger. The cycle of catabolic and anabolic processes is critical for effective adaptation to PRE. The ACSM recommends about 48 hours

Table 5 ▶ Adverse Effects of Anabolic Steroids and Steroid Analogs

On Both Males and Females:

Negative Effects on Behavior

- Hostile and aggressive behavior
- Violent behavior
- Depression and mood swings
- Sleep disturbances
- Personality changes and apathy
- Addiction

Negative Effects on the Body

- Reduced aerobic capacity
- Premature stoppage of bone growth
- Brittle connective tissue
- Increased risk of muscle/bone injury
- Immune system suppression
- Sterility

Negative Impacts on Health

- Increased cancer risk (liver)
- Increased stroke risk
- Increased heart attack risk
- Increased early death risk

Negative Effects on Appearance

- Edema (puffy face)
- Headache and fever
- Acne (face, chest, back, thighs)
- Oily skin
- Hair loss/baldness
- Nose bleeds

On Males Only:

- Testicular atrophy/impotence
- Decreased sperm count
- Breast enlargement
- Prostate enlargement
- Baldness

On Females Only:

- Menstrual irregularity
- Decreased breast size
- Deepened voice
- Uterine atrophy
- Clitoral enlargement

---

between workouts for the same muscle groups (about three workouts a week).

Advanced lifters often train more than 3 days a week, but they typically vary the muscle groups lifted to provide rest between workouts. Serious strength training athletes also employ principles of "periodization" to ensure a proper balance between training and rest. In a periodization plan, the volume and intensity of training are altered to impose different challenges while still keeping the body rested. (See the Concept on performance training.)

There are no *(safe)* shortcuts to strength development or muscle fitness. The use of **anabolic steroids** in sports has received considerable media attention, but more concerning are reports of use among high school youth and young adults. It is important to understand that they are illegal and extremely dangerous. Steroid use directly increases risk for heart disease, liver disease, and early death. It leads to a variety of negative psychological outcomes (e.g., hostility, violence, depression, mood swings, apathy, and addiction) and undesirable body changes such as hair loss, acne, breast enlargement (males), and breast reduction (females). Perhaps more salient to young adults is the fact that steroids lead to adverse sexual/reproductive effects in both males (e.g., testicular atrophy, impotence, and sterility) and females (e.g., uterine atrophy, menstrual irregularities, and sterility). Synthetic "designer" steroids, such as tetrahydrogestrinone

(THG), have the same properties (and risks) of other anabolic steroids. The serious consequences of steroid use are summarized in Table 5.

A number of other dietary supplements are on the market (either legally or illegally) to capitalize on interest in muscular development and sports performance. Contrary to popular belief, they are typically ineffective or dangerous (often both). Details on several common supplements are provided here:

- Prohormone nutritional supplements are marketed as testosterone "prohormones" because they are thought to lead to the production of testosterone and testosterone analogs. Studies have found that these compounds did not produce anabolic or ergogenic effects, and many were found to increase the risk of negative health consequences.

- Androstenedione (andro) is a precursor of naturally occurring testosterone and estrogen. Early studies suggested that andro use did not lead to increases in testosterone levels, but evidence suggests that andro has some anabolic effects at the high doses most likely used by athletes. Andro has

Anabolic Steroids Synthetic hormones similar to the male sex hormone testosterone. They function androgenically to stimulate male characteristics and anabolically to increase muscle mass, weight, bone maturation, and virility.

In the News

Warnings about Muscle-Building Supplements

Many people seek shortcuts to increased muscle strength and size. However, the supplement industry is largely unregulated, and many unsafe and ineffective products are promoted and sold both in stores and online. After receiving 86 reports of illnesses or death from supplements containing DMAA (dimethylamylamine), the Food and Drug Administration (FDA) released warnings about these muscle-building supplements. Even though the FDA warned companies that it is illegal to include DMAA in products, challenges in detection and enforcement have made it difficult to force products off the market. New products containing the related ingredient AMP-citrate have raised similar concerns. The FDA has a website for reporting "adverse events." (See link in Suggested Resources and Readings.)

Are you concerned about the dangers from unregulated supplements, or is it up to consumers to make informed choices?

been found to be associated with most of the same health risks as conventional steroids and is banned by the FDA.

- Human growth hormone (HGH) is produced by the pituitary gland but is also made synthetically. Athletes often use growth hormone in combination with anabolic steroids so they can increase bone strength (the main effect of HGH) along with muscle mass. Athletes assume this will protect them from some of the bone injuries that occur among steroid users. However, these athletes are compounding their health risks, as the use of HGH only adds to the health risks of steroid use.

- Creatine is a nutrient involved in the production of energy during short-term, high-intensity exercise, such as resistance exercise. The body produces creatine naturally from foods containing protein, but some athletes take creatine supplements to increase the amounts available in the muscle. The concept behind supplementation is that additional creatine intake enhances energy production and therefore increases the body's ability to maintain force and delay fatigue. Some studies have shown improvements in athletic performance with creatine, but reviews indicate that it may only help athletes who are already well trained. Studies have demonstrated performance-enhancing effects of creatine on muscle strength, but the benefits are due to the ability to work the muscles harder during an exercise session, not to the supplement itself. At present, creatine usage hasn't been linked to any major health problems, but the long-term effects are unknown

Guidelines for Safe and Effective PRE

Beginners should emphasize lighter weights and progress their program gradually. When beginning a resistance training program, start with light weights so that you can learn proper technique and avoid soreness and injury. Most of the adaptations that occur in the first few months of a program are due to improvements in the body's ability to recruit muscle fibers to contract effectively and efficiently. These neural adaptations occur in response to the movement itself and not the weight that is used. Therefore, beginning lifters can achieve significant benefits from lighter weights. As experience and fitness levels improve, use heavier loads and more challenging sets to continually challenge the muscles.

Use proper technique to reduce the risks for injury and to isolate the intended muscles. An important consideration in resistance exercise is to complete all lifts through the full range of motion using only the intended muscle groups. A common cause of poor technique is using too heavy of a weight. If you have to jerk the weight up or use momentum to lift the weight, it is too heavy. Using heavier weights will provide a greater stimulus to your muscles only if your muscles are actually doing the work. Therefore, it is best to use a weight that you can control safely. By lifting through the full range of motion, you increase the effectiveness of the exercise and maintain good flexibility. Some safety tips are presented in Table 6.

Perform lifts in a slow, controlled manner to enhance both effectiveness and safety. Lifting at a slow cadence provides a greater stimulus to the muscles and increases strength gains. A good recommendation is to take 2 seconds on the lifting phase (concentric) and 3 to 4 seconds on the lowering (eccentric) phase.

Provide sufficient time to rest during and between workouts. The body needs time to rest in order to allow beneficial adaptations to occur. Choose an exercise sequence that alternates muscle groups so muscles have a chance to

Table 6 ▶ How to Prevent Injury

- Warm up 10 minutes before the workout and stay warm.

- Do not hold your breath while lifting. This may cause blackout or hernia.

- Avoid hyperventilation before lifting a weight.

- Avoid dangerous or high-risk exercises.

- Progress slowly.

- Use good shoes with good traction.

- Avoid arching the back. Keep the pelvis in normal alignment.

- Keep the weight close to the body.

- Do not lift from a stoop (bent over with back rounded).

- When lifting from the floor, do not let the hips come up before the upper body.

- For bent-over rowing, lay your head on a table and bend the knees, or use one-arm rowing and support the trunk with your free hand.

- Stay in a squat as short a time as possible and do not do a full squat.

- Be sure collars on free weights are tight.

- Use a moderately slow, continuous, controlled movement and hold the final position a few seconds.

- Overload but don't overwhelm! A program that is too intense can cause injuries.

- Do not allow the weights to drop or bang.

- Do not train without medical supervision if you have a hernia, high blood pressure, a fever, an infection, recent surgery, heart disease, or back problems.

- Use chalk or a towel to keep your hands dry when handling weights.

rest before another set. Lifting every other day or alternating muscle groups (if lifting more than 3 or 4 days per week) provides rest for the muscles.

Include exercises to build muscle fitness of all muscle groups. A common mistake made by many beginning lifters is to perform only a few different exercises or to emphasize a few body parts. Training the biceps without working the triceps, for example, can lead to muscle imbalances that can compromise flexibility and increase risks for injury. In some cases, training must be increased in certain areas to compensate for stronger antagonist muscle groups. Many sprinters, for example, pull their hamstrings because the

quadriceps are so overdeveloped that they overpower the hamstrings. The recommended ratio of quadriceps to hamstring strength is 60:40.

Customize your training program to fit your specific needs. Athletes should train muscles the way they will be used in their skill, using similar patterns, range of motion, and speed (the principle of specificity). If you wish to develop a particular group of muscles, remember that the muscle group can be worked harder when isolated than when worked in combination with other muscle groups. However, a good guideline is to choose exercises that build muscle fitness in the major muscle groups of the body. There are many options of exercises but recommended ones for the major muscle groups are provided in the resource section at the end of the Concept. Table 7 provides eight basic exercises for free weights. Table 8 presents eight basic exercises for resistance machines. For additional options in resistance training, see the eight calisthenic exercises in Table 9 and the eight core strength exercises in Table 10. Since good muscular fitness in the abdominals is important, it is recommended that some abdominal or core training be performed as part of any program.

Using Self-Management Skills

Preparing a muscle fitness exercise plan requires the use of multiple self-management skills. You can use the six steps in program planning outlined in the Concept on self-management to prepare a muscle fitness exercise plan. Preparing a plan requires the use of a variety of self-management skills including self-assessment, goal setting, and self-monitoring. Preparing a plan also helps you manage your time—an important self-management skill. Lack of time is a common reason for not exercising. Preparing a plan helps you fit your activity into your daily schedule.

Practicing self-assessments for muscle fitness can help you determine your strengths and weaknesses. Self-assessment is a critical skill in resistance exercise. Experienced lifters develop a good sense of the appropriate weight for different exercises as well as a sense of when to change the load or the repetitions to fit their training. However, this skill results from careful monitoring and periodic self-assessments of strength and endurance in certain key exercises. The assessments in Lab 10A and Lab 10B allow you to try several different field tests of muscle fitness. Trying all of the tests will help you make an informed choice about which tests will be most useful to you in the future. Trying several self-assessments will also allow you to prepare make a more comprehensive assessment of your current levels of strength, muscular endurance, and power.

Strategies for Action: Lab Information

An important step in taking action for developing and maintaining muscle fitness is assessing your current status. A 1RM test of isotonic strength is described in the Lab Resource Materials. This test allows you to determine absolute and relative strength for the arms and legs. In addition, the 1RM values can be used to help you select the appropriate resistance for your muscle fitness training program. A grip strength test of isometric strength is also provided in the Lab Resource Materias for Lab 10A.

Three tests of muscular endurance and two tests of power are described in the Lab Resource Materials for Lab 10B. It is recommended that you perform the assessments for strength, muscular endurance, and power before you begin your progressive resistance training program. Periodically reevaluate your muscle fitness using these assessments.

Keeping records of progress will help you adhere to a PRE program. Labs 10C and 10D provide activity logging sheets to help you keep records of your progress as you regularly perform PRE to build and maintain good muscle fitness. (A guide to the major muscle groups is presented in the Lab Resource Materials.)

Suggested Resources and Readings

The websites for the following sources can be accessed by searching online for the organization, program, or title listed. Specific scientific references are available at the end of this edition of *Concepts of Fitness and Wellness*.

- ACE Fitness. Reality Check. Are Planks Really the Best Core Exercise? (online article).
- Alvar, B. A, Sell, K., & Deuster, P. A. (2017). *NSCA's Essentials of Tactical Strength and Conditioning.* Champaign, IL: Human Kinetics.
- American College of Sports Medicine. Progression Models for Resistance Training in Healthy Adults (position statement; pdf).
- American College of Sports Medicine. (2018). *ACSM's Guidelines for Exercise Prescription and Testing.* Philadelphia: Wolters Kluwer. Chapter 6, pp. 147–161.
- American College of Sports Medicine. Brochure series: Resistance Training for Health and Fitness (pdf).
- McGuigan, M. (2017). *Developing Power.* Champaign, IL: Human Kinetics.
- NSCA. (2016). *Exercise Technique Manual for Resistance Training* (3rd ed.). Champaign, IL: Human Kinetics.
- Thera-band Academy. Exercises with Theraband (online tool).
- U.S. Food and Drug Administration. MedWatch: The FDA Safety Information and Adverse Event Report Program.
- Westcott, W., & Baechle, T. (2015). *Strength Training Past 50* (3rd ed.). Champaign, IL: Human Kinetics.

Lab Resource Materials: Muscles of the Body (anterior view)

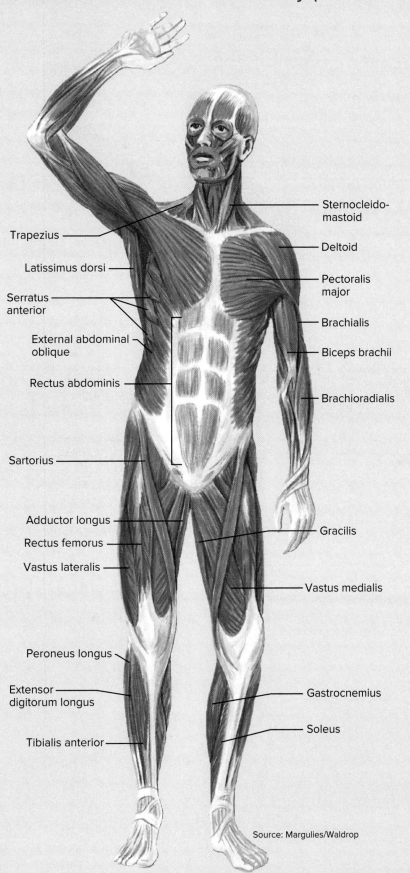

Trapezius

Latissimus dorsi

Serratus anterior

External abdominal oblique

Rectus abdominis

Sartorius

Adductor longus

Rectus femorus

Vastus lateralis

Peroneus longus

Extensor digitorum longus

Tibialis anterior

Sternocleido-mastoid

Deltoid

Pectoralis major

Brachialis

Biceps brachii

Brachioradialis

Gracilis

Vastus medialis

Gastrocnemius

Soleus

Source: Margulies/Waldrop

169

Lab Resource Materials: Muscles of the Body (posterior view)

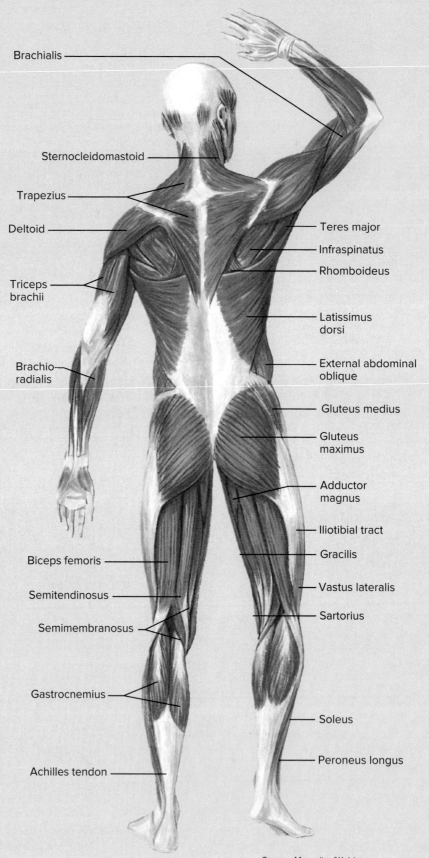

Brachialis

Sternocleidomastoid

Trapezius

Deltoid

Triceps brachii

Brachioradialis

Teres major

Infraspinatus

Rhomboideus

Latissimus dorsi

External abdominal oblique

Gluteus medius

Gluteus maximus

Adductor magnus

Iliotibial tract

Gracilis

Vastus lateralis

Sartorius

Biceps femoris

Semitendinosus

Semimembranosus

Gastrocnemius

Soleus

Peroneus longus

Achilles tendon

Source: Margulies/Waldrop

Lab Resource Materials: Muscle Fitness Tests

Evaluating Isotonic Strength: 1RM

1. Use a weight machine for the leg press and seated arm press (or bench press) for the evaluation.
2. Estimate how much weight you can lift 2 or 3 times. Be conservative; it is better to start with too little weight than too much. If you lift the weight more than 10 times, the procedure should be done again on another day when you are rested.
3. Using correct form, perform a leg press with the weight you have chosen. Perform as many times as you can up to 10.
4. Use Chart 1 to determine your 1RM for the leg press. Find the weight used in the left-hand column and then find the number of repetitions you performed across the top of the chart.
5. Your 1RM score is the value where the weight row and the repetitions column intersect.
6. Repeat this procedure for the seated arm press.
7. Record your 1RM scores for the leg press and seated arm press in the Results section.
8. Next, divide your 1RM scores by your body weight in pounds to get a "strength per pound of body weight" (str/lb/body wt.) score for each of the two exercises.
9. Finally, determine your strength rating for your upper body strength (arm press) and lower body (leg press) using Chart 2.

Chart 1 Predicted 1RM Based on Reps-to-Fatigue

Wt.	Repetitions 1	2	3	4	5	6	7	8	9	10	Wt.	Repetitions 1	2	3	4	5	6	7	8	9	10
30	30	31	32	33	34	35	36	37	38	39	170	170	175	180	185	191	197	204	211	219	227
35	35	37	38	39	40	41	42	43	44	45	175	175	180	185	191	197	203	210	217	225	233
40	40	41	42	44	46	47	49	50	51	53	180	180	185	191	196	202	209	216	223	231	240
45	45	46	48	49	51	52	54	56	58	60	185	185	190	196	202	208	215	222	230	238	247
50	50	51	53	55	56	58	60	62	64	67	190	190	195	201	207	214	221	228	236	244	253
55	55	57	58	60	62	64	66	68	71	73	195	195	201	206	213	219	226	234	242	251	260
60	60	62	64	65	67	70	72	74	77	80	200	200	206	212	218	225	232	240	248	257	267
65	65	67	69	71	73	75	78	81	84	87	205	205	211	217	224	231	238	246	254	264	273
70	70	72	74	76	79	81	84	87	90	93	210	210	216	222	229	236	244	252	261	270	280
75	75	77	79	82	84	87	90	93	96	100	215	215	221	228	235	242	250	258	267	276	287
80	80	82	85	87	90	93	96	99	103	107	220	220	226	233	240	247	255	264	273	283	293
85	85	87	90	93	96	99	102	106	109	113	225	225	231	238	245	253	261	270	279	289	300
90	90	93	95	98	101	105	108	112	116	120	230	230	237	244	251	259	267	276	286	296	307
95	95	98	101	104	107	110	114	118	122	127	235	235	242	249	256	264	273	282	292	302	313
100	100	103	106	109	112	116	120	124	129	133	240	240	247	254	262	270	279	288	298	309	320
105	105	108	111	115	118	122	126	130	135	140	245	245	252	259	267	276	285	294	304	315	327
110	110	113	116	120	124	128	132	137	141	147	250	250	257	265	273	281	290	300	310	321	333
115	115	118	122	125	129	134	138	143	148	153	255	256	262	270	278	287	296	306	317	328	340
120	120	123	127	131	135	139	144	149	154	160	260	260	267	275	284	292	302	312	323	334	347
125	125	129	132	136	141	145	150	155	161	167	265	265	273	281	289	298	308	318	329	341	353
130	130	134	138	142	146	151	156	161	167	173	270	270	278	286	295	304	314	324	335	347	360
135	135	139	143	147	152	157	162	168	174	180	275	275	283	291	300	309	319	330	341	354	367
140	140	144	148	153	157	163	168	174	180	187	280	280	288	296	305	315	325	336	348	360	373
145	145	149	154	158	163	168	174	180	186	193	285	285	293	302	311	321	331	342	354	366	380
150	150	154	159	164	169	174	180	186	193	200	290	290	298	307	316	326	337	348	360	373	387
155	155	159	164	169	174	180	186	192	199	207	295	295	303	312	322	332	343	354	366	379	393
160	160	165	169	175	180	186	192	199	206	213	300	300	309	318	327	337	348	360	372	386	400
165	165	170	175	180	186	192	198	205	212	220	305	305	314	323	333	343	354	366	379	392	407

Source: JOPERD.

Chart 2 Fitness Classification for Relative Strength in Men and Women (1RM/Body Weight)

Age:	Leg Press			Arm Press		
	30 or Less	31–50	51+	30 or Less	31–50	51+
Ratings for Men						
High-performance zone	2.06+	1.81+	1.61+	1.26+	1.01+	.86+
Good fitness zone	1.96–2.05	1.66–1.80	1.51–1.60	1.11–1.25	.91–1.00	.76–.85
Marginal fitness zone	1.76–1.95	1.51–1.65	1.41–1.50	.96–1.10	.86–.90	.66–.75
Low fitness zone	1.75 or less	1.50 or less	1.40 or less	.95 or less	.85 or less	.65 or less
Ratings for Women						
High-performance zone	1.61+	1.36+	1.16+	.76+	.61+	.51+
Good fitness zone	1.46–1.60	1.21–1.35	1.06–1.15	.66–.75	.56–.60	.46–.50
Marginal fitness zone	1.31–1.45	1.11–1.20	.96–1.05	.56–.65	.51–.55	.41–.45
Low fitness zone	1.30 or less	1.10 or less	.95 or less	.55 or less	.50 or less	.40 or less

Evaluating Isometric Strength

Test: Grip Strength

Adjust a hand dynamometer to fit your hand size. Squeeze it as hard as possible. You may bend or straighten the arm, but do not touch the body with your hand, elbow, or arm. Perform with both right and left hands. *Note:* When not being tested, perform the basic eight isometric strength exercises, or squeeze and indent a new tennis ball (after completing the dynamometer test).

©Charles B. Corbin

Evaluating Muscular Endurance

Test: Curl-Up (Dynamic)

Sit on a mat or carpet with your legs bent more than 90 degrees so your feet remain flat on the floor (about halfway between 90 degrees and straight). Make two tape marks 4½ inches apart or lay a 4½-inch strip of paper on the floor. Lie with your arms extended at your sides, palms down and the fingers extended so that your fingertips touch one tape mark (or one side of the paper strip). Keeping your heels in contact with the floor, curl the head and shoulders forward until your fingers reach 4½ inches (second piece of tape or other side of strip). Lower slowly to beginning position. Repeat one curl-up every 3 seconds. Continue until you are unable to keep the pace of one curl-up every 3 seconds. Two partners may be helpful. One stands on the paper strip (to prevent movement); the second ensures that the head returns to the floor after each repetition.

Test: Ninety-Degree Push-Up (Dynamic)
Support the body in a push-up position from the toes. The hands should be just outside the shoulders, the back and legs straight, and toes tucked under. Lower the body until the upper arm is parallel to the floor or the elbow is bent at 90 degrees. The rhythm should be approximately 1 push-up every 3 seconds. Repeat as many times as possible up to 35.

Test: Flexed-Arm Support (Static)
Women: Support the body in a push-up position from the knees. The hands should be outside the shoulders, the back and legs straight. Lower the body until the upper arm is parallel to the floor or the elbow is flexed at 90 degrees.
Men: Use the same procedure as for women except support the push-up position from the toes instead of the knees. (Same position as for 90-degree push-up.) Hold the 90-degree position as long as possible, up to 35 seconds.

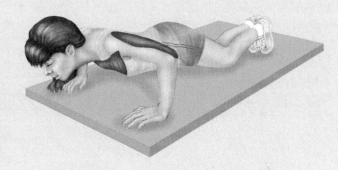

Evaluating Power

Test: Vertical Jump
Hold a piece of chalk so that its end is even with your fingertips. Stand with both feet on the floor and your side to the wall; reach and mark as high as possible. Mark the height of your standing reach with the chalk. Jump upward with both feet as high as possible. Swing arms upward and make a chalk mark on the wall at the peak of your jump. Measure the distance between the reaching height and the jumping height. Your score is the best of three jumps. *Note:* You may use a vertical jump measuring device if available.

Test: Medicine Ball Throw
Place a sturdy chair against a wall. Sit with your back firmly against the back of the chair. Hold a 14-pound medicine ball against your chest with both hands. Keeping your back against the chair, throw (push) the ball as far as possible. Your score is the distance from the spot where the ball landed (nearest edge of ball landing) to the wall.

Chart 3 Isometric Strength Rating Scale (Pounds)

Classification	Left Grip	Right Grip	Total Score
Ratings for Men			
High-performance zone	125+	135+	260+
Good fitness zone	100–124	110–134	210–259
Marginal fitness zone	90–99	95–109	185–209
Low fitness zone	<90	<95	<185
Ratings for Women			
High-performance zone	75+	85+	160+
Good fitness zone	60–74	70–84	130–159
Marginal fitness zone	45–59	50–69	95–129
Low fitness zone	<45	<50	<95

Note: Suitable for use by young adults between 18 and 30 years of age. After 30, an adjustment of .5 to 1 percent per year is appropriate because some loss of muscle tissue typically occurs as you grow older.

Chart 4 Isometric Strength Rating Scale (Pounds)

Age:	17–26		27–39		40–49		50–59		60+	
Classification	Curl-Ups	Push-Ups	Curl-Ups	Push-Ups	Curl-Ups	Push-Ups	Curl-Ups	Push-Ups	Curl-Ups	Push-Ups
Ratings for Men										
High-performance zone	35+	29+	34+	27+	33+	26+	32+	24+	31+	22+
Good fitness zone	24–34	20–28	23–33	18–26	22–32	17–25	21–31	15–23	20–30	13–21
Marginal fitness zone	15–23	16–19	14–22	15–17	13–21	14–16	12–20	12–14	11–19	10–12
Low fitness zone	<15	<16	<14	<15	<13	<14	<12	<12	<11	<10
Ratings for Women										
High-performance zone	25+	17+	24+	16+	23+	15+	22+	14+	21+	13+
Good fitness zone	18–24	12–16	17–23	11–15	16–22	10–14	15–21	9–13	14–20	8–12
Marginal fitness zone	10–17	8–11	9–16	7–10	8–15	6–9	7–14	5–8	6–13	4–7
Low fitness zone	<10	<8	<9	<7	<8	<6	<7	<5	<6	<4

Chart 5 Rating Scale for Static Endurance (Flexed-Arm Support)

Classification	Score in Seconds
High-performance zone	30+
Good fitness zone	20–29
Marginal fitness zone	10–19
Low fitness zone	<10

Chart 6 Rating Scale for Power

Classification	Vertical Jump (inches)		Medicine Ball Throw (inches)	
	Men	Women	Men	Women
High-performance zone	25½+	23½+	186+	121+
Good fitness zone	16½–25	14½–23	171–185	111–120
Marginal fitness zone	12½–16	10½–14	156–170	101–110
Low fitness zone	12 or less	10 or less	155 or less	100 or less

Note: Metric conversions are in Appendix A.

1. Bench Press

This exercise develops the chest (pectoral) and triceps muscles. Lie supine on bench with knees bent and feet flat on bench or flat on floor in stride position. Grasp bar at shoulder level. Push bar up until arms are straight. Return and repeat. Do not arch lower back. *Note:* Feet may be placed on floor if lower back can be kept flattened. Do not put feet on the bench if it is unstable.

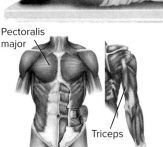

Pectoralis major

Triceps

3. Biceps Curl

This exercise develops the muscles of the upper front part of the arms (biceps). Stand erect with back against a wall, palms forward, bar touching thighs. Spread feet in comfortable position. Tighten abdominals and back muscles. Do not lock knees. Move bar to chin, keeping body straight and elbows near the sides. Lower bar to original position. Do not allow back to arch. Repeat. Spotters are usually not needed. *Variations:* Use dumbbell and sit on end of bench with feet in stride position; work one arm at a time. Or use dumbbell with the palm down or thumb up to emphasize other muscles.

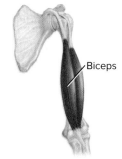

Biceps

2. Overhead (Military) Press

This exercise develops the muscles of the shoulders and arms. Sit erect, bend elbows, palms facing forward at chest level with hands spread (slightly more than shoulder width). Have bar touching chest; spread feet (comfortable distance). Tighten your abdominal and back muscles. Move bar to overhead position (arms straight). Lower bar to chest position. Repeat. *Caution:* Keep arms perpendicular and do not allow weight to move backward or wrists to bend backward. Spotters are needed.

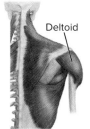

Deltoid

4. Triceps Curl

This exercise develops the muscles on the back of the upper arms (triceps). Sit erect, elbows and palms facing up, bar resting behind neck on shoulders, hands near center of bar, feet spread. Tighten abdominal and back muscles. Keep upper arms stationary. Raise weight overhead, return bar to original position. Repeat. Spotters are needed. *Variation:* Substitute dumbbells (one in each hand, or one held in both hands, or one in one hand at a time).

Triceps

Table 7

Table 7   The Basic Eight for Free Weights

5. Wrist Curl

This exercise develops the muscles of the fingers, wrist, and forearms. Sit astride a bench with the back of one forearm on the bench, wrist and hand hanging over the edge. Hold a dumbbell in the fingers of that hand with the palm facing forward. To develop the flexors, lift the weight by curling the fingers then the wrist through a full range of motion. Slowly lower and repeat. To strengthen the extensors, start with the palm down. Lift the weight by extending the wrist through a full range of motion. Slowly lower and repeat. *Variation:* Both wrists may be exercised at the same time by substituting a barbell in place of the dumbbell.

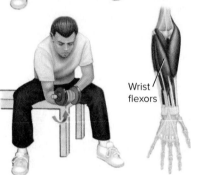

Wrist flexors

6. Dumbbell Rowing

This exercise develops the muscles of the upper back. It is best performed with the aid of a bench or chair for support. Grab a dumbbell with one hand and place opposite hand on the bench to support the trunk. Slowly lift the weight up until the elbow is parallel with the back. Lower the weight and repeat to complete the set. Switch hands and repeat with the opposite arm. *Variation:* The exercise can also be performed with one leg kneeling on the bench.

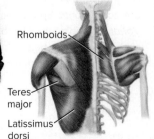

Rhomboids

Teres major

Latissimus dorsi

7. Half Squat

This exercise develops the muscles of the thighs and buttocks. Stand erect, feet shoulder-width apart and turned out 45 degrees. Rest bar behind neck on shoulders. Spread hands in a comfortable position. Begin squat by first moving hips backward, keeping back straight, eyes ahead. By moving first at the hips and then bending knees, shins will remain vertical. Bend knees to approximately 90 degrees. Pause; then stand. Repeat. Spotters are needed. *Variation:* Substitute dumbbell in each hand at sides.

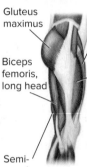

Gluteus maximus

Biceps femoris, long head

Rectus femoris

Vastus lateralis

Semi-membranosus

8. Lunge

This exercise develops the thigh and gluteal muscles. Place a barbell (with or without weight) behind your head and support with hands placed slightly wider than shoulder-width apart. In a slow and controlled motion, take a step forward and allow the leading leg to drop so that it is nearly parallel with the ground. The lower part of the leg should be nearly vertical and the back should be maintained in an upright posture. Take stride with opposite leg to return to standing posture. Repeat with other leg, remaining stationary or moving slowly in a straight line with alternating steps.

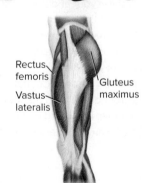

Rectus femoris

Gluteus maximus

Vastus lateralis

The Basic Eight for Resistance Machine Exercises   Table 8

Table 8

connect
VIDEO 7

1. Chest Press

This exercise develops the chest (pectoral) and tricep muscles. Position seat height so that arm handles are directly in front of chest. Position backrest so that hands are at a comfortable distance away from the chest. Push handles forward to full extension and return to starting position in a slow and controlled manner. Repeat. *Note:* Machine may have a foot lever to help position, raise, and lower the weight.

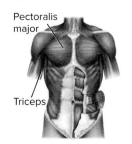

Pectoralis major

Triceps

3. Biceps Curl

This exercise develops the elbow flexor muscles on the front of the arm, primarily the biceps. Adjust seat height so that arms are fully supported by pad when extended. Grasp handles palms up. While keeping the back straight, flex the elbow through the full range of motion.

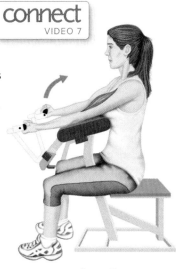

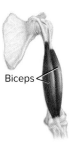

Biceps

2. Overhead Press

This exercise develops the muscles of the shoulders and arms. Position seat so that arm handles are slightly above shoulder height. Grasp handles with palms facing away and push lever up until arms are fully extended. Return to starting position and repeat. *Note:* Some machines may have an incline press.

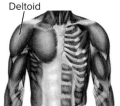

Deltoid

4. Triceps Press

This exercise develops the extensor muscles on the back of the arm, primarily the triceps. Adjust seat height so that arm handles are slightly above shoulder height. Grasp handles with thumbs toward body. While keeping the back straight, extend arms fully until wrist contacts the support pad (arms straight). Return to starting position and repeat.

Triceps

Table 8   The Basic Eight for Resistance Machine Exercises

Table 8

5. Lat Pull-Down

This exercise primarily develops the latissimus dorsi, but the biceps, chest, and other back muscles may also be developed. Sit on the floor. Adjust seat height so that hands can just grasp bar when arms are fully extended. Grasp bar with palms facing away from you and hands shoulder-width (or wider) apart. Pull bar down to chest and return. Repeat.

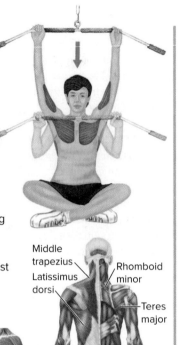

Middle trapezius
Latissimus dorsi
Rhomboid minor
Teres major
Pectoralis major

7. Knee Extension

This exercise develops the thigh (quadriceps) muscles. Sit on end of bench with ankles hooked under padded bar. Grasp edge of table. Extend knees. Return and repeat. *Alternative:* Leg press (similar to half squat). *Note:* The knee extension exercise isolates the quadriceps but places greater stress on the structures of the knee than the leg press or half squat.

Quadriceps

6. Seated Rowing

This exercise develops the muscles of the back and shoulder. Adjust the machine so that arms are almost fully extended and parallel to the ground. Grasp handgrip with palms turned down and hands shoulder-width apart. While keeping the back straight, pull levers straight back to chest. Slowly return to starting position and repeat.

Rhomboid minor
Trapezius
Teres major
Latissimus dorsi

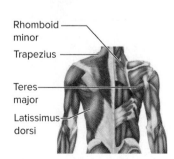

8. Hamstring Curl

This exercise develops the hamstrings (muscles on back of thigh) and other knee flexors. Sit on bench with legs over padded bar, pads contracting lower leg or calf just above the ankles. Grasp handles or edge of seat. Bend knees as far as possible. Return slowly and repeat.

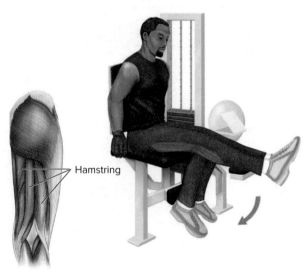

Hamstring

The Basic Eight for Calisthenics   Table 9

Table 9

1. Push-Ups

This exercise develops the muscles of the arms, shoulders, and chest. Lie on the floor, face down with hands under shoulders. Keep body straight from the knees to the top of the head. Push up until the arms are straight. Slowly lower chest to floor. Repeat. *Variation:* If this exercise is too difficult, modify by performing on bent knees.

Variation: Start from the up position and lower until the arm is bent at 90 degrees; then push up until arms are extended. *Caution:* Do not arch back.

Pectoralis minor
Pectoralis major
Triceps brachii

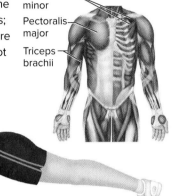

2. Modified Pull-Ups

This exercise develops the muscles of the arms and shoulders. Hang (palms forward and shoulder-width apart) from a low bar (may be placed across two chairs), heels on floor, with the body straight from feet to head. Bracing the feet against a partner or fixed object is helpful. Pull up, keeping the body straight; touch the chest to the bar; then lower to the starting position. Repeat. *Note:* This exercise becomes more difficult as the angle of the body approaches horizontal and easier as it approaches the vertical. *Variations:* Perform so that the feet do not touch the floor (full pull-up). Or, perform with palms turned up. When palms are turned away from the face, pull-ups tend to use all the elbow flexors. With palms facing the body, the biceps are emphasized more.

Trapezius
Rhomboids
Deltoid
Teres major
Latissimus dorsi

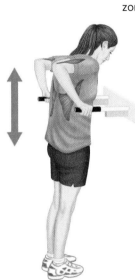

3. Dips

This exercise develops the deltoid, latissimus, rhomboid, and tricep. Start in a fully extended position with hands grasping the bar (palms facing in). Slowly drop down until the upper part of the arm is horizontal or parallel with the floor. Extend the arms back up to the starting position and repeat. *Note:* Many gyms have a dip/pull-up machine with accommodating resistance that provides a variable amount of assistance to help you complete the exercise.

connect
VIDEO 7

Rhomboid major
Deltoid
Triceps
Latissimus dorsi

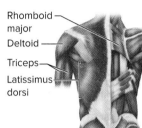

4. Crunch (Curl-Up)

This exercise develops the upper abdominal muscles. Lie on the floor with the knees bent and the arms extended or crossed with hands on shoulders or palms on ears. If desired, legs may rest on bench to increase difficulty. For less resistance, place hands at side of body (do not put hands behind head or neck). For more resistance, move hands higher. Curl up until the shoulder blades leave floor; then roll down to the starting position. Repeat. *Note:* Twisting the trunk on the curl-up develops the oblique abdominals.

Internal abdominal oblique
External abdominal oblique
Rectus abdominis

Table 9

Table 9   The Basic Eight for Calisthenics

5. Trunk Lift

This exercise develops the muscles of the upper back and corrects round shoulders. Lie face down with hands clasped behind the neck. Pull the shoulder blades together, raising the elbows off the floor. Slowly raise the head and chest off the floor by arching the upper back. Return to the starting position; repeat. For less resistance, hands may be placed under thighs. *Caution:* Do not arch the lower back. Lift only until the sternum (breastbone) clears the floor. *Variations:* Arms down at sides (easiest), hands by head, arms extended (hardest).

Back extensors

7. Step-Ups

This exercise develops the muscles of the thighs and buttocks. Stand facing an 8- to 15-inch-high box or stair. Step up, straightening knee. Keep back straight. Slowly lower opposite foot back to the floor by bending the knee. Repeat. *Variation:* Hold onto dumbbells for greater resistance.

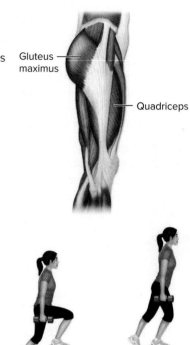

Gluteus maximus

Quadriceps

6. Side Leg Raises

These exercises develop the muscles of the outer and inner thigh. Lie on your side. With knee pointing forward, slowly raise and lower the top leg. Next, bend the top leg and cross it in front of bottom leg for support. Raise and lower the bottom leg. *Variation:* Ankle weights may be added for greater resistance.

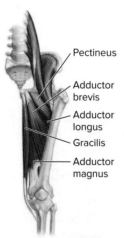

Pectineus

Adductor brevis

Adductor longus

Gracilis

Adductor magnus

Gluteus medius

Tensor fasciae latae

8. Lunge Walk

This exercise develops the muscles of the legs and hips. Stand tall, feet together. Take a step forward with the right foot, touching the left knee to the floor. The knees should be bent only to a 90-degree angle. Rise and step forward with the opposite leg, repeating. *Variation:* Dumbbells may be held in the hands for greater resistance.

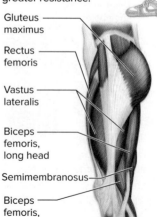

Gluteus maximus

Rectus femoris

Vastus lateralis

Biceps femoris, long head

Semimembranosus

Biceps femoris, short head

Table 10

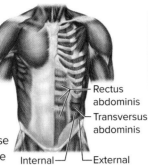 **Exercises for Abdominal Muscle Fitness**   Table 10

1. Crunch

This exercise develops the upper abdominal muscles. Lie on the floor with the knees bent and the arms extended or crossed with hands on shoulders or palms on ears. If desired, legs may rest on bench to increase difficulty. For less resistance, place hands at side of body (do not put hands behind neck). For more resistance, move hands higher. Curl up until shoulder blades leave floor; then roll down to the starting position. Repeat. *Note:* Twisting the trunk on the curl-up develops the oblique abdominals.

Rectus abdominis

Transversus abdominis

Internal oblique (cut)

External oblique (cut)

2. Reverse Curl

This exercise develops the lower abdominal muscles. Lie on the floor. Bend the knees, place the feet flat on the floor, and place arms at sides. Lift the knees to the chest, raising the hips off the floor. Do not let the knees go past the shoulders. Return to the starting position. Repeat.

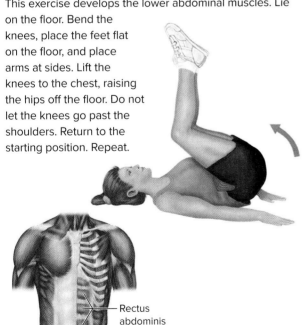

Rectus abdominis

3. Crunch with Twist (on Bench)

This exercise strengthens the oblique abdominals and helps prevent or correct lumbar lordosis, abdominal ptosis, and backache. Lie on your back with your feet on a bench, knees bent at 90 degrees. Arms may be extended or on shoulders or hand on ears (the most difficult). Same as crunch except twist the upper trunk so the right shoulder is higher than the left. Reach toward the left knee with the right elbow. Hold. Return and repeat to the opposite side.

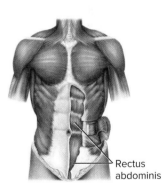

Internal oblique

External oblique

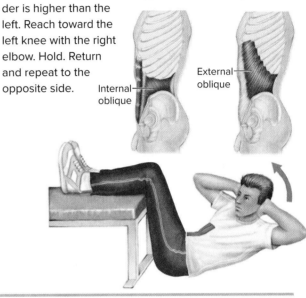

4. Sitting Tucks

This exercise strengthens the lower abdominals, increases their endurance, improves posture, and prevents backache. (This is an advanced exercise and is not recommended for people who have back pain.) Sit on floor with feet raised, arms extended for balance. Alternately bend and extend legs without letting back or feet touch floor.

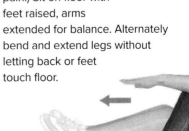

Rectus abdominis

Table 11 Exercises for Trunk Muscle Fitness

Table 11

1. Dynamic Trunk Exercises

(a) Forward curl-up

(b) Curl-up with rotation

(c) Lateral trunk raise

(d) Trunk extension raise

These exercises strengthen the abdominal and back muscles by moving the trunk through a small arc of motion: *(a)* The *forward curl-up* targets the rectus abdominis. Sit on large ball with hands crossed over chest. Recline backward to the point where feet just begin to lose grip on floor. Curl forward. Repeat. *(b)* The *curl-up with rotation* targets the oblique abdominal muscles. Begin with fingertips by ears and trunk reclined approximately 45 degrees. Curl forward with rotation by drawing one shoulder toward opposite knee. Recline back. Curl forward again, rotating trunk in the opposite diagonal. Repeat. *(c)* The *lateral trunk raise* also targets the oblique muscles. Lie side-bent over ball with fingertips by ears. Straighten spine by raising head and shoulders upward. Repeat. *(d)* The *trunk extension raise* targets the back extensor muscles. Lie flexed on stomach over ball with fingertips by ears. Straighten spine by raising head and chest upward, away from ball. Repeat.

Lab 10A Evaluating Muscle Strength: 1RM and Grip Strength

Name	**Section**	**Date**

Purpose: To evaluate your muscle strength using 1RM and to determine the best amount of resistance to use for various strength exercises.

Procedures: 1RM is the maximum amount of resistance you can lift for a specific exercise. Testing yourself to determine how much you can lift only one time using traditional methods can be fatiguing and even dangerous. The procedure you will perform here allows you to estimate 1RM based on the number of times you can lift a weight that is less than 1RM.

Evaluating Strength Using Estimated 1RM

1. Use a resistance machine for the leg press and arm or bench press for the evaluation part of this lab.
2. Estimate how much weight you can lift two or three times. Be conservative; it is better to start with too little weight than too much. If you lift a weight more than 10 times, the procedure should be done again on another day when you are rested.
3. Using correct form, perform a leg press with the weight you have chosen. Perform as many times as you can up to 10.
4. Use Chart 1 in Lab Resource Materials to determine your 1RM for the leg press. Find the weight used in the left-hand column and then find the number of repetitions you performed across the top of the chart.
5. Your 1RM score is the value where the weight row and the repetitions column intersect.
6. Repeat this procedure for the arm or bench press using the same technique.
7. Record your 1RM scores for the leg press and bench press in the Results section.
8. Next divide your 1RM scores by your body weight in pounds to get a "strength per pound of body weight" (1RM/body weight) score for each of the two exercises.
9. Determine your strength rating for your upper body strength (arm press) and lower body (leg press) using Chart 2 in Lab Resource Materials. Record in the Results section. If time allows, assess 1RM for other exercises you choose to perform (see Lab 10C).
10. If a grip dynamometer is available, determine your right-hand and left-hand grip strength using the procedures in Lab Resource Materials. Use Chart 3 in Lab Resource Materials to rate your grip (isometric).

Results

Arm press: Wt. selected [   ]   Reps [   ]   Estimated 1RM [   ]
(or bench press)   (Chart 1, *Lab Resource Materials, page* 171)

Strength per lb body weight [   ]   Rating [   ]
(1RM ÷ body weight)   (Chart 2, *Lab Resource Materials, page* 172)

Leg press: Wt. selected [   ]   Reps [   ]   Estimated 1RM [   ]
                                                   (Chart 1, *Lab Resource Materials, page* 171)

Strength per lb body weight [   ]   Rating [   ]
(1RM ÷ body weight)   (Chart 2, *Lab Resource Materials, page* 172)

Grip strength: Right grip score [   ]   Right grip rating [   ]

Left grip score [   ]   Left grip rating [   ]

Total score [   ]   Total rating [   ]

(Chart 3, *Lab Resource Materials, page* 174)

Seated Press (Arm Press)

This test can be performed using a seated press (see below) or using a bench press machine. When using the seated press, position the seat height so that arm handles are directly in front of the chest. Position backrest so that hands are at comfortable distance away from the chest. Push handles forward to full extension and return to starting position in a slow and controlled manner. Repeat. *Note:* Machine may have a foot lever to help position, raise, and lower the weight.

Leg Press

To perform this test, use a leg press machine. Typically, the beginning position is with the knees bent at right angles with the feet placed on the press machine pedals or a foot platform. Extend the legs and return to beginning position. Do not lock the knees when the legs are straightened. Typically, handles are provided. Grasp the handles with the hands when performing this test.

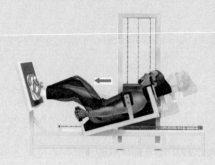

Conclusions and Implications: In several sentences, discuss your current strength, whether you believe it is adequate for good health, and whether you think that your "strength per pound of body weight" scores are representative of your true strength.

Lab 10B Evaluating Muscular Endurance and Power

Name	**Section**	**Date**

Purpose: To evaluate dynamic muscular endurance, static muscular endurance, and power.

Procedures

1. Perform the curl-up, push-up, flexed-arm support, vertical jump, and medicine ball throw tests described in the Lab Resource Materials.
2. Record your test scores in the Results section. Determine and record your rating in Chart 1 on the next page, based on Charts 4, 5, and 6 in the Lab Resource Materials.

1. Curl-up (dynamic muscular endurance)

2. Ninety-degree push-up (dynamic muscular endurance)

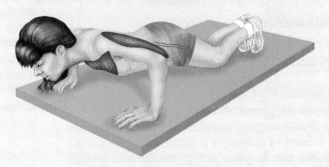

3. Flexed-arm support (static muscular endurance): women in knee position and men in full support position

4. Vertical jump (power)

5. Medicine ball throw (power)

Results

Record your scores below.

Curl-up [   ]   Push-up [   ]   Flexed-arm support (seconds) [   ]

Vertical jump [   ]   Medicine ball throw [   ]

Check your ratings in Chart 1 below.

Chart 1 Rating Scale

	Curl-Up	Push-Up	Flexed-Arm Support	Vertical Jump	Medicine Ball Throw
High	◯	◯	◯	◯	◯
Good	◯	◯	◯	◯	◯
Marginal	◯	◯	◯	◯	◯
Poor	◯	◯	◯	◯	◯

Conclusions and Implications: In several sentences, discuss your current levels of muscular endurance and power. Indicate whether you think you are fit enough to meet your health, work, and leisure-time needs.

Lab 10C Planning and Logging Muscle Fitness Exercises: Free Weights or Resistance Machines

Name		Section	Date

Purpose: To set lifestyle goals for muscle fitness exercise, to prepare a muscle fitness exercise plan, and to self-monitor progress for the 1- to 2-week plan.

Procedures

1. Using Chart 1 below, provide some background information about your experience with resistance exercise, your goals, and your plans for incorporating these exercises into your normal exercise routine.
2. Using Chart 2, select at least eight muscle fitness exercises as directed. Perform the exercises for 3 days over a 1- to 2-week period. Be sure to plan your exercise program so that it fits with the goals you described in Chart 1. If you are just starting out, it is best to start with light weights and more repetitions (e.g., 12–15). For best results, take the log with you during your workout, so that you can remember the weights, reps, and sets you performed.
3. Complete the Results section and then answer the questions in the Conclusions and Implications section.

Chart 1 Muscle Fitness Survey

1. Determine your current stage for resistance exercise. Check only the stage that represents your current activity level.

   ◯ Precontemplation. I do not meet resistance exercise guidelines and have not been thinking about starting.

   ◯ Contemplation. I do not do resistance exercises but have been thinking about starting.

   ◯ Preparation. I am planning to start doing regular resistance exercises to meet guidelines.

   ◯ Action. I do resistance exercises, but am inconsistent or have only recently started being consistent (less than 6 months).

   ◯ Maintenance. I regularly meet guidelines for resistance exercises and have been doing it for more than 6 months.

2. What are your primary goals for resistance exercise?

   ◯ General conditioning   ◯ Improved appearance   ◯ Other_____

   ◯ Sports training   ◯ Avoidance of back pain

Chart 2 Muscle Fitness Exercise Log

Check (√) the exercises you plan to perform in the first column. Choose eight exercises from free weight, machine, or a combination of the two types of exercises. Record the weight (resistance), number of reps, and number of sets you plan to perform. Perform the exercises for 3 days over a period of 1–2 weeks. Write the date (month/day) in the day column for the date you performed the exercise. You may do upper body and lower body exercises on different dates.

Exercises	Exercise Plan			Day 1 _____ (date)			Day 2 _____ (date)			Day 3 _____ (date)		
	Wt.	Reps	Sets	Wt.	Reps	Sets	Wt.	Reps	Sets	Wt.	Reps	Sets
Free Weight Exercises (Table 7, pages 175–176)												
☐ 1. Bench press												
☐ 2. Overhead (military) press												
☐ 3. Biceps curl												
☐ 4. Triceps curl												
☐ 5. Wrist curl												
☐ 6. Dumbbell rowing												
☐ 7. Half squat												
☐ 8. Lunge												
Machine Exercises (Table 8, pages 177–178)												
☐ 1. Chest press												
☐ 2. Overhead press												
☐ 3. Biceps curl												
☐ 4. Triceps press												
☐ 5. Lat pull-down												
☐ 6. Seated rowing												
☐ 7. Knee extension												
☐ 8. Hamstring curl												

Results

Were you able to do your basic eight exercises at least 2 days in the week?   Yes ◯   No ◯

Conclusions and Implications: Do you feel that you will use muscle fitness exercises as part of your regular lifetime physical activity plan, either now or in the future? In the box below, indicate what modifications you would make in your program in the future.

Lab 10D Planning and Logging Muscle Fitness Exercises: Calisthenics, Core Exercises, or Plyometrics

Name	**Section**	**Date**

Purpose: To set lifestyle goals for muscle fitness exercises that can easily be performed at home, to prepare a muscle fitness exercise plan, and to self-monitor progress for a 1-week plan.

Procedures

1. Using Chart 1 below, provide some background information about your experience with calisthenic, core exercise, or plyometrics, and your plans for incorporating these exercises into your normal exercise routine.
2. Using Chart 2, select at least eight calisthenics or core exercises as directed. Perform the exercises for 2 or 3 days. Record the reps and sets performed on each day.
3. Complete the Results section and then answer the questions in the Conclusions and Implications section.

Chart 1 Muscle Fitness Survey

1. What is your level of experience with calisthenic, core, and plyometric exercises? Check a box for each of the 3 types of exercise.

	Inexperienced	Somewhat Experienced	Very Experienced
Calisthenic Exercises	☐	☐	☐
Core Exercises	☐	☐	☐
Plyometric Exercises	☐	☐	☐

2. What are your primary reasons for doing calisthenic or core exercise?

◯ General conditioning   ◯ Improved appearance

◯ Sports training   ◯ Avoidance of back pain

Chart 2 Muscle Fitness Exercise Log

Check (√) the exercises you plan to perform in the first column. Choose eight exercises from the calisthenic, core, and plyometric sections. Record the number of reps and number of sets you plan to perform. Perform the exercises for 3 days over a period of 1–2 weeks. Write the date (month/day) in the day column for the date you performed the exercise. You may do upper body and lower body exercises on different dates.

Exercises	Exercise Plan		Day 1 _____ (date)		Day 2 _____ (date)		Day 3 _____ (date)	
	Reps	Sets	Reps	Sets	Reps	Sets	Reps	Sets
Calisthenic Exercises (Table 9, pages 179–180)								
☐ 1. Push-ups								
☐ 2. Modified pull-ups								
☐ 3. Dips								
☐ 4. Crunch (curl-up)								
☐ 5. Trunk lift								
☐ 6. Side leg raises								
☐ 7. Step-ups								
☐ 8. Lunge walk								
Abdominal and Trunk Exercises (Tables 10 and 11) (Table 10, pages 181–182)								
☐ 1. Crunch (curl-up)								
☐ 2. Reverse curl								
☐ 3. Crunch with twist (on bench)								
☐ 4. Sitting tucks								
☐ 5. Forward curl-up								
☐ 6. Curl-up with rotation								
☐ 7. Lateral trunk raise								
☐ 8. Trunk extension raise								
Plyometric Exercises (See Figure 6 for a sample of Depth Jumps, page 160)								
☐ 1. Rope jumping or hopping								
☐ 2. Medicine Ball (chest pass) Exercise								
☐ 3. Box or Depth Jumps (advanced)								

Results

Were you able to do your planned exercises at least 2 days in the week?　　　Yes ○　　No ○

Conclusions and Implications: Do you feel that you will use these muscle fitness exercises as part of your regular life-time physical activity plan, either now or in the future? Discuss the exercises you feel benefited you and the ones that did not. What modifications would you make in your program for it to work better for you?

Flexibility

LEARNING OBJECTIVES

After completing the study of this Concept, you will be able to:

▶ Identify and explain several misconceptions about flexibility.

▶ List the health benefits of flexibility and stretching.

▶ Describe the various methods of stretching and their advantages and disadvantages.

▶ Determine the amount of exercise necessary to improve flexibility, explain the FIT formulas for the different types of stretching, and describe factors in the "do and don't list for stretching."

▶ Describe a variety of flexibility-based activities for improving flexibility.

▶ Identify some of the guidelines for safe and effective stretching.

▶ Describe several self-assessments for flexibility, select the self-assessments that help you identify personal needs, and plan (and self-monitor) a personal flexibility exercise program.

gular stretching exercises promote flexibility, component of fitness that permits freedom of movement, contribute to ease and economy of muscular effort, allow for successful performance in certain activities, and provide less susceptibility to some types of injuries or musculoskeletal problems.

©Tom Grill/Corbis/Getty Images

Concept 11

Why it Matters!

Flexibility is an important component of functional fitness, but there are many misconceptions about how it contributes to health and how it can be enhanced. It is important to first understand the difference between *stretching* (the principal type of exercise used to build flexibility) and *flexibility* (a component of fitness resulting from stretching). It is also important to distinguish between stretching exercises for building flexibility as part of your workout and stretching as a warm-up. Finally, it is important to understand how much flexibility is needed (some is clearly needed to perform efficiently and effectively in daily life, but excessive flexibility is not desirable). This Concept will clarify the distinctions between flexibility and stretching and provide guidelines for safe and effective ways to include various flexibility-based activities into your program.

Factors Influencing Flexibility

The range of motion in a joint or joints is a reflection of the flexibility at that joint. Clinically, the **range of motion (ROM)** of a joint is the extent *and* direction of movement that is possible. The extent of movement is described by the arc through which a joint moves and is typically measured in degrees using a tool called a goniometer. The direction of movement at a specific joint is determined by the shapes of the bony surfaces that are in contact. Certain types of joints allow for greater movement than others. In fact, flexibility is highly joint specific. An individual may demonstrate optimal flexibility in one region of the body but not in others. For example, a person may have good enough flexibility of the spine, hips, and legs to reach down and touch their toes, but be unable to clasp both hands behind the back due to stiffness of the shoulder joints.

Medical professionals use a specific vocabulary to describe the movement of joints. Figure 1 illustrates some of these movement terms as they relate to hip, knee, or ankle motion. Similar terms are applied in describing movement of the spine and upper body. Note that the same terms (such as *flexion/extension*) can be applied to different joints, while other terms (such as *dorsiflexion/plantar flexion*) are unique to a specific joint like the ankle.

The shape, size, and orientation of a joint greatly influence the amount of motion available. The circular surface of the ball-and-socket joint of the hip, for example, allows for considerable mobility, including movement to the side (adduction and abduction), forward and backward (flexion and extension), and  in and out (internal and external rotation). The hinge joint of the knee is more restrictive and limits movement to primarily forward and backward (flexion and extension). Motion at other joints, such as the ankle, involves the combined

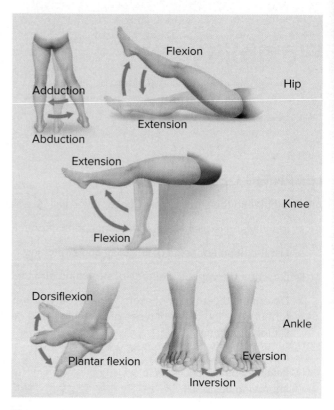

Figure 1 ▶ Ranges of joint motion.

movements of numerous bony surfaces. A hinge-type portion permits the up and down motion of the foot (dorsiflexion and plantar flexion), while a separate planar-type joint allows the side-to-side motion (inversion and eversion) of the foot. A basic understanding of this terminology is important in understanding principles of flexibility and stretching.

Flexibility is influenced by the extensibility of soft tissues such as muscles, tendons, and ligaments. Soft tissues are made up of a number of substances, including fibers called collagen and elastin. These structural building blocks influence the degree of extensibility of tissues such as **ligaments, tendons,** and muscles. Tissues with a greater proportion of collagen fibers tend to be stiffer while those with more elastin tend to bend and stretch more readily. Ligaments contain a greater proportion of collagen and this enhances their function in providing rigidity and stability to a joint and their role in restricting excessive joint motion. Damage to ligaments from repeated sprains can lead to excessive joint **laxity** and increased risk for injuries. Tendons contain a greater proportion of elastin than ligaments, but muscles contain even more and this contributes to their relatively high degree of flexibility. Together, the muscles and tendons are referred to as a **muscle-tendon unit (MTU)** and, due to their connection, they are both stretched together. However, the terms muscles or tissues will generally be used instead of MTU for ease of interpretation.

Viscoelastic properties of muscles have an influence on flexibility. The short-term gains in range of motion immediately following stretching can be attributed, in large part, to viscoelastic properties of the muscle. During a sustained stretch, the viscous (fluid-like) and elastic properties of the muscle allow it to slowly increase in length with less effort. Repeated stretching bouts promote further gains in length (creep) and reduced tension in the muscle (stretch-relaxation). These properties of creep and stretch-relaxation partially explain why a static stretch feels easier the longer it is held. However, these viscoelastic influences on flexibility are relatively short-lived, lasting from just a few seconds up to 2 hours in duration.

Viscoelasticity is also rate-dependent. Rapid, bouncing stretches tend to increase muscle tension more than a slow steady stretch, and this limits the overall extent of elongation. A slower, static stretch avoids this effect and produces more elongation of the muscle. These viscoelastic properties of muscle tissue influence guidelines about the most effective dose (frequency, intensity, time) and type of stretch used to improve flexibility. (Specific guidelines will be covered later in this Concept.)

Short-term changes in muscle flexibility differ from long-term changes. The effectiveness of a flexibility program is largely assessed by its ability to improve ROM. Significant short-term gains in ROM can be achieved by a single (acute) bout of stretching, but a regular, long-term (chronic) stretching program will lead to more sustained gains in flexibility. Research on flexibility suggests that the resulting gains in motion immediately following stretching are due as much to sensory changes in the nervous system as they are to increased muscle length or changes in muscle **stiffness.** Thus, the acute changes in flexibility that occur following a stretch are due to both the viscoelastic properties of muscles and the nervous system's regulation of **stretch tolerance.** Stretch tolerance is the nervous system's way of allowing a person to stretch further towards end range of motion with less perception of pain. Stretch tolerance varies among individuals and can be enhanced by flexibility training.

In contrast to short-term changes, the mechanisms influencing long-term changes in flexibility are considered to be more complex and are not as well understood. Long-term gains in ROM that occur after weeks of participating in a stretching program are believed to be the result of repeated cycles of increased stretch tolerance and changes in muscle length. Increased muscle length is believed to occur when sarcomeres, the building blocks of the muscle fiber, are added to the muscle fiber.

Certain types of muscles are more prone to tightness than others. A number of muscles in the body have a predictable tendency toward tightness. Clinicians refer to these muscles as "tonic" or "postural" muscles because of their tendency to tighten or shorten. Structurally, these muscles tend to be composed of a higher proportion of slow-twitch (Type I) muscle fibers, which tend to be less elastic (stiffer) than fast-twitch (Type II) fibers. Another characteristic of these postural muscles is that they tend to cross more than one joint. Examples include the upper trapezius, the muscles at the base of the skull, the pectorals, hip flexors, back extensors, hamstrings,

adductors, and calf muscles. These muscles typically benefit the most from stretching and therefore are often targeted by common stretching exercises. (Specific exercises for these muscle groups are provided at the end of this Concept.)

Static flexibility is different from dynamic flexibility. The flexibility of a joint differs under static versus dynamic conditions. Static flexibility is the maximum range a joint can achieve under stationary conditions, and it is limited by the structural (viscous and elastic) properties of the muscles. An example of static flexibility would be the amount of hamstring flexibility needed to perform the sit-and-reach test, touching fingertips to toes. Dynamic flexibility is the maximum range a joint can achieve under active conditions, and it is influenced by both structural characteristics and neural factors. Dynamic flexibility refers to the ability of the body to move during functional, real-life movements. An example of dynamic flexibility would be the amount of hamstring flexibility needed to clear a track hurdle with the lead leg during a race. Although good static flexibility is necessary for good dynamic flexibility, it does not ensure it. (Techniques for both static and dynamic stretching are discussed later in the Concept.)

Flexibility is influenced by temperature. Muscle and joint temperature directly influence flexibility with warm muscles being more flexible than cold ones. The higher temperature improves the extensibility of collagen within the joint capsules, muscles, and tendons. Heat also facilitates relaxation by altering the nervous system's response to stretch, making the body less sensitive to the stretch reflex. Thus, a warm shower or heating pad used prior to stretching can help improve flexibility. While the application of an external source of heat has the potential to improve muscle flexibility, an active warm-up is considered to be the most effective method in raising internal temperature of the muscle. In order to prepare the body for exercise or an athletic event, an active warm-up is recommended.

Some people specifically prefer to exercise in warm conditions, possibly because it helps them feel more limber. For example, weight lifters typically prefer to train in a warmer gym.

Range of Motion (ROM) The full motion possible in a joint or series of joints.

Ligaments Bands of tissue that connect bones. Unlike muscles and tendons, overstretching ligaments is not desirable.

Tendons Fibrous bands of tissue that connect muscles to bones and facilitate movement of a joint.

Laxity Motion in a joint outside the normal plane for that joint, due to loose ligaments.

Muscle-Tendon Unit (MTU) The functional union of a skeletal muscle and its associated tendon. Strengthening and stretching affect both elements of the MTU.

Stiffness Elasticity in the MTU; measured by force needed to stretch.

Stretch Tolerance Greater degree of stretch before onset of pain.

Bikram "hot" yoga programs intentionally warm the environment to help promote flexibility. During a typical Bikram yoga session, participants perform 26 poses over 90 minutes of exercise in a room with a set temperature between 95 and 100 degrees and humidity of nearly 40 percent. The hot conditions are part of this yoga form but caution is warranted to avoid overexertion, dehydration, or other heat-related illnesses.

Flexibility varies considerably across the lifespan. Flexibility is generally high in children but declines during adolescence because of the rapid changes in growth—essentially, the bones grow faster than the soft tissues, leading to tightness. In early adulthood, the muscles and tendons catch up to the skeletal system, allowing flexibility to improve (with peaks generally occurring in the mid- to late 20s). With increasing age, range of motion tends to decline, but this is due to both age-dependent (biologic) changes as well as to modifiable lifestyle factors (e.g., sedentary behavior). The intrinsic factors influencing reduced flexibility with age include a loss of elasticity and water content in soft tissues, reduced size of muscle fibers, age-related cross-linkages within the collagen fibers, and more restricted movement of joints. Over the span of their working lives, adults typically lose 3 to 4 inches of lower back and leg flexibility as measured by the common "sit-and-reach" test. Likewise, hip and shoulder ROM have been noted to decrease by approximately 6 degrees per decade in women and men aged 55–86 years old, with the most significant decline noted after age 70.

Decreased flexibility throughout the lifespan has implications for health-related quality of life. For example, reduced leg range of motion can alter gait mechanics and increase risk for falls while reduced flexibility of the spine can increase risk of neck or back pain. Reduced flexibility may also have an impact on functional independence. For instance, reduced joint ROM may adversely affect the ability to perform simple tasks such as bending over to tie shoes or reaching into an overhead cupboard. While loss of flexibility is considered to be a natural part of the aging process, research studies have confirmed that declines in flexibility can be minimized by maintaining regular patterns of physical activity. Thus, adherence to a regular stretching program is one way to somewhat offset declines in function that occur with age.

Gender differences exist in flexibility. Girls tend to be more flexible than boys at young ages, but the gender difference decreases for adults. Greater flexibility of females is generally attributed to anatomical differences (e.g., wider hips) and hormonal influences.

Genetic factors can explain some individual variability in flexibility. Joint **hypermobility** is sometimes referred to as joint laxity. The term *hypermobility* refers to joints that stretch further than normally expected because of increased elasticity in the connective tissues, including ligaments, muscles, and tendons. In some families, the trait for hypermobile joints is passed from generation to generation. Hypermobile joints are

Technology Update

Software Facilitates Stretching at Work

Millions of people have sedentary office jobs that require sitting at a desk all day, and this can be hard on both the body and the mind. Fortunately, there are now many downloadable programs that can help office workers cope with this challenge. Programs such as StretchClock.com and StretchWare.com provide prompts and suggest exercises and stretches that can reduce risks of common maladies caused by excessive sitting (e.g., carpal tunnel syndrome, repetitive stress injury, back pain, shoulder pain). These tools can help remind users to take breaks and to include short stretching breaks during the day.

Would this type of behavioral prompt help you remember to get up and move periodically? Why or why not?

one feature of inherited conditions such as Ehlers-Danlos, Down, and Marfan syndromes. Studies show that people with joint hypermobility may be more prone to injuries including joint subluxations and dislocations, leading to the development of joint pain and premature osteoarthritis.

Flexibility, Injuries, and Rehabilitation

Reduced flexibility may contribute to injuries in some individuals. Reduced flexibility has been commonly viewed as a potential cause of injuries during exercise. A number of studies have reported significant correlations between flexibility deficits and specific types of injuries. For example, reduced hip and ankle range of motion have been  associated with falling in older adults. Similarly, tight hamstring and quadriceps muscles have been associated with knee injuries in soccer players and tight calf muscles have been associated with leg injuries during basic training in army recruits. However, a number of other studies have not reported associations between injury rate and muscle tightness. Therefore, the research is not clear on this subject. While flexibility may influence risk in some cases, the leading predictors of injury risk include a previous strain, age, weakness, novice status, a rapid increase in exercise intensity, and a competitive training history.

Some experts believe that the inconsistent findings on the importance of flexibility may be due to the choices of tests used in past research. They contend that the use of tests such as dynamic movement assessments may provide better clinical utility. In support of this concept, a combination of strength, balance, dynamic, and/or static tests has been shown to be predictive of occupational injuries in football players, firefighters, and military personnel.

Excessive flexibility may contribute to injuries in some individuals with hypermobility. Hypermobility is a condition diagnosed by specific clinical findings. Those with increased ligamentous laxity are often believed to be at risk for injury through overstraining their muscles or joints. For example, studies have documented higher injuries in ballet dancers with excessive flexibility and higher risk of ankle sprains in soldiers with hypermobility disorders. Yet not all persons with excessive flexibility suffer from injuries. Despite excessive joint laxity, it appears that people can learn to control their movements and posture in order to protect joints from harm. Clearly, too little or too much flexibility can increase risk of injury, but it doesn't fully predict its occurrence.

Stretching is used to assist in injury rehabilitation and to prevent future injuries. Physical therapists and athletic trainers frequently prescribe stretching to help patients regain normal range of motion or function after injury. Stretching also helps promote healing by improving the alignment of collagen fibers. Muscle strains and ligamentous sprains are typically responsive to appropriately prescribed stretching exercise. Stretching also helps alleviate joint stiffness, a common problem following surgeries of the shoulder, knee and ankle as well as following use of casts or walking boots. In each case, gentle stretching and range of motion exercises are used to stimulate the healing process and add strength to the healing tissues. Prior to stretching, tissues are warmed up through the use of active exercise, massage techniques, or modalities such as moist heat or ultrasound. Stretching is followed by exercises to increase strength within the newly gained range of motion and neuromuscular activities to restore functional movement patterns. However, once prescribed, the effectiveness of rehabilitation is directly dependent on the willingness of the individual to perform the recommended stretching exercises on their own.

The strongest predictor of future injury is a prior history of injury so proper rehabilitation is critical. Future risks can be reduced by regularly including dynamic stretching before exercise. An advantage of dynamic stretching is that it can improve flexibility without affecting strength or power. Another strategy for reducing future risk of injury is to incorporate stretching as part of a more comprehensive program that incorporates eccentric training, strengthening, and agility training. Specific emphasis on muscle strengthening for activity-specific challenges (e.g., acceleration, deceleration, landing, and changes of direction) is recommended since these movements are associated with greater risk of injury.

Stretching can help with treatment of musculoskeletal pain. Stretching is often one component of a larger treatment plan for addressing low back and neck pain. Because it is rarely used as the sole treatment approach, it is difficult to isolate its effectiveness from other treatments commonly provided. However, stretching has been shown to be as effective as strengthening or massage in the treatment of chronic neck pain. Additionally, movement-based activities such as tai chi have been shown to facilitate movement and reduce low back pain.

Physical therapists and athletic trainers use carefully planned stretching exercise for treatment.
©Royalty-Free/Corbis

Stretching may help relieve muscle cramps and pain associated with myofascial trigger points. Many people experience some form of muscle cramping during or following exercise. A muscle spasm or cramp may result for various reasons, including overexertion, dehydration, and heat stress. Stretching can often help relieve mild cramps but severe cramps are often associated with **Myofascial trigger points.** Trigger points are characterized by taut bands within skeletal muscle that have a nodular texture. They are sensitive to touch and can produce a radiating pain in specific regions of the body when touched. Trigger points can be caused by trauma, but may occur after overuse or from prolonged spasm in the muscles. The application of direct pressure on myofascial trigger points followed by stretching has been shown to help relieve pain. However, stretching has less effect on relieving nonspecific areas of soft tissue tenderness in the body (often called tender points) or delayed onset muscle soreness.

Stretching Methods

Static stretching is the most commonly used method of stretching. Static stretching is done slowly and held for a period of several seconds. The probability of tearing the soft tissue is low if performed properly. However, stretching is recommended when the body is warm, after exercise, or as a separate routine. There is ample evidence that static stretching can have a temporary negative effect on performance in certain athletes requiring speed and power. Strength and power have been shown to decrease by 4 to 30 percent following brief stretching,

Hypermobility Looseness or slackness in the joint and of the muscles and ligaments (soft tissue) surrounding the joint.

Myofascial Trigger Points Tight bands or knots in a muscle or fascia (a sheath of connective tissue that binds muscles and other tissues together). Trigger points often refer pain to another area of the body.

Contrasting Three Methods of Stretching

I. Static Stretch

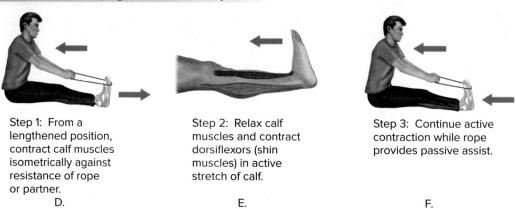

Active
A.

Passive
(Self-Assisted)
B.

Passive
(Gravity Assisted)
C.

II. Pre-Contraction Stretch (e.g., PNF Stretch)

Step 1: From a lengthened position, contract calf muscles isometrically against resistance of rope or partner.
D.

Step 2: Relax calf muscles and contract dorsiflexors (shin muscles) in active stretch of calf.
E.

Step 3: Continue active contraction while rope provides passive assist.
F.

III. Dynamic (Ballistic-type) Stretch

Active
G.

Passive
(Partner Assisted)
H.

Passive
(Gravity Assisted)
I.

Figure 2 ▶ Examples of static, pre-contraction, and dynamic stretches of the calf muscles (gastronemius and soleus). Muscles shown in dark pink are the muscles being contracted. Muscles shown in light pink are those being stretched.

with effects lasting up to an hour. For this reason, static stretching is not recommended immediately prior to athletic competitions involving power, strength, and speed activities.

Static stretches can be performed with **active assistance** or with **passive assistance.** When active assistance is used, the opposing muscle group is contracted to produce a reflex relaxation **(reciprocal inhibition)** in the muscle being stretched. This enables the muscle to be more easily stretched. For example, when doing a calf stretch exercise (see Figure 2A), the muscles on the front of the shin can be contracted to assist in the stretch of the muscles of the calf. However, a limitation of this method is that it is difficult to produce adequate overload by simply contracting the opposing muscles. With passive assistance, an outside force or gravity helps to put the muscle on stretch. In the calf stretch example, passive assistance can be provided by using the hands to pull the foot forward in a sitting stretch (Figure 2B), or with the aid of gravity in a standing stretch (Figure 2C). This type of stretch does not create the relaxation in the muscle associated with active assisted stretch. An unrelaxed muscle cannot be stretched as far, and injury may happen. Therefore, it is best to combine the active assistance with a passive assistance when performing a static stretch. This gives the advantage of a relaxed muscle and a sufficient force to provide an overload to stretch it. A good way to begin static stretching exercises is to stretch until tension is first felt, back off slightly and hold the position several seconds, and then gradually stretch a little farther, back off, and hold. Decrease the stretch slowly after the hold.

Pre-contraction stretching activities such as PNF have proven to be effective at improving flexibility. **Proprioceptive neuromuscular facilitation (PNF)** stretching utilizes techniques to stimulate muscles to contract more strongly (and relax more fully) in order to enhance the effectiveness of stretching. The contract-relax-antagonist-contract (CRAC) technique is the most popular. CRAC PNF involves three specific steps: (1) Move the limb so the muscle to be stretched (agonist) is initially elongated and then contract it isometrically (at 20%–75% maximum voluntary contraction) for several seconds (against an immovable object or the resistance of a partner); (2) relax the muscle; and (3) immediately statically stretch the muscle with the active assistance of the antagonist muscle and passive assist from a partner or gravity. Figures 2D, 2E, and 2F provide an illustration of how this technique is applied to the calf stretch. Research shows that this and other types of PNF stretch are more effective than a simple static stretch.

Dynamic stretching can be safe and effective if performed properly. There are two types of dynamic stretching: active and ballistic. *Active stretching* refers to the gradual controlled movement of body parts through a joint's normal range of motion, with the motion repeated a number of times. Stretches may involve arm or leg swings of increasing reach or increasing speed.

These types of stretches are often incorporated into the warm-up phase of many sport activities as well as functional fitness programs. Compared to static stretching, dynamic techniques have been shown to be equally effective at improving flexibility without impairing measures of athletic performance immediately following their use. The second type of dynamic stretch is *ballistic stretching*. Ballistic techniques involve rapid, alternating movements or bouncing at end range of motion. Due to their speed, they can increase muscle tension and increase the risk of muscle strain. Therefore, ballistic-type stretches are

Dynamic flexibility is important in many sports.
©RubberBall/Alamy Stock Photo

primarily used in sport-specific warm-ups rather than recommended for the general population. Examples of dynamic (ballistic-type) stretching are provided in Figures 2G, 2H, and 2I.

How Much Stretch Is Enough?

Stretching exercises are the primary way to improve flexibility. As mentioned previously, many factors influence flexibility. A factor that is in your control is regular exercise. Normal daily activities, and even other activities from the physical activity pyramid, do relatively little to develop flexibility. For this reason, it is important to perform stretching exercises from step 5 of the pyramid to build flexibility (see Figure 3).

Flexibility is joint specific, so the needed amount of flexibility varies by joint. Norms are available for the amount of flexibility for males and females of different ages, but it is not clear how much is needed for health. For example, there is little scientific evidence to indicate that a person who can reach 2 inches past his or her toes on a sit-and-reach test is less fit (or less healthy) than a person who can reach 8 inches past the toes. The standards presented in the Lab Resource Materials are based on the best available evidence.

Active Assistance An assist to stretch from an active contraction of the opposing (antagonist) muscle.

Passive Assistance Stretch imposed on a muscle with the assistance of a force other than the opposing muscle.

Reciprocal Inhibition Reflex relaxation in stretched muscle during contraction of the antagonist.

Proprioceptive Neuromuscular Facilitation (PNF) A stretching technique that incorporates muscle contraction prior to stretch.

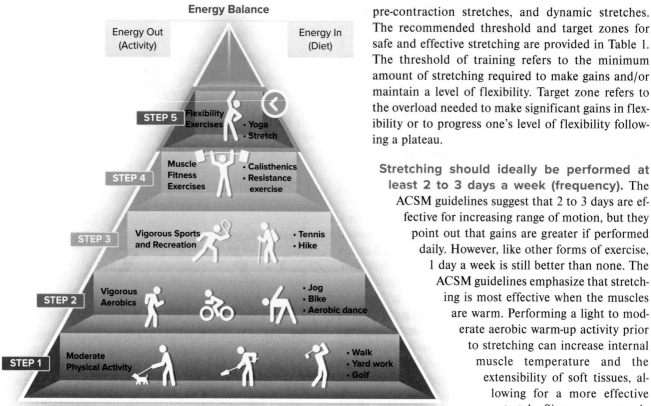

pre-contraction stretches, and dynamic stretches. The recommended threshold and target zones for safe and effective stretching are provided in Table 1. The threshold of training refers to the minimum amount of stretching required to make gains and/or maintain a level of flexibility. Target zone refers to the overload needed to make significant gains in flexibility or to progress one's level of flexibility following a plateau.

Stretching should ideally be performed at least 2 to 3 days a week (frequency). The ACSM guidelines suggest that 2 to 3 days are effective for increasing range of motion, but they point out that gains are greater if performed daily. However, like other forms of exercise, 1 day a week is still better than none. The ACSM guidelines emphasize that stretching is most effective when the muscles are warm. Performing a light to moderate aerobic warm-up activity prior to stretching can increase internal muscle temperature and the extensibility of soft tissues, allowing for a more effective stretch. Since some people do not want to interrupt their workout in the middle, they prefer to stretch at the end. Stretching at the end of the workout serves a dual purpose—building flexibility and cooling down. It is, however, appropriate to stretch at any time in the workout after the muscles have been active and are warm. If you prefer to include it at the beginning of a workout, ease into the stretching gradually after a light warm-up.

To increase the length of a muscle, stretch it more than its normal length but do not overstretch it (intensity). The best evidence suggests that muscles should be stretched to about 10 percent beyond their normal length to bring about an improvement in flexibility. A more practical indicator of the intensity of stretching is to stretch just to the point of tension or slight discomfort. A small overload stimulus is needed in order to increase flexibility. Exercises that do not cause an overload will not increase flexibility. Once adequate flexibility has been achieved, range of motion is best maintained by regular stretching to the desired point of elongation.

To increase flexibility, stretch and hold muscles for an adequate amount of time and for 2–4 repetitions (time). Guidelines suggest that to get the most benefit for the least effort, stretches should be maintained for 10 to 30 seconds and be repeated 2 to 4 times. Holding the stretch for a sustained period is important in overcoming the **stretch reflex** and to enhance the viscoelastic properties of the

Too much flexibility (hyperflexibility) in a joint may increase susceptibility to injury. While an appropriate amount of flexibility is beneficial, too much flexibility can actually compromise the integrity of the joint and make it less stable and prone to injury. Most muscles and tendons can lengthen and return to their normal length after appropriate stretching. However, short, tight muscles and tendons can be easily overstretched (i.e. strained). Even more likely to be injured are the ligaments that connect bone to bone. Ligaments and the joint capsule lack the elasticity and tensile strength of the muscles and tendons. When involuntarily overstretched, they may remain in a lengthened state or become ruptured (i.e. sprained). If this occurs multiple times, the joint loses stability and is susceptible to chronic dislocation, repeated sprains, and excessive wear and tear of the joint surface. This is particularly true of weight-bearing joints, such as the hip, knee, and ankle. Appropriate stretching techniques can increase flexibility without leading to hyperflexibility.

Specific FIT guidelines are established for safe and effective stretching. The guidelines from the American College of Sports Medicine (ACSM) indicate that stretching can be done using static stretches (active or passive),

Table 1 ▶ FIT Formula for Stretching—Thresholds and Target Zones*

	Static		Dynamic		PNF (CRAC)	
	Threshold	**Target**	**Threshold**	**Target**	**Threshold**	**Target**
Frequency	At least 2 to 3 days a week	2–7 days a week	At least 2 to 3 days a week	2–7 days a week	At least 2 to 3 days a week	2–7 days a week
Intensity	Stretch to the point of feeling tightness or slight discomfort.	Add passive assistance. Avoid over-stretching or pain.	Use a gentle swing (active) or bounce (ballistic) to stretch slightly beyond normal length.	Same as dynamic threshold.	Use an active 3- to 6-second contraction prior to an assisted stretch and stretch to point of tightness.	Use a 6-second contraction prior to an assisted stretch to point of tightness.
Time	Perform 2 reps. Hold each for 15–30 seconds. Rest 30 seconds between reps.	Perform 2–4 reps. Hold each for 15–60 seconds. Rest 30 seconds between reps.	Perform 1 set with 30 continuous seconds of motion.	Perform 1–3 sets with 30 consecutive seconds of motion. Rest 1 minute between sets.	Perform 2 reps. Hold each for 10–30 seconds. Rest 30 seconds between reps.	Perform 2–4 reps. Hold each for 10–30 seconds. Rest 30 seconds between reps.
Application	General population as well as rehab from injuries.		Sports and functional fitness.		Rehab from injuries and goal of increased ROM.	

*Optimal volume of stretching is recommended to be 60 seconds of total stretch time for each separate stretch.

muscle and tendon. Repeating the stretch several times is also important, as the muscle will elongate further with each repetition (up to a point) based on the viscoelastic properties. When the muscle is first stretched, neural factors resist the stretch but the reflex contraction subsides, allowing the muscle to be stretched more easily. Repeating the stretch several times is important to gradually increase the overload and promote adaptations. Figure 4 shows the typical responses to a stretched muscle during a series of stretches. Tension in a muscle decreases as the stretch is held over time, with most of the decrease occurring during the first 15 to 30 seconds. The multicolor curves in the figure illustrate that each successive stretch further reduces tension in the muscle, allowing greater stretch. For most people, four repetitions of 10 to 30 seconds is adequate; however, for athletes and older adults, more repetitions of greater length may be used. In older adults, a 30- to 60- second duration stretch may also give greater benefit.

Functional Fitness, Posture, and Flexibility-Based Activities

Functional fitness refers to the ability to function effectively in daily living. Good range of joint motion (flexibility) is necessary to participate in some sports and recreational activities; however, it is also important for a variety of normal daily tasks (e.g., reaching and bending). As we age, flexibility becomes increasingly important for maintaining function and independence including ease with basic tasks such as standing up from a low chair

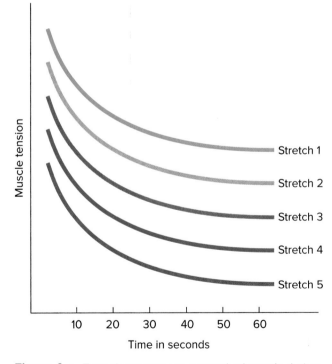

Figure 4 ▶ Typical responses to a stretched muscle during a series of stretches.

Stretch Reflex A reflexive contraction (shortening) of a muscle that occurs when sensory neurons in the MTU perceive a stretch of a muscle. The reflex subsides gradually, allowing the muscle to be stretched beyond resting length.

or bending over to pick up an item from the floor. Properly performed stretching exercise has been shown to improve flexibility in people of all ages and is a key contributor to a broader construct of **functional fitness,** which also incorporates core strength, balance, and agility.

A number of research studies have demonstrated improved functional outcomes in older adults following a stretching program, including improved scores on sit-to-stand time, and walking speed. However, few research studies have directly examined the relationship between older adults' flexibility (ROM) and performance of activities of daily living (ADLs). Therefore, more evidence is needed before recommendations can be made about the role of flexibility exercises in improving daily functioning. It is also not clear whether a flexibility program is superior to other forms of functional fitness such as core strengthening, balance, and agility.

Flexibility is critical for achieving and maintaining optimal posture. Poor posture typically develops over time due to lifestyle choices and/or poor habits. For example, people who sit a lot may develop tightness of the hip flexors. Weight lifters who follow a specific training regimen may develop tightness of the pectoral and biceps muscles. Over time, poor posture can result in muscle imbalance where muscles on one side of a joint become short and "overactive" while muscles on the opposite side become long and "underactive." The nervous system continually reinforces posture through neural programming. Tiny receptors in the skin and joints influence the relative activation of short/tight muscles over inhibited long/"weak" muscles.

Flexibility contributes to postural improvement but may not be enough on its own. Three facets of postural correction include improving the flexibility of the short and "overactive" muscles (for example, the low back), followed by strengthening of the long and "underactive" muscles (for example, the abdominals), and finally incorporating improved body awareness to maintain optimal posture. Stretching is important in this process, but there is little research evidence to support

the idea that stretching or strengthening alone can improve posture. Postural correction appears to be more complicated and may have more to do with the duration of time spent in a faulty posture each day than the positive effects of a short-lived exercise intervention. The most important step in the stretch-strengthen-awareness sequence may be to work on increased awareness and self-correction throughout the day until adoption of a desired posture becomes automatic. This can be achieved through a variety of flexibility-based movement disciplines.

Functional fitness and flexibility-based movement activities continue to be popular among fitness enthusiasts. A recent survey of Worldwide Fitness Trends indicates that of the 20 top trends, 4 relate to flexibility. Included are yoga, functional fitness training, specialized training for older adults, and use of foam rollers (see A Closer Look). The popularity of these activities suggests that people may be more interested in flexibility-related activity when it is presented in an engaging and interactive format. Some of the growth may also be attributed to increased acceptance of these activities by medical professionals. The following sections provide distinctions among these activities.

Tai chi is a relaxing and contemplative martial art with established health benefits. Tai chi (often translated as Chinese shadow boxing) involves the execution of slow, flowing movements called "forms." Tai chi has been shown to improve a wide variety of health outcomes including improved flexibility, improved balance, improved lower leg strength, improved immune capacity, increased bone density, reduced fall

A CLOSER LOOK

Massage Rollers

Massage rollers are specialized devices used to massage sore muscles, alleviate muscle soreness, and improve flexibility. Use of massage rollers is often called "foam rolling" and is considered to be a form of deep soft tissue massage. Massage roller devices come in a variety of sizes, shapes, and textures including the foam roll, massage stick, and massage ball. Research on the purported benefits of roller devices is limited, but studies have demonstrated improvements in range of motion and reduced severity and incidence of delayed onset muscle soreness after their use. Scientists don't fully understand the mechanisms by which rollers work but believe the rollers help by reducing pain thresholds, influencing the central nervous system's modulation of pain, and possibly altering local circulation.

Do you think foam rollers can provide benefits for your stretching program?

HELP   Health is available to Everyone for a Lifetime, and it's Personal

Functional Fitness

The concept of *functional fitness* has generated considerable interest among health and fitness professionals. Many fitness centers offer group classes focused on improving functional fitness and these courses typically involve flexibility and functional movement tasks.

Do you believe that flexibility and functional fitness provide important benefits to your health now, or do you think the benefits may be more relevant as you age?

risk among the elderly, improved cardiovascular function, reduced stress, reduced pain from arthritis, and improved quality of life. For older adults, the improved muscle fitness translates into joint protection and stability as well as improved functional fitness. Younger participants can benefit as well.

Yoga is a popular and diverse mind–body movement discipline. *Yoga* is an umbrella term that refers to a number of yoga traditions. The foundation for most yoga traditions is hatha yoga, which incorporates a variety of asanas (postures). Iyengar yoga is another popular variation. It uses similar asanas as hatha yoga but uses props and cushions to enhance the movements. Emphasis is placed on balance through coordinated breathing and precise body alignment.

The popularity of yoga continues to grow, encompassing numerous yoga forms from gentle and meditative to challenging and sweaty. Although yoga practices are thousands of years old, they are continually reinvented and refreshed, helping them retain popularity with people of diverse ages and interests. While yoga is commonly assumed to be a safe and healthy form of exercise, it is important to remember that, like any other form of exercise, there is potential for injury. Some extreme forms of yoga use contraindicated poses or movements that are potentially harmful to beginning exercisers. Care should be used when performing movements that require unnatural movements of the body or high stress loads placed on small joints. Props such as blocks and straps can be used to ease poses and make yoga gentler on the joints. Likewise, participants of Bikram ("hot") yoga should be aware of symptoms of heat intolerance and avoid overexertion.

Yoga is believed to contribute to a number of health benefits including improvements in flexibility, strength, balance, stress management, cardiovascular health, and pain management. A number of studies support these benefits while others suggest that some claims may be exaggerated. A number of high-quality research studies have provided evidence that yoga has a beneficial effect on improved cardiovascular health markers. Additional research studies have documented

Yoga and other movement classes involving stretching are increasingly popular.
©Ryan McVay/Photodisc/Getty Images

benefits on pain reduction and improved function in those with low back pain. Additional studies are needed to better understand the health-related effects of yoga, to differentiate the effects of varying yoga forms, and to compare the effectiveness of yoga to other exercise interventions (see In the News).

Pilates is a therapeutic regimen that combines strength training with body awareness and flexibility. Pilates differs from yoga in its emphasis on core strengthening and the absence of an overt spiritual or meditative

Functional Fitness The ability to perform activities of daily life.

In the News

Yoga as a Complementary Health Approach

Yoga has been around for thousands of years, but recently it has new advocates among consumers as well as a national scientific committee. Because of its health benefits, the National Center for Complementary and Integrative Health (a division of the National Institutes of Health) has identified yoga as a top 10 complementary health approach. A survey conducted by the National Center for Health Statistics examined Americans' use of alternative or complementary medicine approaches, and yoga was among the strongest

trends. Yoga was also on the list of prominent trends in the most recent ACSM fitness trend report. Experts attribute the wide appeal of yoga to the diversity of disciplines and applications. The positive impacts on health and mental well-being likely also keep people engaged once they try it.

What factors do you think explain the increased popularity of yoga?

component. Created in the 1920s, the Pilates approach has enjoyed a slow growth in popularity. Recent modifications have allowed Pilates to retain novelty and appeal. The health benefits of Pilates are not well researched but are believed to include improvements in strength and flexibility and reduced pain. Despite these claims, current studies have failed to find a relationship between Pilates and improvements in flexibility or posture. In a study on low back pain, Pilates was found to be superior to a general physical activity program in reducing pain and functional disability. Pilates has also been shown to effectively reduce neck pain, with results similar to those of yoga participants.

Guidelines for Safe and Effective Stretching Exercise

Do not confuse the flexibility exercise workout with a stretch warm-up. People who choose to do a stretch warm-up do it to prepare for their workout. Stretching exercises done to build flexibility, as described in this Concept, are performed intentionally as a stand-alone workout or as part of a complete workout. Although similar exercises can be used in both the stretch warm-up and the flexibility workout, each has a different purpose. Both should be preceded by a general or dynamic warm-up.

Stretching is specific to each muscle or muscle group. No single exercise can produce total flexibility. For example, stretching tight hamstrings can increase the length of these muscles but will not lengthen the muscles in other areas of the body. For total flexibility, it is important to stretch each of the major muscle groups and to use the major joints of the body through full range of normal motion and specific to a

functional goal. The guidelines in Table 2 will help you gain the most benefit from your stretching exercises.

A flexibility workout should be done when the body is warmed up and when adequate time is available to perform stretching exercises. Regular stretching is needed to see improvements in flexibility. The consensus is that stretching exercise is most effective when the body is already warmed up. For this reason, some people prefer to perform their stretching routine at the end of a workout when muscles are warm. Others prefer to perform their flexibility workout at a time when they can concentrate specifically on building flexibility. In either case, sufficient time should be allowed to ensure that the exercises are done correctly.

Select exercises that promote flexibility in all areas of the body. For total-body flexibility, 8 to 10 stretching exercises for the major muscle groups of the body are recommended. Table 3 describes some of the most effective exercises for a basic flexibility routine. Individual stretching needs may vary, but the most common areas to target are the trunk, the legs, and the arms. A variety of stretches for these areas are described in Tables 3, 4, and 5. Most are designed for static stretching, but the pectoral stretch and back-saver hamstring stretch use PNF techniques.

Using Self-Management Skills

Preparing a flexibility exercise plan requires the use of multiple self-management skills. You can use the six steps in program planning outlined in the Concept on self-management skills to prepare a flexibility exercise plan. Preparing a plan requires the use of a variety of self-management

Table 2 ▶ Do and Don't List for Stretching

Do	Don't
Do warm muscles before you attempt to stretch them.	Don't stretch to the point of pain. Remember, you want to stretch muscles, not joints.
Do stretch with care if you have osteoporosis or arthritis.	Don't use ballistic stretches if you have osteoporosis or arthritis.
Do use static or PNF stretching rather than ballistic stretching if you are a beginner.	Don't perform ballistic stretches with passive assistance unless you are under the supervision of an expert.
Do stretch weak or recently injured muscles with care.	Don't ballistically stretch weak or recently injured muscles.
Do use great care in applying passive assistance to a partner; go slowly and ask for feedback.	Don't overstretch a muscle after it has been immobilized for a long period of time (such as in a sling or cast).
Do perform stretching exercises for each muscle group and at each joint where flexibility is desired.	Don't bounce muscles through excessive range of motion. Begin ballistic stretching with gentle movements and gradually increase intensity.
Do make certain the body is in good alignment when stretching.	Don't stretch swollen joints without professional supervision.
Do stretch the smaller muscle groups of the arms and legs first; then progress to the larger muscle groups of the trunk and hips.	Don't stretch several muscles at one time until you have stretched individual muscles. For example, stretch muscles at the ankle, then the knee, then the ankle and knee simultaneously.

skills including self-assessment, goal setting, and self-monitoring. Preparing a plan also gives you a chance to practice using these skills. (More information is provided in Strategies for Action: Lab Information.)

Apply consumer skills to ensure you receive good instruction. The popularity of flexibility exercise has led to an increasing array of classes, videos, and on-demand links available for yoga, Pilates, tai chi, and ballet-inspired barre exercises. Be sure to check the credentials of instructors providing these courses.

Apply performance skills by developing better mind–body awareness. Effective stretching requires careful attention to signals from your body. As described, gains in flexibility are influenced by body perceptions and complex stretch reflexes. By paying attention to flexibility and tension in your muscles, you can gain mind–body awareness. Familiarity with your body's capabilities will also help determine safe limits for stretching. Some yoga positions, for example, may be contraindicated exercises that could increase risk for injury in some individuals. For safety, exercises should always be performed within the safe limits, and only you can know how far is too far.

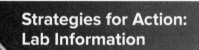

Strategies for Action: Lab Information

An important step for developing and maintaining flexibility is assessing your current status. There are dozens of tests for flexibility. Four tests that assess range of motion in the major joints of the body, that require little equipment, and that can be easily administered are presented in the Lab Resource Materials in this Concept. In Lab 11A, you will get an opportunity to try these self-assessments. Perform these assessments before you begin your regular stretching program and use these assessments to reevaluate your flexibility periodically.

Keeping records of progress will help you adhere to a stretching program. An activity logging sheet is provided in Lab 11B to help you keep records of your progress as you regularly perform stretching exercises to build and maintain good flexibility.

Suggested Resources and Readings

The websites for the following sources can be accessed by searching online for the organization, program, or title listed. Specific scientific

To get the most out of yoga, tai chi, and Pilates classes, find a qualified instructor.
©Comstock/Stockbyte/Getty Images

references are available at the end of this edition of *Concepts of Fitness and Wellness.*

- ACE Fitness. Functional Fitness Specialist (online information).
- ACE Fitness. Practical Application of Functional Assessments: Flexibility Assessment (online articles and assessments).
- American College of Sports Medicine. (2018). *ACSM's Guidelines for Exercise Prescription and Testing.* Philadelphia: Wolters Kluwer. Chapter 6, pp. 147–161.
- Gray Institute Functional Therapy. Functional Flexibility (pdf).
- Mayo Clinic. Functional Fitness. Is It Right for You? (online article).
- McAttee, R., & Charland, J. (2014). *Facilitated Stretching* (4th ed.). Champaign, IL: Human Kinetics (iPad version with video).
- National Center for Complementary and Integrative Health. Yoga for Health (pdf).

Table 3   The Basic Eight for Trunk Stretching Exercises

Table 3

1. Upper Trapezius/Neck Stretch

connect
VIDEO 5

This exercise stretches the muscles on the back and sides of the neck. To stretch the right trapezius, place left hand on top of your head. Gently look down toward your left underarm, tucking your chin toward your chest. Let the weight of your arm gently draw your head forward. Hold. Repeat to the opposite side.

Variations: The stretch above may be modified to stretch the muscles on the front and sides of the neck. Start from the stretch position described above. Tip your left ear near your left shoulder. Turn your head slightly and look up toward the ceiling, lifting your chin 2–3 inches. Hold.

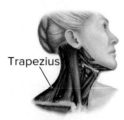

Trapezius

2. Chin Tuck

This exercise stretches the muscles at the base of the skull and reduces headache symptoms. Sit up straight, with chest lifted and shoulders back. Gently tuck in the chin by making a slight motion of nodding "yes." Imagine a string attached to the back of your head, which is pulling your head upward, like a puppet. As your chin draws inward, attempt to lengthen the back of your neck. Hold.

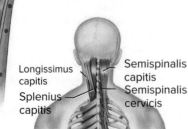

Longissimus capitis
Splenius capitis
Semispinalis capitis
Semispinalis cervicis

3. Pectoral Stretch

This exercise stretches the chest muscles (pectorals).

1. Stand erect in doorway, with arms raised 45 degrees, elbows bent, hands grasping the doorjamb, and feet in front-stride position. Press out on door frame, contracting your arm muscles maximally for 6 seconds. Relax and shift weight forward on legs. Lean into doorway, so that the muscles on the front of your shoulder joint and chest are gently stretched. Do not overstretch. Hold.
2. Repeat with your arms raised 90 degrees.
3. Repeat with your arms raised 135 degrees. This exercise is useful to prevent or correct round shoulders and sunken chest.

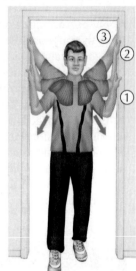

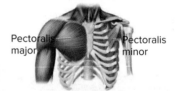

Pectoralis major
Pectoralis minor

4. Lateral Trunk Stretch

This exercise stretches the trunk lateral flexors. Stand with feet shoulder width apart. Stretch left arm overhead to right. Bend to right at waist, reaching as far to right as possible with left arm. Hold. Do not let trunk rotate or lower back arch. Repeat on opposite side.

Trunk lateral flexors

The Basic Eight for Trunk Stretching Exercises Table 3

Table 3

5. Leg Hug

This exercise stretches the hip and back extensor muscles. Lie on your back. Bend one leg and grasp your thigh under the knee. Hug it to your chest. Keep the other leg straight and on the floor. Hold. Repeat with the opposite leg.

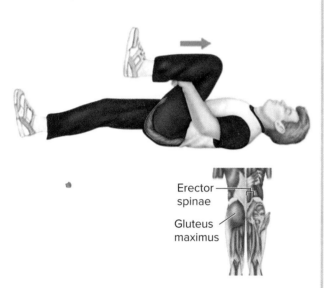

Erector spinae

Gluteus maximus

7. Trunk Twist

This exercise stretches the trunk muscles and the muscles on the outside of the hip. Sit with your right leg extended, left leg bent and crossed over the right knee. Place your right arm on the left side of the left leg and push against that leg while turning the trunk as far as possible to the left. Place the left hand on the floor behind the buttocks. Stretch and hold. Reverse position and repeat on the opposite side.

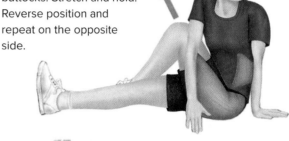

Erector spinae

Gluteals

6. Cobra and Child's Pose

This exercise stretches the back and hips. Begin on stomach with legs extended behind you. Place hands on floor directly under shoulders and fingertips pointed forward. Press tops of feet and thighs into floor. Gently raise head and chest from the ground, straightening the elbows. Hold 30 seconds. Relax. Keeping hands on the ground, sit back toward heels, rounding out low back and lowering forehead toward the floor. Hold for 30 seconds.

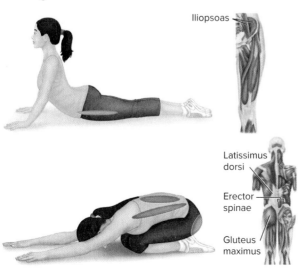

Iliopsoas

Latissimus dorsi

Erector spinae

Gluteus maximus

8. Spine Twist

This exercise stretches the trunk rotators and lateral rotators of the thighs. Start in hook-lying position, arms extended at shoulder level. Cross your left knee over the right. Drop both knees towards the floor on the left side of your body. Keep your arms and shoulders on the floor while moving your legs. Stretch and hold. Reverse leg position and lower your knees to right.

Latissimus dorsi

Erector spinae

Gluteus maximus

Table 4 The Basic Eight for Leg Stretching Exercises

Table 4

1. Calf Stretch

connect
VIDEO 6

This exercise stretches the calf muscles and Achilles tendon. Face a wall with your feet 2 or 3 feet away. Step forward on your left foot to allow both hands to touch the wall. Keep the heel of your right foot on the ground, toe turned in slightly, knee straight, and buttocks tucked in. Lean forward by bending your front knee and arms and allowing your head to move nearer the wall. Hold. Variation: Repeat, bending your right knee, keeping your heel on floor. Stretch and hold. Repeat with the other leg.

Gastrocnemius

2. Shin Stretch

This exercise relieves shin muscle soreness by stretching the muscles on the front of the shin. Kneel on both knees, turn to the right, and press down and stretch your right ankle with your right hand. Move your pelvis forward. Hold. Repeat on the opposite side. Except when they are sore, most people need to strengthen rather than stretch these muscles.

Shin muscles

3. Back-Saver Hamstring Stretch

This exercise stretches the hamstrings and calf muscles and helps prevent or correct backache caused in part by short hamstrings. Sit on the floor with the feet against the wall or an immovable object. Bend left knee and bring foot close to buttocks. Clasp hands behind back. Contract the muscles on the back of the upper leg (hamstrings) by pressing the heel downward toward the floor. Hold, relax. Bend forward from hips, keeping lower back as straight as possible. Let bent knee rotate outward so trunk can move forward. Lean forward keeping back flat; hold and repeat on each leg.

Hamstrings

4. Hip and Thigh Stretch

This exercise stretches the hip (iliopsoas) and thigh muscles (quadriceps) and is useful for people with lordosis and back problems. Kneel on the floor with your left leg behind you and the knee touching the floor. Place your right leg out in front with the right knee directly above your right ankle. If necessary, place your hands on floor for balance.

② ①

1. Tilt the pelvis backward by tucking in the abdomen and flattening the back.
2. Then shift the weight forward until a stretch is felt on the front of the left thigh. Hold. Repeat on the opposite side.
   Caution: Do not bend your front knee more than 90 degrees.

Iliopsoas

Quadriceps

5. Groin Stretch

This exercise stretches the muscles on the inside of the thighs. Sit with the soles of your feet together; place your hands on your knees or ankles and lean your forearms against your knees; resist (contract) by attempting to raise your knees. Hold. Relax and press the knees toward the floor as far as possible. Hold. This exercise is useful for pregnant women and anyone whose thighs tend to rotate inward, causing backache, knock-knees, and flat feet.

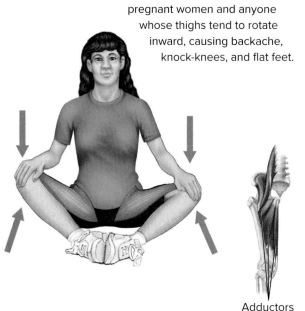

Adductors

7. Inner Thigh Stretch

This exercise stretches the muscles of the inner thigh. Stand with feet spread wider than shoulder-width apart. Shift weight onto the right foot and bend the right knee slightly. Straighten left knee and raise toes of left foot off the floor. Lean forward slightly from the waist, keeping back straight/shoulders back. Shift weight back over the right foot by moving hips diagonally away from the left foot. Hold. Repeat in the opposite direction.

Adductors

6. Lateral Thigh and Hip Stretch

This exercise stretches the muscles and connective tissue on the outside of the legs (tensor fascia lata and iliotibial band). Stand with your left side to the wall, left arm extended and palm of your hand flat on the wall for support. Cross the left leg behind the right leg and turn the toes of both feet out slightly. Bend your left knee slightly and shift your pelvis toward the wall (left) as your trunk bends toward the right. Adjust until tension is felt down the outside of the left hip and thigh. Stretch and hold. Repeat on the other side.

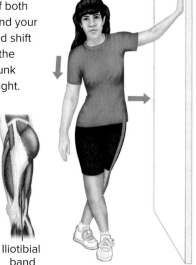

Iliotibial band

8. Deep Buttock Stretch

This exercise stretches the deep buttock muscles, such as the piriformis. Lie on your back with knees bent and one ankle crossed over opposite knee. Grasp thigh of bottom leg and pull gently toward your chest. Hold. Repeat on the other side.

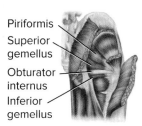

Piriformis
Superior gemellus
Obturator internus
Inferior gemellus

207

Table 5

Table 5   The Basic Four for Arm Stretching Exercises

1. Forearm Stretch

This exercise stretches the muscles on the front and back sides of the lower arm. It is particularly useful in relieving stress from excessive keyboarding activity. Hold your right arm straight out in front, with your palm facing down. Use your left hand to gently stretch the fingertips of your right hand toward the floor. Hold. Turn your right arm over with your palm facing up. Use your left hand to gently stretch the fingertips of your right hand toward the floor. Hold. Repeat on the opposite side.

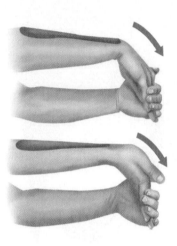

Forearm flexor or extensors

2. Back Scratcher

This exercise stretches the muscles on the front of the shoulder. Stand straight with back of left hand held flat against back. With right hand, throw one end of a towel over right shoulder from front to back. Grab end of towel with left hand. Pull down gently on the towel with right hand, raising left arm in back as high as is comfortable. Hold. Repeat to opposite side.

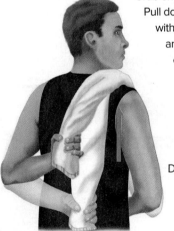

Pectoralis
Deltoid

3. Overhead Arm Stretch

This exercise stretches the triceps and latissimus dorsi muscles. Stretch your arms up overhead. Grasp your right elbow with your left hand. Pull your right elbow back behind your head. Hold. Repeat on opposite side.

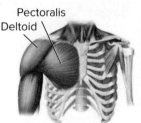

Triceps

Latissimus dorsi

4. Arm Hug Stretch

This exercise stretches the shoulder muscles (lateral rotators and posterior deltoid). Hold onto right arm above the elbow with left hand and gently pull arm across chest.

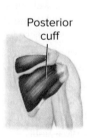

Posterior cuff

Lab Resource Materials: Flexibility Tests

Directions: To test the flexibility of all joints is impractical. These tests are for frequently tight muscle groups that can limit joint flexibility. Follow the instructions carefully. Determine your flexibility using Chart 1.

1. Test: Modified Sit-and-Reach (Flexibility Test of Hamstrings)

   a. Remove shoes and sit on the floor. Place the sole of the foot of the extended leg flat against a box or bench. Bend opposite knee and place the head, back, and hips against a wall with a 90-degree angle at the hips.

   b. Place one hand over the other and slowly reach forward as far as you can with arms fully extended. Keep head and back in contact with the wall. A partner will slide the end of the measuring stick on the bench until it touches the fingertips.

   c. With the measuring stick fixed in the new position, reach forward as far as possible, allowing head and trunk to move away from the wall. Perform three times, holding the position on the third reach for at least 2 seconds while the partner records the distance fingertips slide forward on the ruler. Keep the knee of the extended leg straight (see illustration).

   d. Repeat the test a second time and average the scores of the two trials.

2. Test: Shoulder Flexibility (Zipper Test)

   a. Raise your right arm overhead, bend your elbow, and reach down across your back as far as possible.

   b. At the same time, extend your left arm down and behind your back, bend your elbow up across your back, and try to cross your fingers over those of your right hand as shown in the accompanying illustration.

   c. Measure the distance between fingertips to the nearest half-inch. If your fingers overlap, score as a plus. If they fail to meet, score as a minus. Score as a zero if your fingertips just touch.

   d. Repeat with your arms crossed in the opposite direction (left arm up). Most people will find that they are more flexible on one side than the other.

3. Test: Hamstring and Hip Flexor Flexibility

a. Lie on your back on the floor beside a wall.

b. Slowly lift one leg off the floor. Keep the other leg flat on the floor.

c. Keep both legs straight.

d. Continue to lift the leg until either leg begins to bend or the lower leg begins to lift off the floor.

e. Place a yardstick against the wall and underneath the lifted leg.

f. Hold the yardstick against the wall after the leg is lowered.

g. Using a protractor, measure the angle created by the floor and the yardstick. The greater the angle, the better your score.

h. Repeat with the other leg.

Note: For ease of testing, you may want to draw angles on a piece of posterboard, as illustrated. If you have goniometers, you may be taught to use them instead.

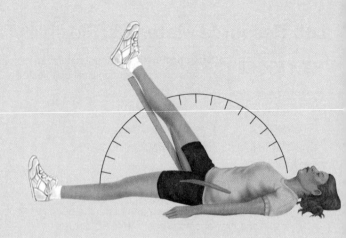

4. Test: Trunk Rotation

a. Tape two yardsticks to the wall at shoulder height, one right side up and the other upside down. Position yardsticks directly over one another.

b. Stand with your left shoulder an arm's length (fist closed) from the wall. Toes should be on the line, which is perpendicular to the wall and even with the 15-inch mark on the yardstick.

c. Drop the left arm and raise the right arm to the side, palm down, fist closed.

d. Without moving your feet, rotate the trunk to the right as far as possible, reaching along the yardstick, and hold it 2 seconds. Do not move the feet or bend the trunk. Your knees may bend slightly.

e. A partner will read the distance reached to the nearest half-inch. Record your score. Repeat two times and average your two scores.

f. Next, perform the test facing the opposite direction. Rotate to the left. For this test, you will use the second yardstick (upside down) so that, **the greater the rotation, the higher the score.** If you have only one yardstick, turn it right side up for the first test and upside down for the second test.

15-inch mark

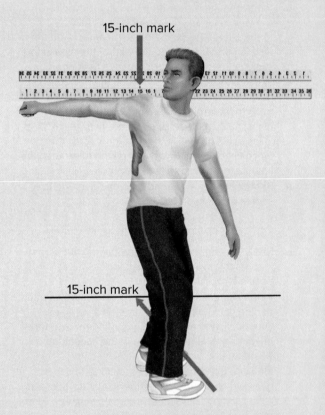

15-inch mark

Chart 1 Flexibility Rating Scale for Tests 1–4

Classification	Men					Women				
	Test 1	Test 2		Test 3	Test 4	Test 1	Test 2		Test 3	Test 4
		Right Up	Left Up				Right Up	Left Up		
High-performance zone*	16+	5+	4+	111+	20+	17+	6+	5+	111+	20.5+
Good fitness zone	13–15	1–4	1–3	80–110	16–19.5	14–16	2–5	2–4	80–110	17–20
Marginal fitness zone	10–12	0	0	60–79	13.5–15.5	11–13	1	1	60–79	14.5–16.5
Low fitness zone	<9	<0	<0	<60	<13.5	<10	<1	<1	<60	<14.5

*Though performers need good flexibility, hypermobility may increase injury risk.

Lab 11A Evaluating Flexibility

Name	Section	Date

Purpose: To evaluate your flexibility in several joints.

Procedures

1. Take the flexibility tests outlined in the Lab Resource Materials.
2. Record your scores in the Results section below.
3. Use Chart 1 in the Lab Resource Materials to determine your ratings on the self-assessments; then place an X over the circle for the appropriate rating.

Results

Flexibility Scores and Ratings

Record Scores

		Record Ratings			
		High Performance	Good Fitness	Marginal	Low
Modified sit-and-reach					
Test 1	Left	◯	◯	◯	◯
	Right	◯	◯	◯	◯
Zipper					
Test 2	Left	◯	◯	◯	◯
	Right	◯	◯	◯	◯
Hamstring/hip flexor					
Test 3	Left	◯	◯	◯	◯
	Right	◯	◯	◯	◯
Trunk rotation					
Test 4	Left	◯	◯	◯	◯
	Right	◯	◯	◯	◯

Do any of these muscle groups need stretching? Check yes or no for each muscle group.

	Yes	No
Back of the thighs and knees (hamstrings)	◯	◯
Calf muscles	◯	◯
Lower back (lumbar region)	◯	◯
Front of right shoulder	◯	◯
Back of right shoulder	◯	◯
Front of left shoulder	◯	◯
Back of left shoulder	◯	◯
Most of the body	◯	◯
Trunk muscles	◯	◯

Conclusions and Implications: In several sentences, discuss your current flexibility and your flexibility needs for the future. Include comments about your current state of flexibility, need for improvement in specific areas, and special flexibility needs for sports or other special activities.

Lab 11B Planning and Logging Stretching Exercises

Name	**Section**	**Date**

Purpose: To set 1-week lifestyle goals for stretching exercises, to prepare a stretching for flexibility plan, and to self-monitor progress in your 1-week plan.

Procedures

1. Using Chart 1, provide some background information about your experience with stretching exercise, your goals, and your plans for incorporating these exercises into your normal exercise routine.
2. Using Chart 2, select at least 8–10 flexibility exercises as directed. Perform the exercises for 3–6 days over a 1-week period. Be sure to plan your exercise program so that it fits with the goals you described in Chart 1. For best results, take the log with you during your workout, so that you can record the exercises you performed.
3. Answer the questions in the Results and Conclusions and Implications sections.

Chart 1 Stretching Exercise Survey

1. Determine your current stage for flexibility exercise. Check only the stage that represents your current activity level.

○ Precontemplation. I do not meet flexibility exercise guidelines and have not been thinking about starting.

○ Contemplation. I do not meet flexibility exercise guidelines but have been thinking about starting.

○ Preparation. I am planning to start doing regular flexibility exercises to meet guidelines.

○ Action. I do flexibility exercises, but I am not as regular as I should be.

○ Maintenance. I regularly meet guidelines for flexibility exercises.

2. What are your primary goals for flexibility exercise?

○ General conditioning

○ Sports improvement (specify sport: _____)

○ Health benefits

3. Are you currently involved in a regular stretching program?

○ Yes

○ No

Results

	Yes	No
Did you do eight exercises at least 3 days in the week?	○	○
Did you notice any changes in flexibility?	○	○

Conclusions and Implications: Do you think you will use stretching exercises as part of your regular physical activity plan, either now or in the future? What modifications would you make in your program in the future?

Chart 2 Stretching Exercise Log

Check (√) the exercises you plan to perform in the first column. Choose 8–10 or more exercises from the three lists (truck, leg, and arm). Be sure to include at least two from each of the three lists. Perform the exercises for 3–6 days over the 1-week period. Write the date (month/day) in the day column for the date you performed the exercise.

Exercises	Day 1	Day 2	Day 3	Day 4	Day 5	Day 6	Day 7
Trunk Stretching Exercises (Table 3, pages 204–205)							
1 Upper trapezius/neck stretch							
2 Chin tuck							
3 Pectoral stretch							
4 Lateral trunk stretch							
5 Leg hug							
6 Cobra and child's pose							
7 Trunk twist							
8 Spine twist							
Leg Stretching Exercises (Table 4, pages 206–207)							
1 Calf stretch							
2 Shin stretch							
3 Back-saver hamstring stretch							
4 Hip and thigh stretch							
5 Groin stretch							
6 Lateral thigh and hip stretch							
7 Inner thigh stretch							
8 Deep buttock stretch							
Arm Stretching Exercises (Table 5, page 208)							
1 Forearm stretch							
2 Back scratcher							
3 Overhead arm stretch							
4 Arm hug stretch							

Body Mechanics: Posture, Questionable Exercises, and Care of the Back and Neck

LEARNING OBJECTIVES

After completing the study of this Concept, you will be able to:

▶ Identify and describe the anatomy and function of the spine.

▶ Identify and describe the anatomy and function of core muscles.

▶ Clarify the causes and consequences of back and neck pain.

▶ Describe how to prevent and rehabilitate back and neck problems.

▶ Explain why posture is important to back and neck health and ways to improve posture.

▶ Explain why good body mechanics is important to back and neck health and ways to improve body mechanics.

▶ Indicate the exercise guidelines for back and neck health and ways to implement the guidelines.

▶ Name questionable exercises and safer alternatives.

▶ Determine self-assessments to identify potential back, neck, and posture problems and risks, and plan a self-monitored personal program that includes exercises for reducing these problems.

e health, integrity, and function of the back and neck are influenced by modifiable as well as nonmodifiable tors. Maintaining a healthy back and neck can be attained by using good sture, good body mechanics, and safe exercise technique.

©Chris Clinton/DigitalVision/Getty Images

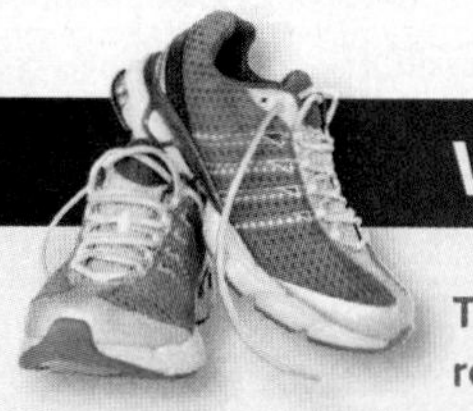

Why it Matters!

The back and neck serve vital roles in supporting the weight of the head and body, producing movements, carrying loads, and protecting the spinal cord and nerves. However, the multiple functions of the spinal column also predispose this area to injuries. To reduce your risks it is important to adopt good posture and to practice good body mechanics. This Concept provides insights into the interrelated functions of the spine and trunk musculature to help you understand how to protect your back and neck. Specific information is provided about harmful exercises and safer alternatives so that you can minimize risks. The content will help you adopt preventive measures that may reduce your risk for back and neck problems.

Anatomy and Function of the Spine

The spinal column is arranged for movement. The bones that make up the spine are called vertebrae. There are 33 vertebrae in the spine, and most are separated from one another by an **intervertebral disc** (see Figure 1). The vertebrae are divided into three main regions commonly referred to as cervical (neck), thoracic (upper back), and lumbar (low back). The fused vertebrae that form the tailbone are called the sacrum and coccyx. The connections among the vertebrae of the cervical, thoracic, and lumbar spine allow the trunk to move in complex ways. The spine is capable of flexion (forward bending), extension (backward bending), side bending, and rotation, but functionally, these movements often occur in combination. For example, in executing a tennis serve, the spine both extends and rotates. The spine is at risk for injury when movements are performed repetitively, performed beyond a joint's healthy range of motion, or performed under conditions of heavy or inefficient lifting.

The spinal column has an important role in bearing loads and protecting the back and neck from injury. The widest portion of each vertebra articulates with the intervertebral disc to form a strong pillar of support extending from the skull to the pelvis. The unique structure of the intervertebral discs is critical in distributing force and absorbing shock. The bony structure of the spine bears loads and provides protection to the spinal cord and spinal nerves. Poor posture and poor body mechanics can damage discs and vertebrae, resulting in pain and disability.

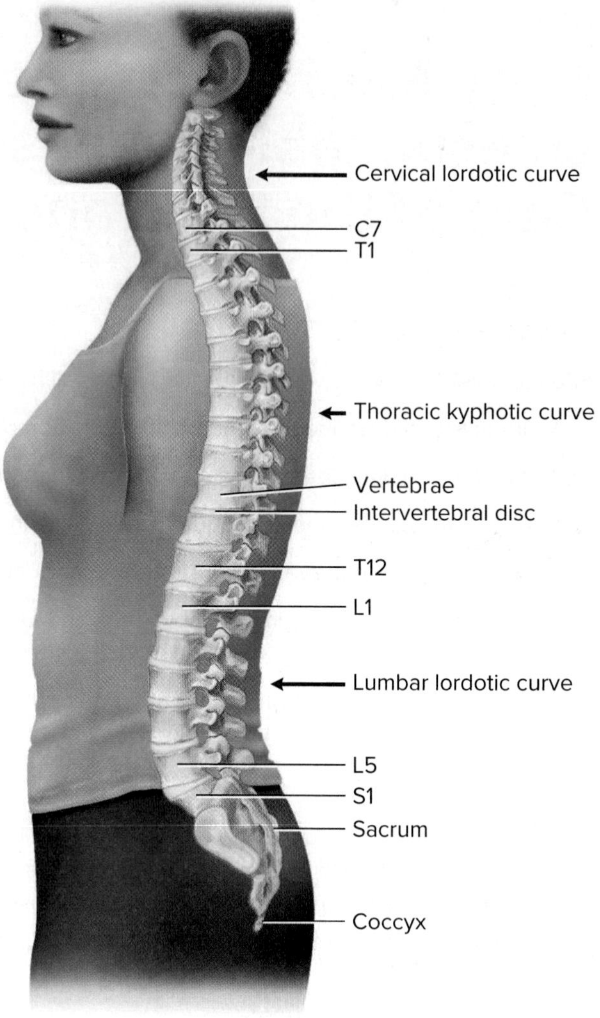
Cervical lordotic curve
C7
T1
Thoracic kyphotic curve
Vertebrae
Intervertebral disc
T12
L1
Lumbar lordotic curve
L5
S1
Sacrum
Coccyx

Figure 1 ▶ Curvatures of the spinal column.

Anatomy and Function of the Core Musculature

The core is composed of an integrated series of muscles. There is no definitive list of muscles belonging to the core. The core can be described as including as few as 6 or as many as 20 different muscle groups, depending on the source. Regardless, the muscles of the core all share common anatomical traits: their location and attachment to the spine, pelvis, or rib cage. Conceptually, the core can be described as a three-dimensional, cylindrical area of the body that encompasses the spine, abdominal cavity, and the body's center of gravity (see Figure 2). Its anatomic boundaries generally include the abdominal muscles (in front), the low back muscles (in back), the diaphragm (across the top), and the pelvic floor and hip muscles (across the bottom). However, it may also be described in broader terms and include other trunk muscles that have attachments to the shoulder or pelvic girdle.

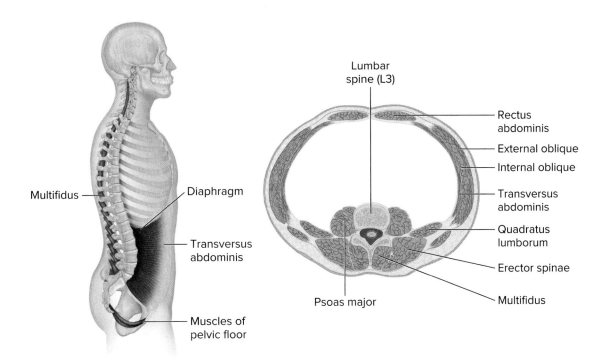

Figure 2 ▶ Cross section showing layers of core musculature.

The core muscles work together to provide the spine with optimal support and function. The core muscles play a key role in improving spinal stability, improving efficiency of movement, and aiding in force transmission. They help you walk, lift heavy objects, swing a bat, or kick a soccer ball. A strong core is believed to help protect the back from harm, improve daily function, and enhance athletic performance. Some describe core stability as the control of movement around a "neutral" postural zone, where the physiological stress and strain on the spine are minimized (e.g., squatting with good body mechanics). Others expand the definition of core stability to include the efficient and coordinated transfer of loads along the kinetic chain (e.g., the coordinated and fluid movement of legs, trunk, and arms during the act of swinging a golf club). The core muscles are essentially active during almost all functional movements.

The various core muscles can be categorized based on function. The core includes both superficial muscles that help move the trunk as well as deeply located muscles responsible for controlling intersegmental movements of the spine. They are often categorized as core mobilizer muscles, core stabilizer muscles, or core transfer muscles, depending on their primary function. The distinctions are described below:

- **Core mobilizer muscles** typically produce concentric (shortening) contractions in order to generate movement of the trunk. Common examples of core mobilizers include the rectus abdominis and erector spinae. These muscles are capable of bending the trunk forward or backward when they contract. Examples of exercises that utilize the core mobilizers include the trunk curl-up and back extension exercises.

- **Core stabilizer muscles** use isometric (holding) and eccentric (braking) contractions to provide stiffness and stability to the spine. The stabilizers keep the individual spinal segments in "neutral" alignment and collectively provide a corset-like stiffness to the trunk. Core activation actually begins in anticipation and in preparation for movement, with muscles of the core contracting before those of the arms or legs. Examples of muscles that provide a role in core stabilization include the lumbar multifidus (the deepest back muscle) and the transverse abdominis (the deepest abdominal muscle). An example of an exercise that utilizes core stabilization is the plank exercise.

- **Core transfer muscles** transfer force from one region of the body to another. The premise is that power comes from a stable foundation. Thus, these muscles help stabilize the trunk in order to generate strong movements of the arms

Intervertebral Discs Spinal discs; cushions of cartilage between the bodies of the vertebrae. Each disc consists of a fibrous outer ring (annulus fibrosus) and a pulpy center (nucleus pulposus).

Core Mobilizer Muscles Superficial core muscles that produce trunk motion and also aid in stabilization.

Core Stabilizer Muscles Deep core muscles that provide stiffness and stability to the spine.

Core Transfer Muscles Superficial core muscles that help integrate trunk and limb function.

Functional Movement Tests

"Functional fitness" and "functional movements" are popular topics in the fitness world. The notion is that functional fitness training techniques better prepare the body to handle the forces, postures, and actions involved in real-life activities and sports and ultimately lead to reduced risk of injuries. Functional movement tests are now commonly used by athletic teams to try to predict which athletes might be at risk for injury. In theory, this type of screening can help identify appropriate exercises that can correct muscle imbalances or weaknesses. Despite the popularity of functional movement training, evidence hasn't fully supported the effectiveness of the screening programs or functional-type exercise for reducing risks of injury. (See link in Suggested Resources and Readings.)

Do you see the potential for this type of screening assessment to reduce injuries?

connect
ACTIVITY

or legs. Examples of muscles involved in force transfer include trunk muscles with attachments to the shoulders or hips (e.g., latisimus dorsi, pectoral, and gluteus maximus muscles). An example of an exercise utilizing core force transfer would be the deadlift in weightlifting.

While this classification scheme is helpful to understanding the basic roles of the core muscles, core function is actually far more complex. For instance, muscles may serve multiple functions or work together in an integrated fashion rather than in an isolated role of "mover" or "stabilizer."

connect
VIDEO 1

Causes and Consequences of Back and Neck Pain

Although back and neck pain are common, many cases stem from lifestyle choices or life experiences. Back and neck pain are common in today's society, with statistics suggesting that nearly 80 percent of Americans will experience an episode of low back pain sometime in life. Back pain is second only to headache as a common medical complaint, and an estimated 30 to 70 percent of the population experiences recurring back problems. The original cause (or causes) of back and neck pain is (are) often hard to identify since damage can build over time. Although back and neck problems can result from an acute injury (e.g., a diving accident or car accident), most are caused by accumulated stresses over a lifetime. These factors include the avoidable effects of poor posture and body mechanics as well as

questionable exercises that put the back at risk. (Exercises to avoid are discussed later in this Concept.)

To reduce risk for back pain, reduce the risk factors that you have control over. Modifiable risk factors (factors you can change) include regular heavy labor, use of vibrational tools, routines of prolonged sitting, smoking, a hypokinetic lifestyle, and obesity. A number of health conditions can also contribute to back problems, including depression, anxiety, cancer, infections, and some visceral diseases (kidney, pelvic organs). You may have some control over these health conditions that contribute to back pain. Nonmodifiable risk factors include a family history of joint disease, age, gender, genetics, congenital anomalies (including some forms of **scoliosis**), and direct trauma (e.g., a fall or rough athletic activity when young). Lab 12A provides a questionnaire for assessing your potential risk for back and neck pain.

The nervous system and various pain-sensitive structures contribute to back pain. Back pain can result from direct or indirect causes. Direct causes are typically the result of mechanical trauma to tissues in or around the spine. Damage to structures of the spinal column can occur slowly over time (degenerative changes) or from a single traumatic event (acute injury). Pain from back problems can arise from a variety of sources including the spine, discs, muscles, and nerves. Indirect causes of back pain can include local cellular changes in and around the injured tissues (e.g., presence of pain-sensitive chemicals) or changes in the type of messages being generated by the nervous system. With chronic pain, the nervous system may continuously resend pain signals in abnormal feedback loops that enhance or maintain the perception of pain, even when the original cause or problem is corrected.

The integrity of the back and neck are jeopardized by excessive stress and strain. Forces are constantly at work to bend, twist, shear, compress, or lengthen tissues of the body. Stress on these tissues may eventually create strain, a change in the tissue's size or dimension. Healthy tissues typically return to their normal state once the force is removed. Injury occurs when excessive stress and strain prevent the tissue from returning to its normal state. A number of specific contributors to stress and strain on the back are listed below:

- *Poor posture can cause body segments to experience stress and strain.* When body segments are in poor alignment (e.g., slouching or forward head positions), the muscles in the back and neck must work hard to compensate. This creates excessive stress and strain in the affected area(s). Over time, tension in these muscles can lead to myofascial trigger points, which can cause headache or **referred pain** in the face, scalp, shoulder, arm, and chest. The chronic stress from poor alignment can also lead to other postural deviations and degenerative changes in the neck.

- *Bad body mechanics contribute to stress and strain on the spine.* Activities that involve heavy lifting, bending, or twisting present risks, as do repetitive motions and those that involve vibrations. The lumbar vertebrae and the sacrum are most vulnerable to this type of injury due to the significant weight they support and the thinner ligaments at this level.

- *Being overweight or obese increases the risk of back pain.* Obesity and overweight status are hard on the body because they overload the bones, discs, tendons, and ligaments. Added wear and tear on joint surfaces can lead to osteoarthritis. Postural changes accompany weight gain and create additional stress and strain on joints. For example, a large protruding abdomen often causes forward tipping of the pelvis and excessive arching of the low back that can lead to back pain. Studies confirm that the risk of back pain increases exponentially with higher levels of body mass. A person who is overweight has a 20 percent greater chance of suffering from back pain than someone of normal weight, and for those with morbid obesity, the rate climbs to 254 percent higher.

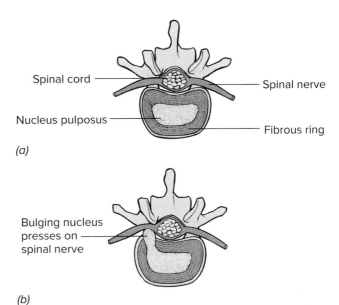

(a)

(b)

Figure 3 ▶ Normal disc (*a*) and herniated disc (*b*).

Some exercises and movements can produce microtrauma, which can lead to back and neck pain. Most people are familiar with acute injuries, such as ankle sprains. These injuries are associated with immediate onset of pain and swelling. **Microtrauma** is a "silent injury"—a subtle form of injury that results from accumulated damage over time. It can result from repetitive motion, repeated forceful exertion, long-term vibration, or working with awkward postures. When microtrauma occurs as the result of activities at work, it is often referred to by the medical terms repetitive stress injury (RSI) or cumulative trauma disorder (CTD). One common example is carpal tunnel syndrome, a painful irritation of the median nerve at the wrist, often brought on by repetitive motion of the wrist during long and extended periods of typing, assembly line tasks, or construction work.

Microtrauma can also result from the repetitive performance of unsafe exercises or contraindicated movements. For example, regular performance of full deep knee squats or full neck circles may irritate the joint surfaces and eventually cause knee or neck pain. Repeated overhead lifting with excessive loads can irritate and damage the rotator cuff tendon of the shoulder. The initial wear and tear from microtrauma is not typically noticed but, over many years, microscopic changes occur in the joint. Examples include swelling, fibrosis of the synovial lining, abnormal thickening of the surrounding joint capsule, calcifications in the tendons, and thinning and roughening of the cartilage cushioning the joint surfaces. Because these changes are unseen and often unfelt, the offending exercise or activity is often viewed as harmless. However, later in life the effects from accumulated microtrauma become more apparent, manifesting in tendonitis, bursitis, arthritis, or nerve compression. Chances are when the injury reaches a painful stage, the cause is not identified and instead is attributed to aging.

The lumbar intervertebral discs are particularly susceptible to injury and herniation. The intervertebral discs located between the vertebrae of the spine are composed of a tire-like outer ring (annulus fibrosus) surrounding a gel-like center (nucleus pulposus). The greatest risk for injury to the discs occurs during excessive loading and twisting motions of the spine. Most people think that disc injuries occur from an acute injury, but herniation typically reflects a degenerative process that takes place over time. With repeated microtrauma, small tears begin to occur in the inner fibers of the annulus. The nucleus begins to move outward (**herniated disc**), much like toothpaste moving within a squeezed tube. Disc herniation is termed *incomplete* or *contained* as long as the migrating edge of the nucleus remains within the fibers of the annulus. As damage continues (often the result of years of cumulative microtrauma), the annular fibers may reach a point of rupture at their periphery (see Figure 3). At this point (termed *disc extrusion*), the nucleus pulposus moves into the space around the spinal cord or nerve root and herniation is termed *complete* or *noncontained.*

Scoliosis A curvature of the spine that produces a sideways curve with some rotation; while typically mild, this condition can sometimes be painful.

Referred Pain Pain that appears to be located in one area, though it originates in another area.

Microtrauma Injury so small it is not detected at the time it occurs.

Herniated Disc The soft center part of the spinal disc that squeezes out through a small tear in the outer boundary of the disc and leaks into the surrounding tissue; also called prolapse.

The risk of disc herniation is greater for younger adults. Disc herniation is frequently listed as a cause of back pain, but studies show that only 5 to 10 percent of persons with herniated discs experience pain. The reason is that pain is often not experienced until complete herniation occurs. Pain is felt as the nuclear material begins to press on pain-sensitive structures in its path. Interestingly, the risk for disc herniation is greatest for individuals in their 30s and 40s. Risk decreases with age as the disc degenerates and becomes less soft and less pliable.

Degenerative disc disease is a common part of aging and a source of back pain. Most adults tend to get shorter with age and this is attributable to degenerative changes within the vertebral bodies and discs. A specific change is the flattening of the discs as a result of lost water content. This reduces the space between vertebrae and increases the compressive forces on the small facet joints and the large vertebral bodies. The decrease in the size of the spinal canal, in turn, increases the likelihood of nerve impingement, bone spur development, and arthritis, all of which can contribute to back pain and disability (see Figure 4).

Injury to the spine negatively affects the function of the core musculature. In contrast to disc herniation, the risk of pain from degenerative disc disease increases with age. One of the more important core muscles, the lumbar multifidus, is adversely affected by back pain. Studies demonstrate that with low back pain, the muscle becomes more inhibited and exhibits decreased levels of activation and increased fatigability. It is also prone to atrophy and becomes infiltrated with fatty deposits with lack of use. In the healthy individual, the multifidus is believed to be responsible for providing more than two-thirds of the dynamic rigidity to the lumbar spine and serves an important role in

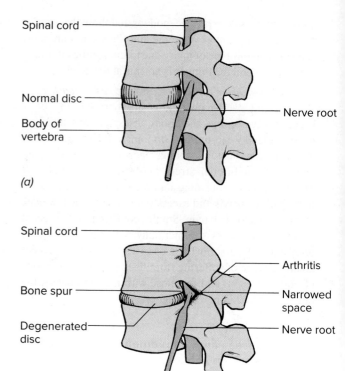

(a)

(b)

Figure 4 ▶ Normal disc (*a*) and degenerated disc with nerve impingement and arthritic changes (*b*).

proprioception and kinesthetic awareness. Research studies have shown specific spinal stabilization exercises to be effective in reversing some of the adverse changes to the multifidus, including positive gains in cross-sectional area/muscle bulk and improved neural recruitment. Participation in a program of core training exercise has also been shown to improve pain tolerance and function. Rehabilitation of the lumbar multifidus appears critical in the recovery period following back pain.

Medical intervention is sometimes needed for neck or back pain. Most cases of back pain resolve spontaneously, with 70 percent having no symptoms at the end of 3 weeks and 90 percent recovered after 2 months. However, medical approaches have been shown to speed up recovery from acute back or neck pain and to improve pain tolerance and function in chronic cases. Conservative treatment typically involves the use of anti-inflammatory medications, muscle relaxants, heat, cryotherapy, traction, or electrical stimulation. It can also include therapeutic exercise, massage, and joint mobilization. When this treatment is unsuccessful, referral to an alternative therapy, such as acupuncture, or to a pain clinic for steroidal anti-inflammatory injections may occur. As a last measure, surgery may be needed for removal of a herniated portion of a disc.

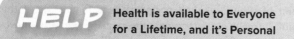

HELP   Health is available to Everyone for a Lifetime, and it's Personal

Is Back Pain in Your Future?

According to the National Institutes of Health, the most common medical problem in the United States is back pain, which is very often caused by degeneration of the discs in the spine. Preventive measures include maintaining a healthy weight over the lifespan, using proper lifting techniques, and engaging in regular exercise, particularly strength training and flexibility exercises.

What steps are you taking today to help prevent back problems later in life?

connect
ACTIVITY

Prevention and Rehabilitation of Back and Neck Problems

Exercise is a frequently prescribed treatment for back or neck pain. The integrity of individual vertebral segments of the spine is often compromised with injury to the back or neck. One or more components of the passive restraint system (ligaments, discs, vertebrae, or joints) may be damaged, creating a weak link in the stabilization system. In addition, optimal function of the dynamic and neural control systems is often adversely affected by injury. This may make a specific segment of the spine more vulnerable to delayed healing or further injury. Core training may enhance stability to the injured area by improving the function of the dynamic and neural control systems. Core training programs are also effective in treating low back pain. Studies have shown significant improvements in pain level and functional status following a program of spinal stabilization exercises, but positive results have also been obtained from more general exercise interventions. Future research may help identify subsets of people who may benefit from one type of exercise program over another.

Both resistance and aerobic exercises have been found to be helpful in treating many types of chronic pain. Exercises that are selected specifically to help correct pain-related problems are classified as therapeutic. These exercises are aimed at correcting the underlying cause of back or neck pain by strengthening weak muscles, stretching short ones, and improving circulation to and nourishment of tissues of the body. Both

Following recommended preventive strategies can reduce the likelihood of back and neck pain.
©George Doyle/Stockbyte/Getty Images

therapeutic and health-related fitness exercises may be considered preventive if done regularly, and with the appropriate FIT guidelines.

Core stabilization training refers to a variety of neuromuscular control exercises aimed at improving core muscle function. Core stabilization training is a popular buzz phrase found in both clinical and fitness-related settings. The phrase refers to a wide variety of interventions designed to improve the strength, endurance, and dynamic control of the core musculature. Core exercises range from the static plank and dynamic curl-up exercise, to functional movements like performing medicine ball lifts in conjunction with active squatting. Beginner-level core stability exercises focus on promoting neuromuscular control and improving body awareness. For example, isometric contractions are first aimed at keeping the spine in "neutral" alignment since this typically requires active engagement of the core stabilizer muscles. As participants gain improved strength and control, exercises can be made more challenging by introducing graduated movements of the arms and legs while maintaining this "neutral" posture of the back. An example is tensing the abdominal muscles while raising one arm and the opposite leg from an all-fours position. This involves engagement of the overall core musculature since it combines mobilization and stabilization.

Use of specific core stabilization exercises can reduce low back pain and functional disability. In the clinical or rehabilitation setting, core training is used to help reduce pain, assist in recovery from injury, and improve function. In fitness and sports enhancement settings, it is used with the goal of improving core strength and athletic performance. The effectiveness of core stabilization exercises has been evaluated most frequently in terms of how well they reduce pain and disability. Core stabilization has been shown to reduce both pain and functional disability in those with low back pain, particularly those with pain lasting longer than 3 months. A recent systematic review demonstrated that stabilization-specific exercises are superior to a general exercise program in reducing pain and disability. However, other studies report no differences between the two forms of intervention. A challenge in this line of research is that there is little consensus regarding the most effective exercise approach.

While core training seems to provide benefits to some, many people continue to suffer from low back pain. Some experts suggest that not all subjects with back pain benefit from the same type of exercise. Future research may help identify subsets of people who may benefit from one type of exercise program over another. Other experts recommend a multimodal approach to treating back pain, one that trains the body to work as an integrated whole using functional movement patterns. Additional research is needed to identify the most successful methods for preventing and treating chronic low back pain.

Movement disciplines like yoga and tai chi can promote body awareness and contribute to back health.
©Thinkstock Images/Stockbyte/Getty Images

Use of mind–body exercise programs, such as yoga, tai chi, and Pilates, can reduce low back pain and functional disability. Muscular exercises can provide benefits for some individuals with low back pain, but the overall effectiveness is rather modest. A possible explanation for the small effect is that exercise-specific treatments do not address other psychosocial correlates of back pain. Exercise programs that incorporate education, breath control, and cognitive components (body awareness, relaxation) may actually be better suited at reducing pain and disability than exercise alone. Both the American College of Physicians and the American Pain Society have supported the use of mind–body exercises in treating chronic low back pain. Yoga and tai chi are theorized to affect back and neck pain by improving body awareness, proprioception, posture, and balance. Studies indicate that nearly 43 percent of those with low back pain who participated in yoga or tai chi found the exercises beneficial. Tai chi has also been shown to reduce depression, a common psychosocial outcome in those with chronic pain.

Correcting muscle imbalances can help address many postural and back problems. If the muscles on one side of a joint are stronger than the muscles on the opposite side, the body part is pulled in the direction of the stronger muscles. Corrective exercises are usually designed to strengthen the long, weak muscles and to stretch the short, strong ones in order to have equal pull in both directions. For example, people with lumbar lordosis may need to strengthen the abdominals and gluteal muscles and also stretch the lower back and hip flexor muscles.

Good Posture Is Important for Back and Neck Health

Posture is important for both health and wellness. Posture is critically important for back and neck health, but there is no universally accepted definition of optimal **posture.** Good posture is unique to each individual and dependent on variations in body structure. Most people know good posture when they see it but often have trouble perceiving their own posture. This has important implications because posture is an important part of nonverbal communication. The first impression a person makes is usually a visual one, and good posture can help convey an impression of alertness, confidence, and vitality. Thus, posture makes important contributions to both health and wellness.

Proper posture allows the body segments to be balanced. Ideal posture is one where forces acting across the body do no harm to the integrity of local body segments. The individual segments of the human body (i.e., the head, shoulder girdle, pelvic girdle, rib cage, and spine) are aligned in a vertical column and are supported by muscles and ligaments. Proper posture helps maintain an even distribution of force across the body, improve shock absorption, and minimize the degree of active muscle tension required to maintain upright posture. When viewed from the side, three normal curvatures of the spine are present, causing the vertebral column to appear S-shaped. These curvatures are created by the **lordotic (inward) curve** of the cervical and lumbar spines and the **kyphotic (outward) curve** of the thoracic spine (see Figure 1). The curves help balance forces on the body and minimize muscle tension. They are also responsible for humans' unique ability to walk upright on two legs while maintaining a forward gaze. The degree of curvature is influenced by the tilt of the pelvis. A forward pelvic tilt increases curvature in the neck and lower back, whereas a backward pelvic tilt flattens the lower back. The most desirable position is a **neutral spine** in which the spine has neither too much nor too little lordotic curvature. The forces across the spine are balanced and muscular tension is at a minimum. Specific guidelines for standing and sitting posture are below:

- When *standing*, the head should be centered over the trunk with forward gaze, the shoulders should be down and back but relaxed, with the chest high and the abdomen flat. The spine should have gentle curves when viewed from the side but should be straight when seen from the back. When the pelvis is tilted properly, the pubis falls directly underneath the lower tip of the sternum. The knees should be relaxed, with the kneecaps pointed straight ahead. The feet should point straight or slightly outward, and the weight should be borne over the heel, on the outside border of the sole, and across the ball of the foot and toes (see Figure 5).

- When *sitting*, the head should be centered over the trunk, the shoulders down and back. If one is using a computer, the screen should be positioned at arm's reach from your

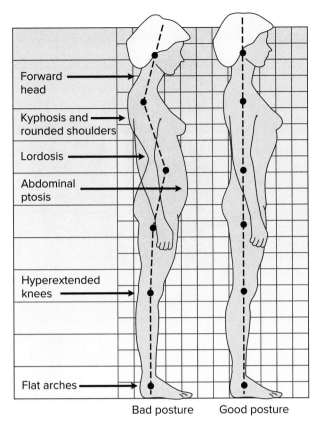

Forward head

Kyphosis and rounded shoulders

Lordosis

Abdominal ptosis

Hyperextended knees

Flat arches

Bad posture   Good posture

Figure 5 ▶ Comparison of bad and good posture.

eyes or a little farther if using a large monitor. (The top of the screen should be 2 to 3 inches above the eyes.) The seat of the chair should be at an angle that allows the knees to be positioned slightly lower than the hips. The feet should be supported on the floor. Good seated posture decreases pressure within the discs of the lower back and reduces fatigue of lower back muscles. A large percentage of our days is spent sitting, so it is important to use good postural habits at work or when studying (see Figure 6).

Poor posture contributes to a variety of health problems. When posture deviates from neutral, weight distribution becomes uneven and tissues are at risk for injury. Examples of common postural deviations are described in Table 1 along with associated health problems. Two of those highlighted are lumbar lordosis (excessive curvature of the lower back) and flat back (reduced curvature of the lower back).

- *Lumbar lordosis posture* occurs when the pelvis is tipped forward from a position of neutral tilt. With this posture, the hip flexor muscles become shortened and tight while the abdominal muscles become weak and long (with a reduced ability to "hold" within inner range). This muscle imbalance shifts body segment alignment toward a

position of uneven loading, increasing pressure on the facet joints of the vertebrae. Over time, degenerative changes may occur, including a narrowing of the openings where spinal nerves exit, thus increasing risk for pain.

- *Flat back posture*, on the other hand, occurs when the pelvis is tipped backward from a position of neutral tilt. With this posture, the lumbar spine is flexed, the lower back muscles are in a lengthened (weak) position, and the hamstring muscles are shortened and tight. A reduced lumbar curvature increases pressure on the intervertebral bodies and decreases shock absorption capabilities. Relative differences in flexibility between tight hamstring and long trunk muscles may also increase risk for injury. Laws of physics demonstrate that the body takes the path of least resistance during a chain of movement (e.g., forward bending), with the most flexible segment (i.e., the back) providing a greater contribution to the total range of movement. It follows that regions of greater movement will experience greater tissue strain. In the case of flat back posture, tight hamstrings may limit the contribution of hip motion during forward bending tasks, thus predisposing the lower back to become the fulcrum for movement and the site of injury.

Poor posture can contribute to back and neck pain, but it also contributes to risks of injury. However, it is important to understand that static posture does not always predict dynamic posture. An example of this would be an elderly person who may be able to stand upright with good posture but, with walking, a forward stoop and lateral limp become apparent. Dynamic conditions typically place greater demands on the musculoskeletal system making it more difficult to control alignment, which increases the risk for injuries. Athletic trainers and coaches routinely evaluate dynamic posture in order to identify problems before injuries occur. For example, the risk of anterior cruciate ligament (ACL) injuries is more likely in individuals with poor dynamic posture of the lower leg. If a person's knee rolls inward excessively in the landing phase of a jump or drop test, it can indicate a greater risk for injury. Postural correction through improved dynamic control is warranted to then reduce the risk.

Posture The relationship among body parts, whether standing, lying, sitting, or moving. Good posture is the relationship among body parts that allows you to function most effectively, with the least expenditure of energy and with a minimal amount of stress and strain on the body.

Lordotic (Inward) Curve The normal inward curvature of the cervical and lumbar spine.

Kyphotic (Outward) Curve The normal outward curvature of the thoracic spine.

Neutral Spine Proper position of the spine to maintain a normal lordotic curve. The spine has neither too much nor too little lordotic curve.

Sitting

- Sit upright with eyes looking straight ahead, chest lifted, shoulders down and back, slight arch in lower back, knees slightly lower than hips, feet supported on a firm surface.
- If you cross your legs, alternate which leg is crossed on top.
- When sitting for longer periods of time, use chair with armrests, an adequate seat cushion, and lumbar support.
- When driving, adjust seat to allow easy reach of foot pedals with slight knee bend; recline seat to allow gentle arch in low back.
- Reading material should be elevated or supported at eye level.
- The office desk should be about 29 to 30 inches high for the average man and about 27 to 29 inches high for the average woman. The computer screen should be positioned at arm's reach from your eyes (or a little farther if using a large monitor) and slightly below eye level.

Elements of Good Posture

Standing

- Stand upright with forward gaze, shoulders down and back, chest raised, stomach pulled up and in, slight arch in the lower back, slight bend in the knees, feet shoulder width apart, and toes pointing straight ahead or slightly outward.
- If you stand with weight shifted to one side, alternate which leg you lean on.
- If you stand in one place for a prolonged time, prop one foot on small step stool.
- Height of work surface should be about 2 to 4 inches below the waist.

Lying

- Use a pillow between the knees when lying on your side and under the knees when lying on the back.
- Choose a pillow that supports the head and neck in neutral alignment.
- Avoid reading in bed.

Figure 6 ▶ Characteristics of good posture for sitting, standing, and lying.

(Sitting): ©Jonathon Ross/Cutcaster; (Standing): ©Mark Ahn Creative Services; (Lying) ©Mark Ahn Creative Services

Table 1 ▶ Health Problems Associated with Poor Posture

Posture Problem	Definition	Health Problem
Forward head	The head aligned in front of the center of gravity	Headache, dizziness, and pain in the neck, shoulders, or arms
Kyphosis	Excessive curvature (flexion) in the upper back; also called humpback	Impaired respiration as a result of sunken chest and pain in the neck, shoulders, and arms
Lumbar lordosis	Excessive curvature (hyperextension) in the lower back (sway back), with a forward pelvic tilt	Back pain and/or injury, protruding abdomen, low back syndrome, and painful menstruation
Flat back	Reduced curvature in the lower back	Back pain, increased risk for injury due to reduced shock absorption
Abdominal ptosis	Excessive protrusion of abdomen	Back pain and/or injury, lordosis, low back syndrome, and painful menstruation
Hyperextended knees	The knees bent backward excessively	Greater risk for knee injury and excessive pelvic tilt (lordosis)
Pronated feet	The longitudinal arch of the foot flattened with increased pressure on inner aspect of foot	Decreased shock absorption, leading to foot, knee, and lower back pain

Correcting postural deviations begins with restoring adequate muscle fitness and muscle length. Lifestyle has a tremendous influence on posture, with most of us having a natu-ral tendency to slouch when sitting and standing. We can correct our posture with conscious effort; however, if poor posture is maintained for very long or very frequent periods of time, the body loses resiliency. Over time, mus-cles on one side of a joint or body segment can become shortened or tight while muscles on the opposite side can become lengthened and weak. Poor posture can also result following muscle injury. This may manifest itself in guarded postures or muscle dysfunction, which eventually leads to muscles on one side of the joint becoming inflexible due to facilitation and muscles on the opposite side becoming weak due to inhibition.

Improving posture can be challenging since it is deter-mined by the body's structure and function, including pas-sive elements (integrity of the joints), active elements (the muscles), and the neural system (signals from the nervous system). Postural correction can be achieved by improving body awareness, increasing flexibility of tight muscles, and improving strength of weak (inhibited) mus-cles. For example, a slouched posture with rounded and forward shoulders can be improved by elongating the pec-toral (chest) and paraspinal (neck) muscles and strength-ening muscles of the upper back. A lumbar lordosis posture can be improved by stretching the hip flexors and back extensors that keep the top of the pelvis tipped forward, followed by strengthening of the abdominal and gluteal muscles that help tip the pelvis backward (see Figure 7).

Awareness of posture is critical for prevention and treatment of back problems. Posture is largely main-tained through the input of small sensors in our skin and

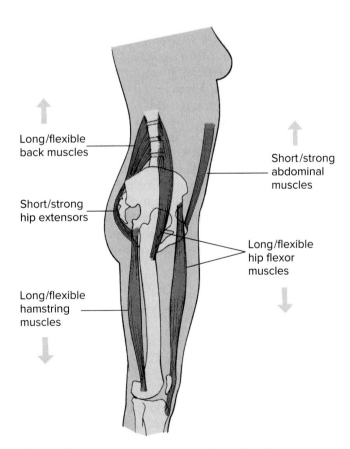

Long/flexible back muscles

Short/strong abdominal muscles

Short/strong hip extensors

Long/flexible hip flexor muscles

Long/flexible hamstring muscles

Figure 7 ▶ Balanced muscle strength and length permit good postural alignment.

Taking a break when using a laptop or tablet helps reduce back and neck strain.
©Ariel Skelley/Blend Images LLC

joints that reinforce our most frequent postures. Postural correction can be achieved by improving body awareness, increasing flexibility of tight muscles, and improving strength of weak (inhibited) muscles. However, in order to be effective, postural correction requires an ongoing use of body awareness and self-correction throughout the day. Studies have demonstrated that a focused stretching and strengthening program can improve posture only a little, at best. What is often missing in these interventions is the use of postural awareness. Poor posture must be corrected regularly in order to overcome the nervous system's memory of the faulty posture and to establish the improved postures as automatic. Both tai chi and yoga have been shown to be effective in improving dynamic postural control, perhaps in part related to the body awareness component of these mind–body disciplines.

Good Body Mechanics Are Important for Back and Neck Health

Proper body mechanics can prevent back and neck injury. Biomechanics is a discipline that applies mechanical laws and principles to study how the body performs more efficiently and with less energy. Good body mechanics, as applied to back care, implies maintaining a neutral spine during activities of daily living. A neutral spine maintains the normal curvature of the spine, thus allowing an optimal balance of forces across the spine, reducing compressive forces, and

minimizing muscle tension. In the following sections, specific recommendations and examples of good body mechanics are provided for a variety of body positions.

Ergnomics is a discipline that uses biomechanical principles to develop tools and workplace settings that put the least amount of strain on the body. Many employers take an active interest in ergonomic principles, since repetitive motion injuries and other musculoskeletal conditions are the leading cause of work-related ill health. One application of ergonomics (also known as human factors engineering) is the design of effective workstations for computer users. Properly fitting desks and chairs and the effective positioning of computer screens and keyboards can minimize problems such as carpal tunnel syndrome.

Good lifting technique focuses on using the legs. The muscles of the legs are relatively large and strong compared with the back muscles. Likewise, the hip joint is well designed for motion. It is less likely to suffer the same amount of wear and tear as the smaller joints of the  spine. When lifting an object from the floor, straddle the object with a wide stance; squat down by hinging through the hips and bending the knees; maintain a slight arch to the lower back by sticking out the buttocks; test the load and get help if it is too heavy or awkward; rise by tightening the leg muscles, not the back; keep the load close to the waist; don't pivot or twist.

Poor body mechanics can increase risks for back pain. A common cause of backache is muscle strain, frequently precipitated by poor body mechanics in daily activities, such as lifting or exercising. If lifting is done improperly, great pressure is exerted on the lumbar discs, and excessive stress and strain are placed on the lumbar muscles and ligaments (see Figure 8). Many popular exercises involve poor body mechanics and should be viewed with caution.

Exercise Guidelines for Back and Neck Health

Some exercises and movements may put the back and neck at risk. The human body is designed for motion. Nevertheless, certain movements can put the joints and musculoskeletal system at risk and should therefore be avoided. With  respect to care of the spine, many **contraindicated** movements involve the extremes of hyperflexion and hyperextension. Hyperflexion causes increased pressure in the discs, potentially leading to disc herniation. Hyperextension causes compressive wear and tear on the facet joints that join

Contraindicated Not recommended because of the potential for harm.

Lifting

Do:
- Keep a slight arch in the lower back, bend with the knees, straddle and test the load, keep load close to body, tighten abdominals, and lift using legs.
- Lower a load using the same principles in reverse.

Don't:
- Bend at the waist.
- Twist.
- Lift more than you can handle.
- Hyperextend the neck or back.

Reaching

Do:
- Use a stool or ladder when working with arms above head level.
- Keep tools within easy reach.
- Choose tools with extended handles.

Don't:
- Keep arms extended out in front or out to the side for long periods of time without rest.
- Hyperextend your neck.

Elements of Good Body Mechanics

Pushing & Pulling

Do:
- Push or pull heavy objects.
- Push rather than pull, if given a choice.

Carrying

Do:
- Keep load midline and close to the body.
- Divide the load if possible, carrying half in each arm/hand.
- Alternate the load from one side of the body to the other when it cannot be divided.
- Carry light to moderate loads in a backpack with straps.

Figure 8 ▶ Characteristics of good body mechanics for different lifestyle tasks.

(Lifting): ©McGraw-Hill Education/Ken Karp, photographer; (Reaching): ©Ingram Publishing/SuperStock; (Pushing & Pulling): ©George Doyle/Stockbyte/Getty Images; (Carrying): ©Creatas Images/Getty Images

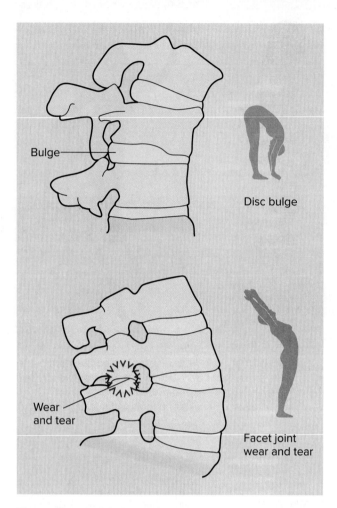

Bulge

Disc bulge

Wear
and tear

Facet joint
wear and tear

Figure 9 ▶ Risks of hyperflexion and hyperextension.

vertebral segments (see Figure 9). Hyperextension of the spine also causes narrowing of the intervertebral canal, potentially causing nerve impingement. Extremes of motion can be harmful to other joints as well. For example, knee hyperextension places excessive stress on structures at the back of the knee, whereas hyperflexion increases compressive forces under the kneecap (patello-femoral joint).

Following established exercise guidelines is important for safe exercise. "Safe" exercises are defined as those performed with normal body posture, mechanics, and movement in mind (see Table 2). They provide the intended benefits without compromising the integrity or stability of another body part. "Questionable" exercises, on the other hand, are exercises that may violate normal body mechanics and place the joints, ligaments, or muscles at risk for injury. No harm may occur from doing the exercise once, but repeated use over time can lead to injury. A number of commonly used exercises are regarded as poor choices (contraindicated) for nearly everyone in the general population due to the reasonable risk for injury over time. A separate category of questionable exercises are poor choices for certain segments of the population because of a specific health issue or known physical problem.

Differentiating exercises as "safe" or "questionable" can be difficult—even experts in the field have different opinions on the subject. These views change over time as new knowledge and research findings reshape our understanding of the effect of exercise on the human body.

When considering the merits and risks of different exercises, it may be necessary to consult an expert. Professionals such as athletic trainers, biomechanists, physical educators, physical therapists, and certified strength and conditioning specialists typically have college degrees and 4 to 8 years of study in such courses as anatomy, physiology, kinesiology, preventive and therapeutic exercise, and physiology of exercise. On-the-job training, a good physique or figure, and good athletic or dancing ability are not sufficient qualifications for teaching or advising about exercise. Most fitness centers hire instructors and personal trainers with appropriate certifications. Unfortunately, certification is not always a requirement. When searching for advice on training or exercise, inquire about an individual's qualifications.

Exercises prescribed for a particular individual differ from those that are good for everyone (mass prescription). In a clinical setting, a therapist works with one patient. A case history is taken and tests are conducted to

 Technology Update

Training Aids Versus Body Weight for Core Training

Core training can be conducted in a variety of ways. Training devices such as rocker boards, air-filled domes, and therapy balls provide ways to work on balance and stability. Other devices such as elastic tubing, stretch cords, vibrating wands, kettlebells, and medicine balls are used to overload the extremities and elicit a corresponding and supportive contraction of the core stabilizers. Although these devices offer engaging options for core training, there has also been a resurgence of interest in "body weight" training which emphasizes using a person's own body weight to provide resistance. No other equipment is required. The exercises utilize pushing and pulling movements to engage multiple muscle groups in a desired task. Examples of body weight exercises include squats, push-ups, sit-ups, and pull-ups. Body weight training naturally engages muscles of the core, forcing the deep muscles to stabilize the trunk in neutral alignment while utilizing the superficial muscles to power movement of the arms and legs. Many advocates appreciate the simplicity of body weight exercises.

Do you prefer training devices for core training or the simplicity of body weight exercises?

determine which muscles are weak or strong, long or short. Exercises are then prescribed for that person. For example, a wrestler with a recent history of shoulder dislocation would probably be prescribed specific shoulder-strengthening exercises to regain stability in the joint. Common shoulder-stretching exercises would likely be contraindicated. In this case, the muscles and joint capsule on the front of the shoulder are already quite lax to have allowed dislocation to occur in the first place.

Exercises prescribed or performed as a group cannot typically take individual needs into account. For example, when a physical educator, an aerobics instructor, or a coach leads a group of people in exercise, there may be little consideration for individual differences. Some of the exercises performed in this type of group setting may not be appropriate for all individuals. Similarly, an exercise that is appropriate for a certain individual may not be appropriate for all members of a group. Since it is not always practical to prescribe individual exercise routines for everyone, it is often necessary to provide general recommendations that are appropriate for most individuals. The classification of exercises in this Concept should be viewed in this context.

The risks associated with physical activity can be reduced by modifying the variables or conditions under which the activity is performed. Although some exercises are clearly contraindicated, risks are often associated with the frequency, intensity, and duration of the movement. *Frequency* may contribute to microtrauma of the back in a gymnast who repeatedly hyperextends the spine. *Intensity* may jeopardize the lower back of the power lifter who pushes too quickly. *Duration* may be a factor in the knee strain of a baseball catcher who spends sustained time in a deep squat. The speed of a movement and the movement quality may also influence the risk. In some cases, changing a single variable (*frequency, duration, intensity, speed,* or *movement quality*) may significantly reduce risk; but in other cases, multiple factors may need to be changed. In some cases, the best strategy may be to look for a safer exercise or to modify the offending activity. (A variety of contraindicated exercises and safer alternatives are presented in Table 2 later in this Concept.)

Risks from exercise can't be avoided completely. Variables that are not always under the direct control of the participant include environmental conditions, such as temperature, humidity, or exercise surface. Likewise, the demands of sports and certain occupations may require individuals to train or work to the maximal limit of these variables (up to or just short of injury). Circumstances may not always permit every variable to be modified to suit an individual. However, making an active effort to adjust variables that are modifiable will make a difference in reducing injury risk.

Some additional general guidelines will help prevent postural, back, and neck problems. In addition to the suggestions for improving body mechanics noted in the previous sections, the following guidelines should be helpful:

- Establish a habit of aerobic activity for overall conditioning of the entire body
- Maintain a healthy weight. The smaller the waistline, the less the strain on the lower back.
- Do exercises to strengthen abdominal and hip extensors and to improve flexibility of the hip flexor and lumbar muscles if they are tight.
- Avoid hazardous exercises.
- Choose an appropriate warm-up before strenuous activity.
- Sleep on a moderately firm mattress or place a 3/4-inch-thick plywood board under the mattress.
- Avoid sudden jerky movements of the trunk, especially twisting.
- Use appropriate back and seat supports when sitting for long periods.
- Maintain good posture when carrying heavy loads; do not lean forward, sideways, or backward.
- Adjust sports equipment to permit good posture; for example, adjust a bicycle seat and handlebars to permit good body alignment.
- Avoid long periods of sitting at a desk or driving; take frequent breaks and adjust the car seat and headrest for maximum support.

In the News

Digital Eye Strain

Excessive sitting may not only lead to back problems. Digital eye strain is a condition characterized by physical eye discomfort felt after two or more hours in front of a digital screen. If unresolved, symptoms can transition to blurred vision, burning eyes, headaches, and disrupted sleep. Approximately two thirds of American adults likely experience symptoms of digital eye strain due to prolonged use of electronic devices like computers, tablets, and cell phones. To break up extended sitting and computer time, ophthamologists recommend the "20/20/20" rule: for every 20 minutes spent using a screen, look away at something that is 20 feet away from you for a total of 20 seconds. This would also be a good time to stand up and move around.

Would you benefit from computer or smartphone apps to remind you to take breaks?

Using Self-Management Skills

Gaining performance skills related to posture and body mechanics is important for reducing risks of back and neck pain. Awareness of body posture is an important self-management skill that takes time to develop. Knowledge about posture and body mechanics is important, but the bigger challenge is to develop the discipline and body awareness needed to make corrections in posture during your daily life. Similarly, it is important to develop good habits and discipline to use good body mechanics when working, lifting, and carrying objects. These types of skills are called "performance skills" since it is important to apply them in practice. Like with other skills, you can improve your awareness and establish better postural habits to decrease your risks for future back and neck problems.

Building knowledge and changing your beliefs can help you avoid harmful exercises. As discussed, back and neck pain can result from accumulated damage (microtrauma) caused by performing unsafe exercises. There are clear risks associated with performing exercises that involve excess hyperflexion and hyperextension movements. Other exercises may put excess load on the spine. Thus, a key self-management skill for back health is to build sufficient knowledge so that you can identify harmful exercises and select safer alternatives. A variety of examples are provided in Table 2 for leg, arms, and trunk exercises. Changing your belief system regarding these exercises is also important. You may have learned these exercises from coaches or teachers, but that doesn't mean they are safe.

Applying self-assessment and self-planning skills can help prevent problems and enhance recovery. The exercises included in this Concept are aimed at building flexibility or promoting strength/muscle endurance; however, each is selected specifically to help correct a postural problem or to remove the cause of back and neck pain. Therefore, these exercises may be classified as therapeutic. The same exercises may be called preventive because they can be used to prevent postural or spine problems. Results from the Healthy Back assessment can help inform needs, and it is important to use the information to identify exercises that can address those needs. The exercises in Tables 3, 4, 5, and 6 depict variations of exercises used to strengthen and stabilize the neck and back. Tables 4 and 5 illustrate core trunk variations that become progressively more difficult throughout the sequence. The beginning pose is appropriate for most people, whereas the last pose is more advanced. You can determine which level of difficulty is appropriate for you and begin there, progressing to the more advanced exercises as you gain better strength and control. Individuals with back and neck pain are encouraged to seek the advice of a physician or physical therapist to guide these decisions.

Strategies for Action: Lab Information

An important step in taking action is assessing your current status. The Healthy Back Tests consist of eight pass or fail items that will give you an idea of the areas in which you might need improvement. The Healthy Back Tests are described in the Lab Resource Materials. You will take these tests in Lab 12A. Experts have identified behaviors associated with potential future back and neck problems. A questionnaire is also provided for assessing these risk factors.

Adopting and maintaining good posture promotes good back health. Lab 12B includes a posture test to help you evaluate your posture. Identify possible postural problems and take appropriate corrective action to reduce stress and strain on your back and neck.

Keep records of progress to maintain a back care program. Lab 12C provides an activity logging sheet for keeping records of your progress as you regularly perform exercises to build and maintain good back and neck fitness.

connect
ACTIVITY

Suggested Resources and Readings

The websites for the following sources can be accessed by searching online for the organization, program, or title listed. Specific scientific references are available at the end of this edition of *Concepts of Fitness and Wellness*.

- Athletic Trainer Plus. Resource app (online information).
- Heid, M. (2016, April 6). Are chiropractors legitimate? *Time* (online article).
- Medline Plus. Low Back Pain Information (online information).
- National Institutes of Health. Low Back Pain Fact Sheet (online information).
- Spine-Health. Low Back Pain Exercises (online resource).
- WebMD. Understanding back pain symptoms (online resource).

Table 2

1. Questionable Exercise: The Swan

This exercise hyperextends the lower back and stretches the abdominals. The abdominals are too long and weak in most people and should not be lengthened further. Extension can be harmful to the back, potentially causing nerve impingement and facet joint compression. Other exercises in which this occurs include cobras, backbends, straight-leg lifts, straight-leg sit-ups, prone-back lifts, donkey kicks, fire hydrants, backward trunk circling, weight lifting with the back arched, and landing from a jump with the back arched.

Safer Alternative Exercise: Back Extension

Lie prone over a roll of blankets or pillows and extend the back to a neutral or horizontal position.

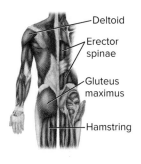

2. Questionable Exercise: Back-Arching Abdominal Stretch

This exercise can stretch the hip flexors, quadriceps, and shoulder flexors (such as the pectorals), but it also stretches the abdominals, which is not desired. Because of the armpull, it can potentially hyperflex the knee joint and strain neck musculature.

Safer Alternative Exercise: Wand Exercise

This exercise stretches the front of the shoulders and chest. Sit with wand grasped at ends. Raise wand overhead. Be certain that the head does not slide forward. Keep the chin tucked, neck straight, and spine erect. Bring wand down behind shoulder blades. Hold. Press forward on the wand simultaneously by pushing with the hands. Relax; then try to move the hands lower, sliding the wand down the back. Hold again. Hands may be moved closer together to increase stretch on chest muscles.

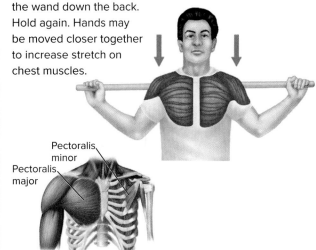

Note: All safer alternative exercises should be held 15 to 30 seconds unless otherwise indicated.

Table 2   Questionable Exercises and Safer Alternatives

Table 2

3. Questionable Exercise: Seated Forward Arm Circles with Palms Down

This exercise (arms straight out to the sides) may cause pinching of the rotator cuff and biceps tendons between the bony structures of the shoulder joint and/or irritate the bursa in the shoulder. The tendency is to emphasize the use of the stronger chest muscles (pectorals) to perform the motion rather than emphasizing the weaker upper back muscles.

Safer Alternative Exercise: Seated Backward Arm Circles with Palms Up

Sit, turn palms up, pull in chin, and contract abdominals. Circle arms backward.

Deltoid

4. Questionable Exercise: Double-Leg Lift

This exercise is usually used with the intent of strengthening the abdominals, when in fact it is primarily a hip flexor (iliopsoas) strengthening exercise. Most people have overdeveloped the hip flexors and do not need to further strengthen those muscles because this may cause forward pelvic tilt. Even if the abdominals are strong enough to contract isometrically to prevent hyperextension of the lower back, the exercise produces excess stress on the discs.

Safer Alternative Exercise: Reverse Curl

This exercise strengthens the lower abdominals. Lie on your back on the floor and bring your knees in toward the chest. Place the arms at the sides for support. For movement, pull the knees toward the head, raising the hips off the floor. Do not let knees go past the shoulders. Return to starting position and repeat.

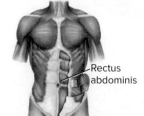

Rectus abdominis

5. Questionable Exercise: The Windmill

This exercise involves simultaneous rotation and flexion (or extension) of the lower back, which is contraindicated. Because of the orientation of the facet joints in the lumbar spine, these movements violate normal joint mechanics, placing tremendous torsional stress on the joint capsule and discs.

Safer Alternative Exercise: Back-Saver Toe Touch

Sit on the floor. Extend leg and bend the other knee, placing the foot flat on the floor. Bend at the hips and reach forward with both hands. Grasp one foot, ankle, or calf depending upon the distance you can reach. Pull forward with your arms and bend forward. Slight bend in the knee is acceptable. Hold. Repeat with the opposite leg.

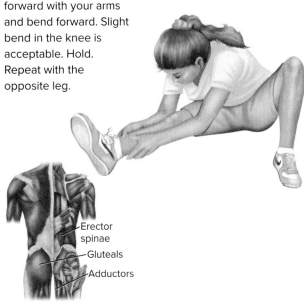

Erector spinae
Gluteals
Adductors

6. Questionable Exercise: Neck Circling

This exercise and other exercises that require neck hyper-extension (e.g., neck bridging) can pinch arteries and nerves in the neck and at the base of the skull, cause wear and tear to small joints of the spine, and produce dizziness or myofascial trigger points. In people with degener-ated discs, it can cause dizziness, numbness, or even precipitate strokes. It also aggravates arthritis and degenerated discs.

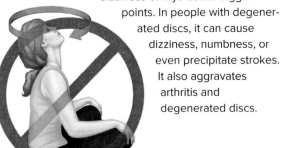

Safer Alternative Exercise: Head Clock

This exercise relaxes the muscle of the neck. Assume a good posture (seated with legs crossed or in a chair), and imagine that your neck is a clock face with the chin at the center. Flex the neck and point the chin at 6:00, hold, lift the chin; repeat point-ing chin to 4:00, to 8:00, to 3:00 and finally to 9:00. Return to center position with chin up after each movement.

Semispinalis capitis
Splenius capitis
Levator scapulae
Sternocleidomastoid
Scalenes
Trapezius

Table 2

Table 2   Questionable Exercises and Safer Alternatives

7. Questionable Exercise: Shoulder Stand Bicycle

This exercise and the yoga positions called the plough and the plough shear (not shown) force the neck and upper back to hyperflex. It has been estimated that 80 percent of the population has forward head and kyphosis (humpback) with accompanying weak muscles. This exercise is especially dangerous for these people. Neck hyperflexion results in excessive stretch on the ligaments and nerves. It can also aggravate preexisting arthritic conditions. If the purpose for these exercises is to reduce gravitational effects on the circulatory system or internal organs, lie on a tilt board with the feet elevated. If the purpose is to warm up the muscles in the legs, slow jog in place. If the purpose is to stretch the lower back, try the leg hug exercise.

Safer Alternative Exercise: Leg Hug

Lie on your back with the knees bent at about 90 degrees. Bring your knees to the chest and wrap the arms around the back of the thighs. Pull knees to chest and hold.

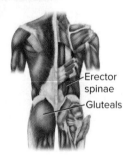

Erector spinae

Gluteals

8. Questionable Exercise: Straight-Leg and Bent-Knee Sit-Ups

There are several valid criticisms of the sit-up exercise. Straight-leg sit-ups can place extra stress on the lower lumbar vertebrae, causing back problems. A bent-knee sit-up creates less shearing force on the spine, but some recent studies have shown it produces greater compression on the lumbar discs than the straight-leg sit-up. Placing the hands behind the neck or head during the sit-up or during a crunch results in hyperflexion of the neck.

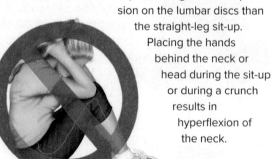

Safer Alternative Exercise: Crunch

Lie on your back with the knees bent more than 90 degrees. Curl up until the shoulder blades lift off the floor, then roll down to starting position and repeat. There are several safe arm positions. The easiest is with the arms extended straight in front of the body. Alternatives are with the arms crossed over the chest or the palms or fist held beside the ears.

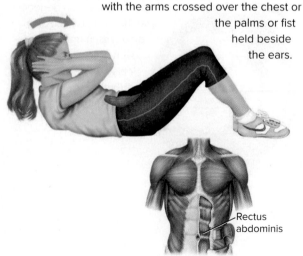

Rectus abdominis

9. Questionable Exercise: Standing Toe Touches or Double-Leg Toe Touches

These exercises—especially when done ballistically—can produce degenerative changes at the vertebrae of the lower back. They also stretch the ligaments and joint capsule of the knee. Bending the back while the legs are straight may cause back strain, particularly if the movement is done ballistically. If performed only on rare occasions as a test, the chance of injury is less than if incorporated into a regular exercise program. Safer stretches of the lower back include the leg hug, the single knee-to-chest, the back-saver hamstring stretch, and the back-saver toe touch.

Safer Alternative Exercise: Back-Saver Hamstring Stretch

This exercise stretches the hamstring and lower back muscles. Sit with one leg extended and one knee bent, foot turned outward and close to the buttocks. Clasp hands behind back. Bend forward from the hips, keeping the low back as straight as possible. Allow bent knee to move laterally so trunk can move forward. Stretch and hold. Repeat with the other leg.

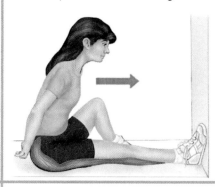 

Hamstring

10. Questionable Exercise: Bar Stretch

This type of stretch may be harmful. Some experts have found that when the extended leg is raised 90 degrees or more and the trunk is bent over the leg, it may lead to **sciatica** and **piriformis syndrome,** especially in the person who has limited flexibility.

Safer Alternative Exercise: One-Leg Stretch

This exercise stretches the hamstring muscles. Stand with one foot on a bench, keeping both legs straight. Hinge forward from the hips keeping shoulders back and chest up. Bend forward until a pull is felt on the back side of the thigh. Hold. Repeat.

Hamstring

> **Sciatica** Pain along the sciatic nerve in the buttock and leg.
>
> **Piriformis Syndrome** Muscle spasm and nerve entrapment in the piriformis muscle of the buttocks region, causing pain in the buttock and referred pain down the leg (sciatica).

Table 2

Table 2 Questionable Exercises and Safer Alternatives

11. Questionable Exercise: Shin and Quadriceps Stretch

This exercise causes hyperflexion of the knee. When the knee is hyperflexed more than 120 degrees and/or rotated outward by an external **torque,** the ligaments and joint capsule are stretched, and damage to the cartilage may occur. *Note:* One of the quadriceps, the rectus femoris, is not stretched if the trunk is allowed to bend forward because it crosses the hip as well as the knee joint. If the exercise is used to stretch the quadriceps, substitute the hip and thigh stretch. For most people it is not necessary to stretch the shin muscles, since they are often elongated and weak; however, if you need to stretch the shin muscles to relieve muscle soreness, try the shin stretch.

Safer Alternative Exercise: Hip and Thigh Stretch

Kneel so that the front leg is bent at 90 degrees (front knee directly above the front ankle). The knee of the back leg should touch the floor well behind the front foot. Press the pelvis forward and downward. Hold. Repeat with the opposite leg forward. Do not bend the front knee more than 90 degrees.

Quadriceps

12. Questionable Exercise: The Hero

Like the shin and quadriceps stretch, this exercise causes hyperflexion of the knee. It also causes torque on the hyperflexed knee. For these reasons the ligaments and joint capsule are stretched and the cartilage may be damaged. For most people it is not necessary to stretch the shin muscles since they are often elongated and weak; however, if you need to stretch the shin muscles, use the shin stretch. If this exercise is used to stretch the quadriceps, substitute the hip and thigh stretch.

Safer Alternative Exercise: Shin Stretch

Kneel on your knees, turn to right and press down on right ankle with right hand. Hold. Keep hips thrust forward to avoid hyperflexing the knees. Do not sit on the heels. Repeat on the left side.

Tibialis anterior

Extensor digitorum longus

Extensor hallucis longus

Torque A twisting or rotating force.

13. Questionable Exercise: Deep Squatting Exercises

This exercise, with or without weights, places the knee joint in hyperflexion, compressing the joint surfaces, stretching certain ligaments, irritating the synovial membrane, and possibly damaging the cartilage. The joint has even greater stress when the lower leg and foot are not in straight alignment with the knee. If you are performing squats to strengthen the knee and hip extensors, try substituting the alternate leg kneel or half squat with free weight or leg presses on a resistance machine.

Safer Alternative Exercise: Half Squat

This exercise develops the muscles of the thighs and buttocks. Stand upright with feet shoulder width apart. Squat slowly by moving hips backward, then bending knees. Keep shins vertical. Bend knees 45–90 degrees. Repeat.

Gluteus maximus

Quadriceps

14. Questionable Exercise: Knee Pull-Down

This exercise can result in hyperflexion of the knee. The arms or hands placed on top of the shin places undue stress on the knee joint.

Safer Alternative Exercise: Single Knee-to-Chest

Lie down with both knees bent, draw one knee to the chest by pulling on the thigh with the hands, then extend the knee and point the foot toward the ceiling. Hold. Pull to chest again and return to starting position. Repeat with other leg.

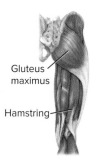

Gluteus maximus

Hamstring

Table 3 Stretching and Strengthening Exercises for the Muscles of the Neck

Table 3

These exercises are designed to increase strength in the neck muscles and to improve neck range of motion. They are helpful in preventing and resolving symptoms of neck pain and for relieving trigger points. Hold stretches for 15–30 seconds.

1. Upper Trapezius Stretch

This exercise stretches the upper trapezius muscle and relieves neck pain and headache. To stretch the right upper trapezius, place left hand on top of head, right hand behind back. Gently turn head toward left underarm and tilt chin toward chest. Increase stretch by gently drawing head forward with left hand. Hold. Repeat to opposite side.

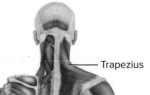

Trapezius

2. Chin Tuck

This exercise stretches the muscles at the base of the skull and reduces headache symptoms. Place hands together at the base of the head. Tuck in the chin and gently press head backward into your hands, while looking straight ahead. Hold.

Deep extensors

3. Head Nod

Lie flat on the back without a pillow. Gently nod the head in a "yes" motion. Motion should result in the tightening of muscles deep in the front of the neck. Place two fingers over the sides of the neck to monitor for the undesirable substitution of stronger muscles in this region. Hold 10–30 seconds (or as long as can be maintained without substitution). Repeat 10 times. Progress this exercise by first nodding "yes" and then lifting the head ¼ inch to ½ inch off the surface.

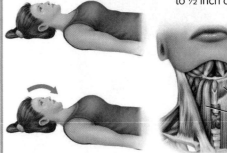

Deep neck flexors

4. Isometric Neck Exercises

This exercise strengthens the neck muscles. Sit and place one or both hands on the head as shown. Assume good head and neck posture by tucking the chin, flattening the neck, and pushing the crown of the head up (axial extension). Apply resistance *(a)* sideward, *(b)* forward, and *(c)* backward. Contract the neck muscles to prevent the head and neck from moving. Hold contraction for 6 seconds. Repeat each exercise up to six times. *Note:* For neck muscles, it is probably best to use a less than maximal contraction, especially in the presence of arthritis, degenerative discs, or injury.

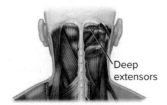

(a)

(b)

(c)

Neck flexors

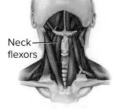

Neck rotator and extensors

Core Stabilization Exercise Variations Table 4

These exercises are designed to help improve the ability of the core muscles to stabilize the trunk during dynamic movements of the arms and legs. The variations depict exercises of progressive difficulty. Many other variations exist along these same themes. Advance to the next exercise in each set only when the preceding level is mastered. Exercises can be performed in 2–3 sets of 10–20 repetitions.

1. Front Plank Variations

(a) Begin by holding a plank position with support through the forearms and toes, keeping back straight and stomach pulled in. Hold for 20–30 seconds. *Variations:* Progress by performing plank with elbows extended and support through palms and feet *(b)*, by adding a single-arm raise with support through opposite forearm and feet *(c)*, or by adding a single-leg raise with support on both forearms *(d)*.

(a)   *(b)*

(c)   *(d)*

2. Side Plank Variations

(a) Begin by holding a side plank position with support through one forearm and lower legs, with knees bent. Lift hips off ground and keep back straight and stomach pulled in. Hold for 20–30 seconds. *Variations:* Progress by performing plank with elbow straight and support through palm *(b)*, by raising one arm straight over head with support through opposite forearm *(c)*, or by raising one leg upward with support through forearm *(d)*.

(a)   *(b)*

(c)   *(d)*

3. Superman Variations

(a) Begin on hands and knees. Tighten stomach and extend one leg behind you until it is parallel with the floor. Don't arch the back. Hold for 5 seconds. Relax and repeat. *Variations:* Progress by raising one arm and opposite leg parallel with the floor. Perform exercise while lying over a medicine ball *(b)*, while positioned on an unstable dome surface *(c)*, or while supported on an extended arm and leg *(d)*.

(a)   *(b)*

(c)   *(d)*

4. Abdominal Bracing Variations

(a) Begin by lying on back with stomach tightened. Raise one foot off the floor until hip and knee are bent 90 degrees and then slowly lower the foot back to the floor without letting back arch. *Variations:* Progress by raising/lowering arms and legs from the floor in alternate fashion, keeping back flat *(b)*; by raising/lowering arms and legs while lying on an unstable surface such as a foam roller *(c)*; or by adding resistance using a medicine ball-lowering ball overhead while extending one leg and then touching ball and knee together over midline *(d)*.

(a)   *(b)*

(c)   *(d)*

Table 4

Table 4   Core Stabilization Exercise Variations

5. Bridge Variations

(a) Begin by lying on back and lifting hips from the floor. Hold 5 seconds. Lower hips slowly and repeat. *Variations:* Progress by performing exercise with only one foot on the floor and opposite leg held in the air, knee bent *(b)*, or by performing exercise with only one foot on the floor and opposite leg extended straight *(c)*. Add complexity by holding a bridge while lying over an unstable medicine ball and moving a weighted ball in an arc overhead *(d)*.

(a)

(b)

(c)

(d)

Exercises for Muscle Fitness of Abdominals and Back Extensors Table 5

These exercises will increase the strength of the abdominal and back muscles. Strong trunk muscles are important for maintaining a neutral pelvis, maintaining good posture, and preventing backache.

Table 5

1. Abdominal Crunch Variations

(a) **Curl-Up** (develops the upper abdominal muscles): Begin by lying on the floor with knees bent. Hands can be progressed from arms extended to cross over chest to palms on ears. Curl up until shoulder blades leave the floor; then roll down. *Variations: (b)* **Crunch with Twist** (strengthens the oblique abdominal): Curl up while bringing one elbow toward opposite knee. Place feet on a bench to increase difficulty. *(c)* **Reverse Curl** (develops the lower abdominal muscles): Lie on back with arms at sides. Left knees to the chest, raising hips from floor. Do not let knees pass the shoulders. *(d)* **Sitting Tucks** (develops the lower abdominal muscles): Sit on the floor with feet raised, arms extended for balance. Alternately bend and extend legs without touching feet or back to the floor.

(a) Curl-Up

(b) Crunch with Twist

(c) Reverse Curl

(d) Sitting Tucks

2. Back Extension Variations

(a) **Arm Lift** (strengthens the scapular adductors): Lie on stomach with arms extended overhead. Raise arms 2–3 inches off the floor. Hold 5 seconds. Relax and repeat. *(b)* **Trunk Lift** (develops the muscles of the upper back and corrects rounded shoulders): Lie face down with hands behind neck. Raise head and chest from the floor. Relax and repeat. *(c)* **Upper Trunk Lift** (strengthens the muscles of the back): Lie over bench with upper half of body over the edge and partner stabilizing legs. Slowly raise trunk parallel to floor. Lower and repeat.

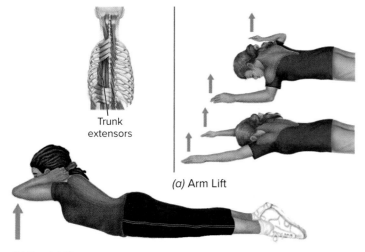

Trunk extensors

(a) Arm Lift

(b) Trunk Lift

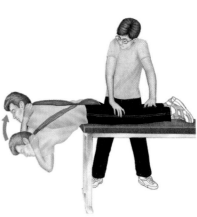

(c) Upper Trunk Lift

Table 6

Table 6 Core Functional Movement Exercises

These exercises are designed to train the muscles of the core, arms, and legs by using functional movement patterns of the trunk and limbs.

1. Pulls and Lifts with Stabilization

(a) **Pulls:** Begin with elastic cord secured above shoulder height. Grasp free end and pull down across body, ending with hand at waist level on opposite side of body. Keep back and neck in a "neutral" posture and stomach tightened throughout. *(b)* **Lifts:** Begin with elastic cord secured below waist height. Cross arms toward opposite side of body and grasp free end. Pull upward, uncrossing arm as it is lifted overhead. Keep back and neck in a "neutral" posture and stomach tightened throughout.

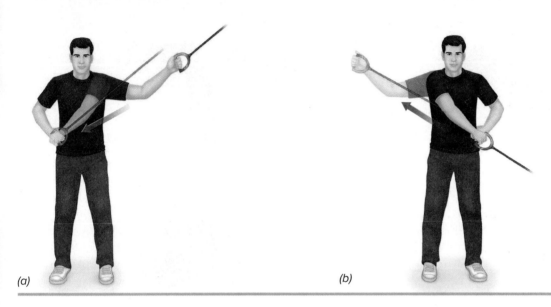

(a)   *(b)*

2. Weighted Lifts and Squats with Stabilization

(a) **Forward Press:** Begin by holding a weight plate at waist level, elbows bent. Tighten stomach and press plate out in front of you by straightening elbows. Return weight to starting position. Maintain low back in a "neutral" posture throughout. *(b)* **Overhead Lift:** Begin by holding weighted ball at chest level while squatting on an unstable surface such as a BOSU. Tighten stomach and lift ball overhead, straightening arms and legs. Return to starting position. Maintain balance and gentle arch in low back throughout.

(a)

(b)

Lab Resource Materials: Healthy Back Tests

Chart 1 Healthy Back Tests

Physicians and therapists use these tests, among others, to make differential diagnoses of back problems. You and your partner can use them to determine if you have muscle tightness that may put you at risk for back problems. Discontinue any of these tests if they produce pain, numbness, or tingling sensations in the back, hips, or legs. Experiencing any of these sensations may be an indication that you have a low back problem that requires diagnosis by your physician. Partners should use *great caution* in applying force. Be gentle and listen to your partner's feedback.

FLEXIBILITY

Test 1—Straight-Leg Lift. Lie on your back with hands behind your neck. The partner on your left should stabilize your right leg by placing his or her right hand on your knee. With the left hand, your partner should grasp your left ankle and raise your left leg as near to a right angle as possible. In this position (as shown in the diagram), your lower back should be in contact with the floor. Your right leg should remain straight and on the floor throughout the test.

If your left leg bends at the knee, this indicates short hamstring muscles. If your back arches and/or your right leg does not remain flat on the floor, this indicates short lumbar muscles or hip flexor muscles. For you to pass the test, each leg should be able to reach approximately 90 degress without the knee or back bending. (Both sides must pass in order to pass the test.)

Test 2—Thomas Test. Lie on your back on a table or bench with your right leg extended beyond the edge of the table (approximately one-third of your thigh off the table). Bring your left knee to your chest and pull your thigh down tightly with your hands. Lower your right leg. Your lower back should remain flat against the table, as shown in the diagram. For you to pass the test, your right thigh should be at table level or lower.

Test 3—Ober Test. Lie on your left side with your left leg flexed 90 degrees at the hip and 90 degrees at the knee. A partner should place your right hip in slight extension and right knee with just a slight bend (~20 degrees flexion). Your partner stabilizes your pelvis with the left hand to prevent movement. Your partner then allows the weight of the top leg to lower the leg to the floor. For you to pass the test, your knee or upper leg should be able to touch the table.

CORE TRUNK ENDURANCE TESTS

Test 4—Leg Drop Test* Lie on your back on a table or on the floor with both legs extended overhead. Flatten your low back against the table or floor by tightening your abdominals. Slowly lower your legs while keeping your back flat.

If your back arches before you reach a 45-degree angle, your abdominal muscles are too weak and you fail the test. A partner should be ready to support your legs if needed to prevent your lower back from arching or strain to the back muscles.

*The Leg Drop Test is suitable as a diagnostic test when performed one time. It is not a good exercise to be performed regularly by most people. If it causes pain, stop the test.

243

Chart 1 Healthy Back Tests (*Continued*)

Test 5—Isometric Abdominal Test. Lie supine with hips bent 45 degrees, feet flat on the floor, and arms by the side. Draw a line 4 1/2 inches beyond fingertips. Tuck chin and curl trunk forward, touching line with fingers. To pass, hold for 30 seconds.

Test 6—Isometric Extensor Test. Lie on a table with upper half of the body hanging over the edge and arms crossed in front of chest. Have a partner stabilize your feet and legs. Raise your trunk smoothly until your back is in a horizontal position parallel to the floor. Do not arch the back. To pass the test, hold this position for 30 seconds.

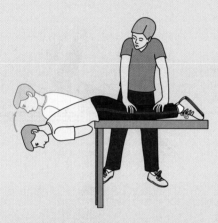

Test 7—Prone Bridge. Support yourself on the floor by resting on forearms and toes, body extended and back straight. Elbows are placed directly underneath shoulders. Look straight down toward hands. Do not arch the back. To pass the test, hold this position for 30 seconds.

Test 8—Quadruped Stabilization. Begin on hands and knees. Place hands directly below shoulders and knees directly below hips. Draw abdominals in. Extend one arm and opposite leg to a horizontal position. Do not allow back to arch or body to sway. To pass, hold position for 30 seconds.

Test 9—Right Lateral Bridge. Lie on your right side with legs extended. Raise pelvis off the floor until trunk is straight and body weight is supported on arm and feet. Do not roll forward or backward. Do not arch back. To pass the test, hold this position for 30 seconds.

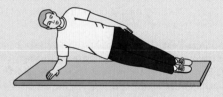

Test 10—Left Lateral Bridge. Lie on your left side with legs extended. Raise pelvis off the floor until trunk is straight and body weight is supported on arm and feet. Do not roll forward or backward or arch back. To pass the test, hold this position for 30 seconds.

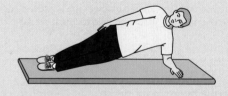

Chart 2 Healthy Back Test Ratings

Classification	Number of Tests Passed
Excellent	8–10
Very good	7
Good	6
Fair	5
Poor	1–4

Lab 12A The Back/Neck Questionnaire and Healthy Back Tests

Name	Section	Date

Purpose: To self-assess your potential for back problems using the Healthy Back Tests and the back/neck questionnaire.

Procedures

1. Answer the questions in the Risk-Factor Questionnaire for Back and Neck Problems (below). Count your points for nonmodifiable factors, modifiable factors, and total score, and record these scores in the Results section. Use Chart 1 to determine your rating for all three scores and record them in the Results section.
2. With a partner, administer the Healthy Back Tests to each other (see Lab Resource Materials). Determine your rating using Chart 2. Record your score and rating in the Results section. If you did not pass a test, list the muscles you should develop to improve on that test.
3. Complete the Conclusions and Implications section.

Risk-Factor Questionnaire for Back and Neck Problems

Directions: Place an X in the appropriate circle after each question. Add the scores for each of the circles you checked to determine your nonmodifiable risk, modifiable risk, and total risk scores.

Nonmodifiable

1. Do you have a family history of osteoporosis, arthritis, rheumatism, or other joint disease?   (0) No   (1) Yes

2. What is your age?   (0) <40   (1) 40–50   (2) 51–60   (3) 61+

3. Did you participate regularly in these sports when you were young: gymnastics, football, weight lifting, skiing, ballet, javelin, or shot put?   (0) No   (1) Some   (3) Regularly

4. How many previous back or neck problems have you had?   (0) None   (1) 1   (2) 2   (5) 3+

Total Nonmodifiable Score = _____

Modifiable

5. Does your daily routine involve heavy lifting?   (0) No   (1) Some   (3) A lot

6. Does your daily routine require you to stand for long periods?   (0) No   (1) Some   (3) A lot

7. Do you have a high level of job-related stress?   (0) No   (1) Some   (3) A lot

8. Do you sit for long periods of time (computer operator, typist, or similar job)?   (0) No   (1) Some   (3) A lot

9. Does your daily routine require doing repetitive movements or holding something (e.g., baby, briefcase, suitcase) for long periods of time?   (0) No   (1) Some   (3) A lot

10. Does your daily routine require you to stand or sit with poor posture (e.g., sitting in a low car seat, reaching overhead with head tilted back)?   (0) No   (1) Some   (3) A lot

11. What is your score on the Healthy Back Tests?   (0) 9–10   (1) 7–8   (3) 5–6   (5) 0–4

12. What is your score on the posture test in Lab 12B?   (0) 0–2   (1) 3–4   (3) 5–7   (5) 8+

Total Modifiable Score = _____

Summary of Healthy Back Tests

	Pass	Fail	If you failed, what exercise should you do?
1. Straight-leg lift	○	○	
2. Thomas test	○	○	
3. Ober test	○	○	
4. Leg drop test	○	○	
5. Isometric abdominal test	○	○	
6. Isometric extensor test	○	○	
7. Prone bridge	○	○	
8. Quadruped stabilization	○	○	
9. Right lateral bridge	○	○	
10. Left lateral bridge	○	○	
Total			

Chart 1 Back/Neck Questionnaire Ratings

Rating	Nonmodifiable Score	Modifiable Score	Total Score
Very high risk	12+	7+	19+
High risk	8–11	5–6	13–17
Average risk	4–7	3–4	7–11
Low risk	0–3	0–2	0–5

Chart 2 Healthy Back Tests Ratings

Classification	Number of Tests Passed
Excellent	8–10
Very good	7
Good	6
Fair	5
Poor	1–4

Results

Back/Neck Questionnaire

Nonmodifiable Score ☐ + Modifiable Score ☐ = Total Score ☐   Rating ☐

Healthy Back Tests

Total Number of Tests Passed ☐   Classification ☐

Conclusions and Implications: In several sentences, discuss your need to do exercises for care of the back and neck. Include steps you might take to prevent future problems. Use your test results to answer.

Lab 12B Evaluating Posture

Name		Section	Date

Purpose: To learn to recognize postural deviations and thus become more posture conscious and to determine your postural limitations in order to institute a preventive or corrective program.

Procedures

1. Wear as little clothing as possible (bathing suits are recommended) and remove shoes and socks.
2. Work in groups of two or three, with one person acting as the subject while partners serve as examiners; then alternate roles.
   a. Stand by a vertical plumb line.
   b. Using Chart 1 and the figure below, check any deviations and indicate their severity using the following point scale (0 = none, 1 = slight, 2 = moderate, and 3 = severe).
   c. Total the score and determine your posture rating from the Posture Rating Scale (Chart 2).
3. If time permits, perform back and posture exercises (see Lab 12C).
4. Complete the Conclusions and Implications section.

Results

Record your posture score (0-18):

Record your posture rating from the Posture Rating Scale in Chart 2:

Chart 1 Posture Evaluation

Side View	Points (0-3)
Forward head	
Rounded shoulders	
Excessive lordosis (lumbar)	
Abdominal ptosis	
Hyperextended knees	
Flat Arches	
Total scores (0–18)	

Chart 2 Posture Rating Scale

Classification	Total Score (0–18)
Excellent	0–4
Very good	5–7
Good	8–10
Fair	11–13
Poor	14 or more

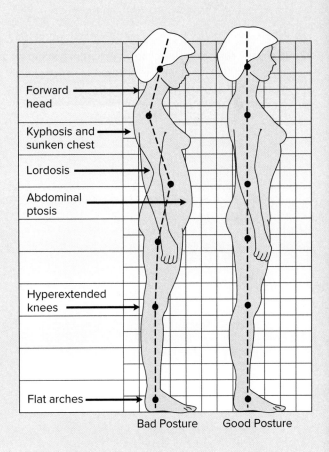

Forward head

Kyphosis and sunken chest

Lordosis

Abdominal ptosis

Hyperextended knees

Flat arches

Bad Posture   Good Posture

Conclusions and Implications

Were you aware of the deviations that were found?   Yes ◯   No ◯

1. List the deviations that were moderate or severe (use several complete sentences).

2. In several sentences, describe your current posture status. Include in this discussion your overall assessment of your current posture, whether you think you will need special exercises in the future, and the reasons your posture rating is good or not so good.

Lab 12C Planning and Logging Core and Back Exercises

Name	**Section**	**Date**

Purpose: To select exercises for the back and neck that meet your personal needs and monitor progress.

Procedures

1. Using Chart 1, provide some background information about your experience with core and back exercise, your goals, and your plans for incorporating these exercises into your normal exercise routine.
2. Using Chart 2 (see next page), choose one variation for each of the nine possible exercises listed. Refer to the core stabilization exercises on Table 4 (page 240), abdominal and back strengthening exercises on Table 5 (page 241), and functional core movements on Table 6 (page 242). Perform the exercises for at least 3 days over a weeklong period. If you are just starting out, it is best to start with the easier variations. If you are more experienced, try the more advanced variations.
3. Answer the questions in the Results and Conclusions and Implications sections.

Chart 1 Core and Back Exercise Survey

1. Determine your current stage for core and back exercise. Check only the stage that represents your current activity level.

   ◯ Precontemplation. I do not do core or back exercises and have not been thinking about starting.

   ◯ Contemplation. I do not do core or back exercises but have been thinking about starting.

   ◯ Preparation. I am planning to start doing core and back exercises.

   ◯ Action. I do core and back exercises but not that regularly.

   ◯ Maintenance. I regularly do core and back exercises.

2. What are your primary goals for core and back exercise?

   ◯ Prevention of back pain.

   ◯ Sports improvement (specify sport:_____)

   ◯ Better functional fitness.

3. Are you currently involved in a regular exercise program that includes resistance exercises?

   ◯ Yes

   ◯ No

Results

Did you do at least 9 exercises at least 3 days in the week?   Yes ◯   No ◯

Conclusions and Implications: Were you able to find variations that provided an appropriate challenge? Do you feel that you will use core and back exercises as part of your regular exercise routine? Use several sentences to answer.

Chart 2 Core and Back Exercise Log

Check (√) at least one exercise variation from each of the nine categories and record the number of sets performed on at least 3 days over a 1-week period. Write the date (month/day) in the day column for the date you performed the exercise.

Table 4 Core Stabilization Exercise Variations

Front Plank Variations	Day 1	Day 2	Day 3	Day 4	Day 5	Day 6	Day 7
☐ A.							
☐ B.							
☐ C.							
☐ D.							
Side Plank Variations							
☐ A.							
☐ B.							
☐ C.							
☐ D.							
Superman Variations							
☐ A.							
☐ B.							
☐ C.							
☐ D.							
Abdominal Bracing Variations							
☐ A.							
☐ B.							
☐ C.							
☐ D.							
Bridge Variations							
☐ A.							
☐ B.							
☐ C.							
☐ D.							

Table 5 Abdominals and Back Extensors Exercise Variations

Abdominal Crunch Variations							
☐ A.							
☐ B.							
☐ C.							
☐ D.							
Back Extension Variations							
☐ A.							
☐ B.							
☐ C.							

Table 6 Core Functional Movement Exercise Variations

Pulls and Lifts with Stabilization							
☐ A.							
☐ B.							
Weighted Lifts and Squats with Stabilization							
☐ A.							
☐ B.							

Performance Benefits of Physical Activity

LEARNING OBJECTIVES

After completing the study of this Concept, you will be able to:

▶ Describe characteristics of high-level performance and the training necessary for high-level performance.

▶ Identify the unique training considerations for cardiorespiratory endurance, speed, muscular strength, muscular endurance, power, functional fitness, and flexibility.

▶ Explain how principles of periodization are used to optimize training effectiveness.

▶ Describe types of ergogenic aids and how they may or may not work to improve performance.

▶ Evaluate your personal skill-related fitness.

▶ Identify and self-assess overtraining symptoms.

Specialized forms of training are needed to optimize adaptations to exercise and performance in sports.

Source: U.S. Air Force photo by Staff Sgt. Desiree N. Palacios

251

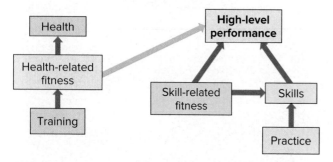

Why it Matters!

Competitive athletics and sports provide opportunities for individuals to explore the limits of their ability and to challenge themselves in competition. Some enjoy competitive aerobic activities, such as running, cycling, swimming, and triathlons. Others enjoy the challenges associated with competitive resistance training activities, such as powerlifting and bodybuilding. The pursuit of high-level performance requires training that is well beyond what is needed for good health and well-being, but many find these endeavors to be very compelling. This Concept will provide insights into the approaches used to train for high-level performance. While the focus is on sports, high-level performance is also a requirement for some types of work, such as fire safety, military service, and police work.

High-Level Performance and Training Characteristics

High-level performance requires health-related and skill-related fitness and the specific motor skills necessary for the performance. Improving performance requires more specific training than the type needed to improve health. **Training** (regular physical activity) builds health-related fitness that enhances both health and high-level performance (see Figure 1). High-level performance is not necessary for all people, only for those who need exceptional performances. A distance runner needs exceptional cardiorespiratory endurance and muscular endurance, a lineman in football needs exceptional strength, and a gymnast needs exceptional flexibility.

Exceptional performance also requires high-level skill-related physical fitness and good physical and motor skills. It is important to understand that skill-related fitness and skills are not the same thing. Skill-related fitness components

are abilities that help you learn skills faster and better, thus the arrow in Figure 1 from skill-related fitness to skills. Skills, on the other hand, are things such as throwing, kicking, catching, and hitting a ball. Practice enhances skills. Practicing the specific skills of a sport or a job can help to improve performance but specific levels of skill-related fitness that influence skills are less amenable to change.

High-level performance requires more focused and structured training. The amount of effort and training required to excel in sports, competitive athletics, or work requiring high-level performance is greater than the amount needed for good health and wellness. Because adaptations to exercise are specific to the type of activity that is performed, training must also be matched to the specific needs of a given activity. Athletes learn to optimize training by carefully planning workouts that maximize adaptations and performance gains. While all principles are important, several are particularly important for high-level training, including overload, progression, specificity, individuality, and rest/recovery.

Success in endurance sports requires a high aerobic capacity. Distance runners, cyclists, and swimmers must be able to perform activity for long periods of time without stopping. These types of performers need high levels of cardiorespiratory endurance, defined as aerobic capacity. In aerobic exercise, adequate oxygen is available to allow the body to rebuild the high-energy fuel the muscles need to sustain performance. Aerobic exercise increases aerobic capacity (cardiorespiratory endurance) by enhancing the body's ability to supply oxygen to the muscles as well as their ability to use it. Slow-twitch muscle fibers are most suited for aerobic exercise, and these fibers adapt most to aerobic training. Activities and events that require sustained, high-intensity aerobic exercise place special demands on the slow-twitch fibers and require a high level of aerobic capacity.

Many types of high-level performance require good anaerobic capacity. While all athletes benefit from aerobic fitness, success in many sports is determined more by speed, strength, and power. The sprinting, jumping, and powerful movements needed in most competitive sports are good examples. Strength competitions and sprint events in running, bicycling, and swimming also require short bursts of high-intensity activity. These activities use more energy than can be provided with aerobic metabolism. Anaerobic processes (i.e., processes that do not require oxygen) provide the additional energy needs, but a by-product of these processes (**lactic acid**) eventually causes the muscles to fatigue.

When you do **anaerobic exercise,** the body cannot supply enough oxygen to sustain performance; so the body uses a high-energy fuel that the body has stored. When the high-energy fuel is used up, you cannot continue to perform. After the exercise, you keep breathing fast and the heart continues to beat fast for a while, because the body needs to take in

Figure 1 ▶ Factors influencing high-level performance.

Performance in most sports requires good levels of fitness (health-related and skill-related) as well as practice to improve skills.
©Jupiterimages

extra oxygen to rebuild the stores of the high-energy fuel used in anaerobic exercise. This is sometimes called **oxygen debt.** The body "borrows" oxygen that it cannot provide when it is using high-energy fuel during anaerobic exercise and then "pays back the debt" by supplying extra oxygen after the anaerobic exercise. The active recovery phase helps break down lactic acid and return the body to its normal resting state. In some ways "borrowing" oxygen during anaerobic exercise, and paying back the oxygen debt later, is like using a credit card to borrow money that is paid back later.

Athletes involved in anaerobic activities typically perform specialized forms of anaerobic exercise to help improve their bodies' ability to produce energy anaerobically and to tolerate higher levels of lactic acid. Using the credit card analogy, this is equivalent to the increases in available credit that are provided to customers who demonstrate they can pay their credit card bills. Fast-twitch muscle fibers are used primarily during intense anaerobic activity, and these fibers are more likely to adapt and respond to anaerobic exercise. Most sports require a combination of aerobic and anaerobic capacity, so it is important to conduct training that is most specific to the needs of a given activity.

Genetics can influence a person's potential for high-level performance. Each person inherits a unique genetic profile, which may predispose him or her to success in different sports and activities. A higher percentage of slow-twitch muscle fibers allows a person to adapt most effectively to aerobic exercise, while a higher percentage of fast-twitch muscle fibers enhance adaptations from and performance in anaerobic exercise. Heredity also influences the dimensions of skill-related fitness, such as balance, coordination, and reaction time, that enhance development of motor skills. The most successful performers are those who inherit good potential for health- and skill-related fitness, who train to improve their health-related fitness, and who do extensive practice to improve the skills needed for the activity or sport.

A CLOSER LOOK

Concussions

The tragic stories about the long-term consequences of concussions have raised many concerns by medical and public health professionals. While football contributes to a large number of concussion cases, it is common in many other sports. Hockey, soccer, and lacrosse also have high rates. Although some mild concussions heal without problems, some head injuries can cause serious and permanent damage. Chronic traumatic encephalopathy (CTE), for example, is a progressive degenerative disorder of the brain found in people who have experienced repeated head trauma. The risks of repeated concussions have led to rule changes, structured screening, and testing programs in many sports to help detect changes and potential risks. The CDC's comprehensive campaign "Heads Up" promotes awareness and education about concussions and head injuries in sports.

Do you think awareness campaigns such as "Heads Up" can help promote better safety and reduce the prevalence of head injuries and concussions in sports?

connect
ACTIVITY

Training for Endurance and Speed

Specific forms of training are needed to optimize endurance performance and speed. Speed and endurance are at opposite ends of the performance continuum. Speed events in running are as short as 100 meters, while endurance events, such as a marathon, last 26 miles. Middle-distance events, such as the mile run, fall between these extremes and present unique challenges, since it is important for athletes to have both speed and endurance. While these examples all involve running, the types of training needed for these events are very different.

A common feature in advanced training programs is the need to continually challenge the body. Involvement in regular

Training Physical activity performed by people interested in high-level performance (e.g., athletes, people in specialized jobs).

Lactic Acid Substance that results from the process of supplying energy during anaerobic exercise; a cause of muscle fatigue.

Anaerobic Exercise *Anaerobic* means "in the absence of oxygen." Anaerobic exercise is performed at an intensity so great that the body's demand for oxygen exceeds its ability to supply it.

Oxygen Debt The oxygen consumed following anaerobic exercise that is used to rebuild the supply of high-energy fuel.

physical activity will lead to increases in cardiorespiratory endurance in most people, but improvements are harder to achieve once a good level of fitness has been attained (the principle of diminishing returns). To maximize performance, it is necessary to perform more specific types of workouts that provide a greater challenge (overload) to the cardiorespiratory system. Serious athletes may exercise 6 or 7 days a week, but easier workouts are generally done after harder and more intense workouts. The hard workouts are generally very specific and are designed to challenge the body in different ways. Supplemental training to improve technique and efficiency are also used to enhance performance.

Long-slow distance training is important for endurance performance. Extended periods of aerobic exercise are needed to achieve high-level endurance performance. Athletes generally refer to this type of training as **long-slow distance (LSD) training.** Emphasis is placed on the overall duration or length of the exercise session rather than on speed. The reason for this is that specific adaptations take place within the muscles when used for long periods of time. These adaptations improve the muscles' ability to take up and use the oxygen in the bloodstream. Adaptations within the muscle cell also improve the body's ability to produce energy from fat stores. Long-slow distance training involves performances longer than the event for which you are performing but at a slower pace. For example, a mile runner will regularly perform 6- to 7-mile runs (at 50 to 60 percent of racing pace) to improve aerobic conditioning, even though the event is much shorter. A marathoner may perform runs of 20 miles or more to achieve even higher levels of endurance. Although this 20-mile distance is shorter than the marathon race distance, research

suggests that ample adaptations occur from this volume of exercise. Excess mileage in this case may just wear the body down. Long-slow distance training should be performed once every 1 to 2 weeks, and a rest day is recommended on the subsequent day to allow the body to recover fully.

Improved anaerobic capacity can contribute to performance in aerobic activities. Many physical activities commonly considered to be aerobic—such as tennis, basketball, and racquetball—have an anaerobic component. These activities require periodic vigorous bursts of exercise. Regular anaerobic training will help you resist fatigue in these activities. Even participants in activities such as long-distance running can benefit from anaerobic training, especially if performance times or winning races is important. A fast start, a sprint past an opponent, and a kick at the end are typically anaerobic.

Interval training can be effective in building both aerobic and anaerobic capacity. High-level performance requires high-level training. **Interval training** is an advanced training technique that helps athletes optimize the effectiveness of their training. The premise behind interval training is that by providing periodic rest you can increase the overall intensity of the exercise session and provide a greater stimulus to the body. Interval training can be performed in different ways to achieve different training goals. It can be done at lower intensities to improve aerobic metabolism or at extremely high intensities to enhance anaerobic capacity. Interval training can be done using a series of shorter intervals that are strung together after short rest or with fewer, but longer, bouts. Examples of interval training options are summarized below:

- *Aerobic intervals improve the efficiency of the aerobic metabolism.* The goal of aerobic intervals is to provide a sustained challenge to the cardiorespiratory system. The intensity should be challenging (but manageable) since the goal is to train the aerobic system to function efficiently over an extended period of time. In general, the pace would be similar to (or slightly slower) than the pace used for a 30- to 40-minute continuous event (about 50 to 70 percent of max heart rate). The body adapts to the pace and becomes better at providing oxygen to the muscles and clearing lactic acid that accumulates during the bout. Aerobic interval training can be done using a series of short 2- to 3-minute intervals (with short 10- to 15-second rests). Alternately, it can be done as a pace workout using a longer continuous bout lasting 15 to 20 minutes. Advanced athletes may repeat the workout after a short recovery period to further enhance the training stimulus.

- *Aerobic/anaerobic intervals help improve maximal aerobic capacity.* To improve aerobic capacity ($\dot{V}O_2$ max) it is necessary to push the body to perform near your aerobic capacity for an extended period of time (4 to 6 minutes is

HELP   Health is available to Everyone for a Lifetime, and it's Personal

Extreme Exercise

Many people have a hard time starting an exercise program while others are drawn to the extreme challenges in sports. Some endurance athletes, for example, seek out greater and greater challenges to see what they can do. A 100 mile "ultra" race used to be the epitome of endurance, but this has only spawned "double ultras" and many other, more extreme endurance challenges. People interested in these events are clearly doing them for reasons other than health; however, a recent study suggested that extreme amounts of activity may actually lead to increased health risks.

Would you still pursue your favorite exercise even if it was bad for you?

Table 1 ▶ Work and Rest Bouts for Different Types of Interval-Training Workouts

Type of Interval	Short-Length Intervals			Long-Length Intervals		
	Intensity	Duration	Frequency	Intensity	Duration	Frequency
Aerobic Intervals (50–70% MaxHR)	50–70%	2–3 minutes 10–15 seconds' rest	Perform 7–8 with rest Repeat after 3–4 minutes (recovery)	50–60%	15–20 minutes	Perform full bout Repeat after 3–4 minutes (recovery)
Aerobic/Anaerobic Intervals (70–90% MaxHR)	75–85%	1–2 minutes 30–60 seconds' rest	Perform 5–6 with rest Repeat after 5–6 minutes (recovery)	70–75%	6–8 minutes	Perform full bout Repeat after 5–6 minutes (recovery)
Anaerobic Intervals (85–95% MaxHR)	90–95%	10–15 seconds 15–120 seconds' rest	Perform 3–4 with rest Repeat after 7–8 minutes (recovery)	85–90%	30–60 seconds 60–240 seconds' rest	Perform 10–12 with rest Repeat after 7–8 minutes (recovery)

a good target). A person's aerobic capacity is reached at intensities above the anaerobic threshold, so this requires a fairly high intensity (typically about 70 to 85 percent maximum heart rate). For runners, a series of repeated mile runs at a faster than normal training pace provides a good challenge to the aerobic system. However, a series of quarter-mile repeats can also achieve the same goal as long as the total time at a high intensity is similar. In this case, the rest intervals for the set must be short enough to allow only partial recovery between intervals. The adaptations here are based on sustaining a high intensity for the 4- to 6-minute period so full recovery is desirable between sets. Similar workouts can be devised for other sports.

- *Anaerobic intervals improve the function of anaerobic energy processes.* This is typically accomplished with a series of high-intensity bouts of activity at 85 to 95 percent of maximum heart rate. In response to this training, the body improves its ability to produce energy anaerobically and to tolerate anaerobic by-products such as lactic acid. A series of 4 to 5 short bouts of activity that are 10 to 15 seconds long at maximum speed provide a good stimulus (e.g., 100-yard dash). Work-to-rest ratios may range from 1:1 to 1:10 depending on the individual's fitness and the goal of the training. Longer intervals (30 to 60 seconds) at a slightly slower speed (85 to 90 percent of maximum heart rate) with more extended rest breaks (60 to 240 seconds) can also be effective.

The purpose of the training session should dictate the intensity, duration, and rest periods with interval training. Examples of aerobic, aerobic/anaerobic and anaerobic intervals are provided in Table 1. A highly fit person may use

shorter rests and repeat the interval session multiple times in a given workout.

Principles of interval training can be adapted for different activities. While athletes have routinely used interval training to optimize their workouts, the use of *high-intensity interval training (HIIT)* has also been promoted for use by fitness leaders in commercial fitness centers. Some people are attracted to HIIT because of the efficiency in the workout, but it also may detract from the enjoyment of the workout by putting too much structure into it.

The principles of interval training can also be integrated into workouts in less structured ways. Runners sometimes use *fartlek* training to break up their workouts. A fartlek run incorporates bursts of higher-intensity running followed by recovery periods of lower intensity. The difference from interval training is that the intermittent bursts in fartlek training are dictated by the nature of the terrain or the feelings of the moment. The term is from a Swedish word meaning "speed play," because the unstructured nature is more relaxed than interval training.

Many competitive sports involve alternating bursts of high-intensity activity followed by periods of recovery.

Long-Slow Distance (LSD) Training Training technique used by marathon runners and other endurance performers that emphasizes slow, sustained exercise rather than speed.

Interval Training A training technique often used for high-level aerobic and anaerobic training which involves alternating periods of high- and low-intensity activity to maximize the quality of the workout.

Training needs to be sport-specific to improve performance.
©Ty Milford/Aurora Open/Getty Images

Strength/power

	Low	Medium	High
Load			
Reps			
Sets			
Volume			
Rest			

Hypertrophy/size

	Low	Medium	High
Load			
Reps			
Sets			
Volume			
Rest			

Muscular endurance

	Low	Medium	High
Load			
Reps			
Sets			
Volume			
Rest			

Figure 2 ▶ Differences in training stimulus for different resistance training programs.

Basketball, for example, involves intermittent sprints and jumps interspersed with periods of short recovery. Similarly, tennis involves bursts of activity separated by short recovery periods between points. To prepare for success in sports, it is important for athletes to incorporate intermittent interval-type training into their conditioning. Simulated games that require repeated sprints up and down the basketball court are a form of interval training specific to basketball players. Tennis players can also incorporate a variety of forward and lateral movements into a high-intensity agility drill to improve conditioning that specifically matches the common challenges in tennis.

Training for Strength, Muscular Endurance, and Power

Specific progressive resistance training programs are needed to achieve high-level muscular performance. A basic progressive resistance program for overall good health might involve performing a single exercise for each major muscle group two or three times a week. This level of training provides a regular stimulus to maintain healthy levels of muscular strength and endurance. However, many people challenge themselves to achieve higher levels of muscular performance. Olympic weight-lifting competitors use free weights and compete in two exercises: the snatch and the clean and jerk. Powerlifting competitors use free weights and compete in three lifts: the bench press, squat, and dead lift.

Bodybuilding competitors use several forms of resistance training and are judged on muscular hypertrophy (large muscles) and **definition of muscle.** Performers in these activities and athletes in strength-related sports need to use more advanced training methods to reach their full potential. The essential goal in high-level training is to provide the optimal stimulus so that the muscles adapt in the desired way. Because the goals are clearly different for athletes interested in strength/power, muscular hypertrophy, or muscular endurance, it is important to follow appropriate programs. The essential aspects of these different training programs are described in the sections that follow. The basic concepts are summarized in Figure 2.

Performers training for high-level strength should use multiple sets with heavier weights. The best stimulus for strength gains is repeated lifts with very heavy loads. Guidelines for intermediate lifters call for multiple sets of 6 to 12 reps performed using 70 to 80 percent of 1RM values. The load and intensity guidelines are higher for advanced lifters

Training for high-level performance requires focus and determination.
©Fuse/Corbis/Getty Images

(1 to 12 reps performed using 70 to 100 percent 1RM) because they may need to use a higher overload to get continued improvements. Rest intervals must be long (2 to 3 minutes) for high-intensity strength training to allow full recovery of the muscles between sets.

Multiple-joint exercises, such as the bench press, have been found to be more effective in strength enhancement, since they allow a greater load to be lifted. The sequencing of exercises within a workout is also an important consideration for strength development. When training all major muscle groups in a workout, large muscle groups should be done before small muscle groups, and multiple-joint exercises should be done before single-joint ones.

Performers training for muscular endurance should emphasize many repetitions with lighter weights. Completing multiple sets of 10 to 25 repetitions is required to build endurance. Short rest periods of 1 to 2 minutes are recommended for high-repetition sets, and periods of less than 1 minute should be used for lower-repetition sets. This challenges the muscles to perform repeatedly and with little or no rest. Variation in the order in which exercises are performed is also recommended to vary the stimulus. Intermediate lifters should aim for two to four times per week, but advanced lifters may perform up to six sessions per week if appropriate variation in muscle groups is used between workouts.

Performers training for bulk and definition often use extra reps and/or sets. Bodybuilders are more interested in definition and hypertrophy than in absolute strength. Gaining both size and definition requires a balance between strength and muscular endurance training. Most bodybuilders use 3 to 7 sets of 10 to 15 repetitions, rather than the 3 sets of 3 to 8 repetitions recommended for most weight lifters. Sometimes definition is difficult to obtain because it is obscured by fat. It should be noted that people with the largest-looking muscles are not always the strongest. The word *tone* is often used inappropriately to explain fitness gains. (More information regarding the misuse of the word *tone* is provided in the Concept on evaluating fitness and wellness products.)

Power reflects the rate at which force can be applied, and it depends on both strength and speed. Some experts consider power to be the most functional mode in which all human motion occurs. Power is exceptionally important in sport activities such as hitting a baseball, blocking in football, putting the shot, and throwing the discus. Power is also essential for good vertical jumping—a movement critical for basketball and many other sports. While power is emphasized in sports training, it is also now viewed as an important attribute for successful aging. A typical progressive resistance exercise program will build sufficient power for normal activities of daily living; however, people interested in high-level performance should consider using additional exercises that specifically develop power. To increase power, you must do more work in the same time or the same work in less time. Increasing one without the other limits power. Some power athletes (e.g., football players) might benefit by achieving less strength and more speed.

Training for power requires highly specific training. If you need power for an activity in which you are required to move heavy weights, then you need to develop *strength-related power* by working against heavy resistance at slower speeds. If you need to move light objects at great speed, such as in throwing a ball, you need to develop *speed-related power* by training at high speeds with relatively low resistance. There are trade-offs between speed and strength-related power

Definition of Muscle The detailed external appearance of a muscle.

Plyometrics are effective at building power.
©Erik Isakson/Blend Images LLC

Table 2 ▶ Safety Guidelines for Plyometrics
• Progression should be gradual to avoid extreme muscle soreness.
• Adequate strength should be developed prior to plyometric training. (As a general rule, you should be able to do a half squat with one-and-a-half times your body weight.)
• The landing surface should be semiresilient, dry, and unobstructed.
• Shoes should have good lateral stability, be cushioned with an arch support, and have a nonslip sole.
• Obstacles used for jumping-over should be padded.
• The training should be preceded by a general and specific warm-up.

• The training sequence should…
  • precede all other workouts (while you are fresh);
  • include at least one spotter;
  • be done no more than twice per week, with 48 hours' rest between bouts;
  • last no more than 30 minutes;
  • include 3 or 4 drills (for beginners), with 2 or 3 sets per drill, 10–15 reps per set, and 1–2 minutes' rest between sets.

Source: Adapted from Brittenham.

training because the heavier the resistance, the slower the movement. Therefore, the focus of training should be on the primary need for the specific sport or activity.

Performers who need explosive power to perform a specific task or event should use training that closely resembles that movement. Jumpers, for example, should jump as a part of their training programs in order to learn correct timing and mechanics. If they use machines, it is better to use the leg press than a knee extension machine because the press more nearly resembles the leg action of the jump. Training adaptations are also specific to the type of training performed. Power exercises done at high speeds will help enhance muscular endurance, whereas power exercises that use heavy resistance at lower speeds will increase strength.

Plyometrics, refer to a specific type of training that is well suited for power development. Plyometric exercises can be customized to help build power for specific performance skills, but typically involve explosive bounding and jumping movements. The eccentric landing phase in the movement is important since it allows the exercise to be maximally loaded and challenged in a dynamic, sport-specific way. However, the eccentric muscle contractions can lead to muscular soreness, so it is important to ease into this type of training to give your body time to adapt. It is also important to have good flexibility before beginning a plyometrics program. Table 2 lists safety guidelines for plyometrics.

Training for cardiorespiratory endurance along with strength or power training can limit adaptations. The body adapts to the type of training that is performed. If too much endurance training is performed, the body tries to

adapt to the needs of aerobic activity, and this makes it more difficult to gain muscle mass or achieve maximal increases in strength. The effect would be an issue only for competitive strength or power athletes and should not deter people from getting the important health benefits associated with moderate amounts of aerobic activity. Regular aerobic activity is considered essential for bodybuilders to help them reduce unwanted body fat.

Training for Functional Fitness and Flexibility

Functional fitness training builds skill-related fitness dimensions such as balance, coordination, and agility as well as muscle fitness and flexibility. Functional fitness training (also called neuromotor training) refers to specific efforts to improve the integration of the body's motor (muscle) system with the neural (sensory) system. This integration can improve the body's ability to perform real-life activities such as bending, squatting, lunging, kicking, climbing, reaching, or lifting. This type of training essentially builds the components of what is more commonly known as skill-related fitness. Neuromotor training is specifically recommended for older adults to promote postural stability and reduce risks of falling. However, it is also important for athletes to build speed and agility for sports.

Functional fitness training can be conducted in a variety of ways, but athletes often use task-specific or sport-specific training regimens such as squatting, tossing a ball against a

Sport-specific training and warm-ups help prepare athletes for the unique demands of their sport.
©Photodisc/Getty Images

rebounder, performing a "grapevine" movement, or running through agility ladders. Resistance needed for building strength comes from the weight of the moving body part(s) or the movement of devices such as kettlebells, medicine balls, or elastic cords. These devices are swung, tossed, caught, stretched, or pulled to provide added resistance to the workout. ACSM guidelines specifically recognize the importance of neuromotor training exercises for the general population. The guidelines recommend that individuals participate in functional fitness activities 20 to 30 minutes/per day at least two to three times per week. The ideal dosage (intensity, repetitions, and sets) has not been determined but would likely depend on the type of functional fitness exercise being performed.

Functional balance training is a specific type of functional fitness training that can promote better body control. Functional balance training involves the execution of skilled movements that improve **proprioception** and promote balance. The unique aspect of this form of training is that exercises typically require movement and stabilization force production at the same time. In other words, one part of the body is in motion while another is stabilized. These actions train the body's many somatic sensory organs to respond and adjust to different postures and positions—thereby improving balance. Functional balance training is frequently performed with exercise balls, balance boards, or BOSU trainers (see the Concept on muscle fitness). It is important to start slowly with easy movements and work up to more challenging positions and movements. This type of training is not recommended for people who have had recent orthopedic injuries, or individuals who have degenerative joint disease or knee instability.

Dynamic stretching provides some advantages for athletes preparing for competition. While static stretching is often recommended for general applications, athletes often need to perform more active (dynamic) stretching to prepare for activity. More dynamic forms of stretching (including ballistic stretching) are considered appropriate for high-level performers because many of the motions of the activities in which they perform require dynamic movements. Although ballistic stretching movements have an associated risk, athletes are trained to tolerate them, and the risk is not as significant. The ballistic movements also better prepare an athlete for the dynamic nature of activities during competition.

Dynamic stretching may provide other advantages for athletes. Static stretching may impair performance if done right before a competition. The reason for this is that the neuromuscular system somewhat fights the stretch with an inhibitory response. The muscles become less responsive and stay weakened for up to 30 minutes after stretching and this is certainly not beneficial for performance. Dynamic forms of stretching that stretch muscles while moving avoid this problem. Dynamic stretching is thought to enhance performance since muscles receive more of a stimulation response rather than an inhibition. Examples of ballistic stretches for

Plyometrics A training technique used to develop explosive power. It consists of isotonic–concentric muscle contractions performed after a prestretch or an eccentric contraction of a muscle.

Proprioception Awareness of body movements and orientation of the body in space; often used synonymously with *kinesthesis.*

sport-related activities include practice swings with a baseball bat, a golf club, or a tennis racquet. In each case, start by swinging backward and forward rhythmically and continuously. Gradually increase the speed and vigor of the swing until it approaches the speed used in the actual movement.

Training for High-Level Performance: Skill-Related Fitness and Skill

Good skill-related fitness is needed for success in many sports. There are five primary components of skill-related fitness: agility, coordination, balance, reaction time, and speed. Having these attributes can make it easier to learn the necessary skills for many competitive sports. Balance and reaction time are critical for hitting a baseball, considered by many to be the toughest skill in sports. Similarly, agility and coordination may help one master advanced dribbling skills for sports such as basketball or soccer. Because skill-related fitness can enhance performance in sports, it is often called **motor fitness** or **sports fitness.** Table 3 summarizes the general skill-related fitness requirements of 44 sport activities. In Lab 13A you will evaluate your skill-related fitness and learn what activities you are most suited for.

Good skills are needed for success in sports and other competitive activities. Skill-related fitness helps you learn skills, but possessing the specific skills of an activity is probably more important. Skill refers to the ability to perform specific tasks. Sports examples include throwing, kicking, striking (as in hitting a baseball), and jumping. A person with good skill-related fitness may learn skills more easily and ultimately be able to achieve a higher level of skills than other people, but with practice anyone can learn skills. High-level performers typically must practice more often than recreational athletes and typically require more coaching on the specific skills of their chosen activity. Feedback from coaches, peers, or video analyses can help improve skill learning and performance if it is provided and utilized appropriately.

Fitness and skills interact to influence high-level performance. The ability to play games or sports is determined by combined abilities in separate skill-related components along with a number of intangible factors. Following are key points about skill-related fitness:

- *Exceptional performers tend to be outstanding in more than one component of skill-related fitness.* Though people possess skill-related fitness in varying degrees, great athletes are likely to be above average in most, if not all, aspects.

- *Excellence in one skill-related fitness component may compensate for a lack in another.* Each individual possesses a specific level of each skill-related fitness aspect. For example, a tennis player may use good coordination to compensate for lack of speed.

Table 3 ▶ Skill-Related Requirements of Sports and Other Activities

Activity	Balance	Coordination	Reaction Time	Agility	Power	Speed
Archery	***	****	*	*	*	*
Backpacking	**	**	*	**	**	*
Badminton	**	****	***	***	**	***
Baseball/softball	***	****	****	***	****	***
Basketball	***	****	****	****	****	***
Bicycling	****	**	**	*	**	**
Bowling	***	****	*	**	**	**
Canoeing	***	***	**	*	***	*
Circuit training	**	**	*	**	***	**
Dance, aerobic	**	****	**	***	*	*
Dance, ballet	****	****	**	****	***	*
Dance, disco	**	***	**	****	*	**
Dance, modern	****	****	**	****	***	*
Dance, social	**	***	**	***	*	**
Fencing	***	****	****	***	***	****
Fitness calisthenics	**	**	*	***	**	*
Football	***	***	****	****	****	****
Golf (walking)	**	****	*	**	***	*
Gymnastics	****	****	***	****	****	**
Handball	**	****	***	****	***	***
Hiking	**	**	*	**	**	*
Horseback riding	***	***	**	***	*	*
Interval training	**	**	*	*	*	**
Jogging	**	**	*	*	*	*
Judo	***	****	****	****	****	****
Karate	***	****	****	****	****	****
Mountain climbing	****	****	**	***	***	*
Pool/billiards	**	***	*	**	**	*
Racquetball	**	****	***	****	**	***
Rope jumping	**	***	**	***	**	*
Rowing, crew	**	****	*	***	****	**
Sailing	***	***	***	***	**	*
Skating	****	***	**	***	**	***
Skiing, cross-country	**	****	*	***	****	**
Skiing, downhill	****	****	***	****	***	*
Soccer	**	****	***	****	***	***
Surfing	****	****	***	****	***	*
Swimming (laps)	**	***	*	***	**	*
Table tennis	**	***	****	**	**	**
Tennis	**	****	****	***	***	**
Volleyball	**	****	****	***	**	**
Walking	**	**	*	*	*	*
Waterskiing	***	***	*	***	**	*
Weight training	**	**	*	*	**	*

* = minimal needed; **** = a lot needed.

In the News

Youth Sports: When Is It Too Much?

Youth sports have become an institution in contemporary society, if not a rite of passage. There are many potentially desirable outcomes from youth sports, such as building character, promoting teamwork, and improving fitness and skills. However, there are also potential concerns. Coaches may not be well trained or they may push children too hard. Parents may also unintentionally put too much pressure on children and cause them to lose interest in sports and activities altogether. The *Time* magazine cover story "How Kids' Sports Became a $15 Billion Industry" exposes the personal, financial, and time commitments families are devoting to youth sports today. (See link in Suggested Resources and Readings.)

Are the pressures and demands of contemporary youth sports too high? Were you involved in sports as a youth? If so, did your experiences have a positive or negative influence on you?

- *Excellence in skill-related fitness may compensate for a lack of health-related fitness when playing sports and games.* Health-related fitness potential tends to decline with age, but experience and good skill-related fitness can help sustain high performance. For example, a baseball pitcher who lacks the power to dominate hitters may rely on a pitch such as a knuckle ball, which depends more on coordination than on power.

High-Level Performance Training

The quality of training is clearly more important than the quantity. A characteristic of high-level performance training is the need to continually challenge the body (overload principle). Involvement in regular physical activity will lead to improvements in fitness for most people, but they are harder to achieve once a good level of fitness has been attained (the principle of diminishing returns). It takes considerably more training to improve fitness than it does to maintain fitness.

To maximize performance, perform more specific types of workouts that provide a greater challenge to the body. Serious athletes may exercise 6 or 7 days a week, but easier workouts are generally done after harder and more intense workouts. The hard workouts are generally very specific and are designed to challenge the body in different ways. The easier workouts provide time to recover while building other dimensions of fitness. Quality is clearly more important than quantity.

Overtraining is a common problem among athletes. Most Americans suffer from hypokinetic conditions resulting from too little activity. Athletes, on the other hand, often push themselves too hard and do not allow adequate time for rest, making them susceptible to a variety of hyperkinetic conditions, such as *overload syndrome.* This condition is characterized by fatigue, irritability, and sleep problems, as well as an increased risk for injuries. Performance can decline sharply in an overtrained status, causing athletes to train even harder and become even more overtrained. Athletes should pay close attention to possible symptoms of overtraining and

back off their training if they notice increased fatigue, lethargy, or unexpected decreases in their performance. Lab 13B helps you identify some symptoms of overtraining.

A slightly elevated morning heart rate (four or five beats more than normal values) is a useful physical indicator of overtraining. The body has had to work too hard to recover from the exercise and isn't in its normal resting mode. To use this indicator, regularly monitor your resting heart rate before getting out of bed in the morning. Another indicator that is increasingly used by elite endurance athletes is compressed or reduced "heart rate variability." A lower beat-to-beat variability indicates fatigue or overtraining, since it reflects sympathetic dominance over the normally dominant parasympathetic system that exists during more rested states. Newer heart rate monitors provide an indicator of heart rate variability.

Rest and a history of regular exercise are both important for reducing the risks for overuse injuries. Adequate rest helps the body recover from the stress of vigorous training—it promotes the physiological adaptations that improve performance and reduces the likelihood of developing overuse injuries.

A history of regular exercise is also important for reducing risks for injury. Research conducted by the military has determined that recruits with a history of regular exercise were less likely to get injured during basic training than recruits without this experience. This suggests that regular exercise can build up the strength and integrity of bones and joints and reduce the risk for injury. While experienced athletes may have less risk for injuries, they often push themselves too hard and develop overuse injuries or other conditions. Listening to your body and getting rest are important for decreasing risk of overtraining.

Motor Fitness Skill-related physical fitness. Also called *sports fitness.*

Sports Fitness See *motor fitness.*

Periodization of training may help prevent overtraining. Athletes must plan carefully to reach peak performance at the right time and to avoid overtraining and injuries. **Periodization** is an advanced training principle that involves manipulating repetition, resistance, and exercise selection so there are periodic peaks and valleys during the training program. The peaks are needed to challenge the body, and the valleys allow the body to recover and adapt fully.

A training program is usually divided into a series of cycles that allow the intensity and volume to change in a systematic way. A hypothetical periodization cycle is depicted in Figure 3. Note that the overall training program (one macrocycle) is made up of three

Figure 3 ▶ Conceptual pattern of cycles within a periodized training program.

mesocycles that are each made up of three microcycles. The intensity increases gradually in each microcycle to provide a progressive training stimulus. Also note that the volume increases somewhat in opposition to the intensity with volume actually decreasing at the higher-intensity phases. The overall training stimulus increases throughout the mesocycle. Rest is a critical point of an effective periodization program as the body needs time to recover from (and adapt to) the challenging training stimulus. The intensity and volume drop to lower levels at the start of each microcycle with larger drops after each mesocycle. Periodization training is usually focused on preparing a person for a competition and, as the competition gets closer, the athlete typically begins a **tapering** plan to ensure a full recovery prior to the event. The tapering plan typically involves reductions in both intensity and volume of training to help facilitate recovery. Following a periodization plan helps an athlete optimize the effectiveness of training while also decreasing the risk of overtraining.

Athletes should be aware of various psychological disorders related to overtraining. Compulsive physical activity, often referred to as activity neurosis or exercise addiction, can be considered a hyperkinetic condition. People with activity neurosis become irrationally concerned about their exercise regimen. They may exercise more than once a day, rarely take a day off, or feel the need to exercise even when ill or injured. One condition related to activity neurosis is an obsession with having an attractive body (body neurosis). Among females, it is usually associated with an extreme desire to be thin, whereas among males it is more often associated with an extreme desire to be muscular. This excessive desire to be fit or thin can negatively affect other aspects of life, threaten personal relationships, and cause extreme stress. Anorexia nervosa, an eating disorder associated with an excessive drive to be thin, has frequently been associated with compulsive exercise.

Technology Update

WHOOP

Rest and recovery are critical for effective training adaptations, but athletes often push themselves too hard. A new device made by a company called WHOOP (www.whoop.com) monitors strain, sleep, and recovery to help athletes ensure that they are getting proper rest. With cooperation from Major League Baseball, the company had a sample of 230 minor league players wear the wrist-band devices. The WHOOP band measured each athlete's heart rate, heart rate variability, environmental temperature, motion and movement, and skin response. The company reported correlations between recovery and performance. For example, recovery was associated with pitch velocity in pitchers and exit velocity for batted balls in hitters. Technology may make it possible to better match training with rest for optimal performance.

Do you see a future for these types of devices for typical consumers or exercisers? Do you believe the results support the importance of rest and recovery?

Performance Trends and Ergogenic Aids

Many athletes look to ergogenic aids as an additional way to improve performance. Athletes are always looking for a competitive edge. In addition to pursuing rigorous training programs, many athletes look for alternative ways to improve their performance. Substances, strategies, and treatments designed to improve physical performance beyond the effects of normal training are collectively referred to as **ergogenic aids.** People interested in improving their appearance (including those with body neurosis) also abuse products they think will enhance their appearance. Ergogenic aids can be classified as mechanical, psychological, and physiological. Each category will be discussed in the subsequent sections.

Mechanical ergogenics may improve efficiency and performance. Mechanical ergogenic aids consist of equipment or devices that aid performance. Examples include oversized tennis racquets, more flexible poles for pole vaulting, spring-loaded ice skates (klap skates), lycra body suits for reducing drag in swimming and running, and carbon fiber bike frames to increase stiffness and force transmission. While mechanical ergogenic aids may help maximize performance, the advantages are probably noticeable only for highly elite athletes. For example, a recreational athlete may not play any better with an expensive tennis racquet or new golf clubs. Expert players, on the other hand, can appreciate subtle differences in equipment and may benefit. Athletes, however, should continue to focus on improving fitness and practicing skills, since these will have bigger impacts on performance.

Psychological ergogenics may improve motivation and concentration and reduce anxiety during competitive activities. Many competitive activities require extreme levels of concentration, motivation, and focus. Athletes who can maintain a mental edge during an event are at a clear advantage over athletes who cannot. Competitive anxiety can impair performance, and psychological ergogenics can help reduce anxiety before and during an event. Psychological ergogenics include mental imagery, hypnosis, performance modeling, and established skill routines, to name but a few.

Physiological ergogenics are designed to improve performance by enhancing various biochemical and physiological processes in the body. Physiological ergogenics are primarily nutritional supplements thought to have a positive effect on various metabolic processes. Because the supplement industry is largely unregulated, many products are developed and marketed with little or no research to document their effects. Producers of these products prey on an athlete's lack of knowledge and concern over performance.

Products with little or no evidence of benefits often have questionable safety. For example, protein supplements are unregulated products for which evidence of effectiveness is lacking. Many strength athletes continue to believe that extra protein in the diet can contribute to strength and muscle mass gains, despite the fact that  this has been clearly refuted in the scientific literature. The aggressive marketing and propaganda in many muscle-related fitness publications convince many people to buy and try unproven supplements. Do not be swayed by ads and unsubstantiated claims. Physiological ergogenics with established performance benefits are described below.

- *Fluid replacement beverages and energy bars.* Fluid replacement beverages, such as Gatorade, Exceed, and Powerade, contain carbohydrates needed for endurance exercise. People exercising for more than an hour can benefit from these supplements, and research shows that they can replace fluid lost in sweat at the same or a faster rate than water. Energy bars (e.g., Power Bars and Clif Bars), energy gels (e.g., GU), or energy chews (e.g., Clif Shot Blocks) also provide valuable energy for extended endurance exercise. Consumers should be wary of other "energy" products that tout energy without calories. These are simply stimulants or caffeine products.

- *Creatine.* The body produces creatine naturally from foods containing protein, but some athletes take creatine supplements (usually a powder dissolved in a liquid) to increase the amounts available in the muscle. The idea behind supplementation is that additional creatine intake enhances energy production and therefore increases the body's ability to maintain force and delay fatigue. Some studies have shown improvements in performance and anaerobic capacity, but recent reviews indicate that the supplement may be effective only for athletes who are already well trained. Products containing creatine do not work by themselves; instead, they only help athletes maximize their training or performance during an event. Effects are not evident unless training is performed while taking the supplements.

Using Self-Management Skills

Use appropriate self-planning skills to take responsibility for your own training program. Coaches handle these tasks for many competitive athletes, but recreational athletes typically have to plan their own program. Although you can contract with a personal trainer to help you, the principles and guidelines described in this Concept (and throughout this edition) provide a strong foundation for effective training. To plan your own program, use the self-planning skills described in the Concept on self-management skills. Brief summaries are below:

1. **Clarify Reasons:** High-level training requires a strong personal commitment, so consider your motives to build your drive.

Periodization A planned sequence of training designed to optimize adaptations and minimize overtraining.

Tapering A reduction in training volume and intensity prior to competition to elicit peak performance.

Ergogenic Aids Substances, strategies, and treatments intended to improve performance in sports or competitive athletics.

2. **Identify Needs:** Critically evaluate your fitness needs using the various self-assessments in this edition or consider more specialized assessments conducted through exercise labs or fitness facilities.

3. **Set Personal Goals:** Use SMART goal principles to set specific, measurable, attainable, realistic, and timely goals. Also, put your goals in writing since a goal really isn't a "goal" unless it is written down.

4. **Select Program Components:** The type of program needs to be designed to specifically help you make progress toward your goals. Training usually needs to be more specifically planned and intentional. It also may necessitate higher-intensity training to challenge the body to continue adapting to the stimuli. Be sure, however, to get adequate rest and consider periodized training to adhere to principles of progression.

5. **Write Out Your Plan:** A written plan provides the needed structure to help you stick with your training program and to stay focused on your goals. Modifications will likely be needed along the way, so you should expect to revisit and adjust the plan as needed.

6. **Evaluate Progress:** Periodic evaluation is a key step to ensure that your program is on the right track. Athletes need to carefully monitor their progress to determine how to adjust their training. Thus, this step really initiates a new cycle of program planning to continue improving. The expression "knowledge is power" certainly applies to health and fitness since knowledge gives you the power to independently take responsibility for your own health, wellness, and fitness.

Use good consumer skills to avoid being a victim of fraud and quackery. The strong interest in training and improved performance makes athletes a primary target for companies selling fraudulent fitness and performance supplements. Many athletes search online for information or visit "nutrition" stores to try to learn how to improve their performance. Unfortunately, there are few (if any) policies that regulate what is communicated in print or online sources. Many companies take small "truths" about fitness or health and then misuse them or apply them incorrectly. The consumer can be hooked by the apparent logic and the company cashes in on the sale. Companies are also not required to document that their products are safe or effective. Therefore, consumers waste millions of dollars a year on fraudulent products that have little or no benefit (and may even be harmful). Caveat emptor (buyer beware)! (Additional information is available in the Concept on consumer awareness.)

Strategies for Action: Lab Information

Select activities that match your abilities. People differ in many factors, including skills and abilities that influence sports and athletic performance. You may be well suited to some sports but not to others. Behavioral scientists have also determined that perceptions of competence are important predictors of long-term exercise adherence. To give yourself the best chance of being successful in sports (and exercise involvement), choose activities that are well matched to your abilities. The assessments in Lab 13A provide a way to get a basic sense of which skill-related fitness dimensions you are stronger in and which ones you are weaker in. Referring to Table 3 can help you determine the sports and activities that best match your individual abilities. These are just conceptual assessments, so the best way to assess your potential in a specific activity is to give it a try.

Get adequate rest and listen to your body. Many athletes make the mistake of training too hard and don't include enough time for rest. Without rest, the body does not have sufficient time to make the needed adaptations, and overtraining syndrome can result. Lab 13B helps you learn how to monitor for signs of overtraining.

connect
ACTIVITY

Suggested Resources and Readings

The websites for the following sources can be accessed by searching online for the organization, program, or title listed. Specific scientific references are available at the end of this edition of *Concepts of Fitness and Wellness.*

- American College of Sports Medicine. Progression Models in Resistance Training for Healthy Adults (pdf).
- American College of Sports Medicine. (2017). *ACSM's Guidelines for Exercise Testing and Prescription* (10th ed.). Philadelphia: Lippincott Williams & Wilkins.

- American College of Sports Medicine Blog. (2017, July 25). Active Voice: Protein Supplementation to Enhance Adaptations to Resistance Exercise Training–Not Supported by Scientific Evidence.
- Gregory, S. (2017, August 24). How kids' sports became a $15 billion industry. *Time.*
- McGuigan, M. (2017). *Monitoring Training and Performance in Athletes.* Champaign, IL: Human Kinetics.
- WHOOP.com. The Advantage of Continuous Physiological Monitoring (white paper, pdf).

Lab Resource Materials: Skill-Related Physical Fitness

Important Note: Because skill-related physical fitness does not relate to good health, the rating charts used in this section differ from those used for health-related fitness. The rating charts that follow can be used to compare your scores with those of other people. You **do not** need exceptional scores on skill-related fitness to be able to enjoy sports and other types of physical activity; however, it is necessary for high-level performance.

Evaluating Skill-Related Physical Fitness

I. Evaluating Agility: The Illinois Agility Run

An agility course using four chairs 10 feet apart and a 30-foot running area will be set up as depicted in this illustration. The test is performed as follows:

1. Lie prone with your hands by your shoulders and your head at the starting line. On the signal to begin, get on your feet and run the course as fast as possible.
2. Your score is the time required to complete the course. Check your rating in Chart 1

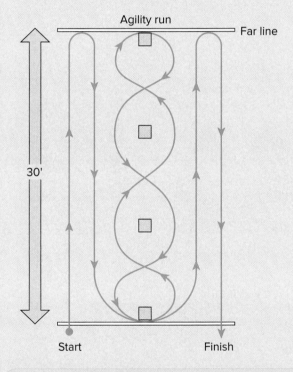

II. Evaluating Balance: The Bass Test of Dynamic Balance

Eleven circles (9½ inches in diameter) are drawn on the floor as shown in the illustration. The test is performed as follows:

1. Stand on the right foot in circle X. *Leap* forward to circle 1, then circle 2 through 10, alternating feet with each leap.
2. The feet must leave the floor on each leap and the heel may not touch. Only the ball of the foot and toes may land on the floor.
3. Remain in each circle for 5 seconds before leaping to the next circle. If you lose balance, reestablish position and count for 5 seconds
4. The score is 50, plus the number of seconds taken to complete the test, minus the number of errors.
5. For every error, deduct 3 points each. Errors include touching the heel, moving the supporting foot, touching outside a circle, and touching any body part other than the supporting foot to the floor. See Chart 2 to check your rating.

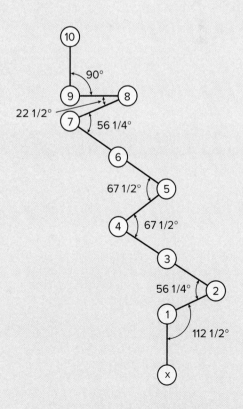

Chart 1 Agility Rating Scale

Classification	Men	Women
Excellent	15.8 or faster	17.4 or faster
Very good	16.7–15.9	18.6–17.5
Good	18.6–16.8	22.3–18.7
Fair	18.8–18.7	23.4–22.4
Poor	18.9 or slower	23.5 or slower

Source: Adams et al.

Chart 2 Balance Rating Scale

Rating	Score
Excellent	90–100
Very good	80–89
Good	70–79
Fair	60–69
Poor	50–59

Chart 3 Coordination Rating Scale

Classification	Men	Women
Excellent	14–15	13–15
Very good	11–13	10–12
Good	5–10	4–9
Fair	3–4	2–3
Poor	0–2	0–1

III. Evaluating Coordination: The Stick Test of Coordination

The stick test of coordination requires you to juggle three wooden sticks. The sticks are used to perform a half flip and a full flip, as shown in the illustrations.

1. *Half flip.* Hold two 24-inch (12 inches in diameter) dowel rods, one in each hand. Support a third rod of the same size across the other two. Toss the supported rod in the air so that it makes a half turn. Catch the thrown rod with the two held rods.
2. *Full flip.* Perform the preceding task, letting the supported rod turn a full flip.

The test is performed as follows:

1. Practice the half flip and full flip several times before taking the test.
2. When you are ready, attempt a half flip five times. Score 1 point for each successful attempt.
3. When you are ready, attempt the full flip five times. Score 2 points for each successful attempt. Check your rating in Chart 3.

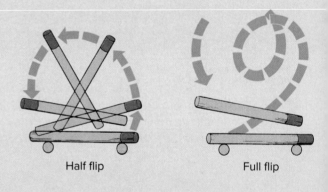

Half flip   Full flip

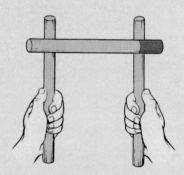

Hand position

IV. Evaluating Reaction Time: The Stick Drop Test

To perform the stick drop test of reaction time, you will need a yardstick, a table, a chair, and a partner to help with the test. To perform the test, follow this procedure:

1. Sit in the chair next to the table so that your elbow and lower arm rest on the table comfortably. The heel of your hand should rest on the table so that only your fingers and thumb extend beyond the edge of the table.
2. Your partner holds a yardstick at the top, allowing it to dangle between your thumb and fingers.
3. The yardstick should be held so that the 24-inch mark is even with your thumb and index finger. No part of your hand should touch the yardstick.
4. Without warning, your partner will drop the stick, and you will catch it with your thumb and index finger.
5. Your score is the number of inches read on the yardstick just above the thumb and index finger after you catch the yardstick.
6. Try the test three times. Your partner should be careful not to drop the stick at predictable time intervals, so that you cannot guess when it will be dropped. It is important that you react only to the dropping of the stick.
7. Use the middle of your three scores (e.g., if your scores are 21, 18, and 19, your middle score is 19). The higher your score, the faster your reaction time. Check your rating in Chart 4.

Chart 4 Reaction Time Rating Scale

Classification	Score
Excellent	More than 21″
Very good	19″–21″
Good	16″–18¾″
Fair	13″–15¾″
Poor	Below 13″

Note: Metric conversions for this chart appear in Appendix A.

Skill-Related Physical Fitness

V. Evaluating Speed: The 3-Second Run

To perform the running test of speed, it will be necessary to have a specially marked running course, a stopwatch, a whistle, and a partner to help you with the test. To perform the test, follow this procedure:

1. Mark a running course on a hard surface so that there is a starting line and a series of nine additional lines, each 2 yards apart, the first marked at a distance 10 yards from the starting line.
2. From a distance 1 or 2 yards behind the starting line, begin to run as fast as you can. As you cross the starting line, your partner starts a stopwatch.
3. Run as fast as you can until you hear the whistle, which your partner will blow exactly 3 seconds after the stopwatch is started. Your partner marks your location at the time the whistle was blown.
4. Your score is the distance you covered in 3 seconds. You may practice the test and take more than one trial if time allows. Use the better of your distances on the last two trials as your score. Check your rating in Chart 5.

Chart 5 Speed Rating Scale

Classification	Men	Women
Excellent	24–26 yards	22–26 yards
Very good	22–23 yards	20–21 yards
Good	18–21 yards	16–19 yards
Fair	16–17 yards	14–15 yards
Poor	Less than 16 yards	Less than 14 yards

Note: Metric conversions for this chart appear in Appendix A.

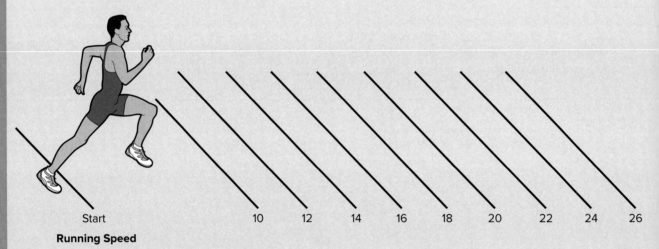

Start   10   12   14   16   18   20   22   24   26

Running Speed

Lab 13A Evaluating Skill-Related Physical Fitness

Name		Section	Date

Purpose: To help you evaluate your own skill-related fitness, including agility, balance, coordination, power, speed, and reaction time; this information may be of value in helping you decide which sports match your skill-related fitness abilities.

Procedures

1. Read the directions for each of the skill-related fitness tests presented in the Lab Resource Materials.
2. Take as many of the tests as possible, given the time and equipment available.
3. Be sure to warm up before and to cool down after the tests.
4. It is all right to practice the tests before trying them. However, you should decide ahead of time which trial you will use to test your skill-related fitness.
5. After completing the tests, write your scores in the appropriate places in the Results section.
6. Determine your rating for each of the tests from the rating charts in the Lab Resource Materials.

Results

Place a check in the circle for each of the tests you completed.

Agility (Illinois run) ◯

Balance (Bass test) ◯

Coordination (stick test) ◯

Reaction time (stick drop test) ◯

Speed (3-second run) ◯

Record your scores and ratings in the following spaces.

	Score	**Rating**	
Agility			(Chart 1)
Balance			(Chart 2)
Coordination			(Chart 3)
Reaction time			(Chart 4)
Speed			(Chart 5)

Conclusions and Implications: In two or three paragraphs, discuss the results of your skill-related fitness tests. Comment on the areas in which you did well or did not do well, the meaning of these findings, and the implications of the results, with specific reference to the activities you will perform in the future.

Lab 13B Identifying Symptoms of Overtraining

Name	Section	Date

Purpose: To help you identify the symptoms of overtraining.

Procedures

1. Answer the questions concerning overtraining syndrome in the Results section. If you are in training, rate yourself; if not, evaluate a person you know who is in training. As an alternative, you may evaluate a person who was formerly in training (and who experienced symptoms) or evaluate yourself when you were in training (if you trained for performance in the past).
2. Use Chart 1 to rate the person (yourself or another person) who is (or was) in training.
3. Use Chart 2 to identify some strategies you can try to treat or prevent overtraining syndrome.
4. Answer the questions in the Conclusions and Implications section.

Results

Answer "Yes" (place a check in the circle) to any of the questions relating to overtraining symptoms you (or the person you are evaluating) experienced.

○ 1. Has performance decreased dramatically in the last week or two?

○ 2. Is there evidence of depression?

○ 3. Is there evidence of atypical anger?

○ 4. Is there evidence of atypical anxiety?

○ 5. Is there evidence of general fatigue that is not typical?

○ 6. Is there general lack of vigor or loss of energy?

○ 7. Have sleeping patterns changed (inability to sleep well)?

○ 8. Is there evidence of heaviness of the arms and/or legs?

○ 9. Is there evidence of loss of appetite?

○ 10. Is there a lack of interest in training?

Chart 1 Ratings for Overtraining Syndrome

Number of "Yes" Answers	Rating
9–10	Overtraining syndrome is very likely present. Seek help.
6–8	Person is at risk for overtraining syndrome if it is not already present. Seek help to prevent additional symptoms.
3–5	Some signs of overtraining syndrome are present. Consider methods of preventing further symptoms.
0–2	Overtraining syndrome is not present, but attention should be paid to any symptoms that do exist.

Conclusions and Implications

Chart 2 lists some of the strategies that may help eliminate or prevent overtraining syndrome. Check the strategies that you think would be (or would have been) most useful to the person you evaluated.

Chart 2 Strategies for Treating or Preventing Overtraining Syndrome

○ 1. Consider a break from training.

○ 2. Taper the program to help reduce symptoms.

○ 3. Seek help to redesign the training program.

○ 4. Alter your diet.

○ 5. Evaluate other stressors that may be producing symptoms.

○ 6. Reset performance goals.

○ 7. Talk to someone about problems.

○ 8. Have a medical checkup to be sure there is no medical problem.

○ 9. If you have a coach, consider a talk with him or her.

○ 10. Add fluids to help prevent performance problems from dehydration.

Discuss overtraining syndrome in general. Elaborate on one or two of the strategies in Chart 2 that you think would be (or would have been) most effective in treating or preventing overtraining syndrome for the person you evaluated.

Body Composition

LEARNING OBJECTIVES

After completing the study of this Concept, you will be able to:

▶ Understand and interpret body composition measures.

▶ Describe common methods of assessing body composition.

▶ List health risks associated with overfatness.

▶ List health risks associated with excessively low body fatness.

▶ Identify and describe the origins of body fatness.

▶ Explain the relationship between physical activity and body composition and apply the FIT formula for achieving and maintaining a healthy body composition.

▶ Evaluate your body composition using several self-assessments and identify personal needs, set goals, and create a plan for achieving and maintaining a healthy body composition.

▶ Self-assess your daily energy expenditure.

Possessing an optimal amount of body fat contributes to health and wellness.

©Comstock Images/Stockbyte/Getty Images

Why it Matters!

The high prevalence of obesity remains a major public health problem. While societal change is exceedingly complicated and difficult, there are things you can do to take control of your own weight status. This Concept provides information about the causes and consequences of obesity as well as how to assess and interpret your body composition status using several indicators. It also covers risks associated with excessively low body fat levels and issues with eating disorders. Having a good understanding of these facts and methods can help you establish lifestyles that are more conducive to establishing and maintaining a healthy weight. Numerous studies have demonstrated that fitness is more important than fatness as far as overall health is concerned. Therefore, instead of focusing on weight, the more important goal is to adopt an active and healthy lifestyle

Understanding the Obesity Epidemic

The term *epidemic* is often used to describe the rapid increases in obesity rates. An epidemic is typically defined as *"an outbreak of disease that spreads quickly and affects many individuals at the same time."* While obesity is not contagious like infectious diseases, it did exhibit epidemic-like characteristics as the prevalence began increasing. For example, 20 years ago, almost no states in the United States had an obesity rate higher than 20 percent, but now almost all (46 out of 50) have adult obesity rates exceeding 25 percent. Half of the states have rates that exceed 30 percent, with five (10 percent) having rates above 35 percent. Obesity rates have been consistently higher in southern states and lower in western ones, but increases have been evident nationwide and in all age groups. Several reports had suggested that the progressive increases were starting to level off, but a new report by the CDC suggests that nearly 40 percent of Americans are classified as obese with approximately 70 percent classified as either overweight or obese. Although these alarming rates are the highest reported, it can be difficult to compare outcomes due to differences in samples and methods. Regardless of the statistics, values remain very high, and evidence suggests that the percentage of people who are extremely obese continues to increase.

The problem is not unique to the United States, since similar trends are evident in almost all developed countries. An international study estimated that there are over 2.1 billion overweight adults worldwide (approximately one-third of the world's population). A similar report by the World Health Organization indicated that the United States

accounted for 13 percent of all obese people while accounting for only 5 percent of the world's population. Thus, Americans tend to have an even greater challenge maintaining a healthy body weight than citizens from other countries. The CDC maintains accessible links and maps of these trends to help promote awareness about the issues. The prominent nonprofit agency Trust for America's Health also releases annual *State of Obesity* reports documenting the issues (see A Closer Look).

A major public health concern is the large disparities in obesity in the population. The overall trends are consistent across different ages, socioeconomic classes, and races, suggesting that the obesity problem is universal, rampant, and widespread. However, the prevalence is higher in some groups than others. For example, obesity rates are highest among 40- to 59-year-old adults (approximately 43 percent) and lowest among 20- to 39-year-old adults (approximately 36 percent). Rates of obesity also vary considerably across ethnic groups. For women, the prevalence is highest for Blacks (55 percent) and Hispanics (51 percent), intermediate for Whites (38 percent), and low for Asians (15 percent). Obesity rates are considerably higher among adults without a college education and those with lower incomes. There are also disparities by urbanicity, with higher rates in rural areas than urban ones. Interestingly, a large national study demonstrated that the disparities between rural and urban settings could be explained by differences in educational attainment at the individual level and by economic and built environmental differences at the neighborhood level. The overall results point out that some segments of the population have a harder time managing weight than others. However, when interpreting these data, it is important to understand that these are population averages and that values do not reflect the reality for all individuals.

The obesity epidemic has had profound financial consequences on our society due to the excess burden on the health-care system. Health-care dollars spent annually on medical conditions associated with obesity are estimated to be between $150 and $190 billion, with projections suggesting that the costs will continue to rise. However, these projections underestimate the true burden since they don't capture billions in lost productivity. Leading public health agencies continue to call for major investment and policy change to address the underlying factors contributing to obesity. Specific emphasis has been placed on policies and programs for youth and community-based programs since these strategies have the greatest long-term potential for positive impact.

Obesity is officially classified as a disease. While obesity is viewed by most people to be largely preventable (with proper attention on healthy lifestyles), it is officially recognized by the American Medical Association (AMA) as a

A CLOSER LOOK

Interpreting the Obesity Epidemic

The trends in the prevalence of obesity are closely monitored by researchers and public health officials in hopes of better understanding the causes. However, it can be difficult to accurately assess the patterns and trends due to differences in the samples and the methods of analyzing data. The Behavioral Risk Factor Surveillance System (BRFSS) used in state-level monitoring relies on *self-reported* height and weight, while the National Health and Nutrition Examination Survey (NHANES) used to assess national trends uses *measured* height and weight. Research has demonstrated that people tend to underreport their body weight, so it is not surprising

that obesity rates are typically 10 percent lower in the BRFSS than in the NHANES data. The prominent nonprofit agency Trust for America's Health publishes an annual summary called the *State of Obesity* that seeks to help promote awareness and understanding of these patterns. The goal is to support stronger health-related policies to help curb the obesity epidemic. (See link in Suggested Resources and Readings.)

Do the alarming trends on the obesity epidemic cause you to be more aware of your own lifestyle?

disease. The designation has considerable implications for how obesity is treated by the medical community as well as the extent to which treatments and prevention methods will be covered by health insurance. This is evidenced by the passage of the Patient Access to Evidence-Based Obesity Services resolution by the AMA which helps improve patient access to evidence-based obesity treatments. Although it legitimizes the public health concerns related to obesity, it is not without controversy. The designation as a disease may, for example, allow some individuals to justify unhealthy lifestyle or dietary practices rather than accepting personal responsibility for their condition.

Body Composition Indicators and Standards

Although body composition is considered a component of health-related fitness, it can also be considered a component of metabolic fitness. Body composition is different from other dimensions of health-related physical fitness in that it is not a performance measure. Cardiorespiratory endurance, strength, muscular endurance, and flexibility can be assessed using movement or performance, such as running, lifting, or stretching. Body composition requires no movement or performance. This is one reason some experts prefer to consider body composition as a component of metabolic fitness. Whether you consider body composition to be a part of health-related or metabolic fitness, it is an important health-related factor.

Standards have been established for healthy levels of body fatness. Fat has important functions in the body, and it is distributed naturally into different tissues and storage depots.

The indicator of **percent body fat** is typically used to reflect the overall fat content of the body. This indicator takes into account differences in body size and allows recommendations to be made for healthy levels of body fatness.

A certain minimal amount of fat is needed to allow the body to function. This level of **essential fat** is necessary for temperature regulation, shock absorption, and the regulation of essential body nutrients, including vitamins A, D, E, and K. The exact amount of fat considered essential to normal body functioning has been debated, but most experts agree that males should possess no less than 5 percent and females no less than 10 percent. For females, an exceptionally low body fat percentage (**underfat**) is of special concern, particularly when associated with overtraining, low calorie intake, competitive stress, and poor diet. **Amenorrhea** may occur, placing the woman at risk for bone loss (osteoporosis) and other health problems. A body fat level below 10 percent is one of the criteria often used by clinicians for diagnosing eating disorders, such as anorexia nervosa.

Figure 1 shows the health-related standards for body composition (percent body fat) for both males and females. Because individuals differ in their response to low fatness, a borderline range is provided above the essential fat (too low) zone. Values in this zone are not necessarily considered to be healthy, but some individuals may seek to have lower body fat levels to enhance performance in certain sports. These levels

Percent Body Fat The percentage of total body weight that is composed of fat.

Essential Fat The minimum amount of fat in the body necessary to maintain healthful living.

Underfat Too little of the body weight composed of fat.

Amenorrhea Absent or infrequent menstruation.

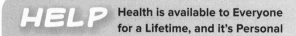

	Too low	Borderline	Good fitness	Marginal	At risk	
Male	5 or less	6–9	10–20	21–25	26+	Body fatness (percent body fat)
Female	10 or less	11–16	17–28	29–35	36+	

	Too low	Borderline	Good fitness	Overweight	Obesity	
Male	12 or less	13–16	17–25	26–30	30+	Body Mass Index (kg/m²)
Female	12 or less	13–16	17–25	26–30	30+	

Figure 1 ▶ Health-related standards for body fatness (percent body fat) and Body Mass Index.

can be acceptable for nonperformers if they can be maintained on a healthy diet and without overtraining. If symptoms such as amenorrhea, bone loss, and frequent injury occur, then levels of body fatness should be reconsidered, as should training techniques and eating patterns.

Fat that is stored above essential fat levels is classified as **nonessential fat.** Just as percent body fat should not drop too low, it should not get too high. The healthy range for body fatness in males is between 10 and 20 percent, while the healthy range for women is between 17 and 28 percent. These levels are associated with good metabolic fitness, good health, and wellness. The marginal zone includes levels that are above the healthy fitness zone but not quite into the range used to reflect **obesity.** The term *obesity* often carries negative connotations and stereotypes, but it is important to understand that it is a clinical term that simply means excessively high body fat. Lab 14A provides opportunities for you to assess your level of body fatness.

Health standards have been established for the Body Mass Index. The **Body Mass Index (BMI)** is a commonly used indicator of **overweight** and obesity in our society but is often misunderstood. The measure of BMI is basically an indicator of your weight relative to your height. It does not provide an indicator of body fatness, although BMI values tend to correlate with body fatness in most people. Because of this association, it is widely used in clinical settings and as a general indicator of body composition.

Because BMI is a frequently used measure, you should know how to calculate and interpret your BMI and your "healthy weight range." Mathematically, BMI is calculated with the following formula: BMI = weight (kg)/(height [m] × height [m]). Instructions for calculating BMI, including the nonmetric formula and rating charts, are provided in the Lab Resource Materials later in this Concept. There are also many BMI calculators on the Internet that make it easy to calculate.

The accepted international standards for defining overweight and obesity are the same for both men and women. BMI values over 25 are used to define overweight, and values over 30 are used to define obesity (see Figure 1). These

HELP   Health is available to Everyone for a Lifetime, and it's Personal

Freshman 15

The *freshman 15* is a term used for the weight gain that often happens to college students during their first year in college. Research has verified that first-year college students do gain weight, though the average gain is closer to 6–9 pounds. Over four years of college the average student gains 10 pounds. Students attribute the gain to factors such as being less active, eating when stressed, and drinking alcohol more. While this is common among college students, the weight proves difficult for many students to lose after college.

What steps can you take to maintain a healthy weight during the college years?

connect ACTIVITY

values are widely used and accepted for general population surveillance but may not be useful for certain individuals. People with high levels of muscle fitness or large muscle mass will often be categorized as overweight or obese using the standard BMI criteria. This is because muscle weighs more than fat. The BMI values are based solely on a person's weight relative to their height so it cannot detect differences in muscle and fat in the body. However, BMI is still a useful indicator for most people.

Methods Used to Assess Body Composition

Methods of body composition assessment vary in accuracy and practicality. Your body is made up of water, fat, protein, carbohydrate, and various vitamins and minerals. However, assessments of body composition

connect VIDEO 2

typically focus on the relative amount of fat in the body. A number of techniques have been developed to assess body composition. They vary in terms of practicality and accuracy, so it is important to understand the limitations of each method. Even established techniques have potential for error. The most common methods are summarized in this section.

Dual-energy X-ray absorptiometry (DXA) has emerged as the accepted "gold standard" measure of body composition. The DXA technique uses the attenuation of two energy sources to estimate the density of the body. A specific advantage of DXA is that it can provide whole-body measurements of body fatness as well as amounts stored in different parts of the body. An additional advantage is that it provides estimates of bone density. For the procedure, the person lies on a table and the machine scans up along the body. While some radiation exposure is necessary with the procedure, it is quite minimal compared with X-ray and other diagnostic scans. Because the machine is quite expensive, this procedure is found only in medical centers and well-equipped research laboratories. The DXA (also called DEXA) procedure provides a highly accurate measure of body composition for research and a criterion measure that has been used to validate other, more practical measures of body composition.

Underwater weighing and Bod Pod are two highly accurate methods. Underwater weighing is another excellent method of assessing body fatness. Before the development of DXA it was considered to be the "gold standard" method of assessment. In this technique, a person is weighed in air and underwater, and the difference in weight is used to assess the levels of body fatness. People with a lot of muscle, bone, and other lean tissue sink like a rock in water because muscle and other lean tissue are dense. Fat is less dense, so people with more fat tend to float in a water environment. A limitation of this method is that participants must exhale all their air while submerged in order to obtain an accurate reading. Additional error from the estimations of residual lung volumes also tends to reduce the accuracy of this approach.

A device called the Bod Pod uses the same principles as underwater weighing but relies on air displacement to assess body composition. The Bod Pod tends to overestimate body fat percentage in thinner participants and underestimate body fat percentage in heavier participants (compared to DXA). Discrepancies are smaller in normal-weight individuals.

Skinfold measurements are a practical method of assessing body fatness. About one-half of the body's fat is located around the various body organs and in the muscles. The other half of the body's fat is located just under the skin, or in skinfolds (Figure 2). A skinfold is two thicknesses of skin and the amount of fat that lies just under the skin. By measuring skinfold thicknesses of various sites around the body, it is possible to estimate total body fatness (Figure 3).

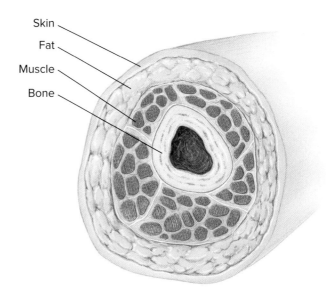

Figure 2 ▶ Location of body fat.

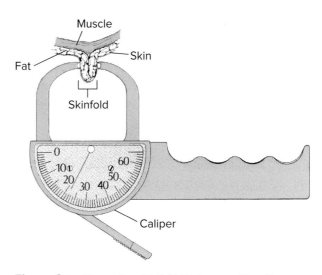

Figure 3 ▶ Measuring skinfold thickness with calipers.

Skinfold measurements are often used because they are relatively easy to do. They are not nearly as costly as underwater weighing and other methods that require expensive equipment. Research-quality skinfold calipers cost more than $100, but consumer models are available for $10 to $20.

Nonessential Fat Extra fat or fat reserves stored in the body.

Obesity A clinical term for a condition characterized by an excessive amount of body fat (or extremely high BMI).

Body Mass Index (BMI) A measure of body composition using a height–weight formula. High BMI values have been related to increased disease risk.

Overweight A clinical term that implies higher than normal levels of body fat and potential risk for development of obesity.

Monitoring weight can be helpful, but measures of body fatness provide a better indication of body composition.
©JGI/Blend Images LLC

In general, the more skinfolds measured, the more accurate the fatness estimate. However, measurements with two or three skinfolds have been shown to be reasonably accurate and can be done in a relatively short period. Two skinfold techniques are used in Lab 14A. You are encouraged to try both to see how they compare. While you might not have access to calipers in the future it is important to understand the concept behind the assessment.

Bioelectric impedance analysis has become a practical alternative for body fatness assessment. Bioelectric impedance analysis (BIA) ranks quite favorably for accuracy and has overall rankings similar to those of skinfold measurement techniques. The test can be performed quickly and is more effective for people high in body fatness (a limitation of skinfolds). The technique is based on measuring resistance to current flow. Electrodes are placed on the body and low doses of current are passed through the skin. Because muscle has greater water content than fat, it is a better conductor and

has less resistance to current. The overall amount of resistance and body size are used to predict body fatness. The results depend heavily on hydration status, so do not test after exercising or immediately after eating or drinking. Accuracy is also affected by the quality of the equipment. Portable BIA scales are available that allow you to simply stand on metal plates to get an estimate of body fatness. These devices are easier to use and are now widely available to consumers. They provide a reasonable estimate but are less accurate than research-grade devices.

Health Risks Associated with Obesity

Obesity contributes directly and indirectly to a number of major health problems. The presence of excess body fat impairs the function of most systems of the body (e.g., the cardiovascular system, the pulmonary system, the skeletal system, the reproductive system, and the metabolic system). It also increases risks for a variety of diseases, including cardiovascular disease and diabetes. And it is linked to a variety of cancers, with one estimate implicating obesity as the cause of 40 percent of all cancer diagnoses. The overall negative impact of excess body fat on the various systems of body is summarized in Figure 4.

Obesity contributes to early death but even greater losses in quality of life. A number of studies have sought to predict the impact of obesity on life expectancy. Results indicate that obesity may cut 8 to 10 years from life, but the absolute impact varies by the severity of the condition as well as by many other social, demographic, lifestyle, and health factors. Public health experts suggest that efforts to estimate risk of mortality are not of much value. They contend that the clear evidence of increased mortality fails to capture the real damage that obesity causes across a lifetime. New statistical models have focused on computing "healthy years lost" rather than total years lost. This distinction is consistent with the shift from the notion of "lifespan" to one of "healthspan."

Physical activity and physical fitness provide protection from the health risks of obesity. A common misconception is that if you are thin, you are fit and healthy, and that if you are overweight, you are unfit and unhealthy. Numerous studies have demonstrated that it is possible to be fit while still being overweight. In fact, the findings consistently show that active people who have a high BMI are at less risk than inactive people with normal BMI levels (see Figure 5). Even high levels of body fatness may not increase disease risk if a person has good metabolic fitness as indicated by healthy blood fat levels, normal blood pressure, and normal blood sugar levels. For this reason, it is important to consider your cardiorespiratory endurance and metabolic fitness levels before drawing conclusions about the effects of high body

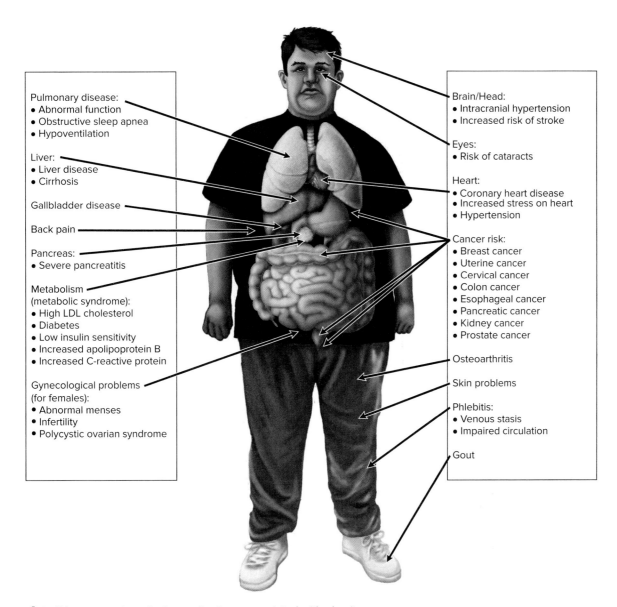

Figure 4 ▶ Diseases and medical complications associated with obesity.

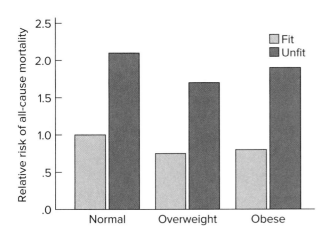

Figure 5 ▶ Risks of fatness versus fitness.

Source: Lee, C. D., et al.

weight or high body fat levels on health and wellness. This information also documents the importance of focusing on adopting and maintaining a habit of regular physical activity.

Excessive abdominal fat and excessive fat of the upper body can increase the risk for various diseases. The location of body fat can influence the health risks associated with obesity. Fat in the upper part of the body is sometimes referred to as "Northern Hemisphere" fat, and a body type high in this type of fat is called the "apple" shape. Upper body fat is also referred to as android fat because it is more characteristic of men than women. Postmenopausal women typically have a higher amount of upper body fat than premenopausal women. Lower body fat, such as in the hips and upper legs, is sometimes referred to as "Southern

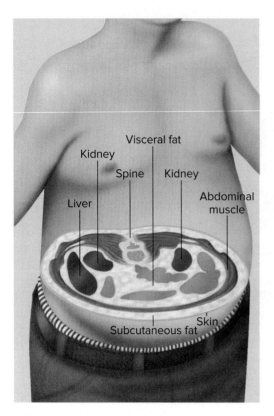

Figure 6 ▶ Visceral, or abdominal, fat is associated with increased disease risk.

Hemisphere" fat. This body type is called the "pear" shape. Lower body fat is also referred to as gynoid fat because it is more characteristic of women than men.

Body fat located in the core of the body is referred to as central fat or visceral fat. Visceral fat is located in the abdominal cavity (see Figure 6), as opposed to subcutaneous fat, which is located just under the skin. Though subcutaneous fat

(skinfold measures) can be used to estimate body fatness, it is not a good indicator of central fatness. Your waist size is a useful indicator of visceral fat distribution. It can be used alone, in combination with BMI, in combination with your gender and height, and/or in combination with hip size (waist-to-hip ratio) to determine health risk (see the Lab Resource Materials). Visceral fat is considered more harmful than other forms and is associated with high blood fat levels as well as other metabolic problems. It is also associated with high incidence of heart attack, stroke, chest pain, breast cancer, and early death.

A number of studies have documented that physical activity tends to promote preferential loss of abdominal body fat. It was assumed that aerobic activity played a bigger role in this effect, but a recent study has shown that resistance exercise may play a more significant role. In this large longitudinal study, individuals who reported regular weight training had less gain in their waistline over a 12-year period compared with those who participated primarily in moderate-to-vigorous aerobic exercise or physical labor from daily life. Both aerobic and resistance activity likely contribute to reductions in abdominal body fat, and this benefit is likely a key reason why physical activity improves health and provides protection against the risks of obesity.

Health effects of obesity may be mediated by circulating "adipokines." Research has recently shown that the fat cell is not only a storage depot, but also an active protein-secreting organ. The biomolecules secreted by adipose tissue are known as adipokines or adipocytokines. A number of adipokines have been identified, including adiponectin, visfatin, resistin, and leptin. Each has an important role, but adiponectin appears to play a particularly important role in energy balance, insulin resistance, and atherosclerosis. Studies show that adiponectin can reduce arterial plaque and clot formation while an adiponectin deficiency appears to

In the News

Is Obesity Really a Disease?

While obesity is clearly a major public health problem, there is considerable debate about the designation of obesity as a disease. A recent report indicates that obesity may soon outpace smoking as the leading cause of cancer, but this can be attributed to the declines in smoking rates as well as the high prevalence of obesity. Another high-profile study confirmed that low body fatness is protective against 13 different types of cancer, but the media tended to

misinterpret this to mean that *obesity causes* these cancers. The designation as a disease has implications for prevention and treatment approaches as well as health care costs. Search "obesity as a disease" to read more about this ongoing debate.

Do you see more positives or negatives associated with the declaration of obesity as a disease?

lead to metabolic dysfunction, insulin resistance, fatty liver disease, and a wide array of cancers. Current evidence suggests that aerobic exercise, alone or combined with a low calorie diet, improves symptoms of the metabolic syndrome, possibly by altering levels of adipokines.

The Origin of Obesity

Obesity is a multifactorial disease that is influenced by both genetics and the environment. The strong evidence of genetic predisposition to obesity certainly played a role in the decision to classify obesity as a disease. There is clear clustering of obesity  within families, and studies have documented similar body composition in identical twins. The role of genetic factors is still not well understood, but genetic mapping studies suggest that a number of genes may work in combination to influence susceptibility to obesity. These *susceptibility genes* may not lead directly to obesity but may predispose a person to overweight or obesity if exposed to certain environmental conditions. Thus, the prevailing model guiding obesity research is that complex genetic and environmental variables interact to increase potential risks for obesity. Future research will allow genetic factors to be integrated with behavioral and environmental data so that the combined effects can be better understood.

Body weight is regulated and maintained through complex regulatory processes. Some scholars have suggested that the human body type, or **somatotype,** is inherited. Clearly, some people have more difficulty than others controlling fatness, and this may be because of their somatotype and genetic predisposition. Regulatory processes appear to balance energy intake and energy expenditure so that body weight stays near a biologically determined **set-point.** The regulation is helpful for maintaining body weight but can be frustrating for people trying to lose weight. If a person slowly tries to cut calories, the body perceives an energy imbalance and initiates processes to protect the current body weight. The body can accommodate to a new, higher set-point if weight gain takes place over time, but there is greater resistance to adopting a lower set-point. Many people lose weight, only to see the weight come back months later. One of the reasons exercise is so critical for weight maintenance is that it may help in resetting this set-point.

In recent years, the mechanisms involved in the regulation of the biological set-point have become better understood. The current view is that there are complex feedback loops among fatty tissues, the brain, and endocrine glands, such as the pancreas and the thyroid. The compound leptin plays a crucial role in altering appetite and in speeding up or slowing down the metabolism. Leptin levels rise during times of energy excess in order to suppress appetite and fall when energy levels are low to stimulate appetite. Resistance to leptin has been hypothesized as a possible contributor to obesity. A number of other compounds also appear to be involved in the complex processes regulating energy balance. Problems with the thyroid gland can lead to impairments in metabolic regulation, but these do not contribute to overfatness in most people.

Changes in basal metabolic rate can be the cause of obesity. Your **basal metabolic rate (BMR)** is the largest component of total daily energy expenditure. BMR is typically expressed in the number of **calories** needed to maintain your body functions under resting conditions. When resting, your body expends calories because your heart is pumping and other body organs are working. Processing the food you eat also expends calories. People with more lean tissue have a higher BMR than those with less lean tissue and greater amounts of body fat. People who are physically active will also have a higher BMR on days they exercise, contributing to long-term weight control.

During childhood and adolescence, BMR is high to support growth and development. This is why teenagers can typically eat more without gaining weight. However, when a person reaches full growth, the BMR decreases and is determined primarily by the amount of muscle mass a person has. Regular physical activity throughout life helps keep the muscle mass higher, which helps to maintain a higher BMR. Evidence suggests that regular exercise can contribute in other ways to increasing BMR. For example, BMR can stay elevated for up to 10 hours following a bout of vigorous physical activity. This boost in BMR helps burn extra calories during the day.

"Creeping obesity" is a problem as you grow older. With age, people tend to become less active, causing declines in BMR. Caloric intake does seem to decrease somewhat with age, but the decrease does not adequately compensate for the decreases in BMR and activity levels. For this reason,

---

Somatotype A term that refers to a person's body type. One simple somatotopic classification system emphasizes three body types: ectomorph (linear), mesomorph (muscular), and endomorph (round).

Set-point A theoretical concept that describes the way the body protects current weight and resists change.

Basal Metabolic Rate (BMR) Energy expenditure in a basic, or rested, state.

Calories Units of energy supplied by food; the quantity of heat necessary to raise the temperature of a kilogram of water 1°C (actually, a kilocalorie, but usually called a calorie for weight control purposes).

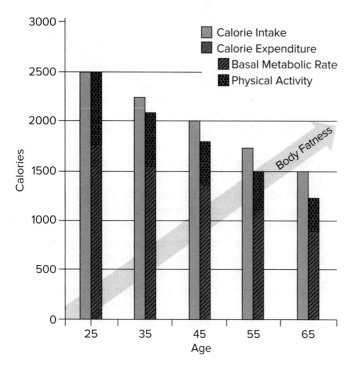

Figure 7 ▶ Creeping obesity.

body fat increases gradually with age for the typical person (see Figure 7). This increase in fatness over time is commonly referred to as "creeping obesity" because the increase in fatness is gradual. For a typical person, creeping obesity can result in a gain of 1/2 to 1 pound per year. People who stay active can keep muscle mass high and delay changes in BMR.

Technology Update

Have Advances in Technology Caused Obesity?

Technology is part of modern life but it may also be contributing to societal problems with weight control and obesity. Research has convincingly documented associations between television viewing and the risk of obesity. Recent research has also demonstrated associations between sedentary behavior and obesity. However, it is still difficult to confirm that the underlying cause of obesity is exposure to "technology." The 25- to 30-year progression in the obesity epidemic largely parallels the evolution of computer and phone technology, which makes the causation seem probable.

Do you see technology as part of the problem or can it be part of the solution to tackling the obesity epidemic?

ACTIVITY

For those who are not active, it is suggested that caloric intake decrease by 3 percent each decade after 25 so that by age 65 caloric intake is at least 10 percent less than it was at age 25. The decrease in caloric intake for active people need not be as great.

Fatness early in life leads to adult fatness. Although there are exceptions, individuals who are overweight or obese as children are more likely to be overweight or obese as adults. One explanation for this is that overfatness in children causes the body to produce more fat cells. Research has even suggested that the neonatal environment that the child is exposed to during development may also influence future risks for obesity. It appears that hormones and lipids circulating in the maternal blood can interact with genetic factors to establish metabolic conditions that contribute to overfatness. Family influences on behavior also play a key role in the tracking of obesity from childhood into adulthood.

While the tracking of obesity over time is a major concern, evidence indicates that there are immediate health risks of childhood obesity. Obese children are at greater risk of developing diabetes, and obese children have a higher than normal risk of premature death, indicating that the effects of obesity can impair health, even for young people. Concerns about the current and future implications of childhood obesity have made it one of the greatest public health concerns facing the United States. Effective prevention programs are clearly the key.

Treatment and Prevention of Overweight and Obesity

Current treatment guidelines for obesity emphasize lifestyle behavior change. The labeling of obesity as a disease led to refinements in the clinical treatment of obesity. One set of guidelines produced by the American Heart Association (AHA), American College of Cardiologists (ACC), and the Obesity Society has increased access to treatment for many individuals. Previous guidelines provided treatment only for individuals with obesity, but the revised guidelines recommend treatment for individuals who are overweight and have at least one risk factor. These clinical guidelines emphasize the use of lifestyle intervention strategies (dietary change, physical activity, and behavioral training) and referral to trained interventionists (e.g., dietitians, psychologists, exercise specialists, and health coaches).

A combination of regular physical activity and dietary restriction is the most effective means of losing body fat. Weight control is based on principles of **caloric balance** (a balance between energy intake and energy expenditure). For optimal results, all weight loss programs should combine a lower energy intake with an enhanced energy expenditure to create a larger caloric deficit. Table 1 presents thresholds of

Table 1 ▶ Threshold of Training and Target Zones for Body Fat Reduction

	Threshold of Training*		Target Zones*	
	Physical Activity	**Diet**	**Physical Activity**	**Diet**
Frequency	Daily activity is best for weight loss and long-term weight control.	Adopt a healthy daily eating pattern.	Daily activity is best for weight loss and long-term weight control.	Adopt a healthy daily eating pattern
Intensity	Moderate intensity activity is best since it can be done comfortably for a longer time.	Aim to cut 250 calories per day from normal intake.	Moderate intensity activity is best since it can be done comfortably for a longer time.	Aim to cut 500 calories per day. Larger cuts can lead to larger weight loss but are hard to sustain.
	Aim for at least 30 minutes a day to expend a reasonable number of calories.	Eating smaller but regular meals is best.	Aim for 60 minutes a day (or more) to maximize daily caloric expenditure.	Eating smaller but regular meals is best.

Note: A gram of fat is 9 calories; thus, a pound is equal to 4,086 calories (9 cal/g × 454 g/pound). However, fat in the body is 10 percent water and contains some protein and minerals that reduce the effective caloric equivalent to 3,500 calories (the accepted standard).

*It is best to combine exercise and diet to achieve the 3,500-calorie imbalance necessary to lose a pound of fat. Using both exercise and diet in the target zone is most effective.

training and target zones for body fat reduction, including information for both physical activity and diet. A general guideline is to try to lose no more than 1 to 2 pounds a week. Because a pound of fat contains 3,500 calories (see note in Table 1), this requires a caloric deficit of approximately 500 calories per day. (See the Concept on weight management for details.)

Physical activity burns calories but also helps maintain lean body mass. National activity guidelines recommend a minimum of 30 minutes of moderate to vigorous activity a day or 150 minutes per week, but these guidelines are based on needs for health and not weight control. More time is often needed either to maintain weight over time or to lose weight. The ACSM guidelines suggest that it may be necessary to work progressively up to 200 to 300 minutes a week to expend enough calories to lose weight. One study found that women who maintained weight across the lifespan average approximately 60 minutes of activity per day. A table showing calories expended in various activities is presented in Table 2 to help promote understanding of how many calories are burned over time.

Physical activity provides advantages for weight maintenance and improved body composition. As discussed in other Concepts, there are limitations associated with trying to lose weight only with changes in **diet.** Weight loss from dieting can come from both fat and muscle. The rate of weight loss also tends to slow because the metabolism slows down when calories are cut. When physical activity and diet are both used in a weight loss program, the same amount of weight may be lost but more of it is from fat.

Physical activity also helps maintain resting metabolic rate at a higher level. This can contribute to further weight loss or facilitate weight maintenance. Individuals who want to increase lean body mass need to increase caloric intake while carefully increasing the intensity and duration of exercise (mainly muscular activity).

Health Risks Associated with Excessively Low Body Fatness

Excessive desire to be thin or low in body weight can result in health problems. In Western society, the near obsession with thinness has been, at least in part, responsible for eating disorders. Eating disorders, or altered eating habits, involve extreme restriction of food intake and/or regurgitation of food to avoid digestion. The most common disorders are anorexia nervosa, binge eating disorder, bulimia, and anorexia athletica. All of these disorders are most common among highly achievement-oriented girls and young women, although they affect virtually all segments of the population. Patterns of "disordered eating" are not the same as clinically diagnosed eating disorders. People who adopt disordered eating, however, tend to have a greater chance of developing an eating disorder.

Caloric Balance Consuming calories in amounts equal to the number of calories expended.

Diet The usual food and drink for a person or an animal.

Table 2 ▶ Calories Expended per Hour in Various Physical Activities (Performed at a Recreational Level)*

Activity	100 lb (46 kg)	120 lb (55 kg)	Calories Used per Hour 150 lb (68 kg)	180 lb (82 kg)	200 lb (91 kg)
Archery	180	204	240	276	300
Backpacking (40-lb. pack)	307	348	410	472	513
Badminton	255	289	340	391	425
Baseball	210	238	280	322	350
Basketball (half-court)	225	255	300	345	375
Bicycling (10 mph)	182	218	273	327	364
Bowling	136	164	205	245	273
Canoeing	227	273	341	409	455
Circuit training	247	280	330	380	413
Dance, aerobics	315	357	420	483	525
Dance, ballet (choreographed)	240	300	360	432	480
Dance, modern (choreographed)	240	300	360	432	480
Dance, social	205	245	307	368	409
Fencing	225	255	300	345	375
Fitness calisthenics	232	263	310	357	388
Football	225	255	300	345	375
Golf (walking)	250	300	375	450	500
Gymnastics	232	263	310	357	388
Handball	450	510	600	690	750
Hiking	225	255	300	345	375
Horseback riding	182	218	273	327	364
Interval training	487	552	650	748	833
Jogging (5 1/2 mph)	487	552	650	748	833
Judo/karate	232	263	310	357	388
Mountain climbing	450	510	600	690	750
Pool/billiards	97	110	130	150	163
Racquetball/paddleball	450	510	600	690	750
Rope jumping (continuous)	525	595	700	805	875
Rowing, crew	615	697	820	943	1025
Running (10 mph)	625	765	900	1035	1125
Sailing (pleasure)	135	153	180	207	225
Skating, ice	262	297	350	403	438
Skating, roller/inline	262	297	350	403	438
Skiing, cross-country	318	382	477	573	636
Skiing, downhill	450	510	600	690	750
Soccer	405	459	540	621	775
Softball (fast-pitch)	210	238	280	322	350
Softball (slow-pitch)	217	246	290	334	363
Surfing	416	467	550	633	684
Swimming (fast laps)	420	530	630	768	846
Swimming (slow laps)	273	327	409	491	545
Table tennis	182	218	273	327	364
Tennis	315	357	420	483	525
Volleyball	262	297	350	403	483
Walking	173	207	259	311	346
Waterskiing	306	390	468	564	636
Weight training	352	399	470	541	558

*Locate your weight to determine the calories expended per hour in each of the activities shown in the table based on recreational involvement. More vigorous activity, as occurs in competitive athletics, may result in greater caloric expenditures.
Source: Corbin and Lindsey.

Body image disorders can influence self-esteem and wellness.
©Ted Foxx/Alamy Stock Photo

Anorexia nervosa is the most severe eating disorder. If untreated, anorexia is life threatening. Anorexics restrict food intake so severely that their bodies become emaciated. The anorexic essentially starves himself or herself and may exercise compulsively or use laxatives to prevent the digestion of food in an attempt to attain excessive leanness. The anorexic's self-image is one of being too fat, even when the person is too lean for good health. Fear of maturity and an "adult figure" are also common symptoms. About 25 percent of those with anorexia exercise compulsively in an attempt to stay lean. Individuals with signs or symptoms of this disorder should obtain medical and psychological help immediately, as the consequences are severe.

Binge eating disorder is the most common eating disorder in the United States. Binge eating disorder (BED) is an increasingly common condition affecting about 2 percent of adults. It is characterized by periods of eating large quantities of food in a short amount of time, often in isolation. Individuals may eat very rapidly until they are uncomfortably full and feel out of control and powerless to stop eating. Clinically diagnosed BED involves recurrent episodes of binge eating at least once a week for 3 months. Treatments are shown to be effective for reversing this condition.

Bulimia is a common eating disorder characterized by bingeing and purging. Disordered eating patterns become habitual for many people with bulimia. A bulimic might binge after a relatively long period of dieting and consume excessive amounts of junk foods containing empty calories. After a binge, the bulimic purges the food by forced regurgitation or the use of laxatives. Another form of bulimia is bingeing on one day and severely restricting calorie intake on the next. The consequences of bulimia include serious mental, gastrointestinal, and dental problems. Bulimics may or may not be anorexic. It may not be possible to use measures of body fatness to identify bulimia, as the bulimic may be lean, normal, or excessively fat.

Anorexia athletica is a more recently identified eating disorder that appears to be related to participation in sports and activities emphasizing body leanness. Studies show that participants in sports such as gymnastics, wrestling, and bodybuilding and activities such as ballet and cheerleading are most likely to develop anorexia athletica. This disorder has many of the symptoms of anorexia nervosa, but not of the same severity. In some cases, anorexia athletica leads to anorexia nervosa.

Female athlete triad is an increasingly common condition among female athletes. The triad refers to the presence of three related and linked symptoms that affect some women athletes (eating disorders/low energy availability, amenorrhea, and decreased bone mineral density). The conditions are linked because low body fat levels lead to the amenorrhea. The alterations in menstrual cycles lead to low levels of estrogen, which subsequently lead to the reduced bone density and risk for osteoporosis.

The female athlete triad is one of the more challenging conditions to treat because it often goes undetected. Once identified or diagnosed, it is hard to change because the three components of the triad are thought to be linked pathophysiologically. The athlete is very serious about performance and has likely developed altered eating patterns to control body weight. Efforts to bring about change often result in resistance, since the compulsion to be thin and perform well overrides other concerns, such as eating well, moderating exercise, and having a normal menstrual cycle. The ACSM recommends regular screening exams to identify those with the triad and rule changes in women's sports to "discourage unhealthy weight loss practices." Nutrition counseling is recommended for those with the triad, and psychotherapy is recommended for athletes with eating disorders.

Many female athletes train extensively and have relatively low body fat levels but experience none of the symptoms of the triad. Eating well, training properly, using stress-management techniques, and monitoring health symptoms are the keys to their success.

Muscle dysmorphia is an emerging problem among male athletes. Muscle dysmorphia is a body dysmorphic disorder in which a male becomes preoccupied with the idea that his body is not sufficiently lean and/or muscular. An athlete with this condition may be more inclined to use performance-enhancing drugs, to exercise while sick, or to have an eating disorder. Additional risks include depression and social isolation.

Fear of obesity and purging disorder are other identified conditions. Fear of obesity is most common among achievement-oriented teenagers who impose a self-restriction on caloric intake because they fear obesity. Consequences include stunting of growth, delayed puberty, delayed sexual development, and decreased physical attractiveness. Purging disorder, a condition that results in purging similar to bulimia, but without the bingeing, has recently been identified. People with these conditions should seek assistance.

Using Self-Management Skills

Self-assessments of body weight can be helpful if done correctly. Many people chronically check their weight on scales, but this is not a good indicator of body composition. Your weight can vary from day to day and even hour to hour, based solely on your level of hydration. Short-term changes in weight are often due to water loss or gain, yet many people erroneously attribute the weight changes to their diet, a

pill they have taken, or the exercise they recently performed. There is some evidence that monitoring weight daily can help normal-weight people from gaining weight. However, for people trying to lose weight, monitoring weight less frequently (maybe once a week) is more useful. When you do weigh yourself, weigh at the same time of day, preferably early in the morning, because it reduces the chances that your weight variation will be a result of body water changes. Of course, it is best to use body composition assessments in addition to those based on body weight.

Self-assessments of body composition should be used and interpreted carefully. Estimates of body composition provide meaningful information about body fatness, but the limitations of the measures need to be considered. Estimates from even the best techniques may be off by as much as 2 to 3 percent. The formulas used to determine body fatness from skinfolds and other procedures are also based on typical body types and non-representative samples. Thus, the estimation errors may be larger for some people than others. View the values as estimates and not as absolute indicators of body fatness. Using the same measuring device each time you assess your body composition is also recommended. This reduces measurement error and allows you to track your progress over time.

Strategies for Action: Lab Information

Doing several self-assessments can help you make informed decisions about body composition. In Labs 14A and 14B you will take various body composition self-assessments. It is important that you take all of the measurements and consider all of the information before making final decisions about your body composition. Each self-assessment technique has strengths and weaknesses to be aware of when you make personal decisions. The importance you place on one particular measure may be different from the importance another person places on that measure. You are a unique individual and should use information that is more relevant for you personally. If doing a self-assessment around other people

VIDEO 6

makes you self-conscious, do the measurement in private. If the measurement requires the assistance of another person, choose a person you trust and feel comfortable with.

Understanding the factors that contribute to energy expenditure can help you determine the number of calories you expend each day. In Lab 14C you will learn how to estimate your basal metabolic rate (BMR) so you can know how much energy you typically expend when you are resting. Use this information together with the information about the energy you expend in activities to help you balance the calories you consume with the calories you expend each day. You will also log the activities you perform in a day and learn how to estimate your total daily energy expenditure.

ACTIVITY

Suggested Resources and Readings

The websites for the following sources can be accessed by searching online for the organization, program, or title listed. Specific scientific references are available at the end of this edition of *Concepts of Fitness and Wellness.*

- Centers for Disease Control and Prevention. Obesity Facts and Trends (online resource).

- Medscape. AMA Declares Obesity as a Disease (online report).
- National Center for Health Statistics. Health, United States, 2016 (online report).
- Trust for America's Health. (2017). State of Obesity 2017: Better Policies for a Healthier America (pdf download).
- World Health Organization. Obesity Facts Worldwide (online report).

Lab Resource Materials: Evaluating Body Fat

General Information about Skinfold Measurements

It is important to use a consistent procedure for "drawing up" or "pinching up" a skinfold and making the measurement with the calipers. The following procedures should be used for each skinfold site.

1. Lay the calipers down on a nearby table. Use the thumbs and index fingers of both hands to draw up a skinfold, or layer of skin and fat. The fingers and thumbs of the two hands should be about 1 inch apart, or 1/2 inch on each side of the location where the measurement is to be made.

2. The skinfolds are normally drawn up in a vertical line rather than a horizontal line. However, if the skin naturally aligns itself less than vertical, the measurement should be done on the natural line of the skinfold, rather than on the vertical.

3. Do not pinch the skinfold too hard. Draw it up so that your thumbs and fingers are not compressing the skinfold.

4. Once the skinfold is drawn up, let go with your right hand and pick up the calipers. Open the jaws of the calipers and place them over the location of the skinfold to be measured and 1/2 inch from your left index finger and thumb. Allow the tips, or jaw faces, of the calipers to close on the skinfold at a level about where the skin would be normally.

5. Let the reading on the calipers settle for 2 or 3 seconds; then note the thickness of the skinfold in millimeters.

6. Three measurements should be taken at each location. Use the middle of the three values to determine your measurement. For example, if you had values of 10, 11, and 9, your measurement for that location would be 10. If the three measures vary by more than 3 millimeters from the lowest to the highest, you may want to take additional measurements.

Skinfold Measurement Methods

You will be exposed to two methods of using skinfolds. The first method (based on the FitnessGram method) uses the same sites for men and women. It was originally developed for use with schoolchildren but has since been modified for adults. The second method (Jackson-Pollock) is the most widely used method. It uses different sites for men and women and considers your age in estimating your body fat percentage. You are encouraged to try both methods.

Calculating Fatness from Skinfolds (FITNESSGRAM Method)

1. Sum the three skinfolds (triceps, abdominal, and calf) for men and women. Use horizontal abdominal measure.

2. Use the skinfold sum and the appropriate column (men or women) to determine your percent fat using Chart 1. Locate your sum of skinfold in the left column at the top of the chart. Your estimated body fat percentage is located where the values intersect.

3. Use the Standards for Body Fatness (Chart 2) to determine your fatness rating.

FITNESSGRAM Locations (Men and Women)

Triceps

Make a mark on the back of the right arm, one-half the distance between the tip of the shoulder and the tip of the elbow. Make the measurement at this location.

Abdominal

Make a mark on the skin approximately 1 inch to the right of the navel. Unlike the Jackson-Pollock method (done vertically), make a horizontal measurement.

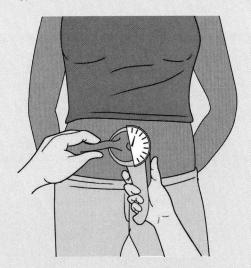

FITNESSGRAM Locations *(continued)*

Calf Skinfold

Make a mark on the inside of the calf of the right leg at the level of the largest calf size (girth). Place the foot on a chair or other elevation so that the knee is kept at approximately 90 degrees. Make a vertical measurement at the mark.

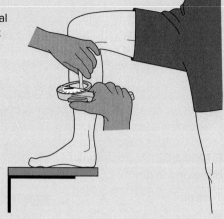

Self-Measured Triceps Skinfold

This measurement is made on the left arm so that the calipers can easily be read. Hold the arm straight at shoulder height. Make a fist with the thumb faced upward. Place the fist against a wall. With the right hand, place the calipers over the skinfold as it "hangs freely" on the back of the tricep (halfway from the tip of the shoulder to the elbow).

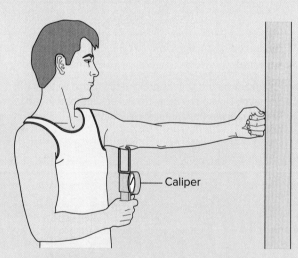

Caliper

Chart 1 Percent Fat for Sum of Triceps, Abdominal, and Calf Skinfolds (FITNESSGRAM)

Men		Women	
Sum of Skinfolds mm	Percent Fat	Sum of Skinfolds mm	Percent Fat
8–10	3.2	23–25	16.8
11–13	4.1	26–28	17.7
14–16	5.0	29–31	18.5
17–19	6.0	32–34	19.4
20–22	6.9	35–37	20.2
23–25	7.8	38–40	21.0
26–28	8.7	41–43	21.9
29–31	9.7	44–46	22.7
32–34	10.6	47–49	23.5
35–37	11.5	50–52	24.4
38–40	12.5	53–55	25.2
41–43	13.4	56–58	26.1
44–46	14.3	59–61	26.9
47–49	15.2	62–64	27.7
50–52	16.2	65–67	28.6
53–55	17.1	68–70	29.4
56–58	18.0	71–73	30.2
59–61	18.9	74–76	31.1
62–64	19.9	77–79	31.9
65–67	20.8	80–82	32.7
68–70	21.7	83–85	33.6
71–73	22.6	86–88	34.4
74–76	23.6	89–91	35.5
77–79	24.5	92–94	36.1
80–82	25.4	95–97	36.9
83–85	26.4	98–100	37.8
86–88	27.3	101–103	38.6
89–91	28.2	104–106	39.4
92–94	29.1	107–109	40.3
95–97	30.1	110–112	41.1
98–100	31.0	113–115	42.0
101–103	31.9	116–118	42.8
104–106	32.8	119–121	43.6
107–109	33.8	122–124	44.5
110–112	34.7	125–127	45.3
113–115	35.6	128–130	46.1
116–118	36.6	131–133	47.0
119–121	37.5	134–136	47.8
122–124	38.4	137–139	48.7
125–127	39.3	140–142	49.5

Chart 2 Standards for Body Fatness (Percent Body Fat)

	Too Low	Borderline	(Healthy) Good Fitness	Marginal	(At Risk) Overfat
	Below Essential Fat Levels	Unhealthy for Many People	Optimal for Good Health	Associated with Some Health Problems	Unhealthy
Males	<5%	6–9%	10–20%	21–25%	>25%
Females	<10%	11–16%	17–28%	29–35%	>35%

Calculating Fatness from Skinfolds (Jackson-Pollock Method)

1. Sum three skinfolds (tricep, iliac crest, and thigh for women; chest, abdominal [vertical], and thigh for men).
2. Use the skinfold sum and your age to determine your percent fat using Chart 3 for women and Chart 4 for men. Locate your sum of skinfold in the left column and your age at the top of the chart. Your estimated body fat percentage is located where the values intersect.
3. Use the Standards for Body Fatness (Chart 2) to determine your fatness rating.

Jackson-Pollock Locations (Women)

Triceps

Same as FitnessGram (see previous instructions).

Iliac crest

Make a mark at the top front of the iliac crest. This skinfold is taken diagonally because of the natural line of the skin.

Thigh

Make a mark on the front of the thigh midway between the hip and the knee. Make the measurement vertically at this location.

Jackson-Pollock Locations (Men)

Chest

Make a mark above and to the right of the right nipple (one-half the distance from the midline of the side and the nipple). The measurement at this location is often done on the diagonal because of the natural line of the skin.

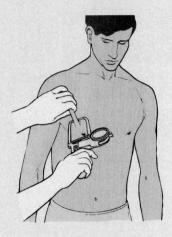

Abdominal

Make a mark on the skin approximately 1 inch to the right of the FitnessGram method.

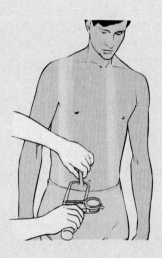

Thigh

Same as for women.

Note: Research has identified other methods that can also be used to calculate body fatness using skinfold measurements. See below.

- Ball, S., Altena, T., & Swan, P. (2004). Accuracy of anthropometry compared to dual energy x-ray absorptiometry: A new generalizable equation for men. *European Journal of Clinical Nutrition,* 58: 1525–1531.
- Ball, S., Swan, P. D., & DeSimone, R. (2004). Comparison of anthropometry compared to dual energy x-ray absorptiometry: A new generalizable equation for women. *Research Quarterly for Exercise and Sports,* 75: 248–258.

Chart 3 Percent Fat for Women (Jackson-Pollock: Sum of Triceps, Iliac Crest, and Thigh Skinfolds)

Sum of Skinfolds (mm)	Age to the Last Year								
	22 and Under	23 to 27	28 to 32	33 to 37	38 to 42	43 to 47	48 to 52	53 to 57	Over 57
23–25	9.7	9.9	10.2	10.4	10.7	10.9	11.2	11.4	11.7
26–28	11.0	11.2	11.5	11.7	12.0	12.3	12.5	12.7	13.0
29–31	12.3	12.5	12.8	13.0	13.3	13.5	13.8	14.0	14.3
32–34	13.6	13.8	14.0	14.3	14.5	14.8	15.0	15.3	15.5
35–37	14.8	15.0	15.3	15.5	15.8	16.0	16.3	16.5	16.8
38–40	16.0	16.3	16.5	16.7	17.0	17.2	17.5	17.7	18.0
41–43	17.2	17.4	17.7	17.9	18.2	18.4	18.7	18.9	19.2
44–46	18.3	18.6	18.8	19.1	19.3	19.6	19.8	20.1	20.3
47–49	19.5	19.7	20.0	20.2	20.5	20.7	21.0	21.2	21.5
50–52	20.6	20.8	21.1	21.3	21.6	21.8	22.1	22.3	22.6
53–55	21.7	21.9	22.1	22.4	22.6	22.9	23.1	23.4	23.6
56–58	22.7	23.0	23.2	23.4	23.7	23.9	24.2	24.4	24.7
59–61	23.7	24.0	24.2	24.5	24.7	25.0	25.2	25.5	25.7
62–64	24.7	25.0	25.2	25.5	25.7	26.0	26.2	26.4	26.7
65–67	25.7	25.9	26.2	26.4	26.7	26.9	27.2	27.4	27.7
68–70	26.6	26.9	27.1	27.4	27.6	27.9	28.1	28.4	28.6
71–73	27.5	27.8	28.0	28.3	28.5	28.8	28.0	29.3	29.5
74–76	28.4	28.7	28.9	29.2	29.4	29.7	29.9	30.2	30.4
77–79	29.3	29.5	29.8	30.0	30.3	30.5	30.8	31.0	31.3
80–82	30.1	30.4	30.6	30.9	31.1	31.4	31.6	31.9	32.1
83–85	30.9	31.2	31.4	31.7	31.9	32.2	32.4	32.7	32.9
86–88	31.7	32.0	32.2	32.5	32.7	32.9	33.2	33.4	33.7
89–91	32.5	32.7	33.0	33.2	33.5	33.7	33.9	34.2	34.4
92–94	33.2	33.4	33.7	33.9	34.2	34.4	34.7	34.9	35.2
95–97	33.9	34.1	34.4	34.6	34.9	35.1	35.4	35.6	35.9
98–100	34.6	34.8	35.1	35.3	35.5	35.8	36.0	36.3	36.5
101–103	35.3	35.4	35.7	35.9	36.2	36.4	36.7	36.9	37.2
104–106	35.8	36.1	36.3	36.6	36.8	37.1	37.3	37.5	37.8
107–109	36.4	36.7	36.9	37.1	37.4	37.6	37.9	38.1	38.4
110–112	37.0	37.2	37.5	37.7	38.0	38.2	38.5	38.7	38.9
113–115	37.5	37.8	38.0	38.2	38.5	38.7	39.0	39.2	39.5
116–118	38.0	38.3	38.5	38.8	39.0	39.3	39.5	39.7	40.0
119–121	38.5	38.7	39.0	39.2	39.5	39.7	40.0	40.2	40.5
122–124	39.0	39.2	39.4	39.7	39.9	40.2	40.4	40.7	40.9
125–127	39.4	39.6	39.9	40.1	40.4	40.6	40.9	41.1	41.4
128–130	39.8	40.0	40.3	40.5	40.8	41.0	41.3	41.5	41.8

Note: Percent fat calculated by the formula by Siri. Percent fat = ([4.95/BD]−4.5) × 100, where BD = body density.
Source: Baumgartner and Jackson, *Evaluation in Physical Education and Exercise Science.* Dubuque, IA: W.C. Brown Publishers (1999).

Chart 4 Percent Fat for Men (Jackson-Pollock: Sum of Thigh, Chest, and Abdominal Skinfolds)

Sum of Skinfolds (mm)	Age to the Last Year								
	22 and Under	23 to 27	28 to 32	33 to 37	38 to 42	43 to 47	48 to 52	53 to 57	Over 57
8–10	1.3	1.8	2.3	2.9	3.4	3.9	4.5	5.0	5.5
11–13	2.2	2.8	3.3	3.9	4.4	4.9	5.5	6.0	6.5
14–16	3.2	3.8	4.3	4.8	5.4	5.9	6.4	7.0	7.5
17–19	4.2	4.7	5.3	5.8	6.3	6.9	7.4	8.0	8.5
20–22	5.1	5.7	6.2	6.8	7.3	7.9	8.4	8.9	9.5
23–25	6.1	6.6	7.2	7.7	8.3	8.8	9.4	9.9	10.5
26–28	7.0	7.6	8.1	8.7	9.2	9.8	10.3	10.9	11.4
29–31	8.0	8.5	9.1	9.6	10.2	10.7	11.3	11.8	12.4
32–34	8.9	9.4	10.0	10.5	11.1	11.6	12.2	12.8	13.3
35–37	9.8	10.4	10.9	11.5	12.0	12.6	13.1	13.7	14.3
38–40	10.7	11.3	11.8	12.4	12.9	13.5	14.1	14.6	15.2
41–43	11.6	12.2	12.7	13.3	13.8	14.4	15.0	15.5	16.1
44–46	12.5	13.1	13.6	14.2	14.7	15.3	15.9	16.4	17.0
47–49	13.4	13.9	14.5	15.1	15.6	16.2	16.8	17.3	17.9
50–52	14.3	14.8	15.4	15.9	16.5	17.1	17.6	18.1	18.8
53–55	15.1	15.7	16.2	16.8	17.4	17.9	18.5	18.2	19.7
56–58	16.0	16.5	17.1	17.7	18.2	18.8	19.4	20.0	20.5
59–61	16.9	17.4	17.9	18.5	19.1	19.7	20.2	20.8	21.4
62–64	17.6	18.2	18.8	19.4	19.9	20.5	21.1	21.7	22.2
65–67	18.5	19.0	19.6	20.2	20.8	21.3	21.9	22.5	23.1
68–70	19.3	19.9	20.4	21.0	21.6	22.2	22.7	23.3	23.9
71–73	20.1	20.7	21.2	21.8	22.4	23.0	23.6	24.1	24.7
74–76	20.9	21.5	22.0	22.6	23.2	23.8	24.4	25.0	25.5
77–79	21.7	22.2	22.8	23.4	24.0	24.6	25.2	25.8	26.3
80–82	22.4	23.0	23.6	24.2	24.8	25.4	25.9	26.5	27.1
83–85	23.2	23.8	24.4	25.0	25.5	26.1	26.7	27.3	27.9
86–88	24.0	24.5	25.1	25.5	26.3	26.9	27.5	28.1	28.7
89–91	24.7	25.3	25.9	25.7	27.1	27.6	28.2	28.8	29.4
92–94	25.4	26.0	26.6	27.2	27.8	28.4	29.0	29.6	30.2
95–97	26.1	26.7	27.3	27.9	28.5	29.1	29.7	30.3	30.9
98–100	26.9	27.4	28.0	28.6	29.2	29.8	30.4	31.0	31.6
101–103	27.5	28.1	28.7	29.3	29.9	30.5	31.1	31.7	32.3
104–106	28.2	28.8	29.4	30.0	30.6	31.2	31.8	32.4	33.0
107–109	28.9	29.5	30.1	30.7	31.3	31.9	32.5	33.1	33.7
110–112	29.6	30.2	30.8	31.4	32.0	32.6	33.2	33.8	34.4
113–115	30.2	30.8	31.4	32.0	32.6	33.2	33.8	34.5	35.1
116–118	30.9	31.5	32.1	32.7	33.3	33.9	34.5	35.1	35.7
119–121	31.5	32.1	32.7	33.3	33.9	34.5	35.1	35.7	36.4
122–124	32.1	32.7	33.3	33.9	34.5	35.1	35.8	36.4	37.0
125–127	32.7	33.3	33.9	34.5	35.1	35.8	36.4	37.0	37.6

Note: Percent fat calculated by the formula by Siri. Percent fat = $([4.95/BD] - 4.5) \times 100$, where BD = body density.
Source: Baumgartner and Jackson, *Evaluation in Physical Education and Exercise Science.* Dubuque, IA: W.C. Brown Publishers (1999).

Calculating Fatness from Self-Measured Skinfolds

1. Sum three skinfolds (tricep, iliac crest, and thigh for women; chest, abdominal [vertical], and thigh for men).

2. Use the skinfold sum and your age to determine your percent fat using Chart 3 for women and Chart 4 for men. Locate your sum of skinfold in the left column and your age at the top of the chart. Your estimated body fat percentage is located where the values intersect.

Height–Weight Measurements

1. *Height*—Measure your height in inches or centimeters. Take the measurement without shoes, but add 2.5 centimeters or 1 inch to measurements, as the charts include heel height.
2. *Weight*—Measure your weight in pounds or kilograms without clothes. Add 3 pounds or 1.4 kilograms because the charts include the weight of clothes. If weight must be taken with clothes on, wear indoor clothing that weighs 3 pounds, or 1.4 kilograms.
3. Determine your frame size using the elbow breadth. The measurement is most accurate when done with a broad-based sliding caliper. However, it can be done using skinfold calipers or can be estimated with a metric ruler. The right arm is measured when it is elevated with the elbow bent at 90 degrees and the upper arm horizontal. The back of the hand should face the person making the measurement. Using the calipers, measure the distance between the epicondyles of the humerus (inside and outside bony points of the elbow). Measure to the nearest millimeter (1/10 centimeter). If a caliper is not available, place the thumb and the index finger of the left hand on the epicondyles of the humerus and measure the distance between the fingers with a metric ruler. Use your height and elbow breadth in centimeters to determine your frame size (Chart 5); you need not repeat this procedure each time you use a height and weight chart.

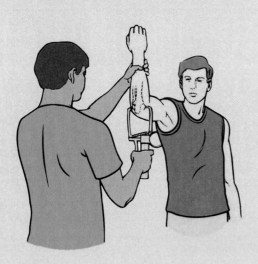

4. Use Chart 6 to determine your healthy weight range. The new healthy weight range charts do not account for frame size. However, you may want to consider frame size when determining a personal weight within the healthy weight range. People with a larger frame size typically can carry more weight within the range than can those with a smaller frame size.

Chart 5 Frame Size Determined from Elbow Breadth (mm)

Height	Elbow Breadth (mm)		
	Small Frame	Medium Frame	Large Frame
Males			
5'2 ½" or less	<64	64–72	>72
5'3"–5'6 ½"	<67	67–74	>74
5'7"–5'10 ½"	<69	69–76	>76
5'11"–6'2 ½"	<71	71–78	>78
6'3" or more	<74	74–81	>81
Females			
4'10 ½" or less	<56	56–64	>64
4'11"–5'2 ½"	<58	58–65	>65
5'3"–5'6 ½"	<59	59–66	>66
5'7"–5'10 ½"	<61	61–68	>69
5'11" or more	<62	62–69	>69

Note: *Height* is given including 1-inch heels.
Source: Metropolitan Life Insurance Company

Chart 6 Healthy Weight Ranges for Adult Women and Men

Height			Height		
Feet	Inches	Pounds	Feet	Inches	Pounds
4	10	91–119	5	9	129–169
4	11	94–124	5	10	132–174
5	0	97–128	5	11	136–179
5	1	101–132	6	0	140–184
5	2	104–137	6	1	144–189
5	3	107–141	6	2	148–195
5	4	111–146	6	3	152–200
5	5	114–150	6	4	156–205
5	6	118–155	6	5	160–211
5	7	121–160	6	6	164–216
5	8	125–164			

Source: U.S. Department of Agriculture and Department of Health and Human Services

Chart 7 Body Mass Index (BMI)

Height \ Weight	100	105	110	115	120	125	130	135	140	145	150	155	160	165	170	175	180	185	190	195	200	205	210	215	220	225	230	235	240	245	250
5'0"	20	21	21	22	23	24	25	26	27	28	29	30	31	32	33	34	35	36	37	38	39	40	41	42	43	44	45	46	47	48	49
5'1"	19	20	21	22	23	24	25	26	26	27	28	29	30	31	32	33	34	35	36	37	38	39	40	41	42	43	43	44	45	46	47
5'2"	18	19	20	21	22	23	24	25	26	27	27	28	29	30	31	32	33	34	35	36	37	37	38	39	40	41	42	43	44	45	46
5'3"	18	19	19	20	21	22	23	24	25	26	27	27	28	29	30	31	32	33	34	35	35	36	37	38	39	40	41	42	43	43	44
5'4"	17	18	19	20	21	21	22	23	24	25	26	27	27	28	29	30	31	32	33	33	34	35	36	37	38	39	39	40	41	42	43
5'5"	17	17	18	19	20	21	22	22	23	24	25	26	27	27	28	29	30	31	32	32	33	34	35	36	37	37	38	39	40	41	42
5'6"	16	17	17	18	19	19	20	21	22	23	24	25	26	27	27	28	29	30	31	31	32	33	34	35	36	36	37	38	39	40	40
5'7"	16	16	17	18	19	20	20	21	22	23	23	24	25	26	27	27	28	29	30	31	31	32	33	34	34	35	36	37	38	38	39
5'8"	15	16	17	17	18	19	20	21	21	22	23	24	24	25	26	27	27	28	29	30	30	31	32	33	33	34	35	36	36	37	38
5'9"	15	16	16	17	18	18	19	20	21	21	22	23	24	24	25	26	27	27	28	29	30	30	31	32	32	33	34	35	35	36	37
5'10"	14	15	16	17	17	18	19	19	20	21	22	22	23	24	24	25	26	27	27	28	29	29	30	31	32	32	33	34	34	35	36
5'11"	14	15	15	16	17	17	18	19	20	20	21	22	22	23	24	24	25	26	26	27	28	29	29	30	31	31	32	33	33	34	35
6'0"	14	14	15	16	16	17	18	18	19	20	20	21	22	22	23	24	24	25	26	26	27	28	28	29	30	31	31	32	33	33	34
6'1"	13	14	15	15	16	16	17	18	18	19	20	20	21	22	22	23	24	24	25	26	26	27	28	28	29	30	30	31	32	32	33
6'2"	13	13	14	15	15	16	17	17	18	19	19	20	21	21	22	22	23	24	24	25	26	26	27	28	28	29	30	30	31	31	32
6'3"	12	13	14	14	15	16	16	17	17	18	19	19	20	21	21	22	22	23	24	24	25	26	26	27	27	28	29	29	30	31	31
6'4"	12	13	13	14	15	15	16	16	17	18	18	19	19	20	21	21	22	23	23	24	24	25	26	26	27	27	28	29	29	30	30

Weight

☐ Low ☐ Normal (good fitness zone) ☐ Overweight ☐ Obese

Body Mass Index (BMI)

Use the steps listed below or use Chart 7 to calculate your BMI.

1. Divide your weight in pounds by 2.2 to determine your weight in kilograms.
2. Multiply your height in inches by .0254 to determine your height in meters.
3. Square your height in meters (multiply your height in meters by your height in meters).
4. Divide your weight in kilograms from step 1 by your height in meters squared from step 3.
5. If you use these steps to determine your BMI, use the Rating Scale for Body Mass Index (Chart 8) to obtain a rating for your BMI.

Chart 8 Rating Scale for Body Mass Index (BMI)

Classification	BMI
Obese (high risk)	Over 30
Overweight	25–30
Normal (good fitness zone)	17–24.9
Low	Less than 17

Note: An excessively low BMI is not desirable. Low BMI values can indicate eating disorders and other health problems.

Formula

$$BMI = \frac{\text{weight in kilograms (kg)}}{\text{(height in meters)} \times \text{(height in meters)}}$$

$$BMI = \frac{\text{weight in pounds (lb)}}{\text{(height in inches)} \times \text{(height in inches)}} \times 703$$

Determining the Waist-to-Hip Circumference Ratio

The waist-to-hip circumference ratio is recommended as the best available index for determining risk for disease associated with fat and weight distribution. Disease and death risk are associated with abdominal and upper body fatness. When a person has high fatness and a high waist-to-hip ratio, additional risks exist. The following steps should be taken in making measurements and calculating the waist-to-hip ratio.

1. Both measurements should be done with a nonelastic tape. Make the measurements while standing with the feet together and the arms at the sides, elevated only high enough to allow the measurements. Be sure the tape is horizontal and around the entire circumference. Record scores to the nearest millimeter or 1/16th of an inch. Use the same units of measure for both circumferences (millimeters or 1/16th of an inch). The tape should be pulled snugly but not to the point of causing an indentation in the skin.

2. Waist measurement—Measure at the natural waist (smallest waist circumference). If no natural waist exists, the measurement should be made at the level of the umbilicus. Measure at the end of a normal inhale.

3. Hip measurement—Measure at the maximum circumference of the buttocks. It is recommended that you wear thin-layered clothing (such as a swimming suit or underwear) that will not add significantly to the measurement.

4. Divide the hip measurement into the waist measurement or use the waist-to-hip nomogram (Chart 9) to determine your waist-to-hip ratio.

5. Use the Waist-to-Hip Ratio Rating Scale (Chart 10) to determine your rating for the waist-to-hip ratio.

Chart 9 Waist-to-Hip Ratio Nomogram

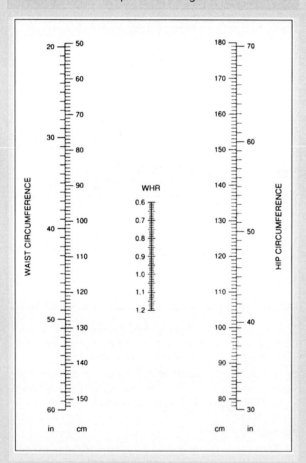

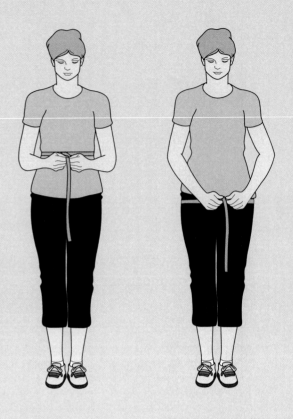

Note: Using a partner or mirror will aid you in keeping the tape horizontal.

Determining Disease Risk Based on BMI and Waist Circumference

Use Chart 11 to determine a BMI and Waist Circumference Rating. In the first column of Chart 11, locate your BMI. Locate your waist circumference in either column 2 or 3 depending on your age. Your rating is located at the point where the appropriate rows and columns intersect.

Chart 11 BMI and Waist Circumference Rating Scale

	Waist Circumference (in)	
BMI	Men, 40 or less Women, 34.5 or less	Men, above 40 Women, above 34.5
Less than 18.5	Normal	Normal
18.5–24.9	Normal	Normal
25.0–29.9	Increased risk	High risk
30.0–34.9	High risk	Very high risk
35.0–39.9	Very high risk	Very high risk
40 or more	Extremely high risk	Extremely high risk

Source: Adapted from ACSM.

Chart 10 Waist-to-Hip Ratio Rating Scale

Classification	Men	Women
High risk	>1.0	>.85
Moderately high risk	.90–1.0	.80–.85
Lower risk	<.90	<.80

Lab 14A Evaluating Body Composition: Skinfold Measures

Name	**Section**	**Date**

Purpose: To estimate body fatness using two skinfold procedures; to compare measures made by an expert, by a partner, and by self-measurements; to learn the strengths and weaknesses of each technique; and to use the results to establish personal standards for evaluating body composition.

General Procedures: Follow the specific procedures for the two self-assessment techniques. If possible, have one set of measurements made by an expert (instructor) for each of the two techniques. Next, work with a partner you trust. Have the partner make measurements at each site for both techniques. Finally, make self-measurements for each of the sites. If you are just learning a measurement technique, it is important to practice the skills of making the measurement. If you do measurements over time, use the same instrument (if possible) each time you measure. If your measurements vary widely, take more than one set until you get more consistent results.

If you have had an underwater weighing, a bioelectric impedance measurement, or some other body fatness measurement done recently, record your results below.

Measurement Technique   **% Body Fat**   **Rating**

1.

2.

Skinfold Measurements (Jackson-Pollock Method)

Procedures for Jackson-Pollock Method

1. Read the directions for the Jackson-Pollock method measurements in the Lab Resource Materials.
2. If possible, observe a demonstration of the proper procedures for measuring skinfolds at each of the different locations before doing partner or self-measurements.
3. Make expert, partner, and self-measurements (see the Lab Resource Materials). When doing the self-measure of the triceps, use the self-measurement technique described in the Lab Resource Materials (women only).
4. Record each of the measurements in the Results section.
5. Calculate your body fatness from skinfolds by summing the appropriate skinfold values (chest, thigh, and abdominal for men; triceps, iliac crest, and thigh for women). Using your age and the sum of the appropriate skinfolds, determine your body fatness using Charts 3 and 4 in the Lab Resource Materials.
6. Rate your fatness using Chart 2 in the Lab Resource Materials.

Results for Jackson-Pollock Method

Skinfolds by an Expert (If Possible)	Skinfolds by Partner	Self-Measurements
Male	**Male**	**Male**
Chest	Chest	Chest
Thigh	Thigh	Thigh
Abdominal	Abdominal	Abdominal
Sum	Sum	Sum
% body fat	% body fat	% body fat
Rating	Rating	Rating
Female	**Female**	**Female**
Triceps	Triceps	Triceps
Iliac crest	Iliac crest	Iliac crest
Thigh	Thigh	Thigh
Sum	Sum	Sum
% body fat	% body fat	% body fat
Rating	Rating	Rating

Make a check by the statements that are true about your measurements.

☐ The person doing measurements has experience with these three skinfold measurements.

☐ Self-measurements were practiced until measurements became consistent.

☐ Results of several trials for each measure are consistent (do not vary more than 2–3 mm).

☐ You are not exceptionally low or exceptionally high in body fat.

The more checks you have, the more likely your measurements are accurate.

Skinfold Measurements (FITNESSGRAM Method)

Procedures for FITNESSGRAM Method

1. Read the directions for the FITNESSGRAM measurements in the Lab Resource Materials.
2. Use the procedures as for the FITNESSGRAM method using the triceps, abdominal, and calf sites described in the Lab Resource Materials. When doing the self-measure of the triceps, use the self-measurement technique shown earlier.
3. Calculate your body fatness from skinfolds by summing the appropriate skinfold values (same for both men and women). Using the sum of the appropriate skinfolds, determine your body fatness using Chart 1 in the Lab Resource Materials.
4. Rate your fatness using Chart 2 in the Lab Resource Materials.

Results for FITNESSGRAM Method

Skinfolds by an Expert (If Possible)

Triceps ____

Abdominal ____

Calf ____

Sum ____

% body fat ____

Rating ____

Skinfolds by Partner

Triceps ____

Abdominal ____

Calf ____

Sum ____

% body fat ____

Rating ____

Self-Measurements

Triceps ____

Abdominal ____

Calf ____

Sum ____

% body fat ____

Rating ____

Make a check by the statements that are true about your measurements.

☐ The person doing measurements has experience with these three skinfold measurements.

☐ Self-measurements were practiced until measurements became consistent.

☐ Results of several trials for each measure are consistent (do not vary more than 2–3 mm).

☐ You are not exceptionally low or exceptionally high in body fat.

The more checks you have, the more likely your measurements are accurate.

Conclusions and Implications: In the space provided below, discuss your current body composition based on the two skinfold procedures and any other measures of body fatness you did. Note any discrepancies in the measurements and discuss which of the measurements you think provide the most useful information. To what extent do you think you need to alter your level of body fatness?

Lab 14B Evaluating Body Composition: Height, Weight, and Circumference Measures

Name	Section	Date

Purpose: To assess body composition using a variety of procedures, to learn the strengths and weaknesses of each technique, and to use the results to establish personal standards for evaluating body composition.

General Procedures: Follow the specific procedures for the three self-assessment techniques. If possible, work with a partner you trust to help with measurements that you have difficulty making yourself. If you are just learning a measurement technique, it is important to practice the skills of making the measurement. If you do measurements over time, use the same instrument (if possible) each time you measure. If your measurements vary widely, take more than one set until you get more consistent results. If possible, have an expert make measurements on you using these procedures.

Height and Weight Measurements

Procedures

1. Read the directions for height and weight measurements in the Lab Resource Materials.
2. Determine your healthy weight range using Chart 6 in the Lab Resource Materials. You may want to use your elbow breadth (Chart 5). People with a smaller frame size should typically weigh less than those with a larger frame size within the healthy weight range. You may need the assistance of a partner to make the elbow breadth measurement.
3. Record your scores in the Results section.

Results

Weight [   ]   Healthy weight range [   ]

Height [   ]

Make a check by the statements that are true about your measurements.

[   ] You are confident in the accuracy of the scale you used.

[   ] You are confident that the height technique is accurate.

The more checks you have, the more likely your measurements are accurate. If you are a very active person with a high amount of muscle, use this method with caution.

Body Mass Index

Procedures

1. Use the height and weight measures from above.
2. Determine your BMI score by using Chart 7 or the directions in the Lab Resource Materials. Determine your rating using Chart 8.
3. Record your score and rating in the Results section.

Results

Body Mass Index [   ]   Rating [   ]

If you are a very active person with a high amount of muscle, use this method with caution.

Waist-to-Hip Ratio

Procedures

1. Measure your waist and hip circumferences using the procedures in the Lab Resource Materials.
2. Divide your hip circumference into your waist circumference, or use Chart 9 in the Lab Resource Materials to calculate your waist-to-hip ratio.
3. Determine your rating using Chart 10 in the Lab Resource Materials.
4. Record your scores in the Results section.

Results

Waist circumference [   ]   Hip circumference [   ]   Waist-to-hip ratio [   ]   Rating

Make a check by the statements that are true about you.

[ ]   I am a male 5'9" or less and have a waist girth of 34 inches or more.

[ ]   I am a male 5'10" to 6'4" and have a waist girth of 36 inches or more.

[ ]   I am a male 6'5" or more and have a waist girth of 38 inches or more.

[ ]   I am a female 5'2" or less and have a waist girth of 29 inches or more.

[ ]   I am a female 5'3" to 5'10" and have a waist girth of 31 inches or more.

[ ]   I am a female 5'11" or more and have a waist girth of 33 inches or more.

If you checked one of the boxes above, the waist-to-hip ratio is especially relevant for you.

BMI and Waist Circumference Rating

Procedures

1. Locate your BMI and waist circumference from previous Results sections in this lab.
2. Use these values to calculate your BMI and Waist Circumference Rating using Chart 11. Record the rating in the Results section.

Results

BMI and Waist Circumference Rating [   ]

Conclusions and Implications: In the space below, discuss your results for the height, weight, and circumference procedures. Note any discrepancies in the measurements. Indicate the strengths and weaknesses of the various methods. Which of the measures do you think provided you with the most useful information? If you also did the skinfold measures (Lab 14A), discuss your body composition based on all the information you have collected (skinfolds and height, weight, and circumference measures).

Lab 14C Determining Your Daily Energy Expenditure

Name	Section	Date

Purpose: To learn how many calories you expend in a day.

Procedures

1. Estimate your basal metabolism using step 1 in the Results section in this lab. First, determine the number of minutes you sleep.
2. Monitor your activity expenditure for 1 day using Chart 1. Record the number of 5-, 15-, and 30-minute blocks of time you perform each of the different types of physical activities (e.g., if an activity lasted 20 minutes, you would use one 15-minute block and one 5-minute block). Be sure to distinguish between moderate (Mod) and vigorous (Vig) intensity in your logging. If you perform an activity that is not listed, specify the activity on the line labeled "Other" and estimate if it is moderate or vigorous. You may want to keep copies of Chart 1 for future use. One extra copy is provided at the end of this section.
3. Sum the total number of minutes of moderate and vigorous activity. Determine your calories expended during moderate and vigorous activity using steps 2 and 3.
4. Determine your nonactive minutes using step 4. This is all time that is not spent sleeping or being active.
5. Determine your calories expended in nonactive minutes using step 5.
6. Determine your calories expended in a day using step 6.

Results

Daily Caloric Expenditure Estimates

Step 1:

Basal calories $= .0076 \times$ [Body wt. (lb)] $\times$ [Minutes of sleep] $=$ [Basal calories] (A)

Step 2:

Calories (moderate activity) $= .036 \times$ [Body wt. (lb)] $\times$ [Minutes of moderate activity] $=$ [Calories in moderate activity] (B)

Step 3:

Calories (vigorous activity) $= .053 \times$ [Body wt. (lb)] $\times$ [Minutes of vigorous activity] $=$ [Calories in vigorous activity] (C)

Step 4:

Minutes (nonactive) $= 1{,}440 \text{ min} -$ [Minutes of sleep] $-$ [Minutes of moderate activity] $-$ [Minutes of vigorous activity] $=$ [Nonactive minutes]

Step 5:

Calories (rest and light activity) $= .011 \times$ [Body wt. (lb)] $\times$ [Nonactive minutes] $=$ [Calories in other activities] (D)

Step 6:

Calories expended (per day) $=$ [(A)] $+$ [(B)] $+$ [(C)] $+$ [(D)] $=$ [**Daily calories**]

Answer the following questions about your daily caloric expenditure estimate.

Yes	No	
☐	☐	Were the activities you performed similar to what you normally perform each day?
☐	☐	Do you think your daily estimated caloric expenditure is an accurate estimate?
☐	☐	Do you think you expend the correct number of calories in a typical day to maintain the body composition (body fat level) that is desirable for you?

Conclusions and Implications: In several paragraphs, discuss your daily caloric expenditure. Comment on your answers to the preceding questions. In addition, comment on whether you think you should modify your daily caloric expenditure for any reason.

Chart 1

Day of Monitoring:					
Physical Activity Category		**5 Minutes**	**15 Minutes**	**30 Minutes**	**Minutes**
Lifestyle Activity		1 2 3 4 5 6	1 2 3 4 5 6	1 2 3	
Dancing (general)	Mod				
Gardening	Mod				
Home repair/maintenance	Mod				
Occupation	Mod				
Walking/hiking	Mod				
Other:	Mod				
Aerobic Activity		1 2 3 4 5 6	1 2 3 4 5 6	1 2 3	
Aerobic dance (low-impact)	Mod				
	Vig				
Aerobic machines (rowing, stair, ski)	Mod				
	Vig				
Bicycling	Mod				
	Vig				
Running	Mod				
	Vig				
Skating (roller/ice)	Mod				
	Vig				
Swimming (laps)	Mod				
	Vig				
Other:	Mod				
	Vig				
Sport/Recreation Activity		1 2 3 4 5 6	1 2 3 4 5 6	1 2 3	
Basketball	Mod				
	Vig				
Bowling/billiards	Mod				
Golf	Mod				
Martial arts (judo, karate)	Mod				
	Vig				
Racquetball/tennis	Mod				
	Vig				
Soccer/hockey	Mod				
	Vig				
Softball/baseball	Mod				
Volleyball	Mod				
	Vig				
Other:	Mod				
Flexibility Activity		1 2 3 4 5 6	1 2 3 4 5 6	1 2 3	
Stretching	Mod				
Other:	Mod				
Strengthening Activity		1 2 3 4 5 6	1 2 3 4 5 6	1 2 3	
Calisthenics (push-ups/sit-ups)	Mod				
Resistance exercise	Mod				
Other:	Mod				

Minutes of moderate activity ☐

Minutes of vigorous activity ☐

Total minutes of activity ☐

Day of Monitoring:

Physical Activity Category		5 Minutes 1 2 3 4 5 6	15 Minutes 1 2 3 4 5 6	30 Minutes 1 2 3	Minutes
Lifestyle Activity					
Dancing (general)	Mod				
Gardening	Mod				
Home repair/maintenance	Mod				
Occupation	Mod				
Walking/hiking	Mod				
Other:	Mod				
Aerobic Activity					
Aerobic dance (low-impact)	Mod / Vig				
Aerobic machines (rowing, stair, ski)	Mod / Vig				
Bicycling	Mod / Vig				
Running	Mod / Vig				
Skating (roller/ice)	Mod / Vig				
Swimming (laps)	Mod / Vig				
Other:	Mod / Vig				
Sport/Recreation Activity					
Basketball	Mod / Vig				
Bowling/billiards	Mod				
Golf	Mod				
Martial arts (judo, karate)	Mod / Vig				
Racquetball/tennis	Mod / Vig				
Soccer/hockey	Mod / Vig				
Softball/baseball	Mod				
Volleyball	Mod / Vig				
Other:	Mod				
Flexibility Activity					
Stretching	Mod				
Other:	Mod				
Strengthening Activity					
Calisthenics (push-ups/sit-ups)	Mod				
Resistance exercise	Mod				
Other:	Mod				

Minutes of moderate activity

Minutes of vigorous activity

Total minutes of activity

Nutrition

LEARNING OBJECTIVES

After completing the study of this Concept, you will be able to:

- ▶ Apply basic guidelines for healthy eating.
- ▶ List and apply dietary recommendations for carbohydrates, fats, proteins, vitamins, minerals, and water.
- ▶ Interpret and use food labels to make healthy decisions.
- ▶ Describe and incorporate sound eating practices.
- ▶ Describe and apply nutrition guidelines for active people and those interested in performance (e.g., sports).
- ▶ Analyze your diet to determine nutrient quality.
- ▶ Compare nutritional quality of various foods.

The amount and kinds of food you eat affect your health and wellness.

©Rolf Bruderer/Blend Images LLC

Why it Matters!

Most people understand the importance of good nutrition for optimal health, but many still find it difficult to maintain a healthy diet. One reason for this is that foods are usually developed, marketed, and advertised for convenience and taste rather than for health or nutritional quality. Another reason is that many individuals have misconceptions about what constitutes a healthy diet. Some misconceptions are propagated by incomplete media reports, others from commercially-oriented marketing efforts, and still others by confusing and often contradictory findings from nutrition research. Although nutrition is an advanced science, many questions remain unanswered. This Concept summarizes the essential principles, guidelines, and recommendations to provide a sound foundation of nutrition knowledge. Strategies are also provided to help you adopt and maintain a healthy diet.

Guidelines for Healthy Eating

National dietary guidelines provide a sound plan for good nutrition. The U.S. Department of Agriculture (USDA) and the U.S. Department of Health and Human Services (DHHS) provide definitive guidelines to help American consumers make healthier food choices. The first guidelines were published in 1980, and federal law requires that these guidelines be updated every five years to incorporate new research findings. The eighth edition of this report (*2015–2020 Dietary Guidelines for Americans*) was released in 2015 and serves as the official guidelines until they are updated again in 2020. Many other countries release similar sets of guidelines specific to their population (e.g., Health Canada's Food Guide).

U.S. dietary guidelines use a model to convey key nutrition concepts. The U.S. dietary guidelines help promote education and awareness about healthy eating. Over the years, a variety of models have been used to illustrate key elements of the guidelines. Although the law requiring new guidelines every five years was not implemented until 1980, models have been used to illustrate the basic food groups since the early 1900s. Early food guide models depicted food groups in a circle or wheel to show the different nutrients. Figure 1 depicts some of the more recent models that utilized a pyramid concept and then switched to a plate.

A common theme in the various models is that each depicts the food groups essential to a healthy diet. The first pyramid used segments of different sizes to illustrate relative amounts of food to be consumed from each food group. For example, the large segment at the bottom of the pyramid depicted carbohydrates—the largest source of calories in the diet. A refinement of the pyramid included a stairway to depict physical activity and colored bands showing the recommended proportion of the food groups. MyPlate uses a plate with four colored areas representing the different food groups (fruits, grains, vegetables, and proteins) and a glass represents the dairy food group (including solid dairy products). A key message conveyed with this image is that half of the plate should be filled with fruits and vegetables. Other countries have developed models for healthy eating as well. For example, Canada uses a rainbow and Japan uses a spinning top to depict food groups. Various organizations have developed their own models. The American Heart Association has used a modified pyramid and a heart-shaped plate to illustrate eating guidelines for heart health. The goal of all the models is to provide consumers with a conceptual way to summarize the principles of healthy eating.

National dietary guidelines provide suggestions for healthy eating. A primary theme in the U.S. dietary guidelines is that it is best to pursue broader changes in overall dietary patterns rather than trying to add or replace specific foods. This approach has been referred to as a "Total Diet Approach" to reflect that the overall pattern of food eaten is the most important goal. From this perspective, there are not

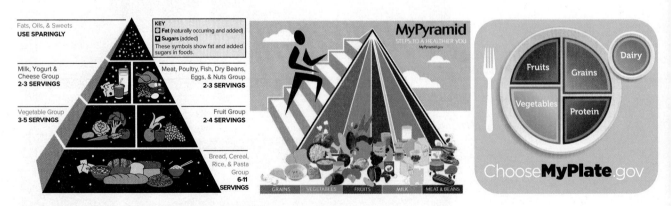

Figure 1 ▶ USDA/DHHS models for healthy eating.

Sources: United States Department of Agriculture (USDA) and the United States Department of Health and Human Services (USDHHS)

"good" or "bad" foods but healthy and unhealthy patterns. Dietary patterns are defined as the quantities, proportions, variety, or combinations of different foods and beverages in diets, and the frequency with which they are habitually consumed. A "healthy dietary pattern" is further characterized by a higher consumption of vegetables, fruits, whole grains, low/nonfat dairy, seafood, legumes, and nuts and a lower consumption of red and processed meat, sugar-sweetened foods and drinks, and refined grains. The rationale for these components is summarized below:

- *Eat the right amount of calories for you.* Effective weight control requires balancing energy intake with energy expenditure. Guidelines are based on average energy intake requirements of about 2,500 calories a day for men and 2,200 for women, but individual needs vary considerably. Factors such as body size, activity level, and personal metabolism all influence daily energy intake needs. Most people underestimate the number of calories they eat, so it is important to learn to regulate your intake to maintain a healthy weight.

- *Consume nutrient-dense foods.* Consuming nutrient-dense foods improves the overall quality of the diet. Examples of nutrient-dense foods include vegetables, fruits, high-fiber whole grains, fat-free or lowfat milk and milk products, seafood, lean meat and poultry, eggs, soy products, nuts, seeds, and oils.

- *Reduce solid fats and added sugars.* Consumption of solid fats and added sugars leads to excessive intake of saturated fat and cholesterol and insufficient intake of dietary fiber and other nutrients. Consuming fewer processed foods (e.g., meats, grains) and sweetened foods and drinks contributes to a healthier dietary pattern.

- *Reduce sodium intake.* Excessive sodium in the diet can increase blood pressure and lead to health problems. Consuming fewer processed foods and snack foods can help reduce overall sodium intake. The goal is to stay below the limit of 2,300 milligrams per day.

Specific Dietary Reference Intakes (DRIs) provide a target zone for healthy eating. About 45 to 50 nutrients in food are believed to be essential for the body's growth, maintenance, and repair. These are classified into six categories: carbohydrates (and fiber), fats, proteins, vitamins, minerals, and water. The first three provide energy, which is measured in calories. Specific dietary recommendations for each of the six nutrients are presented later in this Concept.

In the United States, guidelines specifying the nutrient requirements for good health are developed by the Food and Nutrition Board of the National Academy of Medicine's Institute of Medicine. **Recommended Dietary Allowance (RDA)** historically was used to set recommendations for nutrients, but the complexity of dietary interactions prompted the board to develop a more comprehensive and functional set of dietary intake recommendations. These broader guidelines, referred to as **Dietary Reference Intake (DRI),** include RDA values when adequate scientific information is available and estimated **Adequate Intake (AI)** values when sufficient data aren't available to establish a firm RDA. The DRI values also include **Tolerable Upper Intake Level (UL),** which reflects the highest level of daily intake a person can consume without adverse effects on health. The guidelines make it clear that, although too little of a nutrient can be harmful to health, so can too much. The distinctions are similar to the concept of the target zone used to prescribe exercise levels. The RDA or AI values are analogous to the threshold levels (minimal amount needed to meet guidelines), while the UL values represent amounts that should not be exceeded.

A unique aspect of the DRI values is that they are categorized by function and classification in order to facilitate awareness of the different roles that nutrients play in the diet. Specific guidelines have been developed for B-complex vitamins; vitamins C and E; bone-building nutrients, such as calcium and vitamin D; micronutrients, such as iron and zinc; and the class of macronutrients that includes carbohydrates, fats, proteins, and fiber. Table 1 includes the DRI values (including the UL values) for most of these nutrients.

Nutrition recommendations are flexible, but also highly individualized. The Dietary Guideline Advisory Committee emphasized that healthy dietary patterns can be achieved in many ways and should be tailored to the individual's biological and medical needs as well as sociocultural preferences. The scientific review compiled by this group provided examples of a "Healthy U.S.-Style Pattern," a "Healthy Mediterranean-Style Pattern," and a "Healthy Vegetarian Pattern." However, a consistent theme in the examples was an emphasis on plant-based foods. The comprehensive report specifically stated that a dietary pattern higher in plant-based foods (and lower in animal-based foods) is "more health promoting and is associated with lesser environmental impact than is the current average U.S. diet."

Although plant-based diets were emphasized, a healthful total diet is not a rigid prescription but rather a flexible approach to eating that can be adjusted for a variety of individual tastes and preferences. The

connect VIDEO 1

Recommended Dietary Allowance (RDA) Dietary guideline that specifies the amount of a nutrient needed for almost all of the healthy individuals in a specific age and gender group.

Dietary Reference Intake (DRI) Appropriate amounts of nutrients in the diet (AI, RDA, and UL).

Adequate Intake (AI) Dietary guideline established experimentally to estimate nutrient needs when sufficient data are not available to establish an RDA value.

Tolerable Upper Intake Level (UL) Maximum level of a daily nutrient that will not pose a risk of adverse health effects for most people.

Table 1 ▶ Dietary Reference Intake (DRI), Recommended Dietary Allowance (RDA), and Tolerable Upper Intake Level (UL) for Major Nutrients

	Males	Females	UL	Function
Energy and Macronutrients				
Carbohydrates (45–65%)	130 g	130 g	ND	Energy (only source of energy for the brain)
Fat (20–35%)	ND	ND	ND	Energy, vitamin carrier
Protein (10–35%)	.8 g/kg	.8 g/kg	ND	Growth and maturation, tissue formation
Fiber (g/day)	38 g/day*	25 g/day*	ND	Digestion, blood profiles
B-Complex Vitamins				
Thiamin (mg/day)	1.2	1.1	ND	Co-enzyme for carbohydrates and amino acid metabolism
Riboflavin (mg/day)	1.3	1.1	ND	Co-enzyme for metabolic reactions
Niacin (mg/day)	16	14	35	Co-enzyme for metabolic reactions
Vitamin B-6 (mg/day)	1.3	1.3	100	Co-enzyme for amino acid and glycogen reactions
Folate (µg/day)	400	400	1,000	Metabolism of amino acids
Vitamin B-12 (µg/day)	2.4	2.4	ND	Co-enzyme for nucleic acid metabolism
Pantothenic acid (mg/day)	5*	5*	ND	Co-enzyme for fat metabolism
Biotin (µg/day)	30*	30*	ND	Synthesis of fat, glycogen, and amino acids
Choline (mg/day)	550*	425*	3,500	Precursor to acetylcholine
Antioxidants and Related Nutrients				
Vitamin C (mg/day)	90	75	2,000	Co-factor for reactions, antioxidant
Vitamin E (mg/day)	15	15	1,000	Undetermined, mainly antioxidant
Selenium (µg/day)	55	55	400	Defense against oxidative stress
Bone-Building Nutrients				
Calcium (mg/day)	1,000*	1,000*	2,500	Muscle contraction, nerve transmission
Phosphorus (mg/day)	700	700	3,000	Maintenance of pH, storage of energy
Magnesium (mg/day)	400–420	310–320	350	Co-factor for enzyme reactions
Vitamin D (µg/day)	5*	5*	50	Maintenance of calcium and phosphorus levels
Fluoride (mg/day)	4*	3*	10	Stimulation of new bone formation
Micronutrients and Other Trace Elements				
Vitamin K (µg/day)	120*	90*	ND	Blood clotting and bone metabolism
Vitamin A (µg/day)	900	700	3,000	Vision, immune function
Iron (mg/day)	8	18	45	Component of hemoglobin
Zinc (mg/day)	11	8	40	Component of enzymes and proteins

Note: These values reflect the dietary needs generally for adults aged 19–50 years. Specific guidelines for other age groups are available from the Food and Nutrition Board of the National Academy of Sciences (www.nationalacademies.org; search 'Food and Nutrition Board'). Values labeled with an asterisk (*) are based on Adequate Intake (AI) values rather than the RDA values; ND = not determined.

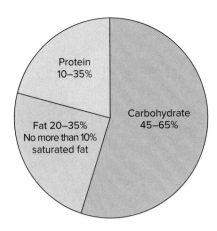

Figure 2 ▶ Dietary Reference Intake values.

flexibility for individual eating patterns is reflected in the wide ranges provided for various DRI categories. The recommended DRI values for carbohydrates range from 45 to 65 percent. The DRI values for protein range from 10 to 35 percent, while the DRI values for fat range from 20 to 35 percent. The broader ranges allow people to make healthy but realistic choices based on their own food preferences and eating patterns. Figure 2 illustrates the recommended DRI distributions for carbohydrates, fats, and proteins. The values are appropriate for most adult men and women, but the USDA has a website (and an app) that calculates personally determined DRI values. You can enter data such as your gender, age, height, weight, and activity level, and the calculator determines your DRI values. (Search "USDA DRI calculator" online.)

Dietary Recommendations for Carbohydrates

Complex carbohydrates should be the principal source of calories in the diet. Carbohydrates have gotten a bad rap in recent years due to the hype associated with low-carbohydrate diets. Carbohydrates have been unfairly implicated as a cause of obesity. It is true that they cause insulin to be released and that insulin, in turn, causes the body to take up and store excess energy as fat. However, this is overly simplistic and doesn't take into account differences in types of carbohydrates. Simple sugars (such as sucrose, glucose, and fructose) found in candy and soda lead to quick increases in blood sugar and tend to promote fat deposition. Complex carbohydrates (e.g., bread, pasta, rice), on the other hand, are broken down more slowly and do not cause the same effect on blood sugar. They contribute valuable nutrients and fiber in the diet and should constitute the bulk of a person's diet. Distinguishing between simple and complex carbohydrates is important, since they are processed differently and have different nutrient values.

A number of low-carb diet books have used an index known as the glycemic index (GI) as the basis for determining if foods are appropriate in the diet. Foods with a high

GI value produce rapid increases in blood sugar, while foods with a low GI value produce slower increases. This may seem to be a logical way to categorize carbohydrates, but it is misleading, since it doesn't account for the amount of carbohydrates in different servings of a food. A more appropriate indicator of the effect of foods on blood sugar levels is called the glycemic load. Carrots, for example, are known to have a very high GI value, but the overall glycemic load is quite low. The carbohydrates from most fruits and vegetables exhibit similar properties.

Despite the intuitive and logical appeal of this classification system, neither the glycemic index nor glycemic load have been consistently associated with body weight. Diets based on low glycemic index diets also don't have advantages for weight loss. There is some evidence linking glycemic load to a higher risk for diabetes so it is wise to still minimize simple carbohydrates.

Reducing dietary sugar can help reduce risk of obesity and heart disease. Minimizing sugar consumption is a good goal, since people who consume high amounts of sugar also tend to consume excess calories. The dietary guidelines specifically recommend decreasing consumption of added sugars to reduce excess calorie consumption and weight gain. The World Health Organization suggests limiting sugars to 5 to 10 percent of total calories consumed.

A variety of foods contribute to daily sugar intake, but soft drinks and sugar-sweetened beverages are the primary sources of added sugars in the American diet. A typical 12-ounce sweetened soft drink contains 150 calories, mostly sugar. Soft drink makers have responded by making smaller sizes and providing alternatives, but personal restraint is still needed to minimize consumption. Reducing consumption of sugar-sweetened beverages is a simple, but important, diet modification.

Increasing consumption of dietary fiber is important for overall good nutrition and health. Diets high in complex carbohydrates and **fiber** are associated with a low incidence of coronary heart disease, stroke, and some forms of cancer. Long-term studies indicate that high-fiber diets may also be associated with a lower risk for diabetes mellitus, diverticulosis, hypertension, and gallstone formation. However, it is not known whether these health benefits are directly attributable to high dietary fiber or other effects associated with the ingestion of vegetables, fruits, and cereals.

It has proven difficult to isolate the effects of dietary fiber, but there is no debate about the benefits. Past guidelines distinguished soluble fiber (typically found in fruits and oat bran) from insoluble fiber (typically found in grains), but this was an oversimplification of the different

Fiber Indigestible bulk in foods that can be either soluble or insoluble in body fluids.

types of fiber as well as how they are processed in the body. From a technical perspective, dietary fibers are defined as carbohydrate molecules that escape digestion in the small intestine and pass into the large intestine, where they are slightly or nearly completely fermented. The fermentation products actually contribute to the many physiological benefits of dietary fiber since they can be absorbed into the bloodstream.

The National Academy of Medicine (formerly the Institute of Medicine) currently distinguishes natural fibers in food from "functional fibers," which are extracted, modified, or synthesized forms of fibers. However, new recommendations have sought to create a more integrated index of dietary fiber. The combination of fibers that we eat interacts to produce health benefits, so the goal is to consume a diverse array of dietary fibers. From this perspective, the additional functional fibers that are added to food are analogous to vitamin-fortified foods that supplement our diets to ensure that we have sufficient amounts and types of fiber in our diet.

Currently, few Americans consume the recommended amounts of dietary fiber. The average intake of dietary fiber is about 15 g/day, which is much lower than the recommended 25 to 35 g/day. Foods in the typical American diet contain little, if any, dietary fiber, and servings of commonly consumed grains, fruits, and vegetables contain only 1 to 3 g of dietary fiber. Therefore, individuals have to look for ways to ensure that they get sufficient fiber in their diet. Manufacturers are allowed to declare a food as a "good source of fiber" if it contains 10 percent of the recommended amount (2.5 g/serving) and an "excellent source of fiber" if it contains 20 percent of the recommended amount (5 g/serving). Because fiber has known health benefits, the dietary guidelines encourage consumers to select foods high in dietary fiber, such as whole-grain breads and cereals, legumes, vegetables, and fruit, whenever possible.

Fruits and vegetables are essential for good health.
Fruits and vegetables are a valuable source of dietary fiber, are packed with vitamins and minerals, and contain many beneficial phytochemicals, which may have positive effects on health. The current guidelines recommend that adults eat 2½ cups of a wide variety of vegetables from all the subgroups of colors and starches a day. A major advantage of this suggestion is that it can make you feel full without eating a lot of calories. The guidelines also suggest that adults eat 2 cups of fruit a day, with half coming in the form of whole fruit. Fruit provides many essential vitamins and most are a good source of fiber as well.

Numerous studies have confirmed the many benefits from fruits and vegetables, but the most powerful documentation is in the detailed report provided by the Dietary Guidelines Advisory Committee. The committee examined numerous health associations with various eating patterns and food groups and provided the following conclusion: "*Vegetables*

Plan ahead for healthy, low-fat snacks when on the run.
©Juice Images/Getty Images

and fruit are the only characteristics of the diet that were consistently identified in every conclusion statement across the health outcomes." These conclusions clearly contributed to the increased emphasis being placed on a plant-based diet in the dietary guidelines.

The popularity of farmers' markets reflects broader interest in fresh fruits and vegetables. However, a challenge in promoting fruit and vegetable consumption is the higher relative cost. Many public health advocates have lobbied for subsidies that would help lower costs of fresh fruits and vegetables. Considerable research is now also focused on understanding factors that influence fruit and vegetable consumption in different segments of the population.

Follow the recommendations to ensure healthy amounts of carbohydrates in the diet. The following list summarizes some key dietary recommendations for carbohydrates:

- Consume a variety of fiber-rich fruits and vegetables.

- Select whole-grain foods when possible.

- Choose and prepare foods and beverages with little added sugars or caloric sweeteners.

Dietary Recommendations for Fat

Fat is an essential nutrient and an important energy source. Humans need some fat in their diet because fats are carriers of vitamins A, D, E, and K. They are a source of essential linoleic acid, they make food taste better, and they provide a concentrated form of calories, which serve as a vital source of energy during moderate to vigorous exercise. Fats have more than twice the calories per gram as carbohydrates.

There are several types of dietary fat. **Saturated fats** come primarily from animal sources, such as red meat, dairy products, and eggs, but they are also found in some vegetable sources, such as coconut and palm oils. **Unsaturated fats** are primarily from vegetable sources, but there are two types: polyunsaturated and monounsaturated. Polyunsaturated fats include a variety of oils categorized as either omega-6 fats (e.g., safflower, cottonseed, soybean, sunflower, and corn oils), or omega-3 fats found in coldwater fish, such as salmon and mackerel. Mono-unsaturated fats are derived primarily from vegetable sources, including olive, peanut, and canola oil.

Consumption of saturated fat should be limited, but the guidelines regarding dietary sources of cholesterol have been relaxed. Health recommendations related to dietary fat have changed over the years, focusing now primarily on risks from saturated fat. Excess saturated fat in the diet is known to increase the level of cholesterol in your blood, which directly increases risk of heart disease and stroke. Therefore, no more than 10 percent of your total calories should come from saturated fats. Dietary guidelines recommend replacing saturated fat with unsaturated fats, especially polyunsaturated fats.

Previous dietary guidelines imposed specific limits on dietary cholesterol (300 mg per day) and this led consumers to carefully minimize consumption of foods high in cholesterol such as eggs. The current guidelines have no limits on cholesterol; however, as noted in the report, "*this change does not suggest that dietary cholesterol is no longer important to consider when building healthy eating patterns.*" It is well established that eating patterns that include a lower intake of dietary cholesterol are associated with reduced risk of

Being an informed and educated consumer can help you make healthier food choices.
©Noel Hendrickson/Blend Images/Getty Images

Saturated Fats Dietary fats that are usually solid at room temperature and come primarily from animal sources.

Unsaturated Fats Monounsaturated or polyunsaturated fats that are usually liquid at room temperature and come primarily from vegetable sources.

cardiovascular disease (CVD) and reduced risk of obesity. Cholesterol (which is found only in animal products) also tends to be found in fatty meats and high-fat dairy products, which are also higher in saturated fats. Therefore, individuals should still consume as little dietary cholesterol as possible while following a healthy eating pattern. Eggs, which were once almost forbidden in diets because of high cholesterol, are now considered to be part of a healthy eating pattern. While they have high cholesterol, they are a good source of protein and are actually low in saturated fat.

Consumption of unsaturated fats (both poly and mono) can be beneficial. Unsaturated fats are a better dietary choice than saturated fats since they are less likely to contribute to CVD, cancer, and obesity. Polyunsaturated fats (mainly omega-6 fats) can reduce total cholesterol and low-density lipoprotein (LDL) cholesterol, but they also decrease levels of high-density lipoprotein (HDL) cholesterol. They are needed in the diet, but should be minimized since they are viewed as *pro-inflammatory* for their cardiovascular effects. Avoiding fried foods (cooked in vegetable oil) and baked goods made with shortening or margarine are ways to reduce excess omega-6 fat consumption.

Omega-3 fatty acids (a special type of polyunsaturated fat found in coldwater fish) are viewed as *anti-inflammatory* and are known to help reduce the risk of cardiovascular disease. Plant source of omega-3 fatty acids (alpha-linolenic acid) found in walnuts, flaxseed, and canola oil may have similar benefits. Thus, increasing omega-3 consumption is recommended while omega-6 consumption should be minimized. Monounsaturated fats (sometimes labeled as omega-9 fats) have also been shown to decrease total cholesterol and LDL cholesterol and increase the desirable HDL cholesterol. Olive oil and canola oil are good sources.

Past guidelines recommended that dietary cholesterol intake be limited to no more than 300 mg/day, but cholesterol intake has not been emphasized in the recent guidelines. The technical report from the Dietary Guidelines Advisory Committee concluded that there are relatively weak relationships between consumption of dietary cholesterol and eventual levels of blood cholesterol. Estimates suggest that only 15 percent of circulating cholesterol is from dietary sources; the remaining amounts are manufactured by the liver as part of fat transport and metabolism. However, restrictions on saturated fat are still important since high fat content requires the liver to produce more cholesterol. Fat should account for 20 to 35 percent of calories in the diet, with no more than 10 percent of total calories from saturated fat. The remaining fat should come from plant-based sources, especially monounsaturated fats.

Trans fats and hydrogenated vegetable oils should be minimized in the diet. For decades, the public has been cautioned to avoid saturated fats and foods with excessive cholesterol. Many people switched from using butter to margarine because margarine is made from vegetable oils that are unsaturated and contain no cholesterol. However, the typical hydrogenation process used to convert oils into solids produces a type of fat (**trans fats**) that was just as harmful as saturated fats, if not more so. Trans fats are known to increase LDL cholesterol and have been shown to contribute to the buildup of atherosclerotic plaque. The FDA initially enacted strong labeling laws to try to minimize consumption of trans fats, but recently issued a declaratory order prohibiting the use of trans fats in foods unless otherwise approved. This order became effective in June of 2018, but it is important to check ingredients for processed foods packaged prior to the ban. The new policy change will improve food quality and hopefully help to reduce cardiovascular disease risk in the population. However, minimizing consumption of processed and high fat foods is still a sound personal dietary habit.

Fat substitutes and neutraceuticals in food products may reduce fat consumption and lower cholesterol. For years, food scientists have sought to develop substitutes that mimic the taste and properties of fat without the negative characteristics. Olestra (often marketed as Olean) is a synthetic fat substitute that passes through the gastrointestinal system without being digested. Unfortunately, trials demonstrated that it tended to also reduce levels of beneficial fat-soluble vitamins and caused abdominal cramping. New products come out regularly with similar goals, but experts from the Dietary Guidelines Advisory Committee specifically advocate "replacement" over "substitution" as strategies to improve the diet. Thus, it is more effective to make alternative food choices than to look for supplements that allow continued consumption of specific foods.

Another class of fat-related supplements can be considered as "neutraceuticals," or "functional foods," because they are a combination of pharmaceuticals and food. The most prominent examples are the various margarines that contain plant sterols and esters designed to help lower total and LDL cholesterol. Trials support the utility of these products, but they must be used regularly and have value only in individuals who have high levels of cholesterol. There is considerable growth (and consumer interest) in functional foods, but consumers also have to be careful about what they believe and buy.

Follow the recommendations to ensure healthy amounts of fat in the diet. The following list summarizes some key dietary recommendations for dietary fat:

- Limit saturated fatty acid intake to less than 10 percent of total calories.

- Emphasize food sources with mono- or polyunsaturated fat sources.

- Avoid trans fatty acids from processed foods (e.g., foods with hydrogenated vegetable oils).

- Consume two servings of seafood per week to provide healthy amounts of omega-3 fatty acids.

connect
VIDEO 3

Dietary Recommendations for Proteins

Protein is the basic building block for the body, but dietary protein constitutes a relatively small amount of daily caloric intake. Proteins are often referred to as the building blocks of the body because all body cells are made of protein. More than 100 proteins are formed from 20 different **amino acids.** Eleven of these amino acids can be synthesized from other nutrients, but 9 **essential amino acids** must be obtained directly from the diet. One way to identify amino acids is the -*ine* at the end of their name. For example, arginine and lysine are two of the amino acids. Only 3 of the 20 amino acids do not have the -*ine* suffix. They are aspartic acid, glutamic acid, and tryptophan.

Certain foods, called complete proteins, contain all of the essential amino acids, along with most of the others. Examples are meat, dairy products, and fish. Incomplete proteins contain some, but not all, of the essential amino acids. Examples include beans, nuts, and rice.

Protein should account for at least 10 percent of daily calorie consumption, which can be met easily with complete (animal) or incomplete (vegetable) sources of protein. For example, a person consuming a 2,000-calorie diet should consume approximately 200 calories from protein. Protein provides 4 calories per gram, so minimum daily protein needs are as low as 50 grams per day. Figure 3 shows the relative protein content of various foods.

To provide more flexibility, dietary guidelines indicate that protein can account for as much as 35 percent of calorie intake. Experts, however, agree that there are no known benefits and some possible risks associated with consuming excess protein, particularly animal protein. High-protein diets are damaging to the kidneys, as the body must process a lot of extra nitrogen. Excessive protein intake can also lead to urinary calcium loss, which can weaken bones and lead to osteoporosis.

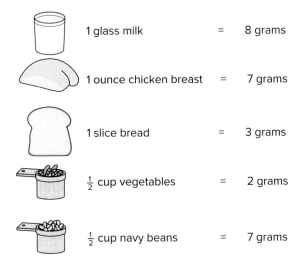

1 glass milk	=	8 grams
1 ounce chicken breast	=	7 grams
1 slice bread	=	3 grams
$\frac{1}{2}$ cup vegetables	=	2 grams
$\frac{1}{2}$ cup navy beans	=	7 grams

Figure 3 ▶ Protein content of various foods.

Source: Williams, M.

People who eat a variety of foods, including meat, dairy, eggs, and plants rich in protein, virtually always consume more protein than the body needs. Because of the negative consequences associated with excess intake, dietary supplements containing extra protein are not recommended for the general population.

An increasing array of soy foods are available to provide alternative sources of protein. Soybeans and soy-based foods are high-quality sources of protein. They may also have beneficial effects on blood pressure and cholesterol levels, possibly contributing to reductions in risk for coronary heart disease. Soy-based foods contain compounds called isoflavones, a phytoestrogen that contributes to bone health, immune function, and maintenance of menopausal health in women. Soy foods that contain at least 6.25 grams per serving can be labeled with FDA-approved health claims.

A variety of soy-based food products are commercially available as alternatives to traditional meat foods. Common options include tofu, tempeh, soy milk, or textured vegetable (soy) protein. Products have been developed to replicate the taste and color of meat products but, until recently, it has proven challenging to replicate the texture. New extrusion

Trans Fats Fats that result when hydrogen is added to liquid oil to make it more solid. Hydrogenation transforms unsaturated fats so that they take on the characteristics of saturated fats, as is the case for margarine and shortening.

Amino Acids The 20 basic building blocks of the body that make up proteins.

Essential Amino Acids The nine basic amino acids that the human body cannot produce and that must be obtained from food sources.

methods are now used to help retain more moisture in the plant proteins which has improved the mouth-feel and taste of alternative meat products. The real advantage of these soy-based alternatives is their enhanced nutritional value. Some "veggie burgers" have more protein than beef, more omega fatty acids than salmon, more calcium than milk, and more antioxidants than blueberries.

Follow the recommendations to ensure healthy amounts of protein in the diet. The following list summarizes some key dietary recommendations for protein:

- As noted in Figure 2, protein should account for 10 to 35% of total calories in the diet. This guideline is designed to allow diet flexibility based on personal needs and interests. For most people, 10–15% of calories consumed as protein is adequate.
- Protein in the diet should meet the RDA of .8 gram per kilogram (2.2 pounds) of a person's weight (about 54 grams for a 150-pound person).
- Protein in the diet should not exceed twice the RDA (1.6 grams per kilogram of body weight). Excess protein can be harmful to the kidneys.
- Vegetarians must eat a combination of foods to ensure an adequate intake of essential amino acids. Vegans should supplement their diet with vitamin B-12.
- Dietary supplements of protein, such as tablets and powders, are not recommended.

Dietary Recommendations for Vitamins

Adequate vitamin intake is necessary for good health and wellness, but excessive vitamin intake is not necessary and can be harmful. Vitamins serve a variety of functions within the body. For example, they serve as co-enzymes for metabolism of different nutrients, contribute to the regulation of energy stores, and assist in immune function. Some vitamins (e.g., B-complex vitamins and vitamin C) are water soluble and are excreted in urine. These vitamins must be consumed on a daily basis. Other vitamins, such as A, D, E, and K, are fat soluble. These vitamins are stored over time, so daily doses of these vitamins are not necessary. Excess consumption of fat-soluble vitamins can actually build to toxic levels and harm cell function and health. The specific DRI values (minimal amounts) for some of the more important vitamins are shown in Table 1, along with the UL values (maximum amounts).

Some vitamins act as antioxidants, but health benefits may depend on other compounds in foods. Carotenoid-rich foods, such as carrots and sweet potatoes, contain high amounts of vitamin A and high amounts of beta-carotene. Diets high in vitamin C (e.g., citrus fruits) and vitamin E (e.g., green, leafy vegetables) are also associated with reduced risk of cancer. Vitamin E has also been associated with reduced risk of heart disease.

Vitamins A, C, and E (as well as beta-carotene) act as **antioxidants** within the body. Antioxidants are substances that are thought to inactivate free radicals (molecules that can cause cell damage and health problems). For this reason, health benefits have been attributed to antioxidant properties. However, several large-scale studies showed no benefit (and some risks) from taking beta-carotene supplements. These results were difficult for scientists to interpret, but it is now known that there may be other substances in foods that contribute health benefits (see the discussion of functional foods later in this Concept). In general, diets containing a lot of fruits and vegetables and whole grains will provide adequate intake of vitamins and other healthy food components.

Fortification of foods has been used to ensure adequate vitamin intake in the population. National policy requires many foods to be fortified. For example, milk is fortified with vitamin D, low-fat milk with vitamins A and D, and margarine with vitamin A. These foods were selected because they are common food sources for growing children. Many common grain products are fortified with folic acid

Fruits and vegetables contain vitamins as well as health-promoting phytochemicals.
©Tetra Images/Shutterstock

because low folic acid levels increase the risk for birth defects in babies. Fortification is considered essential, since more than half of all women do not consume adequate amounts of folic acid during the first months of gestation (before most women even realize they are pregnant).

Vitamin supplements are not necessary for most people but may be beneficial for certain populations. Daily multiple vitamin supplements have not been shown beneficial to the general population. However, there is no current evidence to suggest that they are harmful if taken appropriately. In some cases, health professionals recommend them for specific groups. Health professionals may also recommend specific vitamin supplements for specific individuals or groups. For example, older people may need a vitamin D supplement if they get little exposure to sunlight; folic acid supplements are often recommended for pregnant women. Vitamin supplements at or below the RDA are considered safe; however, excess doses of vitamins can cause health problems. For example, excessively high levels of vitamin C are harmful for a small segment of the population. Excessively high amounts of vitamin D can be toxic, and mothers who take too much vitamin A risk birth defects in unborn children. While supplementation may not be necessary for people with healthy diets, it is acceptable to take a multivitamin or mineral supplements to ensure that your needs are met. (Guidelines are presented in Table 2.)

Follow the recommendations to ensure healthy amounts of vitamins in the diet. Vitamins in the amounts equal to the RDAs should be included in the diet each day. The following guidelines will help you implement this recommendation:

- Eat a diet containing the recommended servings for carbohydrates, proteins, and fats.
- Consume extra servings of green and yellow vegetables, citrus and other fruits, and other nonanimal food sources high in fiber, vitamins, and minerals.
- People with special needs should seek medical advice before selecting supplements and should inform medical personnel as to the amounts and content of all supplements (vitamin and other).

Dietary Recommendations for Minerals

Adequate mineral intake is necessary for good health and wellness, but excessive mineral intake is not necessary and can be harmful. Like vitamins, minerals have no calories and provide no energy for the body. They are important in regulating various bodily functions. Two particularly important minerals are calcium and iron. Calcium is important to bone, muscle, nerve, and blood development and function and has been associated with reduced risk for heart disease. Iron is necessary for the blood to carry adequate oxygen. Other important minerals are phosphorus, which builds teeth and bones; sodium, which regulates water in the body; zinc, which aids in the healing process; and potassium, which is necessary for proper muscle function.

RDAs are established to determine the amounts of each mineral necessary for healthy daily functioning. A sound diet provides all of the RDAs for minerals. Evidence indicating that some segments of the population may be mineral-deficient has led to the establishment of health goals identifying a need to increase mineral intake for some people.

It is relatively easy to obtain recommended amounts of most minerals, but evidence indicates that many individuals do not get recommended amounts of calcium in their diet. Adequate intake is particularly important for pregnant women, postmenopausal women, and people over 65 years of age. The National Institutes of Health (NIH) has indicated that a total intake of 2,000 mg/day of calcium is safe and that adequate vitamin D in the diet is necessary for optimal calcium absorption to take place. Though getting these amounts in a calcium-rich diet is best, calcium supplementation for those not eating properly seems wise. Many multivitamins do

Table 2 ▶ Vitamin and Mineral Supplements

- Limit the use of supplements unless warranted because of a health problem or a specific lack of nutrients in the diet.
- If you decide supplementation is necessary, select a multivitamin/mineral supplement that contains micronutrients in amounts close to the recommended levels (e.g., "one-a-day"-type supplements).
- If your diet is deficient in a particular mineral (e.g., calcium or iron), it may be necessary to incorporate dietary sources or an additional mineral supplement as well, since most multivitamins do not contain the recommended daily amount of minerals.
- Choose supplements that provide between 50 and 100 percent of the AI or RDA, and avoid those that provide many times the recommended amount. The use of supplements that hype "megadoses" of vitamins and minerals can increase the risk for unwanted nutrient interactions and possible toxic effects.
- Buy supplements from a reputable company and look for products that carry a U.S. Pharmacopoeia (USP), Consumer Lab (CL), or NSP International (NSP) designation on the label.

Source: Manore.

Antioxidants Vitamins that are thought to inactivate "activated oxygen molecules," sometimes called free radicals. Free radicals may cause cell damage that leads to diseases of various kinds. Antioxidants may inactivate the free radicals before they do their damage.

not contain enough calcium for some classes of people, so some may want to consider additional calcium. Check with your physician or a dietitian before you consider a supplement because individual needs vary.

Another concern is iron deficiency among very young children and women of childbearing age. Low iron levels may be a special problem for women taking birth control pills because the combination of low iron levels and birth control pills has been associated with depression and generalized fatigue. Eating a well-balanced diet with recommended amounts of fruits, vegetables, and grains can help in meeting the RDA for minerals. Nutrition goals for the nation emphasize the importance of adequate servings of foods rich in calcium, such as green, leafy vegetables and milk products; adequate servings of foods rich in iron, such as beans, peas, spinach, and meat; and reduced salt in the diet.

Reducing salt in the diet can reduce health risks. Salt is common in many processed food products, and most Americans consume way too much. Most meals at fast-food chains provide more than a full day's allotment of salt. Therefore, major public health efforts have focused on encouraging manufacturers to reduce salt content in processed and fast foods. While changes in food supply are important, taking responsibility for lowering salt in the diet is the best way for an individual to make change. Salt intake increases the risk for hypertension, which is a major risk factor for heart disease and stroke. Many people have assumed that salt consumption is not a problem if you are not hypertensive, but this is not the case. Recent studies have shown that sodium intake increases risk of stroke independent of the presence of hypertension. Therefore, reducing salt consumption is important for everyone.

Follow the recommendations to ensure healthy amounts of minerals in the diet. The following list includes basic recommendations for mineral content in the diet:

- Minerals in amounts equal to the RDAs should be consumed in the diet each day.

- Pregnant women and postmenopausal women should consider taking a daily calcium supplement.

- A diet containing the food servings recommended for carbohydrates, proteins, and fats will more than meet the RDA standards.

- Extra servings of green and yellow vegetables, citrus and other fruits, and other nonanimal sources of foods high in fiber, vitamins, and minerals are recommended as a substitute for high-fat foods.

Dietary Recommendations for Water and Other Fluids

Water is a critical component of a healthy diet. Though water contains no calories, provides no energy, and provides no key nutrients, it is crucial to health and survival. Water is a major component of most of the foods you eat, and more than half of all body tissues are composed of it. Regular water intake maintains water balance and is critical to many body functions. Though a variety of fluid-replacement beverages are available for use during and following exercise, replacing water is the primary need.

Beverages other than water are part of many diets, but some beverages can have an adverse effect on good health. Coffee, tea, soft drinks, and alcoholic beverages are often substituted for water. Too much caffeine consumption has been shown to cause symptoms such as irregular heartbeat in some people. Tea has not been shown to have similar effects, though this may be because tea drinkers typically consume less volume than coffee drinkers, and tea has less caffeine per cup than coffee. Many soft drinks also have caffeine, though coffee typically contains two to three times the caffeine of a typical cola drink.

As noted in the U.S. dietary guidelines, alcohol has been used throughout human history to enhance the enjoyment of meals. Evidence has continued to support the benefits of moderate alcohol consumption for reducing risks for forms of cardiovascular disease. However, excessive alcohol consumption is associated with increased risk for heart disease, high blood pressure, stroke, and osteoporosis. Long-term excessive alcoholic beverage consumption also leads to cirrhosis of the liver and to increased risk for hepatitis and cancer. From a nutrition perspective, excessive consumption of alcoholic beverages can have negative health implications because the alcohol often replaces nutrients. Alcohol consumption during pregnancy is associated with low birth weight, fetal alcoholism, and other damage to the fetus. Therefore, it should not be consumed during pregnancy.

Follow the recommendations to ensure healthy amounts of water and other fluids in the diet. The following list includes basic recommendations for water and fluids in the diet:

- Consume about eight glasses (8 ounces each) of water every day. Active people and those who exercise in hot environments require additional water.

- Coffee, tea, and soft drinks should not be substituted for sources of key nutrients, such as low-fat milk, fruit juices, or foods rich in calcium.

- Limit daily servings of beverages containing caffeine to no more than three.

- Limit sugared soft drinks.

- If you are an adult and you choose to drink alcohol, do so in moderation. The dietary guidelines for Americans indicate that moderation means no more than one drink per day for women and no more than two drinks per day for men (one drink equals 12 ounces of regular beer, 5 ounces of wine [small glass], or one average-size cocktail [1.5 ounces of 80-proof alcohol]).

Understanding Contemporary Nutrition Terms, Issues, and Trends

The term *functional foods* is frequently used to refer to foods or dietary components that may provide a health benefit beyond basic nutrition. The current dietary guidelines emphasize the consumption of healthier foods instead of targeting specific nutrient requirements. This is because there are many components of foods that combine to influence our health and well-being (see Table 3).

Table 3 ▶ Examples of Functional Foods and Potential Benefits

Carotenoids	Potential Benefits
Beta-carotene: found in carrots, pumpkin, sweet potato, cantaloupe	May bolster cellular antioxidant defenses
Lutein, zeaxanthin: found in kale, collards, spinach, corn, eggs, citrus	May contribute to healthy vision
Lycopene: Found in tomatoes, watermelon, red/pink grapefruit	May contribute to prostate health

Flavonoids	Potential Benefits
Anthocyanins: found in berries, cherries, red grapes	May bolster antioxidant defenses; may maintain brain function and heart health
Flavanones: found in citrus foods	
Flavonols: found in onions, apples, tea, broccoli	

Isothiocyanates	Potential Benefits
Proanthocyanidins: found in cranberries, cocoa, apples, strawberries, grapes, peanuts	May contribute to maintenance of urinary tract health and heart health
Sulforaphane: found in cauliflower, broccoli, brussels sprouts, cabbage, kale, horseradish	May enhance detoxification of undesirable compounds; may bolster cellular antioxidant defenses

Phenolic Acids	Potential Benefits
Caffeic/ferulic acids: found in apples, pears, citrus fruits, some vegetables, coffee	May bolster cellular antioxidant defenses; may contribute to maintenance of healthy vision

Sulfides/Thioles	Potential Benefits
Sulfides: found in garlic, onions, leeks, scallions	May enhance detoxification of undesirable compounds; may contribute to maintenance of heart health and healthy immune function
Dithiolthiones: found in cruciferous vegetables	

Fruits and vegetables, for example, are loaded with a variety of powerful phytochemicals that have been shown to have potential health benefits. The relative importance to health of each compound is difficult to determine because the compounds may act synergistically with each other (and with antioxidant vitamins) to promote positive outcomes. Other examples of functional foods include the beneficial types of fiber and beta glucan in whole grains, the isoflavones in soy products, the omega-3 fatty acids in coldwater fish, and the probiotic yeasts and bacteria in yogurts and other cultured dairy products. Reports emphasizing the benefits of moderate alcohol consumption, as well as health benefits of chocolate and coffee consumption, are also based on components in these foods that can contribute to good nutrition. It is important to note that most vitamins and minerals are also classified as functional foods, since they have functions beyond their primary role in basic nutrition. The list of compounds in Table 3 should not be viewed as "magic bullets" because research is still accumulating on these compounds. By adopting healthy eating patterns, most people will obtain the benefits from sufficient intake of vitamins and minerals as well as the ancillary benefits from these other functional foods.

Vegetarian diets are endorsed for health benefits, but people adhere to this practice for a variety of reasons. Many people don't understand how vegetarians get sufficient protein or even why a person would choose this eating pattern. Vegetarian diets provide ample sources of protein as long as a variety of protein-rich food sources are included in the diet. According to the Academy of Nutrition and Dietetics, well-planned vegetarian diets "are appropriate for all stages of the life cycle, including during pregnancy and lactation," and can "satisfy the nutrient needs of infants, children, and adolescents." You can get plenty of protein and nutrients on a vegetarian diet. **Vegans** must supplement the diet with vitamin B-12 because the only source of this vitamin is food from animal sources. **Lacto-ovo vegetarians** do not have the same concerns because vitamin B-12 can be obtained in dairy products.

Vegetarian diets are widely endorsed by dietitians and were described in the U.S. dietary guidelines as one of the recommended "healthy eating patterns"; however, vegetarians may choose this pattern for a variety of reasons. Some may choose it for religious, ethical, or animal-rights reasons. Others may choose it for philosophical reasons (e.g., not wanting to eat flesh). Still others may pursue it because of the ancillary benefits on the environment. Societal awareness of vegetarianism is still evolving, but there are now more vegetarian food options in grocery stores and restaurants.

Vegans Strict vegetarians, who exclude not only all forms of meat from the diet but also dairy products and eggs.

Lacto-Ovo Vegetarians Vegetarians who include dairy and eggs in the diet.

Organic foods are more expensive, but some people care about how their food is produced. Organic food differs from conventionally produced food primarily in the way it is grown, handled, and processed. Organic food is produced without conventional pesticides and using natural fertilizers. Organic meat, poultry, eggs, and dairy products come from animals that are given no antibiotics or growth hormones. To be labeled as "organic," a food must be produced by a certified grower that follows USDA guidelines. Currently, a government-approved certifier must inspect the farm where the food is grown or produced to ensure that the farmer is following the rules necessary to meet USDA organic standards. Companies that handle, process, or sell organic food must also be certified, but inspections and certifications are not required for farmers who sell less than $5,000 worth of foods each year. Thus, foods at local farmers' markets may claim to be organic but they may or may not meet standards.

The USDA does not imply that organically produced food is safer or more nutritious than conventionally produced food. A recent review of multiple studies demonstrated that nutrient levels are higher in organic foods, but there is still debate on the issue. However, other reasons that people choose organic foods are to reduce exposure to pesticides and to support more sustainable and environmentally friendly agricultural practices. The higher cost makes it hard to afford them, but greater consumer demand can potentially lead to reduced costs over time.

Gluten intolerance is increasingly common but the cause of this trend is not clear. *Gluten intolerance* is actually an umbrella term that can refer to a number of digestive health problems, including celiac disease and wheat allergies. Gluten is a family of proteins found in certain grains, but most people associate it with wheat. Gluten is responsible for the satisfying texture of baked goods, but some individuals report fatigue, headaches, and abdominal problems after eating foods with gluten. However, many people who think they are gluten intolerant actually are not. One study tested a sample of 400 people who thought they were gluten intolerant; 15 percent were found to be gluten intolerant and 85 percent were not.

While some individuals may not meet the specific criteria for gluten intolerance, there is still a clear increase in the prevalence of this condition. Ten years ago about .04 percent of the population (approximately 1 in 2,500 people) was gluten intolerant, but now the figure is estimated to be almost 1 percent. Various theories have been proposed to explain the increased incidence of gluten intolerance. One is that the peptide structure in wheat today is different (due to genetic modifications aimed at increasing yields) than in the past. Another theory is that the problem reflects limitations in digestion caused by impaired gut flora (i.e., healthy bacteria in our intestines). Regardless of the cause, the issue has had major implications on food production and food preparation. Approximately 30 percent of Americans report trying to avoid gluten, but it is likely that many do so because of misconceptions or because they perceive it to be a healthier choice.

Use of genetically engineered foods is common, but labeling laws remain controversial. A genetically modified organism (GMO) is a plant, animal, or microorganism that has been altered so that its genetic structure (DNA) contains genes not typically found in the organism. GMOs have allowed increased crop yields because the organisms (e.g., corn, wheat, soybeans) are genetically modified to resist diseases, insects, heat, cold, and drought. GMOs have also have been modified to have higher levels of some nutrients (e.g., calcium, folate, protein). They provide us with foods such as seedless grapes and watermelon. Food manufacturers and scientists maintain that the use of genetically modified organisms (GMOs) is completely safe and that the technology is essential to maximize food production for the population. Opponents suggest that insertion of genes not normally found in organisms may alter the functioning of other genes and create novel proteins that can be toxic or lead to allergies. Some opponents point to the recent rise in gluten sensitivity and irritable bowel syndrome as evidence of altered food properties. Others worry

A CLOSER LOOK

Labeling of Genetically Modified Foods

There is currently considerable debate about the issue of whether genetically modified (GM) foods, also referred to as genetically modified organisms (GMOs), should have to be labeled. Current law mandates food labeling when there are clear differences in the characteristics, safety, or nutritional value of a food, but genetic engineering of foods is not currently viewed as being different enough to warrant labeling. Advocates of labeling laws suggest that consumers have a right to know how food is prepared, but opponents view that it is not necessary and that it would add unnecessary cost and regulation. A Pew research study reported that 88 percent of scientists believe that GM foods are safe, but only 37 percent of the general public shares this opinion. Nearly 60 percent of the public remains concerned about their use and wants to be informed when making food choices. This position is supported by several large nonprofit groups (e.g., NonGMOProject.org) that advocate labeling. Some food companies have chosen voluntarily to label their food as "non-GMO," but even this has been controversial. Opponents of labeling suggest it gives these products a marketing advantage because it implies that non-GMO is "better" when science does not currently support such a conclusion.

What is your position about labeling genetically modified foods?

Table 4 ▶ Comparing the Quality of Similar Food Products

Food Product	Less Desirable Option	More Desirable Option	Benefit of More Desirable Option in Nutrition Quality
Bread	White bread	Whole-wheat bread	More fiber
Rice	White rice	Brown rice	More fiber
Juice	Sweetened juice	100% juice	More fiber and less high fructose corn syrup
Fruit	Canned	Fresh	More vitamins, more fiber, less sugar
Vegetables	Canned	Fresh	More vitamins, less salt
Potatoes	French fries	Baked potato	Less saturated fat
Milk	2% milk	Skim milk	Less saturated fat
Meat	Ground beef (high fat)	Ground sirloin (low fat)	Less saturated fat
Oils	Vegetable oil	Canola oil	More monounsaturated fat
Snack food	Fried chips	Baked chips	Less fat/calorie content, less trans fat

that GMOs may lead to antibiotic resistance. However, the real debate is not about the value of GMOs but rather about whether GMO foods should be labeled to inform consumers. Current laws do not require GMO labeling, forcing consumers to rely on voluntary labels that certify products as "GMO free." (See A Closer Look for more information.)

Sound Eating Practices

Consistent eating patterns (with a daily breakfast) are important for good nutrition. Eating regular meals every day, including a good breakfast, is wise. Many studies have shown breakfast to be an important meal but many people still skip it. Skipping breakfast impairs performance because blood sugar levels drop in the long period between dinner the night before and lunch the following day. Eating every 4 to 6 hours is wise.

Minimize your consumption of overly processed foods and foods high in hydrogenated fat or saturated fat. Many foods available in grocery stores have been highly processed to enhance shelf life and convenience. In many cases, the processing of foods removes valuable nutrients and includes other additives that may compromise overall nutrition. Processing of grains, for example, typically removes the bran and germ layers, which contain fiber and valuable minerals. In regard to additives, there has been considerable attention on the possible negative effects of high fructose corn syrup, as well as the pervasive use of hydrogenated vegetable oils containing trans fatty acids. Table 4 compares food quality in each of the main food categories. To improve your diet, you should aim to choose foods in the "more desirable" category instead of those in the "less desirable" category.

Moderation is a good general rule of nutrition. It is likely that some of your favorite foods may not be among the healthiest choices, but it is possible to still enjoy them in moderation. Eating smaller amounts of these foods or eating them less frequently is one way. Balancing out high calorie snacks or desserts with lower calorie foods or meals is another good strategy.

Minimize your reliance on fast foods. Most consumers understand that many fast-food options are relatively poor nutritional choices. Hamburgers are usually high in fat, as are french fries (because they are usually cooked in saturated fat). Even chicken and fish are often high in fat and calories because they may be cooked in fat and covered with high-fat/high-calorie sauces.

Shift toward a plant-based diet. Plant-based diets offer clear advantages for health. Current guidelines recommend that half of your plate should be filled with fruits and vegetables. A population shift toward a plant-based diet would also

Healthy eating on campus requires good decision making.

HELP   Health is available to Everyone for a Lifetime, and it's Personal

What Do "Healthy" and "Natural" Really Mean?

Many food manufacturers label their products as "healthy" or "natural" to attract consumer interest. However, these terms may mean different things to different people. As nutritional guidelines change, the definitions of healthy foods also need to shift. The FDA is currently soliciting broad input from organizations, food companies, and the general public to refine the criteria for these terms. Until it gets changed, consumers should carefully check ingredients to make their own informed choice about the product.

Do the words healthy *or* natural *on a food product catch your attention when you shop?*

connect
ACTIVITY

provide benefits to the environment. Conservative estimates indicate that livestock have a greater negative impact on greenhouse gas emissions than cars and trucks. These benefits were heavily emphasized by the Dietary Guidelines Advisory Committee that developed the overall guidelines.

Make better decisions when choosing snacks. Small snacks of appropriate foods can help maintain energy levels throughout the day. As with your total diet, the best snacks are nutritionally dense. Unfortunately, many widely available snack foods are high in calories, fats, simple sugar, and salt. Even foods sold as "healthy snacks," such as granola bars, are often high in fat and simple sugar. Some common snacks, such as chips, pretzels, and even popcorn, may be high in salt and may be cooked in fat. Look for options lower in salt or fat and consider other healthier snack options such as fresh fruits, vegetables, and nuts.

Nutrition and Physical Performance

Some basic dietary guidelines exist for active people. In general, the nutrition rules described in this Concept apply to all people, whether active or sedentary, but some additional nutrition facts are important for exercisers and athletes. Because active people often expend calories in amounts considerably above normal, they need extra calories in their diet. To avoid excess fat and protein, complex carbohydrates should constitute as much as 70 percent of total caloric intake. A higher amount of protein is generally recommended for active individuals (1.2 grams per kg of body weight) because some protein is used as an energy source during exercise. Extra protein is obtained in the additional calories consumed. Current protein guidelines range from 10 to 35 percent to provide flexibility but intakes above 15 percent are not typically necessary.

Carbohydrate loading before exercise and carbohydrate replacement during exercise can enhance sustained aerobic performances. Athletes and vigorously active people must maintain a high level of readily available fuel, especially in the muscles. Consumption of complex carbohydrates is the best way to ensure this. Prior to an activity requiring an extended duration of physical performance (more than 1 hour in length, such as a marathon), **carbohydrate loading** can be useful. Carbohydrate loading is accomplished by resting 1 or 2 days before the event and eating a higher than normal amount of complex carbohydrates. This helps build up maximum levels of stored carbohydrate (**glycogen**) in the muscles and liver so it can be used during exercise. The key in carbohydrate loading is not to eat a lot but, rather, to eat a higher percentage of carbohydrates than normal.

Ingesting carbohydrate beverages during sustained exercise can also aid performance by preventing or forestalling muscle glycogen depletion. Fluid-replacement drinks containing 6 to 8 percent carbohydrates are very helpful in preventing dehydration and replacing energy stores. A number of companies also make concentrated carbohydrate gels that deliver carbohydrates

Good nutrition is essential for active lifestyles.
©Tony Tallec/Alamy Stock Photo

(generally 80 percent complex, 20 percent simple) in a form the body can absorb quickly for energy. Examples are PowerGel and Gu. Energy bars, such as Powerbars and Clif bars, are also commonly eaten during or after exercise to enhance energy stores. The various carbohydrate supplements have been shown to be effective for exercise sessions lasting over an hour and are good for replacing glycogen stores after exercise. Consuming carbohydrates 15 to 30 minutes following exercise can aid in rapid replenishment of muscle glycogen, which may enhance future performance or training sessions. However, supplements have little benefit before, during, or after shorter bouts of exercise. Because they contain considerable calories, they are not recommended for individuals primarily interested in weight control.

The timing may be more important than the makeup of a pre-event meal. If you are racing or doing high-level exercise early in the morning, eat a small meal prior to starting. Eat about 3 hours before competition or heavy exercise to allow time for digestion. Generally, athletes can select foods on the basis of experience, but easily digested carbohydrates are best. Fat intake should be minimal because fat digests more slowly; proteins and high-cellulose foods should be kept to a moderate amount prior to prolonged events to avoid urinary and bowel excretion. Drinking 2 or 3 cups of liquid will ensure adequate hydration.

Consuming simple carbohydrates (sugar, candy) within an hour or two of an event is not recommended because it may cause an insulin response, resulting in weakness and fatigue, or it may cause stomach distress, cramps, or nausea.

Changes in the frequency and composition of meals are important to gain muscle mass. To increase muscle mass, the body requires a greater caloric intake. The challenge is to provide enough extra calories for the muscle without excess amounts going to fat. An increase of 500 to 1,000 calories a day will help most people gain muscle mass over time. Smaller, more frequent meals are best for weight gain, since they tend to keep the metabolic rate high. The majority of extra calories should come from complex carbohydrates. Breads, pasta, rice, and fruits such as bananas are good sources. Granola, nuts, juices (grape and cranberry), and milk also make good high-calorie, healthy snacks.

Diet supplements are not particularly effective unless used as part of a behaviorally based program. High-fat diets can result in weight gain but may not be best for good health, especially if they are high in saturated fat. If weight gain does not occur over a period of weeks and months with extra calorie consumption, individuals may need to seek medical assistance.

Using Self-Management Skills

Build a strong base of nutrition knowledge to make more informed food choices. Making healthy food choices requires good self-management skills and a commitment to use them. In most cases, the unhealthy choice is the easier, tastier, and cheaper option, so restraint and

self-control are very important. One of the best ways to enhance your nutrition knowledge and improve your eating patterns is to pay attention to food labels at grocery stores and nutrition content posted on restaurant menus.

Reading food labels helps you be more aware of what you are eating and make healthier choices in your daily eating. The new labels make it very easy to find the important information, but you still have to make a commitment to review it. As shown in Figure 4, the label highlights key nutritional information emphasized in the new dietary guidelines and described in this Concept.

Most people underestimate the number of calories they consume daily and the caloric content of specific foods. Therefore, the font size of the calories is considerably larger. Limiting consumption of sugars is a key recommendation in the new guidelines, so a new row indicates the amount of "added sugars" to help promote awareness of this when you are buying foods. It is also important to pay attention to the amounts of saturated fat, trans fat, and salt. The food label also provides this information. When comparing similar food

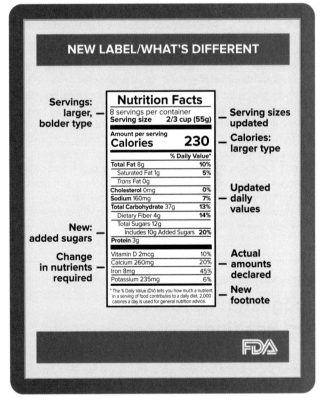

Figure 4 ▶ Conceptual image of the educational features in the new food label.

Source: U.S. Food and Drug Administration

Carbohydrate Loading The extra consumption of complex carbohydrates in the days prior to sustained performance.

Glycogen A source of energy stored in the muscles and liver necessary for sustained physical activity.

products, combine the grams (g) of saturated fat and trans fat and look for the lowest combined amount. The listing of % Daily Value (DV) can also be useful. Foods low in saturated fat generally have % DV less than 5 percent, while foods high in saturated fat have % DV greater than 20 percent.

In addition to the revised labels, the new regulations from the FDA also require fast-food chains and restaurants to provide calorie information on menus and vending machines. These changes are also designed to empower consumers to make healthier food options when eating out. The information is helpful, but discipline and self-management skills are needed to put it to good use

Build confidence and motivation toward healthy eating by making small changes in eating patterns and by learning cooking skills. A key to making lifestyle changes is to focus on small changes that gradually build toward larger changes over time. The many recommendations and nutrition guidelines summarized in this Concept can seem daunting, but

the principles of good nutrition are pretty basic (e.g., eat more fruits and vegetables, minimize consumption of saturated fat, consume less fast food, and eat smaller portions). Making an additional positive change can often lead to one fewer negative choice. Substituting fruit for cookies or snacks helps you gain an extra serving of fruits/veggies while cutting back on high-calorie, processed food. Similarly, cooking one more meal at home can translate to one fewer meal at a fast-food restaurant.

As you make a few small changes you will notice that you may be more open to others. For example, if you start eating brown rice, you might find that it has more flavor and better texture than white rice. Similarly, shifting to products with lower fat (e.g., skim milk instead of 2% milk) or low-added sugar (100% juice instead of juice drinks), you likely shift your palate and preferences to healthier options. By taking small steps to cook for yourself, you can also gain a deeper understanding of food and a greater appreciation for the ingredients that go into it. Like other skills, cooking skills take time to develop, but they can be learned and improved over time with practice.

Strategies for Action: Lab Information

An analysis of your current diet is a good first step in making future decisions about what you eat. Many experts recommend keeping a log of what you eat over an extended period, so you can determine the overall quality of your diet. In Lab 15A, you will have an opportunity to track your diet over several days. In addition to computing the amount of carbohydrates, fats, and proteins, you will also be able to monitor your consumption of fruits and vegetables. A number of online tools and personal software programs can make dietary calculations for you and provide a more comprehensive report of nutrient intake. Whether you use a Web-based tool or a paper-and-pencil log doesn't really matter—the key is to monitor and evaluate the quality of your diet.

Making small changes in diet patterns can have a big impact. Nutrition experts emphasize the importance of making small changes in your diet over time rather than trying to make comprehensive changes at one time. Try cutting back on sweets or soft drinks. Simply adding a few more fruits and vegetables to your diet can lead to major changes in overall diet quality. In Lab 15B, you will be given the opportunity to compare a "nutritious diet" to a "favorite diet." Analyzing two daily meal plans will help you get a more accurate picture as to whether foods that you think are nutritious actually meet current healthy lifestyle goals.

Suggested Resources and Readings

The websites for the following sources can be accessed by searching online for the organization, program, or title listed. Specific scientific references are available at the end of this edition of *Concepts of Fitness and Wellness*.

- Center for Science in the Public Interest. www.cspinet.org.
- Centers for Disease Control and Prevention. Consumption of Added Sugar in Adults (online resource).
- Food Safety Database. www.foodsafety.gov.
- International Food Information Council Foundation. www.ific.org.
- Medscape. AHA Issues "Presidential Advisory" on Harms of Saturated Fat (online resource).
- Non-GMOreport.com. (2015). What is non-GMO? What are genetically modified foods? (online article).
- Park, A. (2015, February 9). Where dietary-fat guidelines went wrong. *Time* (online article).
- Park, A. (2017, March 22). Alcohol is good for your heart—most of the time. *Time* (online article).

- Schiff, W. (2018). *Nutrition Essentials: A Personal Approach* (2nd ed.). St. Louis: McGraw-Hill Higher Education.
- Szabo, L. (2015, February 19). Nutrition panel urges Americans to eat green. *USA Today* (online article).
- U.S. Department of Agriculture. History of Dietary Guidelines (online resource and pdf).
- U.S. Department of Health and Human Services and U.S. Department of Agriculture. (2015, December). *2015–2020 Dietary Guidelines for Americans* (8th ed.) Chapter 1 Summary (online).
- U.S. Food and Drug Administration (website: www.fda.gov):
  - Food Labeling Restaurant Policy Statement (official statement).
  - Food Science Research. Consumer Behavior Research (resource portal).
  - New and Improved Nutrition Facts Label (pdf fact sheet).
  - Standards for Gluten-Free Foods.
- Williams, M., Rawson, E., Branch, D., & Anderson, D. (2017). *Nutrition for Health, Fitness and Sport* (11th ed.). St. Louis: McGraw-Hill Higher Education.

Lab 15A Nutrition Analysis

Name	**Section**	**Date**

Purpose: To learn to keep a dietary log, to determine the nutritional quality of your diet, to determine your average daily caloric intake, and to determine necessary changes in eating habits.

Procedures

1. Record your dietary intake for 2 days using the Daily Diet Record sheets that follow. Record intake for 1 weekday and 1 weekend day. You may wish to make extra copies for future use.
2. Include the actual foods eaten and the amount (size of portion in teaspoons, tablespoons, cups, ounces, or other standard units of measurement). Be sure to include all drinks (coffee, tea, soft drinks, etc.). Include *all* foods eaten, including sauces, gravies, dressings, toppings, spreads, and so on. Determine your caloric consumption for each of the 2 days. Use the calorie guides at the choosemyplate.gov website to assist in evaluating your diet. Calorie and nutrient information is also available in NutritionCalc Plus, a diet analysis tool available in Connect. Launch it by clicking the Nutrition-Calc Plus link on the Resources list on your Connect class home page.
3. List the number of servings from each food group by each food choice.
4. Estimate the proportion of complex carbohydrate, simple carbohydrate, protein, and fat in each meal and in snacks, as well as for the total day.
5. Answer the questions in Chart 1 using information for a typical day based on the Daily Diet Record sheets. Score 1 point for each "yes" answer. Then use Chart 2 to rate your dietary habits (circle rating).
6. Complete the Conclusions and Implications section.

Results

Record the number of calories consumed for each of the 2 days.

Weekday [   ] calories   Weekend [   ] calories

Conclusions and Implications: In several sentences, discuss your diet as recorded in this lab. Explain any changes in your eating habits that may be necessary. Comment on whether the days you surveyed are typical of your normal diet.

Chart 1 Dietary Habits Questionnaire

Yes	No	Answer questions based on a typical day (use your Daily Diet Records to help).
○	○	1. Do you eat at least three healthy meals each day?
○	○	2. Do you eat a healthy breakfast?
○	○	3. Do you eat lunch regularly?
○	○	4. Does your diet contain 45 to 65 percent carbohydrates with a high concentration of fiber?*
○	○	5. Are less than one-fourth of the carbohydrates you eat simple carbohydrates?
○	○	6. Does your diet contain 10 to 35 percent protein?*
○	○	7. Does your diet contain 20 to 35 percent fat?*
○	○	8. Do you limit the amount of saturated fat in your diet (no more than 10 percent)?
○	○	9. Do you limit salt intake to acceptable amounts?
○	○	10. Do you get adequate amounts of vitamins in your diet without a supplement?
○	○	11. Do you typically eat 6 to 11 servings from the bread, cereal, rice, and pasta group of foods?
○	○	12. Do you typically eat 3 to 5 servings of vegetables?
○	○	13. Do you typically eat 2 to 4 servings of fruits?
○	○	14. Do you typically eat 2 to 3 servings from the milk, yogurt, and cheese group of foods?
○	○	15. Do you typically eat 2 to 3 servings from the meat, poultry, fish, beans, eggs, and nuts group of foods?
○	○	16. Do you drink adequate amounts of water?
○	○	17. Do you get adequate minerals in your diet without a supplement?
○	○	18. Do you limit your caffeine and alcohol consumption to acceptable levels?
○	○	19. Is your average caloric consumption reasonable for your body size and for the amount of calories you normally expend?

Total number of "yes" answers

*Based on USDA standards.

Chart 2 Dietary Habits Rating Scale

Score	Rating
18–19	Very good
15–17	Good
13–14	Marginal
12 or less	Poor

Daily Diet Record

Day 1

Breakfast Food	Amount (cups, tsp., etc.)	Calories	Food Servings				Estimated Meal Calories %
			Bread/Cereal	Fruit/Veg.	Milk/Meat	Fat/Sweet	
							☐ % Protein
							☐ % Fat
							☐ % Complex carbohydrate
							☐ % Simple carbohydrate
							100% Total
Meal Total	✕						

Lunch Food	Amount (cups, tsp., etc.)	Calories	Food Servings				Estimated Meal Calories %
			Bread/Cereal	Fruit/Veg.	Milk/Meat	Fat/Sweet	
							☐ % Protein
							☐ % Fat
							☐ % Complex carbohydrate
							☐ % Simple carbohydrate
							100% Total
Meal Total	✕						

Dinner Food	Amount (cups, tsp., etc.)	Calories	Food Servings				Estimated Meal Calories %
			Bread/Cereal	Fruit/Veg.	Milk/Meat	Fat/Sweet	
							☐ % Protein
							☐ % Fat
							☐ % Complex carbohydrate
							☐ % Simple carbohydrate
							100% Total
Meal Total	✕						

Snack Food	Amount (cups, tsp., etc.)	Calories	Food Servings				Estimated Snack Calories %
			Bread/Cereal	Fruit/Veg.	Milk/Meat	Fat/Sweet	
							☐ % Protein
							☐ % Fat
							☐ % Complex carbohydrate
							☐ % Simple carbohydrate
Meal Total							100% Total
Daily Totals	✕						**Estimated Daily Total Calories %**
		Calories	Servings	Servings	Servings	Servings	☐ % Protein
							☐ % Fat
							☐ % Complex carbohydrate
							☐ % Simple carbohydrate
							100% Total

Daily Diet Record

Day 2

Breakfast Food	Amount (cups, tsp., etc.)	Calories	Food Servings				Estimated Meal Calories %
			Bread/Cereal	Fruit/Veg.	Milk/Meat	Fat/Sweet	
							☐ % Protein
							☐ % Fat
							☐ % Complex carbohydrate
							☐ % Simple carbohydrate
							100% Total
Meal Total	✕						

Lunch Food	Amount (cups, tsp., etc.)	Calories	Food Servings				Estimated Meal Calories %
			Bread/Cereal	Fruit/Veg.	Milk/Meat	Fat/Sweet	
							☐ % Protein
							☐ % Fat
							☐ % Complex carbohydrate
							☐ % Simple carbohydrate
							100% Total
Meal Total	✕						

Dinner Food	Amount (cups, tsp., etc.)	Calories	Food Servings				Estimated Meal Calories %
			Bread/Cereal	Fruit/Veg.	Milk/Meat	Fat/Sweet	
							☐ % Protein
							☐ % Fat
							☐ % Complex carbohydrate
							☐ % Simple carbohydrate
							100% Total
Meal Total	✕						

Snack Food	Amount (cups, tsp., etc.)	Calories	Food Servings				Estimated Snack Calories %
			Bread/Cereal	Fruit/Veg.	Milk/Meat	Fat/Sweet	
							☐ % Protein
							☐ % Fat
							☐ % Complex carbohydrate
							☐ % Simple carbohydrate
							100% Total
Meal Total							**Estimated Daily Total Calories %**
Daily Totals	✕						☐ % Protein
		Calories	Servings	Servings	Servings	Servings	☐ % Fat
							☐ % Complex carbohydrate
							☐ % Simple carbohydrate
							100% Total

Lab 15B Selecting Nutritious Foods

Name		Section		Date	

Purpose: To learn to select a nutritious diet, to determine the nutritive value of favorite foods, and to compare nutritious and favorite foods in terms of nutrient content.

Procedures

1. Select a favorite breakfast, lunch, and dinner from the foods list in Appendix B. Include between-meal snacks with the nearest meal. If you cannot find foods you would normally choose, select those most similar to choices you might make. Calorie and nutrient information is also available in NutritionCalc Plus, a diet analysis tool available in Connect. Launch it by clicking the NutritionCalc Plus link on the Resources list on your Connect class home page.
2. Select a breakfast, lunch, and dinner from foods you feel would make the most nutritious meals. Include between-meal snacks with the nearest meal.
3. Record your "favorite foods" and "nutritious foods" in the "Favorite" versus "Nutritious" Food Choices for Three Daily Meals chart that follows. Record the calories for proteins, carbohydrates, and fats for each of the foods you choose.
4. Total each column for the "favorite" and the "nutritious" meals.
5. Determine the percentages of your total calories that are protein, carbohydrates, and fat by dividing each column total by the total number of calories consumed.
6. Comment on what you learned in the Conclusions and Implications section.

Results: Record your results below. Calculate percentage of calories from each source by dividing total calories into calories from each food source (protein, carbohydrates, or fat).

Food Selection Results

Source	Favorite Foods		Nutritious Foods	
	Calories	% of Total Calories	Calories	% of Total Calories
Protein				
Carbohydrates				
Fat				
Total 100%		100%		100%

Conclusions and Implications: In several sentences, discuss the differences you found between your nutritious diet and your favorite diet. Discuss the quality of your nutritious diet as well as other things you learned from doing this lab.

"Favorite" versus "Nutritious" Food Choices for Three Daily Meals

Breakfast Favorite	Food Choices				Breakfast Nutritious	Food Choices			
Food	Cal.	Prot. Cal.	Carb. Cal.	Fat Cal.	Food	Cal.	Prot. Cal.	Carb. Cal.	Fat Cal.
Totals					Totals				

Lunch Favorite	Food Choices				Lunch Nutritious	Food Choices			
Food	Cal.	Prot. Cal.	Carb. Cal.	Fat Cal.	Food	Cal.	Prot. Cal.	Carb. Cal.	Fat Cal.
Totals					Totals				

Dinner Favorite	Food Choices				Dinner Nutritious	Food Choices			
Food	Cal.	Prot. Cal.	Carb. Cal.	Fat Cal.	Food	Cal.	Prot. Cal.	Carb. Cal.	Fat Cal.
Totals					Totals				
Daily Totals (Calories)					Daily Totals (Calories)				
Daily % of Total Calories					Daily % of Total Calories				

Managing Diet and Activity for Healthy Body Fatness

LEARNING OBJECTIVES

After completing the study of this Concept, you will be able to:

▶ Explain the principles for weight control and the concept of energy balance.

▶ Identify the features of an obesogenic environment that influence our behavior.

▶ Outline guidelines for weight loss treatments.

▶ Describe and apply, when appropriate, guidelines for losing body fat.

▶ Utilize healthy shopping and eating strategies and guidelines.

▶ Evaluate fast food options.

Various management strategies for eating and performing physical activity are useful in achieving and maintaining optimal body composition.

©Jack Hollingsworth/Blend Images LLC

Why it Matters!

The fact that more than two-thirds of adult Americans are classified as overweight is evidence that weight control is a vexing problem for the majority of the population. People often resort to fad diets or follow flawed advice or regimens they see online or in consumer magazines. Too much focus is placed on appearance and "weight loss" rather than on health and fat loss. Also, in attempts to lose weight, the energy intake side of the energy balance equation (i.e., eating) is typically emphasized to a greater extent than the energy expenditure side of the equation (i.e., physical activity). Effective long-term weight control requires the adoption of healthy eating patterns *and* regular physical activity. This Concept will separate fact from fiction and provide strategies to help you establish lifestyles conducive to long-term weight control. Following appropriate lifestyle practices may not allow you to achieve the body you want, but it can promote health and wellness and help you attain a size appropriate for your genetics and body type.

Factors Influencing Weight and Fat Control

Long-term weight control requires a balance between energy intake and energy expenditure. The relationships governing energy balance are very simple—the number of calories expended must match the number consumed. There may be subtle differences  on a daily basis, but if intake exceeds expenditure over a period of time, a person will store the extra calories as body fat. The average person gains 1 pound of weight (i.e., fat) for every year over the age of 25. This may sound like a lot, but it represents a calorie difference of only 10 kcal per day (approximately the calories found in a cracker or potato chip). This subtle difference shows the precise regulation of intake and expenditure that is normally in effect when a person maintains his or her body weight. The built-in regulation system is based on our appetite, which guides us when we might be running low on energy.

Figure 1 shows the hypothetical balance between energy intake and expenditure. Energy intake comes from the three major nutrients in our diet (carbohydrates, fats, and proteins) as well as from alcohol. Energy expenditure can be divided into three major components as well. Basal metabolism accounts for the bulk of daily energy expenditure (60 to 75 percent) and this refers to the calories expended to maintain basic body functions while the body is at rest. A second category, called thermogenesis, captures the energy expended processing the food we eat (approximately 10 percent of total daily energy expenditure). The third and most variable component of

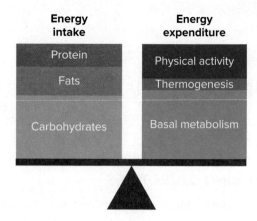

Figure 1 ▶ Components of energy intake must balance components of energy expenditure for weight maintenance.

energy expenditure rate is physical activity (typically accounting for 10 to 30 percent of total energy expenditure in most people). To maintain a healthy weight, a person's overall energy expenditure must offset energy intake. Labs evaluating energy expenditure and energy intake are available in other Concepts.

A basic understanding of your overall calorie needs is important for weight control. Calorie requirements are unique to each person and are influenced by your gender, age, body size, and physical activity level. A simple but crude estimate of basal metabolic rate (BMR) is about 10 calories per pound of body weight; so if you weighed 150 pounds, the contribution of your basal metabolism (as shown in Figure 1) would be approximately 1,500 calories. If you have a moderately active lifestyle, you can multiply your BMR by 1.75 to provide a reasonable estimate of your total daily energy expenditure. Using the example above, your total daily energy needs would be approximately 2,625 calories (i.e. $1,500 \times 1.75 = 2,625$). The World Health Organization refers to this multiplier value as a *"Physical Activity Level"* or PAL. Sedentary people typically have PAL values ranging from 1.4 to 1.7 while moderately active people might have PAL values ranging from 1.7 to 2.0. Your personal needs will depend on your actual activity level which can vary from day to day. This method is intended to just give you a basic estimate to guide weight control efforts. For example, you may think twice about that 1,000-calorie sandwich after realizing that it accounts for almost 40% of your daily calorie needs. To estimate your energy expenditure more precisely, refer to Lab 14C in the Concept on body composition.

Physical activity contributes to energy balance in a number of ways. By maintaining an active lifestyle, you can burn off extra calories, keep your body's metabolism high, and prevent the decline in basal metabolic rate that typically occurs with aging (due to reduced muscle mass). All types of physical activity from the physical activity pyramid can be beneficial to weight control. Moderate physical activity is especially effective because people of all ages and abilities can perform it. It can be maintained for long periods of time and results in significant calorie expenditure. Long-term studies show that 60 or more minutes of moderate activity such as walking is very effective for long-term weight loss and maintenance.

Vigorous physical activity can also be effective in maintaining or losing weight. For some people, especially older adults, vigorous activity may be more difficult to adhere to over a long time. However, for those who stick with it, vigorous activity expends more calories in a shorter time, and for this reason, it can be a very good way to expend calories. Research shows that bouts of vigorous physical activity can lead to increases in basal metabolic rate that persist throughout the day. Therefore, vigorous activity can contribute to additional energy expenditure after the workout is done. There is now considerable evidence showing that muscle fitness exercise also contributes to maintaining a healthy body weight. Muscle fitness exercise expends calories and increases muscle mass, leading to an increase in calories expended at rest. A recent study documented that resistance exercise was more important than aerobic exercise for avoiding progressive increases in abdominal obesity with age. Clearly, all forms of physical activity can contribute to long-term weight control.

The accumulation of light physical activity can help burn extra calories. Most of the emphasis thus far has been on moderate and vigorous forms of physical activity. The category of "light" physical activity falls between rest and moderate physical activity on the energy expenditure continuum (1.5 to 3 METs). Research indicates that light activities may help reduce risks associated with excessive time spent being sedentary (e.g., sitting). The accumulation of light activity can also contribute to weight control by burning more calories. As noted in an earlier Concept, the term *NEAT* (non-exercise activity thermogenesis) is often used to refer to the accumulation of activity from low-intensity movements throughout the day. Light activity may account for as little as 15 percent of total daily energy expenditure in sedentary people and up to 50 percent in people with more active jobs and lifestyles. The weight maintenance benefits of light or NEAT activity are greatest when the activities replace sedentary activities such as sitting (e.g., TV watching and computer use). To further take advantage of NEAT, many people have started using active workstations that allow them to walk slowly on a treadmill or lightly pedal a bike while working at a computer.

Awareness and dietary restraint are needed to avoid excess caloric intake. In our modern society, it is very easy for people to meet their daily energy needs. In fact, considerable willpower is needed to keep energy intake at a manageable level. Having an extra cookie or brownie for a snack may sound like a good idea until you realize you would need to possibly walk between one and two miles to burn it off. Foods high in empty calories are easily available and are frequent selections of college students, who may be responsible for their food selection or preparation for the first time in their lives. Sugar, especially from soft drinks, and beer add calories. Learning to make healthy choices and showing some restraint with food intake are important skills for long-term weight control.

Paying attention to appetite and hunger can help in weight control. The body has built-in regulatory systems that help in weight regulation. Hunger and appetite are the cues that should regulate calorie intake, but many people develop unhealthy habits and eat  when they are not hungry. For example, food is often consumed as a source of comfort when feeling sad, anxious, or bored. This has been termed "emotional eating" since the consumption of food is directly tied to our emotions. Recent research has shown that a number of other factors influence our appetite and our food intake. For example, studies demonstrate that lack of sleep can alter hormones that regulate appetite. These patterns have been implicated as contributing factors to weight gain, but causality can't be assumed. See A Closer Look for details.

A CLOSER LOOK

Does Lack of Sleep Cause Weight Gain?

Numerous reports have emphasized the importance of sleep for good health and wellness. Studies have also implicated a lack of sleep as a contributing factor to obesity. A variety of reasons have been proposed, but the leading explanation is that sleep deprivation may alter key hormones that regulate appetite. However, this doesn't necessarily mean that sleeping more will help you lose weight, as some media outlets have erroneously reported. A comprehensive review paper recently summarized the outcomes from multiple studies that experimentally manipulated sleep under controlled conditions. Interestingly, the results did not support a causal relationship between sleep duration and obesity-related factors. It is possible that the associations are caused by other factors, but it is also possible that the effects are too subtle to be detected in a simulated experimental protocol.

Do you think sleep patterns contribute to your own personal weight management efforts?

Confronting an Obesogenic Environment

An obesogenic environment makes it hard to maintain a healthy weight. Although traditional approaches to weight control have emphasized individual behaviors, public health leaders focus considerable energy on combating *obesogenic environments* that promote excessive eating and inactivity. A variety of social-ecological models have been proposed to summarize and study these environments. A simplified model is depicted in Figure 2 to show the various sectors and settings that shape our environment and ultimately our behavior. The essence of the model is that we are continually confronted with environments that make it easy to consume large quantities of energy-dense food and limit our physical activity. On the energy-intake side, we have easy access to large quantities of low-cost, highly palatable, high-calorie foods almost everywhere we go. The convenience and large portion sizes lead to increases in daily energy intake. On the energy expenditure side, we live in a world dominated by sedentary (computer-based) jobs and lifestyles dominated by automobiles and inactive recreation. These factors lead to reductions in daily energy expenditure. Small increases in energy intake combined with small decreases in energy expenditure lead to the storage of fat. While most people are aware of these general influences, they still find it hard to find ways to overcome them.

Societal changes are needed to create healthier environments. As shown in Figure 2, aspects of our

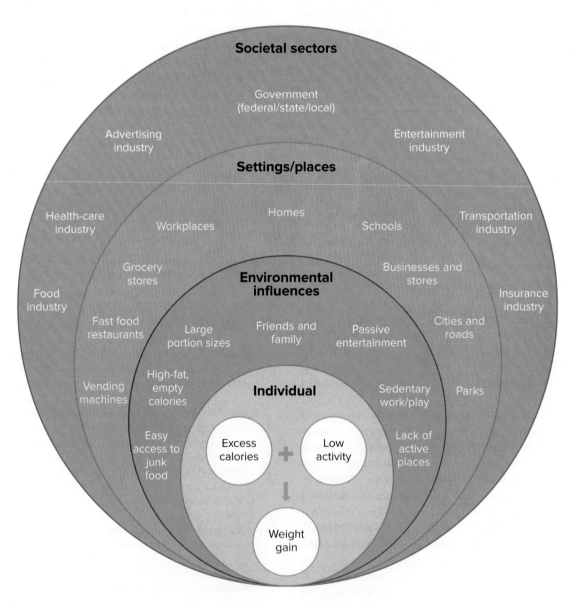

Figure 2 ▶ Social and environmental components of the obesogenic environment.

In the News

Taxes Aimed at Curbing Soft Drink Consumption

A common intervention strategy for obesity prevention is to "make the healthy choice the easy choice." However, policy-based approaches often focus on reducing visibility and increasing barriers to less desirable choices. For example, high taxes on cigarettes contributed to population declines in smoking. The same strategies are now being used to curb soft drink consumption. In Berkeley, California, a penny-per-ounce tax was imposed on sugar-sweetened beverages. This amounts to a 12-cent tax on a 12-ounce can and proportionally larger fees for larger drinks. A well-designed study reported a 21 percent drop in the consumption of soft drinks and other sugary beverages in Berkeley's low-income neighborhoods after this tax was imposed. Similar taxes are now in place in 20 major US cities. A nonprofit group called HealthFoodAmerica estimated that the change would cut diabetes rates by 6 percent in these communities, prevent nearly 115,000 of cases of obesity (out of the 15 million people influenced by the policy), and raise nearly $600 million in funding to go to other needs.

Do you support efforts to curb soft drink consumption with this type of policy-based approach? Why or why not?

environment are influenced by larger societal and economic forces. For example, it is unrealistic to expect changes in menu choices in a local fast food restaurant since it receives its food from the corporate supply chain, which in turn receives ingredients from other larger food conglomerates. To reverse the epidemic of obesity, experts contend that coordinated system-wide approaches are needed. Changes in policy and the business supply chain offer the most promise since they can impact other aspects of the environment. Examples of recent public policy changes that have potential for helping reduce overweight include:

- *Posting food values in restaurants.* New legislation requires chain restaurants to post calorie and other nutrition values for the foods they serve. The FDA also extended the labeling rules to vending machines. Posting food values has been shown to be effective in reducing calorie consumption in people eating at fast food restaurants.

- *Improving access to healthy food in schools.* Policy guidelines from the USDA and the Let's Move initiative improved quality and access to healthy school lunches, imposed restrictions on available foods in vending machines, and banned marketing of junk food in schools and on sports scoreboards. The updated nutrition standards have been implemented by more than 90 percent of schools. Results have shown promising increases in fruit and vegetable consumption with reduced food waste.

- *Implementing an empty-calorie tax (also called a fat tax).* There have been numerous calls and proposals for a tax on foods low in nutritional density, such as sweetened soft drinks, candy, and fast food. Advocates of this type of tax propose that the proceeds go to campaigns to improve nutrition and increase activity levels.

Public support is strong for many of these policies. However, some people argue that policy changes such as "soda taxes" or "fat taxes" infringe on personal liberties. Nevertheless, changes in public policy have resulted in major reductions in smoking and smoking-related deaths over the past 20 years, and experts feel that similar policy changes can decrease obesity in America and reduce associated medical costs. See In the News for details.

Being aware of environmental influences can help reduce risks of overeating. While it may be hard to change aspects of our obesogenic environment, you can exert control over your own environment. Research has suggested that the size of plates and the dimensions of glasses can influence how much we eat. In general, using smaller plates and drinking from taller glasses may trick our minds into thinking that we ate or drank more than we did. By better understanding cues that lead us to eat, we can set habits and create environments that help us eat less.

Guidelines for Losing Body Fat

Following appropriate weight loss guidelines is important for the best long-term results. Fat, weight, and body proportions are all factors that can be changed, but people often set goals that are impossible to achieve. Starting with small goals and aiming for reasonable rates of weight loss (1 to 2 pounds a week) are recommended. Setting unrealistic goals may result in eating disorders, failure to meet goals,

Table 1 ▶ Guidelines for Weight Loss-Common Questions

Questions	Recommendations
Who should consider weight loss?	Individuals with a BMI of >25 or in the marginal or overfat zone should consider reducing their body weight—especially if it is accompanied by abdominal obesity. Individuals with a BMI of >30 are encouraged to seek weight loss treatment.
What types of goals should be used?	Overweight and obese individuals should target reducing their body weight by a minimum of 5 to 10 percent and should aim to maintain this long-term weight loss.
What about maintenance?	Individuals should strive for long-term weight maintenance and the prevention of weight regain over the long term, especially when weight loss is not desired or when attainment of ideal body weight is not achievable.
What should be targeted in a program?	Weight loss programs should target both eating and exercise behaviors, as sustained changes in both behaviors have been associated with significant long-term weight loss.
How should diet be changed?	Overweight and obese individuals should reduce their current intake by 500–1,000 kcal/day to achieve weight loss (<30 percent of calories from fat). Individualized levels of caloric intake should be established to prevent weight regain after initial loss.
How should activity be changed?	Overweight and obese individuals should progressively increase to a minimum of 150 minutes of moderate-intensity physical activity per week for health benefits. However, for long-term weight loss, the program should progress to higher amounts of activity (e.g., 200–300 minutes per week or >2,000 kcal/week).
What about resistance exercise?	Resistance exercise should supplement the endurance exercise program for individuals undertaking modest reductions in energy intake to lose weight.
What about using drugs for weight loss?	Pharmacotherapy (medicine/drugs) for weight loss should be used only by individuals with a BMI >30 or those with excessive body fatness. Weight loss medications should be used only in combination with a strong behavioral intervention that focuses on modifying eating and exercise behaviors.

Source: American College of Sports Medicine.

or failure to maintain weight loss over time. Table 1 provides a summary of weight loss guidelines from the American College of Sports Medicine.

Behavioral goals are more effective than outcome goals. Many people make weight loss goals based on the amount of weight they want to lose or the size they want to attain. However, focusing only on **outcome goals** can lead to frustration if the targets aren't achieved as quickly as hoped. A focus on **behavioral goals** is more effective since it is within your control. By targeting specific diet changes or setting specific goals for physical activity, you will have better long-term success, even if the outcome goal of weight loss comes at a slower rate than desired.

A combination of physical activity and a healthy, low-calorie diet is the best approach for long-term weight control. The most effective diet for fat loss is a low-calorie diet that you can stick with over time. Reduced-calorie diets result in meaningful weight loss, regardless of the composition of the diet (e.g., carbohydrates, fats, proteins). Diets high in grains, fruits, and vegetables are generally recommended because they are typically low in calories

 **HELP** Health is available to Everyone for a Lifetime, and it's Personal

What Is the Secret for Long-Term Weight Control?

The National Weight Control Registry (NWCR) has tracked behaviors and outcomes for more than 10,000 people who have lost significant amounts of weight—and have kept it off. Insights from NWCR annual surveys are used to identify key strategies used by those people who have been successful in maintaining their weight loss. While there are a variety of reported strategies, most success stories include a low-calorie, low-fat diet and a high amount of physical activity. Approximately 78 percent eat breakfast every day, 75 percent weigh themselves at least once a week, 62 percent watch less than 10 hours of TV per week, and 90 percent exercise, on average, about 1 hour per day. Search "National Weight Control Registry" online to learn more.

What strategies do you find most helpful for maintaining a healthy weight?

 connect ACTIVITY

An active, healthy lifestyle is critical for long-term weight control.
©Fancy Collection/SuperStock

and easy to maintain over time. Research also clearly indicates that regular exercise is crucial to long-term fat loss. Weight loss programs that do not include physical activity are likely to fail.

A major advantage of physical activity in a weight loss program is that it can help maintain basal metabolic rate and prevent the decline that occurs with calorie sparing. Studies have shown that programs that include physical activity promote greater loss of body fat than programs based solely on dietary changes. The total weight loss from the programs may be about the same, but a larger fraction of the weight comes from fat when physical activity is included. In contrast, programs based solely on diet result in greater loss of lean muscle tissue. A healthy diet and regular physical activity are both essential for long-term weight control. Small changes, such as eating a few hundred calories less per day or walking for 30 minutes every day, can make a big difference over time. The important point is to strive for permanent changes that can be maintained in a normal daily lifestyle (see Table 1).

Making minor changes in eating patterns can have major benefits. Evidence suggests that small restrictions in caloric intake sustained over time are more effective than drastic short-term changes. This is likely because they can more easily be incorporated into your lifestyle. Other simple and effective changes in eating patterns are listed below:

- *Eat breakfast every day.* Studies show that skipping breakfast is associated with an increased risk of obesity.
- *Consider eating smaller and more frequent meals in a day.* A common strategy in guided weight loss programs is to consume healthy, high-protein snacks to help curb hunger and excess consumption at meals.
- *Eat less fat.* Research shows that a reduction of fat in the diet results not only in fewer calories consumed (fats have more than twice the calories per gram as carbohydrates or proteins) but also in greater body fat loss as well.
- *Increase water consumption.* Drinking more water can help curb your appetite while also helping minimize consumption of sweetened, calorie-laden beverages.
- *Restrict consumption of* **empty calories.** Foods that provide little nutrition often account for an excessive proportion of daily caloric intake. Examples of these foods are candy (often high in simple sugar) and potato chips (often fried in saturated fat).
- *Increase complex carbohydrates.* Foods high in fiber, such as fresh fruits and vegetables, contain few calories for their volume. They are nutritious and filling, and they are especially good foods for a fat loss program.

Make good choices when purchasing, selecting, and preparing food. It has been estimated that we each make over 200 food decisions in a given day. Making good food choices is generally easier at home than when eating at restaurants, at work, or on special occasions. Table 2 provides guidelines for making good selections when purchasing and preparing food at home as well as when you are away from home. Following are some specific steps you can take to improve your eating habits.

VIDEO 4

> **Outcome Goal** Statement of intent to achieve a specific test score or a specific standard associated with good health or wellness—for example, "I will lower my body fat level by 3 percent."
>
> **Behavioral Goal** Statement of intent to perform a specific behavior (changing a lifestyle) for a specific period of time—for example, "I will reduce the calories in my diet by 200 a day for the next 4 weeks."
>
> **Empty Calories** Calories in foods considered to have little or no nutritional value.

Table 2 ▶ Guidelines for Healthy Shopping and Eating in a Variety of Settings	
Guidelines for Shopping	• Shop from a list to avoid purchasing foods that contain empty calories and other foods that will tempt you to overeat. • Shop with a friend to avoid buying unneeded foods. For this technique to work, the other person must be sensitive to your goals. In some cases, a friend can have a bad, rather than a good, influence. • Shop on a full stomach to avoid the temptations of snacking on and buying junk food. • Check labels to avoid foods that are excessively high in fat or saturated fat.
Guidelines for How You Eat	• When you eat, do nothing else but eat. If you watch television, read, or do some other activity while you eat, you may be unaware of what you have eaten. • Eat slowly. Taste your food. Pause between bites. Chew slowly. Do not take the next bite until you have swallowed what you have in your mouth. Periodically take a longer pause. Be the last one finished eating. • Do not eat food you do not want. Some people do not want to waste food, so they clean their plate even when they feel full. • Follow an eating schedule. Eating at regular meal times can help you avoid snacking. Spacing meals equally throughout the day can help reduce appetite. • Leave the table after eating to avoid taking extra, unwanted bites and servings. • Eat meals of equal size. Some people try to restrict calories at one or two meals to save up for a big meal. • Eating several *small* meals helps you avoid hunger (fools the appetite), and this may help prevent overeating. • Avoid second servings. Limit your intake to one moderate serving. If second servings are taken, make them one-half the size of first servings. • Limit servings of salad dressings and condiments (e.g., catsup). These are often high in fat and sugar and can amount to greater caloric consumption than expected.
Guidelines for Controlling the Home Environment	• Store food out of sight. Avoid containers that allow you to see food. Limit the accessibility of foods that tempt you and foods with empty calories. Foods that are out of sight are out of mouth. • Do your eating in designated areas only, such as the kitchen and dining room, so you do not snack elsewhere. It is especially easy to eat too much while watching television. • If you snack, eat foods high in complex carbohydrates and low in fats, such as fresh fruits and carrot sticks. • Freeze leftovers so that it takes preparation to eat them, helping you avoid temptation.
Guidelines for Controlling the Work Environment	• Bring food from home rather than eating from vending machines or catering trucks. • Do not eat while working and take your lunch as a break. Do something active during breaks, such as taking a walk. • Avoid food provided by coworkers, such as snacks in work rooms, birthday cakes, or candy. • Have drinking water or low-calorie drinks available to substitute for snacks.
Guidelines for Eating on Special Occasions	• Practice ways to refuse food. Knowing exactly what to say will help you avoid being talked into eating something you do not want. • Eat before you go out, so you are not as hungry at parties and events. • Do not stand near food sources, and distract yourself if tempted to eat when you are not really hungry. • Limit servings of nonbasic parts of the meal, such as alcohol, soft drinks, appetizers, and desserts.
Guidelines for Eating at Restaurants	• Make healthy selections from the menu. Choose chicken without skin, fish, or lean cuts of meat. Grilled or broiled options are better than fried. Choose healthier options for dessert, as many decadent desserts can have more calories than the whole dinner. • Ask for the condiments (e.g., butter, mayonnaise, salad dressings) on the side, allowing you to determine how much to put on. • Do not feel compelled to eat everything on your plate. Many restaurants serve exceptionally large portions to try to please the customers. • Ask for a to-go box to divide big portions before eating. • Order à la carte rather than full meals to avoid multiple courses and servings. • Avoid supersizing your meals if eating at fast food restaurants, as this can add unwanted calories. Opt for the child-sized meal if possible.

Facts about Fad Diets and Clinical Approaches to Weight Loss

Fad diets and extreme diets are not likely to be effective. Consumers are barraged with products and advertisements that claim easy weight loss solutions. Various fad diets capitalize on the consumer's concern about weight and a general lack of knowledge about diet and exercise. Fad diets often take some small fact about nutrition and claim they have uncovered a magic solution to weight loss that wasn't previously known. Consumers often believe the claims because they have a history of failing with past efforts to control their weight.

A common strategy in some fad diets is to restrict carbohydrates. Because water is required to store carbohydrates, reductions in carbohydrate intake leads to reductions in water storage—and weight. The person who restricts carbohydrates may see a reduction in "weight" (not fat!) and assume the diet worked when it didn't. Regardless of

the approach, fad diets provide little hope since they typically can't be maintained over time. Constant losing and gaining, known as "yo-yo" dieting, is counterproductive and may lead to negative changes in the person's metabolism and unwanted shifts in sites of fat deposition.

Avoid diets that require severe caloric restriction and exercise programs that require exceptionally large caloric expenditure. These plans can be effective in fat loss over a short period but are seldom maintained for a lifetime. Studies show that extreme programs for weight control, designed to "take it off fast," result in long-term success rates of less than 5 percent. One reason extremely low-calorie diets are ineffective is that they may promote "calorie sparing." When caloric intake is 800 to 1,000 or less, the body protects itself by reducing basal and resting metabolism levels (sparing calories). This results in less fat loss, even though the caloric intake is very low. When in doubt, avoid programs that promise fast and easy solutions, extreme diets that favor specific foods or eating patterns, and any product that makes unreasonable claims about easy ways to stimulate your metabolism or "melt away fat." The benefits of sensible, lifestyle-based weight loss programs were documented in a recent comparison of randomized controlled trials of commercial programs. Weight Watchers and Jenny Craig programs yielded the strongest long-term effects.

Artificial sweeteners and fat substitutes do not provide a long-term weight loss solution. Artificial sweeteners are frequently used in soft drinks and food to reduce the calorie content. Because they have few or no calories, these supplements were originally expected to help people with weight control. However, since they were introduced, the general public has not eaten fewer calories and more people are now overweight than before. People consuming these products end up consuming just as many calories per day as people consuming products with real sugar or sweeteners. Similar conclusions have been reached with the use of fat substitutes in foods. These findings reinforce the recommendations in the dietary guidelines that emphasize replacing unhealthy foods with healthier choices (rather than seeking alternative versions with artificial sweeteners or fats).

A variety of appetite suppressants are available, but all of them have limitations. Because long-term weight control is difficult, many individuals seek simple solutions from various nonprescription weight loss products. Many negative reactions and multiple deaths have been attributed to the use of ephedra, and this led the FDA to ban the sale and use of any products containing this compound. A concern among public health officials is that many supplement products are still not labeled accurately. Manufacturers of supplements have recently started selling "ephedra-free" supplements that use other stimulants, but these have been shown to present similar health risks. Consumers should be wary of dietary supplements, due to the unregulated nature of the industry.

Planning ahead for healthy lunches can improve your diet.
©Onoky/SuperStock

A number of prescription drugs have been approved by the FDA for treatment of obesity, but long-term effects aren't known. The various drugs approved for supervised weight loss work in different ways, so it is important to know mechanisms and side effects. Orlistat (used in prescription Xenical and over-the-counter Alli) enhances weight loss by inhibiting the body's absorption of fat. Studies have confirmed that it can help patients lose more weight, but it also blocks the absorption of fat-soluble vitamins. Drugs such as Belviq, Qsymia, and phentermine suppress hunger, whereas others such as Saxenda increase feelings of fullness. The long-term effects of most drugs are not known, and it is noteworthy that earlier drugs such as sibutramine (Meridia) have been pulled from the market. All of the approved prescription medications are considered to be adjuncts to lifestyle modification and are designed for use only by obese patients or overweight adults with other comorbidities.

Using Self-Management Skills

Overcome barriers to weight loss by adopting new ways of thinking about food, eating, and weight control. Although many people struggle with weight control, some of the challenges are self-imposed. By changing your perspectives about food and eating, you can be more successful.

- *View the word* diet *from a lifestyle perspective.* The word *diet* has negative connotations that typically imply caloric restriction and suffering. Avoid thinking of a diet as something temporary that you go "on," since the only place to go is "off." Instead, view your "diet" as a healthy pattern of eating that you possess and live daily.

- *Learn the difference between craving and hunger.* Hunger is a physiological signal that helps promote an organism's drive to eat when energy supply gets low. A craving is simply a desire to eat something, often a food that is sweet or high in calories. When you feel the urge to eat, ask yourself, "Is this real hunger or a craving?"

- *Change your relationship with food.* Too often people consume food simply because it tastes good. While eating is an important part of our culture and a pleasurable experience, it may help to view food primarily for what it provides: sustenance and energy for healthy living.

Technology Update

Can Smartphone Apps Help with Weight Control?

Learning restraint is difficult when confronted with many tempting food options (both at grocery stores and restaurants). New labeling laws will help consumers be more aware of calories of foods, but each person must ultimately learn to make good choices and to balance their caloric intake with caloric expenditure. Many consumer activity monitors contain associated tools or apps to enable people to track energy balance. There are also numerous individual apps on smartphones that can help you make smart choices.

Do you find this type of dietary tracking to be essential, somewhat important, or not helpful at all?

Build and engage your social support network to reinforce behavior change and long-term weight control. Family and friends can help you adopt and maintain healthy eating practices and participate in regular physical activity. However, it is important to ensure that they provide the type of support that you need. Sometimes, friends and family can intervene too much, resulting in the opposite effect if it is perceived as an attempt to control your behavior. Therefore, engage your social support network in ways that reinforce and support your behavior rather that control it.

Adopt relapse prevention strategies to address minor set-backs. It is common for moods and motivations to cycle during efforts to lose weight. Some people become too compulsive in their behaviors and then over-react if they experience a minor setback or revert back to their old ways. For example, giving in and having a dessert or treat can lead some to go completely off their weight loss plan. Don't let one setback lead to relapse. Instead, view it as a minor setback and then get back to your efforts. Long-term weight control requires a lifetime commitment to healthy lifestyles. By following established principles of relapse prevention, you will be better prepared to get back on track.

Strategies for Action: Lab Information

Knowing guidelines for controlling body fat is not as important as following them. The guidelines in this Concept work only if you use them. In Lab 16A, you will identify guidelines that may help you in the future.

Record keeping is important in meeting fat control goals and making moderation a part of your normal lifestyle. It is easy to fool yourself when determining the amount of food you have

eaten or the amount of exercise you have done. Once fat control goals have been set, whether for weight loss, maintenance, or gain, keeping a diet log and an exercise log can help you monitor your behavior and maintain the lifestyle necessary to meet your goals. A log can also help you monitor changes in weight and body fat levels. But remember, avoid too much emphasis on short-term weight changes. Lab 16B will help you learn about the actual content of fast foods, so you can learn to make better choices when eating out.

Suggested Resources and Readings

The websites for the following sources can be accessed by searching online for the organization, program, or title listed. Specific scientific references are available at the end of this edition of *Concepts of Fitness and Wellness.*

- Academy of Nutrition and Dietetics. www.eatright.org.
- Center for Mindful Eating. www.tcme.org.
- Healthy Food America. http://www.healthyfoodamerica.org/.
- Medscape. Implications of New Guidelines for Weight Loss.
- Mindless Eating. http://mindlesseating.org.
- USDA Food and Nutrition Information Center. www.nal.usda.gov/fnic.
- U.S. Food and Drug Administration. Regulations about Restaurant and Vending Machine Labels.

Lab 16A Selecting Strategies for Managing Eating

Name	Section	Date

Purpose: To learn to select strategies for managing eating to control body fatness.

Procedures

1. Read the strategies listed in Chart 1.
2. Check the box beside 5 to 10 of the strategies that you think will be most useful for you.
3. Answer the questions in the Conclusions and Implications section.

Chart 1 Strategies for Managing Eating to Control Body Fatness

✔	Check 5 to 10 strategies that you might use in the future.
	Shopping Strategies
	Shop from a list.
	Shop with a friend.
	Shop on a full stomach.
	Check food labels.
	Consider foods that take some time to prepare.
	Methods of Eating
	When you eat, do nothing but eat. Don't watch television or read.
	Eat slowly.
	Do not eat food you do not want.
	Follow an eating schedule.
	Do your eating in designated areas, such as kitchen or dining room only.
	Leave the table after eating.
	Avoid second servings.
	Limit servings of condiments.
	Limit servings of nonbasics, such as dessert, breads, and soft drinks.
	Eat several meals of equal size rather than one big meal and two small ones.
	Eating in the Work Environment
	Bring your own food to work.
	Avoid snack machines.
	If you eat out, plan your meal ahead of time.
	Do not eat while working.
	Avoid sharing foods from coworkers, such as birthday cakes.
	Have activity breaks during the day.
	Have water available to substitute for soft drinks.
	Have low-calorie snacks to substitute for office snacks.

✔	Check 5 to 10 strategies that you might use in the future.
	Eating on Special Occasions
	Practice ways to refuse food.
	Avoid tempting situations.
	Eat before you go out.
	Don't stand near food sources.
	If you feel the urge to eat, find someone to talk to.
	Strategies for Eating Out
	Limit deep-fat fried foods.
	Ask for information about food content.
	Limit use of condiments.
	Choose low-fat foods (e.g., skim milk, low-fat yogurt).
	Choose chicken, fish, or lean meat.
	Order à la carte.
	Ask early for a to-go box and divide portions.
	If you eat desserts, avoid those with sauces or toppings.
	Eating at Home
	Keep busy at times when you are at risk of overeating.
	Store food out of sight.
	Avoid serving food to others between meals.
	If you snack, choose snacks with complex carbohydrates, such as carrot sticks or apple slices.
	Freeze leftovers to avoid the temptation of eating them between meals.

Conclusions and Implications

1. In several sentences, discuss your need to use strategies for effective eating. Do you need to use them? Why or why not?

2. In several sentences, discuss the effectiveness of the strategies contained in Chart 1. Do you think they can be effective for people who have a problem controlling their body fatness?

3. In several sentences, discuss the value of using behavioral goals versus outcome goals when planning for fat loss.

Lab 16B Evaluating Fast Food Options

Name	Section	Date

Purpose: To learn about the energy and fat content of fast food and how to make better choices when eating at fast food restaurants.

Procedures

1. Select a fast food restaurant and a typical meal that you might order. Then use an online food calculator to determine total calories, fat calories, saturated fat intake, and cholesterol for each food item.
2. Record the values in Chart 2.
3. Sum the totals for the meal in Chart 2.
4. Record recommended daily values by selecting an amount from Chart 1. The estimate should be based on your estimated needs for the day.
5. Compute the percentage of the daily recommended amounts that you consume in the meal by dividing recommended amounts (step 4) into meal totals (step 3). Record the percentage of recommended daily amounts in Chart 2.
6. Answer the questions in the Conclusions and Implications section.

Chart 1 Recommended Daily Amounts of Fat, Saturated Fat, Cholesterol, and Sodium

	2,000 kcal	3,000 kcal
Total fat	65 g	97.5 g
Saturated fat	20 g	30 g
Cholesterol	300 mg	450 mg
Sodium	2,400 mg	3,600 g

Results

Chart 2 Listing of Foods Selected for the Meal

Food Item	Total Calories	Total Fat (g)	Saturated Fat (g)	Cholesterol (mg)
1.				
2.				
3.				
4.				
5.				
6.				
Total for meal (sum each column)				
Recommended daily amount (record your values from Chart 1)				
Calculate % of recommended daily amount (record your calculated %)				

Consult an online fast food calculator to estimate calorie content of menu choices (see www.fastfoodnutrition.org). Calorie and nutrient information is also available in NutritionCalc Plus, a diet analysis tool available in Connect. Launch it by clicking the NutritionCalc Plus link on the Resources list on your Connect class home page.

Conclusions and Implications

1. Describe how often you eat at fast food restaurants and indicate whether you would like to reduce how much fast food you consume.

2. Were you surprised at the amount of fat, saturated fat, and cholesterol in the meal you selected?

3. What could you do differently at fast food restaurants to reduce your intake of fat, saturated fat, and cholesterol?

Stress and Health

LEARNING OBJECTIVES

After completing the study of this Concept, you will be able to:

▶ Identify major sources and types of stress.

▶ Explain the major body responses to stress.

▶ Understand the function of the autonomic nervous system and the HPA axis.

▶ Identify common physical, emotional, and behavioral consequences of stress.

▶ Understand individual differences in both physiological reactivity and appraisals of stressful events.

▶ Describe personal characteristics that influence consequences of stress.

▶ Identify personal sources of stress and your approaches for dealing with stressful life events.

Stress can motivate us to succeed, but it can also overwhelm us and lead to physical and emotional health problems. Understanding personal sources of stress and our unique stress response can help facilitate optimal health.

©dolgachov/123RF

Why it Matters!

Stress affects everyone to some degree. Approximately 75 percent of adults say they have experienced moderate to high levels of stress in the past month, and nearly half report that their level of stress has increased in the past year. This Concept will help you understand the causes and consequences of stress in your life. You will learn about common stressors and the physiological responses to stress. You will also gain a deeper appreciation about the impact of stress on both physical and mental health. Finally, you will gain insights about individual differences in responses to stress and the implications for health and wellness. Having knowledge of the effects of stress can help you adapt, and in some cases, use stressful situations to enhance healthy living.

Sources of Stress

It is important to understand the difference between stress and stressors. **Stress** is defined in this book as a nonspecific response of the body that helps the body maintain equilibrium in response to any demand. **Stressors** are things that cause stress. Stress can be motivating or debilitating. Stressors—those that evoke a stress reaction—come in many forms, and both positive and negative life events can increase our stress levels.

The first step in managing stress is to recognize the causes and to be aware of the symptoms. Identify the factors in your life that make you feel "stressed out." Everything from minor irritations, such as traffic jams, to major life changes, such as births, deaths, or job loss, can be a stressor. A stress overload of too many demands on your time can make you feel that you are no longer in control. Recognizing the causes and effects of stress is important for learning how to manage it.

Stress has a variety of sources. There are many kinds of stressors. Environmental stressors include heat, noise, overcrowding, pollution, and secondhand smoke. Physiological stressors are such things as drugs, caffeine, tobacco, injury, infection or disease, and physical effort.

Emotional stressors are the most frequent and important stressors. Some people refer to these as *psychosocial stressors.* A national study of daily experiences indicated that more than 60 percent of all stressful experiences fall into a few areas (see Table 1).

Stressors vary in severity. Major stressors create major emotional turmoil or require tremendous amounts of adjustment. This category includes personal crises (e.g., major health problems or death in the family, divorce/separation,

Table 1 ▶ Ten Common Stressors in the Lives of College Students and Middle-Aged Adults

College Students	Middle-Aged Adults
1. Troubling thoughts about the future	1. Concerns about weight
2. Not getting enough sleep	2. Health of a family member
3. Wasting time	3. Rising prices of common goods
4. Inconsiderate smokers	4. Home maintenance (interior)
5. Physical appearance	5. Too many things to do
6. Too many things to do	6. Misplacing or losing things
7. Misplacing or losing things	7. Yard work or outside home maintenance
8. Not enough time to do the things you need to do	8. Property, investments, or taxes
9. Concerns about meeting high standards	9. Crime
10. Being lonely	10. Physical appearance

Source: Kanner et al.

financial problems, legal problems) and job/school-related pressures or major age-related transitions (e.g., college, marriage, career, retirement). Daily hassles are generally viewed as shorter term or less severe. This category includes events such as traffic problems, peer/work relations, time pressures, and family conflict. In school, pressures such as grades, term papers, and oral presentations would likely fall into this category. Major stressors can alter daily patterns of stress and impair our ability to handle the minor stressors of life, while daily hassles can accumulate and create more significant problems. It is important to be aware of both types of stressors.

Negative, ambiguous, and uncontrollable events are usually the most stressful. Although stress can come from both positive and negative events, negative ones generally cause more distress because negative stressors usually have harsher consequences and little benefit. Positive stressors, on the other hand, usually have enough benefit to make them worthwhile. For example, the stress of starting a new job may be tremendous, but it is not as bad as the negative stress from losing a job.

Ambiguous stressors are harder to accept than more clearly defined problems. In most cases, if the cause of a stressor or problem can be identified, measures can be taken to improve the situation. For example, if you are stressed about a project at work or school, you can use specific strategies to complete the task on time. Stress brought on by a relationship with friends or coworkers, on the other hand, may be harder to understand. In some cases, it is not possible to determine the primary source or cause of the problem. These situations are more problematic because fewer clear-cut solutions exist. Another factor that makes events stressful is a lack of control. When little can be done to change the situation, we feel powerless.

Stress in Contemporary Society

Americans report high levels of stress. The American Psychological Association (APA) commissions an annual survey (Stress in America) to monitor perceptions of stress in the United States. Although results from this national survey indicate that population levels of stress have decreased in the past eight years, adults continue to report overall levels of stress that they believe are unhealthy, and 29 percent of adults reported increased stress in the past five years, compared to only 18 percent who reported a decrease. Money, work, and the economy continue to be the biggest sources of stress, and the most common symptoms include irritability/anger, feeling nervous or anxious, and lack of interest/motivation. Although the majority of adults recognize that stress management is important, most do not believe they are managing their stress well.

The sources and consequences of stress are similar for men and women, but there are also some important gender differences. Women tend to report higher levels of stress, but they also tend to engage more actively in stress management. In the APA's annual reports, men tend to report less concern about managing stress and are more likely than women to say that they are doing enough to manage their stress. Women, in contrast, tend to report that they feel they are not doing enough despite engaging in more active efforts to cope.

College presents unique challenges and stressors. Although the college years are often thought of as a break from the stresses of the real world, college life has its own stressors. Students are often living independently of family for the first time and face new responsibilities with managing time, money, relationships, and their lifestyles. Unique social pressures evolve through new relationships with roommates, dating partners, friends, and classmates. Academic pressures include keeping up with homework, taking exams, speaking in public, and becoming comfortable with talking to professors. The freedom and autonomy of college life can be empowering and enjoyable, but it also presents additional sources of stress.

In addition to the traditional challenges of college, the new generation of students faces stressors that were not typical for college students in the past. More students now work, and many go back to school after spending time in

Daily hassles can contribute to stress.
©Image Source, all rights reserved.

the working world. According to the U.S. Bureau of Labor Statistics, among high school graduates, 31 percent of those enrolling in college full time also participated in the workforce, with a rate of 74 percent among part-time students. More of today's college students are the first in their family to attend college. Perhaps as a result of some of these factors and the pressures that they create, rates of mental health problems among college students have increased dramatically in recent years. In a survey of campus counseling center directors, 94 percent of respondents indicated that they believed that more students today have severe psychological problems. This impression is substantiated by the 17 percent increase in student use of psychiatric medications since the the 1990s. Student surveys paint a similar picture. For example, a survey of college students found that, at some time in the past year, 54 percent felt overwhelming anxiety, and 33 percent felt so depressed that it was difficult to function. Independent of college issues, evidence suggests that Millennials and Gen Xers have higher levels of reported stress than other age groups (see Figure 1).

Stress The nonspecific response (generalized adaptation) of the body to any demand made on it in order to maintain physiological equilibrium. This positive or negative response results from emotions that are accompanied by biochemical and physiological changes directed at adaptation.

Stressors Things that place a greater than routine demand on the body or evoke a stress reaction.

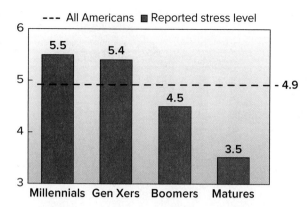

Figure 1 ▶ Reported stress levels by generation.

Source: American Psychological Association

Some sources of stress are shared by entire communities, cultures, or societies. Although the stressors that individuals experience are often unique to their particular circumstances, there are times when entire communities, cultures, or even countries have shared experiences of severe stress. Economic challenges and terrorism can create pressures and stress felt by the entire country. Annual polls such as the Gallup Healthways poll have documented population declines in well-being that correspond with past economic downturns. These patterns document the pervasive and systemic influences of stress on society.

Experiences of discrimination are a significant source of stress. In a meta-analysis of 134 previous studies, researchers found that higher levels of perceived discrimination were associated with both negative physical and psychological health outcomes. Perceived discrimination was also associated with more negative physiological and psychological stress responses, more negative health behaviors (e.g., smoking), and fewer positive health behaviors (e.g., exercise). With respect to physiological response, a study of White and African American women found that higher levels of perceived discrimination were associated with higher levels of visceral fat, a known risk factor for cardiovascular disease. Regarding health risk behaviors, a study of college students found that students who reported more discrimination experiences had more negative moods, were more likely to drink as a way to cope with negative emotions, and were more likely to be heavy drinkers. These findings were consistent across various sub-groups (race/ethnicity, gender, weight, sexual orientation).

Social media and technology keep us connected, but they may also create stress. Advances in technology have changed the way we communicate and connect. This is especially true for young adults as reports suggest that nearly 90 percent own and actively use smartphones. Although smartphones may facilitate organization and time management, excessive use may negatively impact well-being. One recent study found that the more time people spend on their smartphones, the higher their levels of stress. Excessive use in the evenings may be particularly harmful. A study of business managers found that late-night use of smartphones for business purposes was associated with poor sleep quality and quantity and reduced work performance the following day. A study of college students similarly found that those who texted more on their smartphones took longer to fall asleep, got fewer hours of sleep, and reported feeling more tired the following day. (See In the News for a related story.)

HELP Health is available to Everyone for a Lifetime, and it's Personal

Teens and Young Adults Report High Levels of Stress

Although teens and young adults say they are less concerned about the physical and mental health consequences of stress than adults, they report having stress levels that meet or exceed those of older adults—far exceeding what they believe is healthy. Only about half are confident in their ability to manage stress. Millennials report the highest levels of stress, followed by Generation Xers. Millennials also report greater negative effects of stress on health and tend to engage in more sedentary approaches for managing stress, including listening to music, playing video games, and surfing the Internet.

Do you think that you and your friends experience more stress than your parents' generation? What are the sources of stress that are unique to your generation?

Smartphones can keep us connected, but they can also detract from "real" communication.
©Ariel Skelley/Blend Images LLC

Reactions to Stress

All people have a general reaction to stress. In the early 1900s, Walter Cannon identified the fight-or-flight response to threat. According to his model, the body reacts to a threat by preparing either to fight or flee the situation. The body prepares for either option through the activation of the **sympathetic nervous system (SNS).** When the SNS is activated, epinephrine (adrenaline) and norepinephrine are released to focus attention on the task at hand. Heart rate and blood pres- sure increase to deliver oxygen to the muscles and essential organs, the eyes take in more light to increase visual acuity, and more sugar is released into the bloodstream to increase energy level. At the same time, nonessential functions like di- gestion and urine production are slowed. Once the immediate threat has passed, the **parasympathetic nervous system (PNS)** takes over in an attempt to restore the body to homeostasis and conserve resources. The PNS largely reverses the changes initiated by the SNS (e.g., slows heart rate and returns blood from the muscles and essential organs to the periphery).

Sometimes the fight-or-flight, or SNS, response is essen- tial to survival, but when invoked inappropriately or exces- sively it may be more harmful than the effects of the original stressor. Hans Selye, another prominent scientist, was the first to recognize the potential negative consequences of this response. Selye suggested that this system could be invoked by mental as well as physical threats and that the short-term benefits might lead to long-term negative consequences. Based on these ideas, Selye described the general adaptation syndrome, which explains how the autonomic nervous sys- tem reacts to stressful situations and the conditions under which the system may break down (see Figure 2). The term *general* highlights the similarities in response to stressful situ- ations across individuals. Selye's work led him to be referred to as the "father of stress."

The hypothalamic-pituitary-adrenal (HPA) axis plays a key role in the stress response. The chronic activation of the SNS has an influence on the development of physical

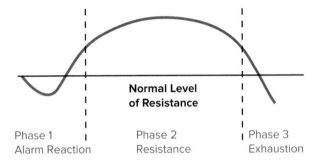

Phase 1: Alarm Reaction
Any physical or mental trauma triggers an immediate set of reactions that combat the stress. Because the immune system is initially depressed, normal levels of resistance are lowered, making us more susceptible to infection and disease. If the stress is not severe or long-lasting, we bounce back and recover rapidly.

Phase 2: Resistance
Eventually, sometimes rather quickly, we adapt to stress, and we tend to become more resistant to illness and disease. The immune system works overtime during this period, keeping up with the demands placed on it.

Phase 3: Exhaustion
Because the body is not able to maintain homeostasis and the long-term resistance needed to combat stress, we invariably experience a drop in resistance level. No one experiences the same resistance and tolerance to stress, but everyone's immunity at some point collapses following prolonged stress reactions.

Figure 2 ▶ Phases and depiction of the general adaptation syndrome.

Sympathetic Nervous System (SNS) The component of the autonomic nervous system that responds to stressful situa- tions by initiating the fight-or-flight response.

Parasympathetic Nervous System (PNS) The component of the autonomic nervous system that helps bring the body to a resting state following stressful experiences.

disease, but negative impacts on health are influenced mainly by a system known as the hypothalamic-pituitary-adrenal (HPA) axis. The HPA axis is activated during stress, leading to the release of corticotropin-releasing hormone (CRH) and secondary activation of the pituitary gland. The pituitary releases a chemical called adrenocorticotropic hormone (ACTH), which ultimately causes the release of an active stress hormone called cortisol. With chronic exposure to stress, the HPA system can become dysregulated, and both over- and underactivation of the system are associated with risk for negative health outcomes.

Stress Effects on Health and Wellness

Excessive stress has a negative impact on health. Moderate stress can motivate us to reach our goals and keep life interesting. However, when stressors are severe or chronic, our bodies may not be able to adapt successfully. Stress beyond the limits of **adaptation** can compromise immune functioning, leading to a host of diseases. In fact, stress has been linked to between 50 and 70 percent of all illnesses. Further, stress is associated with negative health behaviors, such as alcohol and other drug use, and to psychological problems, such as depression and anxiety.

Stress affects immune function and physical health. In addition to preparing the body for fight or flight, the stress-related activation of the SNS and the HPA axis slows down the functioning of the immune response. In the face of an immediate threat, mobilizing resources that will help in the moment is more important to the body than preventing or fighting infection. If the stress response is chronically activated, high levels of adrenaline and cortisol continue to tell the body to mobilize resources at the expense of immune functioning. This contributes to the tendency for people to become sick after experiencing high levels of stress.

Stress can lead to fatigue and can cause or exacerbate a variety of health problems. Exposure to chronic stress or repeated exposure to acute stress may lead to a state of fatigue. Fatigue may result from lack of sleep, emotional strain, pain, disease, or a combination of these factors. Both **physiological fatigue** and **psychological fatigue** can result in a state of exhaustion, with resultant physical and mental health consequences. Chronic stress has been linked to health maladies that plague individuals on a daily basis, such as headaches, indigestion, insomnia, and the common cold. In fact, one study concluded that *"out-of-control"* stress is the leading preventable source of increased health-care costs in the workforce, roughly equivalent to the costs of the health problems related to smoking.

The effects of stress on health are not limited to minor physical complaints. Compelling evidence links psychological stress to a host of serious health problems, including cardiovascular disease, cancer, and HIV/AIDS. Stress may also increase the risk for upper respiratory tract infections, asthma, herpes, viral infections, autoimmune diseases, and slow wound healing. Reduced immune function due to negative emotions and stress appears to be a principal reason for these health problems. Stress may also increase the risk of early death. It is theorized that stress accelerates the aging process by shortening the telomeres in our chromosomes (See resources section and reference list for information on telomeres).

Stress can have mental and emotional effects. The challenges caused by psychosocial stress may lead to a variety of mental and emotional effects. In the short term, stress can impair concentration and attention span. Anxiety is an emotional response to stress characterized by apprehension. Because the response usually involves expending a lot of nervous energy, anxiety can lead to fatigue and muscular tension.

Anxiety may persist long after a stressful experience. For example, adverse childhood experiences (ACEs) such as physical and emotional abuse, neglect, poverty, and family stress can have long-term consequences. According to the CDC, ACEs contribute to risky health behaviors, chronic health conditions, low life potential, and early death. Risks tend to be proportional to the number and severity of ACEs; thus, public health emphasis is placed on preventing them before they happen.

Another long-term consequence of extreme stress is post-traumatic stress disorder (PTSD), a common problem among military veterans. Symptoms of PTSD include flashbacks of the traumatic event, avoidance of situations that remind the person of the event, emotional numbing, and an increased level of arousal. The associated mental health problems contribute to the high rates of depression and suicide among veterans. These consequences underscore the serious health consequences of excess stress.

Stress can alter both positive and negative health behaviors. In addition to direct effects on health, stress can contribute to negative health outcomes indirectly, through increased engagement in negative behaviors, such as smoking, alcohol use, and overeating. Stress may also decrease engagement in health-protective behaviors, such as exercise. During periods of increased stress, people may also get insufficient sleep and have sleep difficulties associated with the causes of stress. For example, an individual experiencing severe stress related to finances may pick up additional shifts at work, leaving less time for sleep. The person may also have difficulty sleeping due to worry associated with the financial situation. Unfortunately, reduced or disrupted sleep may exacerbate the problem. Studies have consistently found a link between sleep difficulties and stress-related physical and mental health problems, including cardiovascular disease and depression, and a recent study found a strong link between stress and sleep disturbances among college students.

Eustress is an optimal amount of stress. We all need sufficient stress to motivate us to engage in activities that make our lives meaningful. Otherwise, we would be in a state

A CLOSER LOOK

Facebook Live and Suicide

Facebook Live is an online feature that allows users to share their lives in real time via live streaming. While it has been used in ways that enhance life's experience (e.g., sharing special family events), it has also been used to portray tragic events. Experts are concerned about the potential problems associated with online live streaming. For example, several live suicides have been broadcasted on Facebook Live and other live streaming sources. Facebook has had an online presence in suicide prevention for some time, including tools to make it easier to report suicides. With the advice of Save.org, Facebook has become even more involved in suicide prevention. As social support is one way to help prevent suicide, Facebook now offers users a chance to report and try to help those who may attempt self-harm live. Some argue that cutting off live streaming is the better option, while others argue that this eliminates opportunities to help.

Do you think that the positives of Facebook Live outweigh the negatives? Explain.

ACTIVITY

One person's stress is another's pleasure.
©Fuse/Getty Images

of **hypostress,** which leads to apathy, boredom, and less than optimal health and wellness. An example of hypostress is a person working on an assembly line. Because the same task is repeated without variation, the level of stimulation is quite low and might lead to a state of boredom and job dissatisfaction. In fact, a certain level of stress, called **eustress,** is experienced positively. In contrast, **distress** is a level of stress that compromises performance and well-being. Each of us possesses a system that allows us to mobilize resources when necessary and seeks to find a homeostatic level of arousal (see Figure 3). Although we all have an optimal level of arousal, it varies considerably. What one person finds stressful another may find exhilarating. For example, riding a roller coaster is thrilling for some people, but stressful and unpleasant for others.

Individual Differences in the Stress Response

Individuals respond differently to stress. Individuals exposed to high levels of stress are most at risk for negative health consequences. However, not everyone exposed to severe or chronic stress will experience negative outcomes. The events that occurred on September 11, 2001, provide a vivid example of the very different reactions that people have to the same or similar stressors. Everyone who witnessed these events, in person or on television, was profoundly impacted. At the same

Adaptation The body's efforts to restore normalcy.

Physiological Fatigue A deterioration in the capacity of the neuromuscular system as a result of physical overwork and strain; also referred to as true fatigue.

Psychological Fatigue A feeling of fatigue, usually caused by such things as lack of exercise, boredom, or mental stress, that results in a lack of energy and depression; also referred to as subjective or false fatigue.

Hypostress Insufficient levels of stress leading to boredom or apathy.

Eustress Positive stress, or stress that is mentally or physically stimulating.

Distress Negative stress, or stress that contributes to health problems.

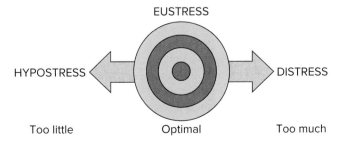

EUSTRESS

HYPOSTRESS ◀   ▶ DISTRESS

Too little   Optimal   Too much

Figure 3 ▶ Stress target zone.

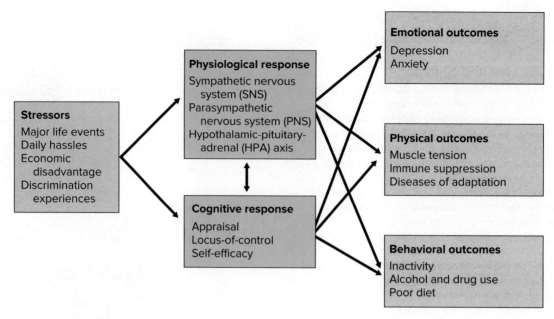

Figure 4 ▶ Reactions to stress.

time, individual reactions varied dramatically. Most felt overwhelming sadness, many felt extreme anger, others felt hopeless or desperate, and yet others felt lost or confused. Undoubtedly, there were some who were simply too shocked to process their emotional experience at all. With time, most Americans began to experience a wave of additional emotions, such as hope and patriotism. Figure 4 depicts the role that stress appraisals play in mediating relations between stress and its emotional, physical, and behavioral consequences.

Reactions to stress depend on one's appraisal of both the event and the subsequent physiological response. Stressors by themselves generally do not cause problems unless they are perceived as stressful. As shown in Figure 4, two specific factors are thought to influence individual susceptibility to negative stress-related outcomes: stress appraisal and stress reactivity.

Stress appraisal refers to an individual's perceptions of a stressor and the person's resources for managing stressful situations. Appraisal usually involves consideration of the consequences of the situation (primary appraisal) and an evaluation of the resources available to cope with the situation (secondary appraisal). If one sees a stressor as a challenge that can be tackled, one is likely to respond in a more positive manner than if the stressor is viewed as an obstacle that cannot be overcome. Individual differences in appraisal are due to inherited predispositions as well as our unique histories of experiencing and attempting to cope with stress.

Individual appraisal of the body's response to a stressful event is also important. Stress reactivity refers to the extent to which the sympathetic nervous system, or fight-or-flight system, is activated by a stressor. The degree of activation

influences how one will react emotionally and behaviorally, but some react more than others. For example, public speaking is a situation that leads to significant autonomic arousal for most people. Those who handle these situations well probably recognize that these sensations are normal and may even interpret them as excitement about the situations. In contrast, those who experience severe and sometimes debilitating anxiety are probably interpreting the same sensations as indicators of fear, panic, and loss of control. The combination of individual differences in stress reactivity and appraisals may lead to characteristic ways of responding to stress that either confer risk or protect against risk for physical and mental health problems. In fact, several different patterns of behavior (or personality styles) associated with stress responses have been clearly identified.

Type A and Type D personalities may increase risk for negative health outcomes. The best-known "personality" style associated with risk for negative health outcomes is the **Type A behavior pattern.** Several decades ago, psychologists Friedman and Rosenman identified a subgroup of goal-oriented, or "driven," patients, whom they believed were at increased risk based on their pattern of behavior. These individuals demonstrated a sense of time urgency, were highly competitive, and tended to experience and express anger and hostility under conditions of stress. In contrast, individuals with the Type B behavior pattern were relatively easygoing and less reactive to stress. Although early research on Type A behavior demonstrated increased risk for heart disease, it now appears that certain aspects of the Type A behavior pattern pose greater risk than others. In particular, hostility and anger appear to be consistently associated with risk for cardiovascular disease. Although most studies have not found time urgency or competitiveness predictive of risk for cardiovascular disease, a recent study found that people who scored high on a measure of impatience were nearly twice as likely to have high blood pressure relative to individuals lower on this trait. At the same time, certain aspects of the Type A behavior pattern (other than hostility) may lead to higher levels of achievement and an increased sense of personal accomplishment. Although the Type A behavior pattern has often been referred to as Type A personality, it was not the intention of those who developed the concept to identify a "personality type."

In contrast, the more recently identified **Type D,** or "distressed," **behavior pattern** is associated with two well-defined personality characteristics based on personality theory. Individuals with Type D personality are characterized by high levels of "negative affectivity," or negative emotion, and "social inhibition," or the tendency not to express negative emotions in social interactions. The combination of these characteristics appears to constitute risk for cardiovascular disease and other negative health outcomes. Converging evidence from recent research on both Type A and Type D behaviors has led some to conclude that negative affectivity, in general, is a more important risk for negative health outcomes than any emotion in particular. In other words, anger and hostility (Type A), as well as anxiety and depressed mood (Type D), pose a health risk. Several other well-established personality traits, including neuroticism and novelty seeking, have also been linked to negative health outcomes.

Several personality traits are associated with resilience in the face of stress. **Resilience** refers not simply to an absence of risk factors, but also to the presence of protective factors that lead to adaptive functioning. The experience of positive emotion is one well-established protective factor. Individuals who experience more positive emotions are more likely to adopt healthy lifestyles, and their physical responses to stress are more adaptive than those who experience less positive emotion. For example, patterns of cortisol response, heart rate, and blood pressure under stress are all more favorable among individuals who experience higher levels of positive emotion. Positive emotion may also be an effective coping mechanism for managing acute stress. Positive moods have been shown to undo some of the cardiovascular effects associated with negative emotions. Individuals who have more positive moods are also more socially integrated and report higher levels of social support, both characteristics associated with health benefits. **Optimism** is a trait associated with more positive emotional experiences and a more positive outlook on the future. Extensive research demonstrates that optimistic individuals have better physical and mental health outcomes than pessimistic individuals.

Resiliency and optimism can help with stress management.
©Mediaphotos/iStockphoto/Getty Images

An individual's **locus of control** can also have a significant impact on how he or she responds to a stressful situation. Research has consistently found that having an internal locus of control is associated with better health outcomes. People with an internal locus of control are more likely to take steps to address the problems that created the stress, rather than avoiding them. Those with an external locus of control tend to use passive methods for managing stress. In

Type A Behavior Pattern Characterized by impatience, ambition, and aggression; Type A personalities may be more susceptible to the effects of stress but may also be more able to cope with stress.

Type D Behavior Pattern Characterized by high levels of negative emotion and the tendency to withhold expression of these emotions.

Resilience Positive outcomes in the face of stress or disadvantage.

Optimism The tendency to have a positive outlook on life or a belief that things will work out favorably.

Locus of Control The extent to which we believe the outcomes of events are under our control (internal locus) or outside our personal control (external locus).

addition, an external locus of control is related to higher perceived levels of stress, lower job satisfaction, and poorer school achievement.

Although an internal locus of control generally promotes health, this is not always the case. This truth is apparent in depressed individuals with a pessimistic explanatory style. They believe that their failures are due to internal factors, squarely placing the control of these events within themselves. Even though they believe stressors are under their control, they don't believe in their ability to initiate change. Thus, for an internal locus of control to be beneficial to well-being, it must be combined with the belief that one is capable of making changes to prevent future problems. The belief in one's ability to reach a desired goal is often referred to as **self-efficacy.** Finally, studies have consistently shown health benefits of **conscientiousness,** the tendency to be organized, thoughtful, and goal directed. Highly conscientious individuals are at decreased risk for a range of negative outcomes, including asthma, stroke, depression, and panic attacks. It appears that conscientiousness contributes to better health outcomes, both through reduced engagement in health risk behaviors like alcohol

use and through more adaptive responses to stressful experiences. For example, individuals higher in conscientiousness are more likely to exercise on days that they experience high levels of stress.

As noted earlier, individuals who possess characteristics that protect them from the negative health consequences of stress are said to be resilient. **Hardiness** is one constellation of characteristics associated with resilience. Hardy individuals are strongly committed to their  goals, view difficult situations as challenges rather than stressors, and find ways to assume control over their problems.

Using Self-Management Skills

Assess common sources of stress and evaluate how you typically respond. The first step to managing stress effectively is to understand the sources of stress in your life. For some, major life events may be the primary sources of stress, whereas for others, chronic everyday stressors may play a more important role. It is also important to understand the unique ways in which you react to stress. This may include both adaptive and maladaptive approaches. Once you know what "stresses you out" and how you typically react to stressful events, you can begin to find more effective ways to combat stress. The labs in this Concept can help with this step.

Learn how to balance your attitudes to moderate stress. While you can't always control your exposure to stressors, you can control your appraisal of stressful events. There are clearly some innate personality differences that may influence how you react to people and to stress. However, there are also a number of characteristics that can be learned, emulated, or nurtured. For example, characteristics of resilience, optimism, conscientiousness, and hardiness all have been shown to help people to become more resistant to stressful experiences. By paying attention to your attitudes and perceptions, you can develop a more stress-resistant personality.

Technology Update

Virtual Reality and Stress: Pros and Cons

Virtual reality (VR) is an emerging technology that is impacting society in a number of ways. VR applications typically involve the use of a computer headset that generates simulated, but seemingly real, experiences. Researchers have used VR technology to study reactions to stressful events and also to prepare individuals to handle stressful situations. Research has also explored methods to employ VR technology to treat individuals with anxiety disorders, PTSD, phobias, and drug addictions. The basis for these applications is that VR puts people with problems into realistic situations, gradually allowing them to learn how to adapt and cope. However, there are concerns that extended exposure to the very real experiences created via VR may create stress and have negative effects on the brain. The very realistic depiction of violence in VR games is a specific concern, since it could desensitize people to violence and potentially impact real interactions.

Do the advantages of VR technology outweigh the cons?

Self-Efficacy The belief in one's ability to take action that will lead to the attainment of a goal.

Conscientiousness Associated with high levels of organization, thoughtfulness, and goal-directed activity.

Hardiness A collection of personality traits thought to make a person more resistant to stress.

Taking an optimistic perspective can build self-confidence and help you cope with stress. Optimists are hopeful about the future, while pessimists expect bad things to happen. Optimists see the glass as half full, while pessimists see the glass as half empty. Research also shows that optimists have a more positive physiological response to stress and respond more effectively to stress than do pessimists (see Figure 4).

If you are already an optimist, you'll reap the health benefits. If you tend to be more of a pessimist, you can take steps to adopt a more optimistic outlook. One way to see things from a more optimistic perspective is to build your self-confidence for handling difficult situations (a self-management skill). Here are some things you can do to increase your self-confidence and have a more optimistic outlook.

- *Set realistic goals for specific tasks.* Over time, setting goals that are too difficult leads to low confidence. Setting goals that are achievable leads to success and improved confidence.

- *Keep trying.* People with low confidence often give up when they don't have early success. They may think, "I can't do it no matter how hard I try." Building self-confidence through continued effort promotes the feeling that "I can." Those who believe that "they can do it" are optimists.

- *Give yourself a break.* It is important to give yourself credit for giving effort. Effort pays off in the long run. Of course, not all attempts at performing a task will be successful. The key is to keep trying even when your initial efforts are unsuccessful.

- *Avoid evaluation when trying something new.* Anyone who has ever given a speech, performed before a large crowd, or taken an important test knows that stress levels increase when you are being evaluated. Trying something new while being evaluated is especially stressful and can undermine self-confidence. When trying something new, practice in private. This builds the confidence that you need prior to being evaluated or performing in public.

- *Don't sell yourself short.* "I'm not big enough to do that." "I have never done that." "I don't think I can do it." Societal stereotypes can make a task seem intimidating. Following the steps suggested above can help you succeed even in tasks that you think "are not for you."

- *Laugh it off.* Laughter has both short-term and long-term benefits for reducing stress and it is associated with both physical and mental health benefits. Some experts recommend watching a TV comedy or telling jokes with friends to create laughter and reduce stress. Give it a try!

Strategies for Action: Lab Information

Self-assessments of stressors in your life can be useful in managing stress. To effectively manage stress, you first must identify the sources of stress in your life. In Lab 17A you will have the opportunity to evaluate your stress levels using the Life Experience Survey.

Learning to appraise stressful events in a more positive way can help you respond to stress more effectively. Personality characteristics have been associated with reactions to stress. Although overall personality structure has proven somewhat resistant to change, it is certainly possible to change your appraisal of stressful events and thereby diminish the resulting emotional, physical, and behavioral outcomes. In Lab 17B you can assess your hardiness and locus of control, characteristics associated with appraising and coping with stress.

Suggested Resources and Readings

The websites for the following sources can be accessed by searching online for the organization, program, or title listed. Specific scientific references are available at the end of this edition of *Concepts of Fitness and Wellness*.

- American Psychological Association. Stress in America: Paying with Our Health (online report pdf).
- American Psychological Association (Help Center). How Stress Affects Your Health (online resource).
- Association for Psychological Science. The Psychological Toll of the Smartphone.
- CBS News (*60 Minutes*). Brain hacking
- Centers for Disease Control and Prevention. Adverse Childhood Experience Study.
- delia Cava, Marco. (2016, February 2). Virtual reality's promise, risk loom large for health researchers. *USA Today*.
- Gallup Poll. Gallup Healthways Well-Being Index.
- Greenberg, J. (2016). *Comprehensive Stress Management* (14th ed.). New York: McGraw-Hill Higher Education.
- Guynn, J. (2017, March 1). Facebook takes steps to stop suicides on Live. *USA Today*.
- McGinigal, K. (2016). *The Upside of Stress: Why Stress Is Good for You, and How to Get Good at It*. New York: Penguin Random House.
- Meyers, L. (2016, March 28). Coping with college. *Counseling Today*.
- National Public Radio. Depression Strikes Today's Teens Especially Hard.
- National Survey of College Counseling Centers. (2014). Stress on Campus.
- Sederer, L. I. (2017, January 22). The Telomere Effect. *Psychology Today Blog* (Therapy, It's More Than Talk).
- Storoni, M. (2017). *Stress Proof: The Scientific Solution to Protect Your Brain and Body*. New York: Penguin Random House.
- Vitelli, R. (2015, May 25). Exploring Facebook depression. *Psychology Today*.
- WebMD. Stress Management Health Center.
- Wingo, M. (2016). *The Impact of the Human Stress Response*. Austin, TX: Roxwell Waterhouse.

Lab 17A Evaluating Your Stress Level

Name	**Section**	**Date**

Purpose: To evaluate your stress during the past year and determine its implications.

Procedures

1. Complete the following Life Experience Survey based on your experiences during the past year. This survey lists a number of life events that may be distressful or eustressful. Read all of the items. If you did not experience an event, leave the box blank. In the box after each event that you did experience, write a number ranging from −3 to +3 using the scale described in the directions. Extra blanks are provided to write in positive or negative events not listed. Some items apply only to males or females. Items 48 to 56 are only for current college students.
2. Add all of the negative numbers and record your score (distress) in the Results section. Add the positive numbers and record your score (eustress) in the Results section. Use all of the events in the past year.
3. Find your scores on Chart 1 and record your ratings in the Results section.
4. Interpret the results by answering the questions in the Conclusions and Implications section.

Results

Sum of negative scores [ ] (distress)   Rating on negative scores [ ]

Sum of positive scores [ ] (eustress)   Rating on positive scores [ ]

Chart 1 Scale for Life Experiences and Stress

	Sum of Negative Scores (Distress)	Sum of Positive Scores (Eustress)
May need counseling	14+	
Above average	9–13	11+
Average	6–8	9–10
Below average	<6	<9

Scoring the Life Experience Survey

1. Add all of the negative scores to arrive at your own distress score (negative stress).
2. Add all of the positive scores to arrive at a eustress score (positive stress).

Conclusions and Implications: In several sentences, discuss your current stress rating and its implications.

Life Experience Survey

Directions: If you did not experience an event, leave the box next to the event empty. If you experienced an event, enter a number in the box based on how the event impacted your life. Use the following scale:

Extremely negative impact	= –3
Moderately negative impact	= –2
Somewhat negative impact	= –1
Neither positive nor negative impact	= 0
Somewhat positive impact	= +1
Moderately positive impact	= +2
Extremely positive impact	= +3

1. Marriage
2. Detention in jail or comparable institution
3. Death of spouse
4. Major change in sleeping habits (much more or less sleep)
5. Death of close family member:
   a. Mother
   b. Father
   c. Brother
   d. Sister
   e. Child
   f. Grandmother
   g. Grandfather
   h. Other (specify) _____
6. Major change in eating habits (much more or much less food intake)
7. Foreclosure on mortgage or loan
8. Death of a close friend
9. Outstanding personal achievement
10. Minor law violation (traffic ticket, disturbing the peace, etc.)
11. Became pregnant or partner became pregnant
12. Changed work situation (different working conditions, working hours, etc.)
13. New job
14. Serious illness or injury of close family member:
   a. Father
   b. Mother
   c. Sister
   d. Brother
   e. Grandfather
   f. Grandmother
   g. Spouse
   h. Child
   i. Other (specify) _____
15. Sexual difficulties
16. Trouble with employer (in danger of losing job, being suspended, demoted, etc.)
17. Trouble with in-laws
18. Major change in financial status (a lot better off or a lot worse off)
19. Major change in closeness of family members (decreased or increased closeness)

20. Gaining a new family member (through birth, adoption, family member moving in, etc.)
21. Change of residence
22. Marital separation from mate (due to conflict)
23. Major change in church activities (increased or decreased attendance)
24. Marital reconciliation with mate
25. Major change in number of arguments with spouse (a lot more or a lot fewer arguments)
26. Change in partner's work (new job, loss of job, retirement, etc.)
27. Major change in usual type and/or amount of recreation
28. Borrowing more than $10,000 (buying a home, business, etc.)
29. Borrowing less than $10,000 (buying car or TV, getting school loan, etc.)
30. Being fired from job
31. Had an abortion or partner had an abortion
32. Major personal illness or injury
33. Major change in social activities, such as parties, movies, visiting (increased or decreased participation)
34. Major change in living conditions of family (building new home, remodeling, deterioration of home or neighborhood, etc.)
35. Divorce
36. Serious injury or illness of close friend
37. Retirement from work
38. Son or daughter leaving home (due to marriage, college, etc.)
39. Ending of formal schooling
40. Separation from spouse (due to work, travel, etc.)
41. Engagement
42. Breaking up with boyfriend/girlfriend
43. Leaving home for the first time
44. Reconciliation with boyfriend/girlfriend

Other recent experiences that have had an impact on your life: list and rate.

45. _____
46. _____
47. _____

For Students Only

48. Beginning new school experience at a higher academic level (college, graduate school, professional school, etc.)
49. Changing to a new school at same academic level (undergraduate, graduate, etc.)
50. Academic probation
51. Being dismissed from dormitory or other residence
52. Failing an important exam
53. Changing a major
54. Failing a course
55. Dropping a course
56. Joining a fraternity/sorority

Source: Sarason, I.G., Johnson, J.H., and Siegel, J.M., Assessing the impact of life changes: development of the Life Experience Survey, *Journal of Consulting and Clinical Psychology.* Vol. 46, issue 5 1978.

Lab 17B Evaluating Your Hardiness and Locus of Control

| Name | | Section | | Date | |

Purpose: To evaluate your level of hardiness and locus of control and to help you identify the ways in which you appraise and respond to stressful situations.

Procedures

1. Complete the Hardiness Questionnaire and the Locus of Control Questionnaire. Make an X over the circle that best describes what is true for you personally.
2. Compute the scale scores and record the values in the Results section.
3. Evaluate your scores using Chart 1, and record your ratings in the Results section.
4. Interpret the results by answering the questions in the Conclusions and Implications section.

Hardiness Questionnaire

	Not True	Rarely True	Sometimes True	Often True	Score
1. I look forward to school and work on most days.	1	2	3	4	
2. Having too many choices in life makes me nervous.	4	3	2	1	
3. I know where my life is going and look forward to the future.	1	2	3	4	
4. I prefer not to get too involved in relationships.	4	3	2	1	
			Commitment Score, Sum 1–4		
5. My efforts at school and work will pay off in the long run.	1	2	3	4	
6. I just have to trust my life to fate to be successful.	4	3	2	1	
7. I believe that I can make a difference in the world.	1	2	3	4	
8. Being successful in life takes more luck and good breaks than effort.	4	3	2	1	
			Control Score, Sum 5–8		
9. I would be willing to work for less money if I could do something really challenging and interesting.	1	2	3	4	
10. I often get frustrated when my daily plans and schedule get altered.	4	3	2	1	
11. Experiencing new situations in life is important to me.	1	2	3	4	
12. I don't mind being bored.	4	3	2	1	
			Challenge Score, Sum 9–12		

Locus of Control Questionnaire

13. Hard work usually pays off.	1	2	3	4	
14. Buying a lottery ticket is not worth the money.	1	2	3	4	
15. Even when I fail I keep trying.	1	2	3	4	
16. I am usually successful in what I do.	1	2	3	4	
17. I am in control of my own life.	1	2	3	4	
18. I make plans to be sure I am successful.	1	2	3	4	
19. I know where I stand with my friends.	1	2	3	4	
			Locus of Control, Sum 13–19		

357

Results

Hardiness

Commitment score [ ]

$+$

Control score [ ]

$+$

Challenge score [ ]

$=$

Total Hardiness score [ ]

Commitment rating [ ]

$+$

Control rating [ ]

$+$

Challenge rating [ ]

$=$

Hardiness rating [ ]

Locus of Control

Locus of control score [ ]

Locus of control rating [ ]

Chart 1 Rating Chart

Rating	Individual Hardiness Scale Scores	Total Hardiness Score	Locus of Control Score
High	14–16	40–48	24–28
Moderate	10–13	30–39	12–23
Low	<10	<30	<12

Conclusions and Implications

1. In several sentences, discuss your commitment, control, and challenge ratings, as well as your overall hardiness rating. Are they what you expected? Do you think they are true indications of your hardiness? Explain.

2. In several sentences, discuss your locus of control rating. Is it what you expected (a high rating indicates an internal locus of control)? Do you think your rating is a realistic indicator of your locus of control? Explain.

Stress Management, Relaxation, and Time Management

LEARNING OBJECTIVES

After completing the study of this Concept, you will be able to:

▶ Describe the stress-buffering effects of physical activity that contribute to positive psychological health.

▶ Identify behaviors that contribute to better sleep hygiene.

▶ Describe the benefits of recreation, leisure, and play to overall quality of life.

▶ Identify a variety of strategies for effective time management.

▶ Understand the unique benefits of cognitive-, emotion-, and problem-focused coping strategies.

▶ Describe the mental health benefits of mindfulness, spirituality, and emotional expression.

▶ Determine several relaxation techniques that can be used to effectively manage stress.

▶ Describe different types of social support and ways in which they facilitate effective stress management.

ough stress cannot be avoided, proper
ress-management techniques can help
educe the impact of stress in your life.

©Caiaimage/Robert
Daly/Getty Images

Why it Matters!

Stress is a normal part of life so it is important to learn how to manage stress effectively. Healthy lifestyle behaviors and self-management skills are important for effective stress management. Exercising regularly is one way to manage stress as are getting sufficient sleep and allowing time for recreation. Time management is another self-management skill for balancing work and school demands and for ensuring that there is time for physical activity, sleep, and recreation. Learning active coping skills is especially important for managing stress and dealing with the demands of daily life. This Concept covers the importance of healthy lifestyle factors and the use of self-management skills for stress management.

Physical Activity and Stress Management

Regular activity can help you adapt to stressful situations. An individual's capacity to adapt to stress is not a static function but fluctuates as situations change. Physical activity is especially important for stress management because it conditions your body to function effectively under challenging physiological conditions. Unfortunately, studies demonstrate that participation in physical activity tends to be lower when people are under high stress. Periods of stress are when you may need physical activity the most. Therefore, it is important to build physical activity into your normal routine to help manage daily stress.

Physical activity can provide relief from stress and aid muscle tension release. Physical activity has been found to be effective at relieving stress, particularly white-collar job stress. Studies show that regular exercise decreases the likelihood of developing stress disorders and reduces the intensity of the stress response. It also shortens the period of recovery from an emotional trauma. Its effect tends to be short term, so exercise regularly for it to have a continuing effect. Whatever your choice of exercise, it is likely to be more effective as an antidote to stress if it is something you find enjoyable.

Regular physical activity reduces reactivity to stress. Physical activity is associated with a physiological response that is similar, in many ways, to the body's response to psychosocial stressors. Individuals who are physically fit have a reduced physiological response to exercise. Therefore, it makes sense that someone who is physically fit would also have a reduced response to psychosocial stressors. Research supports this hypothesis, indicating that regular exercise reduces physiological reactivity to non-exercise stressors. For example, one recent study evaluated the impact of physical activity on responses to social stressors. The stress response was determined by monitoring levels of cortisol, a hormone released during

stress. The social stressor led to a spike in cortisol levels, but the magnitude of the cortisol response to stress was lower among women who more regularly engaged in physical activity. Although regular exercise may protect against elevated cortisol levels, there is some evidence that intensive training and competition may lead to greater overall cortisol exposure. Thus, it appears that regular, but not excessive, exercise is the most beneficial pattern for moderating the response to stress.

Physical activity has direct effects on mental health and also moderates the effect of stress on other health outcomes. Exercise can reduce anxiety, aid in recovery from depression, and assist in efforts to eliminate negative health behaviors, such as smoking. It also appears to buffer the effects of stress on cellular aging. Details about the major benefits on mental health are highlighted below:

- *Physical activity can reduce anxiety and depression.* The 2018 *Physical Activity Guidelines for Americans* report indicates "that regular physical activity not only reduces the risk of clinical depression, but reduces depressive symptoms among people both with and without clinical depression." Other evidence indicates that aerobic exercise is comparable to medication in reducing depressive symptoms among individuals with major depression. Further, those in the exercise intervention were less likely to have a recurrence of depression. A study of formerly depressed individuals found that exercise helped reduce the emotional consequences from negative mood states. This mechanism may explain the ability of an exercise intervention to reduce the recurrence of depression. Physical activity can reduce the severity of those symptoms whether one has only a few or many. The *Physical Activity Guidelines* report also indicates that "regular physical activity reduces symptoms of anxiety, including both chronic levels of anxiety, as well as the acute feelings of anxiety felt by many individuals from time to time." Other research indicates that an exercise intervention can reduce anxiety among individuals with panic disorder.

- *Physical activity buffers the effects of stress on obesity and health.* Recent analyses of data from the National Health and Growth Study found that adolescent girls who reported more stress had larger increases in BMI during adolescence (aged 10 to 19). However stress-related increases were much smaller among those who engaged in regular physical activity.

- *Physical activity can help protect against the effects of stress on memory.* A recent study of older adults found that accumulated stress was associated with decreased volume in the hippocampus, a brain region implicated in memory. Stress effects on the brain were less significant for those who engaged in more frequent exercise. The 2018 *Physical Activity Guidelines* report indicates that physical activity also improves other components of cognition in addition to memory, including processing speed, attention, and academic performance.

- *Physical activity buffers the negative impact of stress on cellular aging.* Stress can reduce the length of telomeres (protective ends of DNA strands), leading to more rapid cell aging. Recent studies suggest that regular physical activity can prevent stress-induced damage to DNA. One recent study found that sedentary individuals showed stress-induced decreases in telomere length, whereas those who engaged in at least 75 minutes of weekly exercise demonstrated no relation between stress and telomere length.

Stress, Sleep, and Recreation

In order to adapt effectively to stressful situations, one must get adequate sleep. Although the number of hours needed varies, the average adult needs between 7 and 8 hours of sleep per night. Teenagers and young adults (those in their early 20s) may need slightly more sleep. Unfortunately, many do not get this extra amount of sleep. Full-time college students get an average of 8.6 hours of sleep on weekday nights. However, more than one-fifth of college students average 7 or fewer hours of sleep on weekdays. Thus, a substantial number of students fail to get adequate sleep. With insufficient sleep, many people resort to caffeine to stay awake, leading to an endless cycle of deficient sleep and caffeine usage and compromised health and wellness. Table 1 presents guidelines for good sleep. The recent *Physical Activity Guidelines for Americans* report indicated that "strong evidence demonstrates that moderate-to-vigorous physical activity improves the quality of sleep. It does so by reducing the length of time it takes to go to sleep and reducing the time one is awake after going to sleep and before arising in the morning. It also can increase the time in deep sleep and reduce daytime sleepiness."

All work and no play can lead to poor mental and physical health. Between 1860 and 1990, the number of hours typically spent working in industrialized countries decreased relatively dramatically. While that trend has continued in most countries, work hours in the United States have increased considerably over the past two decades. A major reason for this increase is that more people now hold second jobs than in the past. Also, some jobs in modern society have increasing rather than decreasing time demands. For example, many medical doctors and other professionals work more hours than the 35 to 44 hours that most people work. Nearly three times as many married women with children work full time now, as compared with 1960.

Experts have referred to young adults as the "overworked Americans" because they work several jobs and maintain dual roles (full-time employment coupled with normal family chores), or they work extended hours in demanding professional jobs. A Gallup poll showed that the great majority of adults have "enough time" for work, chores, and sleep but not enough time for friends, self, spouse, and children. When time is at a premium, the factors most likely to be negatively affected are personal health, relationships with children, and marriage or romantic relationships.

Table 1 ▶ Guidelines for Good Sleep

- Be aware of the effects of medications. Some medicines, such as weight loss pills and decongestants, contain caffeine or other ingredients that interfere with sleep.
- Avoid tobacco use. Nicotine is a stimulant and can interfere with sleep.
- Avoid excess alcohol use. Alcohol may make it easier to get to sleep, but may be a reason you wake up at night and are unable to get back to sleep.
- You may exercise late in the day, but do not do vigorous activity right before bedtime.
- Sleep in a room that is cooler than normal.
- Avoid hard-to-digest foods late in the day, as well as fatty and spicy foods.
- Avoid large meals late in the day or right before bedtime. A light snack before bedtime should not be a problem for most people.
- Avoid too much liquid before bedtime.
- Avoid naps during the day.
- Go to bed and get up at the same time each day.
- Do not study, read, or engage in other activities in your bed. You want your brain to associate your bed with sleep, not with activity.
- If you are having difficulty falling asleep, do not stay in bed. Get up and find something to do until you begin to feel tired, and then go back to bed.

Recreation and leisure are important contributors to wellness (quality of life). Leisure is generally considered to be the opposite of work and includes "doing things we just want to do," as well as "doing nothing." In contrast, **recreation** generally is something that is pursued for a specific purpose. The difference between leisure and recreation often depends on how it is perceived. Many people pursue recreational activities to contribute to fitness goals, but walking can also be a form of leisure for some. Reading and listening to music are common leisure activities, but both can be pursued for recreational purposes (if related to hobbies or for emotional, mental, and spiritual growth). Leisure and recreation both contribute to stress reduction and wellness, although leisure activities are not done specifically to achieve these benefits. The value of recreation and leisure in Western culture is evidenced by the emphasis public health officials place on the availability and accessibility

Leisure Time that is free from the demands of work. Leisure is more than free time; it is also an attitude. Leisure activities need not be means to ends (purposeful) but are ends in themselves.

Recreation *Recreation* means creating something anew. We refer to it as something that you do for amusement or for fun to help you divert your attention and to refresh yourself (re-create yourself).

of recreational facilities in communities. (See A Closer Look for more insight on leisure.)

Play is critical to development, and a sense of play in adult recreation contributes to wellness. Play is distinct from recreation in that it is typically intrinsically motivated and has an imaginative component. Play has been shown to be important to healthy brain development in humans, and there is considerable evidence for physical, social, and cognitive benefits of play. In children, "free play," or unstructured time for play, seems to be particularly important. This type of play has been linked to a number of positive outcomes, including increased attention in the classroom, better self-regulation, and improved social skills and problem solving. Although much less attention has been given to the value of play in adults, a recent literature review identified benefits of play in adults, including mood enhancement, skill development, and enhanced relationships. Clearly, benefits associated with play have the potential both to prevent stress and to facilitate effective coping with stress.

Principles of Stress Management

Stress-management skills can be learned. There is considerable evidence that stress-management training yields both physical and mental health benefits. Positive effects have been noted in a variety of populations. For example, a recent study found that stress-management training for patients with heart disease resulted in improved cardiovascular function, decreased depression, and lower levels of general distress. Similar results were found following a stress-management intervention provided to women following treatment for breast cancer. Interestingly, and perhaps of more relevance to college students, stress-management training has also been shown to improve academic performance.

Stress-management training focuses on teaching active coping strategies. Relaxation training is perhaps the most commonly used approach for stress management, but incorporation of more active **coping** strategies may increase effectiveness. A large meta-analysis of studies of stress-management training in college students found that

cognitive, behavioral, and/or mindfulness-based techniques produced the largest benefits, and these programs often incorporated both relaxation and more active strategies for managing stress. An advantage of cognitive-behavioral training is that it helps a person understand when and how to apply the three types of coping strategies that have been shown to help with stress management.

Active coping strategies are those that attempt to directly affect the source of the stress or to effectively manage the individual's reactions to stress, while passive coping strategies attempt to direct attention away from the stressor. Active coping strategies can be further classified into three basic categories: **appraisal-focused coping, emotion-focused coping,** and **problem-focused coping.** As indicated in Table 2, these coping

Table 2 ▶ Strategies for Stress Management	
Category	**Description**
Appraisal-Focused Strategies	**Strategies That Alter Perceptions of the Problem or Your Ability to Cope Effectively with the Problem**
• Cognitive restructuring	• Changing negative or automatic thoughts leading to unnecessary distress
• Seeking knowledge or practicing skills	• Finding ways to increase your confidence in your ability to cope
Emotion-Focused Strategies	**Strategies That Minimize the Emotional and Physical Effects of the Situation**
• Relaxing	• Using relaxation techniques to reduce the symptoms of stress
• Exercising	• Using physical activity to reduce the symptoms of stress
• Expressing your feelings	• Talking with someone about what you are feeling or writing about your emotional experiences
• Spirituality	• Looking for spiritual guidance to provide comfort
Problem-Focused Strategies	**Strategies That Directly Seek to Solve or Minimize the Stressful Situation**
• Systematic problem solving	• Making a plan of action to solve the problem and following through to make the situation better
• Being assertive	• Standing up for your own rights and values while respecting the opinions of others
• Seeking active social support	• Getting help or advice from others who can provide specific assistance for your situation
Avoidant Coping Strategies	**Strategies That Attempt to Distract the Individual from the Problem**
• Ignoring	• Refusing to think about the situation or pretending no problem exists
• Escaping	• Looking for ways to feel better or to stop thinking about the problem, including eating or using nicotine, alcohol, or other drugs
• Suppressing	• Actively trying to suppress emotional experiences or emotional expression
• Ruminating	• Focusing on your negative emotions and what they mean without taking efforts to address the problem

A CLOSER LOOK

How Do Americans Spend Their Leisure Time?

Leisure is typically defined as "time free from demands." The American Time Use Survey provides indicators of how Americans spend their time, including work tasks and types of leisure. Almost all Americans (96 percent) report engaging in some leisure activities, but the vast majority of time is spent in sedentary activities. More than 78 percent of adults watch TV daily with the average viewing time of 3.5 hours. Much fewer report spending time in physical activity or sports (21 percent) and for much less time (approximately 1.5 hours). Search "American Time Use Survey" online to learn more.

What strategies can you use to decrease sedentary time and increase active recreation?

HELP Health is available to Everyone for a Lifetime, and it's Personal

Dealing with College Stress

Many college campuses have resources available to help students address the various causes of stress. Those resources include academic offices to help with time management and scholastic difficulties as well as counseling centers for anxiety, depression, relationships, and other problems. Additionally, offices such as housing, the medical clinic, health promotion, and financial aid can offer resources to address a variety of other stressors that often come up.

Do you take advantage of the resources that your college provides to aid in your stress management? Why or why not? What stress-management tactics do you use, and how important are they in your lifestyle?

strategies target the cognitive, emotional, physiological, and behavioral aspects of stress. Whereas each of these strategies is effective in various circumstances, the fourth one listed in the table (**avoidant coping** strategies) is likely to be ineffective for almost everyone. This includes futile strategies such as ignoring or escaping the problem or suppressing negative emotions.

Active coping strategies affect stress in different ways. Appraisal-focused coping strategies are based on changing the way one perceives the stressor or changing one's perceptions of resources for effectively managing stress. In contrast, emotion-focused coping strategies attempt to regulate the emotions resulting from stressful events. Both appraisal- and emotion-focused coping can be considered "emotion regulation" strategies, but the difference between the two approaches is in the timing: Appraisal-focused coping attempts to change the initial emotional experience, whereas emotion-focused coping attempts to manage the emotional experiences that follow appraisal. Efforts to positively reappraise stressful experiences can reduce initial emotional reactions to a stressor, but additional strategies may be needed to manage these emotions. Problem-focused strategies act very differently. They do not influence emotional responses to stress but rather focus on helping address or remove the underlying source of the stress.

Effective coping strategies are described in detail in the following section, followed by guidelines on time management and seeking social support. Although you should take steps to minimize stress, it is critical to learn ways to effectively cope with it when it occurs.

Effective Coping Strategies

Coping with most stress requires a variety of thoughts and actions. Stress forces the body to work under less than optimal conditions, yet this is the time when we need to function at our best. Effective coping may require some efforts to regulate the emotional aspects of the stress and other efforts to solve the problem. For example, if you receive a bad grade on an exam, how you view the situation and interpret its meaning will have a major impact on how you feel. You will have to eventually accept your current grade and manage the emotions that accompany this reality. Then, you will need to take active steps to improve your performance on the next exam. It does no good to worry about past events so, instead, you look forward. Thus, coping with this situation can require the use of all three coping strategies.

Play Activity done of one's own free will. The play experience is fun and intrinsically rewarding, and it is a self-absorbing means of self-expression. It is characterized by a sense of freedom or escape from life's normal rules.

Coping A person's constantly changing cognitive and psychological efforts to manage stressful situations.

Appraisal-Focused Coping Adapting to stress by changing your perceptions of stress and your resources for coping.

Emotion-Focused Coping Adapting to stress by regulating the emotions that cause or result from stress.

Problem-Focused Coping Adapting to stress by changing the source or cause of stress.

Avoidant Coping Seeking immediate, temporary relief from stress through distraction or self-indulgence (e.g., use of alcohol, tobacco, or other drugs).

Table 3 ▶ Types of Distorted Thinking

Type	Description
1. All-or-none thinking	You look at things in absolute, black-and-white categories.
2. Overgeneralization	You view a negative event as a never-ending pattern of defeat.
3. Mental filter	You dwell on the negatives and ignore the positives.
4. Discounting the positives	You insist that your accomplishments and positive qualities don't count.
5. Jumping to conclusions	(a) Mind reading—you assume that others are reacting negatively to you when there is no definite evidence of this. (b) Fortune telling—you arbitrarily predict that things will turn out badly.
6. Magnification or minimization	You blow things out of proportion or shrink their importance inappropriately.
7. Emotional reasoning	You reason from how you feel: "I feel like an idiot, so I must be one." "I don't feel like doing this, so I'll put it off."
8. "Should" statements	You criticize yourself or other people with "shoulds" or "shouldn'ts." "Musts," "oughts," and "have tos" are similar offenders.
9. Labeling	You identify with your shortcomings. Instead of saying, "I made a mistake," you tell yourself, "I am a jerk," "a fool," or "a loser."
10. Personalization and blame	You blame yourself for something that you weren't entirely responsible for, or you blame other people and overlook ways that your own attitudes and behaviors might have contributed to the problem.

Source: Burns, D.D., The *Feeling Good Handbook.* Penguin Group (1999).

Appraisal-focused coping strategies can be effective for certain situations. The way you think about stressful situations (see Table 3) can dramatically influence your emotional experiences. Research has demonstrated that cognitive reappraisal leads to down-regulation of the autonomic and endocrine systems, leading to physical and mental health benefits. Fortunately, even those of us who do not typically engage in reappraisal can learn to use this approach. Research on cognitive therapy approaches for treating anxiety and mood disorders has shown that people can readily learn this skill, and learning to change the way you think can reduce emotional distress. Cognitive reappraisal also has benefits for other conditions. In a study of workplace stress, a cognitive-behavioral intervention that targeted appraisal of stress was more effective than a behavioral coping skills intervention that combined emotion- and problem-focused coping strategies. Thus, the way you think about stressful situations can be as important as how you respond to them.

At one time or another, virtually all people have distorted thinking, which can create unnecessary stress. Distorted thinking is also referred to as negative or automatic thinking. To alleviate stress, it can be useful to recognize some common types of distorted thinking (see Table 3). If you can learn to recognize distorted thinking, you can change the way you think and often reduce your stress levels.

If you have ever used any of the 10 types of distorted thinking described in Table 3, you may find it useful to consider different methods of "untwisting" your thinking and change negative thinking to positive thinking (see Table 4). To try

this, think of a recent situation that caused stress. Describe the situation on paper, and see if you used distorted

thinking in the situation (see Table 3). If so, write down which types of distorted thinking you used. Finally, determine if any of the guidelines in Table 4 would have been useful. If so, write down the strategy you could have used. When a similar situation arises, you will be prepared to deal with the stressful situation. Repeat this technique, using several situations that have recently caused stress.

Emotion-focused coping strategies are helpful for issues or problems that are not within your control. Relaxation techniques and/or coping strategies can help reduce the negative impact of both physical and emotional consequences of stress. These ap-

proaches can slow your heart and respiration rate, relax tense muscles, clear your mind, and help you relax mentally and emotionally. Perhaps most important, these techniques can improve your outlook and help you cope better with the stressful situation. In Lab 18B, you will try several relaxation techniques. However, performing the exercises only once will not prepare you to use relaxation techniques effectively. You must practice learning to relax.

Conscious relaxation techniques reduce stress and tension by directly altering the physical symptoms. When you are stressed, heart rate, blood pressure, and

Table 4 ▶ Ten Ways to Untwist Your Thinking

Way	Description
1. Identify the distortion.	Write down your negative thoughts, so you can see which of the 10 types of distorted thinking you are involved in. This will make it easier to think about the problem in a more positive and realistic way.
2. Examine the evidence.	Instead of assuming that your negative thought is true, or if you feel you never do anything right, you can list several things that you have done successfully.
3. Use the double standard method.	Instead of putting yourself down in a harsh, condemning way, talk to yourself in the same compassionate way you would talk to a friend with a similar problem.
4. Use the experimental technique.	Do an experiment to test the validity of your negative thought. For example, if, during an episode of panic you become terrified that you are about to die of a heart attack, you can jog or run up and down several flights of stairs. This will prove that your heart is healthy and strong.
5. Think in shades of gray.	Although this method might sound drab, the effects can be illuminating. Instead of thinking about your problems in all-or-none extremes, evaluate things on a range from 0 to 100. When things do not work out as well as you had hoped, think about the experience as a partial success, rather than a complete failure. See what you can learn from the situation.
6. Use the survey method.	Ask people questions to find out if your thoughts and attitudes are realistic. For example, if you believe that public speaking anxiety is abnormal and shameful, ask several friends if they have ever felt nervous before giving a talk.
7. Define terms.	When you label yourself "inferior," "a fool," or "a loser," ask, "What is the definition of 'a fool'?" You will feel better when you see that there is no such thing as a fool or a loser.
8. Use the semantic method.	Simply substitute language that is less colorful or emotionally loaded. This method is helpful for "should" statements. Instead of telling yourself, "I *shouldn't* have made that mistake," you can say, "It would be better if I hadn't made that mistake."
9. Use reattribution.	Instead of automatically assuming you are "bad" and blaming yourself entirely for a problem, think about the many factors that may have contributed to it. Focus on solving the problem instead of using up all your energy blaming yourself and feeling guilty.
10. Do a cost–benefit analysis.	List the advantages and disadvantages of a feeling (such as getting angry when your plane is late), a negative thought (such as "No matter how hard I try, I always screw up"), or a behavior pattern (such as overeating and lying around in bed when you are depressed). You can also use the cost–benefit analysis to modify a self-defeating belief, such as "I must always be perfect."

Source: Burns, D.D., *The Feeling Good Handbook.* Penguin Group (1999).

muscle tension all increase to help your body deal with the challenge. Conscious relaxation techniques reduce these normal effects and bring the body back to a more relaxed state. These approaches can also help you manage the negative emotions that result from stressors and your appraisal of those stressors. Most techniques use the "three *R*s" of relaxation to help the body and mind relax: (1) reduce mental activity, (2) recognize tension, and (3) reduce respiration. Some relaxation techniques include:

- *Deep breathing and mental imagery.* One of the quickest ways to experience relaxation is through deep breathing. A simple version involves inhaling deeply through your nose for about 4 seconds and then letting the air out slowly through your mouth (for about 8 seconds). Repeating these steps for several minutes can help control your body's reaction to stress and slow your breathing. (See Lab 18B for more detailed instructions about diaphragmatic breathing.) Many relaxation approaches combine deep breathing with mental imagery to maximize the relaxation response. The main advantage of these approaches is that they can be used in any setting, and they take very little time to induce a relaxation response.

- *Jacobson's progressive relaxation method.* You must be able to recognize how a tense muscle feels before you can voluntarily release the tension. In this technique, contract the muscles strongly and then relax. Relax each of the large muscles first and later the small ones. Gradually reduce the contractions in intensity until no movement is visible. The emphasis is always placed on detecting the feeling of tension as the first step in "letting go" or "going negative." Jacobson, a pioneer in muscle relaxation research, emphasized the importance of relaxing eye and speech muscles, because he believed these muscles trigger the reactions of the total organism more than other muscles.

Taking time to relax can help you manage stress.
©Oliver Rossi/Corbis/Getty Images

- *Biofeedback.* Biofeedback training uses machines that monitor certain physiological processes of the body and that provide visual or auditory evidence of what is happening to normally unconscious bodily functions. The evidence, or feedback, is then used to help you decrease these functions. When combined with autogenic training (self-guided relaxation training which involves deep breathing and imagery), subjects can learn to relax and reduce the electrical activity in their muscles, lower blood pressure, decrease heart rate, change their brainwaves, and decrease headaches, asthma attacks, and stomach acid secretion.

- *Stretching and rhythmical exercises.* After working long hours at a desk, release tension by getting up frequently to stretch, taking a brisk walk, or by performing "office exercises." One popular activity that uses stretching and rhythmic exercise (as well as breathing techniques) is yoga. Many find it to be beneficial in reducing stress, and research has found both physical and mental health benefits associated with yoga.

Spirituality and mindfulness can help you cope with stress and daily problems. Besides managing the body's physical response to stress, one must deal with the impact of stress on thoughts and emotions. Although relaxation strategies can affect these dimensions, additional approaches may be necessary to adequately manage these aspects of the stress response.

- *Spirituality.* Studies have shown that spirituality can decrease blood pressure, be a source of internal comfort, and have other calming effects associated with reduced

Technology Update

Online Stress Management Resources

There are many online resources available to help you manage your stress. A training program called SMART (Stress Management and Resiliency Training) provides interactive training exercises that teach users to monitor stress, regulate emotions, relax, think flexibly, be realistic, and take effective action to deal with stressors. Other commercially available devices, such as StressEraser, provide personal biofeedback. Less expensive tools are available as smartphone apps, such as MyCalmBeat and StressCheck.

Would you consider using these types of applications for stress management? Why or why not?

connect
ACTIVITY

distress. It can also provide confidence to function more effectively, thereby reducing the stresses associated with ineffectiveness at work or in other situations. The health benefits of spirituality do not appear to be restricted to prayer, however. Using a more global measure of spirituality, one study of college students found that spirituality moderated the relationship between stress and health outcomes. For those low in spirituality, stress was associated with higher levels of negative emotion and physical symptoms of illness. Among those higher in spirituality, the link between stress and health outcomes was much weaker.

- *Mindfulness meditation.* While most relaxation techniques seek to distract attention away from distressing emotions, mindfulness meditation encourages the individual to experience fully his or her emotions in a nonjudgmental way. The individual brings full attention to the internal and external experiences that are occurring "in the moment." A meta-analysis of stress-management approaches in college students found that mindfulness-based approaches are effective in reducing anxiety and depressive symptoms, as well as cortisol levels. As an example, a study of Koru (a mindfulness approach) found that just four sessions of mindfulness training resulted in increases in mindfulness, decreases in perceived stress, and a reduction in sleep problems. Mindfulness may also be one way of fostering the health-protective effects of spirituality. One study found that changes in mindfulness were directly associated with reported gains in spirituality and quality of life. Benefits have also been demonstrated with medical conditions such as fibromyalgia, cancer, and coronary artery disease. The nonjudgmental aspect of awareness in mindfulness is critical to the success of this approach. Mindfulness tends to counter the tendency for people to focus excessively on negative outcomes (often referred to as rumination). Research has shown that rumination leads to negative psychological adjustment, including increased risk for depression.

Appropriately expressing emotion can help you reduce distress. The ability to control emotional outbursts is an adaptive skill that develops with age. As a society, we socialize our children to develop these skills, as they are critical to adaptive functioning in adulthood. At the same time, complete suppression of emotion has long been recognized as potentially harmful to our health. For example, Freud believed that inhibition of emotion contributed to psychological problems. Although it has taken roughly 100 years since Freud's early writing, recent studies have demonstrated that suppression of emotion indeed leads to negative outcomes. Among college students, emotional suppression has been related to increased anxiety sensitivity, depression, and poor social adjustment. The results demonstrate that to minimize the potential negative impact of our emotions, we need to find appropriate ways to express them.

We often turn to others to provide an outlet for us to "vent" or "get it off our chest." Although this is a perfectly good way to express emotion, we can also benefit from writing about our stressful experiences. Expressive writing has shown benefits for a wide range of outcomes, from faster wound healing to better adaptation following traumatic events. Writing also seems to help mitigate the effects of stress related to discrimination. For example, a recent study of gay male college students found that writing about stresses related to sexual orientation led to better adjustment three months later. Although many of the early studies on the therapeutic benefits of writing focused on traumatic or stressful events, more recent "self-affirmation" approaches focus on writing about personal values. These self-affirmations are believed to counter threats to the self which include threats related to discrimination and physical health problems. In adolescents and college students, self-affirmative writing has been shown to decrease the achievement gap between majority and minority students, and low versus high socioeconomic students. In the health domain, self-affirmative writing has been shown to increase medication compliance and exercise among individuals with hypertension and heart disease. Thus, writing about both challenges and important core values may allow individuals to cope more effectively with stress.

Problem-focused coping is most effective in dealing with controllable stressors. While appraisal- and emotion-focused coping may be the most effective means for coping with situations beyond one's control, a problem under personal control may best be addressed by taking action to solve the problem. A technique called "systematic problem solving" has been shown to improve the likelihood of problem resolution.

The first step is brainstorming, generating every possible solution to the problem. During this stage, do not limit the solutions you generate in any way. Even silly and impractical solutions should be included. After generating a comprehensive list, narrow your focus by eliminating any solutions that do not seem reasonable. Reduce the number of solutions to a reasonable number (four or five), and then carefully evaluate each option. Consider the potential costs and benefits of each approach to aid in making a decision. Once you decide on an approach, carefully plan the implementation of the strategy, anticipating anything that might go wrong and being prepared to alter your plan as necessary.

In some cases, directly addressing the source of stress involves responding assertively. For example, if the source of stress is an employer placing unreasonable demands on your time, the best solution to the problem may involve talking to your boss about the situation. This type of confrontation is difficult for many people concerned about being overly aggressive. However, you can stand up for yourself without infringing on the rights of others.

Many people confuse assertiveness with aggression, leading to passive responses in difficult situations. An aggressive response intimidates others and fulfills one's own needs at the expense of others. In contrast, an assertive response protects your own rights and values while respecting the opinions of others.

Writing about both challenges and important core values can help a person cope with stress.
©Klaus Tiedge/Corbis/Getty Images

Once you are comfortable with the idea of responding assertively, practice or role-play assertive responses with a trusted friend before trying them in the real world. Your friend may provide valuable feedback about your approach, and the practice may increase your self-efficacy for responding and your expectancies for a positive outcome.

Effective Time-Management Skills

Effective time management is a self-management skill that helps you adapt to the stresses of modern living. Lack of time is cited by both the general public and experts as a source of stress and a reason for failing to implement healthy lifestyle changes. For college students, managing time is critical to academic success as well as overall well-being. Managing time effectively has become even more of a challenge for college students in recent years, as more and more students are working part- or full-time jobs to support their education (see Figure 1). The following strategies may help you learn to manage your time more effectively.

- *Prioritize.* Many people feel that there are not enough hours in the day to do everything that needs to be done. The truth is, they are probably right. If you think about all the things that have to get done, it can seem unmanageable. That is why it is important to prioritize. Many time-management experts advocate the ABC approach as a way to prioritize tasks effectively. Create three lists of things you need to do, with list A including the most urgent tasks and list C containing the least urgent. To help you remember the ABC approach, remember that A tasks *A*bsolutely must get done, B tasks had *B*etter get done, and C tasks *C*ould get done. See Table 5 for a brief description of the ABC approach.

- *Plan.* One of the most important steps in effective time management is to plan your daily activities. This includes keeping a daily planner to remember your schedule, tracking important events and deadlines, and maintaining lists (using the ABC approach) to help you remember your goals and priorities. Computers and apps allow you to keep all of this information in one place.

- *Set goals and deadlines.* In addition to knowing how you spend your time, it is important to know what things need to get done. This includes everything from small tasks that need to get done today to important long-term goals. When setting goals, make sure they are attainable and that the time frame for completing them is reasonable. Some tasks may be more easily accomplished if they are broken down into a series of smaller tasks, each with its own deadline. Setting specific deadlines for the completion of goals increases the likelihood that you will follow through.

- *Build recreational activities into your schedule.* Although it may seem that scheduling fun takes away from the enjoyment, you may not find this to be true. By scheduling your free time, you can fully enjoy it rather than worrying about other things you "should" be doing.

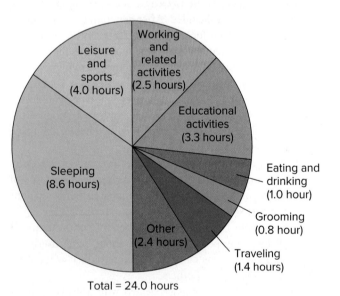

Figure 1 ▶ Time use on an average weekday for full-time university and college students.

Note: Data include individuals, aged 15 to 49, who were enrolled full time at a university or college. Data include averages for non-holiday weekdays.

Source: Bureau of Labor Satistics, American Time Use Survey

Table 5 ▶ The ABC System for Time Management	
Level of Importance	**Description**
A	*A tasks* are those that *must* be done, and soon. When accomplished, A tasks may yield extraordinary results. Left undone, they may generate serious, unpleasant, or disastrous consequences. Immediacy is what an A priority task is all about.
B	*B tasks* are those that *should* be done soon. While not as pressing as A tasks, they're still important. They can be postponed, but not for too long. Within a brief time, though, they can easily rise to A status.
C	*C tasks* are those that *could* be done. These tasks could be put off without creating dire consequences. Some can linger in this category almost indefinitely. Others—especially those tied to distant completion dates—will eventually rise to A or B levels as the deadline approaches.

Source: Mancini, M.

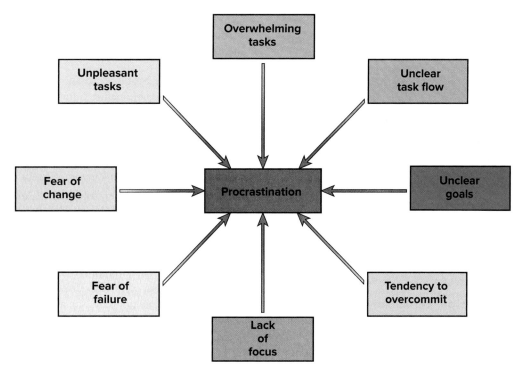

Figure 2 ▶ Causes of procrastination.

Source: Mancini, M., *Time Management* (The McGraw-Hill Companies, Inc., 2003).

- *Make the most of the time you have.* To get the most out of your time, know when you do your best work and under what conditions. If you are sharpest in the morning, schedule the most important work to be done during this time. If you study most effectively when you are alone in a quiet place, schedule your studying at a time when you can create that environment. It is also important not to let time that could be productive go to waste. Try to take advantage of small periods of time (e.g., between classes).

- *Regularly self-assess and monitor your time-management skills in order to manage your time effectively.* Where does your time go? The answer to this question is the first step toward better time management. Most of us are not fully aware of how we spend our time. Periodic self-monitoring of your time usage can help you learn how to focus your time on the most important things and identify where you could spend less time. You probably need to do this for at least a week to get a good indicator. Then reevaluate over time to track your progress, identify areas in need of further improvement, and adapt your plan to improve your chances of success.

- *Avoid procrastination.* Virtually all of us procrastinate at one time or another, but for many, procrastination can significantly decrease performance and increase stress. A number of causes of procrastination have been identified, including both internal and external influences. Understanding the causes of procrastination can help you find ways to prevent it in the future (see Figure 2). Strategies

such as the ABC approach should also help you limit procrastination by getting you to work on the things that are most important first. One of the simplest solutions to procrastination is simply to "get started." The first step toward completing a project is often the most difficult. Once people take the first step, they often find that the task becomes easier.

Effective Social Support

Eliciting social support is an important self-management skill for stress management. Social support can play a role in coping with stress, and it has been linked to better physical and mental health outcomes among individuals with chronic stress-related illnesses. For example, in a large group of patients with coronary artery disease, participation in a social support group was associated with lower systolic blood pressure, better social functioning, and better mental health. Social support may also be critical to managing stress in academic settings. A recent study found that a lack of social support from family, teachers, and peers was associated with a lack of academic motivation and subsequent academic failure.

Social Support The behavior of others that assists a person in addressing a specific need.

Social support is important for stress management.
©Don Hammond/Design Pics

Social support may be particularly important for women. Women may be particularly likely to seek and provide social support when stressed. A paradigm called the "tend or befriend" model suggests that women have a unique stress response. Women respond to stress by tending to others (nurturing) and affiliating with a social group (befriending). This response is helpful in reducing the risk for the negative health consequences of stress.

Social support has various sources. Everyone needs someone to turn to for support when feeling overwhelmed. Support can come from friends, family members, clergy, a teacher, a coach, or a professional counselor. Different sources provide different forms of support. Even pets have been shown to be a good source of social support, with consequent health and quality-of-life benefits. The goal is to identify and nurture relationships that can provide this type of support. In turn, it is important to look for ways to support and assist others.

There are many types of social support. Social support has three main components: informational, material, and emotional. Informational (technical) support includes tips, strategies, and advice that can help a person get through a specific stressful situation. For example, a parent, friend, or coworker may offer insight into how he or she once resolved similar problems. Material support is direct assistance to get a person through a stressful situation—for example, providing a loan to help pay off a short-term debt. Emotional support is encouragement or sympathy that a person provides to help another cope with a particular challenge.

Regardless of the type of support, it is important that it fosters autonomy. Social support that helps you become more self-reliant because of increased feelings of competence is best for developing autonomy. Social support that is controlling or leads to dependence may increase rather than decrease stress over time.

Obtaining good social support requires close relationships. Although we live in a social environment, it is often difficult to ask people for help. Sometimes the nature and severity of our problems may not be apparent to others. Other times, friends may not want to offer suggestions or insight because they do not want to appear too pushy. To obtain good support, one must develop quality personal relationships. Although having a large social support network is helpful, quality is more important than quantity. Many individuals report feeling lonely despite having large social networks, and loneliness is associated with negative health behaviors, including smoking and lack of exercise.

In the News

Social Networking for Social Support

An article in *Review of General Psychology* suggests that extensive exposure to social media such as Facebook can lead to depression. The author indicates that "users of Facebook may be more susceptible to causal triggers for mild depression under the following (specific) circumstances: (a) a large number of online friends; (b) a large amount of time spent reading updates from this wide pool of friends; (c) regular engagement in this activity; and (d) a bragging nature in the updates the individual is reading." Being exposed to Facebook, especially for long periods of time (and when alone), creates the impression that "others are doing better than I am" which may result in negative self-perceptions that can lead to depression. Other recent studies, however, suggest that social networking sites (SNSs) can be a source of social support. For example, a study by Pew Internet (**www.pewinternet.org**) found that SNS users were significantly less likely to be socially isolated and reported a larger number of close social ties. These results suggest that the use of SNSs strengthens rather than weakens social support.

Do social networking sites support or weaken your social network? Do they increase stress or help you manage stress better?

Using Self-Management Skills

Practicing key self-management skills can help you manage stress more effectively. This Concept described a variety of self-management skills that are important for preventing, managing, and coping with stress. Coping skills and time-management skills are considered "enabling factors" that help you adopt healthy lifestyles. As applied to stress management, these skills can help you avoid stress and take effective action to manage or cope with stress. Seeking social support is categorized as a "reinforcing factor" that helps reinforce healthy behaviors. In regard to stress-management, the key is to build your social support network and to learn how to effectively elicit and use support when needed. As you begin to use and practice these self-management skills, try to evaluate how effective they are in managing your stress. Not all approaches will work for all people, so there is no point in continuing to use strategies that do not work for you. If it works, keep practicing until you master the approach.

Sometimes professional help is necessary to deal with problems related to stress. This concept introduces principles for effective stress management, but sometimes stress creates problems that require professional help. If you think you might be suffering from post-traumatic stress disorder or depression, there are well-established treatments that can help you function more effectively. Sometimes, professionals can also be helpful in efforts to change negative health behaviors such as alcohol and drug use or problematic patterns of eating. Thankfully, stigmas associated with these problems have decreased, leading many more people to seek professional services. In addition, new approaches to treatment are now being developed, including online therapy and mail-based interventions. These approaches have the potential to reach even more people in need of professional help.

Practicing key self-management skills can help you manage stress more effectively. This Concept described a variety of self-management skills that are important for preventing, managing, and coping with stress. One useful way to organize these different approaches is to think about their respective roles both prior to and after the experience of a stressful event. *Protective strategies* are those that help prepare your mind and body for a positive response even before a stressful event occurs. Once you have experienced a stressor, you can engage in efforts to directly address the source of the stress (*primary control strategies*) as well as efforts to effectively manage the consequences of the stressor (*secondary control strategies*).

Protective strategies include:

- Time *management*. Learning to prioritize tasks (see Table 5) and plan for effective use of time (see Lab 18A) are effective steps for reducing the amount of stress you experience. Stress is often the result of a failure to plan effectively.

(See the "Effective Time Management Skills" section for more strategies.)

- *Exercise and recreation*. Part of effectively managing stress is about being physically healthy and keeping a work-life balance. Regular physical exercise will allow your body to respond to stress more effectively, and recreation will help with work-life balance.

- *Good sleep hygiene.* Your body will respond most effectively to stress if you get enough good quality sleep. In the busy lives of young people, it can be difficult to find enough time to sleep, but it is essential to do so. Using the time management approaches outlined in this Concept can help leave sufficient time for sleep. Also see Table 1 for tips on good sleep hygiene.

- *Relaxation techniques.* Regular practice of relaxation techniques helps keep the stress systems in the body in homeostasis so that a new stressor does not overwhelm your physical resources. A variety of approaches are available, and several are outlined in the emotion-focused strategies earlier in the Concept.

Primary control strategies include:

- *Systematic problem solving.* Primary control strategies are best employed when there is an opportunity to directly address the source of the stress. For example, a conflict with a coworker may be addressable if you have an effective strategy. The procedures outlined earlier in this Concept can help you engage in a systematic process for finding and implementing the best solution to the problem.

Secondary control strategies include:

- *Re-appraisal.* In many cases the source of stress may not be something you can directly change (e.g., a poor grade or the end of a relationship), but you can always change the way you think about the event. For example, one can let a poor test grade be defeating, or it can be used as a source of motivation to excel on the next exam. Tables 4 and 5 can help you identify self-defeating thoughts and develop approaches to think in ways that lead to more effective responses to stress.

- *Seeking social support.* When you experience events that are beyond your control, just talking to someone who understands your experience can make a big difference. Friends and family can also help you effectively use the other approaches outlined in this Concept. For example, exercising with a companion is often more enjoyable.

- *Protective coping strategies can also help with secondary control.* In addition to preparing your body and mind prior to the experience of a stressor, several of the protective approaches outlined above can help with managing the acute consequences of a stressor. For example, exercise and relaxation techniques can help your body recover from the acute physiological consequences of the stress response.

Although these categories may serve as a useful way to think about which approach to use in different circumstances, it is important to remember that not all strategies will work for all people. So, you have to find the approaches that work best for you. There is no point in continuing to use strategies that are not working. When you find approaches that do work, keep practicing until you master them.

Strategies for Action: Lab Information

Performing a self-assessment of current time use can help you manage time effectively. Lab 18A provides you with an opportunity to take a careful look at your current use of time. The results of the self-assessment can help you develop a schedule that will allow you to focus on your priorities and use your time effectively.

Effectively using relaxation exercises requires practice. Relaxation exercises are a type of performance skill that can be used to manage stress. Like any skill, they require practice to be effective. Lab 18B gives you the opportunity to practice several different relaxation exercises and to perfect the skills for future use in coping with stress.

Assessing your level of social support is the first step in improving it. Lab 18C gives you the opportunity to self-assess your current level of social support. After performing the self-assessment, use your scores to help you find social support if results indicate a need for improvement.

connect
ACTIVITY

Suggested Resources and Readings

The websites for the following sources can be accessed by searching online for the organization, program, or title listed. Specific scientific references are available at the end of this edition of *Concepts of Fitness and Wellness*.

- American Stress Institute (stress information website).
- Blease, C. (2015). Too many "friends," too few "likes"? Evolutionary psychology and "Facebook depression." *Review of General Psychology, 19,* 1–13 (pdf).
- Bureau of Labor Statistics. (2017). American Time Use Survey—2016 Results (pdf).
- Greenberg, J. (2016). *Comprehensive Stress Management* (14th ed.). St. Louis: McGraw-Hill Higher Education.
- Institute of Medicine. The Role of Telehealth in an Evolving Health Care Environment (online report; free pdf available).
- Mayo Clinic. Social Support: Tap This Tool to Beat Stress.
- Mayo Clinic. Spirituality and Stress Relief: Make the Connection.
- McGinigal, K. (2016). *The Upside of Stress: Why Stress Is Good for You, and How to Get Good at It.* New York: Penguin Random House.
- Meyers, L. (2016, March 28). Coping with College. *Counseling Today.*
- Physical Activity Guidelines Advisory Committee Scientific Report. 2018. Online resource.
- Storoni, M. (2017). *Stress Proof: The Scientific Solution to Protect Your Brain and Body.* New York: Penguin Random House.
- Stress Management Society. From distress to de-stress (website).
- Van dam, A., & Maroth, E. (2016, June 24). Changing times: How Americans spend their day reflects a shifting economy and population. *The Wall Street Journal.*
- Vitelli, R. (2015, May 25). Exploring Facebook depression. *Psychology Today.*
- WebMD. 10 Relaxation Techniques That Zap Stress Fast (online information).

Lab 18A Time Management

Name	Section	Date

Purpose: To learn to manage time to meet personal priorities.

Procedures

1. Follow the four steps outlined below.
2. Complete the Conclusions and Implications section.

Results

Step 1: Establish Priorities

1. Check the circles that reflect your priorities in the list below. Add priorities as necessary.
2. Rate each of the priorities you checked. Use a 1 for highest priority, 2 for moderate priority, and 3 for low priority.

Check Priorities	Rating	Check Priorities	Rating	Check Priorities	Rating
◯ More time with family		◯ More time with boyfriend/girlfriend		◯ More time with spouse	
◯ More time for leisure		◯ More time to relax		◯ More time to study	
◯ More time for work success		◯ More time for physical activity		◯ More time to improve myself	
◯ More time for other recreation		◯ Other _____		◯ Other _____	

Step 2: Monitor Current Time Use

1. On the following daily calendar, keep track of daily time expenditure.
2. Write in exactly what you did for each time block.

7–9 A.M.	9–11 A.M.	11 A.M.–1 P.M.	1–3 P.M.

3–5 P.M.	5–7 P.M.	7–9 P.M.	9–11 P.M.

Step 3: Analyze Your Current Time Use by Using the ABC Method (See Table 5 in the Concept)

A Tasks That *Absolutely* Must Get Done	B Tasks That Had *Better* Get Done	C Tasks That *Could* Get Done

Step 4: Make a Schedule: Write in Your Planned Activities for the Day

Time	Activities	Time	Activities
6:00 A.M.		3:00 P.M.	
7:00 A.M.		4:00 P.M.	
8:00 A.M.		5:00 P.M.	
9:00 A.M.		6:00 P.M.	
10:00 A.M.		7:00 P.M.	
11:00 A.M.		8:00 P.M.	
Noon		9:00 P.M.	
1:00 P.M.		10:00 P.M.	
2:00 A.M.		11:00 P.M.	

Conclusions and Implications: In several sentences, discuss how you might modify your schedule to find more time for important priorities.

Lab 18B Relaxation Exercises

Name | **Section** | **Date**

Purpose: To gain experience with specific relaxation exercises and to evaluate their effectiveness.

Procedures

1. Choose two of the relaxation exercises included in Chart 1 of this lab and read through the written instructions until you have a basic understanding of the exercises. Think through the specific aspects of the exercise until you have the process figured out.
2. Find a quiet place to try one of the exercises and follow the procedures as best you can. It is not possible to provide detailed instructions, but the information should be sufficient to give you a basic understanding of the exercises.
3. On another day try a different exercise.
4. Answer the questions in the Results section. Then complete the Conclusions and Implications section.

Results

1. Which of the two exercises did you try? (List them below.)

2. Have you done either of the exercises before? ◯ Yes ◯ No

3. Was one relaxation exercise more effective or better suited to you than the others? If so, which one?

Conclusions and Implications: In several sentences, discuss whether or not you feel that relaxation exercises will be a part of your wellness program. In what ways might you benefit from relaxation training? If you do not think you have a problem with relaxation, explain why.

Chart 1 Descriptions of Relaxation Exercises

A. Progressive Relaxation

Progressive relaxation uses active (conscious) mechanisms to achieve a state of relaxation. The technique involves alternating phases of muscle contraction (tension) and muscle relaxation (tension release). Muscle groups are activated one body segment at a time, incorporating all regions of the body by the end of the routine. Begin by lying on your back in a quiet place with eyes closed. Alternately contract and relax each of the muscles below—following the procedures described below. Begin with the dominant side of the body first; repeat on the nondominant side.

1. Hand and forearm—Make a fist.
2. Biceps—Flex elbows.
3. Triceps—Straighten arm.
4. Forehead—Raise your eyebrows and wrinkle forehead.
5. Cheeks and nose—Wrinkle nose and squint.
6. Jaws—Clench teeth.
7. Lips and tongue—Press lips together and tongue to roof of mouth, teeth apart.
8. Neck and throat—Tuck chin and push head backward against floor (if lying) or chair (if sitting).
9. Shoulder and upper back—Hunch shoulders to ears.
10. Abdomen—Suck abdomen inward.
11. Lower back—Arch back.
12. Thighs and buttocks—Squeeze buttocks together, push heels into floor (if lying) or chair rung (if sitting).
13. Calves—Pull instep and toes toward shins.
14. Toes—Curl toes.

Muscle contraction phase: Inhale as you contract the designated muscle for 3–5 seconds. Use only a moderate level of tension.

Muscle relaxation phase: Exhale, relaxing the muscle and releasing tension for 6–10 seconds. Think of relaxation words such as *warm, calm, peaceful,* and *serene.*

Relax every muscle in your body at the end of the exercise.

B. Diaphragmatic Breathing

This exercise will help improve awareness of using deep abdominal breathing over shallower chest-type breathing. To begin, lie on your back with knees bent and feet on the floor. Place your right hand over your abdomen and left hand over your chest. Your hands will be used to monitor breathing technique. Slowly inhale through the nose by allowing the abdomen to rise under your right hand. Concentrate on expanding the abdomen for 4 seconds. Continue inhaling another 2 seconds allowing the chest to rise under your left hand. Exhale through your mouth in reverse order (for about 8 seconds, or twice as long as inhalation). Relax the chest first, feeling it sink beneath the left hand and then the abdomen, allowing it to sink beneath the right hand. Repeat 4–5 times. Discontinue if you become light-headed.

C. Tai Chi Basic Form

The basic principles of tai chi are to maintain balance, use the entire body to achieve movement, unite movement with awareness (mind) and breathing (chi), and to keep the body upright. Tai chi involves holding the body in specific positions, or "forms." To execute the basic form, stand straight, feet shoulder-width apart and parallel with one another. Your knees should be bent and turned outward slightly with knees over the foot. Your hands are on belly button with palms facing body (men place hands right on left and women left on right), fingers are straight, spread slightly and relaxed.

1. Bring arms in front of body at a 30-degree angle to the plane of the back, palms facing downward. Reach up to shoulder height with arms moving up and to the sides. (Breathe in, allowing belly to move out as you raise arms upward.)
2. When hands reach shoulder height, turn palms up and move hands to head, allowing wrists to drop down. Imagine energy (chi) flowing from palms to top of head. (Continue breathing in.)
3. Imagine energy flowing down through a central line of the body. Follow the energy with hands, point fingers toward one another, palms down, move arms downward in front of the midline of face and chest. (Breathe out as arms lower.)
4. Two inches below belly button stop, cross palms, and move hands together.
5. Lower hands toward sides. (Complete breathing out.)
6. Repeat.

Lab 18C Evaluating Levels of Social Support

Name	**Section**	**Date**

Purpose: To evaluate your level of social support and to identify ways that you can find additional support.

Procedures

1. Answer each question in Chart 1 by placing a check in the box below Not True, Somewhat True, or Very True. Place the number value of each answer in the score box to the right.
2. Sum the scores (in the smaller boxes) for each question to get subscale scores for the three social support areas.
3. Record your three subscores in the Results section on the next page. Total your subscores to get a total social support score.
4. Determine your ratings for each of the three social support subscores and for your total social support score using Chart 2.
5. Answer the questions in the Conclusions and Implications section.

Chart 1 Social Support Questionnaire

These questions assess various aspects of social support. Base your answer on your actual degree of support, not on the type of support that you would like to have. Place a check in the space that best represents what is true for you.

Social Support Questions	Not True 1	Somewhat True 2	Very True 3	Score
1. I have close personal ties with my relatives.				
2. I have close relationships with a number of friends.				
3. I have a deep and meaningful relationship with a spouse or close friend.				
			Access to social support score:	
4. I have parents and relatives who take the time to listen to and understand me.				
5. I have friends or coworkers whom I can confide in and trust when problems come up.				
6. I have a nonjudgmental spouse or close friend who supports me when I need help.				
			Degree of social support score:	
7. I feel comfortable asking others for advice or assistance.				
8. I have confidence in my social skills and enjoy opportunities for new social contacts.				
9. I am willing to open up and discuss my personal life with others.				
			Getting social support score:	

377

Results

Scores and Ratings

(Use Chart 2 to obtain ratings.)

Access to social support score [ ]   Rating [ ]

Degree of social support score [ ]   Rating [ ]

Getting social support score [ ]   Rating [ ]

Total social support score
(sum of three scores) [ ]   Rating [ ]

Chart 2 Rating Scale for Social Support

Rating	Item Scores	Total Score
High	8–9	24–27
Moderate	6–7	18–23
Low	Below 6	Below 18

Conclusions and Implications

1. In several sentences, discuss your overall social support. Do you think your scores and ratings are a true representation of your social support?

2. In several sentences, describe any changes you think you should make to improve your social support system. If you do not think change is necessary, explain why.

The Use and Abuse of Tobacco

LEARNING OBJECTIVES

After completing the study of this Concept, you will be able to:

► Identify the most widely used forms of tobacco and the contents of tobacco products that contribute to negative health outcomes.

► Describe the negative health and economic costs of cigarette and cigar smoking and smokeless tobacco use.

► Describe secondhand smoke and identify the negative health consequences of secondhand smoke exposure.

► Understand trends in the prevalence of tobacco use and concerns about growing interest in e-cigarettes.

► Identify important factors contributing to recent reductions in tobacco use and efforts by the tobacco industry to maintain higher rates of smoking.

► Identify effective prevention and intervention approaches designed to reduce rates of tobacco use.

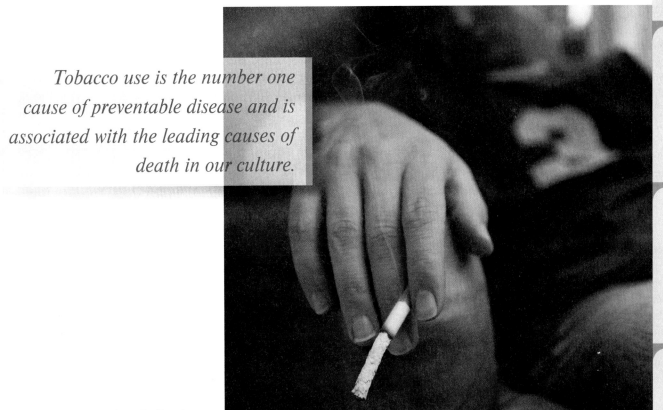

Tobacco use is the number one cause of preventable disease and is associated with the leading causes of death in our culture.

©Flying Colours Ltd/Photodisc/Getty Images

Why it Matters!

Tobacco is the number one cause of preventable death in the United States, and it is linked to most of the leading causes of death. Although rates of smoking in the U.S. have decreased in recent decades due to better awareness and a changed social norm, smoking is still a major public health problem. Nearly 40 million adults in the United States smoke (roughly 15 percent of the population), and nearly 5 million middle and high school students smoke. More than two-thirds of current smokers want to quit, but they find it extremely difficult to succeed. In addition, the use of various forms of e-cigarettes is widespread and the health consequences and risk for nicotine dependence related to these products is largely unknown. This Concept will help you understand risk factors for use and abuse of tobacco products so that you can stay or become tobacco-free.

Tobacco and Nicotine

Tobacco and its smoke contain over 400 noxious chemicals, including 200 known poisons and 50 carcinogens. Tobacco smoke contains both gases and particulates. The gaseous phase includes a variety of harmful gases, but the most dangerous is carbon monoxide. This gas binds onto hemoglobin in the bloodstream and thereby limits how much oxygen can be carried in the bloodstream. As a result, less oxygen is supplied to the vital organs of the body. While not likely from smoking, overexposure to carbon monoxide can be fatal. The particulate phase of burning tobacco includes a variety of carbon-based compounds referred to as tar. Many of these compounds found in tobacco are known to be **carcinogens.** Nicotine is also inhaled during the particulate phase of smoking. Nicotine is a highly addictive and poisonous chemical. It has a particularly broad range of influence and is a potent psychoactive **drug** that affects the brain and alters mood and behavior.

Nicotine is the addictive component of tobacco. When smoke is inhaled, the nicotine reaches the brain in 7 seconds, where it acts on highly sensitive receptors and provides a sensation that brings about a wide variety of responses throughout the body. At first, heart and breathing rates increase. Blood vessels constrict, peripheral circulation slows down, and blood pressure increases. New users may experience dizziness, nausea, and headache. Then feelings of tension and tiredness are relieved.

After a few minutes, the feeling wears off and a rebound, or **withdrawal,** effect occurs. The smoker may feel depressed and irritable and have the urge to smoke again. **Physical dependence** occurs with continued use. Nicotine is one of the most addictive drugs known, even more addictive than heroin or alcohol.

Smokeless chewing tobacco is as addictive as smoking and presents similar risks. Chewing tobacco comes in a variety of forms, including loose leaf, twist, and plug forms. Rather than being smoked, the dip, chew, or chaw stays in the mouth for several hours, where it mixes well with saliva and is absorbed into the bloodstream. Smokeless tobacco contains about seven times more nicotine than cigarettes, and more of it is absorbed because of the length of time the tobacco is in the mouth. It also contains a higher level of carcinogens than cigarettes.

Snuff, a form of smokeless tobacco, comes in either dry or moist form. Dry snuff is powdered tobacco and is typically mixed with flavoring. It is designed to be sniffed, pinched, or dipped. Moist snuff is used the same way, but it is moist, finely cut tobacco in a loose form and is sold in tea-bag-like packets. Regardless of the form, all are harmful.

The Health and Economic Costs of Tobacco

Tobacco use is the most preventable cause of death in our society. The 1964 landmark Surgeon General's report first called attention to the negative health consequences of smoking. It is now well established that tobacco use is the leading cause of death in the United States (accounting for nearly one in five of all deaths), contributing to 7 of the 10 leading causes of death. It is estimated that between 80 and 90 percent of all deaths related to lung cancer and obstructive lung disease are caused by smoking, and risk for coronary disease and stroke is two to four times higher among smokers. Further, new information about health risks continues to emerge. For example, a recent review of the literature on tobacco and dementia by the World Health Organization indicates that as many as 14 percent of Alzheimer disease cases worldwide may be attributed to smoking. The report suggests that exposure to secondhand smoke may be sufficient to increase risk for dementia. Thus, the number of diseases resulting from tobacco use is much more extensive than previously thought (see Figure 1).

One way to highlight the health risks associated with smoking is to examine the health benefits associated with smoking cessation. Estimates suggest that reducing serum cholesterol to recommended levels can increase life expectancy by about 1 week to 6 months. In contrast, smoking cessation may increase life expectancy by 2½ to 4½ years. The earlier people quit, the more years of life they save, with roughly 3 years saved for those who quit at 60 years of age, 6 years for those who quit at 50, and 9 years for those who quit at 40. The most effective way to reduce health risks

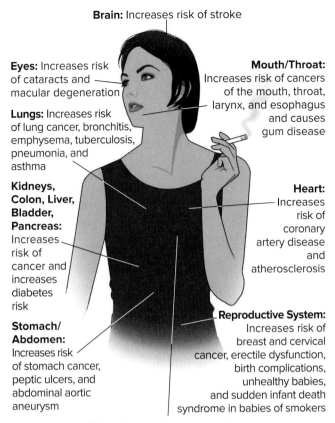

Brain: Increases risk of stroke

Eyes: Increases risk of cataracts and macular degeneration

Lungs: Increases risk of lung cancer, bronchitis, emphysema, tuberculosis, pneumonia, and asthma

Kidneys, Colon, Liver, Bladder, Pancreas: Increases risk of cancer and increases diabetes risk

Stomach/ Abdomen: Increases risk of stomach cancer, peptic ulcers, and abdominal aortic aneurysm

Mouth/Throat: Increases risk of cancers of the mouth, throat, larynx, and esophagus and causes gum disease

Heart: Increases risk of coronary artery disease and atherosclerosis

Reproductive System: Increases risk of breast and cervical cancer, erectile dysfunction, birth complications, unhealthy babies, and sudden infant death syndrome in babies of smokers

Blood: Impairs immune system, increases risk of leukemia, and decreases HDL

Figure 1 ▶ Unhealthy effects of smoking.

associated with smoking is clearly to quit; however, reducing how much one smokes also makes a difference. In one study, rates of lung cancer dropped by 27 percent among those who reduced their smoking from 20 or more to less than 10 cigarettes a day.

Smoking has tremendous economic costs. In addition to the cost of human life, medical costs and lost productivity related to smoking-related illnesses in the U.S. exceed $300 billion annually. Over and above the costs at the societal level, there are significant financial costs for the individual, particularly with increased taxes on tobacco products. In an effort to help smokers appreciate the financial burden of smoking, the Smokefree.gov website has a tool that allows users to see how much they spend on cigarettes. For someone who smokes a pack a day for 10 years, the total would be more than $25,000, based on typical cigarette prices.

The health risks from tobacco are directly related to overall exposure. In past years, tobacco companies denied there was conclusive proof of the harmful effects of tobacco products. Now, in the face of overwhelming medical evidence, tobacco officials have finally conceded that tobacco is harmful to health. It is now clear that the more you use the product (the more doses), the greater the health risk. Several factors determine the dosage: (1) the number of cigarettes smoked, (2) the length of time one has been smoking, (3) the strength (amount of tar, nicotine, etc.) of the cigarette, (4) the depth of the inhalation, and (5) the amount of exposure to other lung-damaging substances (e.g., asbestos). The greater the exposure to smoke, the greater the risk.

While risks clearly increase with the amount of exposure, recent studies suggest that even low levels of smoking have negative consequences. Unfortunately, although overall rates of smoking have decreased in recent years, rates of nondaily smoking have increased. These "chippers" or "social smokers" have lower risk relative to regular smokers, but there are negative health consequences of even low levels of smoking. For example, one study found that smoking one to four cigarettes per day nearly triples the risk of death from heart disease. Short-term physical consequences of smoking include increased rates of respiratory infections and asthma, impairment of athletic performance, and reduced benefits and enjoyment associated with recreational exercise.

Cigar and pipe smokers have lower death rates than cigarette smokers but are still at great risk. Cigar and pipe smokers usually inhale less and, therefore, have less risk for heart and lung disease, but cigarette smokers who switch to cigars and pipes tend to continue inhaling the same way. As the number of cigars smoked and the depth of smoke inhalation increase, the risk for death from cigar smoking approaches that of cigarette smoking. Cigar and pipe smoke contains most of the same harmful ingredients as cigarette smoke, sometimes in higher amounts. It may also have high nicotine content, leading to no appreciable difference between cigarette and pipe/cigar smoking with respect to the development of nicotine dependence. Cigar and pipe smokers also have higher risks for cancer of the mouth, throat, and larynx relative to cigarette smokers. Pipe smokers are especially at risk for lip cancer.

Secondhand smoke poses a significant health risk. When smokers light up, they expose those around them to **secondhand smoke.** Secondhand smoke is a combination of

Carcinogens Substances that promote or facilitate the growth of cancerous cells.

Drug Any biologically active substance that is foreign to the body and is deliberately introduced to affect its functioning.

Withdrawal A temporary condition precipitated by the lack of a drug in the body of an addicted person.

Physical Dependence A drug-induced condition in which a person requires frequent administration of a drug in order to avoid withdrawal.

Secondhand Smoke A combination of mainstream and sidestream smoke.

Technology Update

Are Smokeless Cigarettes "Safer"?

Phillip Morris International (a large cigarette manufacturer) has moved into e-cigarettes and other products to offset declines in the sale of traditional cigarettes. The company is currently developing a new "heat not burn" product called IQOS (pronounced eye-koss). The idea behind the product is to produce an experience that is more like traditional cigarette smoking as compared to e-cigarettes. The company claims that the smoke is what is harmful (IQOS is smokeless), rather than the tobacco or nicotine in cigarettes. To support its claims, it has funded studies demonstrating that IQOS is less harmful than traditional cigarettes. However, critics argue that more and longer-term studies are needed to examine the product's safety.

Do you believe Phillip Morris's claims of "safer" cigarettes or is this just another way to promote addiction to nicotine?

connect
ACTIVITY

mainstream smoke (inhaled and then exhaled by the smoker) and **sidestream smoke** (from the burning end of the cigarette). Because sidestream smoke is not filtered through the smoker's lungs, it has higher levels of carcinogens and is therefore more dangerous. Although the negative consequences of secondhand smoke have been known for some time, a 2006 Surgeon General's report summarized in detail the health dangers of secondhand smoke. The report indicated that there is no risk-free level of exposure to secondhand smoke. Following is a summary of the key conclusions:

- Exposure to secondhand tobacco smoke has been causally linked to cancer, respiratory and cardiovascular diseases, and to adverse effects on the health of infants and children.

- The estimated increase in risk for stroke from exposure to secondhand smoke is about 20 to 30 percent.

- The annual cost of lost productivity from premature death due to exposure to secondhand smoke is more than $5 billion.

- The evidence is sufficient to conclude that smoke-free indoor air policies are effective in reducing exposure to secondhand smoke and lead to less smoking among those covered by these policies.

connect
VIDEO 2

Women and children are especially susceptible to the negative effects of secondhand smoke. Adolescents exposed to secondhand smoke may have five times the risk of developing metabolic syndrome, which increases risk for heart disease, stroke, and diabetes, and they are also at increased risk of becoming smokers themselves. Secondhand smoke can

Awareness about the risks of secondhand smoke has contributed to changed social norms.
©Image Point Fr/Shutterstock

have a negative impact even when smokers try to protect children from exposure. One study found that babies of parents who only smoked outdoors had levels of cotinine (a nicotine by-product) seven times higher than babies of nonsmokers. This has been attributed to "thirdhand" smoke that may cling to clothing and hair. These findings have led to public health efforts to involve pediatricians in smoking cessation efforts, as parents generally see their child's pediatrician more often than their own doctor. Parents may also be more responsive to the message if they learn that smoking can hurt their children.

While not technically considered secondhand exposure, smoking during pregnancy harms a developing fetus. Children of smoking mothers typically have lower birth weight and are more likely to be premature, placing them at risk for a host of health complications. There is also a well-established relation between maternal smoking and risk for sudden infant death syndrome (SIDS). Finally, children of mothers who smoke are at increased risk for later physical problems (respiratory infections and asthma) and behavioral problems (attention deficit hyperactivity disorder). The best way to reduce risk for pregnant mothers and their children is for women to quit smoking altogether. However, there is some evidence that reductions in smoking also have benefits.

Secondhand smoke exposure may also negatively affect mental health. A national survey study found a significant relation between cotinine levels, an indicator of secondhand smoke exposure, and depression. Among those who never smoked, risk for depression was substantially increased for those exposed to cigarette smoke in their home or at work. Exposure to secondhand smoke in both childhood and adulthood has been associated with increased risk for depression and panic disorder 10 years later. Thus, mental health problems can be added to the list of the many negative health consequences of secondhand smoke exposure.

The health risks of smokeless tobacco are similar to those of other forms of tobacco. Some smokers switch to smokeless tobacco, thinking it is a safe substitute for cigarette, cigar, and pipe smoking. While smokeless tobacco does not lead to the same respiratory problems as smoking, the other health risks may be even greater because smokeless tobacco has more nicotine and higher levels of carcinogens. Because it comes in direct contact with body tissues, the health consequences are far more immediate than those from smoking cigarettes. One-third of teenage users have receding gums, and about half have precancerous lesions, 20 percent of which can become oral cancer within 5 years. Some of the health risks of smokeless tobacco are listed in Table 1.

The Facts about Tobacco Use

At one time, smoking was an accepted part of our culture, but the social norm has changed. While smoking has always been a part of our culture, the industrialization and marketing in the middle of the 20th century led to tremendous social acceptance of smoking. As odd as it may sound, cigarettes were once provided free to airline passengers when they boarded planes. The release of the Surgeon General's report on smoking in 1964, aggressive and well-funded antismoking campaigns, and increases in cigarette prices have contributed to reductions in smoking in the United States.

Since the 1950s, the prevalence of smoking has declined steadily from a high of 50 percent. Based on data from the National Health Interview Survey, rates of smoking in the United States dropped from 25 percent in the late 1990s to 15 percent in 2015. Rates among young people (high school students) have dropped even more dramatically, from 36 percent to 8 percent (see Figure 2). These declining trends in youth smoking are encouraging, but there is still much work to be done. Interestingly, while rates have been decreasing in the United States, they have been increasing in many other countries, particularly developing countries. Prevalence rates in China and many European countries greatly exceed those in the United States.

The use of smokeless tobacco is not as prevalent as smoking, but about 3.5 percent of adults (mostly males) are current users. Young people are among the most frequent users, with 6 percent of high school boys reporting smokeless tobacco use.

Table 1 ▶ Health Risks of Smokeless Tobacco

Smokeless tobacco increases the risk for the following:

- Oral cavity cancer (cheek, gum, lip, palate); it increases the risk by 4 to 50 times, depending on length of time used

- Cancer of the throat, larynx, and esophagus

- Precancerous skin changes

- High blood pressure

- Rotting teeth, exposed roots, premature tooth loss, and worn-down teeth

- Ulcerated, inflamed, infected gums

- Slow healing of mouth wounds

- Decreased resistance to infections

- Arteriosclerosis, myocardial infarction, and coronary occlusion

- Widespread hormonal effects, including increased lipids, higher blood sugar, and more blood clots

- Increased heart rate

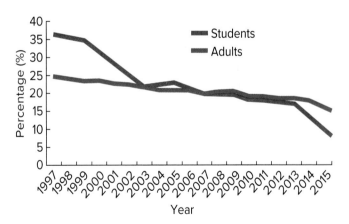

Figure 2 ▶ Trends in cigarette smoking.
Source: Centers for Disease Control and Prevention

Mainstream Smoke Smoke that is exhaled after being filtered by the smoker's lungs.
Sidestream Smoke Smoke that comes directly off the burning end of cigarette, cigar, or pipe.

Most tobacco users begin "using" during adolescence and find it hard to quit. The initiation of smoking is viewed as a pediatric problem by most public health experts. Data from the National Survey on Drug Use and Health indicate that roughly 2,800 adolescents initiate cigarette use each day, with more than 700 becoming daily smokers by age 18. Overall, more than 80 percent of all adult smokers began smoking before the age of 18; and more than 90 percent do so before leaving their teens. Smokeless tobacco use also begins early in life. Almost 50 percent of users report that they started before age 13.

Although most regular smokers begin in adolescence, a significant number start later in life, particularly during early adulthood (ages 18–25). Unfortunately, the number of new smokers over 18 has increased in recent years. The rate of use in the past 30 days is slightly lower among college students than high school seniors, but much lower than the rate of smoking among non–college students of a similar age.

The many types of media play a role in promoting and preventing tobacco use. Much of the blame for tobacco use among youth has been attributed to media campaigns of tobacco companies that have targeted this age group. Fortunately, regulations now prevent companies from direct marketing to anyone under the age of 18. Settlements from lawsuits against tobacco companies have also helped fund smoking prevention programs and public education campaigns (Figure 3). These factors have contributed to decreasing smoking rates in the United States. However, appeals by tobacco companies blocked and delayed full implementation of the planned media campaigns. In late 2017, the court ordered the four major tobacco companies to fund media statements about the health effects of tobacco. Although the companies released TV spots and full-page newspaper ads, public health experts concluded that the ads would not be as effective as those depicted in Figure 3. Consumers need to be aware of continued efforts by tobacco companies to introduce people to smoking and related products.

Public policy can affect tobacco use. A number of states have passed special tax laws to fund anti-tobacco efforts. In addition to efforts at the state level, federal taxes have increased by roughly one dollar per pack. These tax increases have contributed to the dramatic decreases in smoking in recent years. There is, however, wide variability in state taxes resulting in prices of more than $10 a pack in areas of New York, compared to prices of about $5 a pack in many other states. Higher state tax rates have been shown to help reduce smoking rates.

Public health campaigns and policies influencing access have also been very effective in reducing smoking. Four states that have aggressive anti-tobacco campaigns reported a 43 percent decrease in tobacco use—double that reported by other states. According to the Substance Abuse and Mental Health Services Administration (SAMHSA), efforts to cut down on tobacco sales to minors have also been

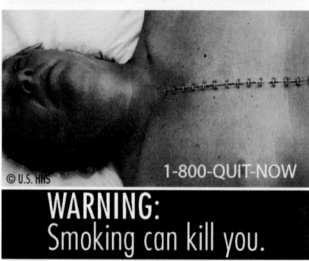

Figure 3 ▶ Warning label images.
©Food Collection/Alamy Stock Photo

extremely effective. The overall reductions in access have been correlated to usage, so the policies seemed to have had a positive effect. Bans on indoor smoking have also been important for reducing access and exposure. A total of 36 states now ban smoking in all restaurants, 31 ban smoking in bars, and 31 ban smoking in the workplace. A total of 28 states now ban smoking in all non-hospitality restaurants, bars, and workplaces and thousands of cities and counties have local mandates that ban indoor smoking. A recent review confirms that public smoking bans decrease rates of heart attacks. Researchers reviewed studies conducted in the United States, Canada, and Europe and found that heart attack rates fell 17 percent within a year after implementing smoking bans.

Most companies have similar policies that discourage smoking at work and encourage employees to quit altogether. Smokers suffer from more physical and mental health problems than non-smokers and this leads to higher health-care

Smoking bans in restaurants create a healthier environment for all.
©monkeybusinessimages/Getty Images

premiums. Efforts to reduce smoking are cheap, by comparison. An evaluation of the "Tips from Former Smokers" public health campaign found that the cost was less than $500 per smoker who quit. A company in Japan recently passed a policy that granted non-smoking staff an additional six days off each year to make up for the time smokers take for cigarette breaks. This type of incentive can be controversial, but it would be a major motivation for employees to quit.

 **HELP** **Health is available to Everyone for a Lifetime, and it's Personal**

Outdoor Smoking Bans

Indoor smoking bans are in place in most states and outdoor smoking bans are becoming increasingly common, particularly on college campuses. There are now more than 1,500 smoke-free campuses in the United States, up from almost 500 in 2010. These policies reflect the changing social norms about smoking.

Is your campus smoke-free? Do you support outdoor smoking bans, or is this going too far?

Tobacco companies are finding new ways to recruit tobacco users. Following the legal settlement, the tobacco industry responded by dramatically increasing its spending on advertising and promotion. Each year tobacco companies spend nearly $25 million per day to  market tobacco products. The vast majority of this spending is for price discounts meant to directly undermine the tax increases that have led to reduced smoking rates. The tobacco industry has also introduced new products and packaging to target young people. First it introduced flavored cigarettes, followed by dissolvable tobacco in pill form (e.g., Camel Orbs). Most recently, the industry has invested heavily in e-cigarettes and other smokeless tobacco products. Although companies manufacturing these products argue that they are a healthy alternative to smoking, the U.S. Food and Drug Administration (FDA) is not convinced, and many people are concerned that e-cigarette use will be a gateway to traditional cigarette use.

Another approach to targeting young people is through Internet-based sales. Although store sales to minors have decreased dramatically in recent years, it is relatively easy for minors to obtain cigarettes online. A Surgeon General's  report noted that 8 out of 10 minors who placed online cigarette orders were able to fill their orders, and only 1 in 10 was asked to provide proof of age.

A CLOSER LOOK

E-Cigarettes: Smoking Cessation Aid or a Gateway to Smoking?

There is considerable controversy about the impact and effects of electronic cigarettes (e-cigarettes). A recent study found that those who used e-cigarettes had a 60 percent higher quit rate (of traditional cigarettes) than those who used nicotine gum or patches. However, reports from national longitudinal studies of risk behavior indicate that rates of e-smoking have increased dramatically in recent years, particularly among young people who have never smoked conventional cigarettes. Moreover, those who had used e-cigarettes were nearly twice as likely to have intentions to try conventional cigarettes compared to those who had not used e-cigarettes.

Are e-cigarettes a healthier alternative or a way for tobacco companies to recruit new customers?

Various factors influence a person's decision to begin smoking. The reasons for starting smoking are varied but are strikingly similar to reasons given for using alcohol and other drugs. Common reasons that influence young people to start smoking include peer influence, social acceptance, or desires to be "mature" or to seem "independent". Some young women begin smoking because they believe it will help them control their weight and negative mood states and current smokers often fear they will gain weight if they quit. Also, those who smoke report higher levels of stress, and stress has been shown to be a maintaining factor among current smokers and a barrier to quitting among those who want to stop

smoking. The stress-management approaches covered in other Concepts may help with managing stress more effectively during attempts to quit.

People who smoke cigarettes also tend to use alcohol, marijuana, and hard drugs. Alcohol has often been considered a gateway to other drug use, and marijuana is often thought of as a gateway to other drugs, such as cocaine and heroine. Although tobacco use has been studied less extensively as a gateway drug, there is strong evidence that smoking is associated with increased risk for the use of both alcohol and illicit drugs. The combination of smoking and drinking is particularly common in college students. Results of a nationally representative study of college students indicated that 97 percent of college smokers drink, while other national data report that 80 percent of all college students drink. Those who drink also report higher levels of smoking. Rates of smoking among college drinkers range from 44 to 59 percent (compared with a national average rate of under 30 percent). The combination of alcohol use and smoking poses an even greater risk to physical health.

The addictive nature of nicotine makes it difficult to quit using tobacco. Salient examples of the power of nicotine addiction are high rates of continued use among those with serious smoking-related health consequences and low rates of success for  quit attempts. In a study in 15 European countries, over half of adults who suffered from serious medical problems known to be associated with smoking (e.g., heart attack, bypass surgery) continued to smoke 1 year later. Data from the CDC found that nearly 7 of 10 smokers want to quit and slightly more that half have tried to quit. Unfortunately, most of these attempts were unsuccessful. Most people make more than three serious attempts before they succeed. Withdrawal

In the News

Teens and Vaping

A variety of nicotine-related products are now marketed as cigarette alternatives (e.g., e-cigarettes, vapes, vaping pens or mods, and hookahs). The ease of access to these products by teens is raising significant concerns. The Juul vaporizer (or JUUL) is a vaping device that looks like a USB flash drive and can deliver very high nicotine content. According to the company that produces it, one JUUL pod contains as much nicotine as a pack of cigarettes. The JUUL can be discreetly plugged into a laptop USB port to

charge, making it a popular choice by high school and college students. Although the FDA is already looking into how to regulate them, it seems likely that companies will continue to develop novel e-cigs that target young users hoping to avoid getting caught with nicotine products.

Should the FDA regulate the use of JUULs to limit access by youth?

symptoms and craving for nicotine are often cited reasons for failed quit attempts. Many former smokers report nicotine craving months and even years after quitting. The good news is that when you quit you may feel better right away and your body will heal. You will feel more energetic, the coughing will stop, you will suddenly begin to taste food again, and your sense of smell will return. Your lungs will eventually heal and look like the lungs of a nonsmoker. Your risk for lung cancer will return to that of the nonsmoker in about 15 to 20 years. If you aren't successful at first, keep trying, as there are now more former smokers in the U.S. than current smokers.

Using Self-Management Skills

Building self-confidence and motivation is important in quitting smoking. Although quitting smoking may be one of the most difficult things a person ever has to do, there are established behavioral strategies that can help you or someone you know succeed. Multiple quit attempts may be necessary, but evidence suggests that people learn valuable behavioral skills through the process and this may help them eventually succeed. Remember, there are now more former than active smokers in the U.S., so millions of people have successfully stopped smoking. Table 2 provides some concrete self-management skills that can be used to successfully quit.

Building knowledge and changing beliefs can help you take action. There are a variety of resources available to help those who want to stop smoking. A number of national organizations provide telephone hotlines to help with quit attempts. These include the American Cancer Society (1-877-YES-QUIT), the National Cancer Institute (1-877-44U-QUIT), and the U.S. Department of Health and Human Services (1-800-QUIT-NOW). In addition, an online smoking program sponsored by several federal agencies is now available at www.smokefree.gov, and the U.S. Public Health Service (USPHS) has published a consumer's guide to quitting smoking (https://dcp.psc.gov/OSG/tobacco/).

Exercise and medication can help overcome barriers to quitting smoking. People trying to adopt healthy lifestyles face many challenges and this is especially true for those trying to quit smoking. Adopting a counter habit of exercise can help shift focus and priorities and facilitate behavior change. Evidence also suggests that physical activity reduces the likelihood of relapse among those who quit. Nicotine replacement products (patches, gum, nasal sprays) and medications such as Zyban and Chantix have also helped many smokers quit. For those who don't like using medications, there are also a variety of behavioral strategies that can help them quit, even without medications.

Developing coping skills can help you stick to your plan to quit smoking. A number of apps and text messaging tools are available to specifically help with smoking cessation. For example, smokefree.gov now includes a text-messaging service (www.smokefree.gov/smokefreetxt). Smokers complete a brief online questionnaire that includes their quit date, and the program sends 1–5 texts per day over a 6- to 8-week period. The text messages provide encouragement, advice, and tips to help the smoker succeed. Users can also text keywords to get additional support. For example, on the day before the identified quit date, the smoker might receive the message *"Tomorrow is quit day! Toss your pack in the trash & get plenty of sleep. For extra support, text these keywords at any time: Crave, Mood, or Slip."* The cues and prompts can help in facing temptations and give smokers the boost they need to quit. The program is provided at no cost to the user other than any data or texting fees from the user's cell phone provider.

Table 2 ▶ Strategies for Quitting Smoking
• You must want to quit. The reasons can be for health, family, money, and so on.
• Remind yourself of the reasons. Each day, repeat to yourself the reasons for not using tobacco.
• Decide how to stop. Methods to stop include counseling, attending formal programs, quitting with a friend, going "cold turkey" (abruptly), and quitting gradually. More succeed with "cold turkey" than with the gradual approach.
• Remove reminders and temptations (ashtrays, tobacco, etc.).
• Use substitutes and distractions. Substitute low-calorie snacks or chewing gum, change your routine, or try new activities.
• Do not worry about gaining weight. If you gain a few pounds, it is not as detrimental to your health as continuing to smoke.
• Get support. Try a formal "quit smoking" program for professional help and seek support from friends and relatives.
• Consider a product that requires a prescription, such as a nicotine transdermal patch, Zyban tablets, or nicotine chewing gum.
• Develop effective stress-management techniques. The single most frequently cited reason for difficulty in quitting smoking is stress.

Strategies for Action: Lab Information

If you are a smoker, an honest assessment of your background and exposure to tobacco is an important first step to quitting. Lab 19A will help you evaluate your potential risks and need for behavior change. If you score in the "high risk" or "very high risk" category, the website smokefree.gov provides a list of questions that can help motivate you to quit (https://smokefree.gov/quitting-smoking/prepare-quit).

Suggested Resources and Readings

The websites for the following sources can be accessed by searching online for the organization, program, or title listed. Specific scientific references are available at the end of this edition of *Concepts of Fitness and Wellness*.

- American Nonsmokers' Rights Foundation (website):
  - Smokefree Colleges and Universities (web resource).
  - Smokefree lists, maps, and data (web resource).
- Campaign for Tobacco-Free Kids (website):
  - Public Education Campaigns Reduce Tobacco Use (pdf).
- Centers for Disease Control and Prevention (CDC):
  - Cigarette Smoking among Adults in the United States (web resource).
  - E-Cigarettes and Young People: A Public Health Concern (web resource).
  - Fact Sheet: Health Effects of Cigarette Smoking (web resource).

- Chaudhuri, S. (2017, October 29). Philip Morris's big smokeless bet. *The Wall Street Journal*.
- Hafner, J. (2017, October 31). Juul e-cigs: The controversial vaping device popular on school campuses. *USA Today*.
- Healthline. Researchers Say E-Cigarettes Can Help You Quit Smoking (online article).
- Mayo Clinic. Thirdhand Smoke and Why It Is a Concern (web resource).
- National Academies of Sciences, Engineering, and Medicine. 2018. Public health consequences of e-cigarettes. Washington, DC: The National Academies Press.
- National Public Radio. Tobacco companies admit they made cigarettes more addictive. (online article)
- Quitnet (free resources to quit smoking).
- SAMHSA. Trends in Smokeless Tobacco Use and Initiation.
- Smokefree.gov (free resources to quit smoking).
- Smokefree.gov. SmokefreeTXT (smokefree texting program).
- WebMD. Smoking Cessation Health Center.
- World Health Organization. Fact Sheet: Tobacco.

Lab 19A Use and Abuse of Tobacco

Name	Section	Date

Purpose: To understand the risks of diseases (such as heart disease and cancer) associated with the use of tobacco or exposure to tobacco by-products.

Procedures

1. Read the Tobacco Use Risk Questionnaire (Chart 1).
2. Answer the questionnaire based on your tobacco use or exposure.
3. Record your score and rating (from Chart 2) in the Results section.

Results

What is your tobacco risk score?　[   ]　(total from Chart 1)

What is your tobacco risk rating?　[   ]　(see Chart 2)

Chart 1 Tobacco Use Risk Questionnaire

Circle one response in each row of the questionnaire. Determine a point value for each response using the point values in the first row of the chart. Sum the numbers of points for the various responses to determine a Tobacco Use Risk score.

	Points				
Categories	**0**	**1**	**2**	**3**	**4**
Cigarette use	Never smoked		1–10 cigarettes a day	11–40 cigarettes a day	>40 cigarettes a day
Pipe and cigar use	Never smoked	Pipe— occasional use	Cigar— infrequent daily use	Cigar or pipe— frequent daily use	Cigar—heavy use
Smoking style	Don't smoke		No inhalation	Slight to moderate inhalation	Deep inhalation
Smokeless tobacco use	Don't use	Occasional use: not daily	Daily use: one use per day	Daily use: multiple use per day	Heavy use: repetitious, multiple use daily
Secondhand or sidestream smoke	No smokers at home or in workplace	Smokers at workplace but not at home	Smokers at home but not workplace	Smokers at home and at workplace	
Years of tobacco use	Never used	1 or less	2–5	6–10	>10

Note: Different forms of tobacco use pose different risks for different diseases. This questionnaire is designed to give you a general idea of risk associated with use and exposure to tobacco by-products.

Chart 2 Tobacco Use Risk Questionnaire
Rating Chart

Rating	Score
Very high risk	16+
High risk	7–15
Moderate risk	1–6
Low risk	0

Conclusions and Implications

1. In several sentences, discuss your personal risk. If your risk is low, discuss some implications of the behavior of other people that affect your risk, including what can be done to change these risks. If your risk is above average, what changes can be made to reduce your risk?

2. In several sentences, discuss how you feel about public laws designed to curtail tobacco use. Discuss your point of view, either pro or con.

The Use and Abuse of Alcohol

LEARNING OBJECTIVES

After completing the study of this Concept, you will be able to:

▶ Understand the effects of alcohol on the body.

▶ Describe different patterns of alcohol use and problems, including alcohol use disorders.

▶ Identify the negative physical, psychological, and behavioral consequences of excess alcohol consumption.

▶ List factors that have contributed to declining rates of driving under the influence of alcohol.

▶ Explain biological and environmental factors associated with increased risk for alcohol problems.

▶ Determine aspects of the college environment that contribute to heavy drinking among students.

▶ Describe effective approaches for preventing and treating alcohol-related problems.

▶ Identify steps you can take to protect yourself and others.

Alcohol is among the most widely used and destructive drugs. Abstaining from alcohol is the surest way to prevent negative consequences, but learning to drink in moderation can significantly reduce risk.

©John Foxx/Media Bakery

Why it Matters!

Alcohol is the most widely used drug in the U.S. and, although moderate drinking may provide some health benefits, excessive drinking is associated with a wide variety of negative consequences. Alcohol use is the third leading health problem and cause of early death in the United States, and some consider alcohol use to be the most destructive because of the devastating results of drinking and driving and the consequences of increased crime, physical and sexual abuse, and destroyed family relationships. Although individuals with alcohol use disorders (AUDs) experience the greatest individual harm, they account for only a small proportion of the overall societal costs. Therefore, it is critical for all to understand the full range of drinking patterns and the factors that lead to hazardous use. This is especially true on college campuses where the environment contributes to high rates of binge drinking and associated consequences. Fortunately, there are both environmental and individual strategies that can be used to prevent and treat alcohol problems. This Concept will help you understand the causes and consequences of hazardous drinking as well as strategies for reducing risks.

Alcohol and Alcoholic Beverages

Alcoholic beverages contain ethanol (ethyl alcohol), an intoxicating and addictive drug that is often misused. The active **drug** in alcoholic beverages (ethanol) is a toxic chemical, but unlike methanol (wood alcohol) and isopropyl (rubbing alcohol), it can be consumed in small doses. As a drug, it is classified as a depressant. However, this classification does not capture the full range of alcohol's effects. The effects experienced by the drinker depend, in part, on whether the drinker's blood alcohol concentration is rising or falling. The sedative effects of alcohol as blood alcohol levels fall are consistent with its classification as a depressant. In contrast, primarily stimulant effects are experienced by the user as blood alcohol concentration rises.

Humans have consumed alcoholic beverages for thousands of years. Unfortunately, many people in our culture view drunkenness as a rite of passage and an expectation. Indeed, there are more synonyms for the word drunk or **intoxication** than for any other word in the English language. This illustrates the importance we give to overconsumption. Fortunately, as people mature and responsibilities such as work and family become more important, most reduce their consumption.

Alcoholic beverages have varying concentrations of alcohol, but many have similar amounts per serving. Beverages are usually served in proportions such that a drink of any one of the three categories (beer, wine, or liquor) contains the same amount of alcohol. Beer is usually served in a

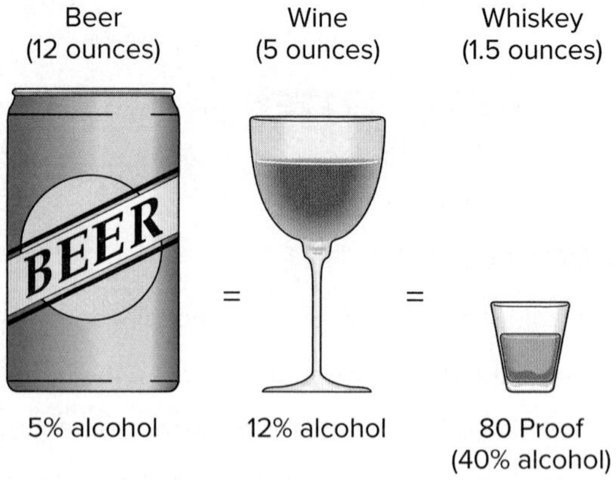

Figure 1 ▶ Alcohol content of drinks.
Source: National Institute on Alcohol Abuse and Alcoholism

12-ounce can, bottle, or mug. A typical glass of wine holds 5 ounces, and a shot of liquor is 1.5 ounces. Even though the percentage of alcohol in the beverages differs, the drinks would be equivalent in alcohol because each would contain about 14 g of alcohol (see Figure 1). Although the amount of alcohol is equivalent across these different drink types, differences in the way they are consumed may lead to differences in blood alcohol concentrations. For example, because liquor is often consumed more quickly than beer or wine, blood alcohol concentrations rise more quickly.

Alcohol's effects on the body depend on many factors. Alcohol is absorbed directly into the bloodstream, primarily in the small intestines. It then concentrates in various organs in proportion to the amount of water each contains. The brain has a high water content, so much of the alcohol goes there. Once it is absorbed, alcohol is metabolized primarily by the liver. An enzyme in the liver, called alcohol dehydrogenase (ADH), converts alcohol to acetaldehyde, which is then converted by acetate and other enzymes into carbon dioxide and water. Individuals differ with respect to their ability to metabolize alcohol, but a healthy adult takes 1 to 2 hours to metabolize one standard drink.

Although the basic processes of alcohol absorption and metabolism are the same for everyone, the effects of alcohol depend on a number of additional factors including stomach contents, body size/weight, rate of consumption, beliefs about alcohol effects, and drinking context (e.g., bar vs. home). There are also important gender differences in alcohol response. Because women have lower amounts of body water, a given amount of alcohol represents a greater percentage of the volume of the blood in their bloodstream. Women also have lower amounts of the enzymes needed to process alcohol.

Because the rate of alcohol consumption is often greater than the rate at which it is processed, the alcohol concentration in the bloodstream begins to increase. The blood alcohol concentration (BAC) is measured as a percentage and is used by law enforcement officials to determine if a driver is legally intoxicated.

Table 1 ▶ Terms and Criteria for Patterns of Alcohol Use

Term	Criteria
Moderate drinking (NIAAA)	Men: ≤2 drinks/day Women: ≤1 drink/day Over 65: ≤1 drink/day
At-risk drinking (NIAAA)	Men: >14 drinks/week or >4 drinks/occasion Women: >7 drinks/week or >3 drinks/occasion
Heavy-episodic drinking/binge drinking (NIAAA)	Men: 5 or more alcoholic drinks consumed in a 2-hour period Women: 4 or more alcoholic drinks consumed in a 2-hour period
Alcohol use disorder (APA)	Maladaptive pattern of alcohol use leading to clinically significant impairment or distress, manifested within a 12-month period by two or more of the following: (mild: 2–3 symptoms, moderate: 4–5 symptoms, severe: 6 or more symptoms) • Use of larger amounts or over a longer time period than intended • Persistent desire or unsuccessful attempts to cut down or control use • Great deal of time spent obtaining, using, or recovering from use • Craving, or a strong desire or urge to use • Recurrent use leading to failure to fulfill role obligations at work, school, or home • Continued use despite alcohol-related social or interpersonal problems • Important social, occupational, or recreational activities given up or reduced due to use • Recurrent use in hazardous situations • Use despite knowledge of alcohol-related physical or psychological problems • Tolerance (either increasing amounts used or diminished effects with the same amount) • Withdrawal (withdrawal symptoms or use to relieve or avoid symptoms)

Note: NIAAA, National Institute on Alcohol Abuse and Alcoholism; APA, American Psychiatric Association.
Source: O'Conner and Schottenfeld.

Alcohol Consumption and Alcohol Abuse

Risks and benefits of alcohol use depend on the amount and pattern of consumption. Making statements about the consequences of alcohol consumption is difficult because the consequences vary depending on the amount consumed and the pattern of consumption. Moderate alcohol consumption has been shown to provide some benefits for reducing risk of heart disease, but considerable risks occur when consumed in excess. Risks for alcohol consumption are not the same for everyone, so it is important to understand the relative risks and benefits of various levels of alcohol consumption.

Patterns of alcohol consumption are characterized in a variety of ways. More than half (56.4 percent) of the U.S. population over the age of 18 report alcohol use in the past 30 days. This makes alcohol the most widely used drug of abuse in this country. Most who choose to drink develop a pattern of light or moderate drinking. The National Institute on Alcohol Abuse and Alcoholism (NIAAA) characterizes "moderate consumption" as one drink per day or less for women and two drinks per day or less for men (see Table 1). Those who exceed these standards are often described as at-risk drinkers. Heavy-episodic

drinking (commonly referred to as binge drinking) is common among at-risk drinkers. It is defined as 5 or more standard alcoholic drinks (for men), and 4 or more for women (see Table 1). Using this standard, approximately 27 percent of the U.S. population over age 18 (more than 65 million people) report binge drinking in the past 30 days.

Binge drinkers account for 85 percent of episodes of drinking and driving, and they are at increased risk for a host of negative outcomes, including development of **alcohol use disorders (AUDs)** (see Table 1 for characteristics). Two key signs of alcohol use disorders are **alcohol tolerance** and **alcohol withdrawal.** Unfortunately, many people seem to think that tolerance is a good sign, as evidenced by

Drug Any biologically active substance that is foreign to the body and is deliberately introduced to affect its functioning.

Intoxication Also referred to as drunkenness; a blood alcohol level of .08 percent.

Alcohol Use Disorder (AUD) A psychiatric condition characterized by alcohol-related problems that cause significant impairment or distress.

Alcohol Tolerance The phenomenon of requiring more and more alcohol over time to achieve the desired effect.

Alcohol Withdrawal Symptoms that occur when alcohol is withdrawn after a period of prolonged heavy use. Symptoms include sweating, anxiety, tremors, and seizures.

statements such as "I can hold my liquor" and "I'm not a lightweight." The reality is that tolerance has mostly negative implications. There is also recent evidence that those who have a natural, or "innate," tolerance to alcohol effects are at increased risk for developing alcohol use disorders. With the heavier use that comes with the development of tolerance, withdrawal symptoms may develop when alcohol is not administered regularly. Withdrawal symptoms include anxiety, increased heart rate, sweating, hand tremor, nausea, and vomiting. In more severe cases, withdrawal can lead to hallucinations and seizures.

Health and Behavioral Consequences of Alcohol Use

Heavy alcohol use is associated with an increased risk for a variety of negative health and social outcomes. The most well-established health risk associated with alcohol consumption is liver disease. Alcohol consumption is the leading cause of disease and death from liver dysfunction, with roughly 47 percent of all liver disease deaths related to excess alcohol consumption. Although the liver is capable of metabolizing moderate amounts of alcohol on a regular basis, persistent, heavy drinking may lead to swollen liver cells, a condition called **fatty liver.** If drinking is stopped or significantly reduced at this point, the damage to the liver is likely reversible. With continued heavy drinking, the individual is likely to develop **alcoholic cirrhosis,** or permanent scarring of the liver.

Heavy drinking is also a risk factor for other life-threatening diseases. Figure 2 depicts all causes of mortality risk as well as mortality risk for several specific diseases by level of alcohol consumption, with values less than 1 reflecting decreased risk and values greater than 1 reflecting increased risk. Although moderate alcohol consumption may protect against coronary heart disease (CHD), as outlined later in this Concept, heavier

use of alcohol may increase the risk for CHD and other cardiovascular disease. Specifically, heavy drinking is associated with increased risk for hypertension, cardiomyopathy, cardiac arrhythmia, and congestive heart failure. Alcohol consumption increases the risk for cancer, including cancer of the oral cavity and pharynx, esophagus, liver, larynx, and female breast. The risk for certain types of stroke (hemorrhagic) is also increased by alcohol, and there is evidence that heavy drinking may impair immune functioning, leading to increased risk for infectious diseases, including pneumonia and tuberculosis. Heavy alcohol use also has both acute and long-term effects on cognitive functions including memory, and increases risk for psychiatric disorders that often occur with alcohol problems (e.g., mood and anxiety disorders).

Although many health risks of alcohol use are directly related to the effects of alcohol on the body, others are related to the intoxicated behavior of the drinker. For example, heavy episodic drinking increases risk for motor vehicle crashes, falls, burns, drownings, interpersonal violence, and sexually transmitted infections. Ambitious public health goals have been set for curtailing binge drinking in the United States, but rates have remained relatively stable.

Women appear to be especially susceptible to the negative health consequences of heavy drinking. At similar levels of alcohol consumption, women are more likely than men to experience liver, cardiovascular, and brain damage from drinking. Alcohol also increases risk of breast cancer and negatively impacts the reproductive system. Pregnant women should avoid alcohol because it can lead to fetal alcohol effects, including fetal alcohol syndrome (FAS), which is associated with low birth weight, physical defects, mental retardation, and stunted growth. In summary, the health risks of alcohol consumption are extensive and must be considered in relation to the potential benefits.

Whereas excessive drinking presents many risks, moderate consumption can provide some health benefits. There is evidence that moderate alcohol consumption (one drink per day for women, up to two drinks per day for men) is associated with decreased risk for CHD, Type 2 diabetes, and certain types of stroke. A recent study that followed more than 300,000 people found that those who were light or moderate drinkers (but not heavy drinkers) were 20 percent less likely to die over an eight-year period. It may be that moderate drinkers are at lower risk based on other characteristics, such as higher education and income, better diet, and more regular exercise. Still, mechanisms for a causal role of alcohol use in protection against CHD are plausible. Recent evidence suggests that moderate alcohol use may also

Figure 2 ▶ Alcohol consumption and death risk.
Source: American Cancer Society

protect against cognitive declines with aging. Although the health benefits of moderate alcohol consumption have largely been attributed to wine consumption, beer appears to have similar benefits. In addition, there is some evidence that beer consumption may benefit bone strength because it has high levels of dietary silicon, which contributes to bone density. Beers with high levels of barley and hops are particularly good sources of silicon.

Although there is evidence of health benefits from moderate alcohol use, there is considerable debate about the extent of these benefits. Also, even moderate alcohol consumption may not be safe for some people. Certain groups are better off not drinking at all, despite potential health benefits (see Table 2). Also note that the pattern of drinking is as important as the absolute level. A woman who has seven drinks one time each week consumes an average of one drink per day but does not receive the same health benefits as a woman who consumes one drink each day. Moderate consumption of alcohol can be safely incorporated into a healthy lifestyle, but heavy drinking cannot.

The greatest danger of alcohol occurs when the drinker gets behind the wheel of a motor vehicle. Alcohol-related traffic crashes are the leading cause of death and spinal cord injury for young Americans. Approximately 31 percent of fatal injury traffic accidents involved at least one driver with a BAC of .08 percent or higher. The driver's likelihood of causing a highway accident increases at a BAC of .04 percent (1–2 drinks for most people). The likelihood of a fatal or serious injury crash is 6 to 12 times higher for an individual with a BAC of .10 percent relative to a person with no alcohol in their system.

In addition to injury risks associated with traffic accidents, those who drink and drive face significant legal, financial, and social costs. Although the short-term costs are significant, the long-term costs of a drunk driving arrest typically far outweigh the immediate financial burden. Having an offense on your record can lead to problems with schools, family, and future employers. Despite the potential short- and long-term costs, a recent survey conducted by the National Highway Traffic Safety Administration (NHTSA) found that about 11 percent of drivers in the United States drove under the influence in the last year. Rates were even higher (roughly 20 percent) among young adults aged 21 to 25. Table 3

Table 3 ► The Effects of Blood Alcohol Concentration (BAC) on Driving Performance and Function

BAC .02%
- Vision is impaired: less ability to see objects in motion; less ability to monitor multiple objects.
- Attention span is lower.
- Reaction time slows.

BAC .05–.06%
- Inhibitions are reduced (unnecessary chances may be taken).
- Visual abilities decrease; side vision is impaired by 30%.
- Judgment is the first function to be impaired.
- Braking distance is extended.
- Coordination is impaired.
- Driving performance is impaired at moderate speed.

BAC .08%
- Vision is seriously impaired, especially at night.
- Driver is overconfident in driving ability.
- Driver is less able to concentrate.
- Judgment is dulled; driver is more careless.
- Muscle control and coordination are hindered.
- Driving performance is impaired at low speeds.
- Driver increases the use of the accelerator and brake.

BAC .15%
- Driver experiences gross motor impairment and lack of physical control.
- Blurred vision and loss of balance occur.

BAC .20%
- Driver is disoriented and has difficulty walking.
- Nausea and vomiting occur.
- Anesthesia occurs.
- Driver may have impaired gag reflex.
- Driver may suffer blackouts.

BAC .30%
- Stupor and decreased respiration occur.
- Driver may lose consciousness.

BAC .40%
- Coma may occur.
- Death is possible, due to respiratory arrest.

Source: Mothers Against Drunk Driving

Table 2 ► People Who Should Consider Abstaining from Alcohol Use

- People under age 21 (legal age)
- Athletes striving for peak performance
- Women trying to get pregnant or who are pregnant or nursing
- Alcoholics and recovering alcoholics
- People with a family history of alcoholism
- People with a medical or surgical problem and/or on medications
- Psychiatric patients or persons experiencing severe psychosis
- People driving vehicles, operating dangerous machinery, or involved in public safety
- People conducting serious business transactions or study

Fatty Liver Swelling of the cells of the liver.

Alcoholic Cirrhosis Permanent scarring of the liver, resulting in reduced blood flow and buildup of toxins in the body.

Table 4 ▶ Approximate BAC Values (%) Based on the Number of Drinks Consumed over a Two-Hour Period

Number of Drinks	Females		Males	
	120-Pound	180-Pound	140-Pound	200-Pound
1	.02	.004	.007	.001
2	.06	.03	.04	.02
3	.10	.06	.07	.04
4	.15	.09	.10	.06
5	.19	.12	.13	.08
6	.23	.15	.16	.10
7	.27	.17	.19	.13
8	.31	.20	.22	.15

Source: National Highway Traffic and Safety Administration (NHTSA), 1994.

who is over the legal limit from starting his or her car. Many states require the interlock devices in the cars of at least some offenders, and studies show that they decrease re-arrest by almost 70 percent. Some states are considering interlock devices for all offenders, and car manufacturers are also working on developing alcohol sensors that can be installed in new cars. This would allow all drivers (not just offenders driving under the influence [DUI]) to know if they are driving impaired. Perhaps in response to stricter laws, many people are testing their own blood alcohol levels before getting behind the wheel. Sales of blood alcohol self-tests have increased dramatically in recent years.

Risk Factors for Alcohol-Related Problems

Early age of drinking onset increases risk for later problems. Those who begin drinking at an earlier age are at risk for the development of alcohol use disorders. Although

summarizes the effects of different BAC values on physical and driving performance.

Awareness of the impact of alcohol on impairment is important for avoiding problems. Table 4 provides estimated BACs for men and women at various weights. Lab 20A provides the formula for calculating BAC for your precise weight.

Stronger policies have contributed to decreases in alcohol-related traffic fatalities. Although alcohol-related traffic fatalities remain a major public health concern, policy changes, such as increasing the legal drinking age to 21 and decreasing the legal limit for intoxication to .08 percent, have led to dramatic decreases in impaired driving over the past 30 years (see Figure 3). Fortunately, new approaches are being developed, including ignition interlock devices that prevent a driver

Choosing not to get behind the wheel is the only responsible choice for those who drink.
©Image Source/Getty Images

A CLOSER LOOK

Impaired Driving and Traffic Fatalities

Rates of impaired driving and their consequences vary considerably from state to state. A Centers for Disease Control and Prevention (CDC) website lets you compare the consequences of driving impaired in your state with other states. The site provides fact sheets for each of the 50 states, allowing you to see rates of drunk driving and alcohol-related traffic fatalities for your state compared to national rates. Understanding and reviewing alcohol policies and penalties

may cause you or a friend to think twice about driving while impaired. Search "CDC state policies on impaired driving" online to learn more.

Are you surprised by the statistics on impaired driving and traffic fatalities in your state? What factors might contribute to higher or lower rates in your state, relative to national levels?

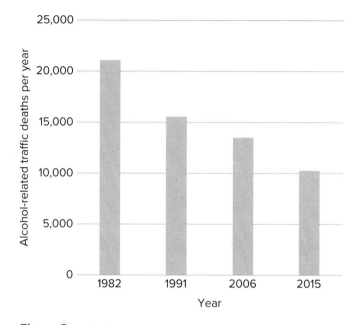

Figure 3 ▶ Declines in alcohol-related traffic fatalities.

Source: Foundation for Advancing Alcohol Responsibility, www.responsibility.org

the nature of the relation between age of onset and later problems is not yet clear, many believe that early use interferes with a critical period of brain development. The part of the brain involved in emotion regulation and impulse control (the frontal lobe) is not fully developed until the mid-20s, so although physical maturation may be complete by age 18, cognitive abilities are still developing during this period. Use of alcohol and other drugs during this important period of brain development may have long-term negative consequences for young people.

Having a family member with an alcohol problem places you at increased risk for developing a problem yourself. Experts have known for some time that the development of alcohol use disorder has a genetic component. Alcohol problems run in families, and it is estimated that genetics account for roughly half of the risk for AUD. In the future, we may find out exactly how genetic differences contribute to risk, but for now we know that genetics are important. Thus, if you have a family history of alcoholism, you should be especially careful about your drinking behavior.

Environment also plays a role in the initiation and escalation of alcohol use. During childhood, parents play a significant role in the socialization process, which includes socialization regarding alcohol use. Parents who talk to their kids about alcohol use, provide social support, and monitor their children's behavior are less likely to have children who drink excessively during adolescence. During adolescence, peers take on a powerful role in the development of alcohol

problems. One of the best predictors of adolescent alcohol use patterns is the pattern of alcohol use among their close friends.

Broader environmental influences also play a key role in the development of alcohol use. The promotion of alcohol as a social lubricant leads to the development of positive beliefs about the effects of alcohol, referred to as "alcohol expectancies." These beliefs have been shown to develop even before personal experience with alcohol. Media portrayals of the benefits of drinking are believed to play an important role in the development of positive expectancies. Adolescents are bombarded with these messages from an early age. In a recent study of 1,000 13- to 20-year-olds, those who did not see any alcohol ads consumed about 14 drinks per month, whereas those who saw ads consumed an average of 33 drinks per month.

Alcohol Use in Young Adults

Excess alcohol consumption is a major problem on most college campuses. Students may view drinking alcohol as a "rite of passage" during college, but it is a very serious public health problem. Alcohol consumption by college students has been associated with hundreds of thousands of cases of injuries, violence, unsafe sexual behavior, sexual assaults, and numerous deaths (over 1,700 annually). About 25 percent of college students report academic problems caused by drinking, including lower grades, poor performance on exams and papers, and missed classes. Grade point average has also been found to be inversely related to the amount of alcohol consumed (see Figure 4).

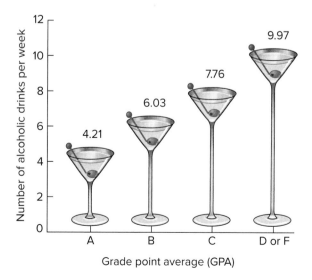

Figure 4 ▶ Average number of alcoholic drinks per week by GPA.

Source: Adapted from Core Institute

Table 5 ▶ Alcohol-Related Problems among College Students

Problems	All Students (%)	Non–Binge Drinkers (%)	Occasional Binge Drinkers (%)	Frequent Binge Drinkers (%)
Did something you regret	36.1	18.0	39.6	62.0
Missed a class	29.9	8.8	30.9	62.5
Drove after drinking	28.8	18.6	39.7	56.7
Forgot where you were or what you did	27.1	10.0	27.2	54.0
Argued with friends	22.5	9.7	23.0	42.6
Got behind in schoolwork	24.1	9.8	26.0	46.3
Engaged in unplanned sexual activities	21.6	7.9	22.3	41.5
Got hurt or injured	12.4	3.9	10.9	26.6
Damaged property	10.8	2.3	8.9	22.7
Had unprotected sex	10.3	3.7	9.8	20.4

Source: Wechsler et al.

The problems associated with alcohol are directly related to the amount consumed. As shown in Table 5, the proportion of various alcohol-related problems is considerably higher for people categorized as *frequent binge drinkers* than for *non-binge drinkers.*

Rates of binge drinking in college have remained high and rates of frequent binge drinking have increased, but there are also signs of progress. There are consistent increases in the number of students who do not drink at all. Over the past 30 years, the percentage of students reporting no alcohol use in the past 30 days has increased approximately 20 percent since the early 1980s. This increase may be due, at least in part, to the greater number of first-generation college students and nontraditional college students returning to college after spending time in the workforce.

The college environment plays a key role in heavy alcohol use among college students. Although many more college students today are not of traditional college age (18 to 25) and/or work full or part time, college remains a period of transition from adolescence to adulthood for many. Because this period is characterized by fewer adult responsibilities, some have referred to it as "extended adolescence" or "emerging adulthood." Regardless of the terminology, the early 20s are clearly a period of heightened risk for engagement in risky behaviors, including alcohol and other drug use. It has been suggested that flexible schedules for college students contribute to this problem. In contrast to emerging adults in the work sector, college students can often avoid morning classes and Friday classes to extend the weekend. In fact, a recent study found that the later students' Friday classes began, the more they drank on Thursday nights, with the heaviest drinking among those with no Friday classes. The authors argue that offering more Friday classes and requiring students to take them may help reduce alcohol use on college campuses.

It's not necessary to consume alcohol to have a good time.
©stockbroker/123RF

Some have argued that the legal drinking age of 21 contributes to alcohol problems in college. A large group of university presidents joined forces to create the "Amethyst Initiative" to urge lawmakers to lower the drinking age from 21 to 18. Those leading the movement argue that current laws are routinely evaded and encourage dangerous binge drinking on campus. The presidents indicate that their movement is designed to stimulate public debate. Some student groups have supported the movement, suggesting that if they are old enough to fight in wars, they are old enough to drink. On the other hand, the organization Mothers Against Drunk Driving (MADD) has argued that lowering the drinking age would lead to more car crashes. In fact, alcohol-related traffic fatalities have decreased dramatically since the legal drinking age was raised to 21. There is also concern that allowing 18-year-olds to possess alcohol legally will facilitate access to those who are under the age of 18, and an earlier age of alcohol use is a well-known risk factor for later problems with alcohol. The debate over the legal drinking age will no doubt continue. As noted in this Concept, there are many factors to be considered.

Drinking games place college students at high risk for negative consequences. Drinking games are common on college campuses, but studies show that students who engage in drinking games reach dangerously high blood alcohol concentrations and experience more negative consequences. Younger students are more  likely to play drinking games and experience negative repercussions. This is probably due to the fact that younger drinkers have less tolerance and are therefore more impaired at comparable blood alcohol levels.

Mixing alcohol and energy drinks puts young people at risk. Alcoholic beverages with high caffeine levels (e.g., Loko and Joose) were popular in young drinkers when they were introduced, but the FDA banned their distribution after several teen deaths and emergency room visits associated with their consumption. Unfortunately, many young people mix alcohol with energy drinks (such as Red Bull or Monster), a combination that is associated with heavier drinking and more alcohol-related problems. One recent study found that those who consumed alcohol with energy drinks reported a stronger desire for more alcohol relative to those who drank alcohol alone. Thus, it appears that mixing alcohol with caffeine may lead to heavier use.

Female college students are at particularly high risk for negative behavioral consequences of drinking. Women are at increased risk for a variety of acute negative behavioral outcomes of drinking, though unprotected or unwanted sexual behavior is perhaps the greatest concern. Risks are particularly high for young women in situations where high blood alcohol levels are likely. For example, women experience more negative consequences of drinking games because they drink at similar levels to men, leading to higher blood alcohol concentrations. Women are also at very high risk for negative consequences during spring break. In a recent online survey, 83 percent of women reported that spring break involved heavier than usual drinking, and 74 percent said sexual activity was increased. Thirteen percent of women said they had sex with more than one partner, and 10 percent said they regretted engaging in public or group sexual activity.

Misperceptions about peer attitudes and drinking behavior contribute to heavy drinking in college. Although increased attention to college drinking problems has led to increased education and prevention, rates of heavy use have changed little.  One contributing factor may be that attention to heavy drinking has led to the perception by college students that their peers are drinking more than they

In the News

Debates about College Drinking and Greek Life

Research has consistently shown that fraternity members have higher rates of binge drinking than non-fraternity members on college campuses. Fraternity parties can create high-risk environments for binge drinking and associated consequences, including physical and sexual assaults and alcohol poisonings. In response to recent drug and alcohol events on some campuses, university leaders have suspended both fraternity and sorority activities. A recent editorial in *Time* recommended that it is time to eliminate fraternities once and for all. Others argue that banning fraternities will do little to change problems like binge drinking and sexual assault, and that using the bad behavior of a small number of fraternity members to condemn organizations that do a lot of good is irresponsible.

Do you believe that fraternities should be banned on college campuses? Would this reduce binge drinking and associated problems like sexual assault?

actually are. Research has shown that college students routinely overestimate use by their peers and that these misperceptions are associated with increases in drinking. In theory, students drink more to keep up with what they perceive to be the norm on campus. In addition to overestimating how much alcohol their peers consume, college students appear to overestimate how much alcohol their peers want them to consume. This may be particularly true for women. A recent study found that 71 percent of women believed men wanted them to consume alcohol excessively, and 17 percent thought that men would find them more sexually attractive if they had five or more drinks. In truth, the percentage of men who endorsed these beliefs was about half of what women perceived it to be.

Much like colleges, the military confronts high rates of alcohol use and abuse. Young men (as a group) are at high risk for heavy drinking and related problems, and the military is a major employer of this demographic (roughly 86 percent of active-duty military are male, and roughly 67 percent are between the ages of 18 and 30). Given these demographics, it is not surprising that active-duty military personnel report levels of binge drinking that are even higher than rates among college students. This risk is exacerbated by the stress associated with deployment and redeployment. Soldiers may turn to alcohol as a means to cope with the stresses of war or with symptoms of post-traumatic stress disorder related to their experiences in the field. For example, one study reported that nearly 15 percent of army soldiers returning from deployments in Iraq or Afghanistan met criteria for an AUD. Another report documented that demand for alcohol treatment programs increased more than 50 percent during the first six years after the beginning of the war in Iraq.

 **Health is available to Everyone for a Lifetime, and it's Personal**

Alcohol Treatment Navigator

Deciding to get treatment for an alcohol problem is an important first step. However, finding effective treatment can also be challenging. The National Institute on Alcohol Abuse and Alcoholism (NIAAA) recently launched the Alcohol Treatment Navigator website (https://alcoholtreatment.niaaa.nih.gov/) that guides users through a step-by-step process to find highly-qualified treatment professionals. It also provides information about the types of treatments (including medications) that have been shown to be most effective.

Do you think medications should be included in treatment of alcohol problems? Why or why not?

Effective Approaches for Alcohol Prevention and Treatment

New approaches to preventing heavy drinking among college students are showing promise. Efforts to prevent heavy drinking among college students have traditionally focused on education. Unfortunately, a task force developed by the NIAAA found that these approaches are largely ineffective. Confrontational approaches do not work well either, particularly with young people. Effective strategies include motivational and skills-based approaches. These approaches encourage young people to examine how their drinking behavior affects their lives and to consider ways that changing their behavior might benefit them. Skills training focuses on teaching young people strategies to moderate their consumption or to maintain abstinence in the face of social pressure to drink. Another promising approach that is increasingly used on college campuses addresses students' misperceptions of drinking behavior on campus. Campuses often provide students with information about actual rates of alcohol consumption on campus to counter erroneous beliefs about heavy drinking. Students may perceive that "everyone" drinks but one study found that about 33% of college students did not report any alcohol use in the past 30 days. Overall, results from the longitudinal Monitoring the Future study show promising declines in various indicators of alcohol use by college students.

The options for treating alcohol use disorders have expanded in recent years. If you think you have (or someone you know has) a problem with alcohol, a number of

 ## Technology Update

Apps for Addiction Treatment

Yes, there is an app for that too. Although some argue that smartphone use has become a new form of addiction, one company, Triggr Health, is trying to harness the power of smartphone apps to cure rather than create addictions. This mobile app uses machine learning (which recognizes patterns of behavior) to analyze your behavior in real time and provide you with the type of support you need when you need it. The app includes 24-hour support and referrals to treatment providers when needed. According to background research by the company, the tool was able to predict regression in substance use behavior with 92 percent accuracy (days before it happened). Although apps like Triggr Health may not be able to help those with severe addictions, they could provide a useful tool for those trying to get a handle on their addictive behavior before it gets out of control.

Would you recommend this type of app to a friend struggling with alcohol problems?

options are available. Self-help groups, such as Alcoholics Anonymous (AA) and Rational Recovery, are widespread in the United States. Treatment centers are also readily available. Most treatment centers focus on abstinence using a 12-step approach consistent with AA. Although this approach works well for many, some are turned off by the strong religious component. A recent multisite clinical trial showed that cognitive-behavioral therapy and motivational enhancement yield similar results to 12-step approaches. These approaches can often be implemented in less time and place more emphasis on personal control over behavior, features that may appeal to young adults in particular. The medication Naltrexone has also been shown to help those trying to abstain from or reduce their alcohol consumption, providing yet another alternative or adjunct to behavioral treatment.

Using Self-Management Skills

Self-monitoring and self-assessment skills are important in reducing your risk for excess drinking. Moderate alcohol consumption is safe for many people and may even have some health benefits. However, many people who drink do so beyond safe levels. As excess alcohol consumption is associated with a number of acute negative consequences (e.g., alcohol poisoning, injuries, unsafe sex, driving accidents), a key self-management strategy is to closely monitor consumption and use behavioral strategies to keep your BAC at a safe level. Protective strategies include eating before you drink, alternating between alcoholic and nonalcoholic drinks, going to a party later and/or leaving earlier, setting a reasonable drink limit that you will not exceed, and avoiding high-risk situations, like drinking games. Studies have shown that students who use these strategies are at much lower risk for experiencing alcohol-related problems.

Honest self-assessment is important in detecting if you or your friends may have alcohol-related problems. The NIAAA created a website called "Rethinking Drinking" (https://www.rethinkingdrinking.niaaa.nih.gov/) to help you evaluate your behaviors and associated risks. The site also provides resources for those who wish to change their drinking behavior. The site is specifically targeted toward young adults with the goal of reducing harm associated with heavy drinking. While some people will need formal intervention to change, it is possible for many with alcohol problems to cut down on their drinking or quit on their own. The following list provides some tips to successfully quit or reduce your alcohol use:

• Make a list of reasons to stop drinking or cut down.
• Set a goal for yourself and make plans to meet it.
• Monitor your drinking—when, where, how much.
• Identify situations that trigger strong urges to drink.
• Spend less time in drinking settings (e.g., bars).
• Establish nondrinking days; offer to be a designated driver.
• Don't try to keep up with others.

Social support is important for avoiding problems associated with alcohol. You can reduce your risks by building a strong and supportive network of friends and by choosing activities that aren't tied to alcohol. If you do have friends that drink, make sure that they understand your preferences and limits. Clearly identify a designated driver if you are out. If you are hosting a party, you have a responsibility to prevent your friends from drinking too much. Equally as—or even more—important you have a responsibility for making sure that they get home safely. Guidelines for being a responsible party host include:

• Have water, nonalcoholic beverages, and food available.
• Do not assume that everyone wants to drink.
• Tactfully remove alcohol from overindulging guests.
• Close the bar an hour or two before the party ends.
• Secure safe transportation for those who are intoxicated.

Strategies for Action: Lab Information

Although one of the greatest risks associated with alcohol use is driving under the influence, drinking to the legal limit for intoxication (.08 g%) is associated with many other negative consequences. This includes physical fights, unwanted sexual behavior, and impaired academic performance. So, knowing how much you can drink without becoming intoxicated is critical. Lab 20A provides a formula to estimate your BAC at different levels of consumption over different periods of time so you can avoid drinking to intoxication.

The first step in protecting yourself from long-term problems with alcohol is to know your level of risk. In college, where students may be exposed to many heavy drinkers, students may underestimate their own levels of risk. Lab 20B provides an opportunity to evaluate your own behavior or the behavior of a friend to determine if a problem may exist. It is always better to identify a problem early and take steps to reduce risk for long-term negative consequences.

Suggested Resources and Readings

The websites for the following sources can be accessed by searching online for the organization, program, or title listed. Specific scientific references are available at the end of this edition of *Concepts of Fitness and Wellness.*

- Amethyst Initiative. Rethinking the Drinking Age (pdf).
- Byrnes, N. (2017, April 17). Treating addiction with an app, *MIT Technology Review.*
- Carroll, L. (2014, July 17). Mixing energy drinks and alcohol can "prime" you for a binge. *USA Today.*
- Centers for Disease Control and Prevention:
  - Alcohol and Public Health.
  - Drinking and Driving.
  - Impaired Driving: Get the Facts.
  - Sobering Facts: Drunk Driving State Fact Sheets.
- Feinstein, L. (2017, November 7). This company wants to "disrupt" alcoholism with an app. *Motherboard.*
- Foundation for Advancing Alcohol Responsibility. (2015). 2015 State of Drunk Driving Fatalities in America (Responsibility.org post).
- Interagency Coordinating Committee on the Prevention of Underage Drinking. STOP Act on Underage Drinking.
- MacMillan, A. (2017, August 14). Having a drink may help you live longer. *Time.*
- Mayo Clinic. Alcohol Use: If You Drink, Keep It Moderate.
- National Institute on Alcohol Abuse and Alcoholism. College Drinking—Changing the Culture.
- National Institute on Alcohol Abuse and Alcoholism. (2017, June). Alcohol Facts and Statistics. (online information).
- Wade, L. (2017, May 19). Why colleges should get rid of fraternities for good. *Time.*
- Wallace, K. (2016, September 9). The more alcohol ads kids see, the more alcohol they consume. *CNN.*

Lab 20A Blood Alcohol Level

Name   Section   Date

Purpose: To learn to calculate your (or a friend's) blood alcohol concentration (BAC).

Procedures

1. Assume a drink is a 12-ounce can or bottle of 5 percent beer, a 5-ounce glass (a small glass) of 12 percent alcohol (wine), or a mixed drink with a 1½-ounce shot glass (jigger) of 80 proof liquor.
   Case A: Assume you consumed two drinks within 40 minutes.
   Case B: Assume you consumed two drinks over a period of 1 hour and 20 minutes.
   Case C: Assume you had two six-packs of beer (12 cans) over 5 hours.
   Case D: Same as C, but, if you weigh less than 150 pounds, assume you weigh 50 pounds more than you now weigh, and, if you weigh more than 150 pounds, assume you weigh 50 pounds less.

2. Divide 3.8 by your weight in pounds to obtain your "BAC maximum per drink," or refer to Table 4 in this Concept. You should obtain a number between .015 and .04 (based on one drink in 40 minutes). Use the formula below to determine BAC over time.

$$\text{Approximate BAC over time} = \frac{(3.8 \times \text{\# of drinks})}{(\text{body weight})} - \frac{[.01 \times (\text{\# min} - 40)]}{40}$$

3. After 40 minutes have passed, your body will begin eliminating alcohol from the bloodstream at the rate of about .01 percent for each additional 40 minutes. Multiply the number of drinks you've had by your "BAC maximum per drink" and subtract .01 percent from the number for each 40 minutes that have passed since you began drinking—but don't count the first 40 minutes. Compute your BAC for cases A, B, C, and D.

   Example: Case A. Mary weighs 100 pounds. $\dfrac{3.8 \times 2}{100} = \dfrac{7.6}{100} = .076\%$ BAC

   Case B. Mary takes 80 minutes. $.076\% - \dfrac{[.01 \times (80 - 40)]}{40} = .066\%$ BAC

4. Record your results below by writing the formula and computing the BAC for each case.

Results

Case A $\dfrac{(3.8 \times \underline{\quad} \text{\# of drinks})}{\underline{\quad} \text{lbs}} = \underline{\quad} - \%$ BAC

Case B $\dfrac{(3.8 \times \underline{\quad} \text{\# of drinks})}{\underline{\quad} \text{lbs}} - \dfrac{[.01 \times (\underline{\quad} \text{\# min} - 40)]}{40} = $ BAC ( ) − ( ) = \underline{\quad}% BAC

Case C $\dfrac{(3.8 \times \underline{\quad} \text{\# of drinks})}{\underline{\quad} \text{lbs}} - \dfrac{[.01 \times (\underline{\quad} \text{\# min} - 40)]}{40} = $ BAC ( ) − ( ) = \underline{\quad}% BAC

Case D $\dfrac{(3.8 \times \underline{\quad} \text{\# of drinks})}{\underline{\quad} \text{lbs}} - \dfrac{[.01 \times (\underline{\quad} \text{\# min} - 40)]}{40} = $ BAC ( ) − ( ) = \underline{\quad}% BAC

Would you (or your friend) be able to drive legally according to your state's laws? Place an X over your answer.

Case A (Yes) (No)

Case B (Yes) (No)

Case C (Yes) (No)

Case D (Yes) (No)

Conclusions and Implications: In several sentences, discuss what you have learned from doing this activity.

Lab 20B Perceptions about Alcohol Use

Name	Section	Date

Purpose: To better understand perceptions about drinking behaviors.

Procedures

1. Think of a person you care about. Do not identify this person on this lab report.
2. Answer each of the questions below as honestly as possible, evaluating the behavior of the person you have identified. Calculate a total score and determine a rating (see Chart 1).
3. At another time, when you do not have to submit your results, you should answer the questions about yourself.
4. Answer the questions in the Conclusions and Implications section.

Results

	Never	Sometimes	Frequently	Too Often	Add Score
1. How often does the person drink?	0	1	2	3	
2. How often does the person have six or more drinks on one occasion?	0	1	2	3	
3. How often do friends of the person drink?	0	1	2	3	
4. How often has the person been unable to stop after starting to drink?	0	1	2	3	
5. How often does the person need a drink to get started in the morning?	0	1	2	3	
6. How often has the person been unable to remember previous events after drinking?	0	1	2	3	
7. How often does the person miss class or work associated with drinking?	0	1	2	3	
8. How often does the person have social or personal problems associated with drinking?	0	1	2	3	
9. How often does the person deny drinking too much (only for those whom you consider to drink too much)?	0	1	2	3	

Total Score ☐

Chart 1 Drinking Behavior Rating Scale

Rating	Score
Alcohol abuse*	18+
Drinking problem	12–17
Potential problem	8–11
Low risk of problem	<8

*Professional help recommended.

☐ **Rating**

Conclusions and Implications

1. In several sentences, discuss the drinking behavior of the person you identified. Do you think your ratings give an accurate picture of the person? Do you think the person you rated has a problem with alcohol?

2. In several sentences, discuss the drinking behavior of the person's friends. Do the friends promote drinking, or not?

3. In several sentences, discuss things you could do to help a friend or loved one solve a drinking problem.

The Use and Abuse of Other Drugs

LEARNING OBJECTIVES

After completing the study of this Concept, you will be able to:

► List the six major classes of illicit drugs and their effects.

► Describe the negative health, financial, and legal consequences of illicit drug use.

► Identify biological, psychological, and social factors that contribute to illicit drug use and abuse.

► Explain differences in prevalence of the various classes of drugs, including both illegal drugs and prescription drugs.

► Describe long-term and recent trends in use of the different drug classes.

► Identify signs of drug problems and available resources for addressing these problems.

Illicit drug abuse has serious health consequences and enormous personal, social, and economic costs. Preventing onset of illicit drug use and providing adequate treatment to individuals with substance use disorders is a public health priority.

©Terry Vine/Blend Images LLC

Why it Matters!

Illicit drug use is associated with a host of personal and societal costs, including overdoses, legal problems, and substance use disorders. Approximately 42 percent of college students report using illegal drugs in the past year. Of particular concern is that rates among young adults are higher than any other age group, with rates among college students even higher than similar-aged young adults not in college. Use of illicit drugs is usually preceded by use of alcohol and/or tobacco. However, other risk factors include exposure to substance-using peers and the belief that drug use will have more positive than negative consequences. This Concept summarizes six distinct categories of illicit drugs: depressants, opiate narcotics, stimulants, hallucinogens, marijuana, and designer drugs. Prevalence and consequences of each drug class are outlined along with risk factors for substance misuse so you can avoid or address these problems.

Classification of Illicit and Prescription Drugs

Psychoactive drugs can be classified in six major groups. Although there are hundreds of illicit drugs, they can generally be classified as depressants, opiate narcotics, stimulants, hallucinogens, marijuana, and designer drugs. Drugs in the same group have similar effects. Narcotics, however, are actually depressants, but because the word *narcotics* is so widely used in law enforcement and in society in general, they are generally given their own category. Across drug classes, effects are classified as either physiological or psychological (primarily affecting the body versus affecting behavior). The effects of these **psychoactive drugs** can vary with each individual and with different doses.

Depressant drugs include alcohol, tranquilizers, and barbiturates. Depressants come in the form of pills, liquids, and injectables (see Table 1). In small doses, they slow heart rate and respiration. In larger doses, they act as a poison and damage every organ system in the body. In large enough doses, they can dramatically depress heart rate and respiration enough to cause death, if quick intervention is not available. In terms of their effect on behavior, the user might at first feel stimulated, despite their depressant effects. Depression, loss of coordination, drop in energy level, mood swings, and confusion occur after prolonged use. Alcohol is the most widely used depressant.

Opiate narcotics include heroin, codeine, morphine, and methadone. Narcotics are smoked, injected, sniffed, or swallowed (see Table 2). Narcotics are often used clinically to treat pain; however, heroin has no legal medical use in the United States and has a high rate of addiction. It is three times stronger than other medicinal narcotics and induces different physiological effects. Narcotics are all opium poppy derivatives or synthetics that emulate them. The *narco-* part of the word derives from the Greek word for "sleep" because of its sleep-inducing properties.

Every narcotic, legal or illegal, is a potential poison. A single dose can be fatal. Deaths related to narcotic abuse are typically caused by overdose, impurities of the drug, or mixing of the drug with other depressants, such as alcohol. The mixing of drugs in the same or similar categories can produce a heightened physiological effect known as synergism, or the **synergistic effect.** The combined use makes drug taking far more dangerous.

Stimulants include cocaine and methamphetamine as well as prescription drugs like Ritalin and Adderall. One of these stimulants—cocaine—comes in powder form (coke) and a rocklike form (crack). The timing and magnitude of effects of cocaine vary depending on whether it is inhaled, injected, or smoked. Combining cocaine and alcohol use leads to production of cocaethylene, which increases risk for overdose. Amphetamines and methamphetamines are also classified as stimulants due to their effects on the central

Table 1 ▶ Depressants ("Downers," Sedatives)

Examples	Physiological Effects	Psychological Effects
Tranquilizers (e.g., Valium, Xanax, meprobamate, sleeping pills, methaqualone) are also called tranks, downers, or candy	In large doses, act as a poison and damage every organ system	Feelings of relaxation and euphoria; after prolonged use: depression, loss of coordination, drop in energy level, mood swings, confusion, euphoria
Barbiturates (e.g., Mebaral, Nembutal)	Quick sedation: vomiting; loss of motor and neurological control; combined with alcohol, can lead to coma and death	Amnesia

Table 2 ▶ Opiate Narcotics

Examples	Physiological Effects	Psychological Effects
Codeine, Morphine, Synthetic opiates (e.g., Vicodin, Oxycontin), Methadone	Narcotics: blockage of pain, chronic constipation, depressed respiration, redness and irritation of nostrils, nausea, lowered sexual drive, impaired immune system	Narcotics (including heroin): euphoria and feeling of pleasure; nontherapeutic doses may result in mental distress, such as fear and nervousness; in heavy users, drowsiness and apathy may occur
Heroin (also called brown sugar, junk, or smack)	Heroin: blood clots, bacterial endocarditis, serum hepatitis, brain abscess, HIV infection (from shared needles); in pregnant users, high risk of miscarriage, stillbirths, birth defects, toxemia, addicted babies	

Table 3 ▶ Stimulants

Examples	Physiological Effects	Psychological Effects
Cocaine (also called coke, blow, snow, or crack)	Cocaine: sore throat, hoarseness, shortness of breath (leads to bronchitis and emphysema), dilated pupils, "lights" seen around objects	Powder cocaine causes an initial response of energy, feeling of confidence; as it wears off: depression, moodiness, irritability, severe mental disorders. Crack causes intense euphoria, then crushing depression, intense feeling of self-hate; as it wears off: depression and sadness, intense anxiety about where to get more drugs, aggressiveness, paranoia
Amphetamines and powder methamphetamines (also called speed, uppers, or black beauties); diet and pep pills, Ritalin	Excite central nervous system; increase blood pressure, respiration, and heart rate (sometimes resulting in convulsions and stroke); reduce appetite; highly addictive; overdose is fatal; with increased use: dizziness, headaches, sleeplessness; with long-term use: progressive brain damage, malnutrition	Initially, feeling of being invincible, alertness, excitement; with increased use: feeling of anxiety; with long-term use: hallucinations, psychosis
Crystal methamphetamine (also called meth, crystal, crank, or ice)	Extreme energy, sleeplessness, seizures, flushed skin, constricted pupils	Euphoria, delusions of grandeur, feelings of invincibility, physical aggression, paranoia, mood swings, psychosis

nervous system. Stimulants are often included in diet pills to reduce appetite; others (e.g., Ritalin) are used clinically to treat attention deficit hyperactivity disorder (see Table 3).

Crystal methamphetamine (also known as ice, meth, or crystal) is a purified methamphetamine that also comes in rock form or powder. As a powder, it is usually smoked in a glass pipe or cigarette. It is a powerful stimulant, with an effect that lasts 8 to 30 hours. Much like crack cocaine, ice is a concentrated form of an already potent stimulant drug that is either smoked or injected. Ice also causes an intense "rush" or "flash," which is experienced as highly pleasurable. Because the initial rush lasts for only a few minutes, users need to administer the drug frequently to maintain the effects.

Drugs that cause the user to have hallucinations are called hallucinogens, or psychedelics. PCP and LSD are common examples of hallucinogens but less-known drugs in this category include mushrooms, or "shrooms," which are

chewed, and peyote cactus buttons, which have been used for ceremonial purposes by some indigenous groups for centuries.

Inhalants are sometimes classified separately from other hallucinogens because their effects are so serious. They reach the brain in seconds, and the effect lasts only a few minutes. There are three types: (1) solvents, such as glue, gasoline, paints, paint thinner, lighter fluid, shoe polish, and liquid wax; (2) aerosols, such as hair spray, air fresheners, insect spray, and spray paint; and (3) nitrites, such as nitrous oxide

Psychoactive Drug Any drug that produces a temporary change in the physiological functions of the nervous system, affecting mood, thoughts, feelings, or behavior.

Synergistic Effect The joint actions of two or more drugs that increase the effects of each.

Table 4 ▶ Hallucinogens (Psychedelics)

Examples	Physiological Effects	Psychological Effects
Lysergic acid diethylamide (LSD, also called acid, boomers, or cubes)	Changes chromosomes and may result in birth defects of babies of users; bad trips, confusion, flashback	Vivid hallucinations, feelings of overlapping/merging of the senses, expanded consciousness and mystical experiences, stimulated awareness and desire, confusion, flashback
Phencyclidine (PCP)	Accumulates in fat cells and may remain in body longer than most drugs; impaired immune system, poor coordination, weight loss, speech problems, heart and lung failure, irreversible brain damage, convulsions, coma, death	Insensitivity to pain can lead to death; euphoria, depersonalization, hallucinations, delirium, amnesia, tunnel vision, loss of control, violent behavior
Inhalants (solvents, aerosols, and nitrites, also known as poppers, rush)	Slow reaction time, headache, nausea, vomiting, seizure, brain damage, suffocation, heart attack, death, double vision, sensitivity to light, dizziness, loss of coordination, weakness, numbness; irregular heartbeat, liver and kidney failure, bone marrow damage	Giddiness, overexcitement, less inhibition, feelings of being all-powerful; powerfulness soon fades and leaves irritability

Table 5 ▶ Marijuana (Subclass of Hallucinogens)

Examples	Physiological Effects	Psychological Effects
Marijuana (containing tetrahydrocannabinol, or THC) is also called pot, grass, weed, blunt, or herb	Long-term use: bronchitis, emphysema and lung cancer, bloodshot eyes, heart disease, infertility, sexual dysfunction, permanent memory loss (brain damage)	May not hallucinate; pleasant, relaxed feeling; giddiness; self-preoccupation; less precise thinking; impaired task performance; inertia; with prolonged use: may be withdrawn and apathetic, have anxiety reactions, paranoia; eventually, decreased motivation and enthusiasm, reduced ability to absorb and integrate effectively, profoundly impaired scholastic performance

(laughing gas) and butyl nitrite (a liquid incense). Table 4 describes the effects of hallucinogens and pyschedelics (drugs that cause **hallucinations**).

Marijuana is classified as a hallucinogenic, but its effects are less dramatic than those of other drugs in this class. The active ingredient in marijuana (delta-9-tetrahydrocannabinol–THC) is technically a hallucinogen (see Table 5). Marijuana use became widespread in the 1960s and, despite decreased use over time, is still the most widely used illicit substance in the United States. Marijuana use leads to a range of experiences, which differ from person to person. Marijuana is generally smoked in a pipe, joint, or bong, although it can also be eaten and is also smoked in hollowed-out cigars called blunts.

Designer drugs, which are made in laboratories, have many of the same properties as the drugs they simulate, such as pain relievers, anesthetics, and amphetamines. Designer drugs are modifications of illegal or restricted drugs made by chemists working illicitly to create

street drugs that are not specifically listed as controlled. They change the molecular structure of an existing drug to create a new substance. Since new drugs are being created all the time, their potential effects and associated risks are often unknown (see Table 6).

Prevalence and Consequences of Illicit Drug Abuse

Use of most illicit substances has decreased in the past decade, but rates of use remain high among adolescents and young adults. In the United States, rates of illicit drug use peaked in the 1970s followed by sharp decreases during the 1980s (see Figure 1). Overall drug use

Hallucinations Imaginary things seen, felt, or heard or things seen in a distorted way.

Table 6 ▶ Designer Drugs

Examples	Physiological Effects	Psychological Effects
Date-rape drugs • Rohypnol • Gamma hydroxybutyrate (GHB) is also called Georgia homeboy or liquid ecstasy • Ketamine (also called Special K)	Depression of the central nervous system, incapacitation, coma, seizures, tremors, nausea, sweating, high blood pressure, and potentially fatal respiratory problems	Negative mood states including depression and anxiety; amnesia and delirium; insomnia and impaired motor function
MDMA (3,4-methylenedioxymethamphetamine; also called ecstasy, or X)	Irregular heartbeat, intensified heart problems, liver and brain damage, depletion of serotonin in the brain, muscle tension, and dry mouth	Initial feelings of calm and euphoria may be followed by exhaustion or psychological burnout; increased risk for psychosis and depression; cognitive impairment
Synthetic cannabinoids (e.g., K2, Spice) and cathinones (bath salts)	Rapid heart rate, vomiting, agitation, confusion, high blood pressure, reduced blood supply to the heart, heart attack, kidney failure, dehydration	Elevated mood, relaxation, altered perception, anxiety, paranoia, hallucinations, panic attacks, delirium

by adolescents spiked upward in the early 1990s, primarily as a result of two- to threefold increases in marijuana use. Rates of illicit drug use then began a steady but gradual decline during the first decade of the new century. Unfortunately, rates of illicit drug use in young adults have increased 6 percent since 2010, representing a proportional increase of nearly 16 percent. Rates have increased even more substantially in college students, from 35 to 42.8 percent. In contrast to other illicit drugs, misuse of prescription drugs peaked in 2001 and rates have remained high among 12th graders through 2013. Fortunately, rates of prescription drug misuse have declined by roughly 24 percent since that time. Still, the current rate of 12.0 percent makes prescription drugs the second most widely used drug class (not including alcohol and tobacco) in young people, trailing only marijuana use.

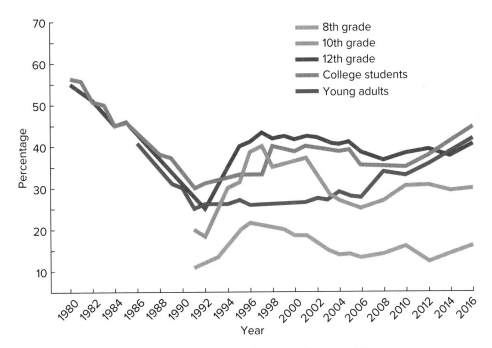

Figure 1 ▶ Trends in annual prevalence of an illicit drug use index across five populations.

Note: Use of "any illicit drugs" includes any use of marijuana, LSD, other hallucinogens, crack, other cocaine, or heroin, or any use that is not under a doctor's orders of other opiates, stimulants, barbiturates, methaqualone (excluded since 1990), or tranquilizers.

Source: National Institute on Drug Abuse

Rates of illicit drug use among college students are among the highest of any age group. High rates of drug use in college are associated with a host of negative consequences, including impaired cognitive abilities and academic performance, increased risk of accidents and injuries, greater incidence of high-risk sexual behavior, and increased risk for substance use disorders. Students who use drugs have less academic motivation and report lower involvement in religion, community service, and extracurricular activities on campus.

Much like alcohol, both direct and indirect peer influences are important predictors of use among college students. Students with friends who use marijuana are more likely to use it themselves. Misperceptions of normative behavior may also influence personal behavior. One study found that 98 percent of students incorrectly believed that the typical student on campus used marijuana at least once per year, despite the fact that most of the students reported no personal use of marijuana. Although both direct and indirect peer influences may contribute to drug use, these same influences can also deter use. One study found that peers exposed to a peer group with strong anti-drug attitudes were likely to conform to this norm.

The development of new drugs contributes to the maintenance of drug use in the United States. New drugs are always being manufactured, and new ways of administering old drugs often lead to a resurgence in use. Designer drugs provide examples of new drugs, and crack cocaine and crystal methamphetamine are examples of old drugs that became popular in new forms. When these new drugs become available, information about their benefits is generally spread immediately by word of mouth. In contrast, the risks associated with use are often unknown until the drug has been used for a number of years. This gives new drugs time to become popular before information that might deter their use is available. Ecstasy and crystal methamphetamine are good examples of this phenomenon. Public campaigns by the National Institute on Drug Abuse and other agencies have provided information about risks and have helped to curb levels of use relatively quickly. Thirty-day prevalence of ecstasy use in high school seniors decreased from 3.6 percent to 1 percent in over a five-year period, and rates of crystal methamphetamine use decreased from 1.2 percent to .5 percent over a similar period of time. Unfortunately, efforts to protect the public are challenged by the constant production of new designer drugs. Recent examples include synthetic cannabinoids and cathinones (bath salts). These drugs emerged around 2010 and quickly led to a large number of calls to poison control centers. (See Table 6 for a description of negative drug reactions.) The Drug Enforcement Administration (DEA) acted swiftly to place bans on these products, and annual rates of synthetic marijuana use subsequently decreased from 11.4 percent in 2011 to 3.5 percent in 2016. Similarly, the use of bath salts has decreased from 1.3 to .8 percent in recent years. In addition to the emergence of new drugs, there is a tendency to forget about the negative consequences of existing drugs after rates decrease—a phenomenon called **generational forgetting.** For example, after dramatic decreases in MDMA use following the peak in 2000, rates began to climb again, nearly doubling between 2005 and 2010.

Social environments and peer pressure can influence decision making and drug behavior.
©Pressmaster/Shutterstock

Drug use takes a human toll in terms of increased morbidity and mortality and lost productivity. Drug abuse leads to over 4 million emergency room visits annually and is the leading cause of injury deaths in the United States, surpassing traffic-related fatalities for the first time in 2011. This does not take into account the indirect effects of drug use on mortality, including deaths from accidents, homicides, and AIDS (acquired via intravenous drug use). Use of illicit drugs also increases risk for the development of **substance use disorders** which often require formal treatment to overcome. Because of problems with low productivity in the workplace, a large percentage of American businesses now conduct employee drug tests to detect usage.

Drug use also has significant economic costs. The economic costs of illicit drug abuse are estimated at approximately $193 billion a year. Approximately 20.2 million adults (about 8.4 percent of the population) in the United States meet criteria for a substance use disorder, but

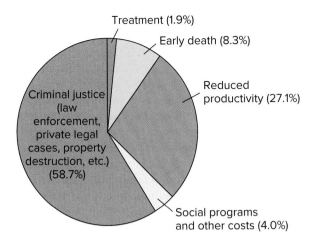

Treatment (1.9%)

Early death (8.3%)

Reduced productivity (27.1%)

Criminal justice (law enforcement, private legal cases, property destruction, etc.) (58.7%)

Social programs and other costs (4.0%)

Figure 2 ▶ The estimated cost of drug abuse (percentage of total costs).

Source: U.S. Department of Justice National Drug Intelligence Center

most of the national economic burden is not related to treatment (3 percent). More than half of the costs are associated with drug-related crime. Figure 2 illustrates the proportion of societal costs resulting from factors such as law enforcement expenditures, social programs, and reduced productivity.

Drug use can lead to significant legal problems, resulting in jail time and substantial fines. State laws regarding the possession and sale of illicit drugs vary considerably, and penalties within states vary based on the amount of the drug, the type of drug, and the type of offense (possession, sales, or production). Although a number of states have decriminalized marijuana, penalties for marijuana possession are still substantial in other states, and all states tend to have more severe penalties for drugs like cocaine, heroin, and methamphetamine. Penalties for the possession of small amounts are the least severe, with penalties for the sale or production of large amounts the most severe. In most states, the maximum jail time for possession ranges from six months to a year for marijuana and from one to seven years for cocaine, methamphetamine, and ecstasy. In addition, fines between $500 and $1,000 for marijuana and between $5,000 and $25,000 for other illicit drugs are typical of most states.

Drug-Specific Prevalence and Consequences

Marijuana is the most widely used (illicit) drug in the United States and is associated with a host of physical health and social consequences. In a national survey, over 22 million Americans, or roughly 8 percent of people

over the age of 12, reported the use of marijuana in the past month. Although many believe it is a relatively safe drug, and some favor decriminalization or legalization, a number of risks are associated with marijuana use. A recent review in the *New England Journal of Medicine* outlines the many risks of marijuana use. With respect to health, chronic marijuana use leads to many of the negative consequences associated with cigarette smoking, including cardiovascular disease and lung cancer. One study showed that marijuana use also increases risk for stroke. Another study found that marijuana use leads to nearly a fivefold increase in acute risk for a heart attack, especially among those with existing cardiovascular risk. Marijuana use is also associated with impaired cognitive

A CLOSER LOOK

Public Health Implications of Marijuana Decriminalization

More than two dozen states now have medical marijuana laws, and more than a dozen have decriminalized marijuana. A total of 8 states and the District of Columbia have now legalized possession of small amounts of marijuana for recreational use. Although it will take some time to determine the consequences of these legal changes, regulation will almost certainly be necessary as it has been for alcohol and tobacco. In particular, there are major concerns about the safety of food products containing marijuana and driving under the influence. In states that have legalized marijuana, poisonings related to marijuana use in young children have increased by 30 percent, though the absolute number of marijuana-related poisonings remains low. With respect to the impact on driving, two recent studies reached conflicting results. One found a small but meaningful increase in crashes in states that legalized marijuana, whereas the other found no increase in traffic fatalities in states that legalized marijuana. It will be critical to closely monitor changes in the public health impact of marijuana as laws change.

Do you support laws that decriminalize marijuana? What do you think are the biggest risks and benefits of this approach?

Generational Forgetting The tendency for individuals to forget about the risks of a particular drug over time, leading to a resurgence in its use.

Substance Use Disorder The use of a drug to the extent that it impairs social, psychological, or physiological functioning.

abilities. For example, adolescents who use marijuana heavily have been shown to have deficits in attention, learning, and processing speed. There is also direct evidence from neuroimaging studies for differences in brain function. In particular, areas of the brain associated with processing of emotional information appear to be affected. These findings are cause for concern, given evidence for increased risk of emotional problems among individuals who use marijuana. For example, a recent study found that marijuana use increased risk for experiencing panic attacks.

Although the debate is ongoing regarding the addictive (physical dependence) potential of marijuana, it is clear that one can become psychologically addicted to the drug. Psychological dependence is characterized by craving for the drug and continued use despite negative consequences. There is also emerging evidence that those who try to quit using marijuana experience withdrawal symptoms. For example, a recent study found that smokers of marijuana experienced withdrawal symptoms that were quite similar to those of tobacco smokers, including irritability, anxiety, and sleep difficulties.

Stimulants are among the most commonly used illicit drugs. Cocaine and methamphetamine are prominent examples of widely used stimulant drugs (see Figure 3). They share common characteristics and have similar effects and risks. First, both come in powder form as well as more concentrated crystal (ice) or rock (crack) forms. Crack cocaine was one of the most abused drugs in the United States during the peak rates of use in the early to mid-1980s, and crystal methamphetamine was at the center of the more recent but less dramatic increase in illicit drug use in the early 1990s. Crack and ice are highly addictive. Because of the intense, short-lived high associated with using these drugs, patterns of repeated use develop quickly, leading to rapid development of dependence. Both drugs are also known to damage dopamine neurons in the brain and lead to a host of short- and long-term health consequences. Short-term effects that occur after the initial high include irritability, anxiety, and paranoia. In terms of long-term risk, cocaine and methamphetamine use lead to increased risk for stroke, respiratory problems (including respiratory failure), irregular heartbeat, heart attacks, and psychiatric symptoms.

Unique physical consequences of methamphetamine use include poor complexion and tooth loss. Ice has added risks associated with its production. Because some of the products used to produce meth (e.g., pseudoephedrine) have legitimate pharmaceutical uses, policies have been put in place to monitor their sale. If you go to your pharmacy to purchase an over-the-counter decongestant, you may be asked to provide identification and a signature. In addition, you may have to purchase your medication at the pharmacy even though it is an over-the-counter drug, and you may be limited to one or two packages.

The continued use of designer drugs is a concern, given strong evidence of their harmful effects. Designer drugs include ecstasy (MDMA), Rohypnol, GHB, ketamine, DOM, DOB, and NEXUS. Ecstasy, a hallucinogen, is inhaled, injected, or swallowed. The drug was initially popular at all-night dance parties called raves, but its use quickly expanded beyond the club scene. Ecstasy alters brain levels of serotonin; negatively impacts memory; and affects the brain regions that regulate sleep, mood, and learning. Recently, a more potent form of ecstasy sold in capsules or as powder has been a major concern in several areas of the country. This type of ecstasy is often referred to as "Molly." The negative effects of ecstasy may last as long as seven years. Dealers often pass off other drugs as ecstasy, and they are often even more dangerous.

Rohypnol and GHB are predominately central nervous system depressants, like the other sedative drugs described previously. These drugs are odorless, colorless, and tasteless, so they can be added to food or beverages without the consumer detecting their presence. Because of these properties, Rohypnol and GHB are known as drug-assisted assault or date-rape drugs. In addition to incapacitating the user, these drugs lead

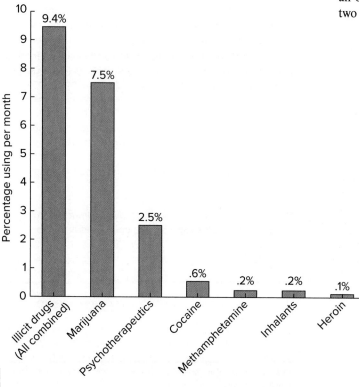

Figure 3 ▶ Illicit drug use among persons 12 and older, by drug (% per month).

Source: Substance Abuse and Mental Health Services Administration

to anterograde amnesia, or the inability to remember events that occur after consumption.

Inhalant use poses a serious risk to physical health, including risk for sudden death. Those who use inhalants are at risk for what is known as "sudden sniffing death." Sniffing inhalants can lead to irregular and rapid heart rhythms that can cause heart failure and rapid death. This can occur from a single episode of sniffing in an otherwise healthy adolescent.

Misuse and abuse of over-the-counter (OTC) and prescription drugs has become an increasing problem. Prescription drugs are often used inappropriately. In fact, psychotherapeutic drugs are now the second most commonly abused class of drugs, trailing only marijuana (See Figure 3). Examples of psychotherapeutic drug misuse include using prescriptions written for other people and using medicines for purposes other than as prescribed. Users may also obtain prescription drugs without prescriptions via the Internet, though most people who misuse prescription drugs indicate that they obtain them for free from friends or family members. Many fail to recognize the potential risks of prescription drug use, assuming that anything prescribed by a physician must be safe. The more commonly abused prescription drugs among college students include Adderall, Ritalin, Valium, Xanax, as well as prescription pain medications such as Percocet, Vicodin, and Oxycontin. Sometimes called "hillbilly heroin," Oxycontin is a painkiller that has received much attention because of its misuse by celebrities and its link to many deaths nationwide. Methadone use without a prescription also appears to be increasing. Methadone has been approved in the United States

Abuse of prescription pain medication can be a difficult habit to break.
©Don Hammond/Design Pics

for the treatment of opiate dependence (primarily heroin) since 1972, but it is increasingly making its way into the hands of those without prescriptions. Although nonprescription use of methadone has not been systematically tracked, methadone-related overdoses have been. Recent data from the CDC indicate a threefold increase in methadone-related deaths in less than a decade, and it is estimated that roughly one-fourth of opioid related overdoses are related to methadone use.

Rates of misuse of ADHD drugs like Ritalin and Adderall are particularly high among young people, particularly college students who often use the drugs in an effort to enhance academic performance. The most recent national data indicate that roughly 10 percent of college students report using Adderall without a prescription in the past year.

In the News

Opioid Abuse Declared a National Public Health Emergency

More than 64,000 people in the U.S. died from drug overdoses in 2016, which represents a doubling in overdoses during the past decade. The CDC has labeled the opioid crisis an epidemic, and the problem is now viewed as a "public health emergency." The Council of Academic Advisors estimates the cost of the opioid epidemic at roughly half a trillion dollars. To help curb abuse, new guidelines by the CDC are in place regarding opioid prescription, but proposed solutions have not been consistently supported. Some argue that the guidelines are not based on sound research and that restricting access to opioids may limit options for physicians. It may also reduce the likelihood that they can prescribe

opioid drugs that are effective in the treatment of opioid dependence (e.g., buprenorphine). Health experts have been critical of the federal government's "underfunding" of efforts to combat the epidemic and some critique proposed ad campaigns to combat drug use citing lack of evidence for the content of proposed ads.

Do you think the CDC's guidelines to reduce opioid prescription are a step in the right direction? What about a media campaign to raise awareness about the issue? What would you recommend as a strategy to combat the opioid epidemic?

Overdoses from misuse of prescription drugs account for the vast majority of drug overdoses in the United States. Drug overdose deaths have nearly tripled in recent years, largely due to increases in opioid use. It is estimated that 60 percent of drug-related emergency room visits are related to prescription narcotics, and roughly 91 people in the U.S. die each day from opioid overdoses. In fact, the recent increases in drug overdoses associated with prescription narcotics are even more dramatic than the increases seen when heroin and crack cocaine were first introduced. This has led major public health organizations, including the CDC, to declare an opioid epidemic in the United States. Although rates are not as dramatic as for prescription narcotics, ER visits related to nonprescription use of tranquilizers like Valium and Xanax have also increased dramatically in recent years.

Accidental misuse of prescription drugs is another common problem. Examples of unwitting misuse of drugs include taking a medicine twice, taking the wrong medicine from unlabeled bottles, using outdated medicines, and taking multiple medications that negatively interact with one another. Thus, it is important to understand the nature of all the medications you are taking (including supplements, prescription drugs, and OTC drugs) and how they interact. Women who are pregnant, are nursing, or want to get pregnant should avoid drug use, including many prescription drugs. The most recent results of the National Pregnancy and Health Survey, conducted by the National Institute on Drug Abuse (NIDA), estimated that 4.7 percent of women who give birth each year in the United States used illegal drugs while they were pregnant. Taking drugs during pregnancy can result in various conditions, including premature separation of the placenta from the womb, fetal stroke, miscarriage, birth defects, low birth weight babies, babies born addicted to substances, and postnatal risks, including SIDS and learning disabilities.

Causes of Illicit Drug Abuse

Drug use generally begins with cigarette smoking and alcohol use. Of course, most people who smoke or drink will not go on to use illegal drugs, but it is rare for people who do not smoke or drink to use illegal drugs. The average age of first use of cigarettes, alcohol, and marijuana is roughly 16 among those who report using prior to age 21. In general, the younger a person is when he or she starts using drugs, including nicotine and alcohol, the more likely that person is to use illegal drugs and become physically dependent on them.

Most experts agree that drug use and abuse are complex phenomena that must be understood within a biopsychosocial model. The biopsychosocial model suggests that biological, psychological, and social factors must be considered in understanding substance use and abuse. From this perspective, the potential for addiction depends on a host of factors, including genetic vulnerability, the type of drug used, the route of administration, attitudes toward drug use, expectations regarding drug effects, peer use, and ease of access.

Technology Update

Digital Tracking Devices in Pills Could Reduce Misuse of Prescription Drugs

The Food and Drug Administration (FDA) recently approved the first prescription medication with a built-in digital tracking device. The drug Abilify has been used for more than a decade to treat severe psychiatric conditions (e.g., bipolar disorder, schizophrenia). However, a new version of the drug labeled with the tag-name MyCite includes an ingestible sensor that records when the medicine is taken. The idea is that it will improve patient compliance in taking the medication. This same technology could also be used to detect overconsumption of prescribed drugs that have a high potential for addiction. Prescription opioids with digital sensors are already being tested in clinical studies.

Do you think that digital sensors are a potentially useful tool for combating opioid misuse, or do you believe this tool violates an individual's privacy? Do you think patients would be willing to use this technology?

HELP Health is Available to Everyone for a Lifetime, and it's Personal

Cyclical Nature of Drug Use in Young Adults

Patterns of use of specific drugs among young adults seem to go up and down in cycles, while overall rates remain relatively stable. As an example, while rates of prescription drug use have decreased substantially in the last decade, there has been a corresponding increase in marijuana use. In addition, new drugs are always emerging to replace those to which access has been restricted.

Do declines in the use of specific drugs simply reflect exploration with new drugs? Which drugs should be targeted to reduce harms associated with illicit drug use?

Connecting with the right social group can help you adopt positive lifestyles and behaviors.
©Radius Images/Alamy Stock Photo

Genetics play a role in susceptibility to drug addiction. Research has suggested that genetic factors explain as much as 50 percent of alcohol and nicotine addiction, and the same is likely true for other drugs of abuse. The effect of genetics (and susceptibility to addiction) depends on how the drug is used and how it affects the brain. Some drugs act on receptors in the brain that are specific to that drug (e.g., cannabanoid receptors for marijuana; opioid receptors for heroin and prescription narcotics), whereas others act on more general neurotransmitters associated with reward (e.g., effects of cocaine and methamphetamine on the dopamine system) and the regulation of mood and behavior (e.g., MDMA effects on the serotonin system). Because both the dopamine and opioid systems are directly related to the experience of reward, drugs like heroin and cocaine that affect these systems are particularly addictive. The route of administration also influences risk for addiction. For example, the likelihood of becoming addicted to methamphetamine is much higher if it is smoked rather than inhaled as powder.

Psychological factors such as personality traits, attitudes, perceptions of risk, and expectations of benefits can influence drug use. Individuals with higher levels of sensation seeking and impulsivity have been shown to be at increased risk for use of a range of illicit drugs. Those who believe drug use is acceptable and affiliate with others with similar views are also more likely to use drugs and to develop problems. These attitudes are influenced by both parental and peer attitudes as well as the attitudes of the broader culture. Perceptions of risk are also a strong predictor of drug use. In fact, national studies have consistently found that shifts in perceptions of risk related to specific drugs precede changes in rates of use of those drugs. Much like alcohol, those who believe drugs will have strong positive effects are more likely to use and abuse them. This is particularly true for those who believe that drug use is an effective way to cope with stress.

Social factors and social norms have important effects on drug use. People who live in areas where drugs are readily available are at increased risk for both use and abuse. Another major influence on drug use in young people is the extent to which their social group engages in drug use. Those who perceive that most of their peers use drugs are likely to use drugs themselves.

Using Self-Management Skills

The best way to avoid problems associated with drug use is not to try illegal drugs and to be careful in the use of legal drugs. This Concept clearly indicates that taking a drug for reasons other than managing your own good health increases the risk of taking more drugs in the future. While most people avoid illegal drugs, almost everyone will take medication sometime in his or her life. Monitor the use of medications to be sure that you are using them as directed and not with other medications that may result in dangerous synergistic effects.

You can also reduce your risk by knowing the true rates of drug use and learning skills to resist peer pressure. In general, college students overestimate the extent to which other students are using illicit drugs, which can lead to drug use in an effort to fit in with one's peers. Knowing true rates of illicit drug use can help protect you from trying to conform to a norm that is not accurate. Current rates of use of the different illicit drugs in U.S. college students are available at www.monitoringthefuture.org. Of course, some peers are actually using drugs and may invite you to join them. So, making responsible decisions about drugs in the face of peer pressure is also an important life skill. To combat peer pressure, the ability to clearly and effectively say no is necessary. One effective strategy is to choose friends whose values support, rather than undermine, your own.

People who have a problem with drugs typically will need support and specific skills to quit using them. People who are struggling with a drug problem need to talk to someone they can trust, perhaps a friend or relative. If you know somebody with a drug problem, you may be able to help them seek assistance from a referral source, such as an employee assistance program, a family or university physician or hospital, or your city or county health department. These sources help get the person into a treatment program or support group. Some of the better-known nationwide programs include Alcoholics (or Narcotics or Cocaine) Anonymous and Al-Anon Family Groups. Another option is to call the Substance Abuse and Mental Health Services Administration (SAMHSA) hotline and someone will direct you to help in your area. SAMHSA also has an online treatment locator to help you find local resources:

- SAMHSA Hotline (1-800-662-HELP)
- SAMHSA Online Treatment Locator (https://findtreatment.samhsa.gov/)

If you think a fellow student might have a problem with illicit or prescription drugs, help is probably available within the counseling center at your school. Most colleges and universities have information on the school's website about available substance abuse services.

Strategies for Action: Lab Information

In order to help yourself or someone else with a drug problem, you first have to know how to identify when a problem exists. In Lab 21A, you will have the opportunity to evaluate the behavior of a friend or loved one to determine if he or she might need help.

Think of somebody you know who uses illicit drugs and complete the lab to see if that person might need your help. At a later time, it might be a good idea to answer the questions in Lab 21A for yourself to determine if you need to reach out for help in managing your own substance use.

Suggested Resources and Readings

The websites for the following sources can be accessed by searching online for the organization, program, or title listed. Specific scientific references are available at the end of this edition of *Concepts of Fitness and Wellness*.

- Berman, R. (2017, November 17). A clear-eyed comparison of alcohol vs marijuana. Big Think.
- Chaverneff, F. (2017, March 18). CDC guideline on prescribing opioids: Some major concerns. Clinical Pain Advisor.
- Governing.com. State Marijuana Laws (web resource).
- Ingraham, C. (2017, June 26). What marijuana legalization did to car accident rates. *The Washington Post*.
- Maldonado, L. New and Designer Drugs. Project Know.
- National Council on Patient Information and Education. "Get the Facts" Prescription Drug Use on College Campuses (pdf).
- National Institute on Drug Abuse. NIDA summarizes research on marijuana's negative health effects (online review of *New England Journal of Medicine* article).
- National Institute on Drug Abuse DrugFacts. Synthetic Cathinones ("Bath Salts") (web resource).
- National Institute on Drug Abuse DrugFacts. What are Synthetic Cannabinoids? (Spice) (web resource).
- NORML. States That Have Decriminalized Marijuana (web resource).
- Perrone, M. (2017, October 27). Donald Trump wants to spend big on anti-drug ads. Here's why they don't work. Yahoo Release.
- Rossman, S. (2017, February 24). Deadly drug overdoses more than doubled since 1999. *USA Today*.
- Superville, D. (2017, November 20). America's opioid epidemic is costing hundreds of billions of dollars. *Time*.
- Wagner, J., Bernstein, L., & Johnson, J. (2017, October 26). Trump declares opioid crisis a public health emergency; critics say plan falls short. *The Washington Post*.

Lab 21A Use and Abuse of Other Drugs

Name	Section	Date

Purpose: To evaluate a friend or family member's behavior and potential for becoming an abuser of drugs; if this report is submitted to an instructor, be sure not to identify by name the person you are evaluating.

Procedures Answer these questions to determine if the person you are evaluating is an abuser of medications. Place an X over the answer that applies.

A. Prescription Drug Abuse

(Yes) (No) 1. Does he/she take more medicine than prescribed per dosage?

(Yes) (No) 2. Does he/she feel more nervous than ever when the medicine wears off?

(Yes) (No) 3. Does he/she hoard medicine?

(Yes) (No) 4. Does he/she hide the amount of medicine taken from friends, family, or his/her doctors?

(Yes) (No) 5. Does he/she fail to provide his/her doctor with a complete list of medications he/she is taking from all sources (dentist, family physician, specialists)?

The more questions to which you answered "yes," the more likely he/she is a drug abuser.

B. Risk Factors for Becoming Addicted (Remember that alcohol is a drug, too.)

(Yes) (No) 1. Have any members of his/her family ever abused drugs?

(Yes) (No) 2. Was he/she abused as a child, or did he/she go through other trauma during childhood?

(Yes) (No) 3. Is he/she now undergoing unusual stress or mental pain?

(Yes) (No) 4. Does he/she have easy access to drugs?

(Yes) (No) 5. Has he/she used or does he/she use drugs recreationally?

(Yes) (No) 6. If he/she has used or now uses drugs recreationally, did or does he/she choose the fastest method of getting a hit?

The more "yes" answers, the greater his/her risk of addiction.

C. Signs and Symptoms That a Problem with Drugs Exists (Remember that alcohol is a drug, too.)

(Yes) (No) 1. Does he/she use drugs as an escape or to cope with a stressful situation?

(Yes) (No) 2. Does he/she become depressed easily?

(Yes) (No) 3. Does he/she use drugs the first thing in the morning?

(Yes) (No) 4. Has he/she ever tried to quit and resumed using again?

(Yes) (No) 5. Does he/she do things under the influence of a drug that he/she would not normally do?

(Yes) (No) 6. Has he/she had any drug-related "close calls" with the police or any arrests?

(Yes) (No) 7. Does he/she think a party or social gathering isn't fun unless drugs are served/available?

(Yes) (No) 8. Does he/she feel proud of an increased tolerance to drugs?

Yes No 9. Does he/she use drugs when alone?

Yes No 10. Has or does he/she use a wide variety of drugs?

Yes No 11. Is he/she constantly thinking about being high?

Yes No 12. Does he/she avoid people or places that oppose usage?

Yes No 13. Have his/her friends, family, teachers, or employer expressed concern about his/her use?

Yes No 14. Is his/her usage causing him/her to neglect responsibilities?

Yes No 15. Has he/she ever had blackouts or lack of memory of drug use or other events?

Yes No 16. Has he/she stolen to get money for drugs?

Yes No 17. Has he/she seriously considered that he/she might have a drug problem?

The more "yes" answers, the more likely he/she is to have a serious problem with drugs.

Results

A. Does he/she abuse prescription drugs? Yes No
   (Questions A: 1–5)

B. Is he/she at considerable risk for addiction? Yes No
   (Questions B: 1–6)

C. Does he/she have a serious problem with drugs? Yes No
   (Questions C: 1–17)

Conclusions and Implications: In several sentences, discuss a plan of action that could be taken by a person who has a problem with the misuse of over-the-counter drugs, prescription drugs, or illegal drugs. Discuss specific things you could do to help a person with a problem. At some point, you may want to answer the questions about yourself.

Preventing Sexually Transmitted Infections

LEARNING OBJECTIVES

After completing the study of this Concept, you will be able to:

▶ Identify the most common sexually transmitted infections (STIs).

▶ Define HIV and AIDS and indicate rates and trends in their prevalence.

▶ Describe common modes of HIV transmission and the HIV replication process.

▶ Understand the importance of testing and early intervention in preventing HIV/AIDS.

▶ Describe symptoms and consequences of common STIs, including HPV, chlamydia, gonorrhea, and syphilis.

▶ Identify less common STIs and their associated health risks.

▶ Describe important factors contributing to increased risk for STIs.

▶ Understand effective approaches to the prevention and treatment of STIs.

Safe sex and sound information about sexually transmitted infections are important to health and wellness.

©Antonio Guillem/Shutterstock

Concept 22

Why it Matters!

Interpersonal relationships and sexual interactions strongly influence our moods and behaviors. They are basic to family life and fundamental to the reproduction of the human species. Approached responsibly, the human sexual experience contributes to wellness and quality of life in many ways. When approached irresponsibly, it can result in disease and personal and interpersonal suffering. Learning and adopting safe sex practices are critical for avoiding unwanted pregnancies and for reducing risks for various infections and diseases. This Concept provides information about the symptoms, causes, and treatments of various infections and diseases transmitted through sexual contact.

Shared interests can help build healthy relationships.
©Glow Images/Superstock

General Facts

The healthy sexual experience can contribute to wellness in many ways. All five wellness dimensions are involved in decisions concerning participation in, the meaningfulness of, and the long-term consequences of the sexual experience. The healthy sexual experience requires sensitive and thoughtful consideration of the conse-

quences. When approached responsibly, sexual behavior can enhance quality of life in important ways. This fact is evident in a recent study of the reasons that college students have sex. The study of over 1,500 college students identified 237 different reasons for engaging in sexual behavior. Although women tended to report more intimacy reasons and men tended to report more reasons related to physical pleasure, 20 of the top 25 reasons overlapped for men and women. The most common reasons across the full sample were love, pleasure, affection, romance, emotional closeness, arousal, excitement, adventure, experience, connection, celebration, curiosity, opportunity, and the desire to please. Although antisocial reasons for sexual behavior were less common, they have the potential for severe negative consequences. For example, one of the very infrequently endorsed reasons for sex was to intentionally infect a partner with an STI, and another was to break up a rival's relationship. Thus, as stated previously, sexual behavior can have both rewarding and costly effects.

Good physical health contributes to an active and satisfying sex life. Two population-based studies in the United States found that individuals who were in good or excellent health were more likely to be sexually active. Among those who were sexually active, good health was associated with greater interest in sex, more frequent sex, and a better-quality sex life. On average, being in good health increased the sexual life expectancy for men by 5 to 7 years and for women by 3 to 6 years.

Sexually transmitted infections is a broad term that refers to a number of different conditions. The term *sexually transmitted disease (STD)* has been used to refer to these conditions, but the broader term of **sexually transmitted infection (STI)** is now more accepted. The term *STI* better reflects the fact that a period of infection typically occurs prior to the emergence of any associated disease symptoms. HIV/AIDS is an example of this, as one can be infected for many years before signs of disease begin to occur. In other cases, STIs never result in identifiable disease symptoms. **Human papillomavirus (HPV)** is an example of this type of STI. Although HPV can lead to cervical cancer in women, most women infected with HPV never experience disease symptoms. While consequences vary, the major risks justify a strong emphasis on prevention of STIs.

Unsafe sexual activity can result in disease, poor health, and much pain and suffering. Until the 1940s, STIs were a leading cause of death. The discovery of penicillin and other antibiotics, and improved public health practices, lowered the death rate from STIs, but they have remained a significant health problem. In 1991, STIs became 1 of the 10 leading causes of death in the United States, principally because of the high death rate from **acquired immune deficiency syndrome (AIDS)** caused by the **human immunodeficiency virus (HIV).** The development of more effective treatments has reduced deaths from HIV/AIDS and moved STIs off the top 10 list.

HIV/AIDS

Of all the STIs, HIV/AIDS poses the greatest health threat to the world. Slightly less than 40,000 people in the United States are infected with HIV annually, with a total of over 1.1 million people currently infected. Worldwide, the problem is even more profound, with roughly 2.1 million people infected each year and a total of more than 36 million people currently living with HIV. The problem of HIV/AIDS is particularly bad in sub-Saharan Africa, which accounts for roughly 70 percent of individuals living with HIV. Only 60 percent are aware of the fact that they are infected, which contributes to the spread of HIV. International health agencies have been working to address the gap in awareness and the limited access to treatments in these parts of the world. Fortunately, these efforts are starting to pay off, with a 40 percent decrease in new HIV infections since 2001. More people are getting HIV medication and the rate of new infections is decreasing.

There are three mechanisms for most HIV transmission. The three primary mechanisms responsible for the transmission of HIV are sexual activity, contact with infected blood (needle sharing), and transmission from an infected mother to her child. Among men in the United States, the greatest number of new cases result from men having sex with men, though a significant number of cases result from heterosexual sex. Among women, risk of transmission is most frequent in heterosexual sex. Worldwide, the most common cause of AIDS is heterosexual sex.

Roughly 6 percent of new cases in the U.S. are the result of using contaminated needles to inject drugs. Transmission from infected mothers to their children used to account for roughly as many HIV infections as IV drug use. However, rates have decreased dramatically since the turn of the century. The latter mode of transmission could be largely prevented through the use of a specific drug (nevirapine) and with a cesarean delivery.

While HIV can be transmitted in multiple ways, it is important to understand that HIV is not transmitted through the air or in saliva, sweat, or urine. It does not spread by hugging, sharing foods or beverages, or casual kissing. Contact with phones, silverware, or toilet seats does not cause the spread of HIV. Although people who had blood transfusions before 1985 had an increased risk of HIV transmission, the safety of the blood supply has increased dramatically since that time, resulting in extremely low rates of risk from transfusion. The routes of transmission of HIV in the United States are summarized in Figure 1.

Incidence of HIV/AIDS is increasing disproportionately in women and minorities. What was once thought to be a disease of males, especially gay men, is now increasingly a female condition. Women now represent roughly one-fourth of those living with HIV in the United States and nearly half of the global cases of HIV. Ethnic minority groups in the United States are also disproportionately affected, with roughly 45 percent of new cases occurring among African Americans and another 24 percent occurring among Hispanics. This discrepancy is largest among women, with a rate among African American women roughly 20 times that of White women.

HIV attacks the immune system and can lead to AIDS. A test of **serostatus** can indicate if a person is seropositive. When a person tests seropositive for HIV, it means that a blood test has indicated the presence of HIV in the body. HIV invades the body's immune system cells, even killing them, which damages the immune system and the body's ability to fight infections. HIV causes immune suppression by directly invading and killing **CD4 helper cells.** When too many of these cells (also called **T helper cells**) are destroyed, the body cannot fight **opportunistic infections** effectively.

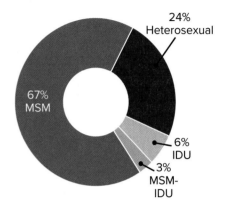

Figure 1 ▶ Routes of transmission for HIV in the United States.

Note: MSM = men who have sex with men; IDU = injection drug users; MSM-IDU = both MSM and IDU.

Source: Centers for Disease Control and Prevention (2016)

Sexually Transmitted Infection (STI) An infection for which a primary method of transmission is sexual activity.

Human Papillomavirus (HPV) A group of more than 150 related viruses that represents the most prevalent STI and a cause of both genital warts and cervical cancer.

Acquired Immune Deficiency Syndrome (AIDS) An HIV-infected individual is said to have AIDS when he or she has developed certain opportunistic infections (for example, pneumonia, tuberculosis, yeast infections, or other infections) or when his or her CD4 cell count drops below 200.

Human Immunodeficiency Virus (HIV) A virus that causes a breakdown of the immune system in humans, resulting in the body's inability to fight infections. It is a precursor to AIDS.

Serostatus A blood test indicating the presence of antibodies the immune system creates to fight disease. A seropositive status indicates that a person has antibodies to fight HIV and is HIV positive.

CD4 Helper Cells (T Helper Cells) Cells that protect against infections and activate the body's immune response. HIV kills these cells, so a high count usually means better health.

Opportunistic Infections Infections that typically do not affect healthy people, but may lead to diseases in people whose immune systems have been compromised.

When T cell counts are low and the **viral load** is high, the immune system cannot function properly, thereby making the seropositive person more susceptible to various types of diseases and disorders. **Antibodies** in the blood that normally fight infections are ineffective in stopping HIV from invading the body.

HIV comes in many forms, creating unique challenges for treatment. There are two primary types of HIV (HIV1 and HIV2). HIV2 appears to be less contagious and to have a longer latency between infection and disease, but the vast majority of cases of AIDS are due to HIV1. There are four groups of HIV1 (M, N, O, and P), with the M, or "Major," type accounting for most cases. Within the M group, there are at least nine different subtypes, though subtype B (predominant in the United States and Europe) and subtypes A and C (predominant in southern and eastern Africa) account for the majority of the global epidemic.

An individual has AIDS when he or she is infected with HIV and develops opportunistic diseases because of impairment of the immune system. Examples of opportunistic diseases associated with AIDS are pneumonia, tuberculosis, **Kaposi's sarcoma,** yeast infections, and cervical cancer. Other symptoms include fatigue, swollen glands, rashes, weight loss, and loss of appetite. Once a person receives a diagnosis of AIDS, the diagnosis is maintained even if the individual becomes nonsymptomatic.

The risk of acquiring HIV/AIDS is reduced if exposure to HIV and to the methods of transmission is avoided. Experts from the National Institutes of Health (NIH) have concluded that HIV transmission could be reduced if legislative barriers to needle exchange programs were lifted, if greater emphasis were given to youth education programs about HIV/AIDS, if greater funding were available for the treatment of people who abuse drugs, and if educational efforts among high-risk populations were increased. Worldwide, the money expended on treatment far exceeds the amounts spent on prevention. Taking personal responsibility for reducing risky behaviors is important for prevention on a personal level. Increasing awareness of these risks is important for national and international prevention.

Early detection is critical for controlling the spread of AIDS. Unfortunately, the majority of adults in the United States have never been tested for HIV. Although rates have increased gradually over the past decade, only about half of adults report having been tested for HIV. Further, the Centers for Disease Control and Prevention (CDC) estimates that about 13 percent of individuals with HIV are unaware that they are infected and that roughly one-third are diagnosed so late that they develop AIDS within a year of their HIV diagnosis. To facilitate early identification of HIV, the CDC now recommends testing for everyone between the ages of 13 and 64 at least once as part of routine health care. The

HELP Health is available to Everyone for a Lifetime, and it's Personal

Talk, Test, and Treat

The CDC has launched a new publicity campaign designed to help prevent the spread of STIs in the United States. The campaign focuses on the three Ts: Talk, Test, and Treat. **T**alk refers to having open discussions about STIs with partners and health-care providers. **T**est refers to getting tested because it is the only way to know for sure if you have an STI. **T**reat refers to seeking medical care to ensure that you have the right medicine for treating your infection. The CDC publicity campaign also emphasizes the dangers of allowing STIs to go untreated, including the increased risk of HIV, inability to get pregnant or pregnancy complications, and long-term pelvic/abdominal pain. For more information, search "CDC and STI Infographics" online.

HELP INTERRUPT THE STEADY CLIMB IN STDS WITH THESE THREE STEPS:

Source: Centers for Disease Control and Prevention.

How effective do you think publicity campaigns are in preventing STIs? What suggestions would you have for reducing STI incidence?

connect
ACTIVITY

American College of Physicians also recommends that physicians encourage all of their patients to get tested for HIV, regardless of their level of risk.

Testing for HIV and other STIs can be either confidential or anonymous. When a test is confidential, there is a written record of the test results, but there is also assurance that this information will be kept private by the health-care provider. An anonymous test is one for which there is no written record, and the results cannot be connected to a name or other identifiable information. Clinics throughout the country provide both confidential and anonymous (in most states) testing at no cost. Self-testing kits can be purchased at drugstores and mailed to labs for analysis so the individual does not have to see a health-care provider. The tests are noninvasive, requiring the use of a swab to collect cells from inside the mouth.

There is no cure for AIDS, but treatments have improved. For those infected with HIV/AIDS, there is no known cure. However, treatments have been developed to

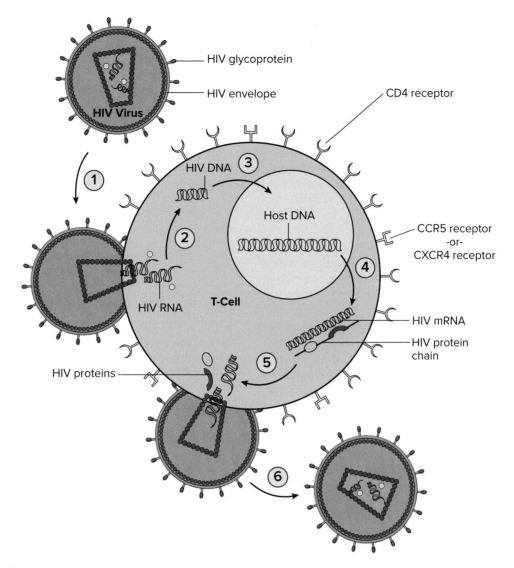

Figure 2 ► HIV replication cycle.

Source: Adapted from U.S. Department of Health and Human Services

suppress or slow the progress of the disease process. HIV is a type of virus (retrovirus) and is treated with drugs called antiretrovirals. These treatments target various stages in the replication process of the HIV virus (see Figure 2). In the first step, the virus must enter T cells in the body (1). Once HIV enters these cells, HIV RNA is translated into DNA through a process called reverse transcription (2). Once the HIV RNA has been converted, an enzyme called integrase facilitates the integration of HIV DNA into the host DNA of the cell (3). The HIV DNA is then able to generate new protein sequences (4) necessary to create new copies of the virus (5). In the final step (6), the HIV protein called protease separates the protein sequence into its components so that these proteins can combine to form new viruses.

There are six classes of antiretroviral (ART) drugs that are used in combination to target different stages in the progression of HIV infection. The three most common are described here. Fusion inhibitors are a class of drugs that operate in the first stage of the process by interfering with the virus's ability to enter the host cell. Reverse transcriptase inhibitors disrupt reverse transcription so that HIV RNA cannot be converted into DNA or integrated into the DNA of the host cell. Finally, protease inhibitors interfere with the protease enzyme, which prevents the HIV DNA from being

Viral Load The level of virus (HIV) in the blood.

Antibodies Proteins in the bloodstream that react to overcome bacterial and other agents that attack the body.

Kaposi's Sarcoma A type of cancer evidenced by purple sores (tumors) on the skin.

separated into its components. This prevents the development of new viruses within the host cell.

A combination of several drugs referred to as "drug cocktails" have been the most common form of HIV treatment, but the FDA has also approved "once a day" pills that combine multiple drugs into a single pill. Some evidence suggests that use of these single-pill treatments leads to better adherence and lower rates of hospitalization. On the down side, it can be difficult to know which of the drugs is creating side effects among those who experience them. Thus, individuals with HIV are encouraged to work closely with their physicians to decide on the best drug or combination of drugs for their particular circumstances.

Early treatment dramatically reduces death rates. Numerous studies have demonstrated the benefits of early treatment for HIV. Public health agencies have responded by promoting and encouraging greater access to treatment. Whereas the CDC used to recommend treatment only for individuals with a CD4 count less than 350, it now recommends treatment for all individuals with HIV, regardless of CD4 count. Similarly, the World Health Organization has moved from recommending treatment at a CD4 count less than 200 to a CD4 count less than 500. It also recommends treatment for all infected children under the age of 5, all pregnant or nursing women, and all HIV-positive individuals with an HIV-positive partner, regardless of CD4 count. It is estimated that these new guidelines could save an additional 3 million lives and prevent 3.5 million new cases of HIV by 2025.

Early treatment with ART may also decrease rates of HIV transmission. Although antiretroviral treatment (ART) does not eliminate the risk for HIV among partners of individuals who are HIV positive, one study found over a 96 percent reduction in risk for infection among the sexual partners of individuals started on ART, relative to those who did not begin ART. A new type of drug, referred to as "pre-exposure prophylaxis" (PrEP), has also proven effective in preventing infection among those at risk (see A Closer Look). Combining the approaches of routine testing, preventive medication, and early treatment may have a particularly dramatic impact. Mathematical models have supported the potential of universal voluntary testing combined with immediate ART for those infected with HIV. Using South Africa as a basis for calculations, the mathematical model suggested that the incidence and mortality associated with HIV could be reduced to 1 in 1,000 cases within 10 years of full implementation. Current incidence rates in South Africa are roughly 1 in 20. Although these are only theoretical models, trials of the test and treat approach are currently under way in sub-Saharan Africa, so we will soon be able to compare these projections to real data.

The search for a vaccine for HIV is well under way, though no vaccine is currently available. HIV medicines and treatments such as ART have allowed individuals

A CLOSER LOOK

HIV Prevention Pill

Preventing the spread of HIV remains an important public health priority. A new type of drug referred to as "pre-exposure prophylaxis" (PrEP) can be taken daily by people who do not have HIV to prevent infection. About 1.2 million Americans who are at high risk for HIV could benefit from the pill sold under the brand name Truvada. Studies show that the pill can reduce the risk of HIV from sex by more than 90 percent and from injected drugs by more than 70 percent. PrEP "on demand" refers to taking several pills before sex and several at regular intervals after sex. Preliminary studies also show benefits of this approach, but more research is needed. Many insurance plans cover the drug and uninsured individuals can get PrEP free via a manufacturer's patient assistance program. Unfortunately, only about 1 percent of those who can benefit currently use the drug.

What groups do you think should be targeted for use of Truvada and what do you think should be done to increase its use in these populations?

living with HIV to stay healthy for many years. However, the ultimate goal is to develop vaccines that can prevent a person from getting HIV in the first place. Vaccines typically work by teaching the body's immune system how to recognize and defend against harmful viruses or bacteria. Successful vaccines have been developed for many diseases, including polio, chicken pox, measles, mumps, rubella, and influenza (flu), but effective vaccines for HIV have proven elusive. More than 100 vaccines have been tested in humans or animals, and many vaccines are currently undergoing clinical trials in the United States and abroad. A study in 2016 provided preliminary evidence that a vaccine could prevent HIV infection, and a new, more robust NIH-supported clinical trial was recently launched to test a modified HIV vaccine. Vaccines have proven to be the safest and most cost-effective way to prevent illness, disability, and death, so there is considerable interest in this work. According to the NIH, "developing safe, effective, and affordable vaccines that can prevent HIV infection in uninfected people is the NIH's highest HIV research priority."

Common Sexually Transmitted Infections

STIs infect about 20 million people in the United States each year. Although HIV is the deadliest of the sexually transmitted infections, it is not among the most common in the United States. Table 1 lists some of the

Table 1 ▶ Rankings of Incidence and Prevalence of Common STIs

STI	Rank of Incidence (Number of New Cases of the Condition)	Rank of Prevalence (Number of People with Condition)
Chlamydia	2	3
Gonorrhea	3	5
Hepatitis B	6	4
Herpes	4	2
HPV	1	1
Syphilis	5	6

Source: Centers for Disease Control and Prevention

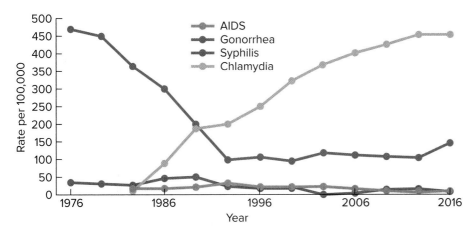

Figure 3 ▶ Trends in STI rates in the United States.

Source: Centers for Disease Control and Prevention

most common STIs in terms of both incidence (new cases) and prevalence (cumulative number of cases). Although rates of HPV have not been tracked by the CDC because the vast majority of individuals with HPV are unaware that they are infected, it is estimated that over 50 percent of sexually active adults will be infected with HPV at some point in their lifetime. Of the STIs that are tracked by the CDC, **chlamydia** has had the highest annual prevalence of new cases for the past two decades.

With improved methods of screening and efforts by the CDC and other agencies to increase screening, rates of identified cases have increased dramatically in the past 25 years despite the fact that most experts believe that rates of infection are not increasing. Gonorrhea had the highest annual prevalence of new cases until the early 1990s and is now

second to Chlamydia among the STIs that are tracked by the CDC. Rates of gonorrhea infection in the United States have decreased dramatically over the past 25 years. Syphilis rates are much lower, though recent increases are cause for concern, particularly among men who have sex with men. Figure 3 provides a graphic depiction of the trends in STI rates over the past 40 years.

The human papillomavirus (HPV) is a very common STI in young people. An estimated 14 million people become infected with HPV each year, making this the most commonly transmitted STI. The virus is responsible for the development of genital warts, but most people do not develop them and are therefore unaware that they are infected. Although the disease is asymptomatic in the short term, it leads to significantly increased risk for cervical cancer in women. In fact, HPV is the leading cause of cervical cancer. Two strains are particularly dangerous, accounting for approximately 70 percent of cases of cervical cancer. There is also recent evidence that oral HPV can be contracted through oral sex, which increases risk for oropharyngeal (throat) cancer. Prevalence of oral HPV is considerably higher for men than women.

Federal guidelines initially recommended that all young girls (aged 11–12) be vaccinated, but the CDC now recommends that all young boys be vaccinated as well. The CDC also recommends the vaccine for gay men and those with compromised immune systems. Catch-up vaccinations are recommended between age 13 and the early 20s for those who do not receive the vaccination in childhood. Several states have mandated vaccinations and a number of other states provide vaccinations at no cost or provide education programs designed to increase vaccination rates.

Advocates argue that vaccinations save lives, whereas opponents have argued that providing the vaccine will encourage casual sexual behavior. A long-term study published in *JAMA Internal Medicine* concluded that "HPV was not associated with increases in STIs in a large cohort of females, suggesting that vaccination is unlikely to promote unsafe sexual activity." Also many females (38 percent) are now fully vaccinated, and rates of HPV in young women decreased dramatically in the early 2000s. In recent years there have been

Chlamydia A bacterial infection, similar to gonorrhea, that attacks the urinary tract and reproductive organs.

gradual decreases in multiple forms of HPV. Rates of vaccination among male adolescents are much lower overall, although they are increasing. It is important to note that the vaccine will not help those already infected with HPV. However, routine Pap tests can identify the early cell changes associated with HPV and help prevent the development of cervical cancer.

Chlamydia is a common STI, but it is often difficult to detect. About 1.6 million new cases of chlamydia are reported in the United States each year. Chlamydia is known as the "silent" STI because about three-fourths of infected women and about half of infected men have no symptoms. Thus, routine screening is essential for detecting most cases of chlamydia. If symptoms do occur, it is typically in the first three weeks following infection. For men who experience symptoms, the most common are discharge from the penis and a burning sensation when urinating. Common symptoms in women include abnormal vaginal discharge, a burning sensation when urinating, lower abdominal or back pain, pain during intercourse, and bleeding between menstrual periods. If chlamydia is left untreated, the health consequences can be extensive, particularly for women. The disease has been linked to increased risk of **pelvic inflammatory disease (PID),** as well as a number of other secondary health problems, including urethritis, cervicitis, ectopic pregnancy, infertility, and chronic pelvic pain.

As a result of the high levels of risk for young women (more than three-fourths of cases in women are among those under age 25), guidelines from the U.S. Preventive Services Task Force suggest that sexually active women under the age of 25 undergo routine screening for chlamydia. Although rates of screening have increased, less than half of women in this age group are screened annually. Fortunately, chlamydia is very treatable, and its long-term health consequences can be prevented if the infection is identified quickly. Treatment with antibiotics can clear up the infection within a week to 10 days.

Early detection is critical for effective treatment of gonorrhea. **Gonorrhea** is a bacterial infection that can be treated with modern antibiotics if detected early. Sexual activity is the principal method of disease transmission. Penile and vaginal gonorrhea are the most common types. Symptoms usually occur within 3 to 7 days after bacteria enter the system. Among men, the most common symptoms are painful urination and penile drip or discharge. Symptoms are less apparent among women, though painful urination and vaginal discharge are not uncommon. Other types of gonorrhea often have fewer symptoms. Chills, fever, painful bowel movements, and sore throat are the most common. Early detection by a culture or smear test at the site or sites of sexual contact is how the disease is diagnosed. Early cure is especially important for females because gonorrhea can lead to PID, which can result in infertility.

Hepatitis B can lead to chronic liver disease. Like other STIs, **hepatitis B** (HPB) is typically spread through unprotected sex with an infected partner, intravenous drug use, or transmission from an infected mother to her baby. Although rare, HPB can be spread through blood transfusion or any other contact with infected blood. Symptoms of HPB include jaundice, fatigue, abdominal pain, loss of appetite, and nausea. Among those chronically infected with the virus, chronic liver disease typically develops, leading to premature death in 15 to 25 percent of cases. Fortunately, a vaccine for HPB has been available since 1982, and rates have decreased since then from over 260,000 cases to less than 4,000 cases in 2015.

Genital herpes is among the most commonly spread STIs because of a lack of awareness of infection. **Genital herpes,** one of the most commonly reported STIs, is caused by the herpes simplex virus (HSV). Although fewer new cases of genital herpes are reported annually than cases of chlamydia, the number of individuals currently infected is much higher. This is because chlamydia is treatable. In contrast, once someone contracts genital herpes, he or she will always carry the virus. Genital herpes causes lesions or blisters on the penis, vagina, or cervix usually occurring 2 to 12 days after infection and often lasting a week to a month. Swollen glands and headache may also occur.

No cure exists for genital sores caused by HSV, though some prescription drugs can help treat the disease symptoms. Episodic antiviral therapy is taken at the first sign of an outbreak, and suppressive antiviral therapy is taken daily to prevent outbreaks from occurring. HSV can remain dormant in the body for long periods, and as a result, symptoms can recur at any time, especially after undergoing stress or illness.

Genital herpes is especially contagious when blisters are present. Condom use or abstinence from sexual activity when symptoms are present can reduce the risk of transmission of the disease. Although genital herpes is less infectious when there are no symptoms present, the infection can still be spread to other partners. Condoms provide some protection, but they are not totally effective in preventing infection because they do not cover all genital areas. Herpes is more dangerous for women than men because of the association between genital herpes and cervical cancer and the risk of transmitting the disease to the unborn.

Syphilis is another serious but less common STI. **Syphilis** was a serious national health problem in the 1940s, when it was 10 times more prevalent than it is now. Cases of syphilis declined 84 percent nationwide during the 1990s. Although rates remain dramatically lower than they were in 1990, rates of primary and secondary syphilis (considered a good index of incidence) in the United States have more than tripled since 2000. This includes an increase of more than 70 percent since 2012. These increases appear to be driven primarily by men who have sex with men, a group that now accounts for more than half of new cases in the U.S. each year. However, it is important to note that rates have been increasing in women since 2013. The CDC also reports that syphilis continues to have a disproportionate effect on African Americans and people living in the southern United States.

Like gonorrhea, syphilis is a bacterial infection that can be effectively treated with antibiotics. The symptoms of syphilis include **chancre** sores that generally appear at the primary site of sexual contact, then change from a red swelling to a hardened ulcer on the skin. Even if not treated, the sores disappear after 1 to 5 weeks. It is important to get treatment even after this primary phase of the disease because the disease is still present and contagious. After several weeks or longer, secondary symptoms occur, such as a rash, loss of hair, joint pain, sore throat, and swollen glands. Even after these symptoms go away, untreated syphilis lingers in a latent phase. Serious health problems may result, including blindness, deafness, tumors, and stillbirth.

Early detection is important and can be diagnosed from chancre discharge or a blood test several weeks after the appearance of chancres. There is an association between syphilis and the spread of HIV. Evidence suggests that the presence of chancres increases the risk of transmitting HIV during sexual activity.

Although health risks are not as severe, lesser-known STIs are highly prevalent and cause significant distress. Genital warts, pubic crab lice, and chancroid are examples of lesser-known but prevalent STIs (see Table 2). Genital warts are caused by the strains of the human papillomavirus, discussed earlier. Fortunately, the strains of HPV associated with genital warts tend to be relatively low risk. The most significant consequence to the individual is often psychological, due to concern about the appearance of the warts and the potential consequences associated with them. Because HPV is so common, the chance of developing genital warts is relatively high, even with a small number of sexual partners. Fortunately, there are several effective treatments for genital warts, including remedies that can be self-administered by patients in their own homes. Pubic lice also tends to be highly distressing to the individual, but effective over-the-counter treatments are available to eliminate pubic lice in a matter of days. Although individuals with genital warts and pubic lice may have few long-term effects from these infections, studies have found that both groups tend to have more sexual partners and are at higher risk for other STIs, including gonorrhea and chlamydia. Therefore, these individuals should be routinely tested for other STIs. Most patients with chancroid in the United States, where it is uncommon, contract it during travels to countries where it is more common. Chancroid is a known risk factor for HIV and should therefore be treated promptly.

Table 2 ▶ Facts about Lesser-Known STIs

Genital Warts (Condylomas)

- Constitute approximately 5 percent of all reported STIs
- Are most prevalent in ages 15 to 24
- Are caused by HPV
- Are hard and yellow or gray on dry skin
- Are soft and pink, red, or dark on moist skin
- Are treated by the prescription drug Podophyllin

Pubic Crab Lice

- Are pinhead-sized insects (parasites) that feed on the blood of the host
- Are transmitted by sexual contact and/or contact with contaminated clothes, bedding, and other washable items
- Have symptoms that include itching, but some people have no symptoms
- Can be controlled by using medicated lotion and shampoos and by washing contaminated bedding
- Do *not* transmit other STIs

Chancroid

- Is caused by bacteria
- Is more commonly seen in men than in women, particularly uncircumcised males
- Has symptoms including one or more sores or raised bumps on the genitals
- Can result in progressive ulcers occurring on the genitals; sometimes the ulcers persist for weeks or months
- Can be successfully treated with certain antibiotics

Pelvic Inflammatory Disease (PID) An infection of the urethra (urine passage), which can lead to infertility among women.

Gonorrhea A bacterial infection of the mucous membranes, including the eyes, throat, genitals, and other organs.

Hepatitis B An infection of the liver caused by the hepatitis B virus, which is often sexually transmitted and can lead to long-term liver disease.

Genital Herpes A viral infection that can attack any area of the body but often causes blisters on the genitals.

Syphilis An infection caused by a corkscrew-shaped bacteria that travels in the bloodstream and embeds itself in the mucous membranes of the body, including those of the sexual organs.

Chancre Sore or lesion commonly associated with syphilis.

Factors That Contribute to Sexual Risks

Sexually explicit media influence teen sexual behavior. There has been considerable concern about the impact of explicit sexual content in the media (music, magazines, television, movies, and Internet) on teen sexual behavior. A recent study found that adolescents exposed to sexually explicit content on the Internet had more permissive attitudes toward sex and were more likely to have multiple sexual partners and to have engaged in anal sex. Another study evaluating exposure to sexually explicit content found that early exposure predicted permissive sexual norms and an increase in oral sex and sexual intercourse two years later. This research shows the powerful impact of media on teen sexual behavior.

Misperceived norms may contribute to sexual risk. Many teens engage in sex because they believe that "everybody is doing it." The media portrayals discussed in the previous section may contribute to these inaccurate beliefs, though they may also be driven by inaccurate communication. In a study of males between ages 15 and 22, 45 percent reported that they were virgins, although 23 percent indicated that they told others they were not.

Healthy relationships depend on trust and good communication.
©Sam Edwards/Glow Images

Overall, 60 percent reported that they lied about something related to sex to appear experienced and more popular. Interestingly, they said that girls who were more sexually experienced were perceived as less popular. Young people need to be aware of the true norms for sexual behavior and not get caught up in perceptions based on inaccurate information.

College students are at risk for HIV and other STIs due to the practice of serial monogamy. Many college students are sexually active, yet most do not use condoms on a consistent basis. This is partly due to perceptions that they are in committed relationships and therefore at low risk for infection. Such perceptions are problematic for several reasons. First, some college students define a regular partner as someone they have been with for as little as one month, and most define a regular partner as someone they have been with for less than six months. Second, most college students do not get tested on a regular basis, if at all. Third, when students perceive that they are in a committed relationship, the likelihood of condom use decreases dramatically. This is particularly true when an alternative form of birth control, primarily birth control pills, is being used. One study found that

Technology Update

"Hook-Up" Apps May Contribute to STIs

Websites like Match.com were originally designed to help users find dating partners, but new smartphone apps are often used to find sexual partners rather than dating partners. Well-known GPS-based apps include Tinder and Grindr (specifically for gay and bisexual men). A recent study found that men who used Grindr and similar smartphone apps were 25 percent more likely to contract gonorrhea and 37 percent more likely to contract chlamydia relative to men who did not use these apps. The risks are not restricted to gay and bisexual men. A recent study of heterosexual college students found that nearly 40 percent reported using dating apps like Tinder, and those who did were more likely to report having sex after using drugs and alcohol as well as unprotected vaginal or anal sex. Developers of these apps argue that the apps could also be used to provide individuals with information and resources to reduce their risk and Tinder, under pressure from sexual health advocates, recently added a free STI testing center locator to its app.

Do you think apps that help people find casual sexual partners should be regulated to prevent harm, or might they provide opportunities to intervene with those at greatest risk?

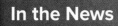

In the News

The "Me Too" Campaign and Sexual Misconduct

The issue of sexual violence on college campuses has received considerable media attention in recent years and rightfully so. One recent analysis by the *Washington Post* found a 50 percent increase in reports of sexual assault on college campuses over a three-year period. Recent high-profile cases of sexual harassment in entertainment and politics have also brought unwanted sexual behavior into the spotlight at levels that are historically unprecedented. Allegations against Hollywood producer and executive Harvey Weinstein have opened the door for women to identify a number of actors, politicians, and other high-profile men as having engaged in sexual misconduct. The "Me Too" campaign in various social media has provided a platform to bring attention to the large percentage of people—both women and men—who have experienced unwanted sexual advances. Many believe that these disclosures have the potential to lead to long-term changes in cultural norms that could reduce the incidence of sexual assault.

Do you think that recent high-profile events related to sexual assault will lead to long-term changes, or will the public quickly forget about these cases as they fade from the headlines?

93.7 percent of sexually active college women were using contraception to prevent pregnancy, but only 23 percent used contraception to prevent STIs. The common result is unprotected sexual intercourse between two people who have known one another for a short time and who are unaware of each other's STI status. Many students go through multiple committed relationships during the college years. This type of serial monogamy places college students at increased risk for HIV and other STIs.

Sexting can have many negative consequences. Though "sexting" (defined as sending or receiving sexually suggestive, nearly nude, or nude photos by text message or email) does not involve physical contact, it has led to problems for many—from teens to prominent politicians. Approximately 50 percent of college students have reported sending explicit pictures or videos to their partners, with a sizable percentage sharing them with strangers. Although the phenomenon may reflect a new social media form of intimacy, many people find the concept of sexting objectionable, and laws in some states make it illegal to send or forward sexually explicit images.

Prevention and Early Intervention of STIs

Early prevention can increase understanding of risk and strategies for practicing safe sex. Some argue that abstinence-only education is best, while others believe that young people also need to be educated about ways to protect themselves in the event that they are or will become sexually active. Between 2001 and 2009, the federal government allocated over a billion dollars to abstinence-only sex education programs. Proponents of this strategy point to decreases in sexual intercourse among teens during this period (from 54 percent in 1991 to 47 percent in 2005). However, most of the decrease occurred before 2001, with virtually no change in the rate between 2001 and 2013. Since 2013, rates have dropped by more than 5 percent. Rates of teen pregnancy also decreased between 2001 and 2009, but again this reduction appears to reflect a general linear decrease that has been ongoing since 1991.

The declines in rates of sexual intercourse and teen pregnancy are encouraging, but studies have not demonstrated conclusively that abstinence-based programming caused the trend. In contrast, evidence does support the effectiveness of comprehensive prevention programs that both promote abstinence and teach safe sex practices. These approaches are shown to be effective in reducing sexual activity, pregnancy, and STIs.

Regular screening and notification of partners who may be infected can reduce the spread of STIs. Because many STIs are treatable with antibiotics, catching them early can reduce the negative health consequences associated with infection. For those who are sexually active with partners of unknown STI status, yearly testing is a good idea.  Even more frequent testing may be appropriate for those at very high risk (e.g., intravenous drug users and those previously diagnosed with an STI). When an individual is identified with a sexually transmitted infection, it is important that he or she notify his or her sexual partners so that they can also receive treatment. This helps reduce the spread of the infection. For more support and information, contact the following national AIDS and STI hotlines:

- AIDS hotline (English): 1-800-342-AIDS (2437)
- AIDS hotline (Spanish): 1-800-344-SIDA (7432)
- CDC STD (STI) hotline: 1-800-232-4636

Using Self-Management Skills

A variety of self-management skills are relevant for preventing STIs. Self-management skills are important for all facets of health, wellness, and fitness, but there are unique considerations with sexual activity since your actions are directly influenced by and linked to others. Abstaining from sexual activity is the safest option, but if you do engage in sex, do so responsibly and with appropriate consideration of both your needs and your partner's. Many people do not fully consider the serious, life-changing consequences of unsafe sex, so it is important to enter into sexual relationships with appropriate care. Remember that condoms are for STI prevention as well as pregnancy prevention, even if your partner is using another form of birth control. Use condoms if your partner has not been tested or you do not know his or her sexual history. Following sound consumer guidelines is recommended to further decrease your risks:

- Talk with your partner about his or her and your own sexual history before initiating sexual behavior.
- Limit sexual activity to a noninfected partner. A lifetime partner who has never had sex with other people and has never used injected drugs (unless medically administered) is the only completely safe partner.

- Avoid sexual activity or other activity that puts you in contact with another person's semen, vaginal fluids, or blood.
- Properly use a new condom (latex) every time you have sex, especially with a partner who is not known to be safe.
- Use a water-based lubricant with condoms because petroleum-based lubricants increase risk for condom failure.
- Abstain from risky sexual activity, such as anal sex and sex with high-risk people (prostitutes, people with HIV or other STIs).
- Use a condom or dental dam when engaging in oral sex.
- Do not inject drugs.
- Never share a needle or drug paraphernalia.

Self-monitoring and regular testing can help detect STIs and reduce complications from these infections. A self-assessment, such as the one provided in Lab 22A, can be helpful in identifying potential STI risk. However, it is not a substitute for medical testing. If symptoms are present, such as those described in this Concept, medical testing is warranted—sooner rather than later. As noted in this Concept, some home tests are available but, in many cases, tests must be performed and interpreted by a health-care professional, and prompt treatment can reduce many of the long-term negative consequences of STIs.

Strategies for Action: Lab Information

The first step in protecting yourself is understanding your level of risk. More than half of all STIs occur in people under age 25. Both teens and college students are at high risk, although they often fail to recognize their level of risk. In Lab 22A, you will evaluate the risk of a friend or loved one. You may also want to evaluate your own risk using the questionnaire in the lab. Adequate knowledge of risk is likely to increase your practice of behaviors that reduce risk for STIs.

Suggested Resources and Readings

The websites for the following sources can be accessed by searching online for the organization, program, or title listed. Specific scientific references are available at the end of this edition of *Concepts of Fitness and Wellness*.

- Centers for Disease Control and Prevention:
  - Contraception (effectiveness)
  - HIV Testing
  - HIV Transmission
  - Human Papillomavirus
  - Sexually Transmitted Diseases
  - Sexually Transmitted Diseases Statistics
  - STIs and HIV Fact Sheet
  - (2013, February). Incidence, Prevalence, and Cost of Sexually Transmitted Infections in the United States (pdf resource).
  - (2016). HIV Surveillance Reports, Online reports.
  - (2017). *Sexually Transmitted Disease Surveillance 2016*. Atlanta: U.S. Department of Health and Human Services (pdf report).

- Codrea-Rado, A. (2017, October 16). #MeToo floods social media with stories of harassment and assault. *The New York Times.*
- Firger, J. (2017, October 17). HPV: Oral sex risks men need to know about. *Newsweek.*
- Hirschler, B. (2017, July 24). HIV fight advances with new drug cocktails, fresh vaccine hopes. Reuters. PrEP HIV Cocktails
- HIV.gov:
  - HIV and Women
  - HIV Treatment
  - HIV Vaccines
  - What Are Vaccines and What Do They Do?
- Szabo, L. (2015, November 24). A daily pill can prevent HIV infection, but few take it. *USA Today.* Daily Pill can Prevent Infection.
- The Hunting Ground. (2017, January 31). The truth about statistics of sexual assault in college. Sexual Assault on Campus.
- Vagianos, A. (2017, April 5). 30 alarming statistics that show the reality of sexual violence in America. *Huffington Post.* Sexual Assault Statistics.
- White, D. (2016, January 22). Tinder adds STD testing center locator to dating app. *Time.*

Lab 22A Sexually Transmitted Infection Risk Questionnaire

Name	Section	Date

Purpose: To help you understand the risks of contracting a sexually transmitted infection.

Procedures

1. Read the Sexually Transmitted Infection Risk Questionnaire (Chart 1).
2. Answer the questionnaire based on information about someone you know who might be at high risk of contracting an STI.
3. Record the scores in the Results section for the person for whom the questionnaire was answered but do *not* include the person's name on the lab sheet. Use the scores to make a rating (Chart 2) and draw conclusions.
4. You may also wish to answer the questionnaire based on your own information but do *not* record your personal results on the lab sheet. Use these scores strictly for your own personal information.

Chart 1 Sexually Transmitted Infection Risk Questionnaire

Place an X over one response in each row of the questionnaire. Determine a point value for each response using the values in the circles. Sum the numbers of points for the various responses to determine an STI risk score.

Categories	0	1	3	5	8
Feelings about prevention	Able to talk with future partner about STIs **(0)**	Finds it hard to discuss STIs with a possible partner **(1)**			
Behaviors	Never engages in sexual activity **(0)**		Sexual activity with one partner, well known to him or her **(3)**	Sexual activity with one partner, not well known to him or her **(5)**	Sexual activity with multiple partners and/or high-risk individuals **(8)**
Behavior of friends	Most friends do not engage in unsafe sexual activity **(0)**	Many friends engage in unsafe sexual activity **(1)**			
Contraception	Not sexually active **(0)**	Would use condom to prevent STI **(1)**		Would sometimes use condom to prevent STI **(5)**	Would never use condom to prevent STI **(8)**
Other	Does not use drugs **(0)**				Uses injected drugs in unsafe manner **(8)**

Points

433

Chart 2 STI Risk Questionnaire Rating Chart

Rating	Score
High risk	9+
Above average risk	7–8
Moderate risk	4–6
Low risk	0–3

Results

What is the person's STI risk score? ☐ (Total from Chart 1)

What is the person's STI rating? ☐ (See Chart 2)

Conclusions and Implications: Of course, risk varies with different types of STIs. However, this questionnaire will give you an idea of an individual's "general" risk for most STIs. Answer the following questions about the risk of the person you scored and rated.

1. In several sentences, explain which STI you think this person should be especially concerned about. Why?

2. What specific recommendations would you have for the person for whom you filled out this questionnaire?

Cancer, Diabetes, and Other Health Threats

LEARNING OBJECTIVES

After completing the study of this Concept, you will be able to:

▶ Describe the general nature of cancer and its various forms and indicate the frequency of each form of cancer in the population.

▶ Outline screening guidelines, lifestyle changes for prevention, and early warning signals for cancer.

▶ Describe the general nature of diabetes and its various forms and indicate the frequency of diabetes in the population.

▶ Outline screening guidelines, lifestyle changes for prevention, and early warning signals for diabetes.

▶ Describe general nature of Alzheimer disease/dementia, and mental health conditions that impact the population.

▶ Identify risks of injuries and other health threats.

▶ Learn self-management skills and self-exams that can help you assess your personal risk for cancer and other health threats.

©Fuse/Getty Images

Many health problems that cause pain, suffering, and premature death are associated with unhealthy lifestyles.

An overarching national health goal is to create a society in which all people live long, healthy lives. Public health programming and our health-care system both contribute to this goal, but ultimately *personal* health and wellness require *personal* responsibility. Many deaths and illnesses can be prevented by adhering to healthy lifestyle choices, but it is also important to follow other established preventive strategies to further reduce your risks. Information on cardiovascular disease and osteoporosis have been covered in earlier Concepts. The focus in this Concept is on guidelines that can help reduce your risk of cancer and diabetes. Information about Alzhiemer disease/dementia, mental health issues, and injury prevention is also provided to promote awareness and prevention of other health threats.

Cancer

Cancer is a group of more than 100 different diseases. According to the American Cancer Society, cancer is a group of many different conditions characterized by abnormal, uncontrolled cell growth that will ultimately invade the blood and lymph tissues and spread throughout the body if not treated. Throughout the body, new cells are constantly being created to replace older ones. For reasons unknown, abnormal cells capable of uncontrolled growth sometimes develop. **Benign tumors** are generally not considered to be cancerous because a protective membrane restricts their growth to a specific area of the body. Treatment is important because any tumor can interfere with normal bodily functioning. Once removed, a benign tumor typically will not return.

Malignant tumors are capable of uncontrolled growth that can cause death to tissue. Approximately 85 percent of malignant tumors are carcinomas, or tumors of the epithelial cells of the inner and outer linings of the body (e.g., lungs, skin). Other malignant tumors include adenocarcinomas (glands such as breast tissue) and sarcomas (bones, muscles, connective tissue, and blood). Malignant cells invade healthy tissues, deplete them of nutrition, and interfere with a multitude of tissue functions. In the early stages of cancer, malignant tumors are located in a small area and can be more easily treated or removed. In advanced cancer, the cells invade the blood or lymph systems and travel throughout the body (**metastasize**). When this occurs, cancer becomes much more difficult to treat.

Figure 1 provides a more detailed illustration of the stages in the spread of cancer. It illustrates how an abnormal cell can divide to form a primary tumor (a), get nourishment from new blood vessels (b), invade the blood system (c), and escape to form a new (secondary) tumor (d). The four stages of cancer range from I to IV, with I being the early stage and IV being most advanced. The early stage is characterized by containment only in the layers of cells where they developed. When cancer spreads beyond the original layers (see Figure 1), it is considered to be invasive and is rated at a higher stage. Early detection is very important in the treatment and cure of cancer. One method of detecting a tumor is to take a **biopsy** of suspicious lumps in the breasts, testicles, or other parts of the body.

Cancer is not only a leading killer but also a cause of much suffering. One of every four deaths in the United States is caused by some form of cancer. Slightly more than one in three women and slightly less than one in two men will have cancer at some time in his or her life, accounting for a large portion of the money spent on health care. Of the over 100 forms of cancer, 4 of them (sometimes referred to as the Big 4) account for approximately half of all illness and death (see Figure 2). Because of the high incidence of these types of cancers (lung, colon-rectal, breast, and prostate), they are discussed in more detail here. In addition, three forms of cancer for which college students have relatively high risk—skin, ovary, and uterus—are discussed.

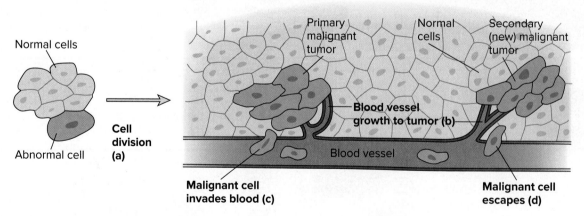

Figure 1 ▶ The spread of cancer (metastasis).

Cancer type

Deaths rank/%		New cases rank/%		Cancer type
1.	27%	2.	14%	lung/bronchus
2.	9%	3.	9%	colon-rectal
3.	8%	1.	19%	prostate
4.	7%	*		pancreas
5.	6%	10.	3%	liver
6.	4%	8.	4%	leukemia
7.	4%	*		esophagus
8.	4%	4.	7%	urinary/bladder
9.	4%	7.	5%	non-Hodgkin's lymphoma
10.	3%	*		brain/nervous system
	*	6.	5%	kidney
	*	5.	6%	skin
	*	9.	4%	thyroid

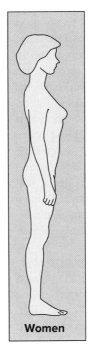

Men   Women

Deaths rank/%		New cases rank/%		Cancer type
1.	25%	2.	12%	lung/bronchus
2.	14%	1.	30%	breast
3.	8%	3.	8%	colon-rectal
4.	7%	9.	3%	pancreas
5.	5%	*		ovary
6.	4%	4.	7%	uterine
7.	4%	8.	3%	leukemia
8.	3%	*		liver
9.	3%	7.	4%	non-Hodgkin's lymphoma
10.	3%	*		brain/nervous system
	*	5.	5%	thyroid
	*	6.	4%	skin
	*	10.	3%	kidney

*Not in top 10.

Figure 2 ▶ Cancer incidence (new cases) and death by site and sex (percentage).

Source: American Cancer Society

While some forms of cancer are equally threatening to both sexes (e.g., lung and colon-rectal), others are more specific to one sex or the other (see Figure 2). It is also important to note that incidence rates are different from death rates. Skin cancer is an example of a form of cancer that is high in incidence (fifth for men and sixth for women) but relatively low in death rate (not in the top 10 for men or women). This is because it can be treated with early detection, and steps can be taken to prevent it. In Lab 23A you will have the opportunity to assess your risk for the major forms of cancer.

Breast Cancer

Breast cancer is the most prevalent form of cancer among women, but lung cancer causes more deaths. Symptoms of breast cancer include lumps and/or thickening or swelling of the breasts. Breast pain may also exist but is more often a symptom of benign tumors. Risk becomes greater as you grow older. Other risk factors include gender (females have higher risk), family history of disease, early menstruation, hormone supplementation, breast implantation, use of oral contraceptives, late childbirth or no children, excessive use of alcohol, poor eating habits, and sedentary living. The discovery of a "breast cancer gene" provides a possible explanation of the hereditary risks. Because a number of factors influence breast cancer risk, follow appropriate screening procedures to detect the possible presence of the disease.

In recent years there have been fewer deaths from breast cancer partly because of improved early diagnosis resulting from screening and more effective treatments. Though breast cancer is not as common among men, both men and women should do regular screening. Like colon-rectal and lung cancers, breast cancer is most prevalent among African Americans (more than twice as frequent) and least prevalent among Asians and Hispanics.

Early detection steps include regular self-exams of the breasts (see Lab 23B), breast exams by a physician, and regular mammograms. In many cases, lumps are present before they can be detected with self-exams. This is one reason for regular **mammograms** (breast X-rays).

There is debate among experts about the recommended frequency of mammograms. The American Cancer Society

Benign Tumors Slow-growing tumors that do not spread to other parts of the body.

Malignant Tumors Malignant means "growing worse." A malignant tumor is one that is considered to be cancerous and will spread throughout the body if not treated.

Metastasize The spread of cancer cells to other parts of the body.

Biopsy The removal of a tissue sample that can be checked for cancer cells.

Mammograms X-rays of the breast.

(ACS) recently changed its recommendation. Rather than recommending that women begin annual mammogram screening at age 40, the ACS now recommends screening at age 45 (see Table 1). The U.S. Preventive Services Task Force (PSTF) recommends "against screen mammography in women aged 40 to 49 years." Both groups indicate that the choice to begin screening at age 40 should be an individual one and take into account both benefits and risks of screening. The primary benefit is early detection of cancer that is very important for aggressive breast tumors. The risks cited by the various organizations include false positives (test results indicate possible cancer when it is not present), unnecessary biopsies, and overtreatment. There is evidence that digital mammography may be more effective than traditional film mammography. Digital "3-D" mammography is still being refined but may cut down on false positive tests. (See In the News for more information.)

Standard "local" treatments for breast cancer include lumpectomy (removal of the tumor and surrounding lymph nodes), mastectomy (removal of breast and surrounding lymph nodes), and local radiation. More "systemic" treatments include chemotherapy, hormone therapy, and targeted therapies which directly target the cells that cause cancer to grow out of control.

Colon-Rectal Cancer

Colon-rectal cancer is the second leading killer of men and third of women. In recent years, colon-rectal cancer rates have declined by about one-third. During this same period, there has been a similar increase in colon-rectal cancer screening, suggesting that testing helps reduce risk. Risk is highest among African Americans; Whites have slightly less risk. Risk among Asians and Hispanics is less than half that of Blacks. Lifestyle risk factors include diet, use of alcohol, family history,

physical activity patterns, and smoking (see Lab 23A). A high-fiber diet and physical activity can decrease the risk.

Colon-rectal cancer is most common among those over 50 years of age. When caught early, 90 percent of colon-rectal

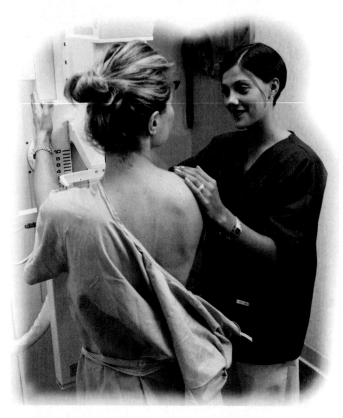

Regular physical activity promotes healthy aging and high quality of life.
©Dynamic Graphics/JupiterImages

In the News

The Mammography Debate Continues

Early detection is critical for effective cancer treatment, but there has been ongoing debate about when women should begin having mammograms to detect breast cancer. A prominent study published in the *New England Journal of Medicine* raised questions about the value of mammograms for detecting dangerous types of cancer among younger women. Despite widespread use of mammography, the detection rates for breast cancer have remained stable in recent decades. This study, and others, led to increases in recommended ages for screening (originally recommended for 40+, the medical guidelines are now set at 45 or 50). The rationale

was largely to avoid unnecessary costs and to minimize false positive tests that may lead to unnecessary concern. However, the guidelines have implications for reimbursements for preventive screening, so some physicians and women's groups have argued in favor of annual screening beginning at age 40. They point out that early detection can save lives and assert that women are not "fragile" and can cope with a false positive test.

What are your views about this debate? Should personal preference outweigh evidence-based guidelines when it comes to preventive care?

Table 1 ▶ Cancer Screening Guidelines

Cancer Type	Test or Procedure	Age	Frequency
Males and Females			
General Cancer-Related Checkup	Exam for thyroid, oral cavity, skin, lymph nodes, testes, and ovaries as part of periodic health exam	20+	With health exam
Colon-Rectal Cancer	Choose Plan 1 or Plan 2		
	Plan 1:	45+	
	Colonoscopy		Every 10 years
	-or-		
	CT colonography (virtual colonoscopy)		Every 5 years (colonoscopy if +)
	-or-		
	Flexible sigmoidoscopy		Every 5 years (colonoscopy if +)
	-or-		
	Double-contrast barium enema		Every 5 years (colonoscopy if +)
	Plan 2:	45+	
	Multi-stool fecal immunochemical test (FIT),		Annual (colonoscopy if +)
	-or-		
	Multi-stool fecal occult blood test (FOBT),		Annual (colonoscopy if +)
	-or-		
	Stool DNA test		Every 3 years (colonoscopy if +)
Skin Cancer[a]	Self-exam	Any age	Monthly
	Exam by health-care provider	Any age	With symptoms
Lung Cancer	Low-dose computed tomography (LDCT) scan	55–74 or high risk	Personal choice after consultation with health-care provider
Females			
Breast Cancer	Breast self-exam	Any age	Know feel and look of breasts; consult health-care provider if changes occur
	Clinical breast exam	Any age	Performed by health-care provider if changes occur
	Mammogram	40–44 45–54 55+	Annual, self-choice Annual Every 2 years
	Breast MRI (for those with high risk)	40+	Consult health-care provider
Cervical Cancer[b]	Pap test Pap and HPV tests Women (normal prior results) Women (history of precancer)	21–29 30–65 65+ 65+	Every 3 years Every 5 years (Pap every 3 years) No tests Continued Pap testing for 20 years
Uterine Cancer	Information about symptoms and risks	Menopause	Consult health-care provider
Males			
Prostate Cancer	Consider pros and cons of testing (2 main options) • Digital rectal exam (DRE) • Prostate-specific antigen (PSA) test	45+ African Americans; 50+ others; Younger with family history	Consult health-care provider; PSA frequency depends on past PSA results
Testicular Cancer[a]	Self-exam	20+	Monthly

[a]The American Cancer Society (ACS) has no current recommendation, but many doctors recommend monthly self-exams.
[b]Exams should begin at age 21; women under age 21 should not be tested.

cancers can be cured. Unfortunately, only 59 percent of adults over the age of 50 report having regular screening. Symptoms include cramping in the lower stomach, change in the shape of the stool, urge to have a bowel movement when there is no need to have one, and blood in the stool. A variety of tests are available for early detection of colon-rectal cancer. All of the tests are designed to detect either the presence of polyps that can turn into cancer, or polyps (or cancers) that are bleeding.

As shown in Table 1, the ACS recommends one of two plans for colon-rectal cancer screening. Plan 1 involves one of four medically focused screening options: a colonoscopy, a virtual colonoscopy, a flexible sigmoidoscopy, or a double-contrast barium enema test. The *colonoscopy* is often considered to be the "gold standard" because it checks for polyps and lesions in the entire colon. If polyps are found during a colonoscopy, they can be removed immediately without an additional procedure. The *virtual colonoscopy* provides a less invasive alternative to the conventional colonoscopy. It uses a CT scan that creates two- and three-dimensional images of the colon. These images allow the colon to be viewed from several different angles, something that is difficult to do with a conventional colonoscopy. Research shows that the procedure identifies 90 percent of large polyps. However, two major disadvantages are that the procedure requires exposure to radiation, and if a positive test occurs (polyps found), a regular colonoscopy must be done to remove them. The *sigmoidoscopy* tests only the lower one-third of the colon, and if polyps are found, a follow-up colonoscopy is recommended. While not as comprehensive as a colonoscopy, a recent study found that having one sigmoidoscopy between the ages of 55 and 64 can cut the risk of colon cancer by 43 percent. The *double-contrast barium enema* test is an X-ray test of the colon and rectum. The colon is filled with a material containing barium and then drained. The barium adheres to the surface of the colon allowing it to be seen on the X-ray. It is also less invasive than a colonoscopy but, if positive, a colonoscopy is still required.

Plan 2 involves more independent screening with follow-up treatment if warranted. A variety of tests are available, but each requires you to wipe stool samples on a test card to be sent to a lab for testing or for home analysis (with home test kits). A simple *fecal immunochemical test (FIT)* detects blood in the stool and does not require any special preparations. A related test called the *fecal occult blood test (FOBT)* requires some dietary modifications and restriction of medication since a specific chemical is used in the detection. A third test called the *stool DNA test* works differently by detecting mutated DNA in the stool, but this test requires a prescription. These screening tests each require follow-up colonoscopies if positive tests occur.

American Cancer Society Guidelines recently changed the age for initial screening from 50 to 45. Details for screening are shown in Table 1. Consult with your physician for advice about screening after age 45.

Lung Cancer

Lung cancer is the leading cause of cancer death in men and women. Lung cancer rates have dropped in the past decade, a change attributable in part to declines in smoking. Smoking rates among youth and young adults have increased, however, suggesting that lung cancer deaths may increase in the years ahead. Incidence and death rates are much higher among African Americans than Whites, with considerably lower rates among Asians and Hispanics.

By far, the greatest risk factor for lung cancer is smoking. Environmental tobacco smoke (ETS) has been shown to be a potent risk factor. According to the ACS, nonsmoking spouses of smokers have a 30 percent greater risk of developing lung cancer than do spouses of nonsmokers. A number of other carcinogens, including radon, asbestos, and pollution, have been linked to lung cancer, so nonsmokers can also get lung cancer.

Symptoms of lung cancer include persistent cough, chest pain, recurring pneumonia or bronchitis, and sputum (spit) streaked with blood. Lung cancer can spread to other organs and tissues before symptoms are evident, so it is important to pay attention to possible symptoms.

A recent study (National Lung Screening Trial) found that screening with low-dose computed tomography (LDCT) scans can lower the risk of dying from lung cancer. The LDCT uses lower doses of radiation than standard CT or CAT scans and does not use intravenous dye. The ACS guidelines reference LDCT but recommend consultation with your health-care provider prior to screening (see Table 1). Like mammograms, LDCT has some risks, including radiation exposure, false positives, and unnecessary additional treatments. Other detection steps include monitoring for symptoms, regular chest X-rays, and analysis of sputum samples. Standard treatments include surgery, radiation, and chemotherapies.

Adopting a healthy diet can help decrease risk for many cancers.
©Fuse/Getty Images

Prostate Cancer

Prostate cancer is one of the most common forms of cancer in men. One of every six men will get prostate cancer. Prostate cancer accounts for 8 percent of all cancer deaths in men (3 percent of all deaths). The death rate among African Americans is five times higher than among Asians, more than three times higher than Hispanics, and more than twice as high as Whites. Risks of prostate cancer increase dramatically after age 50. Symptoms of prostate cancer are urination problems (weak or interrupted stream, inability to start or stop, pain, high frequency of urination at night, and/or presence of blood in the urine).

The two principal screening techniques include a digital rectal exam (DRE) by a physician (to detect an enlarged prostate gland) and a prostate-specific antigen (PSA) blood test. A PSA threshold of 4 nanograms per milliliter was previously used as an indicator of potential risk, but other screening criteria are now being used. Research suggests that year-to-year changes in PSA are a better predictor, even if the score is lower than 4. A new autoantibody signatures test has promise for the future. If future research verifies early findings, this test may be used instead of, or in addition to, the PSA test. Preliminary studies with the new test show that it identifies 82 percent of cancers correctly.

Although research has shown that PSA screening does reduce prostate cancer deaths, there is debate about the age for beginning PSA screening. Some physicians recommend an annual DRE and a yearly PSA beginning at age 50, or earlier for people with a family history or symptoms (e.g., trouble urinating, frequent urination). However, guidelines previously suggested that decisions about testing should be based on symptoms and potential risks. Recent research has prompted the U.S. Preventive Services Task Force (PSTF) to change its position and it now recommends that all men between 55 and 69 should have a discussion with their health-care provider about having a PSA test (even if they have no signs of prostate cancer). The ACS encourages men to begin a dialogue with their physician at age 50 (or by age 45 for African American men and men with a blood relative who had prostate cancer before the age of 65).

The subtle differences among guidelines can cause confusion, particularly in men nearing 50. However, some general recommendations are appropriate. Given that screening has reduced cancer risk, every man should consult with his health-care professional about which methods are best for his unique needs (e.g., age, current symptoms, family history). The discussion should consider the concerns related to testing, including false positives. Although false positives can lead to overtreatment and unnecessary worry (see the In the News discussing mammography), it is clearly a personal decision. As noted earlier, changes in PSA values are more important than absolute values in detecting prostate cancer; thus, an advantage of testing is that it provides a potential baseline measure for purposes of future comparison.

Current treatments for prostate cancer have been shown to be highly effective, and death rates due to prostate cancer have decreased. However, despite the progress, the ACS points out that there is no uniform agreement on treatment. Among the most common treatments is "watchful waiting" with no immediate treating since prostate cancer progresses slowly in some patients. Other treatments include surgery to remove the prostate; hormone therapy; radiation therapy, including implanting of radioactive seeds to kill the tumor; and chemotherapy. One recently approved medication called Provenge uses a patient's own immune system to fight advanced prostate cancer that is no longer responding to hormone therapy.

Uterine and Ovarian Cancers

Combined, uterine and ovarian cancers account for 10 percent of all cancer cases and 9 percent of all deaths among women. Uterine cancer is of two different types: cervical cancer occurs when cancers develop in the cervix, or opening to the uterus, and endometrial cancer occurs when a tumor develops in the inner wall of the uterus. Ovarian cancer occurs when a cancer develops in an ovary. Symptoms of ovarian cancer include abdominal swelling and digestive disturbances. Vaginal bleeding can be a symptom of either uterine or ovarian cancer. Other vaginal discharge may be a symptom of uterine cancer. Understanding the risk factors for these female reproductive system cancers is important for prevention.

Established risk factors for cervical cancer include having sex at an early age, having sex with many partners, and a history of smoking. However, the most important risk factor for cervical cancer is infection by human papillomavirus (HPV), a sexually transmitted infection. The FDA has approved two "cervical cancer" vaccines (Cervarix and Gardasil) that have been shown to prevent the formation of precancerous genital lesions as well as genital warts attributed to HPV infection. While it is not effective against all forms of HPV, it is effective in preventing the form implicated in most cervical cancers and other HPV-related cancers. According to the CDC, each year there are thousands of cases of HPV-related cancer that could be prevented with the HPV vaccine. While HPV-related cancers are twice as common in females, the CDC recommends the HPV vaccine for preteen girls and boys.

The other form of uterine cancer, endometrial cancer, is less common and has a different mechanism of causation. The primary risk factors (early menarche, late menopause, infertility) are all associated with increased exposure to estrogen during the lifespan. However, other risks include obesity and a high-fat diet.

Risk factors for ovarian cancer include age, family history, and lack of pregnancy during the lifetime. One study showed that risk is considerably higher among those who have taken estrogen-progestin therapy, especially those who have taken it for 10 years or more. Those who have had breast cancer or who are at high risk for breast cancer have a relatively high risk for ovarian cancer.

A periodic and thorough pelvic exam is the best method of screening for cervical and ovarian cancers. A **Pap test** is an important part of the exam for detecting cervical cancer. This test (named for Dr. George Papanicolaou, who pioneered it) involves taking scrapings (samples) from the cervix and analyzing them under a microscope. Liquid-based Pap testing (sometimes referred to as ThinPrep) was thought to be more effective than previous Pap testing procedures, but recent research has shown the methods to be equally effective. The liquid-based test is more expensive but is preferred by labs because of the speed and ease of assessment. For this reason, some labs have stopped using the more conventional method. The liquid-based method allows for HPV testing from the same sample, and the ACS indicates that it can be done less frequently. Some home Pap smear kits are available, but these have not been shown to provide accurate information. As noted in Table 1, women should begin Pap testing at age 21 and should be tested every 3 years. Older women can be tested less frequently.

Treatments include surgery to remove one or both of the ovaries and fallopian tubes and/or removal of the uterus (hysterectomy). Radiation and chemotherapy are other options. DNA tests to find cancer-specific genes have been found to predict this form of cancer in a small percentage of the population, but this test has yet to receive governmental approval.

Skin Cancer

While rates of cancer in general have decreased, skin cancer rates have increased in recent years. Each year more than 3 million people are treated for non-melanoma skin cancer. Skin cancer ranks high in new cases (fifth for men and sixth for women), but does not rank high as a cause of death. This is because it can be cured if caught early. Symptoms include darkly pigmented growths, changes in size or color of moles, changes in other nodules on the skin, skin bleeding or scaliness, and skin pain (see Figure 3).

The principal risk factor is exposure to ultraviolet light, such as sun exposure and indoor tanning. Other risk factors include family history, pale skin, exposure to pollutants, and radiation. Some people feel that tanning lights are safe, but research has shown the opposite. Research indicates that tanning dramatically increases risk of skin cancer. A federal tax has been imposed on tanning salons because of the growing evidence of a link between indoor tanning and skin cancer. The effect of sun exposure is illustrated by the fact that significantly more skin cancer is found on the left arm, the arm that is exposed to the sun when driving, than the right arm. **Melanoma** is 10 times more frequent in Whites than African Americans, and a recent study showed an especially high rate of skin cancer among young White women who tan regularly. Unlike many other forms of cancer, skin cancer is not necessarily a disease of older adults. Young people who do not take preventive measures are at risk.

Early detection is essential to treatment, so regular screening is important. Screening techniques include self-exams of the skin followed by a physician's exam of suspicious lesions. A number of different cancer organizations recommend the ABCDE rule for self-exams (see Figure 3). *A* is for asymmetry: Does one half of a growth look different from the other half? *B* is for border irregularity: Are the edges notched, rugged, or blurred? *C* is for color: Is the color uniform, not varying in shades of tan, brown, and black? *D* is for any lesion with a diameter greater than 6 millimeters (about 1/4 inch). Beware of sudden or progressive growth of any lesion. *E* stands for evolution of a lesion (changes in shape or elevation of a lesion, scaliness, pain, itching, or bleeding). Some experts have recommended adding *F* to the list for friend (attentive friends may see changes before you do).

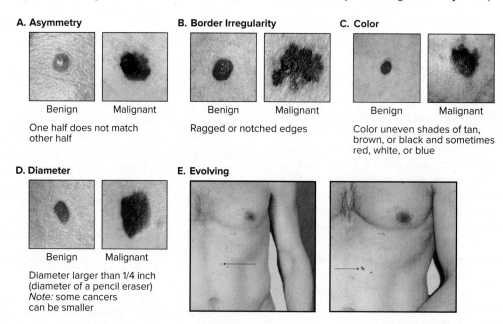

Figure 3 ▶ Warning signs for melanoma: Know your ABCDEs.

(all photos): ©The Skin Cancer Foundation

Nonmalignant basal and squamous cell cancers can be treated in a doctor's office using freezing, heat, or laser procedures. These milder forms of cancer have become more common among younger people in recent years. They occur on the head and neck in 90 percent of cases; however, with the increase in total body exposure and tanning practices, they are now much more common on other parts of the body. Once you have had one of these cancers, your risk of having another is high. Treatment for early melanoma involves the removal of affected cells and surrounding lymph tissues. Advanced cases require radiation and/or chemotherapies, or immunotherapy.

Important preventive measures include limiting exposure to the sun or tanning devices, reducing exposure during midday hours, covering the skin when exposed to the sun (hat, long pants, long-sleeve shirts, high collars on shirts, sunglasses), and using sunscreen that screens for both ultraviolet A radiation (UVA) and ultraviolet B radiation (UVB). Those with a family history of skin cancer and a history of sunburn or extensive sun exposure should be especially careful.

The ACS uses the slogan "Slip, Slop, Slap and Wrap" to encourage safe practices in the sun: slip on a shirt, slop on sunscreen, slap on a hat, and wrap on sunglasses to protect your eyes. For sunscreen, apply it 20 to 30 minutes before

A CLOSER LOOK

FDA Proposes Safety Measures for Indoor Tanning Devices

There are many documented risks associated with the use of indoor tanning beds (e.g., eye injury, skin damage, skin cancer). For example, according to the CDC, use before age 35 increases future risk of melanoma by 75 percent. Although the World Health Organization has labeled indoor tanning devices as "cancer-causing," the public has not been deterred. More than one-third of all Americans say they have used a tanning bed at some point, and 13 percent have used one in the last year. More than 59 percent of college students have used a tanning bed, with 43 percent reporting use in the previous year. To help deter use, the FDA has proposed new safety measures. Previous guidelines required labels on tanning devices indicating that they should not be used by people under age 18. However, new safety guidelines by the FDA will require indoor tanning facilities to inform adult users about the health risks of indoor tanning and to get signed "risk acknowledgment" from users. This rule will also directly prohibit use of indoor tanning facilities by people under 18.

Are these warnings sufficient to influence your feelings about indoor tanning? Do you agree with laws that limit tanning for children and teens?

Figure 4 ▶ SPF 15 broad spectrum sunscreen with FDA guidelines on label.

Source: Food and Drug Administration

going outside, apply it generously (a palmful), cover all body parts, and reapply every 2 hours and after swimming, sweating heavily, or using a towel.

Regulations by the FDA establish standards for the evaluation and labeling of products. Products that pass the test for protecting against both UVA and UVB can be called "broad spectrum" sunscreen, which appears on the front label with the SPF indication. SPF refers to "sun protection factor." According to the ACS, "using an SPF 15 and applying it correctly, you get the equivalent of 1 minute of UVB rays for each 15 minutes you spend in the sun." So, 1 hour in the sun wearing SPF 15 sunscreen is the same as spending 4 minutes totally unprotected. A sunscreen with an SPF of at least 15 can be labeled "broad spectrum." This indicates a base level of protection, but products with higher SPF numbers are generally recommended. Sunscreens with an SPF of less than 15 must include the statement "has only been shown to help prevent sunburn" and may not use the "broad spectrum" designation on the product.

The most recent regulations also require a drug facts label on sunscreen containers (see Figure 4). In addition, they

Pap Test A test of the cells of the cervix to detect cancer or other conditions.

Melanoma Cancer of the cells that produce skin pigment.

prohibit manufacturers from claiming a product is "water proof" or "sweat proof." The regulations require the manufacturer to indicate the length of time that the advertised SPF protection lasts. Two lengths of time, 40 and 80 minutes, will be permitted on labels. The FDA recently outlined a new process for reviewing the safety of the active ingredients of sunscreen products, so additional changes in product development and labeling may occur.

Testicular Cancer

While not a leading cause of death, testicular cancer is a threat to men of all ages, including young men. As noted in Table 1, a monthly testicular self-exam is recommended (see Lab 23B for more information).

Cancer Prevention

Many factors are associated with increased risk for cancer, including unhealthy lifestyles. The malfunction of genes that control cell growth and development is responsible for all cancers. Five to 10 percent of cancers result from an inherited faulty gene. Although genetics can't be altered, a variety of lifestyle and environmental factors also influence cancer. Environments or exposures that may be harmful include exposure to carcinogens at work (e.g., secondhand smoke, coal dust), exposure to geophysical factors (e.g., radon and radiation), exposure to polluted environments (e.g., poor air and water), exposure to certain industrial products (e.g., polychlorinated biphenyls [PCBs] produced in making plastics), and exposure to medical procedures (e.g., X-rays, CT scans). Some risks are hard to avoid, but minimizing exposure to the carcinogens related to environmental factors is an effective strategy for cancer prevention.

Making changes in lifestyles can also be important to cancer prevention. The World Cancer Research Fund (WCRF) and the American Institute for Cancer Research (AICR) released a definitive source of information concerning nutrition and physical activity in cancer prevention. The primary recommendations of this report are included in Table 2. Table 3 summarizes relevant lifestyle changes other than nutrition and physical activity.

Many forms of cancer can now be treated effectively. Cancer death rates (all forms of cancer) have decreased 2 percent for men and 1.6 percent for women each year since the beginning of this century. Many people have lived long, healthy lives after breast, skin, and many other forms of cancer. These people die from other causes, and some observers would consider them to be "cured." Still, what constitutes a cure is elusive. Those who achieve five-year survival after cancer now have a 70 percent survival rate, compared to 49 percent 40 years ago. Though people who survive for five years after detection may not be considered cured, the high survival

Table 2 ▶ Recommendations for Nutrition and Physical Activity to Prevent Cancer
• Be as lean as possible within the normal range of body weight. A Body Mass Index in the healthy range is recommended.
• Be physically active as part of everyday life. At least 30 minutes of moderate activity per day is recommended, with an increase to 60 minutes of moderate activity or 30 minutes of vigorous activity per day as fitness improves.
• Limit consumption of energy-dense foods (including fast foods), and avoid sugary drinks.
• Eat mostly foods from plant origin. Eat 5 to 9 servings of nonstarchy vegetables and fruits every day.
• Limit intake of red meat and avoid processed meat (no more than 30 g per week).
• Limit alcoholic drinks to no more than two drinks a day for men and one for women.
• Limit consumption of salt (less than 1.5 g a day).
• Aim to meet nutritional needs through diet alone. Dietary supplements are not recommended for cancer prevention.

Source: Adapted *from WCRF/AICR*

Table 3 ▶ Other Lifestyle Changes for Cancer Prevention
• Eliminate tobacco use (smoke and smokeless).
• Reduce sun and ultraviolet light exposure: use sunscreen, wear protective clothing, and avoid excess sun and tanning lights.
• Do regular self-screening and medical testing.
• Avoid excessive X-rays.
• Avoid breathing polluted air (e.g., exercise away from freeways and polluted air, check for pollution advisories).
• Minimize occupational and environmental pollutants when possible.

rate illustrates that cancer can be treated, even for those with inherited faulty genes. Much of the increase in the five-year survival rate is attributed to decreases in tobacco use and improved screening and treatment.

Medical consultation is essential when considering hormone replacement therapy. For years, hormone replacement therapy (HRT) was prescribed to women to help prevent loss of bone density, reduce risk for heart disease, and reduce the symptoms of menopause (e.g., hot flashes,

CAUTION

C = Changes in bowel or bladder habits
A = A sore that does not heal
U = Unusual bleeding or discharge
T = Thickening or lump (e.g., breast)
I = Indigestion or difficulty swallowing
O = Obvious change in a wart or mole
N = Nagging cough or hoarseness

Figure 5 ▶ Acronym for monitoring and early detection and treatment of cancer (CAUTION).

sleep disturbances, fatigue, poor concentration, and disruption of work and recreational activities). Research conducted in the early 2000s suggested that HRT increased the risk for some forms of cancer, was not effective in reducing heart disease, and increased the risk for blood clots. As a result, women were cautioned against HRT. The number of HRT prescriptions dropped from nearly 18 million in 2001 to less than 6 million by the late 2000s. However, more comprehensive studies are now providing clarity on the issue. A large study published in the *Journal of the American Medical Association* followed 27,000 women for 18 years. The research showed that women on HRT are *not* at a greater risk for cancer compared with women not on HRT. The risk of breast cancer, however, was slightly higher in the HRT group, but the risk of endometrial cancer was lower.

Unfortunately, the shifting views based on changing evidence are confusing to many women who wonder if HRT is safe for treating the very real symptoms of menopause. Experts agree that each case should be considered individually, with patient and doctor weighing all risks and benefits before choosing a course of action. In addition, other research suggests that low-dose HRT and HRT delivered by gels, patches, and creams may be effective in treating symptoms of menopause and are less likely to cause clotting than oral forms.

Recognizing early warning signals can help reduce the risk of cancer. There are many warning signs and symptoms of cancer. These include unusual fatigue, prolonged fever, abnormal weight loss, and changes in skin. Others are easily remembered using the acronym CAUTION (see Figure 5).

Diabetes

Diabetes presents major health risks, but it can be treated effectively. Diabetes mellitus, typically referred to as diabetes, is a disease that occurs when the blood sugar is abnormally high. The body relies on glucose as the primary source of energy, and complex regulatory processes help regulate levels of blood sugar. Low levels of blood sugar are clearly a problem, but other problems occur if blood sugar is too high. There are as many as 30 different reasons for high blood sugar; therefore, diabetes is really many different diseases, not just one. There is no cure for diabetes, but with proper medical treatment and healthy lifestyle modifications, the condition can be managed effectively.

There are two main forms of diabetes, and it is important to understand the differences. **Type 1 diabetes** is caused by the inability of the body to produce an adequate amount of **insulin,** a hormone produced by the pancreas that regulates glucose levels in the blood. Individuals with Type 1 diabetes must take daily doses of insulin (oral or injection) to help their body regulate blood glucose  levels. This form is more genetically based and is not directly related to obesity or unhealthy lifestyles. A relatively small percentage of diabetics (5 percent) have Type 1 diabetes, and it is typically diagnosed before the age of 30. **Type 2 diabetes** is a far more common form that is caused by a lack of sensitivity to insulin. It is often called "non-insulin-dependent" since the body loses sensitivity to insulin and cannot effectively take up and use the sugar in the blood. Unlike Type 1 diabetes, this form is caused primarily by unhealthy lifestyles (obesity and lack of physical activity). It was previously referred to as "adult-onset diabetes" because it tended to occur later in life, but children and adolescents can also develop the condition. A third and relatively rare form of diabetes is referred to as "gestational diabetes mellitus." This form results when high blood sugar levels occur in pregnant women previously not known to have diabetes. This condition is present in about 3 percent of all pregnancies, can have implications for the fetus, and may or may not result in a diabetic state after pregnancy. Other forms of diabetes are rare.

An understanding of normal blood sugar levels and regulation is important for reducing risk of diabetes. Normal levels range from 50 to 100 mg per 100 mL of blood (measured in a fasted state). A condition known as **pre-diabetes** exists when blood glucose levels range from 101 to 125, and diabetes exists when blood glucose levels regularly exceed 125. Pre-diabetes was formerly known as "impaired glucose

Type 1 Diabetes A chronic metabolic disease characterized by high blood sugar (glucose) levels associated with the inability of the pancreas to produce insulin; also called insulin-dependent diabetes mellitus (IDDM).

Insulin A hormone that regulates blood sugar levels.

Type 2 Diabetes A chronic metabolic disease characterized by high blood sugar, usually not requiring insulin therapy; also called non-insulin-dependent diabetes mellitus (NIDDM).

Pre-diabetes A condition in which fasting blood glucose levels are higher than normal but not high enough to be clinically diagnosed as diabetes.

tolerance," but the name was changed to help focus attention on the seriousness of this condition. Recent research has shown that pre-diabetes can result in long-term damage to the body similar to that of diabetes if not controlled. People who take steps to control pre-diabetes can delay or even prevent the development of Type 2 diabetes. More than 12 percent of all Americans over the age of 20 have diabetes (about 27 million overall), but more than a third of all American adults have pre-diabetes (about 80 million). Millions more are either pre-diabetic or diabetic and do not know it. Early screening is important for detecting and reversing pre-diabetes and diabetes.

Diabetes and related conditions are a leading cause of death in our society. Diabetes is the seventh leading cause of death, and it is a leading killer in other Western nations, including Canada. People with diabetes have a shortened lifespan, as well as many short-term and long-term complications associated with the disease. A study of people in the Netherlands, England, and the United States indicated that longevity after 50 years of age is decreased by 7.5 years for men and 8.2 years for women for diabetics as opposed to nondiabetics.

African Americans and Native Americans are especially at risk for diabetes. Unlike heart disease and cancer, which have shown recent decreases in incidence, the incidence of diabetes has increased in the last decade, with little progress being made in accomplishing national health goals for this disease.

People with diabetes have an increased risk for additional health problems. For example, diabetes is considered to be a risk factor for heart disease and high blood pressure. Diabetics have a higher rate of kidney failure (including the need for kidney  transplants and kidney dialysis), a high incidence of blindness, and a high incidence of lower limb amputation. Women with diabetes also have a high rate of pregnancy complications. A national health goal is to increase the rate of diagnosis and to increase the number of diabetics who get regular blood lipid assessments, blood pressure checks, and eye examinations.

Screening for pre-diabetes and diabetes is essential for diagnosis and treatment. The symptoms of diabetes include frequent urination, excessive thirst, extreme hunger, unusual weight loss, increased fatigue, irritability, and blurry vision. Those who have recently gained large amounts of weight are also at risk. Early diagnosis as a result of attention to the symptoms can expedite treatment. Guidelines recommend screening for pre-diabetes and diabetes using either of two blood tests: a fasting plasma glucose (FPG) test, which measures levels of glucose in the blood after an overnight fast, or a 2-hour **oral glucose tolerance test (OGTT)**, which

Technology Update

Technology in Health Care: Where Should the Money Be Spent?

Technology drives innovation and innovation drives business. Because health care accounts for about 20 percent of the overall economy, considerable efforts are focused on developing new technologies related to health care. For example, researchers from Google (Google X lab) released preliminary information about a "smart contact" lens that has an embedded computer chip and a glucose sensor that can measure sugar levels in tears. The lens continuously monitors glucose levels and alerts diabetics when they are outside of normal ranges. Similarly, a new report highlighted the potential of a blood-based cancer screening test. This new technology would likely help promote early detection, but expensive trials and development are required before it would be available for use. Although these developments clearly offer promise, technology research and development is also a leading contributor to the high cost of health care (e.g., medical inflation continues to exceed overall inflation). The prospects of the technologies are also typically introduced early to the media to draw attention (and potential funding from venture capitalists). But not all will make it into the market, and perhaps funding would be better spent on prevention instead of treatments and screening.

Do you like hearing about new, innovative health technologies, even if they will not be available for many years? Do you feel that technology can help solve or address health problems, or should more funding be directed at prevention?

includes the FPG test but also tests glucose levels 2 hours after a person drinks a standard glucose solution. A blood test called A1C can also be performed. It has the advantage of assessing your average blood glucose level of the past 2 or 3 months as opposed to your blood sugar level on a given day. Also, you do not have to fast prior to the test.

Guidelines recommend regular screening beginning at age 45 for those potentially at risk. Because African Americans, Hispanics, Asians, American Indians, and Pacific Islanders have especially high risk, some experts recommend testing at age 30 or earlier for these groups. Others with diabetes risk factors and those with a Body Mass Index over 25 should also consider testing at an earlier age. Consider using the ADA diabetes risk calculator to see what your risk is. (Search "ADA Diabetes Risk Test" online.)

Lifestyle changes are needed for effective prevention and treatment of diabetes. Although diabetes presents significant health risks, it can be managed effectively.

Table 4 ▶ Lifestyle Changes for Diabetes Prevention and Control
• Maintain a healthy body-fat level. For many, achieving a healthy body-fat level is effective in preventing or reducing Type 2 diabetes symptoms.
• Maintain healthy blood sugar levels. For diabetics, regular testing is necessary.
• Eat well. Limit fats and simple carbohydrates in the diet. Increase complex carbohydrates. Keep total calorie consumption at a level that keeps the body weight at a healthy level.
• Exercise regularly. Physical activity expends calories and helps regulate blood sugar levels.
• Learn to recognize symptoms of diabetes and seek screening.
• If you are diabetic, are pre-diabetic, or have symptoms, seek and adhere to medical advice. Many pre-diabetics do not know that they have a problem. Diabetics need to adhere to a plan for blood sugar regulation.
• Learn stress-management skills to reduce stress and maintain a healthy sleep schedule.

Consultation with a physician is essential to determine appropriate treatment plans for those with both Type 1 and Type 2 diabetes, since most diabetics will require supplemental insulin to manage their condition. However, adopting a healthy lifestyle, including regular physical activity and healthy eating, is central to the prevention of diabetes as well as its management and treatment. (See guidelines in Table 4.)

Alzheimer Disease and Dementia

Alzheimer disease is becoming more frequent and is now among the leading causes of death. Alzheimer disease is a progressive disease of the brain that affects memory as well as cognitive and motor skills. It begins with mild memory loss and, in advanced stages, it has dramatic effects on the ability to function in daily life. It is now the sixth leading cause of death in the United States. Over the last two decades, Alzheimer disease has increased by more than 50 percent, in part due to our aging population. Nearly 6 million people now have Alzheimer disease. Approximately 50 percent of people in nursing homes and 45 percent of hospice patients have Alzheimer disease. (*Note:* The term *Alzheimer disease* is used in this edition, rather than *Alzheimer's disease*, as it is the preferred terminology of leading scholars in the field.)

According to the Alzheimer's Association, "*dementia* is a general term for memory loss and other mental abilities that interfere with daily life." Alzheimer disease accounts for about three-quarters of all types of dementia. There are multiple other forms of dementia (e.g., vascular dementia, Parkinson's disease, frontotemporal dementia). Symptoms of Alzheimer disease (and other types of dementia that become increasingly more serious over time) include asking repetitive questions and making repetitive statements, lacking the ability to perform daily tasks, losing things and getting lost, failing to remember names of family and friends, lacking awareness of time, showing poor judgment, having decreased motor function, and exhibiting changes in mood and personality.

There is no known cure for Alzheimer disease, but healthy lifestyles and medication may delay symptoms. Because there is no known cure, the focus of treatment is on maintaining mental function and slowing the symptoms. The FDA has approved several drugs to help achieve this objective (e.g., cholinesterase inhibitors). They are most effective in the early to moderate stages of the disease. Also approved by the FDA is Namenda®, which is used to treat moderate to severe Alzheimer disease. It is sometimes used in combination with other approved drugs. Healthy lifestyles such as regular physical activity, healthy eating, active social involvement, and involvement in challenging mental tasks all are helpful for those with all forms of dementia. For example, a recent study in the journal *Neurology* indicated that active and fit women are 90% less likely to develop dementia than those who are not active and fit.

Mental Health

Many mental disorders pose threats to health and wellness. The health goals for the nation identify suicide, schizophrenia, and depression as the most serious mental disorders needing attention. Although the U.S. Public Health Service uses the term *mental disorders,* they are sometimes called emotional disorders. Other common mental disorders are panic disorders, alcohol and other drug problems, personality disorders, and phobias.

Statistics from the National Alliance on Mental Illness (NAMI) indicate that more than one in four adults (26 percent) suffer from a diagnosed mental disorder each year.

Oral Glucose Tolerance Test (OGTT) A test used to diagnose diabetes. It consists of a blood sugar measurement following the ingestion of a standard amount of sugar (glucose) after a period of fasting.

About 1 in 5 adults in the United States are affected by a mental illness that limits the ability to function effectively and requires special assistance. The most serious outcome of mental disorders is suicide, the tenth leading cause of death among adults and third leading cause of death in youth and young adults (ages 10 to 24).

Public awareness about mental health issues has improved, but individuals with mental disorders are still frequently stigmatized in society. Concerns about being labelled or judged leads many individuals to not seek treatment. Therefore, one goal of mental health professionals is to alter societal views of mental health and to promote early intervention and treatment for those in need.

Reducing the incidence of suicide and serious injury from suicide attempts is an important national health goal. Progress has been made in reducing suicide, but it is still far too common. Women are about three times more likely to attempt suicide than men, but men are four times more likely to complete a suicide attempt. Among male teenagers, it is the second leading cause of death, and male teenagers with antisocial personality disorders are especially susceptible.

Depression is closely associated with suicide, as are drug and alcohol disorders. Inability to cope with stressful life events may contribute to suicide. Examples of precipitating events are divorce, separation, loss of a loved one, unemployment, and financial setbacks.

The best chance for reducing suicides appears to be early detection and treatment of mental disorders such as depression. As many concerned people as possible should be recruited to help the suicidal individual seek professional assistance. Threats of suicide must be taken seriously.

Depression, a common mental disorder, can usually be treated effectively. Most people occasionally feel depressed or sad. This type of depression is usually not a mental disorder. People with clinical depression (classified as a mental disorder) have chronic feelings of guilt, hopelessness, low self-esteem, and dejection. They might have trouble sleeping, loss of appetite, lack of interest in social activities, lack of interest in sex, and inability to concentrate.

Among the lifestyle changes that can help relieve symptoms are exercising regularly, increasing social contact, setting realistic goals, using stress-management techniques, and removing oneself from situations that contribute to depression. These changes, however, may need to be accompanied by professional therapy and/or medication.

Sleep disorders can often be helped by lifestyle changes. Sleep disorders, especially insomnia (long-term problems with sleep), can result in depression and other dysfunctions. Physiological problems in the brain can cause sleep disorders, but depression, stress, chronic pain, or abuse of alcohol or other drugs are often the source of the problem.

Some sleep disorders require professional help; however, you can take action to prevent insomnia. Create a healthy sleeping environment, avoid excessive caffeine or alcohol, exercise regularly, and establish a sleeping routine.

Injuries and Other Health Threats

Injuries are a major cause of death and suffering. Injuries (accidents) are the fourth leading cause of death among people of all ages, claiming more lives than chronic and infectious diseases among people aged 40 and younger. According to the U.S. Public Health Service, the major causes of injuries are motor vehicle crashes, falls, poisonings, drownings, and residential fires.

Injuries also account for much pain and suffering. Of all hospital stays, one in six results from a nonfatal injury. Injury rates are higher among males than females, and they are quite high among ethnic and racial minority groups. In the past decade, the number of deaths caused by unintentional injuries and work-related injuries has decreased.

Improved occupational safety could help reduce injury rates. Many of the nation's health goals focus on improving occupational safety, especially among construction, health care (e.g., nurses), farm, transportation, and mine workers. It may seem that you have little direct control over occupational safety at your workplace. However, laws do exist to protect workers and you can provide input to employers about these laws and work together to make your workplace safe.

Changes in lifestyles can reduce injury rates. A major conclusion of the Public Health Service is that the prevention of injuries requires the combined efforts of many fields, including health, education, transportation, law, engineering, architecture, and safety science.

The second major conclusion of the Public Health Service is that alcohol is "intimately associated" with the causes and severity of injuries. Other lifestyle behaviors are also associated with reducing injury incidence. Steps that can be taken to reduce risk of injuries are listed in Table 5.

Prompt emergency medical care is critical for saving lives. Paramedics and emergency medical teams provide emergency medical service (EMS) when needed. A survey of medical directors conducted over an 18-month period in the nation's 50 largest cities shows that treatment effectiveness for those needing emergency medical care varies, depending on where you live. In many cities, the EMS responses were slow and less than effective. The study estimates that about 1,000 lives a year could be saved with more effective systems. You may have little control over EMS in your area, but find out what is available so that you get the best possible service in an emergency.

The Cooper Clinic in Dallas, Texas, specializes in preventive medical care. A staff physician (Dr. Tedd Mitchell) has

Table 5 ▶ Steps to Reduce Injuries

Reduce Motor Vehicle Accidents

- Do not drive while under the influence of alcohol.
- Use shoulder seat belts and drive cars that have air bags.
- Reduce driving speed.
- Use motorcycle helmets.
- Increase safety programs for pedestrians and cyclists.
- Establish more effective licensing for very young and older drivers.

Improve Home and Neighborhood Environments

- Require safety controls on handguns.
- Require sprinkler systems in homes with high risk of fire.
- Increase presence of functional smoke detectors in homes.
- Increase injury and poison education in schools.
- Wear effective safety gear in sports.
- Improve pool and boat safety education.
- Learn cardiopulmonary resuscitation.
- Properly mark poisons and prescription drugs.
- Require childproof packaging for poisons and prescription drugs.

Table 6 ▶ Types of People Who Avoid Medical Checkups

- *Gamblers.* These people do not think about their health until a serious problem occurs.
- *Martyrs.* These people are so busy taking care of others that they fail to take care of themselves.
- *Economists.* These people think the cost of preventive exams is too high for the benefits received.
- *Shamans.* These people buy in to the latest health fad and self-diagnose, while avoiding regular medical care.
- *Informers.* These people have an ax to grind with health-care professionals and avoid health care for this reason.
- *Queens of denial (Cleopatra syndrome).* These people do not believe something could be wrong with them or do not want to know if there is.
- *Busy bees.* These people feel they are too busy to take the time to get regular medical care.

Source: Adapted from T. Mitchell, What's Your Excuse?. 2002.

categorized the types of people by the reasons they give for not seeing a doctor or getting a regular medical checkup  (see Table 6). According to Dr. Mitchell, "there is no good reason to avoid your annual visit to the doctor."

Using Self-Management Skills

Self-assessments and medical exams done regularly can help you determine if you need help with various health problems. Just as the fitness assessments you completed earlier helped you build a profile that will help you improve your fitness, regular self-assessments can help you identify and prevent common health problems. Regular medical exams that include the tests outlined in Table 1 as well as those described in other sections of this Concept will help you identify problems that can be treated and cured with early diagnosis.

Staying current with new health information can help you identify and get treatment for health problems. Building knowledge about various health problems changes rapidly as new methods of treatment and prevention become available. The information provided in this edition provides you with good information to get you started but, because new information is rapidly accumulating, it is important to

Health is available to Everyone for a Lifetime, and it's Personal

Get Your Checkup!

Students often think that they are not susceptible to health problems and skip routine medical checkups. Challenges with insurance and transportation often make it difficult to get regular physicals. Students may also ignore warning signs and symptoms for a number of other reasons. See Table 6 for common reasons people skip regular checkups.

Do you recognize yourself in one of the seven descriptions of "checkup avoiders" in Table 6? How can you make regularly scheduled medical checkups or health screenings part of your lifestyle?

learn ways to stay current on health topics. Information presented in the Concept on consumerism will help you develop skills for making good health, wellness, and fitness decisions.

Adhering to sound medical advice is important for disease prevention and treatment. Many conditions described in this Concept, especially cancer and diabetes, can be managed or cured with early diagnosis and proper treatment. Many people ignore early warning signs or symptoms, hoping that problems go away on their own. Some people fear disease and avoid medical advice because of this fear. An important key to good health is to note any irregularities in your health and to seek expert advice when needed. Establishing a regular habit of getting scheduled checkups and/or health screens is part of a healthy lifestyle because it helps ensure that your health is where it should be. Periodic checks can also help detect early signs of heart disease, cancer, diabetes, and other health threats, and this allows for more effective treatment. These checks become increasingly important as you age because people become vulnerable to a wider array of chronic conditions.

Strategies for Action: Lab Information

A risk questionnaire can help you identify your personal risk for diseases such as cancer. In Lab 23A you will have the opportunity to assess your cancer risk. Knowing your current risk level can be of value as you consult with your health-care professional as suggested in Table 1.

Self-assessments can be effective screening tools, but you need to follow up with a health-care provider if positive results are present. In Lab 23B you will learn to do self-exams to help you screen for breast and testicular cancer. A skin self-exam using the ABCDE rule is also advised. Home self-evaluation kits are now available for colon-rectal cancer screening. If irregularities are found, follow-up consultation with a health-care provider is essential.

ACTIVITY

Suggested Resources and Readings

The websites for the following sources can be accessed by searching online for the organization, program, or title listed. Specific scientific references are available at the end of this edition of *Concepts of Fitness and Wellness.*

- American Academy of Dermatologists. SPOT Skin Cancer.
- American Cancer Society. Guidelines for the Early Detection of Cancer.
- American Diabetes Association. Type 2 Diabetes Risk Test.
- American Diabetes Association. Understanding Diabetes.
- Alzheimer's Association. Types of Dementia.
- Bowerman, M. (2017, January 23). Cervical cancer is killing women at a higher rate than previously thought. *USA Today.*
- Centers for Disease Control and Prevention. Alzheimer's Disease.
- Centers for Disease Control and Prevention. Cancer Screening Tests.
- Centers for Disease Control and Prevention. Burden of Mental Illness.
- Fox, M., & Silverman, J. (2017, September 12). HRT does not affect women's death rates. *USA Today.*
- Miller, S. (2017, April 11). Experts shift gears on routine prostate cancer screenings. *USA Today.*
- National Alliance for Mental Illness. Mental Illness Fact Sheets.
- National Alliance for Mental Health. Depression (web resource).
- National Institutes of Health. Hormone Replacement Therapy Information.
- Roberts, C. (2017, Dec 17). Newer Birth Control Methods Linked with Breast Cancer Risk, Study Shows. Consumer Reports.org.
- Szabo, L. (2017, January 9). Mammograms lead to unneeded treatment for some breast cancers. *USA Today.*
- U.S. Food and Drug Administration. Regulations on Indoor Tanning Devices
- U.S. Food and Drug Administration. How to Protect Your Skin from the Sun.
- U.S. Food and Drug Administration. Sun Safety and Your Skin.

Lab 23A Determining Your Cancer Risk

Name	**Section**	**Date**

Purpose: To become aware of your risk for various types of cancer.

Procedures

1. Answer the questions in the six-part questionnaire for the various forms of cancer.
2. Record the number of "yes" answers for each form of cancer in the Results section.
3. Use Chart 1 to determine ratings and record the ratings in the Results section.
4. Answer the questions in the Conclusions and Implications section.

Results: Place an X over your answer to each question.

Skin Cancer Risk Factors

Do you frequently work or play in the sun for long periods?	Yes	No
Do you work or have you worked near industrial exposure (coal mine, radioactivity)?	Yes	No
Do you have a family history of skin cancer?	Yes	No
Do you have fair skin?	Yes	No

Lung Cancer Risk Factors

Do you smoke?	Yes	No
Do you work or have you worked near industrial exposure (coal mine, radioactivity)?	Yes	No
Do you have a family history of lung cancer?	Yes	No
Do you work in a place that allows smoking, such as a bar, or live in a home with smokers?	Yes	No

Colon-Rectal Cancer Risk Factors

Do you eat poorly, abuse alcohol, or smoke?	Yes	No
Are you African American or over 50?	Yes	No
Do you have a family history of colon or rectal cancer?	Yes	No
Have you noticed blood in your stool?	Yes	No

Breast Cancer Risk Factors

Do you have a family history of breast cancer?	Yes	No
Are you sedentary, do you eat poorly, or do you abuse alcohol?	Yes	No
Are you a female over 35 who has not had children?	Yes	No
Have you ever detected lumps or cysts in your breasts?	Yes	No

Uterine/Cervical Cancer Risk Factors* (Females)

Do you regularly have bleeding between periods?	Yes	No
Is your body fat level high?	Yes	No
Did you have early intercourse and multiple sexual partners?	Yes	No
Have you had viral infections of the vagina, such as HPV?	Yes	No

Prostate Cancer Risk Factors (Males)

Do you eat a high-fat or low-fiber diet?	Yes	No
Are you a male over 50 years of age or African American?	Yes	No
Have you had a regular PSA test?	Yes	No
Has a digital rectal exam shown an enlargement of the prostate?	Yes	No

*Because of the personal nature of several questions, do not record results if turned in to an instructor.

Cancer Type	Score	Rating
Skin		
Breast (women)		
Lung		
Uterine/cervical (women)*		
Colon-rectal		
Prostate (men)		

*Do not record results if handed in to an instructor.

Chart 1 Cancer Risk Ratings

Rating	Score
High risk	4
Relatively high risk	3
Lower risk	2
Low risk	0–1

Conclusions and Implications: In several sentences, discuss the type or types of cancer for which you are at greatest risk and why. Also, discuss the lifestyles you could modify to reduce your risk.

Lab 23B Breast and Testicular Self-Exams

Name	**Section**	**Date**

Purpose: To learn to do breast or testicular self-exams.

Procedures

1. If you are female, read the procedures for breast self-exams. *Note:* Males should also be aware of abnormal lumps in their breasts.
2. If you are male, read the procedures for testicular self-exams.
3. After reading the directions, perform the self-exam. If you find lumps or nodules, contact a physician.
4. This procedure should be done monthly. The breast exam is best done a day or two after the end of menstrual flow. For this lab, it can be done at any time.
5. It is not necessary to record your results here. Do answer the questions in the Conclusions and Implications section.

Lying Breast Self-Exam (Men and Women)

1. Lie down with one arm behind your head. You can more easily detect lumps when lying as compared to standing or sitting because when lying the breast tissue is spread more evenly (see illustration).

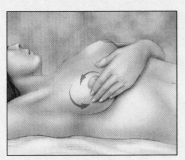

©Brian Evans/Science Source

2. With the tips of the middle three fingers (see illustration) of the hand opposite the one behind your head, feel for lumps in the breast on the side of the raised arm. Use a circular pattern with the fingers. The large arrows illustrate the circular pattern but should be done with overlapping, *dime-sized,* circular motions of the finger pads to feel the breast tissue (see illustration).
3. Identify the spot for the overlapping, dime-sized, circular motions and feel for lumps using three levels of pressure. First apply light pressure to feel for lumps closest to the skin. Then apply medium pressure to feel for lumps deeper below the skin. Finally, to find lumps near the ribs and chest cavity, apply firm pressure. Then move to another spot and repeat the same procedure, applying all three levels of pressure. A firm ridge in the lower curve of each breast is normal. If you have questions about this procedure and how hard to press, talk with your doctor or medical professional.
4. To ensure full coverage of each breast, examine the entire area from your side up and to the middle of the sternum (breastbone) and from the clavicle (collarbone) down to the ribs below the breast.

5. Repeat the exam on the other breast, using the finger pads of the opposite hand.

Standing Breast Self-Exam (Women)

1. Stand in front of a mirror. Press down firmly on your hips with your hands. Look for any changes of size, shape, contour, or dimpling or redness or scaliness of the nipple or breast skin. (Pressing down on the hips contracts the chest wall muscles and enhances any breast changes.)
2. Examine each underarm with your arm slightly raised, so that you can easily feel in this area. Raising your arm straight up (too high) tightens the tissue in this area and makes it harder to examine.

Testicular Self-Exam (Men)

1. Using both hands, grasp one testicle between the thumb and first finger.
2. Roll the testicle gently with the thumb and first finger. Look and feel for lumps or rounded bumps as well as for changes in size, shape, and consistency of testicles.
3. Examine the other testicle using the same procedure.
4. If you find any of the symptoms (see number 2 above), consult a physician. The symptoms may not be associated with disease, but this can be determined only by a physician.

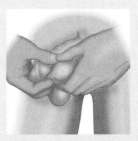

Source: ©Monica Schroeder/ Science Source

Conclusions and Implications: In several sentences, discuss the effectiveness of the procedure you performed. Do you think the directions provided were adequate for you to perform the self-exam effectively? Do you think you will perform this self-exam on a regular basis? Do you believe the screening procedures described in the lab are effective? Why or why not? What could be done to motivate you and others to do regular self-exams?

Additional Self-Exam Information

Several national health agencies maintain websites that include detailed breast and testicular self-exam information. These sites contain both written and pictorial descriptions of both self-exam procedures. For more information, visit the sites listed below.

American Cancer Society
www.cancer.org

Mayo Clinic
www.mayohealth.org

National Cancer Institute
www.nci.nih.gov

Early detection is critical for effective cancer treatment. The ACS notes that a "breast self-exam is an option for women starting in their 20s. Women should be told about the benefits and limitations of BSE. Women should report any changes in how their breasts look or feel to a health expert right away." Men should also be aware of changes in breast tissue. The ACS indicates that many physicians recommend a BSE each month. For those who do a BSE, it is wise to review the technique with a physician or medical professional. According to the ACS, finding a lump in the testicles at an early stage is important. It recommends a regular testicular exam by a physician and indicates that many doctors recommend testicular self-exams.

Evaluating Fitness and Wellness Products: Becoming an Informed Consumer

LEARNING OBJECTIVES

After completing the study of this Concept, you will be able to:

▶ Define quackery and fraud and outline steps that can be taken to avoid being susceptible to them.

▶ Evaluate the effectiveness of different physical activity programs and products.

▶ Select exercise equipment based on effectiveness, safety, and utility.

▶ Assess health clubs and exercise leaders (and their qualifications).

▶ Evaluate body composition and weight loss products for effectiveness and safety.

▶ Evaluate nutrition products for effectiveness and safety.

▶ Detect potentially fraudulent consumer products based on credibility, marketing/ advertising strategies, and the nature of the claims.

©Corbis/VCG/Getty Images

"Let the buyer beware" is a good motto for the consumer seeking advice or planning a program for developing or maintaining health, wellness, and fitness.

Why it Matters!

People have always searched for the fountain of youth and an easy, quick, and miraculous route to happiness and health. In current society, this search is often driven by goals related to fitness, nutrition, weight loss, or improved appearance. Products often promise easy weight loss, better health, or increased fitness—typically with little or no effort. The sale of many, if not most, products can be classified as either quackery or fraud since they simply do not work. The content throughout this edition is designed to help clarify facts and dispute myths. This Concept integrates information to help you build and reinforce your consumer skills so that you can avoid being a victim of quackery and make informed decisions about health, wellness, and fitness products.

Quacks and Quackery

Quacks can be identified by exaggerated claims, frequent use of testimonials, and gimmicks to support their products. The definition of quack is "a pretender of medical skill" or "one who talks pretentiously without sound knowledge of the subject discussed." This implies that the promotion of quackery involves deliberate deception, but quacks often believe in what they promote. The consumer watchdog group Quackwatch defines quackery more broadly as "anything involving overpromotion in the field of health." This definition encompasses questionable ideas as well as questionable products and services. The word *fraud* is reserved for situations in which deliberate deception is involved. Look for these clues to identify quacks, frauds, and rip-off artists:

- Quacks rely on testimonials from paid athletes and celebrities to endorse their products.
- Quacks rely on anecdotal evidence and prey on consumer gullibility.
- Quacks sell products primarily through the mail or the Internet, which does not allow you to examine the products personally.
- Quacks promise quick, miraculous results and money-back guarantees.
- Quacks claim everyone can benefit from the product or service they are selling.

Quacks ignore scientific practice but often pretend to be scientists. Scientific research is a systematic search for truth, and specific procedures are used to control error and minimize bias. The peer-review process used to publish and share findings helps ensure that the design and methods were sound and that the conclusions are appropriate. The standardized process helps ensure that the information in published research studies is scientifically sound and defensible.

Quack products are typically released without any scientific evidence of safety or efficacy. However, quacks know that people value the research process and they often mislead consumers by pretending to follow scientific methods. Occasionally, companies will mention that their product or program has been scientifically tested, but this does not necessarily mean that the results were positive. They may also cite irrelevant findings in obscure journals because they assume (correctly) that most consumers would not check the sources or the nature of the study. Even if a study did show positive results, the study may have been flawed. An article in a prominent scientific journal documented that results of studies, especially small studies that are not well controlled, are often found to be wrong or the effects are not as large as originally thought. The list below summarizes additional unscientific practices used by quacks:

- Quacks mix a little bit of truth with a lot of fiction to try to impress consumers with the use of scientific terms and mechanisms (even if they are not correct in their interpretation).
- Quacks misquote scientific research (or quote out of context) to mislead consumers.
- Quacks quote from individuals, journals, or institutions with questionable reputations.
- Quacks may claim to have the support of "experts," but the experts are not identified.
- Quacks often claim their products are based on "new" experimental discoveries, and they frequently discredit legitimate organizations such as the Food and Drug Administration (FDA) and the American Medical Association (AMA).

Experts have an educated, scientific base and meet other professional criteria. Unlike quacks, experts base their work on the scientific method. Some characteristics of professional experts are an extended education, an established code of ethics, membership in well-known associations, involvement in the profession as an intern before obtaining credentials, and a commitment to perform an important social service. Some experts require a license. Examples of experts in the health, wellness, and fitness area are medical doctors, nurses, certified fitness leaders, physical educators, registered dietitians, physical therapists, and clinical psychologists. In most cases, you can check if a person has the credentials to be considered an expert before obtaining services. The following list includes some things that can be done to determine a person's expertise:

- Determine the source of the person's education and the nature of the degree and/or certification.

- Check with the person's professional association, a government board, licensing agency, or certifying agency to see if there are any complaints against the person; for example, you can contact your state's medical board to check complaints against physicians.
- Check if the person has credentials to provide the service you are seeking (e.g., a registered dietitian is qualified to give nutrition advice but not medical advice).

Physical Activity Quackery

There is no "effortless" way to get the benefits from physical activity. Advertisements for exercise that claim to "get you totally fit in 10 minutes" or "get you fit with little effort" are false. The only way to get fit is to follow the FIT formula for the type of exercise that you choose for meeting specific fitness goals. Claims for exercise that will effortlessly reduce weight or produce significant health benefits are equally false. One example is the false claims made by shoe manufacturers. Reebok International agreed to pay $25 million and Skechers paid $40 million to settle charges related to false claims that their shoes aid weight loss and strengthen and tone buttocks, leg, and abdominal muscles. As noted in previous Concepts, there are specific guidelines for physical activity designed for weight loss or maintenance and for achieving health benefits. Beware of those who claim otherwise.

Claims for many forms of exercise are overstated or unsubstantiated. New exercise programs or routines are often promoted as the complete answer for total fitness or a **panacea** for health. This is very similar to how new fad diets are promoted. With both diet and exercise, it is very unlikely that some new regimen will be discovered to have unique fitness or health benefits. The claims just spin the benefits of exercise in a new way to attract interest.

Similar hype may be used for promoting new pieces of exercise equipment. Each piece of equipment claims to be fun, easy to use, and more effective than other forms of exercise. The benefits from exercise depend on the relative intensity and duration of the activity—and whether it is done regularly over time. The best form of exercise is clearly the one that you are willing and able to do!

Contrary to claims, passive exercises do not provide any benefits for fitness or weight loss. For exercise to be beneficial, the work must be done by contracting skeletal muscles. A variety of **passive exercise** forms have been promoted to try to reduce the effort required to perform regular exercise. Some passive devices have value for people with special needs when administered by a qualified person, such as a physical therapist. However, passive devices sold for use by the general public are ineffective. The goal of sellers is to convince people that there is an effortless way to exercise—there is not. The fallacies associated with many past forms of

It is important to be an informed consumer when selecting a fitness center or joining a program.
©Erik Isakson/Getty Images

passive exercise, such as fat rolling machines (purported to break up and redistribute fat), seem obvious today, but new approaches come out all the time with different marketing and promotions. The following list highlights some of the common forms of physical activity quackery:

- *Vibrating belts.* These wide canvas or leather belts are driven by an electric motor, causing loose tissue of the body part to shake. They have no beneficial effect on fitness, fat, or figure.
- *Toning tables.* Contrary to advertisements, these vibrating tables will not improve posture, trim the body, reduce weight, or develop muscle **tonus.**
- *Continuous passive motion (CPM) tables.* These machines passively move body parts repeatedly through a range of motion. Because the muscles are not doing any work, these tables provide no real benefits. Hospitals and rehabilitation centers may use similar machines to maintain range of motion in patients, but a healthy person has nothing to gain from these devices.

Panacea A cure-all; a remedy for all ills.

Passive Exercise Exercise in which no voluntary muscle contraction occurs; an outside force moves the body part with no effort by the person.

Tonus The most frequently misused and abused term in fitness vocabularies. Tonus is the tension developed in a muscle as a result of passive muscle stretch. Tonus cannot be determined by feeling or inspecting a muscle. It has little or nothing to do with the strength of a muscle.

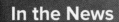

In the News

Illegal Business Practices Drive Fraud and Quackery

Fraud and quackery are driven by clever (and frequently illegal) advertising and marketing practices that prey on consumers' vulnerabilities. An *USA Today* exposé on the dietary supplement industry revealed extensive criminal backgrounds in many "executives" from health supplement companies. Supplement companies also frequently employ multi-level pyramid schemes to entice individuals to help them sell their products. As with most pyramid schemes, people typically make money by recruiting others to sell the products rather than actually selling the products themselves. Friends and family members are often pressured to buy unwanted products or to join the effort to further grow the pyramid. The Federal Trade Commission (FTC) recently charged supplement manufacturer Herbalife with operating this type of multi-level marketing scheme. It is required to pay $200 million in settlements and to restructure its business practices.

Do these stories reinforce or change your perceptions of consumer issues in the health and fitness industry?

- *Motor-driven cycles and rowing machines.* Like all mechanical devices that do the work for the individual, motor-driven machines are not effective in a fitness program. They may help increase circulation and maintain flexibility, but they are not as effective as active exercise.

- *Magnets.* A variety of magnets and ion balance bracelets have been marketed with many claims, but there is no evidence to support any benefits. To date, the FDA has not approved the marketing of any magnets for medical use, and sellers making medical claims for magnets are in violation of the law.

- *Electrical muscle stimulators.* Neuromuscular electrical stimulators cause the muscle to contract involuntarily. In the hands of qualified medical personnel, muscle stimulators are valuable therapeutic devices, but in a healthy person they do not have the same value. The FTC has filed false advertising claims against several firms that market exercise stimulators that promise to build "six-pack abs" and tone muscles without exercise. Spas and clinics often promote various muscle stimulators for fitness enhancement, but they have no value for healthy people.

- *Weighted belts.* Claims have been made that these belts reduce waists, thighs, and hips when worn under the clothing. In reality, they do none of these things and have been reported to cause physical harm.

- *Sauna belts and rubberized suits.* Various garments are marketed to promote weight loss, but they really just promote sweating. If exercise is performed while wearing such garments, the exercise, not the garment, may be beneficial. You cannot squeeze fat out of the pores, nor can you melt it.

- *Body wrapping.* Some reducing salons, gyms, and clubs advertise that wrapping the body in bandages soaked in a magic solution will cause a permanent reduction in body girth. Tight, constricting bands can temporarily indent the skin and squeeze body fluids into other parts of the body, but the skin or body will regain its original size within minutes or hours. Users may temporarily deplete water, but the water is regained quickly. Body fat is not lost.

Considerations with Exercise Equipment

Exercise machines are very useful, but take care when determining the type of machine to use. When deciding which machines are best for you, consider these questions:

- *What is your current state of fitness and your current level of physical activity?* Beginners and people with low fitness will want to choose a different piece of equipment than a more advanced exerciser. For example, exercise on a spinning bike would be appropriate for an advanced exerciser. The beginner might choose a regular exercise bicycle instead.

- *What are your goals?* Make sure the machine will help you meet your goals. For example, a resistance machine would be a good choice for building muscle fitness, and a treadmill or an elliptical machine would be a good choice for building cardiorespiratory endurance.

- *Will you enjoy it?* One limitation of exercise machines is that they may not be as fun as doing sports and some other activities. And some machines may be more fun for you than others. Try several machines and consider one that you enjoy the most.

- *Will you stick with it?* Choose a machine you think you can use consistently. Enjoyment is a factor, but so is difficulty. Find a machine that allows you to easily adjust the intensity so you can find a comfortable intensity and gradually increase it over time.

- *Is it safe?* Exercise machines are the source of more than a few injuries. People with limitations (e.g., knee problems)

Take time to learn the features of exercise equipment.
©Ariel Skelley/Getty Images

may choose a bicycle rather than a treadmill. Get proper instruction on how to use a machine before trying it.

- *Can it be adjusted to fit your body?* Before you begin exercising, adjust the machine to fit your body. For example, adjust the seat on an exercise bicycle. If you are short or tall, some equipment may not fit you.

connect VIDEO 3

Home exercise machines can be very useful, but research your options before making a purchase. Research by the Consumer's Union (*Consumer Reports*) has shown that well-designed and manufactured exercise machines can be used as an effective means to achieving good health-related physical fitness. When using a piece of equipment at a health club, you can change machines if you don't like the one you are using. If you buy the equipment, you are stuck with it even if you don't like it. Before purchasing, consider the questions provided in the previous section as well as the following:

- *Is this the best piece of equipment for you?* Should you buy a resistance machine, a treadmill, an exercise bicycle, or some other equipment? Consider your goals and fitness needs to help you decide what equipment to buy.

- *Do you have space for it?* If you do not have a space where you can put the equipment and leave it, you will probably not use it regularly. Some equipment is "portable" so that it can be stored when not in use, but it is less likely to be used regularly than equipment that is readily available. The more difficult it is to move equipment, the less likely it is to be used. Consider ceiling height, room width, other uses for the space. Also, do you have space for a TV to watch?

- *Is the space appropriate?* More than a few people have bought equipment thinking they will put it in the TV room or the garage. Be sure all members of the family approve of the location of the equipment before purchasing it. Garages may be appropriate for some machines in some locales, but may be unusable in some very hot or cold climates. Also, some equipment such as free weights may take up extra space.

- *Will you use it?* The best time to buy used exercise equipment is in February or March. This is because many people buy equipment in January to fulfill a New Year's resolution to be more active. They don't carefully consider the reasons for their purchase and find that they don't use what they have bought. Try out the equipment before you buy, especially when considering expensive machines.

- *Do you need it?* Are there cheaper alternatives? Can you do the same thing less expensively?

- *Are your sources reliable? Consumer Reports* does regular evaluations of exercise equipment. Consider their ratings and ratings of fitness experts to determine the quality, reliability, and repair records of various machines. Price is also a consideration. In some cases, if you cannot afford a quality machine, it might be wise to wait rather than to buy something that may not last. Finally, consider the product warranty and the cost of repairs if you do not get a warranty.

- *Is the dealer reputable?* Select a company or store that has been in business for a while and is a member of the Better Business Bureau. Compare prices for similar equipment. Beware of dealers who try to sell you extra attachments or accessories you won't use.

Be aware of the limitations of exercise machines and devices. Although exercise machines can be useful in carrying out your personal exercise plan, they are not without limitations. Some of these limitations are described here.

- *Many pieces of equipment are for a single purpose.* A machine that builds cardiorespiratory endurance may do little for muscle fitness or flexibility.

- *Monitors on machines are often inaccurate.* Studies have shown that machines that provide feedback often overestimate energy expenditure (calories expended).

- *Claims for the benefits of some machines are exaggerated.* Claims that machines can get you in the "fat burning zone" or that promise high-calorie expenditure with low effort are examples of quackery and should be discounted.

- *Some home equipment is not cost-effective.* Will you get significant benefits from high-cost items? Consider low-cost equipment, such as exercise bands, exercise balls, and inexpensive weights.

The use of hand weights and wrist weights while walking or bench-stepping is controversial. Carrying weights (not more than 1 to 3 pounds) while doing aerobic dance, walking, and other aerobic activities can increase energy expenditure, but the effect is negligible unless the arms are pumped (bending the elbow and raising the weight to shoulder height and then extending the elbow as the arm swings down). This energy output is comparable to a slow jog. Some experts caution that pumping the arms using weights can increase the risk for injury and suggest that the benefit of added energy expenditure is not worth the added risk for injury.

Those who choose to use weights while doing aerobic activity are at less risk for injury if they use wrist weights rather than handheld weights. Arm movements should be limited to a range of motion below the shoulder level. Coronary patients and people with shoulder or elbow joint problems are advised not to use hand or wrist weights. Ankle weights are not recommended because they may alter your gait and stress the knees.

Technology Update

Online Personal Training Resources

Many people appreciate the convenience (and lower cost) of exercising at home instead of working out at a local fitness center. Companies have responded to this growing market with an array of online products and services. One recent trend is the use of online personal trainers and resources that seek to provide the same type of support and accountability as in-person trainers do. Some sites offer direct personal trainer contact aimed at helping address your individual goals, while other sites provide more generic forms of support. Other online sites provide virtual engagement with other exercisers along with streaming videos. For example, a number of online training resources allow cyclists to bike indoors on virtual courses and to engage in simulated races against other online competitors. The various resources can potentially provide valuable support and motivation, but they also may be expensive and may not help with long-term exercise adherence. Therefore, it is important to carefully consider your needs before making major commitments.

Do you think you would find value in these type of online training resources? How sure are you?

ACTIVITY

Considerations with Health Clubs and Spas

Consider the credentials of a fitness leader or personal trainer before making a selection. Individuals with a college degree in physical education, physical therapy, exercise science, or kinesiology are recommended, as well as certifications from reputable organizations, such as the American College of Sports Medicine (ACSM). The ACSM offers several certifications with differing levels of expertise and education ranging from certified personal trainer to registered clinical exercise physiologist. Not all certifications are equal. Some unreputable and unethical organizations require little more than an application and a fee payment.

Using the sauna, steam room, whirlpool, or hot tub at your local fitness center provides no significant health benefits. Baths do not melt off fat; fat must be metabolized. The heat and humidity from baths may make you perspire, but it is water, not fat, oozing from your pores. Any positive effect is largely psychological, although some temporary relief from aches and pains may result from the heat. Use of these facilities is not advised for people with health problems, such as high or low blood pressure, and should be limited for children, pregnant women, older adults, those who have consumed alcohol, and those who have recently finished a vigorous exercise bout. Skin infections can be spread in a bath; make certain it is cleaned regularly and that the hot tub or whirlpool has proper pH and chlorination. Additional guidelines include:

- Cool down after exercise before using a sauna or tub.
- Take a soap shower before and after use.
- Do not wear makeup, lotion, oil, or jewelry.
- Adhere to the posted temperature guidelines.
- Drink plenty of water before or during use.
- Do not sit on a metal stool; sit on a towel.
- Get out immediately if you become dizzy; feel hot, chilled, or nauseous; or develop a headache.

Sunlamp products, such as tanning beds and various suntanning products, can increase the risk of sun damage and skin cancer. Tanning salons often promise "safe tanning" because they tend to elicit UVA radiation instead of the more intense UVB. It was previously thought that UVA radiation was not as harmful as UVB since it is less intense and penetrates to deeper layers of the skin. However, new evidence suggests that it can significantly damage skin cells called keratinocytes in the basal layer of the epidermis, where most skin cancers occur. The dosage of UVA radiation from salons is also 12 times as strong as that of the sun. Not surprisingly, people who use tanning salons are 2.5 times more likely to develop squamous cell carcinoma than people who don't. As noted previously, the World Health

Staff
- Is the staff well qualified and available when you need help?
- Is the club well run (efficient in day-to-day operations)?

Facilities and Equipment
- Does the club meet your personal needs (e.g., offering equipment, classes, and services you want)?
- Is the facility convenient (near home or work)?
- Is the equipment up-to-date and well maintained?
- Is the facility clean?
- Are towels provided to wipe off machines?
- Are weights replaced after use?
- Are rules posted?
- Is there a time limit for using machines?
- Is there a dress code?

Quackery
- Are quack products sold and pushed?
- Do members speak well of the club and recommend it?
- Are you given promises of quick results?

Memberships
- Can your membership be sold, transferred, or canceled if you move?
- Is there a no-contract or monthly payment option available in case you can change your mind?
- Are there hidden costs associated with membership (e.g., costs for testing, use of personal training)?

Other Important Questions
- Is the club well established (so it won't disappear overnight)?
- Can you make a trial visit during the hours when you would expect to use the facility to determine if it is overcrowded and if you would enjoy the atmosphere?
- Is the club well rated or have there been complaints? (Check the Better Business Bureau.)
- Is this club your best option? Have you investigated programs offered by the YMCA/YWCA, local colleges and universities, and municipal park and recreation departments?

Figure 1 ▶ Questions to answer when choosing a health and fitness club.
©Simone Becchetti/Getty Images

Organization has classified all UV radiation as carcinogenic (cancer causing). The FDA also requires warnings to be placed on a variety of products classified as "suntanning preparations." This includes a variety of gels, creams, liquids, and other topical products marketed to provide cosmetic benefits or the appearance of a tan. The required warning statement conveys the important message for consumers: *"Warning—This product does not contain a sunscreen and does not protect against sunburn. Repeated exposure of unprotected skin while tanning may increase the risk of skin aging, skin cancer, and other harmful effects to the skin even if you do not burn."* It is wise to avoid tanning salons, pills, and other products designed to accelerate tanning.

Consider a number of factors before making decisions about a health or fitness club. In addition to having well-trained experts, there are other guidelines to consider when selecting a health and fitness club. Some of these guidelines are illustrated in Figure 1. You will have the opportunity to

rate a health and fitness club using a comprehensive list of factors in Lab 24B.

Body Composition Quackery

Cellulite is not a special form of fat. Cellulite is ordinary fat with a fancy name. You do not need a special treatment or device to get rid of it. In fact, it has no special remedy. To decrease fat, reduce calories and do more physical activity.

Spot-reducing, or losing fat from a specific location on the body, is not possible. When you do physical activity, calories are burned and fat is recruited from all over the body in a genetically determined pattern. You cannot selectively exercise, bump, vibrate, squeeze, or freeze the fat from a particular spot. If you are flabby to begin with, localized exercise can strengthen the local muscles, causing a change in the contour and the girth of that body part, but exercise affects the muscles, not the fat on that body part. General aerobic exercises are the most effective for burning fat, but you cannot control where the fat comes off.

Surgically sculpting the body with implants and liposuction to acquire physical beauty will not give you physical fitness and may be harmful. Rather than doing it the hard way, an increasing number of people are resorting to surgery and muscle implants to improve their physique. Liposuction is not a weight loss technique but, rather, a contouring procedure. Like any surgery, it has risks, including risks for infection, hematoma, skin slough, other conditions, and death. Muscle implants give a muscular appearance, but they do not make you stronger or more fit. The implants are not really muscle tissue but, rather, silicon gel or saline, such as that used in breast implants or a hard substitute. Some complications can occur, such as infection and bleeding, and some physicians believe that calf implants may put pressure on the calf muscles and cause them to atrophy. A better way to improve physique and fitness is to engage in proper exercise.

Weight loss quackery is the most common form of consumer fraud. The FTC indicates that nearly one-quarter of reported fraud cases involve weight loss products or resources. Space does not allow a listing of all the common weight loss scams; however, following are two current scams that companies use to deceptively market products to gullible consumers:

- *Use of prescription drugs not approved for weight loss.* One example is hCG (human chorionic gonadotropin), a drug for the treatment of fertility. There is no scientific evidence of benefits for weight loss and the FTC and FDA have taken steps against those promoting its use for weight loss.
- *Acai berry scam.* Quacks have set up websites from fake news organizations (with graphics from a real news organization) to promote acai berry supplements for weight loss.

It is difficult for the FDA to keep up with the continual release of new health and weight loss supplements on the market; thus, consumers have to take responsibility for making sound decisions.

Nutrition Quackery

Diets are a major source of quackery. Recommendations for nutrition and healthy eating practices are summarized in established federally approved nutrition guidelines. Beware of diets that do not follow these guidelines. Avoid diets that emphasize one nutrient at the expense of others (unbalanced diets), require the purchase of special products, and are proposed by people lacking sound credentials.

It is not true that if a little of something is "good," more is "better." The marketing of nutrition products often relies on convincing people that additional vitamins,

Vegetables provide many vitamins, minerals, and other essential nutrients.
©LWA/Stephen Welstead/Blend Images LLC

minerals, or enzymes are beneficial. It is true that deficiencies of certain compounds may be harmful, but extra amounts don't always provide added protection or improved health. The myth that vitamin C can cure the common cold is based on the fact that deficiencies of vitamin C can lead to scurvy. The same hype is used to sell consumers many other unnecessary supplements. For example, protein supplements are marketed with convincing (and honest) claims that the body needs amino acids to form muscle. The hidden truth is that the body cannot store or use more than it needs.

Beware of energy drinks with "boosts" sold at smoothie shops and fitness clubs. Many restaurants and shops now promote drinks containing "boosts" (a tablespoon or two of a food supplement). Health clubs that sell drinks with supplements are susceptible to the claim that they are selling products for financial gain rather than the best interests of clients. Even if some supplements are effective, which most are not, taking one dose in a drink would be ineffective and a waste of money.

The designations of "herbal" or "natural" on supplements do not ensure safety or efficacy. Many health and nutrition supplements emphasize the word *herbal* because it relates to plants, and people assume plants, are natural and therefore healthy. There are literally thousands of herbal products, and most medicines are derived from plants. However, the fact that herbs are natural does not mean they are safe. The most prominent example is with the herbal stimulant ephedra, which was used in many weight loss supplements. Over 150 deaths and thousands of adverse reactions were attributed to ephedra use before it could be officially banned. Several other prominent herbal products include saw palmetto, an herbal supplement touted as a preventive for prostate cancer, and echinacea, an herb widely used to reduce symptoms of the common cold. While early studies showed some promise for these products, subsequent studies have not supported claims for these supplements. Consumers are encouraged to be careful about claims made for herbal products.

Some popular supplements from animal sources are also highly touted as having unique benefits. Glucosamine, for example, is made from shellfish, and chondroitin is made from the cartilage of sharks and/or cattle. Glucosamine and chondroitin are two of the most widely used supplements other than vitamins and minerals. They are often used to relieve symptoms and pain from osteoarthritis. Results of one large clinical trial suggested that the two supplements, taken together or separately, were no more effective than a placebo; however, a small group of people who had moderate to severe pain did experience some relief after using the supplements. These products probably do no harm, but they may also do little for clinical relief of joint problems.

Consumer Protections Against Fraud and Quackery

Current legislation makes it difficult to protect consumers against fraudulent dietary supplements. According to the FDA, a dietary supplement is a product taken by mouth that contains a "dietary ingredient" intended to supplement the diet. These ingredients include vitamins, minerals, herbs and other botanicals, amino acids, and other substances, such as enzymes, organ tissues, glandulars, and metabolites. Supplements come in many forms, including powders, tablets, softgels, capsules, gelcaps, and liquids. Consumers assume that supplements that are sold in stores (or online) are both safe and effective, but neither may be true. There are certainly many products sold in stores and online that are safe and effective, but careful research is necessary to be sure. The passage of the Dietary Supplements Health and Education Act (DSHEA) in the 1990s created loopholes that made it easy for companies to promote and sell untested products. Food supplements are typically not considered to be drugs, so they are also not regulated. Unlike drugs and medicines, food supplements need not be proven effective or even safe to be sold in stores. To be removed from stores, they

must be proven ineffective or unsafe. Unfortunately, it takes time and often extended court battles for the FDA and other agencies to get some products off the market.

When the DSHEA was passed in 1994, no provisions were included to ensure that dietary supplements contained the ingredients they claimed to contain. However, the FDA has since instituted a rule requiring supplement manufacturers to provide labels to ensure "a consistent product free of contamination, with accurate labeling." This is important because more than a few cases of product contamination have been reported. Under the new regulations, the manufacturer, not the FDA, has to test products to be sure that they are pure and accurately labeled. However, supplement companies are not required to document that their products are effective or even safe. It is not possible for the FDA to test all possible products so they monitor the safety of supplements through "adverse events monitoring." Thus, the only way that dangerous products and unscrupulous

A CLOSER LOOK

Buyer Be *Very* Aware

Due to the way most supplements are categorized, the FDA can remove products from the market only after obtaining sufficient information to detect risks or problems. Dietary supplements often contain drugs with compounds that have chemical structures similar to banned drugs. The FDA's tainted supplement database lists over 100 companies that have been caught selling hundreds of supplements spiked with drugs and chemicals that are banned or not listed as ingredients (search "FDA and tainted supplements" online). However, as noted on its web page, the FDA is *"unable to test and identify all products marketed as dietary supplements that have potentially harmful hidden ingredients."* Several independent companies now assist the FDA by checking supplements for quality, safety, and compliance with labeling and marketing. The U.S. Pharmacopeial Convention (USP) and NSP International (NSP) are private nonprofit organizations that test supplements, while ConsumerLab (CL) is a for-profit group that also tests supplements. Products containing the USP, NSP, or CL labels provide some additional documentation indicating that the products are what they say they are and contain no unspecified ingredients. However, the labels *do not* suggest that the products are recommended, nor do they provide information about appropriate or inappropriate use of the product.

Would you have more confidence in products that contain one of these labels? Would you consider taking a supplement without a label or without checking to see if there were warnings for the product?

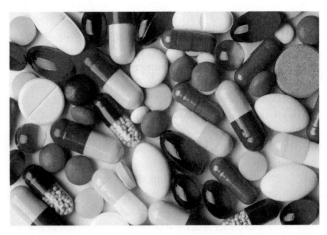
Good consumer skills are important for evaluating health products and for interpreting health claims.
©Didecs/Shutterstock

manufacturers can be identified is if consumers report problems to the FDA. The FDA has established a robust MedWatch alert system that allows consumers to report problems, symptoms, or spurious claims (see HELP feature for details). The "FDA 101" web page also provides information and tips to help avoid being a victim of fraud. (See Suggested Resources and Readings.)

Because supplements do not need approval of the FDA before they are marketed, consumers should very cautious about any products they use. The following list represents a short summary of concerns and issues associated with unregulated supplements:

- Supplements can have unknown risks that are detected later. For example, hundreds of people died from consuming products containing ephedra before it could be banned.

- Supplements may include illegal or banned components. For example, an evaluation of more than 240 supplements detected that over 18 percent contained steroids.

- Supplements often contain drugs with chemical structures similar to banned drugs. For example, many weight loss/muscle supplements contain AMP citrate, a stimulant drug similar in chemical structure to an already banned stimulant known as DMAA.

- Supplements can have negative interactions with medicines or other treatments. For example, St. John's wort (a common herbal supplement used to treat depression) is thought to affect fertility and may lead to birth defects when used during pregnancy.

- Supplements can present unexpected risks due to contamination effects during production. For example, the FDA recently warned consumers about liver injuries and failure following use of the weight loss supplement Lipokinetix.

Most Americans favor increased regulation of the supplement industry. When informed that the FDA does not regulate supplements, more than 80 percent of adults indicate that the FDA should review supplements before they are offered for sale. More than half of adults want more regulation on advertising of supplements and better rules to ensure purity and accurate dosage. Despite the lack of regulation of supplements, nearly half of Americans routinely take supplements and slightly more than half believe in the value of supplements. Interestingly, 44 percent believe that physicians know little or nothing about supplements. More than a few critics point out that self-regulation within the industry has not worked well. They suggest that the public would have more confidence in supplements if the FDA were watching out for their best interests.

Consumers should consult physicians about using vitamin supplements. A panel of experts with the National Institutes of Health (NIH) recently prepared a report noting the value of some vitamin and mineral supplements while not recommending others. Examples of vitamins and mineral that were endorsed include:

connect
VIDEO 5

- Folic acid supplements for women of childbearing age.

- Calcium and vitamin D to protect against osteoporosis for postmenopausal women.

- Specific supplements for those with an eye condition called macular degeneration.

Examples of those that were *not* endorsed for health significant health benefits include:

- Beta-carotene (a form of vitamin A), as it was not found to be effective.

- Daily multivitamins. They were not found to be effective, although no evidence was found that they are harmful.

- Megadoses of vitamins and minerals. The board warned against taking very high levels of vitamins and minerals (megadoses), noting that they are not beneficial and can be dangerous.

These summaries are provided for general information. It is best to check with your physician about your personal needs.

Be wary of claims made for supplements, particularly in free pamphlets and handouts provided in stores. The DSHEA included regulations that prevent companies from making un- substantiated claims on product labels.  Unfortunately, the act failed to limit false claims that are not on the product label. Supplement makers circumvented the spirit of the rule by hinting at effects with clever names, through promotional ads, and most directly through a variety of quack pamphlets and publications. The literature is distributed separately from the product, thus allowing sellers to make unsubstantiated claims for products. (This is protected by free speech laws.) Also, the law does not prohibit unproven verbal claims by salespeople. Many medical experts feel that "alternative treatments" should be subjected to the same type of rigorous scientific testing used to evaluate other medicines. A prominent editorial suggested that "putting customers' health at risk is a high price to pay for a free market in diet supplements." There is clearly need for reform, but as it currently stands, consumers must make their own decisions about the safety and effectiveness of supplements. This is why it is critical to be a well-informed consumer.

Health Literacy and the Internet

Not all books provide information that is sound, reliable, and scientifically accurate. Some material is published on the basis of how popular, famous, or attractive the author is or how sensational or unusual his or her ideas are. Very few movie stars, models, TV personalities, and Olympic athletes are experts in biomechanics, anatomy and physiology, exercise, and other foundations of physical fitness. Having a good figure or physique, being fit, or having gone through a training program does not, in itself, qualify a person to advise others.

After reading the facts presented in this edition, you should be able to evaluate whether or not a book, a magazine, or an article on exercise and fitness is valid, reliable, and scientifically sound. To assist you further, Lab 24A lists 10 guidelines.

Not all websites provide information that is sound, reliable, and scientifically accurate. Currently, approximately three-fourths of all teen and young adult computer users seek health information on the Web. But many health websites contain misinformation. Studies show that Wikipedia is the most common source of health information for the general public. One report showed that as many as one half of doctors surveyed used Wikipedia for health information. Many consumers, and some physicians, do not realize that Wikipedia can be edited by anyone and for this reason can contain erroneous information.

A research study directly compared information provided about prescription drugs on Wikipedia with similar content from a more credible site (Medscape Drug Reference). Not surprisingly, the Wikipedia site had incomplete answers, incorrect information about dosage, and errors of omission about side effects. The authors of the study concluded that Wikipedia should be used only as a supplemental source for drug information.

Improving health literacy is a public health goal. The Internet has made an almost unlimited amount of health information accessible, but it has proven difficult to ensure that the information is used wisely. The U.S. Public Health Service has established goals to improve public health literacy and the quality of health information on the Internet. The two goals are designed to work together: consumers need access to accurate information, but they also need to know how to interpret and use the information (health literacy). The content presented in this Concept provides a foundation for interpreting health information, but some additional guidelines are provided for effectively using the Internet.

One general rule is to consult at least two or more sources to confirm information. Getting confirmation of information from non-Web sources is also a good idea. Perhaps the most important recommendation is to consider the source of information. In general, government sites are valid sources that contain sound information prepared by experts and based on scientific research. Government sites typically include *.gov* as part of the address. Professional organizations and universities can also be good sources of information. Organizations typically have *.org* and universities typically have *.edu* as part of the address. However, caution should still be used with organizations because starting an organization and obtaining an *.org* address is easy. Your greatest trust can be placed in the sites of stable, credible organizations (see Suggested Resources and Readings). The great majority of websites promoting health products have *.com* in the address because these are commercial sites, which are in business to make a profit. Thus, although some contain good information, they may focus on selling products or services. Therefore, it is important to view content from these sites more critically.

Using Self-Management Skills

Reduce your susceptibility to quackery by being an informed consumer. Three characteristics that predispose people to health-related quackery are (1) a concern about appearance, health, or performance; (2) a lack of adequate knowledge; and (3) a desire for immediate results.

Understanding the principles of exercise and nutrition will help you know when something sounds "too good to be true."

When evaluating health-related products or information, carefully consider the quality of your source. Common sources of misinformation are magazines, health food stores, and TV infomercials. These entities all have an economic incentive in promoting the purchase and use of exercise, diet, and weight loss products. Because of freedom of speech laws, it is legal to state opinion through these media. Note, however, that few companies make claims on product labels, since this is false advertising. Follow these additional guidelines to avoid being a victim of quackery:

- Read the ad carefully, especially the small print.

- Do not send cash; use a check, money order, or credit card so you will have a receipt.

- Do not order from a company with only a post office box, unless you know the company.

- When making decisions about products or services, begin your investigation well in advance of the day when a decision is to be made.

- Do not let high-pressure sales tactics make you rush into a decision.

- When in doubt, check out the company through the Better Business Bureau.

Understanding principles of persuasion can help you make more informed decisions. Making good consumer decisions requires critical thinking skills and discipline. Advertising and marketing campaigns can be highly persuasive; thus, it is important to learn to identify the strategies that companies (and quacks) use to manipulate your beliefs and impulses. Robert Cialdini, a leading expert in consumerism, emphasizes that *"persuasion is no longer just an art, it's an out-and-out science."* For example, evidence clearly documents that individuals are more likely to follow through on a decision after they develop a personal commitment or internalized belief. Companies know this and frequently lure consumers with low-ball prices or promises that then are later retracted or softened. Once a person makes a preliminary decision to take an action, they tend to follow through, even after the costs (or value) of performing that action have been changed. Fortunately, evidence also suggests that awareness of these influences can help individuals detect when they are being influenced or manipulated into a decision or a purchase.

Strategies for Action: Lab Information

Being a good consumer requires time, information, and effort. Taking the time to investigate a product will help you save money and avoid making poor decisions that affect your health, wellness, and fitness. In Lab 24A you will evaluate an exercise device, a food supplement, a book, a magazine article, or a website. In Lab 24B you will evaluate a health, wellness, or fitness club to gain experience in what to look for.

Suggested Resources and Readings

The websites for the following sources can be accessed by searching online for the organization, program, or title listed. Specific scientific references are available at the end of this edition of *Concepts of Fitness and Wellness.*

- American Psychological Association. (2017, August 7). Understanding how persuasion works can make consumers more savvy. *ScienceDaily.*
- Berezow, A. (2017, July 21). Call junk science by its rightful name: Fake news. *USA Today.*
- Bomey, N., & McCoy, K. (2016, July 15). Herbalife agrees to $200M FTC settlement. *USA Today.*
- Center for Science in the Public Interest. Consumer protection information.
- Federal Trade Commission. Health & Fitness.
- Federal Trade Commission. Scam Alerts.
- Healthfinder. Link to trusted health information.
- Informed-Choice.org. Quality Assurance for Sport Nutrition Products.
- Johnson, L. (2017, April 25). FDA: Avoid fake "miracle" cancer treatments sold on Internet. *U.S. News & World Report.*
- MedlinePlus. Consumer health resources.
- National Council Against Health Fraud. Consumer fraud protection website.
- Perrone, M. (2015, April 21). FDA official says increased popularity, safety issues led to review of unproven remedies. *USA Today.*
- Quackwatch. Consumer fraud protection website.
- Rosenbaum, M., et al. (2015, April 23). Columbia medical faculty: What do we do about Dr. Oz? *USA Today.*
- U.S. Consumer Information Center. Bureau of Consumer Protection.
- U.S. Food and Drug Administration:
  - FDA 101 information page.
  - MedWatch page.
  - Requirements for tanning products.
  - Tainted supplements page.
- Young, A. (October 22, 2015). Oregon AG accuses retailer GNC of selling drug-spiked dietary supplements. *USA Today.*

Lab 24A Practicing Consumer Skills: Evaluating Products

Name   **Section**   **Date**

Purpose: To evaluate an exercise device, a book, a magazine article, an advertisement, a food supplement, or a website.

Procedures

1. Select an appropriate product or promotional item to review from one of the following four categories: 1. Exercise Device, 2. Food Supplement, 3. Book, Article, or Advertisement, or 4. Website.
2. Complete Chart 1 to provide details of the product/item you reviewed. You should provide the specific name and manufacturer (if you selected an exercise device or food supplement) or a title/source/reference (if you reviewed a book, article, advertisement, or website), then the specific citation or source for a book, article, advertisement, or website. Finally, provide a description of the product in your own words.
3. Complete Chart 2 to evaluate the specific characteristics or qualities of the product or tool that you reviewed. Fill in circles for items that are "True" for the product or promotion you are evaluating.
4. Total the number of true statements out of 10 and report the total to compute an overall score for the item being evaluated. The higher the score, the more likely it is to be safe and/or effective.
5. Answer the questions in the Conclusions and Implications section.

Chart 1 Product Category _____ (I,2,3, or 4)

Name, Manufacturer, Source, or Reference	Brief Description of Product, Item, Book/article/advertisement, or Website

---

Conclusions and Implications: In several sentences, give your assessment of the product (be sure to refer to specific questions in Chart 2 that influenced your conclusion). Did it score well? Would you use/buy the product? Explain.

Results: Place an X over the circle by each true statement and summarize your score at the bottom by tallying the number of true statements.

Lab 24A — Practicing Consumer Skills: Evaluating Products

Chart 2

Exercise Device

1. The exercise device requires effort consistent with the FIT fomula.
2. The exercise device is safe and the exercise done using the device is safe.
3. There are no claims that the device uses exercise that is effortless.
4. Exercise using the device is fun or is a type that you might do regularly.
5. There are no claims using gimmick words, such as *tone, cellulite, quick,* or *spot fat reduction.*
6. The seller's credentials are sound.
7. The product does something for you that cannot be done without it.
8. You can return the device if you do not like it (the seller has been in business for a long time).
9. The cost of the product is justified by the potential benefits.
10. The device is easy to store or you have a place to permanently use the equipment without storing it.

Food Supplement

1. The seller is not the prime source of product information.
2. The seller has been in business for a long time and has a good reputation.
3. There is scientific evidence of product effectiveness.
4. There is clear evidence about the side effects of the active ingredients.
5. The long-term effectiveness and safety of the product are cited.
6. You are sure of the content of the product.
7. You have information that the manufacturer is reputable.
8. The known benefits are worth the cost.
9. There is evidence that you can get benefits from this product that cannot be obtained from good food.
10. There are no claims that use quack words or claims about conspiracies against the product by reputable organizations.

Book/Article/Advertisement

1. The credentials of the author are sound. He or she has a degree in an area related to the content of the book or magazine.
2. The facts in the article are consistent with the facts described in *Concepts of Fitness and Wellness.*
3. The author does not claim "quick" or "miraculous" results.
4. There are no claims about the spot reduction of fat or other unfounded claims.
5. The author/advertisement is not selling a product.
6. Reputable experts are cited.
7. The article does not promote unsafe exercises or products.
8. New discoveries from exotic places are not cited.
9. The article/advertisement does not rely on testimonials by nonexpert, famous people.
10. The author/advertisement does not make claims that the AMA, the FDA, or another legitimate organization is trying to suppress information.

Website

1. The site does not sell products associated with information provided.
2. The provider is a person, an organization (.org), or a governmental agency (.gov) with a sound reputation.
3. The site does not use quack words.
4. The site does not try to discredit well-established organizations or governmental agencies.
5. The site does not rely on testimonials, celebrities, or people with unknown credentials.
6. The site is endorsed by, or linked to, credible agencies, associations, or experts.
7. The site has a history of providing good information.
8. The site provides complete information that is documented by research.
9. No claims of quick cures or miracle results are made.
10. The site provides information consistent with content provided in this Concept.

Summary Score: Total the number of Xs for the device, book/magazine, advertisement, food supplement, or website:

468

Lab 24B Evaluating a Health, Wellness, or Fitness Club

Name	**Section**	**Date**

Purpose: To practice evaluating a health club (various combinations of the words *health, wellness,* and *fitness* are often used for these clubs).

Procedures

1. Choose a club and make a visit.
2. Listen carefully to all that is said and ask many questions.
3. Look carefully all around as you are given the tour of the facilities. Ask what the exercises or the equipment will do for you, or ask leading questions such as, "Will this take inches off my hips?"
4. As soon as you leave the club, rate it using Chart 1.

Chart 1 Health Club Evaluation Questionnaire

Place an X over a "yes" or "no" answer.	Yes	No	Notes
1. Were claims for improvement in weight, figure/physique, or fitness realistic?	○	○	
2. Was a long-term contract (1 to 3 years) encouraged?	○	○	
3. Was the sales pitch high-pressure to make an immediate decision?	○	○	
4. Were you given a copy of the contract to read at home?	○	○	
5. Did the fine print include objectionable clauses?	○	○	
6. Did the club representative ask you about medical readiness?	○	○	
7. Did the club sell diet supplements as a sideline?	○	○	
8. Did the club have passive equipment?	○	○	
9. Did the club have cardiovascular training equipment or facilities (cycles, track, pool, aerobic dance)?	○	○	
10. Did the club make unscientific claims for the equipment, exercise, baths, or diet supplements?	○	○	
11. Were the facilities clean?	○	○	
12. Were the facilities crowded?	○	○	
13. Were there days and hours when the facilities were open but would not be available to you?	○	○	
14. Were there limits on the number of minutes you could use a piece of equipment?	○	○	
15. Did the floor personnel closely supervise and assist clients?	○	○	
16. Were the floor personnel qualified experts?	○	○	
17. Were the managers/owners qualified experts?	○	○	
18. Has the club been in business at this location for a year or more?	○	○	

Results

1. Score the chart as follows:

   A. Give 1 point for each "no" answer for items 2, 3, 5, 7, 8, 10, 12, 13, and 14 and place the score in the box.

   Total A [ ]

   B. Give 1 point for each "yes" answer for items 1, 4, 6, 9, 11, and 18 and place the score in the box.

   Total B [ ]

   Total A and B above and place the score in the box.

   Total A and B [ ]

   C. Give 1 point for each "yes" answer for items 15, 16, and 17 and place the score in the box.

   Total C [ ]

2. A total score of 12–15 points on items A and B suggests the club rates at least fair, compared with other clubs.
3. A score of 3 on item C indicates that the personnel are qualified and suggests that you could expect to get accurate technical advice from the staff.
4. Regardless of the total scores, you would have to decide the importance of each item to you personally, as well as evaluate other considerations, such as cost, location, and personalities of the clients and the personnel, to decide if this would be a good place for you or your friends to join.

Conclusions and Implications: In several sentences, discuss your conclusion about the quality of this club and whether you think it would fit your needs if you wanted to belong.

Toward Optimal Health and Wellness: Planning for Healthy Lifestyle Change

LEARNING OBJECTIVES

After completing the study of this Concept, you will be able to:

▶ Assess inherited health risks.

▶ Describe how to access and use the health-care system effectively.

▶ Explain the importance of environmental influences on lifestyle (as well as the impact of our lifestyles on our environment).

▶ List the key healthy lifestyles that influence health and wellness.

▶ Explain how personal actions and interactions influence the adoption of healthy lifestyles.

▶ Apply behavioral skills to plan and follow personal health and fitness programs.

In addition to healthy lifestyles, other factors such as heredity, health care, the environment, cognitions and emotions, and personal actions and interactions contribute to good health, wellness, and fitness.

©Image Source

Why it Matters!

The broad vision of the national health goals is to create "a society in which all people live long, healthy lives." The focus is on *healthspan* (having many years of good health, wellness, and fitness), as well as *lifespan* (living a long life). Earlier, you were introduced to a comprehensive model that explained the many determinants of health, wellness, and fitness (see Figure 1). You learned that you have the most control over the lifestyles you lead, reasonable control over your cognitions and emotions, some control over your environment and use of health care, but relatively little control over heredity factors. Lifestyle behaviors are emphasized because they are under your control. Self-management skills are also emphasized because they help you learn how to adopt and sustain healthy behaviors over time. This final Concept revisits the determinants model to enable you to address the many factors that influence your health, wellness, and fitness.

Understand Inherited Risks and Strengths

Learn about your family health history and take stock of inherited risk. Many health conditions and risks are linked to or influenced by your genetics. If members of your immediate or extended family have had specific diseases or health problems, you may have a greater risk or likelihood of the same condition. Your DNA contains the instructions for building the proteins that control the structure and function of all the cells in your body. Abnormalities in DNA can provide the wrong set of instructions and lead to faulty cell growth or function. There are clear genetic influences on risks for obesity, cardiovascular disease risk factors, diabetes, and many forms of cancer. At present it is not possible for people to truly know their genetic risk profile, but it may be possible in the future with more comprehensive genetic testing.

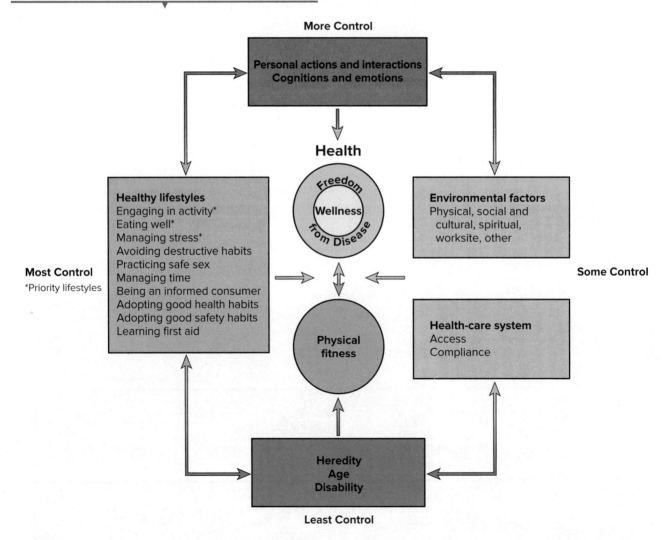

Figure 1 ▶ Determinants of health, wellness, and fitness.

Take action to diminish risk factors for which you have a predisposition.  As mentioned, research shows strong familial aggregation of certain chronic disease risk factors (e.g., obesity, diabetes, cholesterol, blood pressure) as well as some cancers. While you cannot change your heredity risks, you can take steps to reduce your risks for certain inherited conditions. Specifically, adopting healthy lifestyles may significantly reduce inherited risks for certain diseases. Researchers have computed obesity risk scores based on the presence or absence of 32 genes known to increase weight status. The genetic risk score was associated with an individual's inherited risk for being overweight, but risk was influenced by lifestyle behaviors. An active lifestyle (marked by the presence of a brisk daily walk) reduced the genetic influence by 50 percent, while a sedentary lifestyle (marked by watching television 4 hours a day) increased the genetic influence by 50 percent. Eating a healthy diet, managing stress, and not smoking are other important lifestyles that would likely contribute to lowering inherited risks for disease.

Technology Update

Direct-to-Consumer Genetic Testing

Genetics have a major influence on health, and advances in genetic technology may make it possible for individuals to better understand inherited health risks as well as potential risks to offspring. A company called 23andMe provides a "DNA analysis service" that allows individuals to learn about and explore their DNA. Until recently, the company was able to provide only general information about genetic variants, but the FDA recently approved of "direct-to-consumer" genetic testing. The current approval is for "carrier testing," which determines whether a healthy person has a genetic variation that could lead to an offspring inheriting a potentially serious disorder. With this step, the FDA acknowledged that, in some cases, consumers should not have to go through a licensed medical provider to obtain information about their personal genetic information. The change will likely spur additional innovation and may open the door to broader access to genetic testing. However, reports from established public health agencies, such as the CDC, warn consumers about the limitations of these tests (see the article "Direct to Consumer Genetic Testing: Think Before You Spit" in the Suggested Resources and Readings).

Do you support the use of this type of testing, or could it just lead to potential quackery? Would you value learning about your genetic predisposition if the information were available? Why or why not?

Make Effective Use of Health Care

Follow sound medical advice and recommendations. The medical system can provide individuals with supportive, personalized health care, but people have to seek consultation and follow advice for it to be effective (see Table 1). Some basic strategies for accessing the medical system effectively are summarized below:

- *Get medical insurance.* People who think they save money by avoiding the payment of insurance premiums place themselves (and their families) at risk and may not really save money.

- *Consider a health savings account (HSA).* An HSA, typically employee funded, allows you to set aside a portion of your earnings to pay future medical expenses. You do not pay tax on the money you set aside as long as you follow the rules. An HSA can save you money and encourages prevention and medical treatment.

- *Investigate and then identify a hospital and regular doctor.* Check with other physicians you know and trust for referrals. Check with your state medical board and national directories (e.g., Directory of Board Certified Medical Specialists, www.abms.org) for specialist certifications or fellowships. Choose an accredited emergency center near your home and a hospital that is accredited and grants privileges to your personal doctors.

- *Get periodic medical exams.* Do not wait until something is wrong before you seek medical advice. A yearly preventive physical exam is recommended for adults over the age of 40. Younger people should have an exam at least every two years.

- *Follow appropriate screening recommendations.* Many illnesses and chronic conditions can be treated effectively if they are identified early in the disease process. Following

Table 1 ► Facts about Health Care Use

- More women than men have a regular physician.
- More than half of young men have no personal doctor.
- Three times more women than men have visited a doctor in the past year.
- Women are more aware of health issues than men.
- Nearly half of men wait a week or more to see a doctor when ill.
- Many men see sickness as "unmanly."
- Married men see doctors more frequently than single men because their wives prompt them.
- Lack of health insurance results in fewer doctor's visits, less frequent health screening, and less access to prescribed medicine.

cancer screening guidelines is particularly important (e.g., mammograms for women and prostate tests for men). Breast and testicular self-exams are also important for detection.

- *Ask questions.* Do not be afraid to speak up. Prepare questions for doctors and other medical personnel. The American College of Surgeons suggests several questions before surgeries: What are the reasons for the surgery? Are there alternatives? What will happen if I don't have the procedure? What are the risks? What are the long-term effects and problems? How will the procedure impact my quality of life and future health?

- *Understand effects of medications.* Seek out information about medicines and supplements so you understand their intended effect. Read the inserts that come with the medicine and ask your doctor and pharmacist about correct dosage and information concerning when to take the medication. The FDA recently simplified drug inserts to help you understand the information that comes with medicine. Track your medicine and supplement use and share it with your physician.

- *Consider potential side effects of medicines you take.* Most medications are tested for use with certain populations, and they may not be safe or effective for all people. Consider the safety and potential risks. Side effects from preventable adverse reactions to medicines account for more than 1.5 million deaths each year. When medicine is prescribed, ask for details. Ask why the medicine was prescribed and the nature of side effects. Ask if the medicine interacts with other medicines or supplements.

- *If you have doubts about medical advice, get a second opinion.* Some estimates indicate that as many as 30 percent of original diagnoses are incorrect or differ from second opinions. Don't worry about offending your doctor by getting another opinion. Good doctors encourage this.

- *Make your wishes for health care known.* Have a medical power of attorney. This document spells out the treatments you desire in the case of severe illness. Without such a document, your loved ones may not be able to make decisions consistent with your wishes. Be sure your loved ones have a similar document so that you can also help them carry out their wishes.

Become a wise health- and medical-care consumer. Medical illiteracy and lack of health-care information are linked to higher than normal death rates. This is why improving medical literacy is such a high priority for public health officials. Some strategies for becoming a better health- and medical-care consumer are listed here.

- *Become familiar with the symptoms of common medical problems.* If symptoms persist, seek medical help. Many deaths can be prevented if early warning signs of medical problems are heeded.

- *Practice good hygiene.* The consensus among health experts is that hand washing is effective in flu prevention and is among the best defenses against the common cold and other respiratory illnesses. Always wash hands before preparing food or eating and after using the toilet, touching animals, handling garbage, coughing, or blowing your nose. Avoid sharing cups and utensils, and use hand sanitizers when you don't have access to water.

- *Stay home when you are sick.* Most companies urge sick employees to stay home to prevent spreading illness to others. Sickness (especially the flu) can spread rapidly in worksites or group settings so use your "sick days" or avoid interactions with others if possible. Sick workers are less productive, and working when sick lengthens recovery time.

A CLOSER LOOK

Patients with Female Doctors Fare Better

Research published in *JAMA Internal Medicine* found that patients who were cared for by female doctors got better results and were less likely to die than those treated by male doctors. The researchers examined outcomes from over 1.5 million older adults on Medicare who were hospitalized. The study reported a reduced likelihood of being readmitted to the hospital if patients were treated by a female doctor. However, researchers did not have definitive answers as to why. Some have speculated that female doctors are better listeners and communicators and show more empathy when caring for patients. It is also possible that they promoted healthier lifestyles after

release, since previous research has demonstrated that female doctors encourage preventive practices more often than male doctors. The researchers indicated that the study did not mean that males were not good doctors; but it could benefit all doctors to know why female doctors saw better results in this study.

Why do you think female doctors had better outcomes? Does your doctor listen carefully, communicate well, and encourage preventive practices? Would you look for these traits in a doctor?

- *Carefully review the credibility and accuracy of new health information.* There are many examples of misleading claims and fraud in the health and fitness industry. Even news reports from credible scientific studies can exert too much influence on consumer decisions. It takes years for scientific consensus to emerge, so carefully review new health claims.

Consider Environmental Influences on Your Health

Understand how environmental factors shape your behaviors. As described throughout this edition, environmental factors influence your health and well-being (see Figure 2). The term *obesogenic environments* has been used to describe

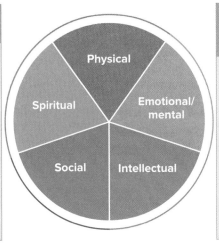

A positive *physical* environment helps make the healthy choice the easy choice.

- **Access to physical activity and healthy foods:** A healthy environment supports efforts to adopt healthy lifestyles by making it easier to be active and to eat healthy. Parks, trails, and green spaces provide opportunities to be active. Farmers' markets, health sections of grocery stores, and food co-ops make it easier to select healthy food.
- **Safe and clean communities:** A pleasant, clean, and safe environment encourages healthy living and the adoption of healthy lifestyles. Clean water and clean air are critical for good health.

A positive *spiritual* environment helps to support spiritual fulfillment.

- **Opportunities for spiritual development:** Reading spiritual materials, prayer, meditation, and discussions with others provide opportunities to clarify and solidify spiritual beliefs.
- **Access to spiritual community and leadership:** Finding a community for worship provides comfort and a path to fulfillment for many. Consider consultation with those with experience and expertise.

A positive *emotional* environment can help with adopting healthy lifestyles and managing stress.

- **Supportive personal relationships:** Support by others, especially family members, can help in managing stress and in adopting healthy lifestyles. Unhealthy relationships have the opposite effect.
- **Stress-management skills:** Friends, families, and coworkers can provide emotional support to assist in coping and stress management.

A healthy *social* environment enhances quality of life and supports wellness.

- **A sense of community:** Being a part of the greater community is important to social and mental health. Community-based groups are also important for planning and promoting healthy lifestyles for residents.
- **Social support:** A strong support network can help in times of need and provide advice, assistance, or support when needed.

A stimulating *intellectual* environment fosters learning and critical thinking.

- **Access to accurate information:** Whether the source is formal education or self-learning, access to accurate information is essential. Of course, good information is beneficial only if used.
- **Build and maintain cognitions:** A stimulating intellectual environment can promote self-discovery, build cognitive skills, and promote critical thinking.

Figure 2 ▶ The influence of environmental factors on dimensions of wellness.

In the News

Access to Health Care and Insurance

The rising costs of health care make health insurance more important than ever. However, recent CDC statistics indicate that young adults are most likely to be uninsured. Uninsured rates are highest for those aged 25–34 and second highest among those 18–24. However, data from the U.S. Department of Health and Human Services indicates that coverage for young adults has increased since enactment of a provision of the Affordable Care Act (ACA) that allows them to remain on their parent's health care plans until age 26. The ACA originally mandated that people who do not have an approved health plan must pay a penalty when filing taxes. Recently the individual mandate was repealed (effective in 2019). Some experts fear that the lack of a mandate will reduce the number of people who are insured, especially young people. Changes in health-care legislation will likely continue to occur for years to come and consumers are encouraged to stay informed. Search "Access to Health Services" on the *Healthy People* website to learn more about the issue.

Why do you think young adults have the highest uninsured rates?

specifically how aspects of our environment contribute to overeating and lack of physical activity. To live healthy, it is important to understand how environmental settings and factors influence our lifestyles. Figure 2 summarizes the broad impact of physical, spiritual, social, intellectual, and emotional environments on personal health and wellness. Specific environmental strategies that you can use for each dimension of wellness are listed below:

- *Strategies for the physical environment.* Living healthy in our modern society can be challenging, but this can be overcome with good planning. Think ahead about ways to be sitting less during the day and how to add daily physical activity (e.g., commuting and walk breaks). Plan your meals and dining choices to ensure you can make healthier food choices. Avoid smoke-filled establishments, highly-polluted environments, and use of toxic products.

- *Strategies for the social and emotional environments.* Find a social community that accommodates your personal and family needs; get involved in community affairs, including those that affect the environment; build relationships with family and friends; provide support for others so that their support will be there for you when you need it; and use time-management strategies to help you allocate time for social interactions.

- *Strategies for the spiritual environment.* Pray, meditate, read spiritual materials, participate in spiritual discussions, find a place to worship, provide spiritual support for others, seek spiritual guidance from those with experience and expertise, keep a journal, experience nature, honor relationships, and help others.

- *Strategies for the intellectual environment.* Make decisions based on sound information, question simple solutions to complex problems, and seek environments that stimulate critical thinking.

Choose to live and work in places that support healthy living. Environmental factors are often out of a person's control. However, you do have some autonomy regarding where you choose to live and work. If physical activity is important to you, find a community with parks and playgrounds and accessible sidewalks, bike paths, jogging trails, swimming facilities, a gym, or health club. Avoid environments that have only fast food restaurants. Find a social environment that reinforces healthy lifestyles. If possible, work in businesses or settings that support healthy lifestyles. Ideally, the work environment should have adequate space, lighting, and freedom from pollution (tobacco smoke), as well as a healthy physical, social, spiritual, and intellectual environment. Considerable attention has been given recently to characteristics that define healthy work sites, communities, cities, and states. This is encouraging because the increased demand for healthy resources could lead to increased supply.

Being open to new experiences is important for optimal wellness.
©Vision SRL/Getty Images

Adopt and Maintain Healthy Lifestyles

Consider strategies for adopting healthy lifestyles. Statistics show that more than half of early deaths are caused by unhealthy lifestyles. For this reason, changing lifestyles has been our focus as we have emphasized "priority" healthy lifestyles, such as being regularly active, eating well, managing stress, avoiding destructive behaviors, and practicing safe sex, because they are factors over which we have some control, and if adopted, they have considerable impact on health, wellness, and fitness (see Figure 1). Being an informed consumer is another healthy lifestyle we have emphasized since it enables you to understand health information and take appropriate action. Other healthy lifestyles include adopting good health and safety habits and learning first aid. Examples of healthy lifestyles in these domains are highlighted in Table 2.

Consider the impact of your lifestyle on the health of the environment. The environment clearly influences your lifestyle, but your lifestyle can also have a damaging effect on the environment. Consider our use of fossil fuels. Burning fossil fuels has contributed to depletion of the ozone layer and the associated patterns of climate change. The changes in weather along with the pollution of our air and water compromise our agricultural systems, which in turn threatens our food and water supply. These are just a few examples of the complex ecological systems going on in the world. A number of promising strategies are being implemented to address these problems, including the use of alternative energy

Make it a priority to find ways to remain active throughout your life.
©Purestock/SuperStock

Table 2 ▶ Other Healthy Lifestyles

Lifestyle	Examples
Adopting good personal health habits. Many of these habits, important to optimal health, are considered to be elementary because they are often taught in school or in the home at an early age. In spite of their importance, many adults regularly fail to adopt these behaviors.	• Brush and floss teeth. • Bathe and wash hands regularly. • Get adequate sleep. • Take care of ears, eyes, and skin. • Limit exposure to loud sounds, including live and recorded music. • Limit sun exposure (e.g., wear protective clothing, hats, and sunglasses) and use sunscreen with high SPF to reduce exposure to ultraviolet rays from the sun.
Adopting good safety habits. Thousands of people die each year and thousands more suffer disabilities or problems that detract from good health and wellness. Not all accidents can be prevented, but we can adopt habits to reduce risk.	• *Automobile accidents.* Wear seat belts, avoid using the phone while driving, do not drink and drive, and do not drive aggressively. • *Water accidents.* Learn to swim, learn cardiopulmonary resuscitation (CPR), wear life jackets while boating, and do not drink while boating. • *Others.* Store guns safely, use smoke alarms, use ladders and electrical equipment safely, and maintain cars, bikes, and motorcycles properly.
Learning first aid. Many deaths could be prevented and the severity of injury could be reduced if those at the sites of emergencies were able to administer first aid.	• Learn CPR. New research shows that chest compression alone saves lives even without mouth-to-mouth breathing. • Learn the Heimlich maneuver to assist people who are choking. • Learn basic first aid.

sources to reduce our consumption of fossil fuels. While technology can solve some of the problems, we cannot completely heal the environment without major efforts from large segments of the population. Individually we can't change the world, but if each person makes small changes, we can together have a big impact. For example, individual efforts to use your car less, recycle, and use less paper can add up to larger changes in society.

Importance of Personal Actions and Interactions

Consider strategies for taking action and benefiting from personal interactions. The diagram in Figure 1 includes a box labeled "Personal actions and interactions" at the very top of the image. It is at the top for a reason—ultimately, it is what you do that counts. You can learn everything there is to know about health, wellness, and fitness, but if you do not take action and take advantage of your interactions with people and your environments, you will not benefit. As described in this Concept (and throughout this edition), your actions and interactions have a major influence on all aspects of wellness.

Commit to using this information to help plan your approaches for healthy living (see Table 3). People who plan are not only more likely to act, they are also more likely to act effectively and more proactively. Many people put off health and wellness, believing they will eventually be able to get control over their lives and their lifestyles. Delaying action will only make it harder to change in the future. It is much easier to maintain a healthy weight than it is to lose weight after it is gained. This applies to all aspects of healthy living. "Do not put off until tomorrow what you can do today." We've discussed information to help you create plans for healthy living, but the decision to follow them is up to you.

Consider your cognitions and emotions when planning strategies for action. Much of the information in this edition is designed to help you make good decisions about health, wellness, and fitness. Using the guidelines and your self-management skills can help you make good decisions. It is also important to consider your emotions when making decisions. Consider these guidelines:

- *Collect and evaluate information before you act.* Become informed before you make important decisions. Get information from reliable sources and consult with others you trust.

- *Emotions will influence certain decisions but should not detract from sound decision-making processes.* Fear and anger are two emotions that can affect your judgment and influence your ability to make decisions. Even love for another person can influence your actions. Get control of your emotions, or seek guidance from others you trust, before making important decisions in emotionally-charged situations.

- *Resist pressure to make quick decisions when there is no need to decide quickly.* Salespeople often press for a quick decision to get a sale. Take some time to think before making a quick decision that may be based on emotion rather than critical thinking. Of course, some decisions must be made when emotions are charged (e.g., medical care in an emergency), but, when possible, delaying a decision can be to your advantage.

- *Use stress-management techniques to help you gain control when you must make decisions in emotionally-charged situations.* Practice stress-management techniques so that you can use them effectively when needed.

- *Honor your beliefs and relationships.* Actions and interactions that are inconsistent with basic beliefs and that fail to honor important relationships can result in reduced quality of life.

Table 3 ▶ Actions and Interactions That Influence Wellness

Dimension of Wellness	Influential Factors
Physical wellness	Pursuing behaviors that are conducive to good physical health (being physically active and maintaining a healthy diet)
Social wellness	Being supportive of family, friends, and coworkers and practicing good communication skills
Emotional wellness	Balancing work and leisure and responding proactively to challenging or stressful situations
Intellectual wellness	Challenging yourself to continually learn and improve in your work and personal life
Spiritual wellness	Praying, meditating, or reflecting on life
Total wellness	Taking responsibility for your own health

Health is available to Everyone for a Lifetime, and it's Personal

Importance of Optimism

Optimism is a positive predictor of good physical health. This is the conclusion of a statistical review of 83 different studies on the topic. The analysis considered several physical health topics, including cardiovascular, immune system, and cancer conditions as well as chronic pain, pregnancy symptoms, and other physical symptoms. In all cases, optimism was a predictor of positive health outcomes. Being optimistic, by itself, is not a treatment or a cure for physical health symptoms. However, maintaining an optimistic outlook and applying the HELP philosophy ("Health is available to Everyone for a Lifetime, and it's Personal") can go a long way toward maintaining health, wellness, and fitness throughout life.

Are you an optimistic person? Do you think that optimism can play a role in your future health, wellness, and fitness?

criteria rather than comparative criteria. Adhering to the HELP philosophy can help you adopt a new way of thinking. This philosophy suggests that each person should use health (*H*) as the basis for making decisions rather than comparisons with others. This is something that everyone (*E*) can do for a lifetime (*L*). It allows each of us to set personal (*P*) goals that are realistic and possible to attain.

- *Allow for spontaneity.* The reliance on science we have emphasized can help you make good choices. But if you are to live life fully, you sometimes must allow yourself to be spontaneous. In doing so, the key is to be consistent with your personal philosophy so that your spontaneous actions will be enriching rather than a source of future regret.

- *Believe that you can make a difference.* As noted previously, you make your own choices. Though heredity and several other factors are out of your control, the choices that you make are yours. Believing that your actions make a difference is critical to taking action and making changes when necessary, allowing you to be healthy, well, and fit for a lifetime.

- *Seek help from others and provide support for others who need your help.* As already noted, support from friends, family, and significant others can be critical in helping you achieve health, wellness, and fitness. Get help. Do what you can to be there for others who need your help.

- *Consider using professional help.* Most colleges have health center programs that provide free, confidential assistance or referral. Many businesses have employee assistance programs (EAPs), providing counselors who will help you or your family members find ways to solve a particular problem. Other programs and support groups help with lifestyle changes. For example, most hospitals and many health organizations have hotlines that provide referral services for establishing healthy lifestyles.

Consider your personal beliefs and philosophy when making decisions. Though science can help you make good decisions and solve problems, most experts tell you that there is more to it than that. Your personal philosophy and beliefs play a role. The following are factors to consider:

- *Clarify your personal philosophy and consider a new way of thinking.* Health, wellness, and fitness are often subjective. Making comparisons to other people can result in setting personal standards impossible to achieve. For example, achieving the body fat level of a model seen on TV or performing like a professional athlete is not realistic for most of us. For this reason, the standards for health, wellness, and fitness in this edition are based on health

Having a belief that "you can" increases chances of adherence.
©Sam Edwards/Getty Images

Using Self-Management Skills

Learning and adopting self-management skills can predispose and enable you to adhere to lifelong healthy behaviors and reinforce the behaviors once they are acquired. You have learned about the different self-management skills that help you adopt healthy lifestyles. For your review, these self-management skills are listed in Table 4. Some skills are most useful to get you started (predisposing), others help you make the changes (enabling), and others help you maintain changes in behaviors (reinforcing). While each type of skill may be most influential at certain stages, *all* can be beneficial at any stage of change. For example, self-assessment is considered to be a predisposing factor because it provides you with the information about your

personal needs. However, self-assessment can also be valuable in reinforcing behavior by providing a positive indicator of progress. Another example is using social support, which is considered to be reinforcing because having the support of friends and family can help you stick with a health behavior (e.g., regular exercise, healthy eating). But social support can also help you get started in exercise (predisposing). Explanations of how to apply various self-management skills have been included throughout the "Using Self-Management Skills" sections, but the summary in Table 4 will help remind you of the relevance of each one for lifestyle change.

Self-management skills, like all skills, must be practiced to be used effectively. All skills are best acquired through good practice.

connect
VIDEO 5

Table 4 ▶ Self-Management Skills and Relevance to Lifestyle Change

Self-Management Skill	Relevance to Lifestyle Change
Predisposing Factors	
Overcoming Barriers	Adopting healthy lifestyles requires discipline, but you can learn to overcome barriers that make it difficult.
Building Confidence and Motivation	Focusing your efforts and progress can increase your confidence and motivation to change.
Balancing Attitudes	Adopting positive attitudes (and fighting negative ones) can increase the likelihood of making healthy changes.
Building Knowledge and Changing Beliefs	Distinguishing myths from facts can help with planning and behavior change.
Enabling Factors	
Goal-Setting Skills	Learning to set and follow reasonable goals can enable behavior change.
Self-Assessment Skills	Assessing your health, wellness, and fitness can help in determining needs and evaluating progress.
Self-Monitoring Skills	Learning to monitor your lifestyle behaviors can help you make healthier choices over time.
Self-Planning Skills	Following effective planning guidelines can increase your chances of being successful at behavior change.
Performance Skills	Applying and practicing various performance skills can increase your chances of success.
Coping Skills	Developing new ways of thinking can help you adapt to changing life circumstances.
Consumer Skills	Thinking critically about health, wellness, and fitness information can help you make better decisions.
Time-Managing Skills	Using time effectively can reduce stress and provide more time for physical activity and other healthy lifestyles.
Reinforcing Factors	
Using Social Support	Building strong support networks with friends and family members can help you adhere to and reinforce healthy habits.
Preventing Relapse	Preparing for challenges can increase your chance of overcoming them.

Good information, including good instruction with quality feedback, helps practice be effective. Many of the lab activities in this edition are aimed at helping you practice self-management skills so that you can improve and perfect them. However, if you don't practice them regularly, your skills will eventually deteriorate. For this reason, regular use and practice of the self-management skills are encouraged.

Formal steps for self-planning can become less formal with experience. Throughout this edition, we have presented a structured approach to self-planning that is designed to help you practice the various self-management skills required for effective planning (e.g., self-assessment,  goals setting, self-monitoring). It is important to learn this process, but it is likely that you will eventually adopt less formalized procedures on your own. Few of us will go through life doing formal fitness assessments every month, writing down goals weekly, or self-monitoring activity daily. However, the more a person does self-assessments, the more he or she is aware of personal health, wellness, and fitness status. This awareness reduces the need for frequent testing. For example, a person who does regular heart-rate monitoring knows when he or she is in the target zone without counting heart rate every minute. The same is true of other self-management skills. With experience, you can use the techniques less formally to manage your lifestyle in the future.

Building knowledge (a self-management skill) does not guarantee adherence to healthy behaviors, but it does provide the basis for making good decisions about future health behaviors. Throughout this edition, you have been provided with information that can be beneficial in making sound decisions about health, fitness, and wellness. But having the facts does not always lead to healthy decisions. For example, surveys consistently show that virtually all smokers know that tobacco use is unhealthy and leads to premature death. Yet people continue to start using tobacco, often at an early age and continue using throughout life. This example illustrates several important points. First, we sometimes make decisions at young ages, before we have all of the facts and when social and environmental factors have a larger impact on our decisions. We may know the facts, yet still not believe they "really will affect me." Second, when unhealthy behaviors are adopted, they are often very difficult to change. Finally, we know that behaviors can change. With the use of self-management skills, even addictive behaviors can be changed. For example, social support from friends, loved ones, and professionals can help people, even smokers, change their behavior.

It is our hope that you will use the information (and self-management skills) learned from *Concepts of Fitness and Wellness* to help you adopt and sustain healthy behaviors throughout your life. Adopting a healthy lifestyle can be challenging, but you can hopefully rely on the strategies presented here to gradually shift your lifestyles toward behaviors more conducive to good health. We also hope that you will use your self-management skills to become a diligent and literate health consumer, seeking out the best and most current information about health, wellness, and fitness. New information becomes available daily, and being aware is critical to continuing to make sound decisions in the future.

Strategies for Action: Lab Information

Doing a self-assessment of the factors that influence health, wellness, and fitness can identify needs for lifestyle change. The questionnaire in Lab 25A includes perceptions of your needs related to each of the 5 determinants described in Figure 1. An honest assessment of these items will help you determine factors that might be most important to change.

Following sound program planning skills can help you prepare a plan. In Lab 25B, you will have the opportunity to use the information gained from the self-assessment in Lab 25A to create a personal plan for appropriate changes aimed at improving health, wellness, and fitness. The lab guides you through appropriate steps to increase your chance of success.

Using the six steps in program planning can help you to prepare a comprehensive personal physical activity plan. In previous Concepts, you have had the opportunity to prepare plans for each of the different types of physical activity in the activity pyramid. Lab 25C provides you with the opportunity to use the self-management skills used in preparing these plans to provide a comprehensive plan for all types of physical activity.

Suggested Resources and Readings

The websites for the following sources can be accessed by searching online for the organization, program, or title listed. Specific scientific references are available at the end of this edition of *Concepts of Fitness and Wellness*.

- American College Health Association. Mental Health resources.
- American College of Sports Medicine. American Fitness Index.
- Centers for Disease Control and Prevention. (2016, February 18). 1 in 3 adults don't get enough sleep (online article).
- Centers for Disease Control and Prevention. (2017, April 18). Direct to consumer genetic testing–Think before you spit (online resource).
- Feibus, M. (2017, December 7). New health trackers warn of heart-attack risks, discretely. *USA Today.*
- Gallup-Sharecare. Well-Being Index.
- IQVIA Institute. The Growing Value of Digital Health (pdf).
- Painter, K. (2016, December 19). Don't want to die before your time? Get a female doctor. *USA Today.*
- Painter, K. (2017, November 29). "Scary" prediction for U.S. kids: 57% of youth could be obese by age 35. *USA Today.*
- Robert Wood Johnson Foundation. County Health Rankings & Roadmaps.
- Robert Wood Johnson Foundation. (2015, July 16). New research: Children with strong social skills in kindergarten more likely to thrive as adults.
- Stobbe, M. (2017, November 21). Nearly half of US cancer deaths blamed on unhealthy behavior. *U.S. News & World Report.*
- Trust for America's Health. Blueprint for a Healthier America.

Lab 25A Assessing Factors That Influence Health, Wellness, and Fitness

Name	Section	Date

Purpose: To assess the factors that relate to health, wellness, and fitness.

Chart 1 Assessment Questionnaire: Factors That Influence Health, Wellness, and Fitness

Factor	Very True	Somewhat True	Not True At All	Score
Heredity				
1. I have checked my family history for medical problems.	③	②	①	
2. I have taken steps to overcome hereditary predispositions.	③	②	①	
			Heredity Score =	
Health Care				
3. I have health insurance.	③	②	①	
4. I get regular medical exams and have my own doctor.	③	②	①	
5. I get treatment early, rather than waiting until problems get serious	③	②	①	
6. I carefully investigate my health problems before making decisions.	③	②	①	
			Health-Care Score =	
Environment				
7. My physical environment is healthy.	③	②	①	
8. My social environment is healthy.	③	②	①	
9. My spiritual environment is healthy.	③	②	①	
10. My intellectual environment is healthy.	③	②	①	
11. My work environment is healthy.	③	②	①	
12. My environment fosters healthy lifestyles.	③	②	①	
			Environment Score =	
Lifestyles				
13. I am physically active on a regular basis.	③	②	①	
14. I eat well.	③	②	①	
15. I use effective techniques for managing stress.	③	②	①	
16. I avoid destructive behaviors.	③	②	①	
17. I practice safe sex.	③	②	①	
18. I manage my time effectively.	③	②	①	
19. I evaluate information carefully and am an informed consumer.	③	②	①	
20. My personal health habits are good.	③	②	①	
21. My safety habits are good.	③	②	①	
22. I know first aid and can use it if needed.	③	②	①	
			Lifestyles Score =	
Personal Actions and Interactions				
23. I collect and evaluate information before I act.	③	②	①	
24. I plan before I take action.	③	②	①	
25. I am good about taking action when I know it is good for me.	③	②	①	
26. I honor my beliefs and relationships.	③	②	①	
27. I seek help when I need it.	③	②	①	
			Personal Actions/Interactions Score =	

Procedures

1. Answer each of the questions in Chart 1. Consider the information in this Concept as you answer each question. The five factors assessed in the questionnaire are from Figure 1.
2. Calculate the scores for heredity (sum items 1 and 2), health care (sum items 3–6), environment (sum items 7–12), lifestyles (sum items 13–22), and personal actions/interactions (sum items 23–27).
3. Determine ratings for each of the scores using the Rating Chart.
4. Record your scores and ratings in the Results chart. Record your comments in the Conclusions and Implications section.

Results

Factor	Score	Rating
Heredity		
Health care		
Environment		
Lifestyles		
Personal Actions/Interactions		

Rating Chart

Factor	Healthy	Marginal	Needs Attention
Heredity	6	4–5	Below 4
Health care	11–12	9–10	Below 9
Environment	16–18	13–15	Below 13
Lifestyles	26–30	20–25	Below 20
Personal Actions/ Interactions	13–15	10–12	Below 10

Conclusions and Implications

1. In the space below, discuss your scores for the five factors (sums of several questions) identified in Chart 1. Use several sentences to identify specific areas that need attention and changes that you could make to improve.

2. For any individual item on Chart 1, a score of 1 is considered low. You might have a high score on a set of questions and still have a low score in one area that indicates a need for attention. In several sentences, discuss actions you could take to make changes related to individual questions.

Lab 25B Planning for Improved Health, Wellness, and Fitness

Name	**Section**	**Date**

Purpose: To plan to make changes in areas that can most contribute to improved health, wellness, and fitness.

Procedures

1. Experts agree that it is best not to make too many changes all at once. Focusing attention on one or two things at a time will produce better results. Based on your assessments made in Lab 25A, select two areas in which you would like to make changes. Choose one from the list related to health care and environment and one related to lifestyle change. Place a check by those areas in Chart 1 in the Results section. Because Lab 25C is devoted to physical activity, it is not included in the list. You may want to make additional copies of this lab for use in making other changes in the future.
2. Use Chart 2 to determine your stage of change for the changes you have identified. Since you have identified these as an area of need, it is unlikely that you would identify the stage of maintenance. If you are at maintenance, you can select a different area of change that would be more useful.
3. In the appropriate locations, record the change you want to make related to your environment or health care. State your reasons, your specific goal(s), your written statement of the plan for change, and a statement about how you will self-monitor and evaluate the effectiveness of the changes made. In Chart 3, record similar information for the lifestyle change you identified.

Results

Chart 1

Check one in each column.

Area of Change	✓	Area of Change	✓
Health insurance		Eating well	
Medical checkups		Managing stress	
Doctor selection		Avoiding destructive habits	
Physical environment		Practicing safe sex	
Social environment		Managing time	
Spiritual environment		Becoming a better consumer	
Intellectual environment		Improving health habits	
Work environment		Improving safety habits	
Environment for lifestyles		Learning first aid	

Chart 2

List the two areas of change identified in Chart 1. Make a rating using the following diagram.

Identified Area of Change	Stage of Change Rating
1.	
2.	

Maintenance "Regular participation for at least 6 months"

Action "Regular participation but less than 6 months"

Preparation "Some participation but not on a regular basis"

Contemplation "Thinking about doing this but have not done it yet"

Precontemplation "Don't want to change"

Note: Some of the areas identified in this lab relate to personal information. It is appropriate not to divulge personal information to others (including your instructor) if you choose not to. For this reason, you may choose not to address certain problems in this lab. You are encouraged to take steps to make changes independent of this assignment and to consult privately with your instructor to get assistance.

Chart 3 Making Changes for Improved Health, Wellness, and Fitness

Describe First Area of Change (from Chart 1)	Describe Second Area of Change (from Chart 1)
Step 1: State Reasons for Making Change	**Step 1: State Reasons for Making Change**
Step 2: Do Self-Assessment of Need for Change List your stage from Chart 2.	**Step 2: Do Self-Assessment of Need for Change** List your stage from Chart 2.
Step 3: State Your Specific Goals for Change State several specific and realistic goals.	**Step 3: State Your Specific Goals for Change** State several specific and realistic goals.
Step 4: Identify Activities or Actions for Change List specific activities you will do or actions you will take to meet your goals.	**Step 4: Identify Activities or Actions for Change** List specific activities you will do or actions you will take to meet your goals.

Step 5: Write a Plan; Include a Timetable
Expected start date:

Expected finish date:

Mon.	Tue.	Wed.	Th.	Fri.	Sat.	Sun.

Location: Where will you do the plan?

Step 6: Evaluate Your Plan
How will you self-monitor and evaluate to determine if the plan is working?

Step 5: Write a Plan; Include a Timetable
Expected start date:

Expected finish date:

Mon.	Tue.	Wed.	Th.	Fri.	Sat.	Sun.

Location: Where will you do the plan?

Step 6: Evaluate Your Plan
How will you self-monitor and evaluate to determine if the plan is working?

Lab 25C Planning Your Personal Physical Activity Program

Name	**Section**	**Date**

Purpose: To establish a comprehensive plan of lifestyle physical activity and to self-monitor progress in your plan. (*Note:* You may want to reread the Concept on planning for physical activity before completing this lab.)

Procedures

Step 1. Establish Your Reasons

In the spaces provided below, list several of your principal reasons for doing a comprehensive activity plan.

1.

2.

3.

4.

5.

6.

Step 2. Identify Your Needs Using Fitness Self-Assessments and Ratings of Stage of Change for Various Activities

In Chart 1, rate your fitness by placing an X over the circle by the appropriate rating for each part of fitness. Use your results obtained from previous labs or perform the self-assessments again to determine your ratings. If you took more than one self-assessment for one component of physical fitness, select the rating that you think best describes your true fitness for that fitness component. If you were unable to do a self-assessment for some reason, check the "No Results" circle.

Chart 1 Rating for Self-Assessments

	Rating				
Health-Related Fitness Tests	**High-Performance Zone**	**Good Fitness Zone**	**Marginal Fitness Zone**	**Low Fitness Zone**	**No Results**
1. Cardiorespiratory: walking test (Chart 1, page 125)	◯	◯	◯	◯	◯
2. Cardiorespiratory: step test (Chart 2, page 125)	◯	◯	◯	◯	◯
3. Cardiorespiratory: bicycle test (Chart 5, page 127)	◯	◯	◯	◯	◯
4. Cardiorespiratory: 12-minute run (Chart 6, page 127)	◯	◯	◯	◯	◯
5. Cardiorespiratory: swim test (Chart 7, page 128)	◯	◯	◯	◯	◯
6. Strength: isometric grip (Chart 3, page 174)	◯	◯	◯	◯	◯
7. Strength: 1RM upper body (Chart 2, page 172)	◯	◯	◯	◯	◯
8. Strength: 1RM lower body (Chart 2, page 172)	◯	◯	◯	◯	◯
9. Muscular endurance: curl-up (Chart 4, page 174)	◯	◯	◯	◯	◯
10. Muscular endurance: 90-degree push-up (Chart 4, page 174)	◯	◯	◯	◯	◯
11. Muscular endurance: flexed-arm support (Chart 5, page 174)	◯	◯	◯	◯	◯

Chart 1 Rating for Self-Assessments, *continued*

Health-Related Fitness Tests	Rating				
	High-Performance Zone	Good Fitness Zone	Marginal Fitness Zone	Low Fitness Zone	No Results
12. Power: vertical jump (Chart 6, page 174)	◯	◯	◯	◯	◯
13. Power: medicine ball throw (Chart 6, page 174)	◯	◯	◯	◯	◯
14. Flexibility: sit-and-reach test (Chart 1, page 210)	◯	◯	◯	◯	◯
15. Flexibility: shoulder flexibility (Chart 1, page 210)	◯	◯	◯	◯	◯
16. Flexibility: hamstring/hip flexibility (Chart 1, page 210)	◯	◯	◯	◯	◯
17. Flexibility: trunk rotation (Chart 1, page 210)	◯	◯	◯	◯	◯
18. Fitness rating: skinfold (Chart 1, page 286–291)	◯	◯	◯	◯	◯
19. Body Mass Index (Chart 7, page 292–293)					

Skill-Related Fitness and Other Self-Assessments	Excellent	Very Good or Good	Fair	Poor	No Results
1. Fitness of the back (Chart 2, page 246)	◯	◯	◯	◯	◯
2. Posture (Chart 2, page 247)	◯	◯	◯	◯	◯
3. Agility (Chart 1, page 265)	◯	◯	◯	◯	◯
4. Balance (Chart 2, page 266)	◯	◯	◯	◯	◯
5. Coordination (Chart 3, page 266)	◯	◯	◯	◯	◯
6. Reaction time (Chart 4, page 267)	◯	◯	◯	◯	◯
7. Speed (Chart 5, page 268)	◯	◯	◯	◯	◯

Summarize Your Fitness Ratings Using the Results Above	High-Performance Zone	Good Fitness Zone	Marginal Fitness Zone	Low Fitness Zone	No Results
Cardiorespiratory	◯	◯	◯	◯	◯
Flexibility	◯	◯	◯	◯	◯
Strength	◯	◯	◯	◯	◯
Muscular endurance	◯	◯	◯	◯	◯
Body fatness	◯	◯	◯	◯	◯
Power	◯	◯	◯	◯	◯

	Excellent	Very Good or Good	Fair	Poor	No Results
Skill-related fitness	◯	◯	◯	◯	◯
Posture and fitness of the back	◯	◯	◯	◯	◯

Rate your stage of change for each of the different types of activities from the physical activity pyramid. Place an X over the circle beside the stage that best represents your behavior for each of the five types of activity in the lower three levels of the pyramid. A description of the various stages is provided below to help you make your ratings.

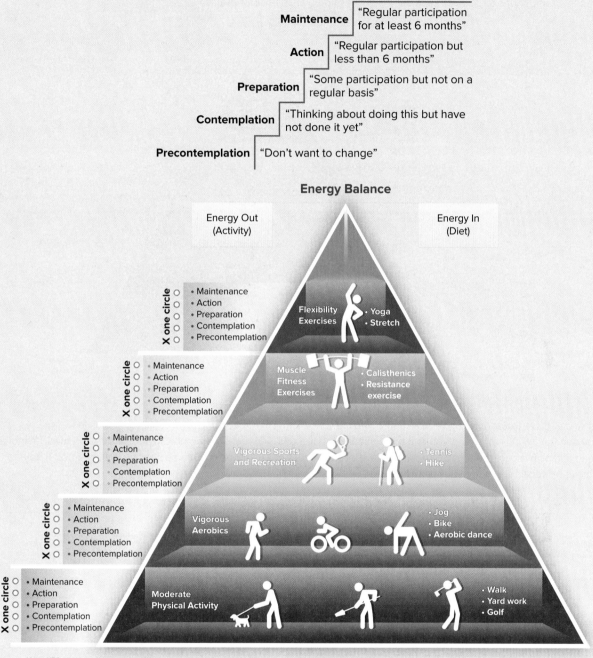

Maintenance — "Regular participation for at least 6 months"

Action — "Regular participation but less than 6 months"

Preparation — "Some participation but not on a regular basis"

Contemplation — "Thinking about doing this but have not done it yet"

Precontemplation — "Don't want to change"

Energy Balance

Energy Out (Activity)

Energy In (Diet)

X one circle
• Maintenance
• Action
• Preparation
• Contemplation
• Precontemplation

Flexibility Exercises — • Yoga • Stretch

X one circle
• Maintenance
• Action
• Preparation
• Contemplation
• Precontemplation

Muscle Fitness Exercises — • Calisthenics • Resistance exercise

X one circle
• Maintenance
• Action
• Preparation
• Contemplation
• Precontemplation

Vigorous Sports and Recreation — • Tennis • Hike

X one circle
• Maintenance
• Action
• Preparation
• Contemplation
• Precontemplation

Vigorous Aerobics — • Jog • Bike • Aerobic dance

X one circle
• Maintenance
• Action
• Preparation
• Contemplation
• Precontemplation

Moderate Physical Activity — • Walk • Yard work • Golf

Note: *150 minutes of moderate or 75 minutes of vigorous activity per week is recommended; moderate and vigorous activity can be combined to meet guidelines.

Avoid Inactivity

Source: Charles B. Corbin.

In step 1, you wrote down some general reasons for developing your physical activity plan. Setting goals requires more specific statements of goals that are realistic and achievable. For people who are at the contemplation or preparation stage for a specific type of activity, it is recommended that you write only short-term physical activity goals (no more than 4 weeks). Those at the action or maintenance level may choose short-term goals to start with, or if you have a good history of adherence, choose long-term goals (longer than 4 weeks). Precontemplators are not considered because they would not be doing this activity.

Step 3. Set Specific Goals

Chart 2 Setting Goals

Physical Activity Goals. Place an X over the appropriate circle for the number of days and weeks for each type of activity. Write the number of exercises or minutes of activities you plan in each of the five areas.

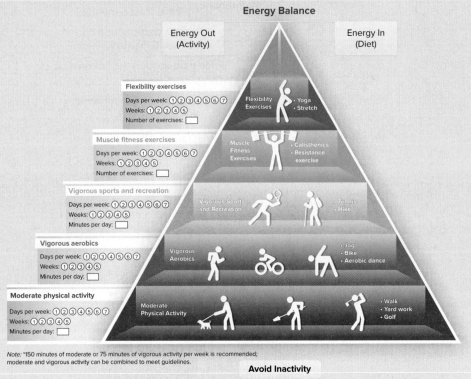

Energy Balance

Energy Out (Activity)

Energy In (Diet)

Flexibility exercises
Days per week: ① ② ③ ④ ⑤ ⑥ ⑦
Weeks: ① ② ③ ④ ⑤
Number of exercises: ☐

Muscle fitness exercises
Days per week: ① ② ③ ④ ⑤ ⑥ ⑦
Weeks: ① ② ③ ④ ⑤
Number of exercises: ☐

Vigorous sports and recreation
Days per week: ① ② ③ ④ ⑤ ⑥ ⑦
Weeks: ① ② ③ ④ ⑤
Minutes per day: ☐

Vigorous aerobics
Days per week: ① ② ③ ④ ⑤ ⑥ ⑦
Weeks: ① ② ③ ④ ⑤
Minutes per day: ☐

Moderate physical activity
Days per week: ① ② ③ ④ ⑤ ⑥ ⑦
Weeks: ① ② ③ ④ ⑤
Minutes per day: ☐

Flexibility Exercises • Yoga • Stretch

Muscle Fitness Exercises • Calisthenics • Resistance exercise

Vigorous Sports and Recreation • Tennis • Hike

Vigorous Aerobics • Jog • Bike • Aerobic dance

Moderate Physical Activity • Walk • Yard work • Golf

Note: *150 minutes of moderate or 75 minutes of vigorous activity per week is recommended; moderate and vigorous activity can be combined to meet guidelines.

Avoid Inactivity

Source: Charles B. Corbin.

Physical Fitness Goals (for People at Action or Maintenance Only). Write specific physical fitness goals in the spaces provided below. Indicate when you expect to accomplish the goal (in weeks). Examples include improving the 12-minute run to a specific score, being able to perform a specific number of push-ups, attaining a specific BMI, and being able to achieve a specific score on a flexibility test.

Part of Fitness	Description of Specific Performance	Weeks to Goal

Step 4. Select Activities

In Chart 3, indicate the specific activities you plan to perform from each area of the physical activity pyramid. If the activity you expect to perform is listed, note the number of minutes or reps/sets you plan to perform. If the activity you want to perform is not listed, write the name of the activity or exercise in the space designated as "Other." For moderate activities, active aerobics, and active sports and recreation, indicate the length of time the activity will be performed each day. For flexibility, muscle fitness exercises, and exercises for back and neck, indicate the number of repetitions for each exercise.

Chart 3 Lifetime Physical Activity Selections

✓	Moderate Activities	Min/Day	✓	Active Aerobics	Min/Day	✓	Active Sports and Recreation	Min./Day
	Active housework			Aerobic exercise machines			Basketball	
	Bicycling to work or store			Bicycling			Bowling	
	Gardening			Circuit training or calisthenics			Golf	
	Occupational activity			Dance or step aerobics			Karate/judo	
	Social dancing			Hiking or backpacking			Mountain climbing	
	Walking			Jogging or running (or walking)			Racquetball	
	Wheeling in wheelchair			Skating/cross-country skiing			Skating	
	Yard work			Swimming			Softball	
	Other:			Water activity			Skiing	
	Other:			Other:			Soccer	
	Other:			Other:			Volleyball	
	Other:			Other:			Other:	
	Other:			Other:			Other:	
	Other:			Other:			Other:	
	Other:			Other:			Other:	

✓	Flexibility Exercises	Reps/Sets	✓	Muscle Fitness Exercises	Reps/Sets	✓	Exercises for Back and Neck	Reps/Sets
	Calf stretch			Bench or seated press			Back saver stretch	
	Hip and thigh stretch			Biceps curl			Single knee to chest	
	Groin stretch			Triceps curl			Spine twist	
	Hamstring stretch			Lat pull-down			Hip/thigh stretch	
	Back stretch (leg hug)			Seated rowing			Cobra/child's pose	
	Trunk twist			Wrist curl			Bridge variation	
	Pectoral stretch			Knee extension			Superman variation	
	Arm hug stretch			Side leg raise			Abdominal brace	
	Overhead arm stretch			Half squat			Neck rotation	
	Other:			Lunge			Isometric neck exercise	
	Other:			Push-up			Chin tuck	
	Other:			Crunch or reverse curl			Trapezius stretch	
	Other:			Plyometrics			Other:	
	Other:			Other:			Other:	
	Other:			Other:			Other:	

Step 5. Prepare a Written Plan

In Chart 4, place a check in the shaded boxes for each activity you will perform for each day you will do it. Indicate the time of day you expect to perform the activity or exercise (Example: 7:30 to 8 A.M. or 6 to 6:30 P.M.). In the spaces labeled "Warm-Up Exercises" and "Cool-Down Exercises," check the warm-up and cool-down exercises you expect to perform. Indicate the number of reps you will use for each exercise.

Chart 4 My Physical Activity Plan

✓	Monday	Time	✓	Tuesday	Time	✓	Wednesday	Time
	Moderate activity			Moderate activity			Moderate activity	
	Active aerobics			Active aerobics			Active aerobics	
	Active sports/rec.			Active sports/rec.			Active sports/rec.	
	Flexibility exercises*			Flexibility exercises*			Flexibility exercises*	
	Muscle fitness exercises*			Muscle fitness exercises*			Muscle fitness exercises*	
	Back/neck exercises*			Back/neck exercises*			Back/neck exercises*	
	Warm-up exercises			Warm-up exercises			Warm-up exercises	
	Other:			Other:			Other:	

✓	Thursday	Time	✓	Friday	Time	✓	Saturday	Time
	Moderate activity			Moderate activity			Moderate activity	
	Active aerobics			Active aerobics			Active aerobics	
	Active sports/rec.			Active sports/rec.			Active sports/rec.	
	Flexibility exercises*			Flexibility exercises*			Flexibility exercises*	
	Muscle fitness exercises*			Muscle fitness exercises*			Muscle fitness exercises*	
	Back/neck exercises*			Back/neck exercises*			Back/neck exercises*	
	Warm-up exercises			Warm-up exercises			Warm-up exercises	
	Other:			Other:			Other:	

✓	Sunday	Time	✓	Warm-Up Exercises	Reps	✓	Cool-Down Exercises	Reps
	Moderate activity			Walk or jog			Walk or jog	
	Active aerobics			Grapevine			Calf stretch	
	Active sports/rec.			Knee stride and reach			Hamstring stretch	
	Flexibility exercises*			High skip and reach			Leg hug	
	Muscle fitness exercises*			Inchworm			Sitting side stretch	
	Back/neck exercises*			Calf stretch or hamstring stretch			Zipper	
	Warm-up exercises			Leg hug or seated side stretch			Other:	
	Other:			Other:			Other:	

*Perform the specific exercises you checked in Chart 3.

Step 6. Keep Records of Progress and Evaluate Your Plan

Make copies of Chart 4 (one for each week that you plan to keep records). Each day, make a check by the activities you actually performed. Include the times when you did the activities in your plan. Periodically check your goals to see if they have been accomplished. At some point, it will be necessary to reestablish your goals and create a revised activity plan.

Results

After performing your plan for a specific period of time, answer the question in the space provided.

How long have you been performing the plan? Please provide a short statement about your previous experience.

Conclusions and Implications

1. In several sentences, discuss your adherence to the plan. Have you been able to stick with the plan? If so, do you think it is a plan you can do for a lifetime? If not, why do you think you are unable to do your plan?

2. In several sentences, discuss how you might modify your plan in the future.

3. In several sentences, discuss your goals for your program. Do you think you will meet your goals? Why or why not?

Appendix A
Metric Conversion Charts

Chart 1 Traditional/Metric Measurement Conversions

	Metric to Traditional	Traditional to Metric
Length	centimeters to inches: cm × .39 = in	inches to centimeters: in × 2.54 = cm
	meters to feet: m × 3.3 = ft	feet to meters: ft × .3048 = m
	m to yards: m × 1.09 = yd	yards to meters: yd × .92 = m
	kilometers to miles: km × .6 = mi	miles to kilometers: mi × 1.6 = km
Weight (Mass)	grams to ounces: g × .0352 = oz	ounces to grams: oz × 28.41 = g
	kilograms to pounds: kg × 2.2 = lb	pounds to kilograms: lb × .45 = kg
Volume	milliliters to fluid ounces: ml × .03 = fl oz	fluid ounces to milliliters: fl oz × 29.573 = ml
	liters to quarts: l × 1.06 = qt	quarts to liters: qt × .95 = l
	liters to gallons: l × .264 = gal	gallons to liters: gal × 3.8 = l

Chart 2 Isometric Strength Rating Scale (kg)—page 174

	Men			Women		
Classification	Left Grip	Right Grip	Total Score	Left Grip	Right Grip	Total Score
High-performance zone	57+	61+	118+	34+	39+	73+
Good fitness zone	45–56	50–60	95–117	27–33	32–38	59–72
Marginal fitness zone	41–44	43–49	84–94	20–26	23–31	43–58
Low fitness zone	<41	<43	<84	<20	<23	<43

Suitable for use by young adults between 18 and 30 years of age. After 30, an adjustment of .5 to 1 percent per year is appropriate because some loss of muscle tissue typically occurs as you grow older.

Chart 3 Rating Scale for Power—page 174

	Vertical Jump (centimeters)		Medicine Ball Throw (centimeters)	
Classification	Men	Women	Men	Women
High-performance zone	65+	60+	472+	307+
Good fitness zone	42–64	37–59	434–471	281–306
Marginal fitness zone	32–41	27–36	391–433	256–280
Low fitness zone	31 or less	26 or less	390 or less	255 or less

Chart 4 Reaction Time Rating Scale—page 267

Classification	Score in Inches	Score in Centimeters
Excellent	>21	>52
Very good	19–21	48–52
Good	16–18 ¾	41–47
Fair	13–15 ¾	33–40
Poor	<13	<33

Chart 5 Speed Rating Scale—page 268

	Men		Women	
Classification	Yards	Meters	Yards	Meters
Excellent	24+	22+	22+	20+
Very good	22–23	20–21.9	20–21	18–19.9
Good	18–21	16.5–19.9	16–19	14.5–17.9
Fair	16–17	14.5–16.4	14–15	13–14.4
Poor	<16	<14.5	<14	<13

Appendix B

Calories of Protein, Carbohydrates, and Fats in Foods

Food Choice	Total Calories	Protein Calories	Carbohydrate Calories	Fat Calories
Breakfast				
Scrambled egg (1 lg.)	111	29	7	75
Fried egg (1 lg.)	99	26	1	72
Pancake (1-6 inch)	146	19	67	58
Syrup (1 T)	60	0	60	0
French toast (1 slice)	180	23	49	108
Waffle (7-inch)	245	28	100	117
Biscuit (medium)	104	8	52	44
Bran muffin (medium)	104	11	63	31
White toast (1 slice)	68	9	52	7
Wheat toast (1 slice)	67	14	52	6
Peanut butter (1 T)	94	15	11	68
Yogurt (8 oz plain)	227	39	161	27
Orange juice (8 oz)	114	8	100	6
Apple juice (8 oz)	117	1	116	0
Soft drink (12 oz)	144	0	144	0
Bacon (2 slices)	86	15	2	70
Sausage (1 link)	141	11	0	130
Sausage (1 patty)	284	23	0	261
Grits (8 oz)	125	11	110	4
Hash browns (8 oz)	355	18	178	159
French fries (reg.)	239	12	115	112
Donut, cake	125	4	61	60
Donut, glazed	164	8	87	69
Sweet roll	317	22	136	159
Cake (medium slice)	274	14	175	85
Ice cream (8 oz)	257	15	108	134
Cream cheese (T)	52	4	1	47
Jelly (T)	49	0	49	0
Jam (T)	54	0	54	0
Coffee (cup)	0	0	0	0
Tea (cup)	0	0	0	0
Cream (T)	32	2	2	28
Sugar (t)	15	0	15	0
Corn flakes (8 oz)	97	8	87	2
Wheat flakes (8 oz)	106	12	90	4
Oatmeal (8 oz)	132	19	92	21
Strawberries (8 oz)	55	4	46	5
Orange (medium)	64	6	57	1
Apple (medium)	96	1	86	9
Banana (medium)	101	4	95	2
Cantaloupe (half)	82	7	73	2
Grapefruit (half)	40	2	37	1
Custard pie (slice)	285	20	188	77
Fruit pie (slice)	350	14	259	77
Fritter (medium)	132	11	54	67
Skim milk (8 oz)	88	36	52	0
Whole milk (8 oz)	159	33	48	78
Butter (pat)	36	0	0	36
Margarine (pat)	36	0	0	36
Lunch				
Hamburger (reg. FF)	255	48	120	89
Cheeseburger (reg. FF)	307	61	120	126
Doubleburger (FF)	563	101	163	299
¼ lb burger (FF)	427	73	137	217
Doublecheese burger (FF)	670	174	134	362
Doublecheese baconburger (FF)	724	138	174	340
Hot dog (FF)	214	36	54	124
Chili dog (FF)	320	51	90	179
Pizza, cheese (slice FF)	290	116	116	58
Pizza, meat (slice FF)	360	126	126	108
Pizza, everything (slice FF)	510	179	173	158
Sandwich, roast beef (FF)	350	88	126	137
Sandwich, bologna	313	44	106	163
Sandwich, bologna-cheese	428	69	158	201
Sandwich, ham-cheese (FF)	380	91	133	156
Sandwich, peanut butter	281	39	118	124
Sandwich, PB and jelly	330	40	168	122
Sandwich, egg salad	330	40	109	181
Sandwich, tuna salad	390	101	109	180
Sandwich, fish (FF)	432	56	147	229
French fries (reg. FF)	239	12	115	112
French fries (lg. FF)	406	20	195	191
Onion rings (reg. FF)	274	14	112	148
Chili (8 oz)	260	49	62	148
Bean soup (8 oz)	355	67	181	107
Beef noodle soup (8 oz)	140	32	59	49
Tomato soup (8 oz)	180	14	121	45
Vegetable soup (8 oz)	160	21	107	32
Small salad, plain	37	6	27	4
Small salad, French dressing	152	8	50	94
Small salad, Italian dressing	162	8	28	126
Small salad, bleu cheese	184	13	28	143
Potato salad (8 oz)	248	27	159	62

The principal reference for the calculation of values used in this appendix was the *Nutritive Value* of Foods, published by the United States Department of Agriculture, Washington, DC, Home and Gardens Bulletin, No. 72, although other published sources were consulted, including Jacobson, M., & Fritschner, S. (1986). *The fast-food guide*. New York: Workman.

Notes:
1. FF by a food indicates that it is typical of a food served in a fast food restaurant.
2. Your portions of foods may be larger or smaller than those listed here. For this reason, you may wish to select a food more than once (e.g., two hamburgers) or select only a portion of a serving (i.e., divide the calories in half for a half portion).
3. An ounce equals 28.35 grams.
4. T = tablespoon and t = teaspoon.

Food Choice	Total Calories	Protein Calories	Carbohydrate Calories	Fat Calories
Cole slaw (8 oz)	180	0	25	155
Macaroni and cheese (8 oz)	230	37	103	90
Beef taco (FF)	186	59	56	71
Bean burrito (FF)	343	45	192	106
Meat burrito (FF)	466	158	196	112
Mexican rice (FF)	213	17	160	36
Mexican beans (FF)	168	42	82	44
Fried chicken breast (FF)	436	262	13	161
Broiled chicken breast	284	224	0	60
Broiled fish	228	82	32	114
Fish stick (1 stick FF)	50	18	8	24
Fried egg	99	26	1	72
Donut	125	4	61	60
Potato chips (small bag)	115	3	39	73
Soft drink (12 oz)	144	0	144	0
Apple juice (8 oz)	117	1	116	0
Skim milk (8 oz)	88	36	52	0
Whole milk (8 oz)	159	33	48	78
Diet drink (12 oz)	0	0	0	0
Mustard (t)	4	0	4	0
Catsup (t)	6	0	6	0
Mayonnaise (T)	100	0	0	100
Fruit pie	350	14	259	77
Cheesecake (slice)	400	56	132	212
Ice cream (8 oz)	257	15	108	134
Coffee (8 oz)	0	0	0	0
Tea (8 oz)	0	0	0	0
Dinner				
Hamburger (reg. FF)	255	48	120	89
Cheeseburger (reg. FF)	307	61	120	126
Doubleburger (FF)	563	101	163	299
¼ lb burger (FF)	427	73	137	217
Doublecheese burger (FF)	670	174	134	362
Doublecheese baconburger (FF)	724	138	174	412
Hot dog (FF)	214	36	54	124
Chili dog (FF)	320	51	90	179
Pizza, cheese (slice FF)	290	116	116	58
Pizza, meat (slice FF)	360	126	126	108
Pizza, everything (slice FF)	510	179	173	158
Steak (8 oz)	880	290	0	590
French fried shrimp (6 oz)	360	133	68	158
Roast beef (8 oz)	440	268	0	172
Liver (8 oz)	520	250	52	218
Corned beef (8 oz)	493	242	0	251
Meat loaf (8 oz)	711	228	35	448
Ham (8 oz)	540	178	0	362
Spaghetti, no meat (13 oz)	400	56	220	124
Spaghetti, meat (13 oz)	500	115	230	155
Baked potato (medium)	90	12	78	0
Cooked carrots (8 oz)	71	12	59	0
Cooked spinach (8 oz)	50	18	18	14
Corn (1 ear)	70	10	52	8
Cooked green beans (8 oz)	54	11	43	0
Cooked broccoli (8 oz)	60	19	26	15
Cooked cabbage	47	12	35	0
French fries (reg. FF)	239	12	115	112
French fries (lg. FF)	406	20	195	191
Onion rings (reg. FF)	274	14	112	148
Chili (8 oz)	260	49	62	148
Small salad, plain	37	6	27	4
Small salad, French dressing	152	8	50	94
Small salad, Italian dressing	162	8	28	126
Small salad, bleu cheese	184	13	28	143
Potato salad (8 oz)	248	27	159	62

Food Choice	Total Calories	Protein Calories	Carbohydrate Calories	Fat Calories
Cole slaw (8 oz)	180	0	25	155
Macaroni and cheese (8 oz)	230	37	103	90
Beef Taco (FF)	186	59	56	71
Bean burrito (FF)	343	45	192	106
Meat burrito (FF)	466	158	196	112
Mexican rice (FF)	213	17	160	36
Mexican beans (FF)	168	42	82	44
Fried chicken breast (FF)	436	262	13	161
Broiled chicken breast	284	224	0	60
Broiled fish	228	82	32	114
Fish stick (1 stick FF)	50	18	8	24
Soft drink (12 oz)	144	0	144	0
Apple juice (8 oz)	117	1	116	0
Skim milk (8 oz)	88	36	52	0
Whole milk (8 oz)	159	33	48	78
Diet drink (12 oz)	0	0	0	0
Mustard (t)	4	0	4	0
Catsup (t)	6	0	6	0
Mayonnaise (T)	100	0	0	100
Fruit pie (slice)	350	14	259	77
Cheesecake (slice)	400	56	132	212
Ice cream (8 oz)	257	15	108	134
Custard pie (slice)	285	20	188	77
Cake (slice)	274	14	175	85
Snacks				
Peanut butter (1 T)	94	15	11	68
Yogurt (8 oz plain)	227	39	161	27
Orange juice (8 oz)	114	8	100	6
Apple juice (8 oz)	117	1	116	0
Soft drink (12 oz)	144	0	144	0
Donut, cake	125	4	61	60
Donut, glazed	164	8	87	69
Sweet roll	317	22	136	159
Cake (medium slice)	274	14	175	85
Ice cream (8 oz)	257	15	108	134
Softserve cone (reg.)	240	10	89	134
Ice cream sandwich bar	210	40	82	88
Strawberries (8 oz)	55	4	46	5
Orange (medium)	64	6	57	1
Apple (medium)	96	1	86	9
Banana (medium)	101	4	95	2
Cantaloupe (half)	82	7	73	2
Grapefruit (half)	40	2	37	1
Celery stick	5	2	3	0
Carrot (medium)	20	3	17	0
Raisins (4 oz)	210	6	204	0
Watermelon (4" × 6" slice)	115	8	99	8
Chocolate chip cookie	60	3	9	48
Brownie	145	6	26	113
Oatmeal cookie	65	3	13	49
Sandwich cookie	200	8	112	80
Custard pie (slice)	285	20	188	77
Fruit pie (slice)	350	14	259	77
Gelatin (4 oz)	70	4	32	34
Fritter (medium)	132	11	54	67
Skim milk (8 oz)	88	36	52	0
Diet drink	0	0	0	0
Potato chips (small bag)	115	3	39	73
Roasted peanuts (1.3 oz)	210	34	25	151
Chocolate candy bar (1 oz)	145	7	61	77
Chocolate almond candy bar (1 oz)	265	38	74	164
Saltine cracker	18	1	1	16
Popped corn	40	7	33	0
Cheese nachos	471	63	194	214

Appendix C
Eating Well: Canada's Food Guide

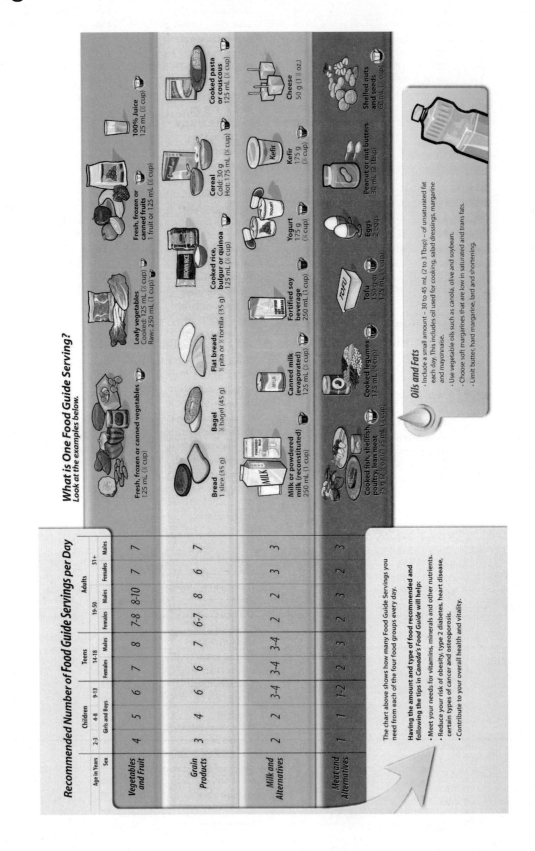

Recommended Number of Food Guide Servings per Day

Age in Years	Children			Teens		Adults			
	2-3	4-8	9-13	14-18		19-50		51+	
Sex	Girls and Boys			Females	Males	Females	Males	Females	Males
Vegetables and Fruit	4	5	6	7	8	7-8	8-10	7	7
Grain Products	3	4	6	6	7	6-7	8	6	7
Milk and Alternatives	2	2	3-4	3-4	3-4	2	2	3	3
Meat and Alternatives	1	1	1-2	2	3	2	3	2	3

The chart above shows how many Food Guide Servings you need from each of the four food groups every day.

Having the amount and type of food recommended and following the tips in *Canada's Food Guide* will help:
- Meet your needs for vitamins, minerals and other nutrients.
- Reduce your risk of obesity, type 2 diabetes, heart disease, certain types of cancer and osteoporosis.
- Contribute to your overall health and vitality.

What is One Food Guide Serving?
Look at the examples below.

Fresh, frozen or canned vegetables 125 mL (½ cup)

Leafy vegetables Cooked 125 mL (½ cup) Raw: 250 mL (1 cup)

Fresh, frozen or canned fruits 1 fruit or 125 mL (½ cup)

100% Juice 125 mL (½ cup)

Bread 1 slice (35 g)

Bagel ½ bagel (45 g)

Flat breads ½ pita or ½ tortilla (35 g)

Cooked rice, bulgur or quinoa 125 mL (½ cup)

Cereal Cold: 30 g Hot: 175 mL (¾ cup)

Cooked pasta or couscous 125 mL (½ cup)

Milk or powdered milk (reconstituted) 250 mL (1 cup)

Canned milk (evaporated) 125 mL (½ cup)

Fortified soy beverage 250 mL (1 cup)

Yogurt 175 g (¾ cup)

Kefir 175 g (¾ cup)

Cheese 50 g (1 ½ oz.)

Cooked fish, shellfish, poultry, lean meat 75 g (2 ½ oz.)/125 mL (½ cup)

Cooked legumes 175 mL (¾ cup)

Tofu 150 g or 175 mL (¾ cup)

Eggs 2 eggs

Peanut or nut butters 30 mL (2 Tbsp)

Shelled nuts and seeds 60 mL (¼ cup)

Oils and Fats
- Include a small amount – 30 to 45 mL (2 to 3 Tbsp) – of unsaturated fat each day. This includes oil used for cooking, salad dressings, margarine and mayonnaise.
- Use vegetable oils such as canola, olive and soybean.
- Choose soft margarines that are low in saturated and trans fats.
- Limit butter, hard margarine, lard and shortening.

Make each Food Guide Serving count...
wherever you are – at home, at school, at work or when eating out!

▸ **Eat at least one dark green and one orange vegetable each day.**
- Go for dark green vegetables such as broccoli, romaine lettuce and spinach.
- Go for orange vegetables such as carrots, sweet potatoes and winter squash.

▸ **Choose vegetables and fruit prepared with little or no added fat, sugar or salt.**
- Enjoy vegetables steamed, baked or stir-fried instead of deep-fried.

▸ **Have vegetables and fruit more often than juice.**

▸ **Make at least half of your grain products whole grain each day.**
- Eat a variety of whole grains such as barley, brown rice, oats, quinoa and wild rice.
- Enjoy whole grain breads, oatmeal or whole wheat pasta.

▸ **Choose grain products that are lower in fat, sugar or salt.**
- Compare the Nutrition Facts table on labels to make wise choices.
- Enjoy the true taste of grain products. When adding sauces or spreads, use small amounts.

▸ **Drink skim, 1%, or 2% milk each day.**
- Have 500 mL (2 cups) of milk every day for adequate vitamin D.
- Drink fortified soy beverages if you do not drink milk.

▸ **Select lower fat milk alternatives.**
- Compare the Nutrition Facts table on yogurts or cheeses to make wise choices.

▸ **Have meat alternatives such as beans, lentils and tofu often.**

▸ **Eat at least two Food Guide Servings of fish each week.***
- Choose fish such as char, herring, mackerel, salmon, sardines and trout.

▸ **Select lean meat and alternatives prepared with little or no added fat or salt.**
- Trim the visible fat from meats. Remove the skin on poultry.
- Use cooking methods such as roasting, baking or poaching that require little or no added fat.
- If you eat luncheon meats, sausages or prepackaged meats, choose those lower in salt (sodium) and fat.

Enjoy a variety of foods from the four food groups.

Satisfy your thirst with water!

Drink water regularly. It's a calorie-free way to quench your thirst. Drink more water in hot weather or when you are very active.

* Health Canada provides advice for limiting exposure to mercury from certain types of fish. Refer to www.healthcanada.gc.ca for the latest information.

References

This edition of *Concepts of Fitness and Wellness* incorporates the latest updates in research as well as new developments in public health, medicine, and technology related to health, wellness, and fitness. Resources new to this edition include the following.

Concept 1

Bennett, D. A., Bisanzio, D., Deribew, A., Gething, P. W., Hay, S. I., & Ali, R. (2017). Global, regional, and national under-5 mortality, adult mortality, age-specific mortality, and life expectancy, 1970-2016: A systematic analysis for the Global Burden of Disease Study 2016. Lancet. 390 (No 10100, p1084-1150.

Dwyer-Lindgren, L., Bertozzi-Villa, A., Stubbs, R. W., Morozoff, C., Mackenbach, J. P., van Lenthe, F. J., . . . & Murray, C. J. (2017). Inequalities in life expectancy among US counties, 1980 to 2014: Temporal trends and key drivers. *JAMA Internal Medicine, 177*(7), 1003-1011.

Kanesarajah, J., Waller, M., Whitty, J. A., & Mishra, G. D. (2018). Multimorbidity and quality of life at mid-life: A systematic review of general population studies. *Maturitas, 109*, 53-62.

National Academies of Sciences, Engineering, and Medicine. (2017). *Global health and the future role of the United States.* Washington, DC: National Academies Press.

National Center for Health Statistics. (2017). *Health, United States, 2016: With chartbook on long-term trends in health.* Hyattsville, MD: Author.

Concept 2

James, C. V. (2017). Racial/ethnic health disparities among rural adults—United States, 2012-2015. *MMWR Surveillance Summaries, 66.*

James, W., & Cossman, J. S. (2017). Long-term trends in Black and White mortality in the rural United States: Evidence of a race-specific rural mortality penalty. *Journal of Rural Health, 33*(1), 21-31.

Paige, S. R., Krieger, J. L., & Stellefson, M. L. (2017). The influence of eHealth literacy on perceived trust in online health communication channels and sources. *Journal of Health Communication, 22*(1), 53-65.

Paige, S. R., Stellefson, M., Chaney, B. H., Chaney, D. J., Alber, J. M., Chappell, C., & Barry, A. E. (2017). Examining the relationship between online social capital and eHealth literacy: Implications for Instagram use for chronic disease prevention among college students. *American Journal of Health Education, 48*(4), 264-277.

Sallis, J. F., Conway, T. L., Cain, K. L., Carlson, J. A., Frank, L. D., Kerr, J., . . . & Saelens, B. E. (2018). Neighborhood built environment and socioeconomic status in relation to physical activity, sedentary behavior, and weight status of adolescents. *Preventive Medicine.*

Singh, G. K., Daus, G. P., Allender, M., Ramey, C. T., Martin, E. K., Perry, C., . . . & Vedamuthu, I. P. (2017). Social determinants of health in the United States: Addressing major health inequality trends for the nation, 1935-2016. *International Journal of MCH and AIDS, 6*(2), 139.

Yang, S. C., Luo, Y. F., & Chiang, C. H. (2017). The associations among individual factors, eHealth literacy, and health-promoting lifestyles among college students. *Journal of Medical Internet Research, 19*(1).

Concept 3

Khalesi, S., Irwin, C., & Sun, J. (2018). Lifestyle and self-management determinants of hypertension control in a sample of Australian adults. *Expert Review of Cardiovascular Therapy.*

Oliver, J. E., & Wood, T. (2014). Medical conspiracy theories and health behaviors in the United States. *JAMA Internal Medicine, 174*(5), 817-818.

Stulberg, B. (2014). The key to changing individual health behaviors: Change the environments that give rise to them. *Harvard Public Health Review, 2,* 1-6.

van der Vaart, R., & Drossaert, C. (2017). Development of the digital health literacy instrument: Measuring a broad spectrum of health 1.0 and health 2.0 skills. *Journal of Medical Internet Research, 19*(1).

Young, S. (2014). Health behavior change in practical settings. *Permanente Journal, 18*(4), 89-92.

Concept 4

Casa, D. J., Hosokawa, Y., Belval, L. N., Adams, W. M., & Stearns, R. L. (2017). Preventing death from exertional heat stroke—The long road from evidence to policy. *Kinesiology Review, 6,* 99-109.

Heidbuchel, H. (2017, December 13). The athlete's heart is a proarrhythmic heart, and what that means for clinical decision making. *EP Europace.*

van den Bekerom, M. P. J., Struijs, P. A. A., Blankevoort, L., Welling, L., van Dijk, C. N., & Kerkhoffs, G. M. M. J. (2012). What is the evidence for rest, ice, compression, and elevation therapy in the treatment of ankle sprains in adults? *Journal of Athletic Training, 47*(4), 435-443.

Whitfield, G. P., Riebe, D., Magal, M., & Liguori, G. (2017). Applying the ACSM preparticipation screening algorithm to US adults: National Health and Nutrition Examination Survey 2001-2004. *Medicine and Science in Sports and Exercise, 49*(10), 2056-2063.

Concept 5

Carter, S., Hartman, Y., Holder, S., Thijssen, D. H., & Hopkins, N. D. (2017). Sedentary behavior and cardiovascular disease risk: Mediating mechanisms. *Exercise & Sport Sciences Reviews, 45*(2), 80-86.

Crump, C., Sundquist, J., Winkleby, M. A., & Sundquist, K. (2017). Interactive effects of aerobic fitness, strength, and obesity on mortality in men. *American Journal of Preventive Medicine, 52*(3), 353-361.

Kraschnewski, J. L., & Schmitz, K. H. (2017). Exercise in the prevention and treatment of breast cancer: What clinicians need to tell their Patients. *Translational Journal of the ACSM, 2*(15), 92-96.

Kyu, H. H., Bachman, V. F., Alexander, Lily, T., et al. (2016, August 9). Physical activity and risk of breast cancer, colon cancer, diabetes, ischemic heart disease, and ischemic stroke events: Systematic review and dose-response meta-analysis for the Global Burden of Disease Study 2013. *British Medical Journal.*

Sallis, R. E. (2017). Exercise in the treatment of chronic disease: An underfilled prescription. *Current Sports Medicine Reports, 16*(4), 225-226.

Wanigatunga, A. A., Tudor-Locke, C., Axtell, R. S., Glynn, N. W., King, A. C., Mcdermott, M. M., . . . & Manini, T. M. (2017). Effects of a long-term physical activity program on activity patterns in older adults. *Medicine and Science in Sports and Exercise, 49*(11), 2167-2175.

Concept 6

García-Hermoso, A., Saavedra, J. M., Ramírez-Vélez, R., Ekelund, U., & Pozo-Cruz, B. (2017). Reallocating sedentary time to moderate-to-vigorous physical activity but not to light-intensity physical activity is effective to reduce adiposity among youths: A systematic review and meta-analysis. *Obesity Reviews, 18*(9), 1088-1095.

Edwards, M. K., Addoh, O., & Loprinzi, P. D. (2017, May). Predictive validity of a fitness fatness index in predicting cardiovascular disease and all-cause mortality. *Mayo Clinic Proceedings, 92*(5), 851).

Kennedy, A. B., Lavie, C. J., & Blair, S. N. (2018). Fitness or fatness: Which is more important? *JAMA, 319*(3), 231-232.

Lee, P. G., Jackson, E. A., & Richardson, C. R. (2017). Exercise prescriptions in older adults. *American Family Physician, 95*(7), 425-432.

Moholdt, T., Lavie, C. J., & Nauman, J. (2017). Interaction of physical activity and Body Mass Index on mortality in coronary heart disease: Data from the Nord-Trøndelag Health Study. *American Journal of Medicine, 130*(8), 949-957.

O'Donovan, G., Lee, I., Hamer, M., & Stamatakis, A. (2017). Association of "Weekend Warrior" and other leisure time physical activity patterns with risks for all-cause, cardiovascular disease, and cancer mortality. *JAMA Internal Medicine, 177*(3), 335-342.

Riebe, D., Franklin, B. A., Thompson, P. D., Garber, C. E., Whitfield, G. P., Magal, M., & Pescatello, L. S. (2015). Updating ACSM's recommendations for exercise preparticipation health screening. *Medicine and Science in Sports and Exercise, 47*(8), 2473-2479.

Varma, V. R., Dey, D., Leroux, A., Di, J., Urbanek, J., Xiao, L., & Zippunnikov, V. (2017). Re-evaluating the effect of age on physical activity over the lifespan. *Preventive Medicine, 101*, 102-108.

Concept 7

Alinia, P., Cain, C., Fallahzadeh, R., Shahrokni, A., Cook, D., & Ghasemzadeh, H. (2017). How accurate is your activity tracker? A comparative study of step counts in low-intensity physical activities. *Journal of Medical Internet Research mHealth and uHealth, 5*(8).

Biswas, A., Oh, P. I., Faulkner, G. E., Bajaj, R. R., Silver, M. A., Mitchell, M. S., & Alter, D. A. (2015). Sedentary time and its association with risk for disease incidence, mortality, and hospitalization in adults: A systematic review and meta-analysis. *Annals of Internal Medicine, 162*(2), 123-132.

Carter, S., Hartman, Y., Holder, S., Thijssen, D. H., & Hopkins, N. D. (2017). Sedentary behavior and cardiovascular disease risk: Mediating mechanisms. *Exercise and Sport Sciences Reviews, 45*(2), 80-86.

Chau, J. Y., Daley, M., Dunn, S., Srinivasan, A., Do, A., Bauman, A. E., & van der Ploeg, H. P. (2014). The effectiveness of sit-stand workstations for changing office workers' sitting time: Results from the Stand@Work randomized controlled trial pilot. *International Journal of Behavior, Nutrition and Physical Activity,* 11, 127.

Creasy, S. A., Rogers, R. J., Byard, T. D., Kowalsky, R. J., & Jakicic, J. M. (2016). Energy expenditure during acute periods of sitting, standing, and walking. *Journal of Physical Activity and Health, 13*(6), 573-578.

Diaz, K. M., Howard, V. J., Hutto, B., Colabianchi, N., Vena, J. E., Safford, M. M., . . . & Hooker, S. P. (2017). Patterns of sedentary behavior and mortality in US middle-aged and older adults: A national cohort study. *Annals of Internal Medicine.*

Ding, D., Lawson, K. D., Kolbe-Alexander, T. L., Finkelstein, E. A., Katzmarzyk, P. T., van Mechelen, W., . . . & Lancet Physical Activity Series 2 Executive Committee. (2016). The economic burden of physical inactivity: A global analysis of major non-communicable diseases. *The Lancet, 388*(10051), 1311-1324.

Dohrn, M., Kwak, L., Oja, P., Sjöström, M., & Hagströmer, M. (2018). Replacing sedentary time with physical activity: A 15-year follow-up of mortality in a national cohort. *Clinical Epidemiology, 10*, 179.

Peterson, N. E., Sirard, J. R., Kulbok, P. A., DeBoer, M. D., & Erickson, J. M. (2018). Sedentary behavior and physical activity of young adult university students. *Research in Nursing & Health, 41*(1), 30-38.

Phillips, C. M., Dillon, C. B., & Perry, I. J. (2017). Does replacing sedentary behaviour with light or moderate to vigorous physical activity modulate inflammatory status in adults? *International Journal of Behavioral Nutrition and Physical Activity, 14*(1), 138.

Tremblay, M. S., Aubert, S., Barnes J. D., Saunders, T. J., Carson, V., Latimer-Cheung, A.E., . . . & SBRN Terminology Consensus Project Participants. (2017). Sedentary Behavior Research Network (SBRN)—Terminology Consensus Project process and outcome. *International Journal of Behavioral Nutrition and Physical Activity, 14*(1), 75.

Concept 8

Alinia, P., Cain, C., Fallahzadeh, R., Shahrokni, A., Cook, D., & Ghasemzadeh, H. (2017). How accurate is your activity tracker? A comparative study of step counts in low-intensity physical activities. *Journal of Medical Internet Research mHealth and uHealth, 5*(8).

Bushman, B. A. (2014). Determining the I (intensity) for a FITT-VP aerobic exercise prescription. *ACSM's Health and Fitness Journal, 18*(3), 4-7.

Dohrn, M., Kwak, L., Oja, P., Sjöström, M., & Hagströmer, M. (2018). Replacing sedentary time with physical activity: A 15-year follow-up of mortality in a national cohort. *Clinical Epidemiology, 10*, 179.

Eckel, R. H., et al. (2013). 2013 AHA/ACC guideline on lifestyle management to reduce cardiovascular risk. *Circulation, 129*(suppl. 2), S76-S99.

Fan, W., et al. (2017). PPARδ promotes running endurance by preserving glucose. *Cell Metabolism, 25*(5), 1186-1193.

Lee, P. G., Jackson, E. A., & Richardson, C. R. (2017). Exercise prescriptions in older adults. *American Family Physician, 95*(7), 425-432.

Lear, S. A., Hu, W., Rangarajan, S., Gasevic, D., Leong, D., Iqbal, R., . . . & Rosengren, A. (2017). The effect of physical activity on mortality and cardiovascular disease in 130,000 people from 17 high-income, middle-income, and low-income countries: The PURE study. *The Lancet, 390*(10113), 2643-2654.

Peterson, N. E., Sirard, J. R., Kulbok, P. A., DeBoer, M. D., & Erickson, J. M. (2018). Sedentary behavior and physical activity of young adult university students. *Research in Nursing & Health, 41*(1), 30-38.

Phillips, C. M., Dillon, C. B., & Perry, I. J. (2017). Does replacing sedentary behaviour with light or moderate to vigorous physical activity modulate inflammatory status in adults? *International Journal of Behavioral Nutrition and Physical Activity, 14*(1), 138.

Concept 9

Decker, E. S., & Ekkekakis, P. (2017). More efficient, perhaps, but at what price? Pleasure and enjoyment responses to high-intensity interval exercise in low-active women with obesity. *Psychology of Sport and Exercise, 28*, 1-10.

Dishman, R. K., McIver, K. L., Dowda, M., & Pate, R. R. (2018). Declining physical activity and motivation from middle school to high school. *Medicine and Science in Sports and Exercise.*

Hermsen, S., Moons, J., Kerkhof, P., Wiekens, C., & De Groot, M. (2017). Determinants for sustained use of an activity tracker: Observational study. *Journal of Medical Internet Research mHealth and uHealth, 5*(10).

Lee, D. C., Brellenthin, A. G., Thompson, P. D., Sui, X., Lee, I. M., & Lavie, C. J. (2017). Running as a key lifestyle medicine for longevity. *Progress in Cardiovascular Diseases, 60*(1), 45-55.

Maher, C., Ryan, J., Ambrosi, C., & Edney, S. (2017). Users' experiences of wearable activity trackers: A cross-sectional study. *BMC Public Health, 17*(1), 880.

Zenko, Z., Ekkekakis, P., & Ariely, D. (2016). Can you have your vigorous exercise and enjoy it too? Ramping intensity down increases postexercise, remembered, and forecasted pleasure. *Journal of Sport and Exercise Psychology, 38*(2), 149-159.

Concept 10

Gill, A., Kok, G., Peters, G. J. Y., Frissen, T., Schols, A. M., & Plasqui, G. (2017). The psychological effects of strength exercises in people who are overweight or obese: A systematic review. *Sports Medicine,* 1-13.

Gordon, B. R., McDowell, C. P., Lyons, M., & Herring, M. P. (2017). The effects of resistance exercise training on anxiety: A meta-analysis and meta-regression analysis of randomized controlled trials. *Sports Medicine, 47*(10), 1-12.

Law, T. D., Clark, L. A., & Clark, B. C. (2016). Resistance exercise to prevent and manage sarcopenia and dynapenia. *Annual Review of Gerontology & Geriatrics, 36*(1), 205.

Scott, B. R., Duthie, G. M., Thornton, H. R., & Dascombe, B. J. (2016). Training monitoring for resistance exercise: Theory and applications. *Sports Medicine, 46*(5), 687-698.

Suchomel, T. J., Nimphius, S., Bellon, C. R., & Stone, M. H. (2018). The importance of muscular strength: Training considerations. *Sports Medicine,* 1-21.

Concept 11

Geremia, J. M., Iskiewicz, M. M., Marschner, R. A., Lehnen, T. E., & Lehnen, A. M. (2015). Effect of a physical training program using the Pilates method on flexibility in elderly subjects. *Age, 37*(6), 119.

Junior, R. M., Berton, R., de Souza, T. M. F., Chacon-Mikahil, M. P. T., & Cavaglieri, C. R. (2017). Effect of the flexibility training performed immediately before resistance training on muscle hypertrophy, maximum strength and flexibility. *European Journal of Applied Physiology, 117*(4), 767-774.

Kongkaew, C., Lertsinthai, P., Jampachaisri, K., Mongkhon, P., Meesomperm, P., Kornkaew, K., & Malaiwong, P. (2018, February 13). The effects of Thai yoga on physical fitness: A meta-analysis of randomized control trials. *Journal of Alternative and Complementary Medicine.*

McCrary, J. M., Ackermann, B. J., & Halaki, M. (2015). A systematic review of the effects of upper body warm-up on performance and injury. *British Journal of Sports Medicine, 49*(14), 935-942.

Papadimitriou, K., Loupos, D., Tsalis, G., & Manou, B. (2017). Effects of proprioceptive neuromuscular facilitation (PNF) on swimmers leg mobility and performance. *Journal of Physical Education and Sport, 17*(2), 663.

Concept 12

Bidonde, J., Busch, A. J., Schachter, C. L., Overend, T. J., Kim, S. Y., Góes, S. M., ... & Foulds, H. J. (2017). Aerobic exercise training for adults with fibromyalgia. *The Cochrane Library*.

Budhrani-Shani, P., Berry, D. L., Arcari, P., Langevin, H., & Wayne, P. M. (2016). Mind-body exercises for nurses with chronic low back pain: An evidence-based review. *Nursing Research and Practice*.

Dsa, C. F., Rengaramanujam, K., & Kudchadkar, M. S. (2014). To assess the effect of modified pilates compared to conventional core stabilization exercises on pain and disability in chronic non-specific low back pain-randomized controlled trial. *Indian Journal of Physiotherapy and Occupational Therapy, 8*(3), 202.

Gomes-Neto, M., Lopes, J. M., Conceição, C. S., Araujo, A., Brasileiro, A., Sousa, C., ... & Arcanjo, F. L. (2017). Stabilization exercise compared to general exercises or manual therapy for the management of low back pain: A systematic review and meta-analysis. *Physical Therapy in Sport, 23*, 136–142.

Kapetanovic, A., Jerkovic, S., & Avdic, D. (2016). Effect of core stabilization exercises on functional disability in patients with chronic low back pain. *Journal of Health Sciences, 6*(1).

Prieske, O., Muehlbauer, T., & Granacher, U. (2016). The role of trunk muscle strength for physical fitness and athletic performance in trained individuals: A systematic review and meta-analysis. *Sports Medicine, 46*(3), 401–419.

Wieland, L. S., Skoetz, N., Pilkington, K., Vempati, R., D'Adamo, C. R., & Berman, B. M. (2017). Yoga treatment for chronic non-specific low back pain. *The Cochrane Library*.

Concept 13

Brachman, A., Kamieniarz, A., Michalska, J., Pawłowski, M., Słomka, K. J., & Juras, G. (2017). Balance training programs in athletes—A systematic review. *Journal of Human Kinetics, 58*(1), 45–64.

Cunanan, A. J., DeWeese, B. H., Wagle, J. P., Carroll, K. M., Sausaman, R., Hornsby, W. G., ... & Stone, M. H. (2018). The General Adaptation Syndrome: A foundation for the concept of periodization. *Sports Medicine*, 1–11.

Hartmann, H., Wirth, K., Keiner, M., Mickel, C., Sander, A., & Szilvas, E. (2015). Short-term periodization models: Effects on strength and speed-strength performance. *Sports Medicine, 45*(10), 1373–1386.

Kiely, J. (2017). Periodization theory: Confronting an inconvenient truth. *Sports Medicine*, 1–12.

Lichtenstein, M. B., Emborg, B., Hemmingsen, S. D., & Hansen, N. B. (2017). Is exercise addiction in fitness centers a socially accepted behavior? *Addictive Behaviors Reports, 6*, 102–105.

Pierce, J. R., DeGroot, D. W., Grier, T. L., Hauret, K. G., Nindl, B. C., East, W. B., ... & Jones, B. H. (2017). Body Mass Index predicts selected physical fitness attributes but is not associated with performance on military relevant tasks in US Army Soldiers. *Journal of Science and Medicine in Sport, 20*, S79–S84.

Concept 14

Dalene, K. E., Andersen, L. B., Steene-Johannessen, J., Ekelund, U., Hansen, B. H., & Kolle, E. (2017). Cross-sectional and prospective associations between physical activity, Body Mass Index and waist circumference in children and adolescents. *Obesity Science & Practice*.

Flegal, K. M., Kruszon-Moran, D., Carroll, M. D. Fryar, C. D., & Ogden, C. L. (2016). Trends in obesity among adults in the United States, 2005 to 2014. *JAMA, 315*(21), 2284–2291.

Gibbs, B. B., Gabriel, K. P., Carnethon, M. R., Gary-Webb, T., Jakicic, J. M., Rana, J. S., ... & Lewis, C. E. (2017). Sedentary time, physical activity, and adiposity: Cross-sectional and longitudinal associations in CARDIA. *American Journal of Preventive Medicine, 53*(6), 764–771.

Kim, D. D., & Basu, A. (2016). Estimating the medical care costs of obesity in the United States: systematic review, meta-analysis, and empirical analysis. *Value in Health, 19*(5), 602–613.

Ng, M., Fleming, T., Robinson, M., Thomson, B., Graetz, N., Margono, C., ... & Abraham, J. P. (2014). Global, regional, and national prevalence of overweight and obesity in children and adults during 1980–2013: A systematic analysis for the Global Burden of Disease Study 2013. *The Lancet, 384*(9945), 766–781.

Stoner, L., & Cornwall, J. (2014). Did the American Medical Association make the correct decision classifying obesity as a disease? *Australasian Medical Journal, 7*(11), 462.

St-Onge, M. P. (2017). Sleep–obesity relation: Underlying mechanisms and consequences for treatment. *Obesity Reviews, 18*(S1), 34–39.

Tatsukawa, Y., Misumi, M., Kim, Y. M., Yamada, M., Ohishi, W., Fujiwara, S., ... & Yoneda, M. (2018). Body composition and development of diabetes: A 15-year follow-up study in a Japanese population. *European Journal of Clinical Nutrition, 1*.

Wen, M., Fan, J. X., Kowaleski-Jones, L., & Wan, N. (2017). Rural–urban disparities in obesity prevalence among working age adults in the United States: Exploring the mechanisms. *American Journal of Health Promotion, 32*(2).

Concept 15

Bell, S., Daskalopoulou, M., Rapsomaniki, E., George, J., Britton, A., Bobak, M., ... & Hemingway, H. (2017). Association between clinically recorded alcohol consumption and initial presentation of 12 cardiovascular diseases: Population based cohort study using linked health records. *BMJ, 356*, j909.

Evans, C. E. L. (2017). Sugars and health: A review of current evidence and future policy. *Proceedings of the Nutrition Society, 76*(3), 400–407.

Freeland-Graves, J. H., & Nitzke, S. (2013). Position of the academy of nutrition and dietetics: Total diet approach to healthy eating. *Journal of the Academy of Nutrition and Dietetics, 113*(2), 307–317.

Gibson, S., Ashwell, M., Arthur, J., Bagley, L., Lennox, A., Rogers, P. J., & Stanner, S. (2017). What can the food and drink industry do to help achieve the 5% free sugars goal? *Perspectives in Public Health, 137*(4), 237–247.

Lamothe, L. M., Lê, K. A., Samra, R. A., Roger, O., Green, H., & Macé, K. (2017). The scientific basis for healthful carbohydrate profile. *Critical Reviews in Food Science and Nutrition*, 1–13.

Miller, L. S., Sutter, C. A., Wilson, M. D., Bergman, J. J., Beckett, L. A., & Gibson, T. N. (2017). An evaluation of an eHealth tool designed to improve college students' label reading skills and feelings of empowerment to choose healthful foods. *Frontiers in Public Health, 5*, 359.

Miller, L. M. S., Beckett, L. A., Bergman, J. J., Wilson, M. D., Applegate, E. A., & Gibson, T. N. (2017). Developing nutrition label reading skills: A web-based practice approach. *Journal of Medical Internet Research, 19*(1).

Taylor, C. A., Watowicz, R. P., Spees, C. K., & Hooker, N. H. (2018, February 7). Shelf to health: Does product innovation change national estimates of dietary impacts? *Journal of Food Science*.

Concept 16

Capers, P. L., Fobian, A. D., Kaiser, K. A., Borah, R., & Allison, D. B. (2015). A systematic review and meta-analysis of randomized controlled trials of the impact of sleep duration on adiposity and components of energy balance. *Obesity Reviews, 16*(9), 771–782.

Cheatham, S. W., Stull, K. R., Fantigrassi, M., & Motel, I. (2017). The efficacy of wearable activity tracking technology as part of a weight loss program: A systematic review. *Journal of Sports Medicine and Physical Fitness*.

Ekkekakis, P., Vazou, S., Bixby, W. R., & Georgiadis, E. (2016). The mysterious case of the public health guideline that is (almost) entirely ignored: Call for a research agenda on the causes of the extreme avoidance of physical activity in obesity. *Obesity Reviews, 17*(4), 313–329.

Falbe, J., Thompson, H. R., Becker, C. M., Rojas, N., McCulloch, C. E., & Madsen, K. A. (2016). Impact of the Berkeley excise tax on sugar-sweetened beverage consumption. *American Journal of Public Health, 106*(10), 1865–1871.

Kerrigan, S. G., Call, C., Schaumberg, K., Forman, E., & Butryn, M. L. (2018). Associations between change in sedentary behavior and outcome in standard behavioral weight loss treatment. *Translational Behavioral Medicine*.

Khera, R., Murad, M. H., Chandar, A. K., Dulai, P. S., Wang, Z., Prokop, L. J., ... & Singh, S. (2016). Association of pharmacological treatments for obesity with weight loss and adverse events: A systematic review and meta-analysis. *JAMA, 315*(22), 2424–2434.

Tierney, M., Gallagher, A. M., Giotis, E. S., & Pentieva, K. (2017). An online survey on consumer knowledge and understanding of added sugars. *Nutrients, 9*(1), 37.

Yeung, C. H. C., Gohil, P., Rangan, A. M., Flood, V. M., Arcot, J., Gill, T. P., & Louie, J. C. Y. (2017). Modelling of the impact of universal added sugar reduction through food reformulation. *Scientific Reports, 7*(1), 17392.

Concept 17

Blackburn, E., & Epel, E. (2017). *The telomere effect: Living younger, longer and healthier.* New York: Grand Central Publishing.

Brailovskaia, J., & Margraf, J. (2018). What does media use reveal about personality and mental health? An exploratory investigation among German students. *PLOS ONE, 13*(1), e0191810.

Disabato, D. J., Kashdan, T. B., Short, J. L., & Jarden, A. (2017). What predicts positive life events that influence the course of depression? A longitudinal examination of gratitude and meaning in life. *Cognitive Therapy and Research, 41*(3), 444–458.

Lin, J. S., Lee, Y. I., Jin, Y., & Gilbreath, B. (2017). Personality traits, motivations, and emotional consequences of social media usage. *Cyberpsychology, Behavior, and Social Networking, 20*(10), 615–623.

Owens, H., Christian, B., & Polivka, B. (2017). Sleep behaviors in traditional-age college students: A state of the science review with implications for practice. *Journal of the American Association of Nurse Practitioners, 29*(11), 695–703.

Twomey, C., & O'Reilly, G. (2017). Associations of self-presentation on Facebook with mental health and personality variables: A systematic review. *Cyberpsychology, Behavior, and Social Networking, 20*(10), 587–595.

Wolf, E. J., Maniates, H., Nugent, N., Maihofer, A. X., Armstrong, D., Ratanatharathorn, A., . . . & Workgroup, V. M. A. M. (2017). Traumatic stress and accelerated DNA methylation age: A meta-analysis. *Psychoneuroendocrinology.*

Concept 18

Blackburn, E., & Epel, E. (2017). *The telomere effect: Living younger, longer and healthier.* New York: Grand Central Publishing.

Dvořáková, K., Kishida, M., Li, J., Elavsky, S., Broderick, P. C., Agrusti, M. R., & Greenberg, M. T. (2017). Promoting healthy transition to college through mindfulness training with first-year college students: Pilot randomized controlled trial. *Journal of American College Health, 65*(4), 259–267.

Hayat, T. Z., Brainin, E., & Neter, E. (2017). With some help from my network: supplementing eHealth literacy with social ties. *Journal of Medical Internet Research, 19*(3).

Karatekin, C. (2017). Adverse childhood experiences (ACEs), stress and mental health in college students. *Stress and Health.*

Lee, R. A., & Jung, M. E. (2018). Evaluation of an mHealth app (DeStressify) on university students'

mental health: Pilot trial. *Journal of Medical Internet Research Mental Health, 5*(1), e2.

Mak, W. W., Chio, F. H., Chan, A. T., Lui, W. W., & Wu, E. K. (2017). The efficacy of Internet-based mindfulness training and cognitive-behavioral training with telephone support in the enhancement of mental health among college students and young working adults: Randomized controlled trial. *Journal of Medical Internet Research, 19*(3).

Manigault, A. W., Woody, A., Zoccola, P. M., & Dickerson, S. S. (2018). Trait mindfulness predicts the presence but not the magnitude of cortisol responses to acute stress. *Psychoneuroendocrinology, 90,* 29–34.

Ng, Feng, V. N., Greer, C. S., & Frazier, P. (2017) Using online interventions to deliver college student mental health resources: Evidence from randomized clinical trials. *Psychological services, 14*(4), 481.

Oh, B., Lee, K. J., Zaslawski, C., Yeung, A., Rosenthal, D., Larkey, L., & Back, M. (2017). Health and well-being benefits of spending time in forests: Systematic review. *Environmental Health and Preventive Medicine, 22*(1), 71.

Regehr, C., Glancy, D., & Pitts, A. (2013). Interventions to reduce stress in university students: A review and meta-analysis. *Journal of Affective Disorders, 148*(1), 1–11.

Windle, M., Haardörfer, R., Getachew, B., Shah, J., Payne, J., Pillai, D., & Berg, C. J. (2018, February). A multivariate analysis of adverse childhood experiences and health behaviors and outcomes among college students. *Journal of American College Health.*

Yang, E., Schamber, E., Meyer, R. M., & Gold, J. I. (2018, February 8). Happier healers: Randomized controlled trial of mobile mindfulness for stress management. *Journal of Alternative and Complementary Medicine.*

Concept 19

General, S. (2014). *The health consequences of smoking—50 years of progress: A report of the surgeon general.* US Department of Health and Human Services. Retrieved from https://www.surgeongeneral.gov/library/reports/50-years-of-progress/index.html.

Hair, E. C., Romberg, A. R., Niaura, R., Abrams, D. B., Bennett, M. A., Xiao, H., . . . & Vallone, D. (2018). Longitudinal tobacco use transitions among adolescents and young adults: 2014–2016. *Nicotine & Tobacco Research.*

Jamal, A., Gentzke, A., Hu, S. S., et al. (2017). Tobacco use among middle and high school students—United States, 2011–2016. *MMWR 66,* 597–603.

Nguyen, A. B., Henrie, J., Slavit, W. I., & Kaufman, A. (2018). Beliefs about FDA tobacco regulation, modifiability of cancer risk, and tobacco product comparative harm perceptions: Findings from the HINTS-FDA 2015. *Preventive Medicine.*

Roods, K. (2018). Trends in hookah use among New York City middle and high school students, 2008–2014. *Preventing Chronic Disease, 15.*

Yao, T., Sung, H. Y., Wang, Y., Lightwood, J., & Max, W. (2017). Healthcare costs attributable to secondhand smoke exposure at home for US adults. *Preventive Medicine.*

Concept 20

Bartone, P. T., Johnsen, B. H., Eid, J., Hystad, S. W., & Laberg, J. C. (2017). Hardiness, avoidance coping, and alcohol consumption in war veterans: A moderated-mediation study. *Stress and Health, 33*(5), 498–507.

Daube, M. (2015). Alcohol's evaporating health benefits. *BMJ, 350,* h407.

Iwamoto, D. K., Corbin, W., Takamatsu, S., & Castellanos, J. (2018). The association between multidimensional feminine norms, binge drinking and alcohol-related problems among young adult college women. *Addictive Behaviors, 76,* 243–249.

McGrath, E. L., Gao, J., Kuo, Y-F., Dunn, T. J., Ray, M. J., Dineley, K. T., Cunningham, K. A., . . . & Wu, P. (2017). Spatial and sex-dependent responses of adult endogenous neural stem cells to alcohol consumption. *Stem Cell Reports, 9,* 1–15.

National Institute on Alcohol Abuse and Alcoholism. *Alcohol use disorder: A comparison between DSM-IV and DSM-5.* Retrieved from https://pubs.niaaa.nih.gov/publications/dsmfactsheet/dsmfact.pdf.

Schulenberg, J. E., Johnston, L. D., O'Malley, P. M., Bachman, J. G., Miech, R. A., & Patrick, M. E. (2017). *Monitoring the Future national survey results on drug use, 1975–2016: Volume II, College students and adults ages 19–55.* Ann Arbor: Institute for Social Research, University of Michigan.

Substance Abuse and Mental Health Services Administration. *2015 National Survey on Drug Use and Health (NSDUH),* Table 2.46B—Alcohol use, binge alcohol use, and heavy alcohol use in past month among persons aged 12 or older, by demographic characteristics: Percentages, 2014 and 2015. Retrieved from https://www.samhsa.gov/data/sites/default/files/NSDUH-DetTabs-2015/NSDUH-DetTabs-2015-NSDUH-DetTabs-2015.htm#tab2-41b.

Concept 21

Ali, M. M., Dowd, W. N., Classen, T., Mutter, R., & Novak, S. P. (2017). Prescription drug monitoring programs, nonmedical use of prescription drugs, and heroin use: Evidence from the National Survey of Drug Use and Health. *Addictive Behaviors, 69,* 65–77.

Baraa, O., Barreiro, A. E., Bradshaw, Y. S., Chui, K. K. H., & Carr, D. B. (2016). Durations of opioid, nonopioid drug, and behavioral clinical trials for chronic pain: Adequate or inadequate? *Pain Medicine, 17,* 2036–2046.

Centers for Disease Control and Prevention. (2016, March 15). CDC releases guideline for prescribing opioids for chronic pain. Retrieved from https://www.cdc.gov/media/releases/2016/p0315-prescribing-opioids-guidelines.html

Center for Behavioral Health Statistics and Quality. (2016). *Key substance use and mental health indicators in the United States: Results from the*

2015 National Survey on Drug Use and Health (HHS Publication No. SMA 16-4984, NSDUH Series H-51). Retrieved from http://www.samhsa.gov/data/.

Faul, M., Bohm, M., & Alexander, C. (2017). Methadone prescribing and overdose and the Association with Medicaid preferred drug list policies—United States, 2007-2014. *MMWR, 66*, 320-323.

Jean, H., Wiese, C., Piercey, R. R., & Clark, C. D. (2018). Changing prescribing behavior in the United States: Moving upstream in opioid prescription education. *Clinical Pharmacology & Therapeutics.*

Jones, C. M. (2018). Trends and key correlates of prescription opioid injection misuse in the United States. *Addictive Behaviors, 78*, 145-152.

Lipari, R. N., Williams, M. R., Copello, E. A. P., & Pemberton, M. R. (2016). Risk and protective factors and estimates of substance use initiation: results from the 2015 national survey on drug use and health. *NSDUH Data Review.* Retrieved from http://www.samhsa.gov/data.

Marsh, J. C., Park, K., Lin, Y. A., & Bersamira, C. (2018). Gender differences in trends for heroin use and nonmedical prescription opioid use, 2007-2014. *Journal of Substance Abuse Treatment.*

National Academies of Sciences, Engineering, and Medicine. (2017). *The health effects of cannabis and cannabinoids: Current state of evidence and recommendations for research.* Washington, DC: National Academies Press.

National Academies of Sciences, Engineering, and Medicine. (2017). *Pain management and the opioid epidemic: Balancing societal and individual benefits and risks of prescription opioid use.* Washington, DC: National Academies Press.

Rudd, R. A., Seth, P., David, F., & Scholl, L. (2016), Increases in drug and opioid-involved overdose deaths—United States, 2010-2015. *MMWR, 65,*1445-1452.

Schulenberg, J. E., Johnston, L. D., O'Malley, P. M., Bachman, J. G., Miech, R. A., & Patrick, M. E. (2017). *Monitoring the Future national survey results on drug use, 1975-2016: Volume II, College students and adults ages 19-55.* Ann Arbor: Institute for Social Research, University of Michigan.

Concept 22

Hyde, J., & DeLamater, J. (2017). *Understanding human sexuality* (13th ed.). St. Louis: McGraw-Hill Higher Education.

Jena, A. B., Goldman, D. P., & Seabury, S. A. (2015). Incidence of sexually transmitted infections after human papillomavirus vaccination among adolescent females. *JAMA Internal Medicine, 175*(4), 617-623.

McKee, R., Gilbert, T., & GeLarz, J. (2017). *Taking sides: Clashing views in human sexuality* (124th ed.). St. Louis: McGraw-Hill Higher Education.

National Center for Health Statistics. (2017). *Health, United States, 2016: With chartbook on long-term trends in health.* Hyattsville, MD: Author.

National Institute of Allergy and Infectious Diseases. (2016, November 28). First new HIV vaccine efficacy study in seven years has begun. Retrieved from https://www.hiv.gov/blog/first-new-hiv-vaccine-efficacy-study-in-seven-years-has-begun.

Concept 23

Ackermann, R. T. (2017). From programs to policy and back again: The push and pull of realizing type 2 diabetes prevention on a national scale. *Diabetes Care, 40*(10), 1298-1301.

Horder, H. et al. (2018). Midlife cardiovascular fitness and dementia: A 44-year longitudinal population study in women. Neurology.

Holtermann, A., Gyntelberg, F., Bauman, A., & Jensen, M. T. (2017). Cardiorespiratory fitness, fatness and incident diabetes. *Diabetes Research and Clinical Practice, 134*, 113-120.

Mørch, L. S., Skovlund, C. W., Hannaford, P. C., Iversen, L., Fielding, S., & Lidegaard, Ø. (2017). Contemporary hormonal contraception and the risk of breast cancer. *New England Journal of Medicine, 377*(23), 2228-2239.

Nwose, E. U., Digban, K. A., Anyasodor, A. E., Bwititi, P. T., Richards, R. S., & Igumbor, E. O. (2017). Development of public health program for type 1 diabetes in a university community: Preliminary evaluation of behavioural change wheel. *Acta Bio Medica Atenei Parmensis, 88*(3), 281-288.

Concept 24

Akabas, S. R., Vannice, G., Atwater, J. B., Cooperman, T., Cotter, R, & Thomas, L. (2016). Quality certification programs for dietary supplements. *Journal of the Academy of Nutrition and Dietetics, 116*(9), 1370-1379.

Berezow, A. (2017). *Little black book of junk science.* New York: Thomas Dunne Books.

Piper, C. E. (2016). *Healthcare fraud: Investigation guidebook.* Boca Raton, FL: CRC Press.

Concept 25

Aceijas, C., Waldhäusl, S., Lambert, N., Cassar, S., & Bello-Corassa, R. (2017). Determinants of health-related lifestyles among university students. *Perspectives in Public Health, 137*(4), 227-236.

Barber, R. M., Fullman, N., Sorensen, R. J., Bollyky, T., McKee, M., Nolte, E., . . . & Abd-Allah, F. (2017). Healthcare access and quality index based on mortality from causes amenable to personal health care in 195 countries and territories, 1990-2015: A novel analysis from the Global Burden of Disease Study 2015. *The Lancet, 390*(10091), 231-266.

Loiselle, C. G., & Ahmed, S. (2017). Is connected health contributing to a healthier population? *Journal of Medical Internet Research, 19*(11).

Patrode, C. D., Evans, C. V., Senger, C. A., Redmond, N., & Lin, J. S. (2017). *Behavioral counseling to promote a healthful diet and physical activity for cardiovascular disease prevention in adults without known cardiovascular disease risk factors: Updated systematic review for the U.S. Preventive Services Task Force.* Evidence Synthesis No. 152. AHRQ Publication No. 15-05222-EF-1. Rockville, MD: Agency for Healthcare Research and Quality.

Maruta, T., Colligan, R. C., Malinchoc, M., & Offord, K. P. (2000, February). Optimists vs pessimists: Survival rate among medical patients over a 30-year period. *Mayo Clinic Proceedings, 75*(2), 140-143.

Monroe, C. M., Turner-McGrievy, G., Larsen, C. A., Magradey, K., Brandt, H. M., Wilcox, S., . . . & West, D. S. (2017). College freshmen students' perspectives on weight gain prevention in the digital age: Web-based survey. *Journal of Medical Internet Research Public Health and Surveillance, 3*(4).

Tsugawa, Y., et al. (2017). Comparison of hospital mortality and readmission rates for Medicare patients treated by male vs female physicians. *JAMA Internal Medicine, 177*(2), 206-213.

Stulberg, B. (2014). The key to changing individual health behaviors: Change the environments that give rise to them. *Harvard Public Health Review, 2,* 1-6.

Young, S. (2014). Health behavior change in practical settings. *Permanente Journal,18*(4), 89-92.

Index

Note: Page numbers in **boldface** refer to glossary terms; those followed by "f" refer to figures; those followed by "t" refer to tables

A

A1C blood test, 72, 446
ABC system for time management, 368, 368t
ABCDE self-exam, 442, 442f
abdominal exercises. *See* core training
abdominal (visceral) fat, 280, 280f, 331
abdominal muscles, 169f, 170f
abdominal ptosis, 223f, 225t
abduction, 192, 192f
absolute muscle fitness, 154, **155**
ACA (Patient Protection and Affordable Care Act), 20, 475
academic performance
  alcohol use and, 397, 397f
  physical activity and, 75
  stress management and, 362
acai berry scam, 462
accidental injuries, 448–449, 449t
acclimatization, 48–49
ACEs (adverse childhood experiences), 348
acetaminophen (Tylenol), 53
achilles tendon, 170f
acquired aging, 66
Acquired immune deficiency syndrome (AIDS). *See* HIV/AIDS
ACSM. *See* American College of Sports Medicine
ACTH (adrenocorticotropic hormone), 348
action stage, 28f, 29
active assistance, in stretching, 196–197, **197**
active stretching, 197. *See also* stretching
activity. *See* physical activity
activity monitoring apps, 104, 143
activity neurosis, 262
activity patterns
  by age group, 140–141, 140f
  for cardiovascular endurance, 119
  during college, 123
  moderate physical activity, 88–89, 88t, 98
  vigorous physical activity, 140–141
adaptations
  to aerobic exercise, 115
  defined, **349**
  limitations on, 258
  stress and, 348

Adderall, 408, 415
addiction. *See also* alcohol use and abuse; drug use and abuse; tobacco use
  biopsychosocial model, 416
  exercise, 262
  genetics and, 19, 417
  nicotine, 386
  treatment apps, 400
adduction, 192, 192f
adductor brevis, 180
adductors
  adductor longus, 169f
  adductor magnus, 170f
  exercising, 180, 233
  stretching, 207
adenocarcinomas (malignant tumors), 436
Adequate Intake (AI), 307, **307**
adherence questionnaire, 145–146
adipokines, 280–281
adolescents
  alcohol use, 397
  drug use, 411, 411f
  secondhand smoke susceptibility, 382
  smoking, 383–384
  stress, 346
adrenocorticotropic hormone (ACTH), 348
adverse childhood experiences (ACEs), 348
advocacy, for safe and healthy environments, 23, 104
AED (automated external defibrillator), 47
aerobic activities. *See also* moderate physical activity; vigorous physical activity
  continuous versus intermittent, 137, **137**
  defined, 135
  using hand weights during, 460
aerobic capacity (VO$_2$ max)
  anaerobic capacity and, 254
  defined, **113, 115**
  for high-level performance, 252
aerobic fitness. *See* cardiorespiratory endurance
aerobic intervals, 254, 255t
aerobic/anaerobic intervals, 254–255, 255t
Aerobics (Cooper), 135
aerosols (inhalants), 410t
age and aging
  bone density changes, 73f
  calcium intake, 315
  creeping obesity, 281–282, 282f
  degenerative disc disease, 220
  flexibility, 194
  functional fitness, 157, 258
  as health determinant, 19, 31

muscle fitness, 66, 154
  physical activity effects on, 65–66, 360–361
  physical activity guidelines, 101
  physical activity patterns, 88–89, 88t, 98, 140–141, 140f
  power and, 257
  stress effect on, 348
  target heart rate zone and, 121f
agility, 11f, 94, 265
agonist muscles, 153, **153,** 153f
AI (Adequate Intake), 307, **307**
AIDS. *See* HIV/AIDS
air pollution, and physical activity, 51–52
alarm reaction phase, 347f
alcohol expectancies, 397
alcohol tolerance, 393–394, **393**
alcohol use and abuse
  accidents and, 448
  beverage contents, 392, 392f
  blood alcohol concentration, 392, 396t, 403–404
  in college students, 397–400, 397f, 398t
  consumption guidelines, 316
  consumption patterns, 393–304, 393t
  drug classification, 392, 408
  effects on body, 392
  empty calories from, 331
  excessive intake, 316
  as gateway drug, 416
  health risks and benefits, 394–395, 394f
  impaired driving and, 395–396, 396t, 397f
  in military personnel, 400
  people who should abstain, 395t
  perceptions about, 405–406
  prevention and treatment, 400–401
  problem drinking risk factors, 397
  public health goals, 5
  self-monitoring, 401
  smoking and, 386
alcohol use disorders (AUD), 393, **393,** 393t
alcohol withdrawal, 393–394, **393**
alcoholic cirrhosis, 394, **395**
all-or-none thinking, 364t
altitude, and physical activity, 51
Alzheimer disease, 75, 447
amenorrhea, 275, **275**
American College of Sports Medicine (ACSM)
  Exercise is Medicine program, 76
  FITT-VP, 84
  screening guidelines, 44